American
HORIZONS

American HORIZONS

U.S. HISTORY IN A GLOBAL CONTEXT WITH SOURCES

Volume I | To 1877

Second Edition

Michael Schaller
University of Arizona

Robert Schulzinger
University of Colorado, Boulder

John Bezís-Selfa
Wheaton College

Janette Thomas Greenwood
Clark University

Andrew Kirk
University of Nevada, Las Vegas

Sarah J. Purcell
Grinnell College

Aaron Sheehan-Dean
Louisiana State University

New York Oxford
OXFORD UNIVERSITY PRESS

Oxford University Press is a department of the University of Oxford.
It furthers the University's objective of excellence in research, scholarship,
and education by publishing worldwide.

Oxford   New York
Auckland   Cape Town   Dar es Salaam   Hong Kong   Karachi
Kuala Lumpur   Madrid   Melbourne   Mexico City   Nairobi
New Delhi   Shanghai   Taipei   Toronto

With offices in
Argentina   Austria   Brazil   Chile   Czech Republic   France   Greece
Guatemala   Hungary   Italy   Japan   Poland   Portugal   Singapore
South Korea   Switzerland   Thailand   Turkey   Ukraine   Vietnam

For titles covered by Section 112 of the US Higher Education
Opportunity Act, please visit www.oup.com/us/he for the
latest information about pricing and alternate formats.

Published in the United States of America by
Oxford University Press
198 Madison Avenue, New York, NY 10016
http://www.oup.com

Library of Congress Cataloging-in-Publication Data

CIP data is on file at the Library of Congress.

ISBN: 978-0-19-938933-9

Printing number: 9 8 7 6 5 4 3 2 1

Printed in the United States of America
on acid-free paper

DEDICATION

To all of our students.
The individual authors would also like to dedicate this book to the following people.
Michael Schaller: *to GS, N, G, & D*
Robert D. Schulzinger: *to MES & EAS*
John Bezís-Selfa: *to PCZ & JBS*
Janette Thomas Greenwood: *to M, E, & S*
Andrew Kirk: *to L, H, & Q*
Sarah J. Purcell: *to H, E, & M*
Aaron Sheehan-Dean: *to M, L, & A*

Brief Contents Volume I: To 1877

Contents

CHAPTER 4
Accelerating the Pace of Change, c. 1690–1730 · 111

CHAPTER 13
A House Dividing, 1844–1860 · 433

CHAPTER 14
The Civil War, 1860–1865 · 467

Maps

Preface

American Horizons is a text for the course in American history that views the development of America in the context of global history.

For more than 400 years, North America has been part of a global network centered on the exchange of peoples, goods, and ideas. Human migrations—sometimes freely, sometimes forced—have continued over the centuries, along with the evolution of commerce in commodities as varied as tobacco, sugar, and computer chips. Europeans and Africans came or were brought to the continent, where they met, traded with, fought among, and intermarried with native peoples. Some of these migrants stayed, whereas others returned to their home countries. Still others came and went periodically. This initial circulation of people across the oceans foreshadowed the continuous movement of people, goods, and ideas that made the United States. These are the forces that have shaped American history, both dividing and unifying the nation. American "horizons" truly stretch beyond our nation's borders, embracing the trading networks established during and after the colonial era to the digital social networks connecting people globally today.

American Horizons tells the story of the United States by exploring this exchange on a global scale and placing it at the center of that story. By doing so, we provide a different perspective on the history of the United States, one that we hope broadens the horizons of those who read our work and are ever mindful of the global forces that increasingly and profoundly shape our lives. At the same time, American Horizons considers those ways in which U.S. influence reshaped the lives and experiences of people of other nations.

U.S. history is increasingly perceived, interpreted, and taught as part of a global historical experience. The mutual influence of change—of global forces entering the United States and of American ideas, goods, and people moving out through the world—has been a consistent feature since the 16th century. Although most Americans today are aware that their influence is felt abroad and are increasingly aware of the influence of events abroad on their own lives, they tend to think of these as recent developments. In fact, those earliest exchanges of beliefs and products some 500 years ago established a pattern of interaction that continues today.

We have written a narrative that encourages readers to consider the variety of pressures that spurred historical change. Some of these pressures arose within America and some came from outside its borders. In the 1820s, the global market for whale oil shaped labor conditions throughout New England. At the same time, the American political system was transformed by the unique inheritance of the American Revolution and the relative abundance of land in North America. In the 1940s and 1950s, the federal government designed a unique set of policies to help World War II veterans readjust to civilian life, whereas the Civil Rights Movement unfolded within a global context of decolonization in Africa and Asia. Topics such as these help us ask the reader to consider the relationship between local and global forces that shaped American history.

This book was conceived as an opportunity to present the nation's history as more than a mere sequence of events for the student to memorize. The approach of *American Horizons* reflects this. Although adhering to the familiar chronological organization of this course, our narrative style and structure provide the flexibility of shifting emphasis from time to time to the global aspects of American history. Although the story of the United States is always at the center of the story, that story is told through the movement of people, goods, and ideas into, within, or out of the United States.

What qualities make the United States unique? What accounts for the diversity of dialect and lifestyle across this country? How did the United States become a major player on the world stage of nations? History includes many story lines that contribute to this narrative. *American Horizons* is the story of where this nation came from and how it has been shaped by its own set of shared values as well as its interaction with the rest of the world. It recognizes that many of the significant events in American history had causes and consequences connected to developments elsewhere and presents those events accordingly. *American Horizons* depicts this intersection of story lines from many nations that influenced, and were influenced by, the United States of America.

As readers engage the text, we encourage them to think explicitly about what makes history. What matters? What forces or events shaped how people lived their lives?

The Development Story

The seven coauthors of this book specialize in a variety of time periods and methodologies. Based on our research and teaching, we all share the idea that the nation's history can best be understood by examining how, from the colonial era forward, the American experience reflected the interaction of many nations, peoples, and events. We present this idea in a format that integrates traditional narrative history with the enhanced perspective of five centuries of global interaction.

About the Second Edition

This new edition of *American Horizons* is comprehensive yet concise enough for instructors who prefer a more economical option for their students without sacrificing the primary advantages of a traditional, longer text. This has been achieved without sacrificing the kinds of features, images, tables, maps, or figures expected in this course.

A GUIDED TOUR OF *AMERICAN HORIZONS*

American Horizons is distinguished by three elements: a global theme, innovative scholarship, and learning features that encourage active learning.

CHAPTER INTRODUCTIONS

Each chapter of *American Horizons* begins with a compelling story at the core of each chapter theme.

GLOBAL THEME

American Horizons seamlessly incorporates connections to global history throughout the text, including discussion rarely found in other books.

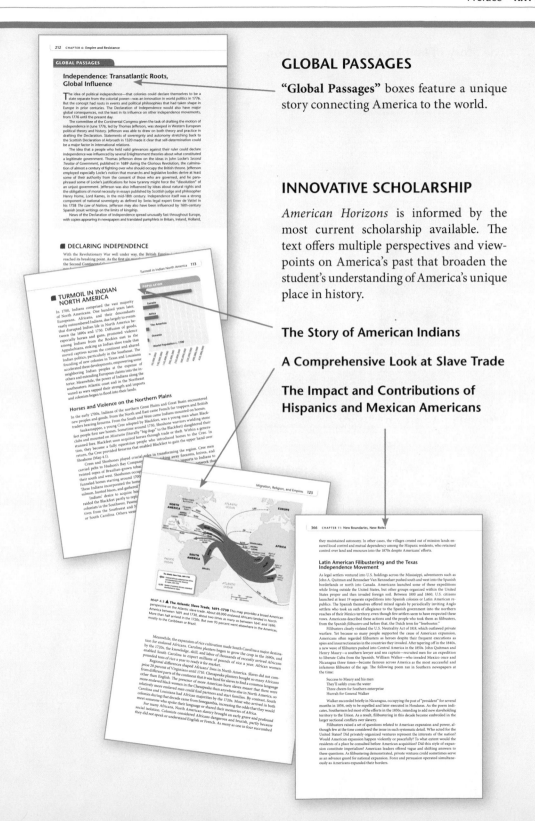

GLOBAL PASSAGES

"Global Passages" boxes feature a unique story connecting America to the world.

INNOVATIVE SCHOLARSHIP

American Horizons is informed by the most current scholarship available. The text offers multiple perspectives and viewpoints on America's past that broaden the student's understanding of America's unique place in history.

The Story of American Indians

A Comprehensive Look at Slave Trade

The Impact and Contributions of Hispanics and Mexican Americans

The Story of Immigration and Migration

Women in American History

LEARNING FEATURES

American Horizons offers vivid features to help students read, comprehend, and analyze key information, often using innovative visual aids.

Maps and Infographics

A rich graphics program explores essential themes in new ways.

Timeline in Every Chapter

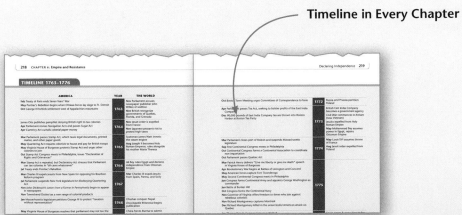

America in the World

At the conclusion of each chapter, this visual summarizes the key themes of exchange discussed in the chapter: the exchange of peoples, goods, and ideas between America and other nations.

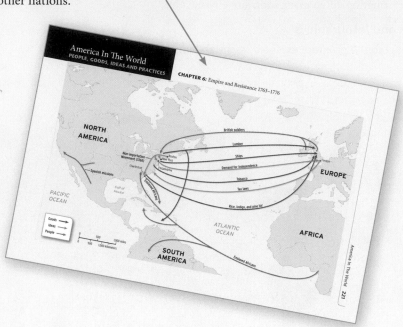

Primary Source Documents

Key primary source documents are located after each chapter. These selected documents and visual artifacts help the student understand the chapters by examining supplementary original sources, each provided with a contextual introduction and review questions.

WHAT'S NEW IN THE SECOND EDITION?

Two new learning tools highlight the changes to *American Horizons*. Every chapter includes the following:

- **NEW Timelines**—Timelines highlighting significant happenings in North America *and* the rest of the world, presented in parallel, provide the student with a global context for American events.
- **NEW America in the World**—An annotated geographic feature, found at the conclusion of each chapter, reinforces the key themes of exchange between America and other nations.
- **NEWLY Integrated Primary Source Documents**—*American Horizons* now includes primary source materials to help tell the story of the United States through carefully selected original documents and visual artifacts. These are organized to follow each chapter. Each source document begins with an introduction to place the material in context and concludes with several probing questions for the student.

NEW GLOBAL PASSAGES BOXES

Global Passages boxes are found in each chapter and feature a unique story connecting America to the world. For the second edition, the following boxes have been refreshed with new examples of key global connections. New Global Passages boxes:

- Chapter 6: Independence: Transatlantic Roots, Global Influence
- Chapter 9: Francisco de Miranda, the United States, and Latin American Independence
- Chapter 12: Celebrating the Black Atlantic
- Chapter 15: Irish Americans and the Fenian Struggle

OTHER NEW AND REVISED CHAPTER CONTENT

Chapter 3:

- Expanded discussion of the Barbados slave code's influence on the Anglo-Atlantic world.
- Expanded discussion of Kateri Tekakwitha's role between 17th-century Jesuits and Native Americans.

Chapter 6:

- Inclusion of new section highlighting the reciprocal relationship between Jefferson's drafting of the Declaration of Independence and Enlightenment theories in 17th-century Europe, with emphasis placed on the document's global implications.
- Expanded discussion of Spain's difficulty in taking control of Louisiana in the wake of French authority.

Chapter 9:

- New chapter opener discusses Magdelaine La Framboise, whose ascendancy of the social ladder through the fur trade symbolized the movement that abounded in North America at the turn of the 19th century.

- Inclusion of new section covering Francisco de Miranda, an ex-colonel in the Spanish army who attempted to infuse America's revolutionary spirit into Latin America.

Chapter 11:

- Expanded discussion of men's and women's roles in different parts of the antebellum United States.

Chapter 12:

- Expanded coverage of slave rebellion leader Denmark Vesey's use of religion to radicalize and mobilize communities, a tactic that drew on established precedents.
- Inclusion of new section discussing how the disparate Haitian and British West Indian emancipations inspired African Americans hoping to one day undergo the same process.

Chapter 14:

- Inclusion of new section focusing on European involvement in the American Civil War, and the Emancipation Proclamation's effect on a global scale.

Chapter 15:

- Inclusion of new section attributing Irish American involvement in the American Civil War to the Fenians, a group of late-19th-century Irish dissidents who challenged the British Empire.

SUPPLEMENTS

FOR STUDENTS

Oxford University Press offers a complete and authoritative package of supplementary materials for the student, including print and new media resources designed for chapter review, primary source reading, essay writing, test preparation, and further research.

Student Companion Web site at www.oup.com/us/americanhorizons

The open access Online Study Center designed specifically for *American Horizons* helps students to review what they have learned from the textbook as well as explore other resources online. Note-taking guides help students focus their attention in class, whereas interactive practice quizzes allow them to assess their knowledge of a topic before a test.

- **Online Study Guide,** including
  - Note-taking outlines
  - Multiple-choice and identification quizzes (two quizzes per chapter, 30-question quizzes—*different* from those found in the Instructor's Manual/Test bank)

- **Primary Source Companion & Research Guide**, a brief online Research Primer, with a library of annotated links to primary and secondary sources in U.S. history.
- **Interactive Flashcards**, using key terms and people listed at the end of each chapter; these multimedia cards help students remember who's who and what's what.
- *Oxford Homework Online (www.oup.com/us/schaller)*. Designed to be simple, intuitive, and mobile *Oxford Homework Online* offers you a simple, nationally hosted, online learning course—including study, review, interactive and assessment materials—in an easy to use system requiring less than 15 minutes to master. Assignment and assessment results flow into a straightforward gradebook allowing professors a clear view into students' progress. And the system works on every major platform and device, including mobile devices!

OXFORD FIRST SOURCE

Oxford First Source is an online database—with custom print capability—of primary source documents for the U.S. History Survey Course.

These documents cover a broad variety of political, economic, social, and cultural topics and represent a broad cross section of American voices. Special effort was made to include as many previously disenfranchised voices as possible. The documents in this collection are indexed by date, author, title, and subject, allowing instructors to identify and select documents best suited for their courses. Short documents (one or two pages) are presented in their entirety while longer documents have been carefully edited to highlight significant content.

Each document is introduced with a short explanatory paragraph and accompanied with study questions. The collection includes an *Introduction to Reading and Interpreting Primary Documents*, which introduces students to the concept of primary documents and explains several methods for reading, interpreting, and understanding them. It also explains how to set documents into their historical context and how to incorporate primary documents into papers, exams, and other assignments.

FOR INSTRUCTORS

For decades, American history professors have turned to Oxford University Press as the leading source for high-quality readings and reference materials. Now, when you adopt *American Horizons*, the Press will partner with you and make available its best supplemental materials and resources for your classroom. Listed here are several series of high interest, but you will want to talk with your Sales Representative to learn more about what can be made available and about what would suit your course best.

Ancillary Resource Center (ARC) at **www.oup-arc.com** is a convenient, instructor-focused single destination for resources to accompany your text. Accessed online through individual user accounts, the ARC provides instructors with access to up-to-date ancillaries at any time while guaranteeing the security of grade-significant resources. In addition, it allows OUP to keep instructors informed when new content becomes available. The following are available on the ARC:

- Digital copy of **Instructor's Manual**
- Computerized **Test Bank** including:

- **Quizzes** (two per chapter, one per half of the chapter, content divided somewhat evenly down the middle of the chapter: 25 multiple-choice questions each)
  - **Tests** (two per chapter, each covering the entire chapter contents, offering 10 identification/matching; 10 multiple choice; five short answer, two essay)
- Chapter-by-chapter **PowerPoint Presentations** with images and videos to illustrate important points
- **Sample Syllabi**
- **Chapter Outlines**
- **In-Class Discussion Questions**
- **Lecture Ideas**
- **Oxford's Further Reading List**

A complete **Course Management cartridge** is also available to qualified adopters. Instructor's resources are also available for download directly to your computer through a secure connection via the instructor's side of the companion Web site. Contact your Oxford University Press Sales Representative for more information.

OTHER OXFORD TITLES OF INTEREST FOR THE U.S. HISTORY CLASSROOM

Oxford University Press publishes a vast array of titles in American history. Listed following is just a small selection of books that pair particularly well with *American Horizons*. Any of the books in these series can be packaged with *American Horizons* at a significant discount to students. Please contact your Oxford University Press Sales Representative for specific pricing information or for additional packaging suggestions. Please visit www.oup.com/us for a full listing of Oxford titles.

NEW NARRATIVES IN AMERICAN HISTORY

At Oxford University Press, we believe that good history begins with a good story. Each volume in this series features a compelling tale that draws on a sustained narrative to illuminate a greater historical theme or controversy. Then, in a thoughtful Afterword, the authors place their narratives within larger historical contexts, discuss their sources and narrative strategies, and describe their personal involvement with the work. Intensely personal and highly relevant, these succinct texts are innovative teaching tools that provide a springboard for incisive class discussion as they immerse students in a particular historical moment.

- *Escaping Salem: The Other Witch Hunt of 1692*, by Richard Godbeer
- *Sleuthing the Alamo: Davy Crockett's Last Stand and Other Mysteries of the Texas Revolution*, by James E. Crisp
- *In Search of the Promised Land: A Slave Family in the Old South,* by John Hope Franklin and Loren Schweninger
- *The Making of a Confederate: Walter Lenoir's Civil War*, by William L. Barney
- *"They Say": Ida B. Wells and the Reconstruction of Race*, by James West Davidson
- *Wild Men: Ishi and Kroeber in the Wilderness of Modern America*, by Douglas Cazaux Sackman

- *The Gentle Subversive: Rachel Carson, Silent Spring, and the Rise of the Environmental Movement*, by Mark Hamilton Lytle
- *"To Everything There is a Season": Pete Seeger and the Power of Song*, by Allan Winkler
- *Tales from a Revolution: Bacon's Rebellion and the Transformation of Colonial America*, by James D. Rice

PAGES FROM HISTORY

Textbooks may interpret and recall history, but these books **are** history. Each title, compiled and edited by a prominent historian, is a collection of primary sources relating to a particular topic of historical significance. Documentary evidence includes news articles, government documents, memoirs, letters, diaries, fiction, photographs, advertisements, posters, and political cartoons. Headnotes, extended captions, sidebars, and introductory essays provide the essential context that frames the documents. All the books are amply illustrated, and each includes a documentary picture essay, chronology, further reading, source notes, and index.

- *Encounters in the New World* (Jill Lepore)
- *Colonial America* (Edward G. Gray)
- *The American Revolution* (Stephen C. Bullock)
- *The Bill of Rights* (John J. Patrick)
- *The Struggle Against Slavery* (David Waldstreicher)
- *The Civil War* (Rachel Filene Seidman)
- *The Gilded Age* (Janette Thomas Greenwood)
- *The Industrial Revolution* (Laura Levine Frader)
- *Imperialism* (Bonnie G. Smith)
- *World War I* (Frans Coetzee and Marilyn Shevin-Coetzee)
- *The Depression and the New Deal* (Robert McElvaine)
- *World War II* (James H. Madison)
- *The Cold War* (Allan M. Winkler)
- *The Vietnam War* (Marilyn B. Young)

CRITICAL HISTORICAL ENCOUNTERS

The volumes in this Oxford University Press book series focus on major critical encounters in the American experience. The word "critical" refers to formative, vital, transforming events and actions that have had a major impact in shaping the ever changing contours of life in the United States. "Encounter" indicates a confrontation or clash, oftentimes but not always contentious in character, but always full of profound historical meaning and consequence. The Critical Historical Encounters series emphasizes formative episodes in America's contested history. Each volume contains two fundamental ingredients: a carefully-written narrative of the encounter and the consequences, both immediate and long-term, of that moment of conflict in America's contested history.

- *For Ourselves and Our Posterity: The Preamble to the Federal Constitution in American History* (Peter Charles Hoffer)
- *Marching Across the Color Line: A. Philip Randolph and Civil Rights in the World War II Era* (David Welky)

- *Pennsylvania Hall: A 'Legal Lynching' in the Shadow of the Liberty Bell* (Beverly Tomek)
- *The Battle of Ole Miss: Civil Rights v. States' Rights* (Frank Lambert)
- *The Making of a Patriot: Benjamin Franklin at the Cockpit* (Sheila L. Skemp)
- *The Jerry Rescue* (Angela F. Murphy)

ACKNOWLEDGMENTS

A book as detailed as this draws on the talents and support of many individuals. Our first thanks must certainly go to our families for their support and patience during the development of this textbook. We also wish to thank Christina Snyder, associate professor, Committee on Native American and Indigenous Studies, Indiana University, who contributed significantly to a review of the first five chapters of the text. We would also like to acknowledge the team at Oxford University Press for their support in making this book a reality. Thanks go first to our editor, Brian Wheel, who encouraged and challenged us at every step of the process. Oxford publisher John Challice supported the project at an early stage and spurred us to think broadly about how we envisioned it. We appreciate the able assistance of development manager Thom Holmes, development editor Naomi Friedman, and development assistant Paul Longo. Editorial assistant Taylor Pilkington and Brianna Provenzano were especially helpful in wrangling the photo, map, and figure program for the book. We thank the Oxford production team, led by managing editor Lisa Grzan, for their encouragement and help in generating this book and shaping its final form. The interior and cover design were created by art director Michele Laseau. The innovative map program was created by International Mapping.

MANUSCRIPT REVIEWERS

We have greatly benefited from the perceptive comments and suggestions of the many talented scholars and instructors who reviewed the manuscript of *American Horizons*. Their insight and suggestions contributed immensely to the published work.

EXPERT REVIEWERS FOR THE SECOND EDITION

Ian J. Aebel
Virginia State University

Bill Mauzey
Metropolitan Community College

Karen Miller
Oakland University

Chad Parke
University of Louisiana Lafayette

Mary Ellen Rowe
University of Central Missouri

Cynthia Counsil
Florida State College at Jacksonville

Diane C. Vecchio
Furman University

Felicia Viator
San Francisco State University

Christopher Jones
College of William and Mary

Thomas Humphrey
Cleveland State University

Larry Grubbs
Georgia State University

Jeremy Neely
Missouri State University

Brittany Fremion
Central Michigan University

EXPERT REVIEWERS OF THE FIRST EDITION

Stanley Arnold
Northern Illinois University

Shelby M. Balik
Metropolitan State College of Denver
University of Colorado

Eirlys M. Barker
Thomas Nelson Community College

Toby Bates
University of Mississippi

Carol Bender
Saddleback College

Wendy Benningfield
Campbellsville University

Katherine Benton-Cohen
Georgetown University

Angela Boswell
Henderson State University

Robert Bouwman
North Georgia College & State
University

Jessica Brannon-Wranosky
Texas A&M University—Commerce

Blanche Brick
Blinn College

Howard Brick
University of Michigan

Margaret M. Caffrey
University of Memphis

Jacqueline B. Carr
University of Vermont

Dominic Carrillo
Grossmont College

Brian Casserly
Bellevue College

Cheryll Ann Cody
Houston Community College--Southwest
College

Elizabeth Collins
Triton College

Edward M. Cook, Jr.
University of Chicago

Cynthia Gardner Counsil
Florida State College—Jacksonville

C. David Dalton
College of the Ozarks

David Dzurec
University of Scranton

Brian J. Els
University of Portland

Kevin Eoff
Palo Verde College

Richard M. Filipink
Western Illinois University

Joshua Fulton
Moraine Valley Community
College

David Garvin
Highland Community College

Glen Gendzel
San José State University

Tiffany Gill
University of Texas—Austin

Aram Goudsouzian
University of Memphis

Larry Gragg
Missouri University of Science and Technology

Jean W. Griffith
Fort Scott Community College; Labette Community College

Mark Grimsley
Ohio State University

Elisa M. Guernsey
Monroe Community College

Aaron Gulyas
Mott Community College

Michael R. Hall
Armstrong Atlantic State University

David E. Hamilton
University of Kentucky

Peggy J. Hardman
Eastern New Mexico University

Kristin Hargrove
Grossmont College

Claudrena N. Harold
University of Virginia

Edward Hashima
American River College

Robin Henry
Wichita State University

John Herron
University of Missouri—Kansas City

L. Edward Hicks
Faulkner University

Matt Hinckley
Richland College

D. Sandy Hoover
East Texas Baptist University

Jerry Hopkins
East Texas Baptist University

Kelly Hopkins
University of Houston

Kenneth W. Howell
Prairie View A&M University

Raymond Pierre Hylton
Virginia Union University

Bryan M. Jack
Winston-Salem State University

Brenda Jackson-Abernathy
Belmont University

Volker Janssen
California State University—Fullerton

Lawrence W. Kennedy
University of Scranton

William Kerrigan
Muskingum University

Andrew E. Kersten
University of Wisconsin

Todd Kerstetter
TCU

Patricia Knol
Triton College

Jeffrey Kosiorek
Hendrix College

Peter Kuryla
Belmont University

Peggy Lambert
Lone Star College—Kingwood

Ian Lehmann
Blinn College

Carolyn Herbst Lewis
Louisiana State University

Christopher J. Mauceri
Farmingdale State College of New York

Derrick McKisick
Fairfield University

Marian Mollin
Virginia Tech

Linda Mollno
Cal Poly Pomona

Michelle Morgan
Missouri State University

Susan Rhoades Neel
Utah State University

Caryn E. Neumann
Miami University

Jeffrey Nichols
Westminster College

Christopher H. Owen
Northeastern State University

Jeffrey Pilz
North Iowa Area Community College

Amy M. Porter
Georgia Southwestern State University

William E. Price
Kennesaw State University

Emily Rader
El Camino College

Matthew Redinger
Montana State University—Billings

Yolanda Romero
North Lake College

Jessica Roney
Ohio University

Walter L. Sargent
University of Maine—Farmington

Robert Francis Saxe
Rhodes College

Jerry G. Sheppard
Mount Olive College

Robert Sherwood
Georgia Military College

Terry L. Shoptaugh
Minnesota State University—Moorhead

Jason H. Silverman
Winthrop University

Nico Slate
Carnegie Mellon University

Jodie Steeley
Merced Community College

Jennifer A. Stollman
Fort Lewis College

James S. Taw
Valdosta State University

Connie Brown Thomason
Louisiana Delta Community College

Kurt Troutman
Muskegon Community College

Stanley J. Underdal
San José State University

David Voelker
University of Wisconsin–Green Bay

Charles Waite
University of Texas—Pan American

R. Stuart Wallace
NHTI-Concord's Community College
University of New Hampshire—Manchester

Pamela West
Jefferson State Community College

William Benton Whisenhunt
College of DuPage

Louis Williams
St. Louis Community College Forest Park

Scott M. Williams
Weatherford College

Mary Montgomery Wolf
University of Georgia

Bill Wood
University of Arkansas Community College—Batesville

Melyssa Wrisley
Broome Community College

Charles Young
Umpqua Community College

Nancy L. Zens
Central Oregon Community College

About the Authors

Michael Schaller (Ph.D., University of Michigan, 1974) is Regents Professor of History at the University of Arizona where he has taught since 1974. His areas of specialization include U.S. international and East Asian relations and the resurgence of conservatism in late-20th century America. Among his publications are: *Altered States: The United States and Japan Since the Occupation* (Oxford University Press, 1997), *The U.S. and China into the 21st Century* (Oxford University Press, 2002), *Right Turn: American Life in the Reagan-Bush Era* (Oxford University Press, 2007), and *Ronald Reagan* (Oxford University Press, 2011).

Robert D. Schulzinger is College of Arts and Sciences Professor of Distinction of History and International Affairs at the University of Colorado, Boulder. He specializes in 20th-century U.S. history and U.S. diplomatic history. Books include *A Time for War: The United States and Vietnam, 1941–1975* (Oxford University Press, 1997), *U.S. Diplomacy since 1900* (Oxford University Press, 2002), and *Present Tense* (Houghton Mifflin, 2004).

John Bezís-Selfa is an Associate Professor of History at Wheaton College (Ph.D. at the University of Pennsylvania). He specializes in the history of the early Americas and teaches U.S., Latin American, and Latino/a history. Books include *Forging America: Ironworkers, Adventurers, and the Industrious Revolution* (Cornell University Press, 2004).

Janette Thomas Greenwood is Professor of History at Clark University (Ph.D. at the University of Virginia); she specializes in African American history and history of the U.S. South. Books include *The Gilded Age: A History in Documents* (Oxford University Press, 2000), *Bittersweet Legacy: The Black and White "Better Classes" in Charlotte, 1850–1910* (University of North Carolina Press, 1994), and *First Fruits of Freedom: The Migration of Former Slaves and Their Search For Equality in Worcester, Massachusetts, 1862–1900* (University of North Carolina, 2010).

Andrew Kirk is Professor of History at University of Nevada, Las Vegas (Ph.D. at the University of New Mexico) and specializes in the history of the U.S. West and environmental history. Books include *Collecting Nature: The American Environmental Movement and the Conservation Library* (University of Kansas Press, 2001) and *Counterculture Green: The Whole Earth Catalog and American Environmentalism* (Lawrence: University Press of Kansas, 2007).

Sarah J. Purcell is Professor of History at Grinnell College (Ph.D. at Brown University); she specializes in the Early National period, Antebellum United States, popular culture, politics, gender, and military history. She also directs the Rosenfield Program in Public Affairs, International Relations, and Human Rights. Books include *Sealed with Blood: War, Sacrifice, and Memory in Revolutionary America* (University of Pennsylvania Press, 2002), *The Early National Period* (Facts on File, 2004), and *The Encyclopedia of Battles in North America, 1517–1916* (Facts on File, 2000).

Aaron Sheehan-Dean is the Fred C. Frey Professor at Louisiana State University (Ph.D. at the University of Virginia); he specializes in Antebellum United States and the U.S. Civil War. Books include *Why Confederates Fought: Family and Nation in Civil War Virginia* (The University of North Carolina Press, 2007), *The View from the Ground: Experiences of Civil War Soldiers* (The University Press of Kentucky, 2006), and *Concise Historical Atlas of the U.S. Civil War* (Oxford University Press, 2008).

American
HORIZONS

North America Encounters the Atlantic World

On June 4, 1539, a tattooed man carrying a bow and arrow boldly approached a group of Spanish soldiers who had just landed near Tampa Bay, Florida. In broken Spanish, he pleaded to a shocked audience: "Sirs, for the love of God and of St. Mary, do not kill me; I am Christian, like you, and I am a native of Seville, and my name is Juan Ortiz."

It took Ortiz nearly a week to summon enough Spanish to explain how he came to Florida and survived. About 12 years earlier, he and at least 20 other soldiers had arrived to join an army led by Pánfilo de Narváez. Ortiz and a companion volunteered to swim ashore from their boat to retrieve a sheet of paper affixed to a stick—what they hoped was a letter that would tell them where Narváez's expedition had gone. But Indians from the nearby town of Ozita had planted the letter as bait. They killed Ortiz's companion and took Ortiz hostage. The chief of Ozita had good reason to want Ortiz. Soldiers from the Narváez expedition had lopped off the tip of the chief's nose and thrown one of his wives to their dogs. Ozita planned to exact revenge by burning Ortiz alive, but one of the chief's wives and his daughters intervened and saved his life. Ortiz endured three years of enslavement in Ozita before finding refuge with Mocozo, who led a nearby rival chiefdom. Mocozo hoped to use Ortiz as a means of building an alliance with the Spanish. When Hernando de Soto landed in Tampa Bay, Mocozo sent Ortiz to meet de Soto's fleet.

To de Soto, Ortiz was a sign that God had "taken this enterprise in His especial keeping." He needed a guide and translator. "This interpreter," de Soto wrote, "puts new life into us, for without

< *Monumenta Cartographia* by Alberto Cantino, c. 1502.

3

him I know not what would become of us." He presented Ortiz with a horse, arms, and a suit of clothes. Because Ortiz had become so accustomed to Indian attire, three weeks passed before he could bring himself to wear it.

Ortiz served de Soto for nearly three years as the Spanish-led force slashed and pillaged its way through the Southeast. Ortiz died in present-day Arkansas in March 1542, leaving de Soto and his men with another captive Indian guide who barely spoke Spanish. De Soto died a few weeks later. His men sunk his body in the Mississippi River and later rafted down to the Gulf of Mexico. Then they built boats and sailed for Mexico, staggering ashore in the summer of 1543.

The fate of Juan Ortiz and of the de Soto mission was not atypical. Over the course of thousands of years, Indians had spread across and adjusted to an ecologically diverse continent. Outsiders like Ortiz who adapted to Indian ways and served Indian needs survived. Those who did not, particularly Ortiz's fellow Spanish conquistadors who stormed in from the Caribbean and Mexico, often perished. All of what is today the mainland United States remained entirely in Indian hands until 1565, decades after much of the rest of the Americas had fallen to the Spanish sword. Still, men like Ortiz and de Soto laid the groundwork for the subsequent European colonization of North America.

◼ NORTH AMERICA TO 1500

The human history of North America began when peoples from northeast Asia arrived more than 10,000 years ago. During centuries of climate change, they discovered what they could hunt, fish, and gather from wild plants. They began cultivating local wild plants and established trade. Many peoples adopted and adapted transplants from Mexico. The most significant Mexican transplant—corn—transformed the lives of peoples in the Southwest, the Plains, and across all of Eastern North America. By the time the Europeans and Africans arrived, the inhabitants of North America had well-established cultures, economies, and societies.

The Three Waves of Migration

The findings of archeologists, linguists, and geneticists indicate that Indians' ancestors left northeast Asia for North America in three distinct waves. The first and largest most likely walked from Siberia to Alaska during the last Ice Age at least 15,000 years ago, probably following game along paths now submerged by the Bering Sea. Most Indians descend from those migrants, who dispersed across the Americas. However, some archaeologists disagree with this time frame, suggesting that the first wave of Indian settlements could be 20,000 years old or older. The next wave crossed by water, arriving 8,000 to 10,000 years ago. Most of these migrants spoke a Na-Dene language and settled first in Alaska and northwestern Canada. The last wave of Indians traveled by boat about 5,000 years ago. These were the ancestors of the peoples we know as Inuit and Aleuts. Those who became Inuit claimed the Arctic shoreline from Alaska east to Labrador and Greenland. Meanwhile, ancestors of Aleuts settled the Aleutian Islands. Both groups subsisted by fishing and hunting marine mammals.

Many Indian peoples consider migration a formative part of their past. Diné (Navajo) history includes the story of their ancestors moving among four worlds. Ojibwa say that they, along with Ottawa and Potawatomi, descend from one people who lived near the "Great Salt Sea" in northeastern North America before moving to the Great Lakes, where they parted ways to become three distinct nations. Choctaw recall an exodus east to their homeland in what is today Mississippi. The West, they remembered, was the direction of death, a place that barred spirits from entering the afterworld.

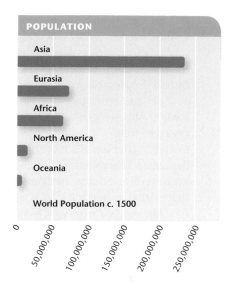

Farmers, Hunters, and Gatherers

The first Americans grappled with environmental changes that would profoundly alter their cultures. It took thousands of years for global warming to end the Ice Age; most of the glacial ice that had covered much of the continent had melted by 8,000 BCE. Two-thirds of the continent's animal species that weighed 100 pounds or more went extinct, including the ancestors of the modern horse and camel. Indian hunters may have accelerated such extinctions, though to what extent is controversial among scholars and Indians.

MIWOK ACORN GRANARIES, CALIFORNIA, 1870s Miwoks interlaced branches and grass to build structures like these to store acorns. They and many other California peoples harvested acorns, a staple of their diets, from oak groves that they maintained. Indians' skillful use of California's varied ecologies enabled them to become some of North America's densest populations.

Environmental changes transformed Indians' relationship to the land and to one another over the next 7,000 years. Hunters in most of North America set their sights on smaller game, such as deer, rabbits, and squirrels, while on the Plains and in the interior Northwest, they teamed up to hunt bison. Peoples who lived near rivers and estuaries came to rely more heavily on fish and shellfish as sources of animal protein. The appearance of stone artifacts—slabs with hollowed-out depressions and mortars, used to grind seeds or nuts—suggests that locally available wild plants, most likely harvested and processed by women, played a more significant role in Indian diets. As Indian bands learned to make better use of a more diverse range of local resources, their populations became denser, and they confined their annual movements to smaller areas. This encouraged greater cultural differentiation, which included the rise of many of the language families that existed in North America when Europeans arrived.

About 5,000 years ago, Indian women in North America began to tend gardens to which they returned yearly. Around 3,500 years ago, southwestern peoples began to cultivate corn, a plant that originated in central Mexico. Over the next thousand years, they would develop strains that fared well in the colder and more arid conditions in which they lived. By 1000 CE, most people who inhabited what is today the mainland United States cultivated plants wherever the climate permitted. California, the Great Basin, and the Pacific Northwest were exceptions. California's staggering variety of microclimates and ecological zones in close proximity to one another enabled Indians to subsist on what they could hunt, fish, and gather. The Great Basin was too arid to sustain agriculture, but the people there gathered and processed acorns and other plants and hunted deer, rabbits, and other game. Salmon fishing, hunting marine mammals, and gathering wild plants enabled Indians in the Pacific Northwest to avoid agriculture and devote more time and energy to other activities, such as intricate wood carving.

By 1000 CE, most North Americans grew corn, beans, and squash. Beans came from Mexico. Indians in most of the Southwest grew them by 200 CE. Women in the East had domesticated four indigenous seed plants: lamb's quarter, marsh elder, squash, and sunflower. Corn entered eastern North America around 200 CE, but centuries passed before it became the region's dominant crop. By 900 CE, Indian women had created a frost-resistant variety of corn called Northern flint. This variety could be harvested in parts of the northeast and Great Lakes where growing seasons were at least 120 days long. Southeastern women later developed a different variety, Southern dent. Most varieties of hybrid corn grown today originated from Northern flint or Southern dent.

Corn offered clear advantages over the crops that Europeans introduced to the Americas. Corn provided higher yields than European grains: 1 grain of wheat might yield 15 new grains when harvested, but a kernel of corn produced many ears, each bearing 200 kernels. Indian agriculture also required less labor and caused less damage to the soil. Europeans usually planted rows, plots, or fields of the same species, a technique that depleted soil more quickly and encouraged weeds. Indians planted corn, beans, and squash together in small hills. Corn stalks supported climbing bean tendrils, and nodules in the beans' roots fixed nitrogen, restoring some fertility to the soil. Squash and beans created ground cover that crowded out weeds, discouraged erosion, and saved labor. The three crops were a good dietary combination as well. When eaten together, corn and beans supply a full range of essential amino acids, and squash is rich in vitamins. In short, Indian North American agriculture offered a good diet for less labor with a smaller environmental footprint than did traditional European practices.

Indian diets also differed markedly from Europeans' diets in their sources of animal protein. Aside from turkeys, North American Indians did not domesticate animals for food. Unlike Europe, Asia, and Africa, the Americas had few animals small and tame enough to domesticate; and Indians had little reason to raise animals because game usually provided all the animal protein that they needed. European observers noted that Indians set fires to maintain prairies or to burn away underbrush in mature forests to make it easier to hunt game and to maintain sunny clearings that attracted deer and other favored species. Even Indians who grew corn used most of their territory to hunt and fish. In time, new technology made hunting a bit easier. Inuit initiated the use of the bow and arrow, an advance that spread to all parts of the continent north of Mexico as of 700 CE.

Because most Indians relied on wild sources of animal protein, they did not suffer from many of the illnesses that plagued Europeans, Africans, and Asians. Many virulent diseases have resulted from millennia of microbial exchange between humans and domesticated animals. Cowpox is a close relative of smallpox, and pigs and ducks act as reservoirs for influenza viruses that mutate within humans. Indians raised few animals, so they did not develop immunity to these virulent germs. That left them highly vulnerable to disease when the Europeans and Africans arrived.

The Rise and Decline of Urban Indian North America

The rise of agriculture encouraged the creation of urban centers in North America that thrived on long-distance trade in rare commodities. The largest were in the Southwest and the Mississippi Valley. Two urban peoples arose in the Southwest by 1000 CE—Hohokam and Anasazi. Both groups owed their success to irrigation systems. The Hohokam began to build canals to divert river water to their fields around 800 CE. Over the next four centuries, they created thousands of miles of canals that supported a population of tens of thousands. The modern city of Phoenix has a canal system that was virtually superimposed on the one Hohokam constructed. Contact and exchange between cities helps to explain the appearance of ball courts like those found in central Mexico in Snaketown, a principal Hohokam settlement. The Hohokam probably overtaxed their environment. They stopped building ball courts after 1150. A flood destroyed most of the canal network two centuries later. Meanwhile, irrigated soils became saltier and increasingly poisonous to crops. By 1400, the Hohokam had dispersed and combined with nearby peoples to become O'odham. The Spanish called them Pima and Papago, as do most outsiders.

As Hohokam made more of modern-day Arizona bloom, the Anasazi developed a commercial hub in New Mexico. In 1100, Chaco Canyon contained as many as a dozen towns that together housed up to 11,000 people. Chaco anchored a network of at least 70 communities that stretched over 25,000 square miles, many linked to Chaco by straight roads totaling more than 400 miles in length. Chaco residents specialized in making turquoise, which they exchanged for shells from the Gulf of California and copper bells, macaws, and feathers from Mexico. Global cooling caused severe droughts that compelled people to abandon Chaco. By 1300, many Anasazi descendants had migrated to the Rio Grande Valley and settled into small towns built of adobe, located in defensible places near reliable sources of water. These became the Hopi, Zuni, and other diverse peoples whom the Spanish collectively named Pueblos in the 1540s. Pueblos

KACHINA, KIVA WALL PAINTING, KUAUA PUEBLO, c. 1450   Kachinas are ancestral spiritual beings that Pueblo peoples believe bring rain, fertility, communal harmony, and well-being. Note the seeds, bolt of lightning, and rainbow emanating from the eagle's mouth. All symbolize fertility. Anasazi peoples constructed and settled in Kuaua Pueblo in central New Mexico during the 1300s.

spoke six distinct languages, but they were united by a shared belief in **kachinas**, ancestral beings believed to bring rain and communal harmony.

Cultivation of corn also transformed the Mississippi Valley, where what scholars call "Mississippian" societies began to form around 700 CE. **Mississippian societies** peaked between 1100 and 1300, stretching from Georgia west to Oklahoma and north to Wisconsin. Mississippians built on fertile floodplains, constructing cities with temples, earthen burial mounds, and large plazas for ceremonies and ball games like those in the Southwest and Mexico. All had paramount (supreme) hereditary chiefs who collected tribute and demanded labor on public works as well as military service. Chiefs mediated between their people and the sun, the source of life and their principal deity, and lived in wooden temples built atop earthen pyramids. When a chief died, his wives and servants were sometimes killed and entombed, along with rare goods, to accompany him into the afterlife (Map 1.1).

The most famous Mississippian society peaked around 1100 at Cahokia, near today's East St. Louis, Illinois. As many as 10,000 people lived in Cahokia proper and up to 30,000 in the villages around it. Cahokia's central mound occupied 16 acres and stood 100 feet high. Located just south of where the Missouri and Mississippi Rivers met, Cahokians traded widely. They obtained copper from the Great Lakes, shells from the Atlantic coast, and obsidian (volcanic glass) from the Rockies, all items that filled the graves of chiefs and nobles.

MAP 1.1 ▲ Trade and Selected Urbanized Indian Societies in North America, c. 700 to c. 1450 This map shows major trade routes and the goods transported along them c. 1450. Overlaid are the areas in the Southwest where the Anasazi and Hohokam settled and areas in the Mississippi River Valley in which Mississippian societies flourished between roughly 700 and 1450 CE. Modern political boundaries are included to provide orientation.

Two centuries later, Cahokia was a ghost town. The city probably demanded more than the region and its people could provide, especially as the climate cooled and crop yields plummeted. Meanwhile, other major Mississippian chiefdoms endured at Spiro in Oklahoma, Moundville in Alabama, and Etowah in Georgia. Spiro declined after 1350, when its Caddoan-speaking residents and tributaries stopped erecting temples or burial mounds. The city was abandoned by 1450.

The spread of corn cultivation to the northeast sparked profound changes among the Owasco, the most likely immediate ancestors of the Iroquois of upstate New York and Canada. As corn became the main source of food, Owasco women—responsible for cultivating the crop—gained importance. The rise of the longhouse during the 1100s enhanced women's status as well. Several families, all related by blood to a matriarch, occupied a longhouse where they coordinated farming, cooking, and child rearing.

Meanwhile, Owasco relocated to villages situated on hilltops and surrounded by ditches and palisades for protection from attacks by other Owasco peoples. Villages that shared an enemy and, increasingly, a common language, banded together. Five such alliances gradually took shape sometime before the 1400s. They became Seneca, Cayuga, Onondaga, Oneida, and Mohawk.

Indian North America in the Century before Contact

In 1492, scholars estimate that between 43 and 65 million people, about one-fifth of humanity, inhabited the Americas. Somewhere between 7 million and 10 million lived north of Mexico. They spoke at least 375 distinct languages representing 21 language families. California was the most densely populated and culturally diverse area within what is today the United States. There were as many as 400,000 Californians, who spoke 50 different languages belonging to at least six language families. By contrast, five language families—Algonquian, Iroquoian, Muskogean, Caddoan, and Siouan—were dominant among Indian groups from the Mississippi River Valley east to the Atlantic (Map 1.2). North America was one of the world's most diverse places prior to the arrival of Europeans and Africans.

Migration enhanced North American diversity. Bands of Na-Dene may have introduced the bow and arrow, as well as shields, to the northwestern Plains by 700 CE. Seven centuries later, Na-Dene were settling in the Southwest, where they became Apaches and Navajo. Their arrival affected trade and diplomacy. Na-Dene hunted growing bison herds

HURON WOMAN POUNDING CORN INTO MEAL, 1657
This image of a Huron woman at work in front of a longhouse comes from a map drawn by an Italian Jesuit who lived among Huron in the 1640s. It illustrates the centrality of women, their labor, and their roles in Huron and Iroquois societies.

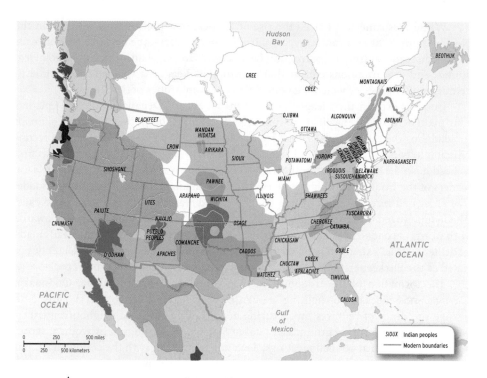

MAP 1.2 ▲ Linguistic Map of Indian North America with Select Indian Peoples Included North America's Indians spoke nearly 400 different languages when Europeans first arrived. Shown here are the continent's linguistic boundaries, along with locations for a number of Indian peoples, both of which reflect the time when Europeans first made sustained contact with peoples in that region.

in the southern Plains. They replaced Caddo and Wichita as the Pueblos' main providers of bison meat and hides, receiving corn and cotton blankets in return and helping to create the Southwest that Europeans and Africans encountered in the 1540s.

Meanwhile, relatively recent arrivals were also transforming central Mexico. They called themselves *Mexica*. Their legends held that they had fled south from their ancestral homeland Aztlán (hence the name "Aztecs" by which Mexica are often known), finding refuge on an island in Lake Texcoco. There, around 1325, the Mexica founded their capital Tenochtitlán. By the early 1400s, Mexica warriors had made Tenochtitlán a formidable power. Mexica were ruled by *tlatoani*, which literally translates as "the one who speaks," but whom the Europeans called "emperors." Under Itzcoatl and Moctezuma I, the Mexica became Mesoamerica's dominant power in the 1460s. They collected tribute from millions, many of whom, like Mexica, spoke Nahuatl. Tenochtitlán soon had over 100,000 residents and a skyline dominated by two massive pyramids, one devoted to the Mesoamerican rain god Tlaloc and the other to Mexica patron deity Huitzilopochtli. The Mexica fought battles to seize captives who were sacrificed to Huitzilopochtli to ensure that the sun would again rise and to keep death at bay. Demands for tribute and captives created many enemies for Mexica and stiffened the resolve of city-states like Tlaxcala to remain independent.

While Mesoamericans faced the rise of Mexica, new polities were forming in the Northeast. By 1500, two confederacies of Iroquoian speakers—the Great League of Peace (known hereafter as Iroquois or **Iroquois League**) and **Huron**—had formed. Archeological studies and oral traditions concur that the Iroquois League developed in response to centuries of destructive violence among different communities of the Owasco.

Iroquois explain their league's origins in the **epic of Deganawidah**. The epic has four main actors: Deganawidah, a woman named Jikonsahseh, the Onondaga shaman Thadadaho, and the Onondaga chief Hiawatha. Deganawidah bore a message of reconciliation to end warfare between Iroquoians of upstate New York. Jikonsahseh was first to heed it, so she became the "mother of nations." Women earned the right to choose the leaders of the Iroquois through her. Hiawatha and Thadadaho were harder to persuade. The chief had recently buried three daughters and was consumed by grief and rage. Thadadaho urged him to seek revenge by going to war. Deganawidah soothed Hiawatha with words of condolence and conveyed his sincerity with a gift of wampum, beads made of drilled seashells strung together. He then focused on Thadadaho, who was later designated as the Firekeeper, the first chief appointed to Deganawidah's league of peace.

The formation of the Iroquois League prompted Mohawk, Oneida, Onondaga, Cayuga, and Seneca to stop fighting "**mourning wars**" against each other: skirmishes to avenge the death of relatives by capturing or killing members of neighboring tribes. Members shared hunting grounds. A total of 50 chiefs, each chosen by women, represented each nation at council meetings. Each meeting began with the condolence ceremony and recitation of the epic. League councils could not make decisions until delegates had reached consensus and operated mainly to preserve harmony among the five peoples of the Iroquois, each of which was composed of autonomous villages. A council could not compel obedience from them, even when at war with outsiders.

Outsiders could be friend or foe, but could never be trusted unless they became kin. For Iroquois, as for most Indians, war was mainly a matter of exacting revenge on outsiders. The main objective was to seize captives and adopt them, not to kill or wound as many as possible. For adult male captives, that often meant ritual torture and execution. For women and children, it usually meant adoption to replace loved ones who had died. Adoption often meant enslavement. Indians practiced slavery widely and often considered slaves kin, although that did not prevent a lively slave trade between peoples that persisted well into the 1800s in North America, particularly in the Southwest. There were some exceptions. In the Southeast, adopted people were never slaves; slaves were a special category of people who were stigmatized by their lack of kin ties.

Deganawidah's epic also reveals meanings that Indians attached to exchange of goods. Deganawidah offered Hiawatha wampum because doing so told Hiawatha that he had something with spiritual power that he was willing to share. Wampum meant serious purpose, friendship, and generosity. The gift bound Hiawatha to reciprocate. Strings of shells, like other exotic portable items such as copper or turquoise, were considered otherworldly objects that conferred prestige and spiritual power on those who received them and on whoever gave them away. Most chiefs were expected not to amass such goods but to redistribute them. Indians considered trade a form of diplomacy. Friends traded with friends and did so by following customary protocols (rather than, say, a market price). Exchange of goods and people symbolized, reenacted, and maintained friendship between trading parties. That was the American way before the arrival of Europeans and Africans brought Indians into an emerging global network.

◼ MAKING AN ATLANTIC WORLD, 1400–1513

During the 1400s, western Europeans developed technologies that enabled them to cross the Atlantic and return home. The Spanish and Portuguese discovered new sources of wealth and new allies in sub-Saharan Africa and Asia. They initiated trade in enslaved Africans that encouraged the spread of plantation agriculture to new Iberian (Spanish and Portuguese) colonies off Africa's coast. Spanish mariners brought and extended that new **Atlantic world** to the Americas in 1492, an act that had the most immediate impact on people of the Caribbean island of Española.

Western Europe in the 15th Century

As the 1400s dawned, western Europe was a relatively poor region on the fringe of a prosperous Mediterranean world. Ottomans and Venetians controlled access to luxury goods—gold and ivory from sub-Saharan Africa and silks, gems, and spices from east, southeast, and south Asia. They made hefty profits as the middlemen. Merchants of the port city of Genoa, Italy, specialized in transporting bulk goods such as grains and wine.

Western Europeans had many interconnected reasons to venture beyond the world that they knew. Some sought to spread Christianity and make new allies for what they believed was a spiritual and ideological struggle against Islam. Many Christian Europeans feared the growing power of Ottoman Turks to their west and south and the Islamic emirates in parts of southern Spain. Monarchs in England, France, Portugal, and Spain sought revenue to fund armies and consolidate power over nobles. Ambitious men of ordinary birth saw acquisition of wealth as a path to social mobility. They concluded that the best way to become richer quick was to circumvent the Mediterranean networks that brought them luxury goods and deal directly with Africans and east and south Asians.

By 1450, Europeans had the technology to sustain long-distance maritime commerce. The Christian conquest of Gibraltar in the late 1200s facilitated direct trade between the North Sea, the Baltic, and the Mediterranean. Iberian and Genoese shipyards produced a new kind of ship, the caravel. Caravels combined the strength and durability required of vessels that plied stormy waters off northern Europe with the speed and maneuverability of those that operated in the relatively calm Mediterranean. They could sail in protected coastal waters or on the open ocean. Most caravels had at least three masts. The front and center masts supported the large square sails long used in oceangoing vessels. Mariners attached a triangular sail—like those used in Mediterranean ships—to the rear mast, enabling a vessel to tack against the wind and return to shore from the open sea.

Europeans also had most of what they needed to orient themselves at sea. Compasses indicated which way was north. Hourglasses permitted rough calculations of

NOVA REPERTA This image, from *Nova Reperta*, a book published in Antwerp in 1600, illustrates how Europeans identified their "discovery" of the Americas with technologies that they had modified and mastered. At the center a cannon, flanked by shot and barrels of gunpowder, takes aim at a printing press.

velocity. **Astrolabes** and quadrants helped to determine latitude. Long before 1400, Mediterranean mariners used portolan charts, maps with detailed images of coastlines, to decide on the best route between two ports. They also employed classical knowledge. A Latin translation of Ptolemy's *Geography* appeared in 1406. It summarized the Greek world's understanding of geography circa 100 CE and offered guidance on how to represent Earth's spherical shape on a flat map. Subsequent editions added maps created during the 1400s.

Meanwhile, ideas coursed more rapidly thanks to Europeans' adaptation of two Chinese inventions. One was a technique for making paper. Arabs introduced it to Spain, and it diffused slowly to most of Europe in the early 1400s. The other was block printing, inspired by a Chinese technique whereby characters carved into wood were dipped in ink and pressed onto paper. In the 1450s, German artisans brought together movable metal typecasts of each letter of the alphabet, ink, and a machine to press inked type against paper. The printing press revolutionized access to information. Scholars could refer to standardized texts rather than inaccurate transcriptions made by hand. Books became cheaper and more widely available. As of 1500, Europe's printers had turned out some six million books, probably more than had appeared in the previous 1,000 years.

In the 1450s, Europeans had also developed techniques of warfare to support expansion. They obtained gunpowder from China by 1250, and about 70 years later used it to propel missiles. In 1400, Europeans were producing firearms, especially artillery, used for sieges. By 1500, soldiers carried arquebuses, the ancestor of the musket, into battle, although their primitive design made them inaccurate. Surging metal production met the demand for more weaponry. Improvements in mining and to blast furnaces enabled Europeans to make five times more iron in 1530 than in 1460. Much of it was forged into steel and beaten into pikes and swords, which remained indispensable in combat.

Christian kingdoms of the Iberian Peninsula spearheaded western European expansion during the 1400s. Those that formed modern Spain had entered the final stage of a centuries-long process of evicting Islamic emirates from Iberia. Their *reconquista* (reconquest) combined religious, economic, and political goals. Christians saw themselves as crusaders who were reclaiming Iberia for their faith. Monarchs could not afford to mount military campaigns themselves, so they licensed private entrepreneurs who shared the spoils of conquest. Those who succeeded received *encomiendas*—grants of land that they had conquered. **Isabel of Castile**'s marriage to **Ferdinand of Aragon** in 1469 united two principal Christian kingdoms; 13 years later, Christian forces launched the conquest of Granada, Iberia's last emirate. The conflict drew volunteers from all over Europe. In January 1492, the last Muslim settlement capitulated. The victorious Christians, seeking religious conformity, soon decreed that Muslims or Jews should accept baptism or leave Spain in a matter of months.

Meanwhile, the Portuguese gazed south and west. Unlike Spain, England, or France, Portugal was a united kingdom at peace with its neighbors for most of the 1400s. It was also a relatively poor one with a long coastline that drew thousands of Portuguese to the sea. Located near northwest Africa and thrust far out into the Atlantic, Portugal was poised to use the ocean to link the two continents.

Iberians, Africans, and the Creation of an Eastern Atlantic World

Europeans and Africans created an eastern Atlantic world over the course of the 15th century, largely by connecting western Africa directly to the outside world. That laid a foundation for the conquest and colonization of the Americas and for the enslavement of millions of Africans.

Portugal's expansion into Africa began in 1415 with the conquest of Ceuta, a Muslim city in Morocco. Portuguese mariners soon began to map Africa's northwest coast by inching south, trading with or raiding whomever they encountered, and returning home to report on their exploits and split the profits. Their efforts, sponsored by Prince Henry, the younger son of King John I, had three linked objectives. One was to challenge Muslim powers in North Africa. Another was to make direct contact and ally with the Christian kingdom of Ethiopia, which had begun to send emissaries to Europe in the early 1400s. Europeans hoped for a Christian African-European alliance against a common Muslim foe. The third objective, gold, mattered most to the Portuguese. North African Muslims controlled the flow of West African gold across the Sahara and into the Mediterranean. The Portuguese wanted to divert that stream into their pockets by trading directly with West Africans. They established their first *feitoria*

MAP 1.3 ▲ Global Trade, Africa, and the Making of the Eastern Atlantic World, 15th Century The Mediterranean Basin linked Europe to Africa and Asia for thousands of years through a combination of oceanic and overland routes. Portuguese seafaring along Africa's Atlantic coast during the 15th century brought West Africa into maritime global trade networks and launched the Atlantic slave trade.

(fortified trading post) at Arguim in 1445. In 1482, the Portuguese built a feitoria at Elmina, on Africa's Gold Coast, because of its proximity to mines (Map 1.3). To obtain African cooperation and consent, the Portuguese employed locals to operate them and paid rent to their rulers.

Portuguese mariners launched the **Atlantic slave trade**. The first cargo of enslaved people shipped directly from Africa arrived in Portugal in 1441. At first, the Portuguese raided for slaves, but they soon found it easier and more profitable to buy slaves from African captors. The Portuguese lacked the military might or the physical constitution to impose their will on African rulers. Like other Europeans, they had little immunity to diseases endemic to West Africa.

Slavery was already common in West and West Central Africa when the Portuguese arrived. Slaves were the only form of private, revenue-producing property that legal systems widely recognized. Those condemned to slavery in Africa were usually criminals, war captives, or debtors. They did not inherit their status, nor did they pass it on to their children.

Africans were also already engaging in long-distance slave trading. Thousands were driven across the Sahara or transported up the Red Sea to North Africa and the Middle East annually between 800 and 1600. In Europe, the Ottoman conquest of Constantinople, today's Istanbul, in 1453 made it harder for Europeans to purchase Slavs (hence the word "slave") from the Black Sea, a key source of enslaved labor to northern and western Europe for centuries. So, these countries began to purchase African slaves available through the Mediterranean slave markets.

At first, relatively few entered the Atlantic slave trade—about 800 a year during the 1450s and 1460s and over 2,000 by the 1490s. By 1550, however, Africans comprised about 10 percent of Lisbon's population, a reflection of Portuguese dominance of the Atlantic slave trade until the late 1500s.

The Atlantic slave trade affected how Europeans viewed Africans. By the late 1400s, Christian Europeans seldom enslaved one another, mainly for religious reasons. Muslims who ruled Iberia had distinguished between slaves on the basis of skin color: they considered darker-skinned people from sub-Saharan Africa inferior and most suitable for enslavement. Christian Iberians came to hold similar views of sub-Saharan Africans, partly because they also associated dark-skinned Africans with Muslims, whom they condemned as infidels. Demographic changes in the slave trade during the 1400s reinforced such beliefs. Ottoman control of the eastern Mediterranean and the Atlantic slave trade meant that dark-skinned Africans soon became the majority of Christian Europe's slaves, leading more Europeans to associate black skin with servility. Prejudice based on skin color arose before Europeans reached the Americas.

As the Atlantic slave trade began, Iberians were already colonizing islands off Africa's northwest coast. The most significant of these were the Canary Islands and Madeira. The Canaries, known to the Romans, were rediscovered in the early 1300s. Their conquest began in 1402. The islands' indigenous people, Guanches, probably descended from Berbers of North Africa. Guanches became targets of slaving raids and fell victim to diseases to which they had no acquired immunity. There were virtually no Guanches left by the 1490s.

Meanwhile, Portuguese colonists established sugar plantations off northwest Africa's coast on the Madeira islands. Europeans first encountered cultivation of sugar cane in the Middle East during the Crusades. For the next few centuries, Cyprus and Sicily supplied European markets with sugar, from plantations staffed by enslaved Slavs, Tatars, and Mediterranean captives. Genoese merchants brought sugar-making technology from Sicily to Iberia, and by the 1450s Sicilians ran sugar mills on Madeira. Genoese merchants financed many of them and had the sugar hauled back to Europe. By 1500, about 2,000 slaves, mostly Africans, toiled on Madeira's plantations. They became one of western Europe's main sources of sugar, along with Spanish plantations on the Canaries.

The imperative to spread Christianity helped to propel and justify Portuguese expansion into Africa. Papal decrees issued between 1442 and 1456 granted Portugal the right to colonize islands off Africa's coast and monopolize trade between West Africa and Europe. In exchange, Portugal agreed to establish Catholic missions in Africa. One decree permitted Portuguese to buy African captives if doing so meant that they might become converts.

The Portuguese saw missionaries as a way to forge diplomatic and commercial ties in Africa, a view that African rulers sometimes shared. To them, conversion offered a way to gain a powerful ally and bolster their own authority. In 1491, Portuguese soldiers helped the Kongolese king, Nzinga a Nkuwu, put down a rebellion; and on Christmas Day, he and his family were baptized. For the next 15 years, Kongolese fought over who should rule them. In 1506, the victor, Afonso, committed Kongo to an alliance with the Portuguese. His son Henrique studied in Portugal, became a priest in 1518, and was appointed the first sub-Saharan African bishop two years later. Thousands of Kongolese accepted baptism and gradually infused Christianity with their traditions.

By the time the Kongolese had begun to Africanize Western Christianity, the Portuguese were about to open a direct water route to the Indian Ocean. In 1487, Bartolomeu Dias rounded the Cape of Good Hope and entered the Indian Ocean. Eleven years later, an Arab pilot guided Vasco da Gama across the Indian Ocean to India. Da Gama returned to Lisbon with spices. King Manoel fired off a letter to Ferdinand and Isabel trumpeting da Gama's achievement and pledging to force Muslim merchants to relinquish control of the Indian Ocean's spice trade to Portugal.

The Portuguese never made good on Manoel's boast, but they did dominate the eastern water route to Asia for over a century. A chain of feitorias down Africa's Atlantic coast, their cannon facing the ocean, backed Portugal's claim. But the Portuguese could not monopolize knowledge of winds and currents gleaned from thousands of voyages to Africa, Madeira, and the Canaries, and this knowledge suggested that one might reach Asia by crossing the Atlantic.

Columbus and the First Encounter

The man most responsible for extending the Atlantic world to the Americas emerged from the intersection of Mediterranean, Iberian, and eastern Atlantic networks. **Christopher Columbus** was born in Genoa around 1450. Columbus likely began his maritime career in the early 1470s. He soon moved to Lisbon, drawn by opportunities offered by the city's Genoese merchants. He had ties to Portugal's royal court and supervised the colonization of one of the Madeira islands. By the early 1480s, Columbus had visited Ireland, Iceland, Madeira, the Canaries, and Elmina. He knew the eastern Atlantic well.

Columbus also studied geography, sold books, and made maps. He pored over Ptolemy's *Geography*, which postulated that one could sail across the Atlantic to Asia. Ptolemy thought the distance between the continents was so great that no ship or crew could reach Asia and return. Access to the royal court alerted Columbus to a more optimistic alternative. In 1474, the Florentine cosmographer Paolo dal Pazzo Toscanelli had written the king of Portugal to claim that 5,000 miles separated the Canaries and China—still a great distance but one that sounded more feasible.

Columbus needed financial and legal backing to get to Asia. He tried and failed to interest John II of

PORTUGUESE INFLUENCE IN WEST AFRICA   This brass casting, probably made by an African artist at the royal court of Benin in the late 1500s or early 1600s, illustrates Portuguese influence in West Africa. It depicts a Portuguese mercenary fighting for the oba (king) of Benin. He carries a firearm, which the Portuguese introduced to the region.

SEVILLE   This view of Seville, attributed to Alonso Sánchez Coello and painted in the late 1550s, captures the city's status as Spain's main gateway to the Americas. In the foreground, an expedition prepares to set off for the Americas.

Portugal, so Columbus moved to Spain in 1485. He spent the next seven years lobbying Ferdinand and Isabel for support. They had reasons to expand their influence into the Atlantic: the ongoing conquest of the Canaries, competition with Portugal, and a need for new sources of gold. Ferdinand and Isabel approved Columbus's proposal shortly after the conquest of Granada and put up more than half the money for the voyage. The monarchs also granted him noble status and the offices of admiral, viceroy, and governor-general. Columbus had to provide one-quarter of the financing, most of which he borrowed from Italian merchants.

With three ships and 90 men under his command, Columbus departed Spain in early August 1492. After a stop in the Canaries, trade winds propelled them west. In mid-October, the crew made landfall on an island in the Bahamas. The Lucayan Taínos who lived there called it "Guanahaní." Columbus, thinking he had landed near the Indian Ocean's eastern edge, called them "Indians." His account of their first encounter stressed how little clothing the Taínos wore. Europeans of Columbus's time used clothing as a benchmark to judge individuals' social status and the level of civilization that a society had attained. Columbus also interpreted Taínos's lack of clothing as a sign of their innocence. Their willingness to trade whatever they had for glass beads, coins, and copper bells was another. Both suggested to Columbus that Taínos might make suitable converts and good workers. He took seven people from Guanahaní to serve as guides and interpreters. The three ships then sailed south in search of Asian ports as well as gold and other commodities that would sell in Europe. Along the way they overtook a Taíno in a canoe who was carrying a string of glass beads and some small coins. News of the strangers and items that they had brought were circulating just four days after they arrived.

After exploring Cuba, Columbus reached an island that the Taínos called Quisqueya. He renamed it "La Isla Española"—the Spanish island, now Haiti and the Dominican Republic. On Española, the visitors met Taínos who seemed more like themselves. The ancestors of these natives had migrated from South America over a thousand years earlier. These Taínos wore gold jewelry and lived in villages of up to 2,000 people governed by chiefs called caciques. They subsisted mainly on what they grew in conucos— plots that they had slashed and burned from the forest. They grew cassava, from which they made bread. One of the Taínos' two main deities was Yúcahu, god of cassava and of the sea. Taíno gods took physical form as zemis—carved idols that occupied places of honor in villages and homes. Taínos had a profound impact on how Europeans viewed the Americas and Indians. Many Arawak (the Taíno language) words entered Spanish and English, including "canoe" and "hammock." The word "Taíno" means "good" or "noble" in Arawak. Taínos used it to distinguish themselves from Caribs, who inhabited most of the Lesser Antilles. Taínos told Columbus that Caribs were a vicious warlike people who ate their enemies. Columbus was inclined to accept how the Taínos portrayed their foes, largely because it enabled him and the Spanish to pose as Taíno protectors, seek alliances with caciques, and claim that the Spanish were the Taínos' rightful rulers. Columbus later had a violent encounter with Caribs, which in his mind reinforced what the Taínos told him. An account of Columbus's first voyage distinguished between "good noble" Indians and violent savage ones. It circulated widely in Europe and molded European perceptions of Indians, including the belief that many were "cannibals"—a corruption of the word "Carib."

Columbus touted Española as a paradise. It had gold and a large population that farmed and lived in villages. After spending a few weeks along the island's north coast, Columbus loaded two ships with gold, chilies, tobacco, a canoe, a hammock, and seven Taínos. He left 39 men behind, sailed north, and discovered winds that blew east. Columbus reached Spain in March 1493 and headed to Barcelona to brief Ferdinand and Isabel and display the Taínos. He arrived to learn that a published account of his trip had beaten him there by two weeks. By December, versions of the story sold in Paris, Florence, and Rome. Some debated what Columbus had found. A few thought he had reached the Antilles, islands where legend had it that Christian Iberians fleeing Muslim rule had taken refuge centuries earlier. Columbus insisted that he had reached Asia and that Japan and China could not be far beyond. Pope Alexander VI believed that he had found people who required evangelization and awarded Spain sovereignty over the lands Columbus had visited. This sat poorly with the Portuguese. In 1494, Spain and Portugal signed the **Treaty of Tordesillas**, by which they divided the world between them. The Americas, excepting Brazil, ended up on the Spanish side of the line (Map 1.4).

An Italian named **Giovanni Caboto** was visiting Spain when Columbus returned. Like Columbus, he had lobbied the monarchs of Portugal and Spain to sponsor a voyage to Asia. Caboto moved to England and settled in Bristol, a home port for fishermen who sailed beyond Iceland. He obtained the backing of Henry VII and crossed the ocean in 1497. After exploring the coasts of Labrador and Newfoundland, Caboto returned with stories of seas full of fish and of a land that must be near Asia. The following year, Caboto embarked with five vessels laden with goods to trade. Only one made it home, without Caboto. English interest in Western ventures dimmed for nearly a century. Caboto had publicized the marine resources of Newfoundland and Canada, places that soon formed the northwestern edge of the Atlantic world. But the Caribbean, especially Española, attracted more attention from powerful and ambitious Europeans.

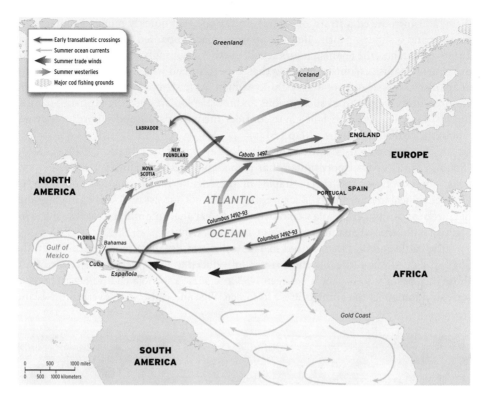

MAP 1.4 ▲ Summer Winds and Currents, Fishing Banks, and Two Early Transoceanic Crossings of the North Atlantic Mariners who sailed the Atlantic needed a good understanding of the ocean's winds and currents to navigate it successfully. Columbus and Giovanni Caboto were the first to learn how to return to Europe from the Americas. Note the major cod fishing grounds where cold and warm currents collided.

The Atlantic World Invades the Caribbean

In November 1493, Columbus returned to Española with about 1,500 men. He hoped to create a colony built around a feitoria, with colonists as company employees. Columbus soon discovered that the men he had left behind were dead. Disease had claimed some, and Taínos killed the rest because they had demanded gold or raped Taíno women.

Relations between the colonists and Taínos deteriorated as Columbus lost control of his men. They had come to Española for gold and conquest, not a salary. In 1495, colonists provoked a war with most of Española's main caciques. Columbus, who had earlier proposed trading enslaved "cannibals" for livestock to Ferdinand and Isabel and had been rejected, shipped over 500 Taínos to Spain to show that Española could be profitable. He justified their enslavement on the grounds that they had rebelled. Meanwhile, colonists abandoned the site that Columbus chose. In 1496, they founded Santo Domingo, the first permanent European town in the Americas.

Columbus's return to Española in 1493 set in motion several developments. First, it ensured the permanence of the "**Columbian exchange**," what historians call the movement of people, plants, animals, and pathogens between the Americas and the rest of the world. One form of exchange, sex between European men and Taíno women, began in 1492. It introduced a strain of syphilis to Europe that quickly mutated into a more virulent and disfiguring form. Because no women accompanied the second expedition, Taíno women became Spanish men's sexual partners, willingly or not. A 1514 census of prominent Spanish colonists indicates that 37 percent had wives, although the majority of Spanish colonists did not marry Taíno women. At first, many fathers recognized the children that resulted from such unions and most colonists considered them Spanish. But by the 1530s, the Spanish began to consider them a separate and subordinate group whom they called "mestizos" (Map 1.5).

As Spanish colonists settled the island, they hoped to remake Española into a "Spanish land" by transporting familiar plants and livestock. However, wheat, chickpeas, grapes, olives, and sheep, staples of the Mediterranean diet, fared poorly in Caribbean heat and humidity. Because they could not subsist on locally grown grains of European origin, Española's colonists had to eat the unfamiliar cassava. By 1496, Spanish authorities demanded cassava of Taínos as tribute.

The cattle and pigs that arrived in 1493 colonized Española more quickly than the Spanish did. All the cattle that the Spanish introduced to the Americas descended from those they brought to Española between 1493 and 1512. Española had no natural predators, so colonists let the animals loose to forage. Pigs and cattle soon overran the island

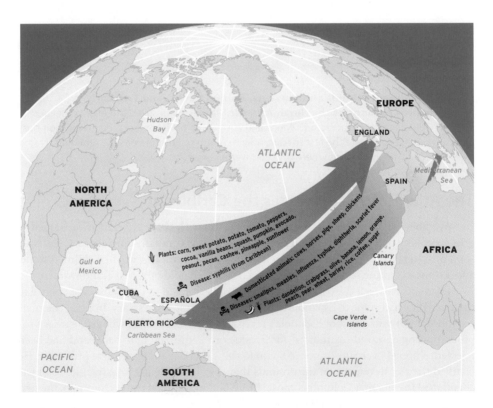

MAP 1.5 ▲ The Columbian Exchange Columbus's second voyage established a permanent exchange of plants, animals, and microbes between the Americas and the rest of the world. In some cases, it took centuries for Europeans, Africans, and Asians to adopt American crops. The impact of Eurasian microbes on American Indians was immediate and devastating.

and diminished its biodiversity. By 1508, authorities sought to protect the conucos that fed Española by permitting hunters to kill feral swine. After 1519, the island's two main exports were hides and sugar from cane, which the Spanish also introduced in 1493. Enslaved West Africans, Spaniards, and Indians herded, slaughtered, and skinned the animals.

Animal and human colonists also introduced Taínos to pathogens to which they had little or no acquired immunity and made them more vulnerable to those that had long infected them. Pigs from Columbus's second voyage probably brought influenza to the Americas. Gold mining overworked Taínos and crowded them together. The Taínos population declined and the Spanish responded by forcing Taínos into fewer but larger settlements so that they could be counted, taxed, put to work, and converted to Christianity more easily. These became death traps. Smallpox reached Española in January 1519, the first documented pandemic clearly of European origin to hit the Americas. By then, however, most Taínos had died. Perhaps 400,000 people inhabited Española in 1492. Spanish officials counted only 11,000 in 1518.

Spaniards stormed the Caribbean in search of new conquests, riches, and slaves. Between 1508 and 1513 they overran Cuba, Puerto Rico, and Jamaica, establishing encomiendas and shipping Taínos to Española. In 1509, Spanish mariners raided the Bahamas. They practically emptied those islands of people in just four years (Map 1.6).

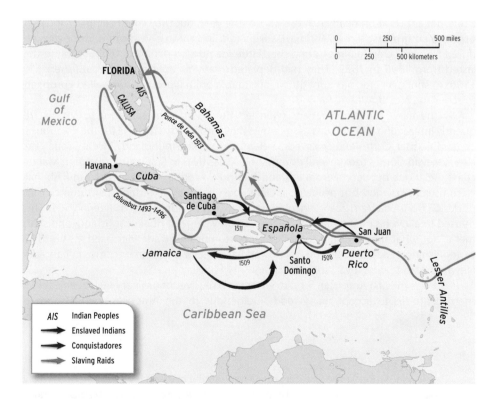

MAP 1.6 ▲ Española and Spanish Conquests in the Caribbean, 1493–1515 The depopulation of Española's Taínos caused by microbes that the Spanish brought and by Spanish abuses spurred conquistadores and slave raiders to invade nearby islands, a process that led the Spanish to Florida in 1513.

Cod

In 1497, Giovanni Caboto journeyed to Newfoundland and reported that "the sea there is swarming with fish." Word spread quickly. By the 1540s, more than 100 vessels carrying thousands of men left France each year for waters off Newfoundland, Labrador, and Nova Scotia. They wanted cod, which soon comprised over half the fish eaten in Europe.

Cod is a meaty, white-fleshed fish. It prefers waters between 34° and 50° F, where it devours the marine life that thrives wherever warm and cold currents meet on either side of the North Atlantic. Cod was ideal for a time when people had no refrigeration. Less than 1 percent fat, the fish can be preserved by drying it in the sun and wind.

During the late medieval era, wind-dried cod and ling (a fish related to cod) became Europe's first mass-produced food. At first Scandinavia was Europe's supplier of dried cod. Growing demand pushed fishermen to seek the fish in open water. By 1350, dried cod was Iceland's principal export and a staple on European tables—a cheap, portable, and durable source of protein.

Religion, war, and environmental change boosted demand for cod. Devout Catholics could not eat meat on nearly half the days of the year, but they could eat fish. Monarchs provisioned growing armies and navies with cod, largely to save money. Europeans endured frequent crop failures during the "Little Ice Age," a period of global cooling that lasted from 1300 to 1850. They had depleted many of their own coastal fisheries by 1500. In short, a voracious appetite for affordable animal protein compelled Europeans to scour the North Atlantic for cod.

By the early 1500s, Europeans swarmed the coast from Labrador to Maine, frequently interacting with Indians. Sometimes they targeted them. In 1501, the Portuguese captain Gaspar Corte-Real enslaved 57 Beothuk on Newfoundland. Twenty-four years later, Estevão Gomes took several dozen Abenaki captives to Spain after mapping Maine's coast. Relations between Europeans and Beothuk, Montagnais, Micmac, and Abenaki were usually guarded but peaceful. Indians soon became discerning consumers of imports. Giovanni da Verrazzano encountered a group of Abenaki in Maine in 1524. They refused to allow his men to land and accepted only "knives, hooks for fishing, and sharp metal" for what they brought to barter. Opportunities for trade increased in the 1540s as cod fishing expanded and the French and Basques set up summer camps in Labrador, Newfoundland, and Nova Scotia to salt and dry cod.

Cod was the first American food to enter the daily lives of ordinary Europeans. It took them centuries to accept many foods indigenous to the Americas such as corn or

The depopulation of the Greater Antilles spurred a missionary-led campaign to end the worst abuses of the conquest. In 1511, the friar Antonio de Montesinos enraged Santo Domingo's elite by delivering a sermon in which he threatened that God would punish them for their cruelty toward Indians. In 1512, his efforts helped lead to the enactment of regulations to protect Indians. They went mostly unenforced in the potatoes, but they knew cod and had ventured across the Atlantic to catch it. Fishermen were the first Europeans to have regular and sustained contact with North American Indians. From such contact arose a transatlantic trade in animal skins based on Indian labor, one that became a mainstay of North America's economy for centuries. In the early 1600s, word that New England's coast teemed with cod spurred the English to colonize there.

- What prompted Europeans to cross the Atlantic in pursuit of cod?
- What impact did European fishermen's visits have on Indians? What impact did the cod that they caught have on Europe?

EARLY MODERN EUROPEANS FISHING AND PROCESSING COD, 1690s Just above the legend is a depiction of onshore drying, the most common method for preserving cod in the 1500s and the one that brought European fishermen into regular contact with Indians. Here also is shown the "green" or "wet" method of preserving cod on board ships that developed later.

Americas. A Montesinos disciple, **Bartolomé de las Casas**, a priest and former Cuban encomendero, was an even harsher critic of the abuse of Indians. He focused his ire on colonists and conquistadors, but never questioned Spain's right to rule in the Americas.

The decimation of the Taíno and missionaries' efforts to stem it facilitated the extension of African slavery and plantation agriculture to the Americas. The first shipment of enslaved Africans arrived in Española in 1502. Fourteen years later, las Casas proposed enslaved Africans as an alternative to Indian labor on humanitarian grounds, a position that he later bitterly regretted. That year, a colonist built Española's first functional mill to crush sugar cane, extract the juice, and boil it down to make sugar. During the 1520s, Española witnessed the first sugar boom in the Americas. At first, most who toiled in the cane fields were enslaved Indians, with artisans from the Canaries, Italy, and Portugal supervising the mills. By the late 1520s, enslaved Africans had mostly replaced Indians on plantations. As of 1540, 15,000 slaves had been sent to Española and the island had an African majority—some of whom had escaped slavery to found the first free black communities in the Americas. Española remained an important source of sugar to Europe until the 1580s, when sugar production boomed in Brazil.

The devastation of the Greater Antilles led conquistadors to look to the American mainland. The Caribbean served as the gateway for invasions of Central America, Mexico, and Florida. An expedition from Española seeking gold and slaves in Panama became the first group of Europeans to set eyes on the Pacific Ocean in 1513. Meanwhile, Juan Ponce de León, who led the conquest of Puerto Rico, made the first recorded European visit to Florida. Ais and Calusa Indians assumed that he led a group of slavers and repelled the expedition. In 1521, Ponce de León returned to conquer and colonize Florida. The Calusa again turned the invaders back. Ponce de León died in Cuba, wounded by a Calusa arrowhead. The Atlantic world, however, represented mainly by Europeans seeking fish, passages to Asia, Indians to enslave, and lands to conquer, had reached North America.

STUDY QUESTIONS FOR MAKING AN ATLANTIC WORLD, 1400–1513

1. What factors led to the creation of the eastern Atlantic world?
2. What were the consequences of the Spanish conquest and colonization of Española?

◼ THE ATLANTIC WORLD ENTERS NORTH AMERICA, 1513–1565

Knowledge that the Americas had wealthy indigenous empires and that the world's oceans are connected intensified European interest in North America. Mariners mapped the continent's coasts as Spanish-led expeditions invaded its interior in search of Indian empires to conquer and pillage. Europeans soon realized that there were few riches to be had easily in North America. Nevertheless, the continent became a stage for European imperial rivalries and religious conflicts that led the Spanish to establish the first colony in what would become the United States.

The Fall of Mexica

In September 1519, **Hernán Cortés**, leader of a Spanish expedition to Mexico, persuaded the leaders of Tlaxcala to join him against the Mexica. Scholars have long sought to explain how fewer than a thousand Spaniards could have toppled a mighty empire of millions. Most agree that technology played an indispensible role. But Cortés could not have prevailed without Indian allies such as Tlaxcalans or his translator and advisor **Malintzín**. The Spanish conquest of Mexico was also an Indian conquest of Mexica.

Cortés acquired Malintzín and 19 other enslaved women from the Chontal Maya in 1519. The Spanish baptized them, renamed them, and parceled them out to provide sexual services. Malintzín was a Nahua (speaker of Nahuatl, the language of the Mexica and millions of others in central Mexico) who probably grew up in a noble's household. Her knowledge of Nahua culture and politics helped to win allies against Mexica. Bernal Díaz, a soldier in Cortés's expedition, wrote of Malintzín: "After Our Lord God, it was she who caused New Spain (what the Spanish renamed Mexico after the conquest) to be won."

Malintzín knew that Mexica demands for tribute and captives had alienated many Nahua peoples, including Tlaxcalans. When the Spanish arrived, Tlaxcala clung to independence, surrounded by city-states allied with or subject to Mexica. One Tlaxcalan faction fought the Spanish and lost badly. Thereafter, Tlaxcalans presented themselves as Spain's most loyal allies. Several thousand escorted Cortés when he entered Tenochtitlán in 1519. They suffered the brunt of the casualties when Mexica reclaimed the city the following year. The Spanish found sanctuary in Tlaxcala and used it as a base to recruit more allies. In 1521, tens of thousands of Tlaxcalans, along with warriors from other Nahua city-states, joined 900 Spaniards in besieging Tenochtitlán and taking the city two months later.

Technology indeed played a key role in the conquest. Horses afforded the Spanish advantages in speed, mobility, and height. They proved especially effective when those who rode them wielded swords and wore armor. Nahua memories of the conquest stressed two forms of technology. One was metal, especially steel blades and armor. The other was the ability of the Spanish to summon help from lands overseas. Ironically, the Spanish maritime network benefitted Cortés even when his superiors did not intend it to. Cortés disobeyed the orders of the Spanish governor of Cuba when he chose to embark on the conquest of Mexica. In 1520, the governor sent Pánfilo de Narváez and several hundred men to force Cortés to surrender. Cortés persuaded most to defect by promising them a share of the spoils of Tenochtitlán. The Cuban governor's failed plan to control Cortes inadvertently helped him to succeed. When Narváez retreated to Cuba, having lost an eye in battle, the defectors reinforced Cortés's army. They also brought smallpox to Mexico. Lacking immunity to the virus, the people of Tenochtitlán were devastated by the disease.

The most important Nahua allies of the Spanish, Malintzín and Tlaxcalans, retained their ties to the conquerors after the fall of Tenochtitlán. Not long after the Mexica surrendered, Malintzín gave birth to Martín Cortés, Hernán's son. She later married another Spaniard, with whom she had a daughter, Maria. In 1535, Charles V granted Tlaxcala special rights as a reward for helping to conquer Tenochtitlán, Guatemala, and western Mexico. Tlaxcalans were to answer directly to Spanish monarchs and never be put under the authority of anyone else. They also continued to act as coconquerors of the Americas. Tlaxcalans claimed that they accompanied **Francisco de Coronado** to New Mexico in 1540 and participated in an aborted Spanish colony in southeastern North America in the early 1560s. Malintzín, Tlaxcalans, and other Indians were crucial in remaking Mexico into New Spain.

Efforts to convert Mexico's Indians into Christians also helped to create New Spain. Twelve **Franciscans** arrived in Mexico from Española in 1524. The friars followed strict vows of poverty and viewed Europe as corrupt and sinful. They saw in Mexico a chance to recreate the original Christian communities. Once they had preached the gospel in every language, "The Twelve" believed, Jesus would return to earth, determine who was saved and who was damned, and bring on the end of the world. The eagerness with which Indians sought baptism, sometimes by the thousands at a time, seemed to confirm their vision. To convert more Indians, Franciscans and other missionaries burned most of the histories that Nahuas and Maya had written before the conquest and had most of their temples demolished. Franciscans studied Indian languages and wrote detailed accounts of Indian cultures and histories in hopes of facilitating conversion of Indians. They developed a Romanized alphabet for Nahuatl that many Indians soon mastered. A monk, Peter of Ghent, helped to write the first instruction manual in Nahuatl. Another, Bernardino de Sahagún, in 1547 directed Nahuas to gather information about Mexico before and during the conquest. The result was the Florentine Codex. Compiled mainly from Nahua interviews, it is invaluable to scholars who study Mexico. Franciscans' zeal faded, partly because most Indian converts blended their beliefs and rituals with Christianity. Their successors looked for other Indians to convert. A few decades later, they believed that they had found them in Florida and New Mexico, where Franciscans followed the conversion strategies they had learned in Mexico.

The conquest of Mexico also triggered more Spanish invasions. In 1532, 160 men led by Francisco Pizarro intervened in a civil war over who should rule the Inca Empire based in modern-day Peru. The intruders took one claimant to the throne, Atahualpa, hostage and ransomed him for enough gold and treasure to fill the room in which they imprisoned him. Pizarro's men melted down the ornaments and artwork that they extorted into nearly 20 tons of gold and silver before murdering Atahualpa. The Spanish had decapitated the Inca Empire. It took 40 more years and the help of Indian allies to conquer it. From the Spanish perspective, Mexico and Peru yielded the best of treasures, precious metals. Mexico and Peru became the hubs of the Spanish empire and the main destinations for Spanish immigrants for centuries.

Invasions of North America and the Rise of Imperial Competition

Dreams of conquering wealthy Indian empires and of finding quicker routes to Asia lured Europeans to North America between the early 1520s and the early 1540s. Explorers in the service of Spain and France mapped the coasts. Spanish and French entrepreneurs tried to establish outposts in the Southeast and Northeast. Meanwhile, three Spanish-led expeditions invaded the interior. Indians rebuffed every incursion.

Europeans first charted the Gulf of Mexico and then began to map the eastern seaboard. Most sought a channel to the Pacific, a possible North American counterpart to the one that Ferdinand Magellan's fleet had used to pass through South America in 1520 and to circumnavigate the globe two years later, a journey that proved that the oceans are connected. Meanwhile, the small fleet of Juan Rodríguez Cabrillo, veteran of the conquests of Cuba and Mexico, hugged the California coast in the early 1540s (Map 1.7). The voyages exposed more Indians to Europeans, as traders or as captors, laying a foundation for more intensive migration and exchange. This contact also furnished Indians with information to resist European invasions.

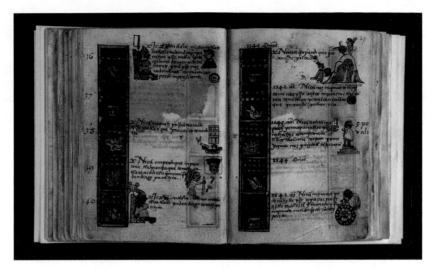

THE TENOCHCA JOURNEY NORTH   Over 1,000 Indians from Mexico accompanied Coronado to the Southwest, including many Tenochca. The entry for 1539, recorded as "39" and as the glyph "[year] 8 ácatl [reed]," reads, "[It was] at this time they departed for the new land; the Tenochca went." Note the figure with a walking stick beside the inscription.

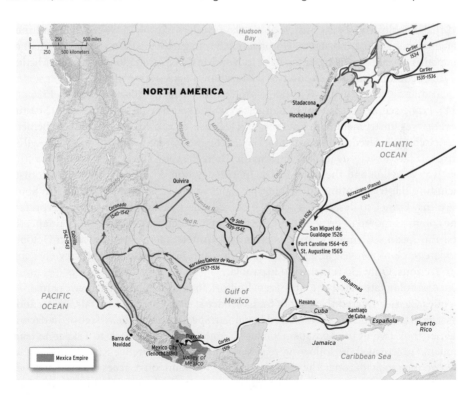

MAP 1.7 ▲ The Spanish and French Invade North America, 1519–1565 The conquest of Mexico sparked greater European interest in North America. Spanish incursions into the Southeast and Southwest sought riches and the expansion of Spain's empire. France saw North America as a good place to challenge Spanish power.

Meanwhile, three groups of conquistadors pushed into the Southeast and Southwest. The leader of the first, Pánfilo de Narváez, lost Mexico to Cortés in 1520. Hernando de Soto, who commanded the second, was an officer to Pizarro. His incursion into the Southeast was described at the beginning of this chapter. Francisco de Coronado headed the third expedition, which followed a model established by the conquest of Mexico. Most of the nearly 2,000 men whom Coronado led into the Southwest and onto the Great Plains were Mexican Indians. None of the expeditions found riches or a powerful empire. Indians did not ally en masse with the Spanish as Nahuas had against Mexica. Instead, the invaders quickly exhausted whatever welcome they received. Coronado's army took food from Pueblos who had little to spare. De Soto's men extorted huge quantities of corn and enslaved hundreds of Indians to shoulder their gear and booty as they plundered the Southeast.

Indian resistance ensured that such incursions failed. News of the invaders traveled far and fast. Indians repeatedly deflected them, often toward their enemies, with tales that the gold and riches they sought were somewhere else. The greedy Spanish took the bait and invariably got lost, far from reinforcements. Indians controlled the flow of information, especially because the Spanish had to depend on Indian interpreters whose loyalty they often doubted. Coronado's men met an enslaved Indian whom they called El Turco (The Turk) at Pecos Pueblo. He spoke Nahuatl (as did many Indians who marched with Coronado) and a Plains Indian sign language. El Turco promised to lead the expedition to Quivira, a town on the Great Plains, where the Spanish would find what they wanted. Quivira turned out to be a modest Wichita village. El Turco admitted that Pueblos had asked him to guide the invaders to a place where they and their horses would get lost and starve. Coronado had him garroted. The expedition, adrift on the plains, spent months trudging back to New Mexico. Coronado retreated to Mexico, leaving behind some Indians and two friars whom Pueblos soon killed.

Indians also scuttled two initiatives to colonize North America between 1526 and 1543. Francisco de Chicora, an Indian seized on the southeast Atlantic coast by Spanish slavers, was instrumental in the rise and demise of the first European settlement. Francisco took revenge on his captors by accompanying Nicolás Vázquez de Ayllón, Española lawyer and sugar planter, to Spain. There, he spun stories of his homeland that captivated Ayllón and the royal court. In 1526, Ayllón, Francisco, and 600 colonists, including the friar Antonio de Montesinos and some African slaves, landed in South Carolina. Francisco deserted, as did the other Indians Ayllón brought as interpreters. The colonists moved to present-day Georgia and founded **San Miguel de Gualdape**, the first European settlement in today's mainland United States. They arrived in October, too late to plant. Disease and cold killed Ayllón and many others as the survivors split into factions. Only 150 returned to Española.

A similar fate befell the first French effort to colonize North America. In 1534, **Jacques Cartier** entered the Gulf of St. Lawrence seeking precious metals, gems, and a passage to the Pacific. He encountered Iroquoian speakers from the village of Stadacona. Cartier took two of the Indians, Domagaya and Taignoagny, back to France to learn French. He returned the following year, sailed up the St. Lawrence River, and returned the two men to Stadacona. The villagers, hoping to monopolize access to French goods, tried to dissuade Cartier from proceeding upriver. Cartier ignored them and proceeded to Hochelaga, a village on the site of present-day Montreal. Iced in until April 1536, several French died of scurvy before Domagaya showed them how to brew a tea from cedar bark and needles that contained the vitamin C that they needed. Five years later, Cartier led colonists to Canada, where they erected a fort. By 1543, the French left after suffering harsh winters and two more bouts with scurvy. It added insult to injury that samples that Cartier had carried to France and touted as gold and diamonds turned out to be worthless. "This is a Canadian diamond" soon became a French expression to describe something without value.

Indians turned back European invasions at a profound cost. The French returned to Stadacona and Hochelaga in the late 1500s to find them abandoned. Disease and warfare had forced their residents to flee. De Soto's expedition accelerated the decline of Mississippian chiefdoms. Spaniards returned to the Southeast interior in the 1560s to find most towns deserted. Historians debate why this happened. Some contend that de Soto's army, especially the pigs that they brought along to eat, spread diseases that killed thousands. Others argue that the invasion disrupted Indian societies by slaughtering thousands, causing food shortages that were exacerbated by a cooling climate, and undermining the chiefs' authority. By the early 1700s, only the Natchez followed Mississippian ways closely. Other descendants of the peoples whom de Soto encountered would in time become Choctaw, Chickasaw, and Creek.

Religious Reformation, Imperial Rivalries, and Piracy

In the 1550s, European rivalries in the Americas became entrenched in religious conflict. It began in 1517 when a monk named **Martin Luther** nailed his *Ninety-five Theses* to the door of a church in Germany. He challenged the propriety and ability of church officials to confer forgiveness of sins and salvation on others. Only personal faith, Luther argued, could save one's soul. Those who concurred came to be known as Protestants for their protests against the Catholic Church's authority.

Protestantism was part of a broader reform movement that swept Christianity in western Europe in the 1500s. All reformers, Protestant or Catholic, held that church members should be more pious and know basic Christian doctrine. They agreed that Christians should reject folk beliefs that reformers considered pagan superstition or even satanic. Most demanded that government enforce religious conformity. Protestants denied the authority of the pope and the Catholic Church on the grounds that both were corrupt and violated God's will. They believed that the Bible should be accorded more authority and that its verses should be made more accessible by translating them from Latin into languages such as English or German. Defying Catholic doctrine, Luther asserted that faith mattered more than deeds for salvation. This left ample room for Protestants to disagree. They differed, sometimes violently, on matters such as infant baptism; the degree to which they should reject Catholic ritual, iconography, and theology; how they should govern their churches; and what was the proper relationship between church and state.

Religious groups that arose during the western European reformation played a key role in conflicts over the Americas. One was the Catholic Reformation, which created new organizations to win converts, renewed insistence on religious orthodoxy, and bolstered Spanish determination to uphold Catholicism. In 1534, Ignatius Loyola, a Basque priest, founded the **Society of Jesus**. One main goal of the Jesuits, as they were popularly known, was to make new converts overseas and in Europe. By 1550, they operated in India and Brazil. **Jesuits (Society of Jesus)** also sought to spread Catholic doctrine by founding and operating schools. Meanwhile, the Spanish proclaimed themselves Catholicism's staunchest defenders and Protestantism's worst enemy.

A second group that played a major role in the Americas were the Calvinists, products of the Protestant Reformation. In 1534, Parliament passed the **Act of Supremacy**,

TIMELINE PREHISTORY–1565

AMERICA	YEAR	THE WORLD
Nomadic hunters from East Asia enter Alaska and migrate south and east	c. 13,000–12,000 BCE	Global temperatures rise, causing rising sea levels and flooding that diminish resources but contribute to fishing in Japan and Southeast Asia
	10,000 BCE	Africa is largely populated by hunter-gatherers
Na-Dene speakers cross Bering Sea into Alaska	c. 6,000–8,000 BCE	Conditions become suitable for farming communities to grow and spread in Asia
Peoples in central Mexico begin to cultivate ancestor of corn	c. 7,000 BCE	Farming communities appear in Europe
Aleut and Inuit ancestors begin to arrive in Alaska	c. 3,000 BCE	Egyptian communities build irrigation channels centered around the Nile, leading to establishment of the First Dynasty
Southwestern peoples begin to cultivate corn	c. 1500 BCE	
Mississippian chiefdoms emerge in Mississippi River Valley and in Southeast Bow and arrow has spread throughout North America	c. 700 CE	
Anasazi culture peaks in Southwest	c. 900–1300	Medieval Warm Period occurs European economy grows, thanks to increased population, monetarization, and developing markets
Cahokia reaches its zenith	c. 1100–1200	
Drought plagues Indian peoples in Mississippi Valley, Plains, and Southwest	c. 1200–1300	Mongol Empire, founded by Temujin, expands westward
Na-Dene–speaking ancestors of Navajos and Apaches arrive in Southwest	c. 1200–1400	
Drought and raids compel Anasazi to abandon towns in Southwest	c. 1300	
Cahokia abandoned	1300s	Plague peaks in Europe
Iroquois Great League of Peace and Huron Confederacy founded	c. 1400	
	1415–1469	Portuguese forces capture Ceuta in North Africa Portuguese mariners launch Atlantic slave trade Papal decrees authorize Portuguese conquests in Africa and Atlantic slave trade Marriage of Isabel and Ferdinand creates foundation for modern Spain
	1487	Bartolomeu Dias navigates past Cape of Good Hope
Jan Muslim forces surrender Granada, completing Iberian Christians' reconquest of the peninsula **Apr** Christopher Columbus contracts with Ferdinand and Isabel to sail west across Atlantic **Aug** Columbus's expedition departs Spain **Oct** Columbus's expedition makes landfall in Bahamas	1492	
Jan Columbus departs Española for Spain **Mar** Columbus returns to Spain **Nov** Columbus returns to Española and introduces cattle, pigs, and sugar cane to the Americas	1493	
	1494	Treaty of Tordesillas divides most of world into territories claimed by Spain or Portugal

Santo Domingo, first permanent European settlement in the Americas, founded on Española	**1496**	
Giovanni Caboto explores Newfoundland on behalf of England	**1497**	
	1498	Portuguese mariner Vasco da Gama arrives in India
Enslaved Africans arrive in Española European women arrive in Americas First shipment of cod from North America to Europe	**1502**	
	1508–1513	Spanish conquer Puerto Rico, Jamaica, and Cuba
Spanish slaving raids depopulate Bahamas and likely start targeting Florida	**1509–1513**	
Juan Ponce de León leads first recorded European visit to Florida	**1513**	
	1517	Martin Luther releases *Ninety-five Theses* against Church indulgences; Protestant Reformation begins
Dec First recorded smallpox epidemic reaches the Americas	**1518**	
	1519–1522	Voyage originally led by Ferdinand Magellan circumnavigates globe
Feb Spanish expedition led by Hernán Cortés reaches Yucatán Peninsula **Oct** Spanish-Nahua forces enter Tenochtitlán	**1519**	
Jul Spanish-Nahua forces conquer Tenochtitlán	**1521**	
First Franciscan missionaries arrive in Mexico	**1524**	
Spanish colonists found and abandon San Miguel de Gualdape in Georgia	**1526**	
Spanish expedition becomes first European group to enter interior of what is today the United States	**1528–1536**	
	1532	Spanish expedition launches conquest of Peru
Spanish expedition led by Hernando de Soto invades southeastern North America	**1539–1543**	
Spanish expedition invades southwestern North America and southern Great Plains	**1540–1542**	
Spanish expedition led by Juan Cabrillo explores California's coast	**1542–1543**	
	1540–1558	Spanish begin to exploit silver deposits in Mexico and Bolivia "Elizabethan Settlement" brings religious peace to England
French privateers and pirates step up attacks on Spanish shipping in Caribbean	**1550s to early 1560s**	
French attempt to establish colonies in southeastern North America	**1562–1565**	William Shakespeare born in England, 1564
Sep Spanish forces defeat French and found St. Augustine, FL	**1565**	

which abolished papal authority over England and made King **Henry VIII** head of the **Church of England**. Henry's Protestant daughter **Elizabeth I** established a religious moderation that satisfied most English, but alienated a minority who sought to purge England of all vestiges of Catholicism. Critics labeled these more extreme Protestants "puritans." **Puritans** followed the teachings of **John Calvin**, a theologian based in Geneva. He argued that God had already determined who would be saved or damned. People might recognize God's elect by their professions of faith that God had saved them and by their conduct. Calvin thought that a body composed of ministers and elders should oversee church affairs and that local officials should uphold religious orthodoxy. By 1560, **Calvinism** had spread to England, Scotland, the Netherlands, Germany, and France, where its followers were known as **Huguenots**.

Although both Catholic, France and Spain fought a series of wars starting in the 1520s. French kings authorized private vessels to seize Spanish ships and sell their cargoes. Such **privateers**, many of them Huguenots, began to prowl the Caribbean in the 1530s, capturing ships laden with gold and silver and raiding Spanish settlements. When peace came, some privateers continued to operate without official license as corsairs or pirates. Spain responded in the 1540s by starting to provide military escorts for vessels traveling to and from the Caribbean. The toll on Spanish America and on Spain's coffers was immense. Between 1556 and 1561, French privateers and pirates made off with more than half of the royal revenues from Spanish America.

As Huguenots attacked Spanish shipping, bloodier religious violence in France encouraged them to seek refuge. Admiral Gaspard de Coligny, a Huguenot who financed privateers, directed the founding of a colony in Brazil in 1555. Factionalism and poor relations with Indians sapped the outpost, located near today's Rio de Janeiro. The Portuguese destroyed it five years later. Florida seemed a good alternative. It was relatively safe and most Spain-bound ships rode the Florida Current up the peninsula's coast. Florida could be an ideal base for French who sought to get rich and wound Catholicism's most militant champion.

The Founding of Florida

By the early 1560s winds, currents, shoals, religion, and piracy had made the Florida peninsula a global crossroads. Florida Indians had endured countless Spanish slaving raids and four Spanish colonization ventures. Ais and Calusa Indians had also absorbed hundreds of people who were left behind or whose ships had run aground or sunk and salvaged the wrecks, trading the gold and other items that they recovered with other Indians. Soon Florida became the first European battleground for North America and the first permanent European outpost in the mainland United States.

In 1562, the French Admiral Coligny sent Huguenot captain Jean Ribault and 150 men, mostly Huguenots, to North America to establish a colony. Ribault quickly returned to France, where a religious war had just erupted. He fled to England, where he proposed a joint Anglo-French venture to found a Protestant colony in Florida. The men Ribault left behind built a fort in present-day South Carolina. They soon alienated their Guale hosts and most abandoned the colony. In 1564, another Huguenot fleet under the command of René de Laudonnière arrived with 300 colonists, including Jacques Le Moyne, hired to paint illustrations of Florida to promote the colony in France. They erected Fort Caroline near present-day Jacksonville. The Saturiwa welcomed them until the French began to demand more food than they were able or willing to provide. Colonists saw that Saturiwas had silver and gold, which suggested that there were mines inland.

Many left to find them, unaware that the precious metals had come from shipwrecks. Meanwhile, other French commandeered vessels and sailed off to prey on Spanish shipping. Fort Caroline teetered on the brink of collapse when John Hawkins, an English pirate, slave trader, and smuggler, showed up in 1565 with provisions and a boat. Ribault's fleet brought reinforcements a few weeks later.

The Spanish monitored developments in Florida. Pedro Menéndez de Avilés, who had escorted several fleets across the Atlantic, battled French privateers and corsairs, and knew eastern North America's coastline well, thought that the future of the Spanish Empire hung in the balance. If the French had a base in Florida, Menéndez argued, pirates could attack the Spanish at will. Worse, Menéndez warned **Philip II**, French colonists might forge alliances with Florida Indians and convince African slaves in Cuba and Española to rebel. Philip appointed Menéndez governor of Florida and subsidized his expedition of 800 soldiers, mariners, and colonists.

They landed near a Timucuan village on the feast-day of Saint Augustine. Seloy, the village chief, permitted them to found **St. Augustine**, calculating that the Spanish were a better risk than the French. Over the next three months, the Spanish seized Fort Caroline and found most of the members of Ribault's fleet. Menéndez executed most of the French on grounds that they were pirates and Protestant heretics. He spared women, children, and Catholics. Laudonnière and Le Moyne escaped. In the 1580s, each published an account that perpetuated the myth that eastern North America contained precious metals, animating English readers who dreamed of riches like those the Spanish enjoyed.

The founding of St. Augustine signaled that Europeans and Africans were in North America to stay. The colonial history of what would become the mainland United States had begun, more than 70 years after Spaniards and Taínos first met in the Bahamas.

STUDY QUESTIONS FOR THE ATLANTIC WORLD ENTERS NORTH AMERICA, 1513–1565

1. What explains the conquest of Mexica?
2. Europeans became very interested in North America in the 1520s and lost interest two decades later. Why?
3. How did religious changes in Europe and piracy lead to the founding of St. Augustine?

Summary

- By 1500, Indians in North America had settled the continent, transformed its landscape, and created hundreds of diverse societies capable of adapting to political, social, and environmental change.
- In the 1400s, Europeans and Africans created networks that accelerated the flow of people, goods, and ideas between them and enabled Europeans to colonize the Caribbean and establish a foothold in the Americas by the 1510s.
- In the 1520s, new conquests and new knowledge spurred Europeans to explore North America's coasts and invade its interior, efforts that Indians successfully resisted until the 1560s when imperial rivalries and religious conflicts led Spain to begin colonizing Florida.

Key Terms and People

Reviewing Chapter 1

1. In what ways did environmental changes shape Indian life before 1565?
2. Europeans had conquered Mexico, Central America, and much of South America by 1565. But they had conquered none of North America north of Mexico. Why?
3. "A whole chapter devoted to events before 1565 in a U.S. history textbook! What for? It was so long ago and nothing much happened." Please take issue with this statement, using specific examples from this chapter.

Further Reading

Abulafia, David. *The Discovery of Man: Atlantic Encounters in the Age of Columbus.* New Haven and London: Yale University Press, 2008. An excellent synthesis that places the European "discovery" of the Americas within the context of the formation of the Atlantic world.

Fagan, Brian. *Fish on Friday: Feasting, Fasting, and the Discovery of the New World.* New York: Basic Books, 2006. Ties growing European demand for fish to religious and political changes in Europe and presents fishing as key to European expansion across the North Atlantic and into North America.

Northrup, David. *Africa's Discovery of Europe, 1450–1850.* New York: Oxford University Press, 2002. A concise overview of relations between Europeans and Africans that emphasizes African perspectives and motives.

Pauketat, Timothy R. *Cahokia: Ancient America's Great City on the Mississippi.* New York: Viking, 2009. Brings together the latest historical and archeological scholarship on the premiere example of a Mississippian chiefdom in one compact and readable package.

Reséndez, Andrés. *A Land So Strange: The Epic Journey of Cabeza de Vaca: The Extraordinary Tale of a Shipwrecked Spaniard Who Walked across America in the Sixteenth Century.* New York: Basic Books, 2007. A beautifully written account of Cabeza de Vaca's journey that strives to capture Indian as well as Spanish perspectives on a North America that was about to change drastically as a result of Spanish incursions.

Townsend, Camilla. *Malintizin's Choices: An Indian Woman in the Conquest of Mexico.* Albuquerque: University of New Mexico Press, 2006. A sensitive account of Malintzín and her world that explains how and why so many Nahuas chose to join Cortés in attacking Mexica, an act that enabled the Spanish to conquer Mexico.

America In The World
PEOPLE, GOODS, IDEAS AND PRACTICES

CHAPTER 1: North America Encounters the Atlantic World, Prehistory–1565

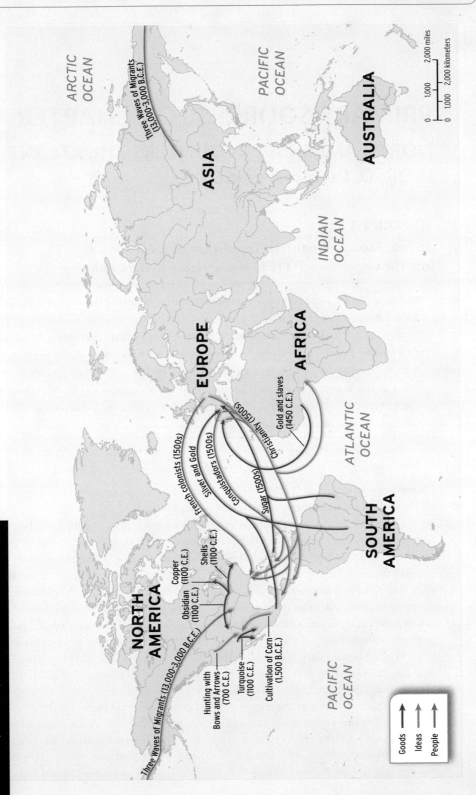

PRIMARY SOURCES FOR CHAPTER 1

NORTH AMERICA ENCOUNTERS THE ATLANTIC WORLD, Prehistory–1565

SOURCE 1.1

Acoma, Excerpts from "The Emergence of the Acoma into the Upper World" (1930 and undated oral traditions)

Acoma, a Keresan-speaking town in New Mexico, is one of the oldest continuously settled areas of what is today the United States. What follows are excerpts from a modern version of an Acoma creation story by Richard Erdoes and Alonso Ortiz, based on a legend that C. Daryll Forde reported in 1930 and a number of oral accounts. The work focuses on two sisters, Ia'tik ("bringing to life") and Nao'tsiti ("more of everything in the basket"), who were born and raised underground before ascending to the surface bearing baskets that contained images of the plants and animals that they were to bring to life.

Source: Carla Mumford, ed., *Early American Writings* (New York: Oxford University Press, 2002), 18–22.

Emergence into the Upper World

. . . They prayed and sang the creation song, and for the first time they asked Tsitctinako why they had been created. The spirit replied, "It was not I but your father, Utc'tsiti, who made you. He made the world, the sun, the sky, and many other things, but he is not yet satisfied. For this reason he has made you in his image. You will rule over the world and create the things he has given you in the baskets."

. . . When it became dark at the end of the first day, the sisters were frightened. They thought that Tsitctinako had betrayed them, but she explained, "This is the way it will always be. The sun will go down and a new sun will come up in the east tomorrow. Rest and sleep while it is dark." So the sisters slept, and the next day the sun rose. Happy to feel its warmth, they prayed to it as they had been taught. . . .

The sun was too bright for Ia'tik; it hurt her eyes. She tilted her head sideways so that her hair hung as a sunscreen, producing a reddish shade on her face. "The sun has not appeared for you," Tsitctinako observed. "See how it shines on Nao'tsiti, and how white she looks." Hastily Ia'tik also bared her face to the sun. But it did not make her as white as Nao'tsiti, and Ia'tik's mind was slowed down, while Nao'tsiti's was made quick. Even so, both always remembered to do everything Tsitctinako taught them.

"From now on," Tsitctinako told the sisters, "you will rule in every direction, north, west, south, and east. Bring everything in your baskets to life for Utc'tsiti has created you to help him complete the world. Now is the time to plant the seeds."

So far the sisters had not eaten food, and they did not understand what the seeds in their baskets were for. "First plant the corn, and when it grows, it will produce a part that you can eat," Tsitctinako said. Highly interested, the two women watched the growing corn every day. The spirit showed them where the pollen formed so that they could continue to offer pollen and cornmeal every morning to the sun. And they always did, though sometimes Nao'tsiti was a little lazy.

After a while the corn turned hard and ripe. Ia'tik carefully picked two ears without hurting the plant; Nao'tsiti yanked two off, and Ia'tik told her to handle it more gently. Tsitctinako had said that the corn must be cooked, but the sisters did not understand what "cooked" meant until a red light dropped from the sky that evening. Explaining that it was fire, the spirit taught them to scoop some of the flames up on a flat rock and feed them with branches from the pine tree.

Following Tsitctinako's directions, they roasted the corn and seasoned it with salt from their baskets. Nao'tsiti grabbed some and ate it, exclaiming how good it was. Then she gave a piece to Ia'tik, and so it was that the two women had their first meal. "You have been fasting for a long time, and your father has nourished you," the spirit told them. "Now you will eat in order to live."

The sisters learned to give life to their salt by praying to the earth, whereupon salt appeared in each of the four directions. Then Tsitctinako taught them their first song for creating an animal—a mouse. When they had sung it, they said, "Come to life, mouse," and their mouse image breathed. "Go and increase," they told it, and it ran away and soon bred many offspring. Tsitctinako showed them how to take one back, kill it, and roast it with the corn and salt. They prayed to their father and offered him little pieces of the meal before they ate. There was not much food on the mouse, but they thought it was good.

Looking into their baskets for larger animals to eat, the women found images of a rat, a mole, and a prairie dog. "Before you give life to them," Tsitctinako said, "you must plant grass for their food." The sisters took grass seed and scattered it north, west, south, and east—and grass immediately covered the ground. Then they gave life to the animals, telling each its name as it began to breathe. Before commanding them to run away and increase, they told the three creatures to live in the ground, because there was no shade on earth.

"Now we are going to make the mountains," Tsitctinako said, and showed them how to throw a certain stone from the basket toward the north while speaking certain words. There a large mountain arose. They did the same in the other directions, and mountains appeared all around them. "Now that you have the mountains," the spirit said, "you must clothe them with growing things." From the trees they had planted underground the sisters took seeds, which they scattered in all the directions. "These will be tall trees," Tsitctinako said, "and large enough to form the logs you will use to build houses."

There were many seeds left in their baskets. The women planted the food-yielding trees—piñon, cedar, oak, and walnut—with the prayer, "Grow on this mountain and yield fruit for food. Your places are in the mountains. You will grow and be useful." They planted other seeds, such as pumpkin, squash, and beans, that Tsitctinako said would be important to them. As these crops ripened, she showed them which parts to eat.

The sisters too were growing, and they needed more food. They began to bring the larger animals to life: first rabbits, jackrabbits, antelope, and water deer; then deer, elk, mountain sheep, and buffalo. They told the buffalo to live in the plains, the elk and deer in the mountains, and the sheep on the very high mountain slopes. They ate their meat and enjoyed the new tastes, and always they prayed to their father before they began a meal.

The sisters made mountain lions, wolves, wildcats, and bears—strong beasts that hunted the same game the humans used. They made birds—eagles and hawks, which hunted small game, and little birds whose bright colors beautified the country. They made the wild turkey and told it not to fly. They told the smaller birds to eat various seeds on the mountains and plains.

Tsitctinako pointed out that there were still fish, snakes, and turtles to be created, and the sisters gave life to all these and tried them for food. They found that some were good to eat and others were not, but whenever they ate they prayed first to their father. So it happened that many animals came alive in the world.

. . . Both sisters were now having selfish thoughts. Nao'tsiti was full of plans to outwit Ia'tik, but Ia'tik watched her and anticipated everything. Nao'tsiti saw that Ia'tik was not happy; Ia'tik noticed that Nao'tsiti wandered off alone.

Tsitctinako had told them that their father forbade them to think about having children. She promised that other humans would be born to them at the appropriate time. But now Nao'tsiti met a snake who said, "Why are you sad? If you bore a child in your likeness, you wouldn't have to be lonely just because you and your sister don't get along."

"What can I do?" Nao'tsiti asked.

"Go to the rainbow; he will show you."

Soon afterward Nao'tsiti was sitting alone on a rock when it rained. It was so hot that the rain cracked on the ground, and she lay on her back to receive the drops. As the water dripped into her, the rainbow did his work and she conceived without knowing it. Ia'tik

noticed that her sister was growing very fat, and after a time Nao'tsiti bore two children, both boys.

Very angry, Tsitctinako came to them. "Why have you disobeyed your father?" she said. "For your sin, he is taking me away. You are alone now."

Tsitctinako left them, but instead of feeling sorry, the two sisters found that they were happier. It turned out that Nao'tsiti disliked one of her children, so Ia'tik took him and brought him up. The two women still did not get along, but they were so busy with the children that it hardly mattered.

When the children were almost grown, Nao'tsiti said to her sister, "We aren't really happy together. Let's divide what remains in our baskets and separate. I still have many things, though they require a lot of work." Nao'tsiti pulled out sheep and cows, seeds for wheat and vegetables, and many metals. But Ia'tik refused them, saying they would be too difficult to take care of. Nao'tsiti looked again in her basket and found something written. She offered it, but Ia'tik did not want the gift of writing either. "You should have taken some of the things I offered," Nao'tsiti said. "In a long time we will meet again, and then you will desire my possessions. We'll still be sisters, but I'll have the better of you again."

Taking the boy she had brought up, Nao'tsiti disappeared into the east. Ia'tik said to the other boy, "We will continue to live here with everything our father has given us." The years passed, and Tia'muni, as she called him, grew up to become her husband. Ia'tik bore him a girl, who was entered into the clan of her sister, the Sun clan. After the fourth day of the baby's birth, Ia'tik put some pollen and sacred cornmeal into its hands and took it to pray to the sun. And with the many children that Ia'tik bore afterwards, she followed this same ritual that she herself had been taught when she came up into the light. . . .

WORKING WITH SOURCES

1. Acoma's extended kinship system is matrilineal, meaning that one inherits one's status from one's mother. In what ways does this story demonstrate Acoman society's matrilineal nature?

2. In what ways does this creation story reflect and explain the Acomans' encounter with Europeans and the goods and ideas that they brought?

SOURCE 1.2

Letters from Afonso, King of Kongo, to João Iii, King of Portugal (1526)

The Catholic convert Afonso I assumed the throne of Kongo with Portuguese support in 1506 and ruled until 1543. Unfortunately, by the 1520s Kongo had little to pay for the imports that flooded the kingdom or provide for the Portuguese craftsmen, missionaries, arms specialists, and teachers whom Afonso invited—except enslaved captives, most of whom were shipped to Portuguese sugar plantations on the island of São Tomé, located off the coast of Africa. The excerpted letters that follow, originally written in Portuguese in 1526, are among the few surviving documents written by an African during the 16th century. Basil Davidson translated them from transcripts of the original letters printed in *História do Congo: Obra Posthuma do Visconde de Paiva Manso* (Lisbon, 1877).

Source: Basil Davidson, *The African Past: Chronicles from Antiquity to Modern Times* (Boston: Little, Brown, 1964), 191–93. Davidson translated the letters from *História do Congo: Obra Posthuma do Visconde de Paiva Manso* (Lisbon, 1877).

[1526] Sir, Your Highness [of Portugal] should know how our Kingdom is being lost in so many ways that it is convenient to provide for the necessary remedy, since this is caused by the excessive freedom given by your factors and officials to the men and merchants who are allowed to come to this Kingdom to set up shops with goods and many things which have been prohibited by us, and which they spread throughout our Kingdoms and Domains in such an abundance that many of our vassals, whom we had in obedience, do not comply because they have the things in greater abundance than we ourselves; and it was with these things that we had them content and subjected under our vassalage and jurisdiction, so it is doing a great harm not only to the service of God, but the security and peace of our Kingdoms and State as well.

And we cannot reckon how great the damage is, since the mentioned merchants are taking every day our natives, sons of the land and the sons of our noblemen and vassals and our relatives, because the thieves and men of bad conscience grab them wishing to have the things and wares of this Kingdom which they are ambitious of; they grab them and get them to be sold; and so great, Sir, is the corruption and licentiousness that our country is being completely depopulated, and Your Highness should not agree with this nor accept it as in your service. And to avoid it we need from those [your] Kingdoms no more than some priests and a few people to teach in schools, and no other goods except wine and flour for the holy sacrament. That is why we beg of Your Highness to help and assist us in this matter, commanding your factors that they should not send here either merchants or wares, because it is *our will that in these Kingdoms there should not be any trade of slaves nor outlet for them*.[1] Concerning what is referred above, again we beg of Your Highness to agree with it, since otherwise we cannot remedy such an obvious damage. Pray Our Lord in His mercy to have Your Highness under His guard and let you do for ever the things of His service. I kiss your hands many times.

At our town of Congo, written on the sixth day of July. João Teixeira[2] did it in 1526. The King. Dom Afonso

[*On the back of this letter the following can be read:* To the most powerful and excellent prince Dom João, King our Brother.]

The Origins of Slaving

[1526] Moreover, Sir, in our Kingdoms there is another great inconvenience which is of little service to God, and this is that many of our people [*naturaes*], keenly desirous as they are of the wares and things of your Kingdoms, which are brought here by your people, and in order to satisfy their voracious appetite, seize many of our people, freed and exempt men;

and very often it happens that they kidnap even noblemen and the sons of noblemen, and our relatives, and take them to be sold to the white men who are in our Kingdoms; and for this purpose they have concealed them; and others are brought during the night so that they might not be recognized.

And as soon as they are taken by the white men they are immediately ironed and branded with fire, and when they are carried to be embarked, if they are caught by our guards' men the whites allege that they have bought them but they cannot say from whom, so that it is our duty to do justice and to restore to the freemen their freedom, but it cannot be done if your subjects feel offended, as they claim to be.

And to avoid such a great evil we passed a law so that any white man living in our Kingdoms and wanting to purchase goods in any way should first inform three of our noblemen and officials of our court whom we rely upon in this matter, and these are Dom Pedro Manipanza and Dom Manuel Manissaba, our chief usher, and Gonçalo Pires our chief freighter, who should investigate if the mentioned goods are captives or free men, and if cleared by them there will be no further doubt nor embargo for them to be taken and embarked. But if the white men do not comply with it they will lose the aforementioned goods. And if we do them this favor and concession it is for the part Your Highness has in it, since we know that it is in your service too that these goods are taken from our Kingdom, otherwise we should not consent to this. . . .

---

[1] Emphasis in the original.
[2] Probably, from the evidence, a Congolese secretary educated by Portuguese missionaries at Mbanza Congo (S. Salvador). See J. Cuvelier, *L'Ancien Royaume de Congo* (Brussels: Desclée de Brouwer, 1946), 294.

WORKING WITH SOURCES

1. In what terms does Afonso characterize the influence of imported goods on his subjects? What does he propose that João do to regulate trade with Kongo? What actions does Afonso take to restrict the impact of the slave trade on Kongo?

2. In what ways did Afonso's Christian beliefs shape the message that he sent to João and what he asked of the Portuguese king?

SOURCE 1.3
Pedro Menéndez de Áviles, Memorandum to Philip II, King of Spain (1565)

In early 1565, Philip II requested that Pedro Menéndez de Áviles report on his knowledge of French designs on eastern North America, the threat that such designs posed to the Spanish Empire, and what the Spanish might do to safeguard their claims to North America. Menéndez, a naval commander who had explored the Atlantic coast of North America and sailed with the royal fleet that protected Spanish shipping from French privateers, responded with the following message. Shortly after receipt of this memorandum, Philip authorized Menéndez to organize an invasion of Florida to oust the French and colonize "La Florida," the term that the Spanish then used to refer to areas along the Atlantic and Gulf coasts north of the Rio Grande.

Source: A. M. Brooks, ed., *The Unwritten History of Old St. Augustine*, trans. Annie Averette (St. Augustine: The Record Co., 1909[?]), 5–10.

To His Catholic Royal Majesty Pedro Menendez says: That what he sends your Majesty is what he declares to know of the coast and lands of Florida, and of the corsairs whom it is said have gone to populate it and seize the vessels coming from the Indias[3]—and the damage they may do, and the remedy to be used in cases where they should have settled. Give them no quarter, and appropriate the coast and lands so that they can be the more easily turned out—that your Majesty can send to spread the Gospel, prevent the damages that can be done the vessels coming from the Indias is as follows: If . . . the English, French or any other nation should feel disposed to go and settle any part of Florida, it would be very damaging to these kingdoms, because on said coast of Florida and in said strait of the Bahamas, they could settle and fortify themselves in such a way, that they could have galleons and vessels of war to capture the fleets and other private vessels that came from the Indias, and pass through there, as they would run great risk of being captured.

---

[3]The term that the Spanish used to refer to their overseas colonies, including those in the Americas.

Also, that if last summer the French and English went to Florida as we are certain they did, and should have settled and built a fort in any port, and summered there, giving notice to their home government as to how they are situated, and should they be supplied this summer before we can raid upon them, and turn them out, it would be very difficult to do so on account of the friendship formed by them with the natives who would help them in such a way as to cause serious difficulty, and even should we finally succeed the natives would remain our enemies, and this would be extremely disadvantageous. Should they be supplied this summer the merchantmen which we expect from the Indias would also run great risk of being captured. Also, that it would be very annoying to have the above mentioned or others settle in Florida. Considering the proximity of the Islands of Santo Domingo, Puerto Rico and Cuba, where there are such vast numbers of negroes and mulattoes of bad disposition, there being in each of these islands more than thirty negroes to each Christian. And it is a land in which this generation multiplies with great rapidity. In the power of the French and English, all these slaves would be freed, and to enjoy their freedom would help them even against their own masters and lords and there would be an uprising in the land, and with the help of the negroes it would be easy to capture us. As an example of this, take Jaques de Soria, France, which in the year fifty-three[4], with one boat of a hundred tons and eighty men, by simply freeing the negroes,

took and plundered the Islands of Margarite and Saint Martha, and burned Carthagena, plundered Santiago de Cuba and Havana, although at the time there were two hundred Spaniards there. They took the Fort with all it contained, and twelve pieces of bronze artillery and carried them all off. I consider these negroes a great obstacle to having the French or English settle in Florida or to have them so near, even though they should not be in favor with these two nations, there is danger of an uprising as there are so many cunning and sagacious ones who desire this liberty that I feel sure the design of those who should settle in Florida is to domineer over those islands, and stop the navigation with the Indias, which they can easily do by settling in said Florida. Also he says: That on account of these dangers and many others, it seems to him it would be to the service of God Our Lord, and your Majesty for the general good of your Kingdoms the Indies it would be well for your Majesty to try and domineer over these lands and coasts, which on account of their position, if other nations should go on settling and making friends with the Indians, it would be difficult to conquer them, especially if settled by French and English Lutherans[5], as they and the Indians having about the same laws, they would be friendly, and being near could rule and each year send out a thousand vessels to easily treat and contract with these lands which are said to be fertile and prolific for sugar plantations, which they so much need and are supplied from these Kingdoms. There might also be many cattle good for

---

[4]1553.

[5]Spaniards of the era often referred to Protestants as "Lutherans."

their tallow and wool and other necessities. What seems to him that your Majesty should do in the service of God and your Majesty's and for the salvation of so many souls, and the aggrandizement of your kingdoms and your royal estates, is as follows:

As there are neither French nor English nor any other nation to disturb them, that your Majesty should send five hundred persons, sailors, laborers, etc., and that among them should be one hundred master carpenters, blacksmiths, plasterers and builders of mud walls, all with their implements and appurtenances for every thing, with their arms of defense, such as arquebuses, cross-bows, etc. That among this number of five hundred people should be four Friars, four teachers and twelve Christian children, so that the principal Indians would send their children to school to learn to read and learn the doctrine of Christianity. There should be three surgeons who would go about in small boats, canoes or row boats with supplies for one year—go straight to Santa Elena and from there find all the paths, rivers and ports most suited and best, by land and water. See the condition of the land for planting and settle two or three towns in the best vicinity, build their fort, to be able to defend themselves against the Indians, that each of these forts should have artillery and ammunition. All this supply with the cost of the voyage will amount to eighty thousand ducats or more. There will be left vessels enough to carry a number of cattle. These must be sent from Spain, because in the Indias we could not find suitable vessels nor head workmen of the necessary qualifications and it could not give the desired results, besides the delay would cause much damage. It would be difficult to find the proper kind of people, and even if found the cost would be very much greater, as head workmen gain very large wages in those parts, as do also laborers and sailors. From Havana it would be still more impossible to bring them, as there are none to be obtained, and if they have to settle they must go a long way 'round, as they cannot enter the mouth of the Bahama Channel, it being as easy and quick to come from Spain as from Havana. . . .

Pedro Menendez

WORKING WITH SOURCES

1. On what grounds does Menéndez advocate that the Spanish conquer and colonize Florida? In what ways does Menéndez use the knowledge of North America and the Caribbean that he acquired through his travels around the Atlantic world to make his case?

2. What kind of relationship does Menéndez envision existing between Spanish colonists and Florida's Indians? In what ways does his memorial acknowledge Indian power in Florida?

SOURCE 1.4

Visual Document: Texas Fragment, "Arrival of Cortés and Malintzín in Atlihuetzyan" (1530s or 1540s)

Long before the Spanish arrived in Mexico, Nahuas (Nahuatl-speaking Indians) recorded or commemorated events and agreements by painting them in stylized ways. Shortly after central Mexico came under Spanish rule, Nahuas continued and

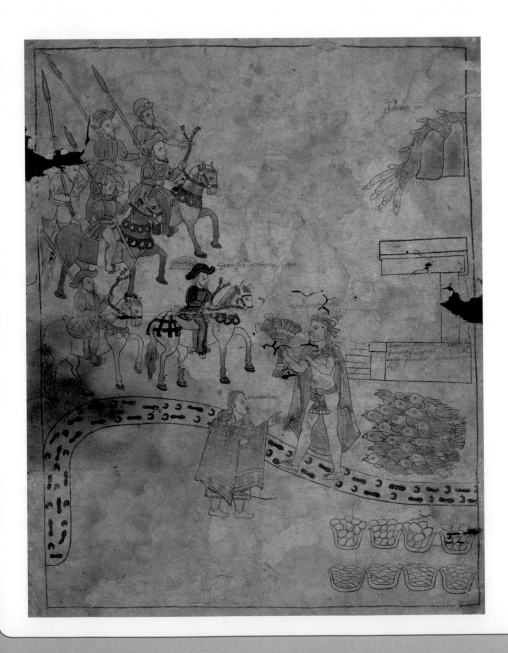

modified this tradition to provide their own perspective on their histories, including their memories of the Spanish conquest. Artists of Tlaxcala, one of Cortés's principal allies against the Mexica, created the painting featured below. It was probably completed in the 1530s or 1540s and depicts the arrival of Cortés, Malintzín (with her hand raised to indicate that she is speaking), and a party of Spanish soldiers on horseback to Atlihuetzyan in Tlaxcala. Tepolouatecatl, a noble member of Tlaxcalan leader Xicotencatl's family, greets the visitors and offers them birds, bread, and corn, all of which are intended as tribute.

Source: Courtesy of the Nettie Lee Benson Collection of the University of Texas Library.

WORKING WITH SOURCES

1. The road with footprints proceeding in one direction traditionally signified travel in such paintings. In what way did Tlaxcalan artists modify this sign to reflect the arrival of the Spanish?

2. Malintzín occupies a central place in this scene. Why?

3. The scene depicted here clashes with non-Tlaxcalan accounts, which indicate that many Tlaxcalan leaders decided to fight the invaders. Among the last holdouts against the Spanish was Xicotencatl's son. For what reasons did the Tlaxcalan artist(s) choose to portray the initial reception of the Spanish as peaceful?

Their greene

Corne newly sp

The place of Solemne prayer

Their sitting at meate

...ose wherin the Tombe of their Herounds standeth

SECOTON

A ceremony in their strange iesturs and son
aboute posts carued on

Colonists on the Margins

1565–1640

In 1616, the **Virginia Company of London** found itself in dire financial straits. Nine years had elapsed since **Jamestown's** founding and the firm had yet to turn a profit. Reports from Virginia of hard winters, starving colonists, and frequent hostilities with the Algonquian Indians of Tsenacommacah, the chiefdom that claimed the land on which the English were building Jamestown, scared off investors. The company badly needed good publicity, which was fortuitously provided by the visit of an Algonquian "princess," her English husband, their infant son, and an Indian priest to London.

The "princess" Matoaka was better known by one of her nicknames, **Pocahontas**, or "playful one." She was the daughter of **Powhatan**, the paramount chief of Tsenacommacah. Pocahontas had been baptized, a fact that the Virginia Company trumpeted to assure nervous English investors that it could convert Algonquians into Anglicized Christian subjects. The visit was important to the Virginia Company's well-being, so the hosts had every reason to make the Indians' stay in London as pleasant as possible.

Instead, the English deeply offended their Algonquian guests by repeatedly deviating from protocols that Algonquians normally followed with their allies. Pocahontas reprimanded **John Smith**, a former colonist who initiated relations between Jamestown and Tsenacommacah and who Pocahontas believed should have known better: "You did promise Powhatan what was yours should be his, and he the like to you." She addressed Smith as "father," using the language of kinship to indicate that they were allies and request his assistance. Pocahontas reminded Smith that he had called Powhatan "father, being in his land a stranger, and by the same reason so must I do you." For eastern Algonquians, fathers were

< Algonquian village of Secotan by John White.

not stern authority figures. Instead, uncles, especially maternal ones, were the male disciplinarians to children. Algonquian fathers behaved more like what the English would consider indulgent uncles. Uttamatomakkin, the Indian priest, exploded when Smith told him that he had just met **James I**, king of England and Scotland. Uttamatomakkin could not believe it. A paramount chief would have offered him a gift. James did not. "You gave Powhatan a white Dog, which Powhatan fed as himself," he scolded Smith, "but your King gave me nothing, and I am better than your white Dog."

The English had to obey their own social and cultural norms, especially in England. Smith, a commoner, could not allow a princess to call him "father." His English peers and social superiors would find that unseemly and presumptuous. Smith might have explained to Uttamatomakkin that a king outranked everyone in his realm. Subjects normally paid him tribute, and James certainly considered Pocahontas and Uttamatomakkin his subjects.

Still, the Virginia Company reaped good publicity from their visit. Pocahontas, however, fell ill, died, and was buried in England in 1617. Her husband **John Rolfe** returned to Virginia, leaving their son Thomas behind for his kin to raise and educate. Uttamatomakkin also sailed home to tell a grieving Powhatan what he had learned from his visit. Meanwhile, thousands of English poured into Tsenacommacah, most of them to burn the woods and plant tobacco amidst the ashes and charred stumps. Soon hundreds would die at the hands of Tsenacommacah warriors.

The first European settlers clung to the edge of an Indian continent. Their survival usually depended on how well they met Indian needs and heeded Indian ways. The Spanish created North America's first permanent European colonies by intimidating and converting Indians. The French also evangelized Indians, but emphasized cooperation and commerce rather than coercion. English and Dutch colonists expended far less effort on making Christians of Indians and far more on resettling their lands. The strategic alliances that colonists forged with Indians linked North American networks to those that extended across the Atlantic. By the early 1640s, Europeans' ability to draw on their overseas ties enabled their colonies to take root despite often fierce Indian resistance.

◼ CONQUEST BEGINS AND TRADE EXPANDS, 1565–1607

The conquest and colonization of what became the United States began as Latin America expanded north. Spanish soldiers and friars struggled to colonize Florida and expand Mexico by conquering New Mexico. An unlikely kingdom, England, emerged as Spain's main European rival in North America. Meanwhile, European fishermen flooded northeastern North America with goods that intensified competition among Indians and began to transform their cultures.

Spain Stakes Claim to Florida

After founding St. Augustine and defeating the French, Pedro Menéndez had an ambitious vision for Florida. The Spanish, supported by a network of coastal garrisons, could protect sea lanes and salvage shipwrecks more easily. The governor hoped that Indians, awed by Spanish might, would become allies and subjects. In 1566, Menéndez married a Calusa chief's sister. Baptized as Doña Antonia, she accompanied Menéndez to Havana. Jesuit missionaries arrived that same year to cement Hispanic-Indian alliances by converting Florida Indians and sending chiefs' sons to Havana to be schooled alongside sons of prominent Cuban colonists. Menéndez also planned a road between his capital, Santa Elena, founded in today's Georgia in 1566, and the mines of Zacatecas in Mexico so that the Spanish Empire could move silver overland and bypass the pirate-infested Caribbean.

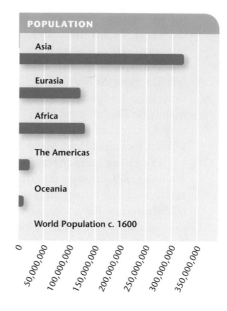

Little of his vision became reality. Menéndez ran out of money and lost interest in Florida once he became governor of Cuba in 1567. He had also badly underestimated the distance between Georgia and Mexico. Two expeditions headed west to launch his far-fetched plan. They built small garrisons along the way and returned to Santa Elena. Indians killed off or absorbed each.

Indian resistance and European attacks nearly finished off Florida too. Timucua and French soldiers teamed up to destroy one Spanish fort. Santa Elena and St. Augustine,

FRANCIS DRAKE SACKS ST. AUGUSTINE, 1586 War between Spain and England in the 1580s accelerated English attacks on Spanish-American colonies. St. Augustine, besieged by English forces, is at the upper left, while more English ships lurk in the Atlantic. Drake, then en route to Roanoke, had raided Santo Domingo and Cartagena before attacking St. Augustine.

the last outposts standing by 1574, barely weathered repeated Indian attacks. Thirteen years later, the Spanish abandoned Santa Elena and retreated to a St. Augustine that had just been destroyed by an English raid led by Francis Drake. Enslaved Africans owned by **Philip II**, king of Spain, assisted recovery efforts, which included construction of a stone fort like those the Spanish were building in their major Caribbean ports to protect them from their European foes. St. Augustine had but 500 residents in 1600 who subsisted mainly on food shipped from Havana. More than half were officers, soldiers, or mariners. Officers and imperial officials had Spanish wives. Soldiers and sailors wed Indian women, including Doña Maria Meléndez, a female chief.

Franciscan friars pursued Indian converts outside St. Augustine. They replaced the Jesuits in 1573, the same year that Philip II issued the **Royal Orders for New Discoveries**. He decreed that missionaries should play the principal role in exploring, pacifying, and colonizing new territories. Philip also mandated that baptized Indians should live on missions and be hispanized, which is, learn to speak Spanish, keep livestock, cultivate European crops, and use European tools to master European crafts. Franciscans began to intensify their efforts in 1595, focusing on Timucua and Guales along the Georgia coast.

Timucuans became indispensable Spanish allies. Guales rebelled. The Franciscans insisted that was because they had barred a chief's heir from having more than one wife, a traditional sign of his authority. Guales killed nearly all the friars before Spanish-Timucua raids compelled some chiefs to surrender in 1600. Within four years, the southernmost mission reopened. Guales soon paid tribute to the Spanish by sending corn and laborers to St. Augustine.

New Spain into the Southwest

As Florida's Indians held Spanish colonists at bay, Pueblo Indians in what is today New Mexico faced a series of Spanish-led invasions. Franciscans sought souls, while colonists drawn north from central Mexico by silver strikes in and around Zacatecas sought riches. In 1581, a small group of friars and soldiers arrived and renamed the region New Mexico. Pueblos soon killed the missionaries. Indians endured three more Spanish incursions before an expedition led by **Juan de Oñate** arrived in 1598.

Visions of riches and glory in Mexico motivated Oñate to conquer New Mexico. Pueblos were still nursing the wounds that they had endured from previous Spanish-led invasions, so they decided to receive Oñate peacefully.

New Mexico's conquerors won little glory or wealth, but they spilled plenty of Pueblo blood. Spanish soldiers, frustrated that New Mexico had few of the riches that Mexico did, plotted mutiny. Pueblos offered them scarce food and clothing as gifts. When the soldiers did not get what they wanted, they extorted, raped, and murdered. Acoma's residents fought back, killing eleven Spanish soldiers. Oñate's men slaughtered 800 Acomans, including 300 women and children. They enslaved 500 women and children. Every Acoman between 12 and 25 years old was sentenced to 20 years' servitude. Children under age 12 became servants to monasteries or Spanish households. Every Acoman man over age 25 had one foot cut off. Such brutality dissuaded most Pueblos from challenging Spanish authority for decades. In 1998, someone commemorated the conquest's 400th anniversary by severing the right foot from Oñate's statue in Santa Fé.

New Mexico served as a base for Spanish expeditions in the region. Oñate journeyed to the southern Great Plains and found little there that interested him. Three expeditions

INDIAN PICTOGRAPH OF SPANIARDS ON HORSEBACK Indians drew this image on the walls of Cañón del Muerto. Note how prominently the artist(s) displayed horses and the lances that their riders wielded. The figure in black with a white cross is probably a missionary.

searched for the Pacific. The last, in 1604–1605, found it by marching through Arizona and following the Colorado River to the Gulf of California.

Oñate wanted to reach the Pacific in part because the Spanish were considering a California outpost to facilitate trade with East Asia and ward off European rivals. In 1565, Spanish mariners discovered a route from the Philippines to Acapulco. The journey took four to five months, so mariners needed a port to stop for repairs and provisions. The Mexican-Filipino trade was lucrative. Mexican silver bought Chinese silks and porcelain in Manila. Francis Drake's raids along the Pacific coast in 1579 and the English capture of an Acapulco-bound ship off Baja California in 1587 stoked Spanish interest in California. Sebastián Vizcaíno explored its coast in 1602–1603, inadvertently sailed past San Francisco Bay, and concluded that Monterey Bay would best harbor a Spanish port. But New Spain's viceroy decided that a California base would lure English and French smugglers to a remote place that they would otherwise ignore. As a result, Spain showed little interest in California until the 1760s (Map 2.1).

Franciscan lobbying prevented Spain from abandoning New Mexico. Friars' enthusiastic accounts claimed that 7,000 Pueblos had already converted and that more sought baptism. New Mexico remained a poor remote satellite of Mexico that drew few Spanish immigrants. As in Florida, friars held most of the power as they dispersed to found missions among Indians.

England Enters Eastern North America

Three European powers contested Spanish claims to North America and the Caribbean during the last quarter of the 16th century: France, the Netherlands, and England.

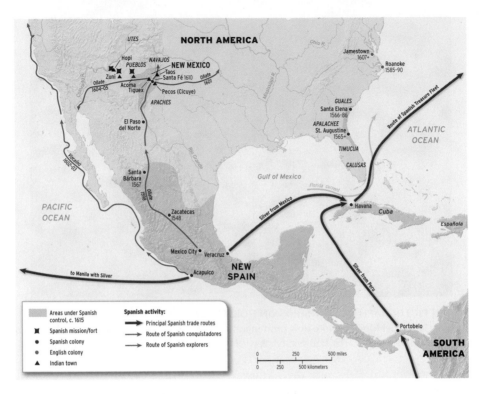

MAP 2.1 ▲ European Invasions of the Southwest and Southeast, 1565 to c. 1610
Florida and New Mexico were the first European outposts in North America. European colonization
of what is today the United States began from the Caribbean and Mexico and was oriented toward
those regions. Note the location of Roanoke, chosen largely to give English privateers better access
to Spanish shipping leaving the Caribbean and sailing up Florida's coast.

The French and Dutch were wealthier and better able to finance colonizing ventures
than the English but faced religious and political strife at home. Seven civil wars between Catholics and Huguenots (French Calvinist Protestants) convulsed France
between 1562 and 1580. France did not enjoy peace until 1598, when Henry IV became
king and granted limited toleration to Huguenots with the **Edict of Nantes**. The Dutch,
under direct Spanish rule since 1519, rebelled in the 1570s, an effort led by Calvinists.
The two sides did not negotiate a cease-fire until 1608.

By contrast, England enjoyed relative political stability that helped it to emerge
as Spain's main rival in the West Indies and North America. Elizabeth I's moderate
policies had ended domestic religious strife and enabled the English to focus on other
challenges. England's population nearly doubled from three million to around five million between 1500 and 1650, but its economy could not create enough jobs to keep pace.
To make matters worse, prominent landlords fenced off **commons** (lands previously
open to all residents) to graze sheep and grow grain. This accelerated the concentration
of land ownership, pushed those of more modest means off the land, and increased
unemployment.

Meanwhile, some English merchants pursued new markets by obtaining licenses for monopolies on commerce with Eastern Europe, the Mediterranean, or Asia. The Muscovy Company formed in 1555 to operate in Russia. Its success encouraged the creation of the Levant Company to trade with the Middle East in 1582 and the East India Company, chartered in 1600. These **joint-stock companies** offered a model for financing colonial ventures. Investors bought shares and hoped to earn dividends. Joint-stock companies later owned and directed English colonies in Virginia, Plymouth, and Massachusetts Bay. Many who invested in the Virginia Company also held shares in the East India Company and the Levant Company.

England's renewed interest in the Americas focused first on the Caribbean and on diverting the Spanish Empire's wealth into English hands. John Hawkins tried to enter the lucrative slave trade, dominated by Spanish merchants. He led three expeditions from West Africa to the Caribbean to smuggle enslaved Africans to Spanish colonists in the 1560s. The last ended in 1568 when Spanish vessels destroyed two of Hawkins's ships. The English largely abandoned the Atlantic slave trade until the 1640s and instead focused on seizing Spanish ships and raiding Spanish colonies. Francis Drake became famous in 1573 for capturing a Spanish silver fleet in Panama. Eight years later, Elizabeth knighted Drake after he raided Spanish ports in the Pacific and circumnavigated the globe. When England and Spain went to war in 1585, Elizabeth licensed privateers (privately owned armed ships) to attack Spanish vessels and divide the spoils. Over 200 English privateering vessels prowled the Caribbean between 1585 and 1603. Privateers boosted the English economy; the goods that they seized accounted for up to 10 percent of England's imports during the 1590s. After James I became king of England in 1603, he made peace with Spain and temporarily halted privateering.

Some English touted colonization as a way to oppose Spain and Catholicism and solve many of England's social and economic problems. In the 1570s, English forces conquered more of Catholic Ireland, which soon lured thousands of land-hungry English colonists and investors such as **Walter Raleigh** who hoped to profit from their labor. The translation and publication in 1583 of Bartolomé de las Casas's writings fueled belief in a "**Black Legend**" of the Spanish conquest in which Spaniards indiscriminately slaughtered Indians, tyrannized them, and imposed Catholic "superstition" on them. Raleigh, an explorer and confidant of Elizabeth, cited las Casas often and claimed that the English would deliver Indians from Spanish and Catholic "tyranny" and convert them into grateful subjects and Protestants.

Privateering and opposition to Spain led to England's first sustained attempt to colonize North America. Investors wanted a coastal base a safe distance from St. Augustine so that privateers could safely sail the Caribbean most of the year. To that end, Raleigh sent an expedition to present-day North Carolina in 1584. The explorers recommended Roanoke on the Outer Banks and brought home two Indian men, **Manteo** and Wanchese, to learn English. They taught the scientist **Thomas Harriot** to speak Carolina Algonquian. The following year, Raleigh sent a hundred men, including Harriot and the painter **John White**, who were to study the area and its peoples. The English stopped in Española to buy livestock and set sail for Roanoke. Their flagship ran aground and seawater ruined their food supply. The English pressed Roanoke Indians for food, but they had little to spare. Convinced that Roanokes would attack, the colonists killed Roanoke chief Wingina and stuck his head on a pole. Drake arrived in 1586, having just torched St. Augustine in hopes of preventing a Spanish attack on Roanoke. Panicked colonists swarmed aboard his ships. Drake made room for them by stranding hundreds of Africans and Indians he had picked up in the Caribbean.

Raleigh did not give up on the colony, sending a second group composed mostly of families in 1587. Elenor Dare, daughter of painter and governor John White, gave birth to Virginia, the first English child born in North America. Manteo accepted baptism and White named him lord of Roanoke. Envisioning that colonists would govern the area's Indians through Manteo, White returned to England. Harriot's report of his 1585 visit, illustrated with engravings of White's paintings, was published in 1588 to drum up support for the Roanoke colony in England. The report circulated widely. It profoundly shaped English views of Algonquians and of North America. War with Spain kept the English from returning to Roanoke until 1590. They found the colony abandoned and a post with the word "CROATOAN" (probably the name of the island where Manteo's people lived) carved into it. The "lost" colonists likely became Algonquian adoptees who lived on North Carolina's Outer Banks or moved north to Chesapeake Bay. Meanwhile, most English interest in colonization stayed focused on Ireland, which attracted far more English migrants than North America did until the 1640s.

Events at Roanoke and English interpretations of them established key patterns in English colonization of the Americas. The display of Wingina's severed head belied Raleigh's assertion that the English would be kinder and gentler colonists than the Spanish. But the English presentation of themselves as more humane than the Spanish took root. It still shapes how many in the United States view the nation's colonial past and distinguish it from Latin America's.

Imports and a Changing Indian Northeast

Long before St. Augustine's founding, Indians in eastern Canada had regular contact with Europeans fishing offshore for cod. By the 1530s, Europeans hunted whales, processing the carcasses onshore. By 1580, as many as 20,000 Europeans journeyed across the North Atlantic and back each year. More ships sailed between Europe and Canada than between Spain and its American colonies during the late 1500s. Europeans traded glass beads, metal tools, kettles, and woolen cloth to Indians for small quantities of furs. The imports circulated among Indians via established routes that stretched hundreds of miles inland.

In the early 1580s, French merchants began to specialize in acquiring beaver pelts from the St. Lawrence Valley. They sought to meet growing demand in Europe for felted beaver hats. Indian men were happy to bring more pelts; they found beaver less taxing to hunt than other fur-bearing animals. The **fur trade**, like the fishing and whaling industries that gave rise to it, ensured that the St. Lawrence River remained the main gateway for European goods into North America well into the 1600s (Map 2.2).

The imports initially reinforced traditional Indian beliefs and practices. Before 1600, relatively few Indians had steady access to such goods, so they seldom used or viewed them in ways that Europeans did. Instead, Indians incorporated imports into their world on their own terms. Most brass or copper kettles were broken apart and the pieces put to other uses. Many were reworked into arrowheads, whereas others became amulets that chiefs wore to display their connection to sources of such valued items. Copper and brass, along with iron goods and glass beads, accompanied prominent people to their graves, indicating the spiritual power that Indians believed infused such objects.

BEAVER HUNTING　This illustration shows the various ways that Indians hunted beaver and some of the animal's habits, such as how it constructs dams. Beaver pelts were New France's chief export. Trade in them was key to relations between European colonists, their descendants, and Indians in northern North America well into the 1800s.

MAP 2.2 ▲ Trade in the Indian Northeast, c. 1580–1607　The St. Lawrence River Valley and the Indian trade routes that ran through it helped to make the region the chief entry point for European goods into North America. The Huron Confederacy, located at the intersection of many trade routes, had a relatively easy time acquiring imports, while the Iroquois League's peoples, whose lands lay outside those routes, had far more difficulty.

Although Indians assimilated most new goods in traditional ways, trade with Europeans brought important changes. Susquehannocks moved south to the Lower Susquehanna Valley to escape Iroquois and be closer to goods that trickled north from Chesapeake Bay. The region's two main Iroquoian-speaking confederacies, Iroquois (Seneca, Cayuga, Onondaga, Oneida, and Mohawk) League and Huron, operated to secure better access to trade routes. By the 1570s, Mohawks and Oneidas were at war with Montagnais and Algonquians, who funneled imports inland. That gave Iroquois foes an advantage: better weapons. Brass arrowheads outperformed stone-tipped ones. They were lighter, easier to aim, and penetrated wooden armor. Iroquois warriors adapted as best they could by shedding their wooden armor and raiding in small parties to minimize casualties. But as late as 1610, Iroquois still fought with stone-tipped hatchets, spears, and arrowheads and found themselves on the losing end of a regional arms race.

By then, more Indians with direct and steady access to European goods used them as their manufacturers intended. The imports made life easier, especially for women. Steel axes simplified gathering firewood, and metal kettles were more durable and versatile than ceramic or wooden ones. Refashioning woolen cloth into traditionally styled garments took less work than it did to dress skins and furs.

Indians in the Northeast gradually became more dependent on such imports. By the early 1600s, Montagnais had stopped building birch bark canoes and instead bought French-made longboats. Micmacs, who lived too far north to grow corn or much else themselves, became so devoted to gathering beaver pelts that they required French imports to eat. Their situation was an extreme example of the future that awaited most Indians who ventured too far into the Atlantic marketplace.

STUDY QUESTIONS FOR CONQUEST BEGINS AND TRADE EXPANDS, 1565–1607

1. In what ways did the Spanish colonization of Florida and New Mexico differ? In what ways did Indian responses to Spanish colonization differ in Florida and New Mexico?

2. By what means and for what reasons did England become Spain's chief rival in North America?

3. What impact did the fur trade and trade goods have on Indians in the Northeast?

◼ EUROPEAN ISLANDS IN AN ALGONQUIAN OCEAN, 1607–1625

Algonquians from the St. Lawrence River to Chesapeake Bay cautiously welcomed the thousands of strangers who arrived between the 1600s and 1620s and began to occupy their lands. A minority of them spoke French or Dutch, came in small numbers to the lands of Algonquians, Montagnais, and Mahicans, and devoted themselves to trading with their neighbors. The vast majority of the foreigners spoke English and staked claim to large quantities of land, which they soon divided among themselves and began to farm. Most of these disembarked in Tsenacommacah along the estuaries of Chesapeake Bay. The rest landed in Massachusetts Bay in territory claimed by Wampanoags. All the newcomers depended on native-grown corn and knowledge to survive their first years in North America. They traded with Indians to make their colonies financially viable. But the English decided rather quickly that they needed the locals less than they needed their land. Their refusal to honor Indian ways led to wars with the Tsenacommacah and tension along the shores of Massachusetts Bay (Map 2.3).

MAP 2.3 ▲ European Islands in an Algonquian Ocean, 1607–1626 An Algonquian-speaking world surrounded the European outposts at Quebec, New Netherland, Plymouth, and Virginia; sustained them; and sometimes threatened them. Algonquian-made wampum enabled a regional trade that benefitted New Netherland and New England. Virginia's encroachments on Tsenacommacah, driven mainly by a tobacco boom, led to two bloody wars, one in 1622 and the other in the 1640s.

Tsenacommacah and Virginia

In May 1607, 144 English colonists founded Jamestown on a marshy triangle of land that jutted into the James River. The location offered protection from Indian land attacks and possible Spanish sea attacks. The Virginia Company of London's royal charter gave it exclusive rights to colonize from New England south to Virginia. Its directors and investors hoped to turn a quick profit. But the hardships of establishing a new colony and the lack of gold or anything else of value in the area dimmed English hopes. Hunger, disease, and cold claimed all but 38 Jamestown residents by the spring of 1608.

Peoples of Tsenacommacah watched warily as they tried to determine the strangers' motives. Tsenacommacah had expanded over the previous four decades under the leadership of Wahunsonacock. As Powhatan (paramount chief), he had used diplomacy, marriage, intimidation, and warfare to gain the allegiance of other Algonquian bands and collect tribute from them. By the time the English strangers arrived, Tsenacommacah included almost all Algonquians who lived in Virginia's tidewater region.

Powhatan decided to incorporate Jamestown into Tsenacommacah. In December 1607, warriors seized John Smith, one of the colony's leaders, and delivered him to Powhatan. Powhatan's nine-year-old daughter Pocahontas helped to stage Smith's mock execution. As most Americans know the story, Pocahontas demonstrated her love for Smith by throwing herself on top of him to save his life. Powhatan probably intended the event to symbolize the death of Smith's former identity and the Jamestown leader's rebirth as a chief who led another village that paid him tribute.

Smith either did not understand or refused to accept the role. Neither did his superiors in the Virginia Company, who believed that Tsenacommacah was subject to

INDENTURE OF RICHARD LOWTHER, 1627 By this indenture (contract), Lowther agreed to serve a Virginia plantation owner for four years, after which he was to receive 50 acres of land. Lowther differed from most English indentured servants who went to the Americas in that he signed his indenture, an indication that he was probably literate.

Virginia and James I and not the other way around. In 1608, Christopher Newport arrived from England with orders to make Powhatan James's vassal. Powhatan saw no reason to submit. Their English subjects subsisted on corn that Tsenacommacah's women grew. Warriors attacked Jamestown shortly after John Smith departed in October 1609, initiating nearly five years of intermittent warfare that starved Jamestown. When Smith left, there were 490 colonists. When Thomas Gates arrived as governor in May 1610, only 60 remained.

Pocahontas helped Powhatan monitor events in Jamestown by acting as his emissary and keeping lines of communication open. In 1613, colonists took her hostage. John Rolfe, a prominent immigrant, fell in love with her, and the following year, Pocahontas, only 16, married Rolfe and was baptized as Rebecca. The marriage halted the war between Tsenacommacah and Virginia. A tense peace bought the colony some time.

Meanwhile, officials on both sides of the Atlantic concluded that only drastic action could save the colony and the Virginia Company. In 1612, the firm tried to lure more investors by putting governance in stockholders' hands. It also added the island of Bermuda to its jurisdiction. In Virginia, reforms focused on breaking English dependence on Indians. Gates and his successor, Thomas Dale, both military men, put Jamestown under martial law. Dale tried to make Jamestown more self-sufficient by renting land to former company servants in exchange for one month of service and some of the corn that they harvested. Meanwhile the company's defenders in England pleaded for patience. It would take time to turn a profit.

The Virginia Company never earned one, even though colonists learned to cultivate tobacco, a valuable export crop that enabled Virginia to survive. In 1611, John Rolfe planted seeds of a sweeter-smelling variety of West Indies tobacco that he obtained in England. Virginia began to export tobacco three years later as the English learned how to cure it.

Virginia colonists also adapted English labor systems to meet their needs. In England, families or magistrates regularly bound adolescents and young adults by a practice known as **indentured servitude**. Young servants might learn a skill and cease to be financial burdens on kin or on England's poor relief system. In Virginia, indentured servants, most of them men between 18 and 26 years old, agreed to serve from three to seven years in exchange for passage overseas. They mainly did the hard work of growing, harvesting, and curing tobacco. They could be bought and sold against their will. The Virginia Company encouraged immigration and the colony's expansion in 1617 by promising 50 acres of land for every free adult who went to Virginia and another 50 for each servant imported.

Two years later, company officials sent 90 young women to become planters' wives. They hoped that married men would stay rather than return to England. Persuading English women to emigrate proved a challenge. A shortage of labor and the tobacco boom compelled colonists to put English women, be they servants or wives, to work in the fields, an arrangement that fit Algonquian gender norms but violated those of the English.

The need for labor also led Virginia colonists to purchase Africans. In 1619, the privateer *White Lion* brought the first unfree Africans to enter English North America. At first, colonists considered some Africans to be slaves and others to be indentured servants whom they freed after completing their terms. African slavery emerged gradually over the course of decades in Virginia.

The most significant changes to Virginia Company policy came in the late 1610s when officials decided to let colonists own land and govern themselves. The right to own land drew tens of thousands of men, mostly indentured servants, to Virginia over the next several decades. Land was increasingly scarce in England. To English men, land ownership brought respect, economic independence, and political rights such as serving on a jury, voting, or holding office. In 1619, the Virginia Company established English America's first representative assembly, the **House of Burgesses**. The firm also replaced martial law with English **common law**, setting in motion the development of county courts. The fields that they cleared and on which they planted tobacco steadily encroached on Tsenacommacah.

This alarmed Powhatan's kinsman and successor Opechcancanough, who made plans to finish off the colony. In March 1622, Tsenacommacah warriors stormed Virginia, killing more than one in four colonists. The English counterattacked brutally, but the war dragged on for 10 years.

The war finished off the Virginia Company, which had never earned a profit and faced charges that its mismanagement had cost thousands of English lives. About 1,200 colonists lived in Virginia in 1622, just one-third of the number of immigrants who had arrived in the previous three years. Most succumbed to disease. In 1624, James I revoked the bankrupt company's charter and put Virginia under royal rule. Virginians' refusal to honor Algonquian ways had nearly led to their colony's demise. Company reforms that empowered colonists to own land, form militias, and elect representatives to govern themselves offered other English colonies a blueprint to follow. But thickening ties to the Atlantic world and England, sustained mainly by European demand for tobacco, ultimately saved Virginia.

New France, New Netherland, New Indian Northeast

As English immigrants struggled to turn Tsenacommacah into Virginia, the French and Dutch claimed the St. Lawrence and Hudson River valleys, respectively. In 1603, Pierre de Gua received a 10-year monopoly on the Acadia and St. Lawrence fur trade. His associate **Samuel de Champlain** charted the coast from Nova Scotia to Cape Cod for France, established alliances with Micmac and Abenaki, and learned of growing English interest in the cod-rich coastal waters of New England. In 1608, Champlain founded what became Quebec City. Built on the site of the abandoned Iroquoian town Stadacona, the new French village controlled water access inland. But New France's immediate future looked dim. Only 8 of 28 colonists survived their first Canadian winter.

Indians who forged ties to New France for their own purposes saved the colony. In 1609, Algonquians, Montagnais, and Hurons persuaded Champlain to help them attack Mohawks, a member of the Iroquois League. He brought his arquebus, an early musket, which, like other firearms of the time, was wildly inaccurate. With some lucky shooting, Champlain managed to kill three Mohawks. The rest fled, having never seen firearms. Six years later, Champlain joined Huron and Algonquian warriors as they invaded Iroquois League territory, cementing an alliance with the Huron Confederacy, a longtime Iroquois League foe. Hurons became the principal Indian middlemen in New France's fur trade, gathering pelts from peoples to their north and west and taking them to Quebec. They and other Indian allies sustained New France's economy.

Champlain lobbied for more support from France, but internal political turmoil and the Thirty Years' War left France with little money and few people to spare. The Catholic

Church proved more receptive. In 1615, four French Récollet priests arrived, followed a decade later by Jesuit missionaries. An English attack the following year forced Champlain to surrender Quebec and send the Jesuits home. They returned when England ceded Quebec to France.

By then, Dutch entrepreneurs had established a colony on the Hudson. In 1609, Henry Hudson, an English captain hired by the Dutch East India Company, sailed up-river in search of a water route to Asia, trading with Algonquians along the way. Five years later, the Dutch founded a trading post, Fort Nassau, now Albany, New York, on Mahican land. Fort Nassau's residents emulated the French by allying with their neighbors. In 1615, they joined a Mohawk-Mahican raid on Susquehannocks. By the early 1620s, the Dutch expanded their commercial network to both sides of Long Island Sound and the Delaware Valley.

They did so by catering to Indian beliefs and needs. The Dutch learned of wampum's spiritual and material value to the northeast's Indians. Wampum manufacturing, simplified by imported iron tools that reshaped shells into beads and bored holes through them, soon spread to Narragansett Bay and Long Island Sound. Algonquian women incorporated gathering shells and fashioning them into wampum into their winter routines. Pequots and Narragansett, two peoples well positioned to make wampum, emerged as southern New England's main powers, partly because wampum soon became currency among Indians in New Netherland and New England. English and Dutch merchants used it to lure the business of Indians, particularly those who sold pelts to the French. Meanwhile, Mohawks feared that they might get cut off from the imports that enabled them to fight off their enemies. In 1624, they forced Mahicans to move, linking Iroquois lands to New Netherland.

Like New France, New Netherland at first was a satellite of its Indian neighbors. In 1621, Dutch officials awarded the **Dutch West India Company** (DWIC) a monopoly on commerce between the Americas, West Africa, and the Netherlands and charged it to establish colonies. The firm focused mainly on the Caribbean and South America. It sent no colonists to New Netherland until 1624. Two years later, the company purchased Manhattan from Indians and founded its local headquarters, New Amsterdam, on the island to coordinate commerce with Indians. New Netherland remained a low priority for the DWIC. In 1630, it had just 300 colonists.

Pilgrims and Algonquians

In 1620–1621, Algonquians watched English immigrants weather their first New England winter. The 102 newcomers called themselves "Pilgrims." Delayed by storms and blown well north of their intended destination—Virginia—they sighted Cape Cod in November. Pilgrims spent a month searching for a suitable site, which they named Plymouth. Some aboard the *Mayflower* argued that the location of their new home nullified the royal charter under which they were to settle. They questioned who should govern them. Their leaders responded with the Mayflower Compact, an agreement that all free adult male passengers signed. They promised to obey laws enforced by the officials whom they chose. The Pilgrims arrived too late to plant and failed to bring enough to eat. Barely half survived the winter, mainly by devouring corn that Indians had buried.

Angela's Ordeal, the Atlantic Slave Trade, and the Creation of African North American Cultures

In 1620, an African woman named Angela arrived in Jamestown. Her Christian name indicates that Angela was baptized. Like Angela, most Africans brought to North America before 1660 came from West Central Africa. They spoke one of two closely related Bantu languages, Kikongo or Kimbundu. Many probably knew some Portuguese too. Most had been baptized and many considered themselves Christian.

Angela had been captured during a Portuguese-Imbangala war against the Kingdom of Ndongo in Angola. She and about 350 others boarded the *São João Bautista*, one of the Portuguese-registered vessels that ferried the vast majority of Africans to the Americas until 1650. Nearly 700,000 enslaved Africans crossed the Atlantic between 1600 and 1650. More than three-quarters of them departed West Central Africa as Angela did, but most West Central Africans who left between 1616 and 1625 were taken to Brazil or Central America. Angela's intended destination was Mexico. But two privateers, each commanded by an English captain, intercepted the *São João Bautista* in the Gulf of Mexico. The privateers seized Angela and over 50 others, divided them, and sailed for Virginia. The *White Lion* arrived first and sold 20 people in Jamestown.

Until 1670, fewer than 5 percent of Virginians were Africans. Angela's background and experience matched those of the first Africans shipped to English and Dutch North America before 1660. Most came as a result of English or Dutch piracy on Spanish shipping (Portugal and Spain were united under Spanish rule between 1581 and 1640). English ships transported fewer than 2,000 Africans across the Atlantic in any decade until the 1640s, when sugar cultivation boomed on Barbados.

No one bid on Angela, who landed in Virginia in February 1620. She became one of William Pierce's four "servants" and probably spent most of her time tending to livestock. Angela joined 32 African Virginians and about 900 other colonists. Among them were Antonio and Isabel, who by 1625 had their son William baptized. A generation later they were free and had become the Johnsons, the most prosperous African American family in English North America, one that owned slaves who grew tobacco. In 1667,

Plymouth's leaders were religious dissidents from England who had just spent 12 years in the Netherlands. They followed principles articulated by the reformer John Field, who argued that the Church of England was too Catholic. It did not allow believers to choose their own leaders or even whether they wished to belong to the Church of England at all. Puritans believed that Anglican clergy dishonored God by preventing the faithful from disciplining and excluding those who did not believe or practice what the church preached. The Pilgrims who founded Plymouth believed that they could only save themselves by leaving the Anglican Church. Pilgrims enjoyed freedom their son John bought 44 acres and named the estate "Angola" to honor his parents' origins.

About one-quarter of the Africans whose names appear in Virginia's public records between 1635 and 1650 had Iberian names such as Antonio, Manuel, or Maria. Before 1640, most lived and worked alongside at least five other Africans. We do not know when Angela died or if she ever became free. We do know that Angela and other Africans shared much in common that helped them to weather their bondage and sometimes escape it during the first decades of Afro-Virginian history.

- In what ways did the struggle between England and Spain for supremacy in the Americas shape Angela's ordeal and English participation in the Atlantic slave trade?
- In what ways did shared origins in West Central Africa likely shape the lives of Angela and other Africans in early Virginia?

BAPTISM   West Central African leaders often saw baptism as a tool of diplomacy. Here Njinga Mbandi, sister and representative of King Ngola Mbandi of Ndongo, receives baptism during a visit to Angola's Portuguese governor that aimed to end wars that decimated Ndongo and enslaved thousands of West Central Africans, including Angela.

of worship in the Netherlands but worried that their children would become Dutch or marginalized if they stayed there.

Meanwhile, an epidemic decimated the Algonquians who lived near Massachusetts Bay. Fishermen from England and Virginia frequented their waters in the 1600s and 1610s in pursuit of cod. They introduced an unknown disease between 1616 and 1618 that killed up to 90 percent of the peoples who lived nearby. Massasoit, chief of the decimated Pokanoket Wampanoags, had to submit to the Narragansetts and pay them tribute. **Tisquantum**, often known as Squanto, paid a higher price. In 1614, an English captain seized him and tried to sell him into slavery in Spain. Tisquantum escaped and somehow made his way to London and Newfoundland. He arrived home in 1619, only to find that disease had killed most of his people, the Patuxet.

Eurasian diseases that killed Indians made Plymouth's survival more likely. People felled by the epidemic had buried the corn that saw Pilgrims through their first winter. Colonists did not have to clear land their first spring; Algonquians had done so before they died. As at Jamestown, corn grown by Algonquian women fed Plymouth for its first four years, fruit of a treaty forged with Massasoit in 1621. Massasoit hoped that friendship with Plymouth would allow his people to escape Narragansett control by securing a powerful ally and better access to imported goods. Pilgrims envisioned that Plymouth would become southeastern New England's most powerful village, with Massasoit collecting tribute from other Algonquians as Plymouth shipped beaver pelts to England to pay off company investors. Tisquantum would live in Plymouth and serve as the Pilgrims' guide and interpreter.

Tensions rose as colonists and Indians interpreted the agreement differently. Tisquantum aimed to reconstitute the Patuxet under his leadership by stoking English mistrust of Massasoit, who soon learned that Plymouth's leaders viewed him and his people as subjects. By the summer of 1621, colony officials prohibited Wampanoag social visits and allowed only Massasoit or his designated representative to enter Plymouth. Word of the English-Algonquian war in Virginia led Plymouth colonists to fear a massive conspiracy between Tsenacommacah and New England Algonquian peoples against all English. They embarked on building a fort and sent armed expeditions to nearby villages to extort corn and intimidate their residents. Plymouth soon sought more autonomy from Indians by ending the system of communal production that had been in place since the colony was founded. Ironically, the new system made Plymouth resemble an Algonquian village. Each family received a parcel to plant, although the land remained company property. Colonists grew corn mostly, with women and children performing much of the field labor. Within two years, Plymouth fed itself and had corn left over.

The surplus of corn strengthened the colony's position strategically and financially. In 1625, its merchants began to exchange corn for beaver pelts with Maine's Kennebec Abenaki. Plymouth also joined the Dutch-Algonquian wampum network.

Still, Plymouth never prospered. In 1627, colonists bought out English shareholders and divided up the livestock and land among male heads of household. They built a relatively obscure society of a few thousand small farmers who scratched out a living on poor soil. But the English had put down roots in New England, an accomplishment that owed much to the Algonquians' intensified contact with Europeans—and with the goods and microbes that they brought to North America.

STUDY QUESTIONS FOR EUROPEAN ISLANDS IN AN ALGONQUIAN OCEAN, 1607–1625

1. In what ways did Indians, particularly Algonquians, influence the development of European colonies in eastern North America between 1607 and 1625?

2. The stories of Pocahontas and the Pilgrims are two founding myths of the United States. Does viewing their stories from Algonquian perspectives change your understanding of them? Explain.

SEEKING GOD, SEIZING LAND, REAPING CONFLICT, 1625 TO C. 1640

As small European outposts grew in three corners of the continent, new patterns emerged and old ones became entrenched. Faith and fear of growing English and Dutch influence moved missionaries in New Mexico and New France to intensify their efforts to convert Indians. Political and religious turmoil in England and western Europe encouraged thousands to seek refuge in New Netherland and in the new English colonies in New England and Maryland. Meanwhile, thousands more flooded into Virginia to plant tobacco and seek land. New arrivals who hoped to create a harmonious and prosperous society in New England multiplied rapidly but quickly divided into factions. Heavy immigration and colonial expansion intensified pressure on Algonquians from New England south to Chesapeake Bay, resulting in wars that prompted Indians to think of themselves in new ways.

Missionaries and Indians in New France and New Mexico

In the late 1620s and early 1630s, Catholic missionaries brought new zeal to their efforts to evangelize Indians in New France and New Mexico. Jesuits served as New France's principal emissaries to Indian allies and the colony's most vocal promoters in France. Meanwhile, Franciscans preached to new groups of Indians on New Mexico's borders while sparring with governors over who should have more power over colonists and Indians. Missionaries studied the cultures of Indians whom they evangelized. However, New France's Jesuits proved more willing to meet converts part way than New Mexico's Franciscans.

Jesuits embarked on two related tasks when they returned to New France in 1632. One was to establish missions among Montagnais and Hurons. The other was to promote

PORTRAIT OF FATHER PAUL LE JEUNE, FROM ENGRAVING FROM RENÉ LOCHON, 1665 Le Jeune served as Jesuit superior in New France from 1632 to 1639. He noted that Montagnais audiences laughed at him because "I pronounce the Indian as a German pronounces French" but were impressed that he could interpret dreams. Le Jeune edited the first 11 editions of the *Jesuit Relations*.

their work, seek financial support for it, and recruit colonists. They sought to achieve these goals by gathering reports from Jesuits in New France and publishing them in France. Historians call these narratives, compiled and distributed annually between 1632 and 1673, the *Jesuit Relations*. Many study them closely for their detailed if heavily biased observations of the Indians whose souls Jesuits aspired to save.

Jesuits focused on Hurons, who were easier to reach most of the year because they lived and farmed in large villages. Most Indians who traded with the Hurons spoke their language, so Jesuits who learned it could preach to Huron allies as well. Two-thirds of the pelts that New France exported between 1616 and 1629 passed through Huron hands. Trade with the French shored up Huron power, particularly against the Iroquois League. That was why Huron leaders had to accept Jesuit missions when Champlain renegotiated the colony's alliance with them in 1633.

Jesuits found Hurons to be grudging hosts, partly because the priests often behaved like rude and annoying guests. At first, the Jesuits demanded that converts become culturally French. They expected Indians to renounce their faith in dreams as revelations of the future and become monogamous. To Hurons, Jesuits, with their short hair and beards, looked beastly, smelled bad, could neither hunt nor fight, and labored to speak their language. Christian concepts such as sin or eternal punishment after death did not exist in Huron religion. Most Hurons found the promise of a heaven that excluded kin who were not Christian repellent. Jesuits' practice of baptizing dying infants and children led many Hurons to conclude that the priests were sorcerers.

Despite these conflicts, the Huron valued their alliance with France and spared Jesuit lives. Hurons also admired many Jesuit qualities. Unlike other French men, the priests cared little about land, pelts, or sex with Indian women. Viewing their mission as a chance to become martyrs for bringing the gospel of Christ to North America, Jesuits often showed a warrior's stoic courage in the face of captivity, torture, and death. They also seemed to possess special powers. Their ability to read and write at first astonished Indians. Astronomical charts enabled the priests to predict solar and lunar eclipses. Perhaps most importantly, Jesuits possessed some immunity to diseases that ravaged Indians.

Epidemics and Jesuits' increasing willingness to compromise with converts saved their missions. A smallpox outbreak in 1640 pushed over 1,000 Hurons to seek baptism. Many hoped that the sacrament would heal or spare them. Jesuits soon tried to build on beliefs that Catholics and Hurons shared, such as the power of prayer and the immortality of souls. They created prayer books and catechisms in the Huron language and employed Huron assistants to explain doctrine. Priests encouraged converts to substitute crucifixes, medallions, and rosaries for the stone amulets that Hurons traditionally wore. Relatively few Hurons identified themselves as Christians; only 500 did so in 1646. But Jesuits established a foothold in Huron territory, sealing the alliance between that confederation and New France and making themselves targets for Iroquois warriors.

As Jesuits prepared to return to New France, Franciscans in New Mexico expressed a renewed sense of optimism. Eight friars arrived in 1629 and promptly founded missions among the Acoma, Zuni, and Hopi. The head of New Mexico's missions, Fray **Alonso de Benavides**, eagerly anticipated the conversion of Na-Dene–speaking peoples who lived on the borders between Pueblo and Apache territory. In 1630, Benavides published a report in Madrid that boasted that friars had baptized 86,000 Indians in New Mexico.

Benavides celebrated that thousands of Pueblos lived within New Mexico's missions, but misinterpreted why many did. Life outside the missions was hard. Spanish officials often seized corn from Pueblos who did not live on missions, disrupting trade with Indians who supplied bison and other game in exchange for Pueblo corn. Missions offered cattle, pigs, and sheep for butchering as well as some protection from Apache raids and Spanish governors.

These benefits came at a price. Mission Indians endured campaigns to remake them into hispanized Christians. Friars confiscated and destroyed their religious symbols and built crosses over **kivas**—the sacred cave-like structures in which Pueblos re-enacted their creation and honored their gods. Friars undermined systems of Pueblo authority. They adopted the role of Pueblo hunting chiefs by supplying livestock and meat to baptized Indians. Franciscans targeted children for baptism and catechization, luring them with gifts of seed and livestock and taking on the role of both parents as their providers and protectors. They inverted Pueblos' gendered division of labor to match Hispanic norms by compelling men to build homes and women to weave. Pueblo peoples were traditionally **matrilineal** (meaning that they inherited social identity and property through the female line), but Pueblo women lost their exclusive rights to land, seeds, and children to men wherever missions took root.

By the early 1640s, Pueblos found themselves besieged by Apaches. The Spanish had introduced horses to Pueblo peoples, who began to trade them to the Apaches in 1601. Horses facilitated Apache raids and reinforced Apache ways by making them more mobile and facilitating their hunts. Growing herds of Apache horses exhausted pastures, forcing Apaches to move more often, strengthening each band's autonomy, and encouraging more raids on Pueblos and colonists. Meanwhile, the Diné, whom the Spanish at first called "Apaches Navaju," traded and raided for sheep as well as horses. Raising sheep and weaving wool soon became central to Navajo culture and the foundation of the Navajo economy.

Indians also raided New Mexico to avenge kin captured and enslaved by Spanish-led incursions. Governor Luis de Rosas saw Indian slavery as a way to profit from his office. Some slaves worked in colonists' households, others in Rosas's textile factory in Santa Fé to make blankets to trade to Plains peoples. The rest were sold to Mexican mines. In 1638, Rosas attacked Plains Apaches, killing 100 and enslaving as many. A raid on Utes the following year yielded 80 more slaves. Apaches retaliated by raiding the lightly defended colony. Between 1639 and 1640, they destroyed stores of corn, leaving the disease-ravaged Pueblos weaker and hungrier. About 80,000 Pueblos lived in 150 towns in 1598. By 1640, fewer than half as many inhabited just 43 towns.

Migration and the Expansion of Dutch and English North America

Heavy immigration between the mid-1620s and 1640 caused the New Netherland and English colonies in the Chesapeake, New England, and the Caribbean to grow rapidly. Demand for labor in North America and the West Indies, recruitment by company officials, and events in Europe and the South Atlantic rim channeled migrants across the Atlantic. Political and religious conflict in England prompted the creation of two new mainland colonies, Massachusetts Bay in 1629 and Maryland in 1634, founded to provide a haven for Puritans and Catholics, respectively. The new colonies attracted thousands of migrants who helped to anchor English claims to North America.

By contrast, the DWIC did relatively little to promote New Netherland to prospective colonists. The firm's directors considered the Hudson River valley a northern outpost of a global Dutch empire that by the early 1640s linked New Netherland to south and southeast Asia, northeastern Brazil, Angola, and the West Indies. Nearly all offered more lucrative opportunities than New Netherland. In addition, few Dutch had reason to leave Holland, where they enjoyed a prosperous economy, low unemployment, and religious toleration.

As a result, New Netherland became a Dutch colony composed mostly of people who were not Dutch. In 1629, the DWIC copied what the Virginia Company did in the 1610s to boost immigration. Directors encouraged private investment by offering patroonships, large land grants along the Hudson, to those who brought at least 50 immigrants with them. Rensselaerswyck, the only patroonship to succeed by 1640, attracted English, Norwegian, and German migrants during the 1630s. In 1638, a group opposed to company rule left New Netherland, settled near what later became Philadelphia, and recruited colonists from Sweden. Susquehannocks protected them in exchange for imported goods. In 1640, the DWIC issued a **Charter of Freedoms and Exemptions**. It granted 200 acres to whoever brought five adults to New Netherland, and it promised prospective colonists religious freedom and local self-governance, guarantees that lured English Puritans from Massachusetts to eastern Long Island. New Netherland became the most ethnically—and religiously—diverse colony yet seen in North America. In 1644, the French Jesuit Isaac Jogues visited New Amsterdam and heard 18 languages spoken on its streets.

New Netherland also grew because African bondage took root there sooner than in English North America. Africans and their American-born children comprised 30 percent of New Amsterdam's 100 residents in 1638 and 20 percent of nearly 2,000 in 1664. The DWIC's ties to Africa, Brazil, and the Caribbean and its need for labor, largely to build and maintain fortifications and conduct commerce, drove the growth of the African population. In 1648, the DWIC ended its monopoly over the African slave trade to and from New Netherland but remained the colony's largest importer and buyer of Africans.

New Amsterdam's Africans created the first urban African American community north of St. Augustine. Like their peers in Virginia, New Amsterdam's Africans shared similar origins and experiences. In 1644, 11 men petitioned company director **Willem Kieft** for their freedom. He permitted them to work for themselves and live where they wished, but Kieft required that the men pay the DWIC and bind themselves and their children to serve the company. Such "half-freedom" exemplified the discrimination that New Amsterdam's Africans confronted. But many Africans and African Americans earned real freedom. By 1664, one in five in New Netherland had done so. Africans in New Amsterdam also participated in church life, accounting for 28 percent of marriages in New Amsterdam's Dutch Reformed church between 1639 and 1652. Almost one in three people baptized in the 1640s was African.

Although DWIC reforms enabled New Netherland's population to increase rapidly, the Dutch failed to keep pace with the English. The number of people who lived in New Netherland nearly doubled between 1638 and 1643 to 2,000. By 1664, the colony had 10,000 residents. But Virginia had 40,000 and New England 50,000.

Between 1560 and 1640, emigrants departed England, Wales, and Scotland in droves. Most went to Ireland. However, migration to America soared during the 1630s. Thousands went to five colonies (St. Christopher, Barbados, Nevis, Providence Island,

and Antigua) that the English had recently founded in the West Indies. Thousands more left for the tobacco fields of Maryland and Virginia. Meanwhile, 13,000 headed for New England in the most concentrated and targeted movement of people across the Atlantic and into North America yet. The wave of immigrants during the 1630s swelled the population of English North America and the West Indies from 9,500 in 1630 to 54,000 ten years later. English colonists vastly outnumbered their French, Dutch, and Spanish counterparts from then on, giving England a huge advantage over its European rivals in North America.

Most English who went to the Chesapeake or the West Indies were young single men who sought economic independence. Landless and unemployed, they poured into London and other cities seeking work. Tobacco planters, who desperately needed labor, lured such men to the colonies. One in four died of malaria or another disease within a year of landing in the Chesapeake, but those who survived their American servitude stood a good chance of becoming landowners. About half the men who left London for Maryland or Virginia in 1635 managed to acquire land. The immigrants entered a colonial world in which men vastly outnumbered women; most died young, and few were American born. Deaths outnumbered births among whites in the Chesapeake region until the 1690s. This increased demand for servants and increased survivors' chances of owning land and enjoying upward social mobility. With so many men available, English women could be choosier about whom they wished to marry. Those who outlived their husbands owned a large share of land in the Chesapeake colonies and often attracted many suitors.

An array of forces pushed people out of England and drew them to Puritan colonies in America during the 1630s. A worsening economy in eastern England in the 1620s made migration look more attractive. **Charles I**'s decision to suspend Parliament in 1629 cut off the main avenue for peaceful expression of dissent. Some Puritan leaders and London merchants organized the **Massachusetts Bay Company** in 1629 and recruited emigrants by promising them the opportunity to create godly communities in America. Some 3,000 people fled for New England in 1635 after William Laud became Archbishop of Canterbury, Anglicanism's second highest-ranking official after the monarch, and targeted Puritan reformers.

Those who moved to New England prospered and multiplied. Almost all adult English men there owned land during the 1600s. Many kept moving until they found a town with religious views that agreed with their own and with enough land for themselves and their heirs. The number of colonists in New England grew by 66 percent during the 1640s, almost entirely through births, largely because women and children comprised a large share of migrants during the 1630s. White women in New England on average gave birth to eight children (compared to seven in England) and more of them reached adulthood. Most of those American-born children knew their grandparents; most people lived past age 60. Such rapid population growth put additional strain on southern New England's Algonquians and made it harder to achieve the social harmony that Puritans sought to create in America.

Dissent in the "City upon a Hill"

In 1630, Massachusetts Bay Colony's first governor, **John Winthrop**, articulated the principles on which he and his fellow Puritans would build a new society. He reminded

SILVER BADGE GIVEN TO "KING OF THE MACHOTICK INDIANS," VIRGINIA, c. 1662–1677 The 1646 treaty between Tsenacommacah and Virginia required Indians to wear a striped coat to enter English territory. In 1662, Virginia required Indians to carry metal passports. Chiefs needed a silver badge like this one presented to the chief of the Machodoc. Other Indians had to use copper badges.

them that they had entered into a **covenant** with God that required them to translate their faith into actions that obeyed God's will as revealed in the Bible. If colonists stayed united and honored their word to God and one another, they would set the standard for others to follow. "We shall be as a city upon a hill," Winthrop exhorted; "the eyes of all people are upon us." But if colonists violated the covenant, they would invite divine wrath on themselves and "open the mouths of enemies to speak evil of the ways of God." God, Winthrop argued, had charged them to create a new and godly England in America for the whole world, especially England, to see and emulate.

Winthrop drew deeply from Calvinist beliefs. His shipmates thought that each congregation should decide how it should operate and who should belong to it. Church members should be those whom God had designated for salvation, those who truly believed in God and acted accordingly. The Church of England made no such distinction. It presumed that all English were members because Anglicanism was the realm's official faith. Winthrop and most who accompanied him argued that they could still reform the Anglican Church from within, but had to move to New England to do so. There the faithful could honor their covenant with God by purging their churches and communities of sin.

To sustain their "city upon a hill," Massachusetts Bay Puritans tried to ensure that only God's elect were church members and that God's elect held political power. To accomplish the first goal, they developed a "**conversion test**" in the 1630s. Prospective members had to appear before those already deemed elect, testify to their relationship with God, and offer proof that God had saved them. Members judged whether candidates had received saving grace and merited full admission to their congregation. Men who were not church members were barred from voting or holding office, a form of exclusion adopted nowhere else. Other Puritans did adopt the conversion test, which spread from Massachusetts Bay through New England and then to England.

Religious convictions also led Massachusetts Bay Puritans to create a well-educated society. All believers merited direct access to God's will as written in the Bible, so they needed to know how to read. Persecution of Puritans in England meant that New England had to supply its own ministers. In 1636, reformers founded Harvard College to educate colonists' sons and train ministers. Harvard operated Anglo America's first printing press, which rolled off its first publication in 1639. Three years later, Massachusetts Bay magistrates required that parents teach children to read. By 1647, six towns had started grammar schools, and a new law mandated that every community with more than 100 households have one. A college, a printing press, and an educated public positioned New England Puritans to generate ideas and broadcast them to the Anglo-Atlantic world.

Reforms inspired by Puritanism also reshaped marriage and family life. Puritans in North America made marriage, a sacrament within the Church of England, a civil ceremony. That made it easier for couples to divorce, although few did. Courts regularly addressed domestic violence, whether complaints were generated by victims or neighbors, and prosecuted male offenders. Authorities also granted parents more power over children. In 1647, Massachusetts Bay became the first place in the Anglo-Atlantic world to give parents power over whom their adult children could marry. New laws empowered fathers and husbands most of all.

As Massachusetts Bay's founders labored to make a model English society, they also proclaimed that they would convert Algonquians and live alongside them peacefully. "Come over and help us" declared the Indian depicted on the colony's seal. A campaign to convert Indians did not begin until the mid-1640s. Instead, Puritans imagined that they would set examples that would encourage their Indian neighbors to become Christian and adopt English ways, including English gender norms. In 1634, William Wood published *New England's Prospect* to encourage more Puritans to sail to New England. He cast Algonquian men as lazy tyrants who did little but hunt as they "forced" Algonquian women to grow corn, trap lobsters, and build wigwams—all "man's" work in English eyes. English women, Wood thought, offered good role models for Algonquian women. Meanwhile, John Winthrop argued that Algonquians did not deserve their lands because they did not cultivate or develop them permanently. He drew from an emerging body of international law to assert that Algonquian New England was *vacuum domicilium*—empty of "settlement." English who farmed, grazed livestock, claimed land as personal property, and erected permanent structures on it had a far more legitimate claim, Winthrop insisted.

To Winthrop's chagrin, Indians' rights became a controversial issue, largely because the minister **Roger Williams** made it one. Williams arrived in 1631 and quickly moved to Plymouth, where most shared his belief that Puritans should separate from the Anglican Church. Williams forged ties to Wampanoags and Narragansetts and began to learn their dialects of Algonquian. He returned to Massachusetts Bay after authoring a tract that argued that the patent Charles I gave the Massachusetts Bay Company did not entitle colonists to Indian land. Indians rightfully owned their land and could only cede it voluntarily. Massachusetts Bay leaders condemned Williams and had his work burned. Williams threw fuel on the fire. He even wrote Charles I to criticize the patent that he had issued to Massachusetts Bay. The colony's officials responded by banishing Williams in 1636. He moved to Narragansett Bay, founding Providence on land that Narragansetts granted him.

There Williams established the principle of separation of church and state in English America. Use of government power to compel conformity of belief, Williams argued, corrupted religion. Authorities instead should allow what Williams called "soul liberty," the freedom to believe and worship as one wished. Williams practiced what he preached by cofounding the Americas' first Baptist church in 1639. He also maintained close ties to Algonquians that protected Providence and enabled him to author an Algonquian-English dictionary. Providence became the first of four English towns, each founded by Massachusetts Bay exiles, that joined to form Rhode Island in 1644.

Anne Hutchinson was, after Williams, Rhode Island's second most notorious resident. She was 43 when she sailed to Boston with her husband and 11 children and was admitted to a congregation. Hutchinson soon began to hold meetings for women at her home at which she reviewed the sermons of John Cotton, her spiritual mentor in England and a Boston minister. Before long, Hutchinson, her adversaries charged, was preaching her own views and insisting that good works had no bearing on salvation or on others' knowledge of it. Her enemies, Winthrop among them, abhorred her alleged emphasis on faith alone as evidence of salvation. It challenged how Massachusetts Bay Puritans determined church membership and who should exercise political power. By developing her own theology and preaching it, Hutchinson had also claimed a public role that magistrates thought belonged to men alone. Hutchinson was tried in court and exiled. She recanted her views before heading for Rhode Island. Dozens followed her there.

Puritans' tendency to resolve disputes through exile or migration accelerated colonial New England's expansion in the 1630s. The founders of Hartford, Connecticut, considered the criteria for church membership in Massachusetts Bay too restrictive and thought that its congregations had too much power over government. By contrast, the founders of New Haven Colony left Massachusetts Bay because they considered its union of church and state too loose and permissive. They constructed a theocracy in which ministers made the rules. Rhode Island, Hartford, and New Haven were all fruits of the tension between individual conscience and conformity within Puritanism. Their creation put even more pressure on Algonquians (Map 2.4).

Colonist-Algonquian Wars

Wars, triggered mainly by immigrant demand for land, erupted between colonists and Algonquians in New Netherland, New England, and Virginia between 1636 and 1644. Each resulted in the decimation, relocation, or subjugation of Algonquians who lived on the borders of English and Dutch North America.

New Netherland generally enjoyed amicable relations with Munsee-speaking Algonquian peoples of the lower Hudson Valley until Willem Kieft arrived in 1638 to oversee Dutch West India Company operations. He aggressively acquired land north and east of Manhattan. Colonists who resettled those areas turned cattle and pigs loose to forage and devour crops that Munsee women planted. Kieft fanned Munsee resentment by demanding tribute to bolster New Amsterdam's defenses. Indians, provoked by the Dutch militia, attacked Staten Island in 1641. The war raged for four years, forcing colonists to seek shelter within New Amsterdam. Indians soon vacated most of the lower Hudson Valley and western Long Island.

As war raged around Manhattan, another conflict engulfed Virginia and Tsenacommacah. The colony's expansion, driven by English immigrants and their desire for

MAP 2.4 ▲ Colonization of New England, 1635–1675 Religious dissent among Puritans and their habit of migrating as families accelerated English invasions of lands that belonged to Algonquian peoples. Connecticut, New Haven Colony, and Rhode Island, all colonies founded by dissenters who left Massachusetts Bay, expanded rapidly after 1635, a process enabled partly by the Pequot War.

more land for tobacco, provoked Algonquian warriors to attack in 1644. They killed 500 colonists. Virginia militiamen retaliated by storming Algonquian villages and massacring their inhabitants. Two years later, they captured and killed the elderly paramount chief, Opechcancanough. Officials forced his successor Necotowance to sign a peace treaty that declared that his people were English subjects. Indians could no longer enter English communities without passes. Necotowance and those under his authority had to return guns, Africans, and runaway Indian servants. Thomas Rolfe,

TIMELINE 1555–1640

AMERICA	YEAR	THE WORLD
	1555	English merchants found Muscovy Company to trade with Russia
Spanish mariners discover route from Philippines to North America	1565	
	1568	**May** Eighty Years' War begins
	1573	Philip II of Spain issues Royal Orders for New Discoveries
French merchants establish trade in beaver pelts with Indians in Canada	1580s	
English launch colony at Roanoke	1585	
Sir Francis Drake attacks and destroys St. Augustine	1586	
English abandon Roanoke colony	1587	
Guales rebel against Spanish in Florida	1597–1601	
Spanish forces conquer New Mexico	1598	Edict of Nantes grants tolerance to France's Huguenots
Apaches begin to acquire horses from Pueblo peoples	1601	
Sebastián Vizcaíno explores and maps coast of California	1602–1603	
May Employees of Virginia Company found Jamestown **Dec** Tsenacommacah warriors take John Smith captive	1607	
Spanish officials decide to remain in Florida and New Mexico **Jul** French colonists found Quebec	1608	
First Virginia–Tsenacommacah war	1609–1613	
French colonists ally with the Montagnais, Algonquian, and Huron against the Mohawks Henry Hudson sails up river that bears his name and founds New Netherland	1609	**Apr** Treaty of Antwerp introduces Twelve Years' Truce in Eighty Years' War between the Netherlands and Spain
Santa Fé, New Mexico founded	1610	
Virginia planters begin to export tobacco	1614	
Bermudans purchase first unfree Africans brought to English America	1616	**Apr** William Shakespeare dies
Disease decimates Algonquians along New England coast	1616–1618	
Virginia Company permits colonists to own land	1618	Thirty Years' War begins in Europe
Virginia planters purchase the first unfree Africans shipped to mainland English North America Virginia Company permits colonists to establish first representative assembly in English North America	1619	
Nov Adult male Pilgrims sign Mayflower Compact **Dec** Pilgrims found Plymouth Colony	1620	
Dutch West India Company founded and charged to govern New Netherland	1621	
Second Virginia-Tsenacommacah War	1622–1632	

Dutch merchants create wampum industry	**1622**	
James I puts Virginia under direct royal rule Colonization of St. Christopher, first permanent English colony in the West Indies, begins	**1624**	
Jesuits arrive in New France	**1625**	
New Amsterdam (now New York City) founded	**1626**	
English begin to colonize Barbados	**1627**	
English begin to colonize Nevis	**1628**	
English Puritans found Massachusetts Bay Colony	**1629**	**Oct** Plague arrives in Milan, Italy; one of the last major European outbreaks
More than 13,000 English emigrate to New England in "Great Migration"	**1630–1642**	
Providence Island Company forms and begins to plan colonization of Providence Island in Caribbean	**1630**	
Jesuit Relations begins publication English begin to colonize Antigua	**1632**	
French–Huron alliance renegotiated to require Jesuit missions within Huron Confederacy	**1633**	
Maryland founded	**1634**	
Connecticut founded	**1635**	Sakoku Edict issued, locking Japan's borders to Japanese and Europeans; restricts Catholicism and limits trade
Roger Williams banished from Massachusetts Bay and founds Providence, Rhode Island Suffrage in Massachusetts Bay restricted to adult male church members Harvard College founded	**1636**	
Pequot War in New England	**1636–1637**	
New Haven Colony founded	**1637**	
Anne Hutchinson banished from Massachusetts Bay	**1638**	
Printing press at Harvard, English America's first, begins operating	**1639**	
Dutch West India Company issues Charter of Freedoms and Exemptions for New Netherland	**1640**	
Massachusetts Bay becomes first English North American colony to recognize slavery as a legal institution	**1641**	Epidemic in China spreads along Grand Canal; kills up to 90% of population in some towns
Miantonomi attempts to organize Indian alliance against New England	**1641–1643**	
Kieft's War rages in New Netherland	**1641–1645**	
United Colonies of New England forms	**1643**	

Pocahontas's son, fought for Virginia. His service earned him an appointment to run a fort in Chickahominy territory, a position that enabled him to acquire hundreds of acres.

The most complex conflict pitted Pequots against Massachusetts Bay, Connecticut, Narragansetts, and Mohegans. Pequot control over the wampum trade and access to European goods antagonized the Mohegans and the Narragansetts. A smallpox epidemic weakened Pequots. Desperate for allies, Pequots offered Massachusetts officials title to the Connecticut River valley before approaching Narragansetts to propose an alliance against the English. Narragansetts rejected them, thanks partly to their friendship with Roger Williams. Massachusetts Bay's leaders, reeling from the conflict that swirled about Anne Hutchinson, saw war as a way to unite a fractious society and slake demand for land.

The **Pequot War** erupted in 1636. Its bloodiest chapter came in May 1637, when an English-Narragansett-Mohegan force surrounded a Pequot village on Mystic River in Connecticut, populated by hundreds of women, children, and elderly men. The Indian allies set fire to the village, and the English shot whoever fled. English and Algonquian forces mopped up Pequot resistance over the next few months. They executed many Pequot men and permitted a small autonomous community of Pequots to remain in their homeland.

Colonists and Indians divided the remaining Pequots. Narragansetts and Mohegans adopted or executed some; colonists bound the rest as servants or sold them into slavery in the West Indies and Providence Island. In exchange, New England received enslaved Africans. In 1641, Massachusetts Bay soon became English North America's first colony to legalize slavery.

English and Algonquians drew different lessons from the war. Most immigrants rejoiced; it opened more land and demonstrated English might. Indians responded in a variety of ways. In 1638, Quinnipiacs, outnumbered by residents of New Haven Colony, agreed to surrender most of their land and confine themselves to a reservation. No outsiders could visit without the permission of New Haven authorities. In return, Quinnipiacs received promises of protection, the right to hunt and fish off the reservation as long as they did not bother colonists, and some coats and tools. The Mohegans, led by **Uncas**, concluded that it was better to side with the English than fight them. Narragansetts found the new balance of power disturbing. They had expected the war to confirm them as southern New England's largest power. Instead, the English claimed land, influence, and Pequot captives that Narragansetts considered rightfully theirs. The English treated the Narragansetts as subjects.

The Narragansett chief **Miantonomi** was particularly offended. By the early 1640s, he had concluded that the English had become too powerful for one Indian nation to contain, so he began to recruit Mohawks and Algonquians throughout southern New England and Long Island to ally against the foreigners. In 1642, Miantonomi urged that Montauks should see themselves as nearly all English saw them, as *Indians* first and foremost, who shared more in common with each other than they did with the newcomers. He explained, "We must be one as they are, otherwise we shall be all gone shortly."

Miantonomi's words fell mostly on deaf ears among the Indian peoples he had hoped to reach, but colonists paid rapt attention. In 1643, Massachusetts Bay, Plymouth, Connecticut, and New Haven formed the **United Colonies of New England** for their mutual defense. Its commissioners urged Uncas to capture Miantonomi, who was killed while in Mohegan custody later that year. Uncas had played, and would continue to play, a role similar to that which Massasoit filled for Plymouth in the 1620s. To most Mohegans, that seemed the best way to meet the challenges they faced. Some Narragansetts chose a different path. They teamed up with Rhode Islanders, excluded from the United Colonies, to take their case straight to Charles I. In a 1644 letter, Canonicus and Pessacus, Miantonomi's uncle and brother, requested protection from English colonists as his loyal subjects and as their equals. Charles was then facing a rebellion in which most Puritans on both sides of the Atlantic sought to overthrow him. He could not have paid the petition much mind. Still, like Miantonomi's proposition, it was a novel way in which Indians employed imported ideas in a bid to regain control over a world that three generations earlier had been entirely theirs.

STUDY QUESTIONS FOR SEEKING GOD, SEIZING LAND, REAPING CONFLICT, 1625 TO C. 1640

1. England's North American colonies grew more rapidly than New Netherland or New France. Why? What impact did such rapid growth have on Indians?

2. How did different Indian tribes respond to the colonization of their lands and violent conflicts with the English?

Summary

- The Spanish Empire initiated the colonial era of what became the mainland United States by clinging to Florida and New Mexico, while England emerged as Spain's main rival in North America and the Northeast's Indians became more integral participants in Atlantic trade networks.
- In 1607, English, French, and Dutch immigrants began to colonize small areas on the Atlantic coast in lands dominated by Algonquians, with whom they had tense relationships usually marked by mutual misunderstanding and from whom they sought land, knowledge, and goods to send overseas for profit.
- Missionary activity among Indians in New Mexico and New France intensified after 1625, as did English, Dutch, and African migration to North America, which led to the creation of new colonies, the expansion of older ones, and greater demands on Indians that led to war and the subjugation of some Algonquian peoples by the 1640s.

Key Terms and People

Benavides, Alonso de *58*

Black Legend *45*

Champlain, Samuel de *52*

Charles I *61*

Charter of Freedoms and Exemptions *60*

common law *52*

commons *44*

conversion test *62*

covenant *62*

Dutch West India Company (DWIC) *53*

Edict of Nantes *44*

fur trade *46*

Harriot, Thomas *45*

House of Burgesses *52*

Reviewing Chapter 2

1. In what ways did the movement of people, goods, and ideas shape North America between 1565 and the 1640s?
2. Cultural differences were mainly responsible for conflicts between Europeans and Indians. Is this statement correct? If so, why? If not, why not?
3. In what ways did religion influence events in North America between 1565 and 1640?

Further Reading

Brewer, Holly. *By Birth or Consent: Children, Law, and the Anglo-American Revolution in Authority*. Chapel Hill: University of North Carolina Press, 2005. A fascinating account that accords a central role to Puritans in the shaping of modern Anglo-American concepts of rights, be they children's, spouses', or parents' rights.

Calloway, Colin G. *One Vast Winter Count: The Native American West before Lewis and Clark*. Lincoln: University of Nebraska Press, 2003. An overview of Indian history from the arrival of humans to the early 1800s that focuses on Southwestern and Plains peoples and how they adapted to European invaders.

Games, Alison. *Migration and the Origins of the English Atlantic World*. Cambridge, Mass.: Harvard University Press, 1999. Tracks English men and women who migrated through London in the 1630s to North America and the Caribbean and examines how they fared in their new homes.

Kupperman, Karen Ordahl. *The Jamestown Project*. Cambridge, Mass.: Belknap Press of Harvard University Press, 2007. A comprehensive history published on the 400th anniversary of the founding of Jamestown that argues that early Virginia provided a successful model to the English for how to colonize the Americas.

Townsend, Camilla. *Pocahontas and the Powhatan Dilemma*. New York: Hill and Wang, 2004. A sensitive account of Pocahontas and her world that clearly spells out the challenges that English colonization posed for her and for Tsenacommacah's residents.

Van Zandt, Cynthia J. *Brothers Among Nations: The Pursuit of Intercultural Alliances in Early America, 1580–1660*. New York: Oxford University Press, 2008. A pathbreaking exploration of the ties that Europeans and Indians forged to one another and of the significance of such ties for early European efforts to colonize eastern North America.

America In The World
PEOPLE, GOODS, IDEAS AND PRACTICES

CHAPTER 2: Colonists on the Margins, 1565–1640

EUROPE

AFRICA

NORTH
AMERICA

SOUTH
AMERICA

ATLANTIC
OCEAN

ATLANTIC
OCEAN

PACIFIC
OCEAN

Gulf of
Mexico

Jamestown

St. Augustine

Dutch colonists (1624)

French colonists (1603)

Metal tools, woven cloth, firearms (1530s on)

Fur (1530s on)

Puritanism

English colonists (1607)

Conquistadors and Franciscan priests (1500s)

Catholicism

Conquistadors and
Franciscan priests (1598)

Enslaved Africans

Goods
Ideas
People

| 0 | 500 | 1,000 miles |
| 0 | 500 | 1,000 kilometers |

PRIMARY SOURCES FOR CHAPTER 2
COLONISTS ON THE MARGINS, 1565–1640

SOURCE 2.1

Fray Alonso de Benavides, Excerpts from "Petition to Restrict Indian Tribute and Personal Service" (c. 1630)

One of the principal sources of friction between friars and governors in Florida and New Mexico concerned the amount of tribute and personal service that Indians owed and to whom, friars or colonists, they owed that tribute and service. The friar Alonso de Benavides, who oversaw New Mexico's missions from 1626 to 1629, likely wrote the petition excerpted below. Benavides composed his petition shortly after he returned to Spain in 1630 and addressed it to the King of Spain. It appears that Benavides's efforts succeeded. In 1635, a royal decree exempted Indians in New Mexico who converted to Christianity from paying tribute or rendering personal service for ten years.

Source: Frederick W. Hodge, George P. Hammond, and Agapito Rey, eds., *Fray Alonso de Benavides: Revised Memorial of 1634 with Numerous Supplementary Documents Elaborately Annotated* (Albuquerque: University of New Mexico Press, 1945), 168–77.

Through royal decrees it is ordered that no tributes or personal services be imposed on the Indians of New Mexico until after they have been baptized. Before any can be levied against them, the governor of the province and the custodian must notify the viceroy and the royal *audiencia*[1] of Mexico stating the reasons why they should be imposed, this to be done by the viceroy himself and the royal *audiencia*, and in no other way. At present everything is done in just the opposite manner; even before the pueblos are converted, the governor himself gives them out in *encomienda*[2] without notifying the custodian or the viceroy. Even before they are converted and baptized, when they are only pacified, they [Spaniards] constrain them to pay tribute and to do personal service, taking them far from their pueblos and treating them badly. As a result, the heathen Indians who have not yet been converted or even pacified say that they do not want to become converted, or even pacified, that they do not want to become Christians, in order not to pay tribute or serve. They have even been sent to be sold as slaves in New Spain[3], as was the practice. They escape these and other abuses as long as they remain free and do not become Christians.

---

[1]A group of judges headquartered in Mexico City who had jurisdiction over cases from New Mexico.
[2]A grant to a prominent colonist of control over the services of Indians.
[3]In this case, Benavides probably means what we today would call Mexico.

Wherefore your Majesty is entreated to order, under severe penalties, that the Indians of New Mexico be not given in *encomienda* by the governors of New Mexico until five years after the whole pueblo has been baptized, and in order to be given in *encomienda*, the said governor and the custodian there must notify the viceroy and the *audiencia*, reporting that the five years have passed, so that they may be authorized to do it; that the *encomenderos*[4] of the said pueblos should have no other power or rights over the pueblos and Indians than the tribute owed them; that the Indians must remain always as tributary vassals of your Majesty, in whose name they pay the tribute to their *encomenderos*, without owing them any more obligations than to those who are not *encomenderos*; that neither the *encomenderos* nor any other Spaniards be allowed to live in their pueblos without the consent of the Indians themselves; that they may not have houses in the pueblos for their employment or other gain, by which they cause much harm to the pueblos and the Indians.

Likewise, it has been established by the first governors of New Mexico, and is being continued by order of the viceroy that each house pay a tribute consisting of a cotton blanket, the best of which are about a yard and a half square, and a *fanega*[5] of corn. This is understood to be for each house and not for each Indian, even though many Indian families live in such houses. It often happens that the pueblos increase or decrease in houses, or, if one tumbles down, its dwellers move to that of their relatives, and none of these pay tribute, except for the house in which they live. This works against the increase in houses, as tribute is collected as soon as the owners occupy them.

The *encomenderos* compel the Indians whose houses may have fallen down, or which they may have lost for other reasons, to pay tribute, even though they live in someone else's house. It is requested of your Majesty that the Indians of New Mexico do not pay tribute by the person, but by the house, as has always been done; that, as the *encomendero* is ready to receive the tribute of houses added to their pueblos, he should also be ready to lose and cease taking tribute from abandoned houses, even though the owners live in someone else's house.

It is requested that the Indians who, of their own will, move to live in other pueblos, being free, as they are, must not be hindered by their *encomenderos*, the governors, or other persons; that they may live freely in whatever pueblo they wish, and that, after they have established residence there for one year and a day, they become taxpayers at the place like the others of the same pueblo to the *encomendero* with whom they live. For the Indians suffer much harm when, if they do not get along with the *encomendero* in a pueblo where they do not find as good facilities for their work and farming as in some other one, they are forced to live there for the accommodation of the *encomendero*, whether they like it or not. If they have this freedom, the *encomenderos* will help and accord good treatment to their tributary Indians so that they will not leave their pueblos and their tributes diminish.

It is requested that all the *caciques*[6], chief captains, governors, *alcaldes*[7], and *fiscales*[8] of the churches, on account of the big tasks they perform for the republic and the service of your Majesty, be exempt from tribute and personal service while they hold these offices.

---

[4]Individuals to whom a grant of *encomienda* had been given.
[5]Approximately 2 cubic feet, or just over a bushel and a half.
[6]What Taíno peoples in the Caribbean called their chiefs, a term that the Spanish subsequently used to refer to Indian chiefs in North America, Mexico, Central America, and parts of South America.
[7]Indian magistrates who often oversaw the apprehension of criminals, among other duties.
[8]*Fiscales* acted as assistants to priests, helping with the management of parishes and the discipline of those who violated church teachings.

They are so busy in their offices that even their planted fields are cared for by others, as they are unable to do it themselves. The native lords and chieftains resent very much that they are compelled to pay tribute. Likewise, all the Indians who are choir singers and assistants in the churches are free only from personal service, but not from tribute, because of their regular attendance in church and in the schools.

It is requested that the Spanish governors be forbidden to issue warrants or permits to take Indian boys or girls from the pueblos on the pretext that they are orphans, and take them to serve permanently in the houses of the Spaniards where they remain as slaves. As a matter of fact, the orphans are well cared for at the homes of their grandparents or other relatives where they are brought up as if they were their own children. In case there should be any one without a home, the governor should not issue warrants without the consent of the ecclesiastical minister, who lives alone with the Indians and knows their needs and relieves them as much as he is able. This must be done so that the destitute Indian orphans may live freely with their relatives. The governors often take from the Spaniards some Indians who are serving the Spaniards well, in order to keep them for themselves. They take them without compensation, or, in payment, give them a permit to go to the pueblos to look for other boys and girls and to take them by force.

It is requested that the Indians taken in wars, whatever their nation, may not be given as slaves or sentenced to personal service outside of New Mexico, as is prescribed by royal decrees. On the contrary, they should be placed in convents of the friars or in houses of Spaniards or Indians of exemplary conduct so that they may be taught our holy Catholic faith with all kindness in order that they may become Christians. If any of them should run away they will tell the people of their nations of the good treatment accorded them and they will become inclined to our life and religion. This assignment to a convent may not be in the nature of a sale, transfer, or any other material consideration or period of time, but simply as an act of charity to instruct and convert them, which is the only purpose for which we have gone there. They must always be free in their lands, as they are often taken in wars and on other occasions, placed with an individual for many years who then transfers them to another individual for a consideration for the remainder of the time the assignment is to last. This is often done by the governors through a third party, and under this pretext they take many Indians, both men and women, to Mexico and other places to be sold.

It is requested that the Spanish governors be forbidden from depriving any native Indian chief of his post or authority, because of the fact that the Indians greatly resent seeing their leaders and chieftains mistreated.

WORKING WITH SOURCES

1. For what reasons does Benavides request restrictions on the amount of tribute and personal service that governors could demand of Indians? For what reasons does he request greater regulation of the Indian slave trade to and through New Mexico?

2. What kind of relationship among friars, governors, and Indians does Benavides seek?

3. What can you learn about Pueblo life and politics from Benavides's petition?

SOURCE 2.2

William Simmonds, Excerpts from *The Proceedings of the English Colonie in Virginia* (1612)

The difficulties that the Virginia Company of London encountered in trying to establish a colony at Jamestown and turn a profit from it generated a great deal of commentary on both sides of the Atlantic. The excerpt below comes from a narrative that William Simmonds published in Oxford, England, in 1612. A large portion of the work, which mostly provided an account of events in Virginia, came from John Smith himself and was sent to Simmonds by three friends of Smith, all of whom were in Virginia. At the beginning of the excerpt, these men have just finished recounting the difficulties that the English encountered in securing corn from Tsenacommacah's Algonquians to feed Jamestown.

Source: William Simmonds, The Proceedings of the English Colonie in Virginia since Their First Beginning from England in the Yeare of our Lord, 1606 till This Present 1612, with All Their Accidents that Befell Them in the Journies and Discoveries (Oxford, 1612), 76–78. Taken from Edward Arber, ed., Captain John Smith: Works, 1608–1631, (Birmingham, 1884), 147–48.

Those temporall proceedings, to some maie seeme too charitable, to such a dailie daring trecherous people; to others unpleasant that we washed not the ground with their blouds, nor shewed such strange inventions in mangling, murdering, ransaking, and destroying (as did the Spaniards) the simple bodies of those ignorant soules; nor delightful, because not stuffed with relations of heaps and mines of gold and silver, nor such rare commodities as the Portugals[9] and Spaniards found in the East and West Indies. The want wherof hath begot us, that were the first undertakers, no lesse scorne and contempt, than their noble conquests and valiant adventures (beautified with it), praise and honor. Too much, I confesse, the world cannot attribute to their ever memorable merit. And to cleare us from the worlds blind ignorant censure, these fewe words may suffise to any reasonably understanding.

It was the Spaniards good hap[10] to happen in those parts where were infinite numbers of people, whoe had manured the ground with that providence that it afforded victuall at all times; and time had brought them to that perfection [that] they had the vse of gold and silver, and [of] the most of such commodities as their countries affoorded: so that what the Spaniard got was only the spoile and pillage of those countrie people, and not the labours of their owne hands.

But had those fruitfull Countries beene as Salvage, as barbarous, as ill-peopled, as little planted laboured and manured, as *Virginia*; their proper labours, it is likely would have produced as small profit as ours. But had *Virginia* bin peopled, planted, manured, and adorned with such store of pretious Jewels and rich commodities as was the Indies: then, had we not gotten and done as much as by their examples might bee expected from us, the world might then have traduced us and our merits, and have made shame and infamy our recompence and reward.

[9]Portuguese.
[10]Luck.

But we chanced in a lande, even as God made it. Where we found only an idle, improvident, scattered people, ignorant of the knowledge of gold, or silver, or any commodities; and carelesse of anything but from hand to mouth, but for ba[u]bles of no worth; nothing to encourage us but what accidentally wee found nature afforded. Which ere wee could bring to recompence our paines, defray our charges, and satisfie our adventurers; we were to discover the country, subdue the people, bring them to be tractable civil and industrious, and teach them trades that the fruits of their labours might make us recompence, or plant such colonies of our owne that must first make provision how to live of themselves ere they can bring to perfection the commodities of the countrie: which doubtless will be as commodious for England as the west Indies for Spaine, if it be rightly managed; notwithstanding all our home-bred opinions that will argue the contrarie, as formerly such like have done against the Spaniards and Portugals.

But to conclude, against all rumor of opinion I only say this for those that the three first yeares began this plantation: notwithstanding al their factions, mutenies, and miseries, so gently corrected and well prevented, peruse the Spanish *Decades*, the relations of *Master Hacklu[y]t*; and tell mee how many ever, with such smal meanes as a barge of 2 Tunnes, sometimes with 7. 8. 9, or but at most 15 men, did ever discover so many faire and navigable rivers, subject so many severall kings people and nations to obedience and contribution, with so little bloud shed.

And if in the search of those Countries, wee had hapned where wealth had beene, we had as surely had it, as obedience and contribution; but if wee have overskipped it, we will not envy them that shall chance to finde it. Yet can wee not but lament it was our ill fortunes to end, when wee had but only learned how to begin, and found the right course how to proceed.

WORKING WITH SOURCES

1. In what terms do the authors discuss the Spanish conquest of much of the Americas? In what ways does their discussion reflect the "Black Legend" of Spanish conquest that was then circulating in the Anglo-Atlantic world? Does their discussion undermine the "Black Legend" in some way? If so, how so? If not, why not?

2. In what ways did the precarious finances of the Virginia Company and concerns about the reputation of its employees in Virginia influence the tone and content of the narrative you've just read?

SOURCE 2.3

John Winthrop, Excerpts from "A Modell of Christian Charity" (1630)

In 1630, John Winthrop, first governor of the Massachusetts Bay Company and occasional lay preacher in England, delivered the sermon "A Model of Christian Charity" to Puritans who were migrating to New England. We do not know whether Winthrop gave the sermon to departing colonists in England or en route to New England. Indeed, no written record of a person claiming to have heard it survives. It is likely that no one published Winthrop's sermon during the 17th century because few of the ideas would have struck its original audience as unusual or particularly noteworthy. Below are excerpts from the concluding section of the sermon, which has become one of the most famous examples of colonial literature.

Source: Collections of the Massachusetts Historical Society, 3rd Series, vol. 7 (Boston: Charles C. Little and James Brown, 1838), 33–48.

God Almighty in his most holy and wise providence, hath soe disposed of the condition of mankind, as in all times some must be rich, some poore, some high and eminent in power and dignitie; others mean and in submission. . . .

It rests now to make some application of this discourse, by the present designe, which gave the occasion of writing of it. Herein are 4 things to be propounded; *first* the persons, 2ly the worke, 3ly the end, 4thly the meanes. 1. For *the persons.* Wee are a company professing ourselves fellow members of Christ, in which respect only though wee were absent from each other many miles, and had our imployments as farre distant, yet wee ought to account ourselves knitt together by this bond of love, and, live in the exercise of it, if wee would have comforte of our being in Christ. This was notorious in the practise of the Christians in former times; . . . 2nly for the *worke* wee have in hand. It is by a mutuall consent, through a speciall overvaluing providence and a more than an ordinary approbation of the Churches of Christ, to seeke out a place of cohabitation and Consorteshipp under a due forme of Government both civill and ecclesiasticall. In such cases as this, the care of the publique must oversway all private respects, by which, not only conscience, but meare civill pollicy, dothe binde us. For it is a true rule that particular Estates cannot subsist in the ruin of the publique. 3ly The *end* is to improve our lives to doe more service to the Lord; the comforte and encrease of the body of Christe, whereof we are members; that ourselves and posterity may be the better preserved from the common corruptions of this evill world, to serve the Lord and worke out our Salvation under the power and purity of his holy ordinances. 4thly for the *meanes* whereby this must be effected. They are twofold, a conformity with the worke and end wee aime at. These wee see are extraordinary, therefore wee must not content ourselves with usuall ordinary meanes. Whatsoever wee did, or ought to have done, when wee lived in England, the same must wee doe, and more allsoe, where wee goe. That which the most in theire churches mainetaine as truthe in profession onely, wee must bring into familiar and constant practise; as in this duty of love, wee must love brotherly without dissimulation, wee must love one another with a pure hearte fervently. Wee must beare one anothers burthens. We must not looke onely on our owne things, but allsoe on the things of our brethren. Neither must wee thinke that the Lord will beare with such faileings at our hands as he dothe from those among whome wee have lived; and that for these 3 Reasons; 1. In regard of the more neare bond of mariage between him and us, wherein hee hath taken us to be his, after a most strickt and peculiar manner, which will make them the more jealous of our love and obedience. Soe he tells the people of Israell, *you onely have I knowne of all the families of the Earthe, therefore will I punishe you for your Transgressions.* 2ly, because *the Lord will be sanctified in them that come neare him.* We know that there were many that corrupted the service of the Lord; some setting upp altars before his owne; others offering both strange fire and strange sacrifices allsoe; yet there came noe fire from heaven, or other sudden judgement upon them, as did upon Nadab and Abihu, whoe yet wee may think did not sinne presumptuously. 3ly When God gives a speciall commission he lookes to have it strictly observed in every article, When he gave Saule a commission to destroy Amaleck, Hee indented with him upon certain articles, and because hee failed in one of the least, and that upon a faire pretense, it lost him the kingdom, which should have beene his reward, if hee had observed his commission. Thus stands the cause betweene God and us. We are entered into Covenant with Him for this worke. Wee haue taken out a commission. The Lord hath given us leave to drawe our own articles. Wee have professed to enterprise these and those accounts, upon these and those ends. Wee have hereupon besought Him of favour and blessing. Now if the Lord shall please to heare us, and bring us in peace to the place we desire, then hath hee ratified this covenant and sealed our Commission, and will expect a strict performance of the articles contained in it; but if wee shall neglect the observation of these articles which are the ends wee have propounded, and, dissembling with our God, shall fall to embrace this present world and prosecute our carnall intentions, seeking greate things for ourselves and our posterity, the Lord will surely breake out in wrathe against us; be revenged of such a [sinful] people and make us knowe the price of the breache of such a covenant.

Now the onely way to avoyde this shipwracke, and to provide for our posterity, is to followe the counsell of Micah, *to doe justly, to love mercy, to walk humbly with our God.* For this end, wee must be knitt together, in this worke, as one man. Wee must entertaine each other in brotherly affection. Wee must be willing to abridge ourselves of our superfluities, for the supply of other's necessities. Wee must uphold a familiar commerce together in all meekeness, gentlenes, patience and liberality. Wee must delight in eache other; make other's conditions our oune; rejoice together, mourne together, labour and suffer together, allwayes haueving before our eyes our commission and community in the worke, as members of the same body. Soe shall wee *keepe the unitie of the spirit in the bond of peace.* The Lord will be our God, and delight to dwell among us, as his oune people, and will command a blessing upon us in all our wayes. Soe that wee shall see much more of his wisdome, power, goodness and truthe, than formerly wee haue been acquainted with. Wee shall finde that the God of Israell is among us, when ten of us shall be able to resist a thousand of our enemies; when hee shall make us a prayse and glory that men shall say of succeeding plantations, "the Lord make it likely that of *New England.*" For wee must consider that wee shall be as a citty upon a hill. The eies of all people are uppon us. Soe that if wee shall deale falsely with our God in this worke wee have undertaken, and soe cause him to withdrawe his present help from us, wee shall be made a story and a by-word through the world. Wee shall open the mouthes of enemies to speake evill of the wayes of God, and all professors for God's sake. Wee shall shame the faces of many of God's worthy servants, and cause theire prayers to be turned into curses upon us till wee be consumed out of the good land whither wee are a goeing.

WORKING WITH SOURCES

1. What kind of relationship does Winthrop posit between his audience and God? In what ways does that relationship help to explain Massachusetts Bay colonists' belief that they should police each other's behavior?

2. Based on Winthrop's sermon, in what sense did colonists believe that they were about to create a "New" England in North America?

SOURCE 2.4

Visual Document: Simon Van de Passe and Compton Holland, Portrait of Pocahontas (1616)

In 1616, Pocahontas, along with her husband John Rolfe, their infant son Thomas, an advisor to Powhatan named Uttamatomakin, and at least six Algonquian attendants, visited England. Officials of the struggling Virginia Company saw an opportunity to publicize the firm's work and shore up its precarious finances. They commissioned a Dutch-German artist, Simon Van de Passe, to sketch Pocahontas's portrait, from which Compton Holland made the engraving shown below. The English inscription underneath the engraving translates the Latin words that surround her image and also identifies her as a Christian convert married to John Rolfe and her father as "Emperor of Attanoughs-komouck," which the English usually called Tsenacommacah. Although the engraving claims that she was 21 years old at the time of its making, she was probably only 19.

Source: Virginia Historical Society, Richmond, Virginia, USA/The Bridgeman Art Library.

WORKING WITH SOURCES

1. In what ways does Pocahontas's portrait differ from that of Eiakintomino in Chapter 2 of the text? Remember that the Virginia Company either used or sought to use both images for promotional purposes, and that its officials considered Pocahontas to be "nobility."

2. Did Pocahontas influence how Van de Passe portrayed her? What elements of the portrait and its captions suggest that she did?

Forging Tighter Bonds

"Who is the father?" the midwife demanded of Anne Orthwood, an indentured servant who was in the throes of labor in the summer of 1664. The young woman identified him as John Kendall, one of Virginia's most prominent men and her former master. Orthwood gave birth to twins before suffering an agonizing death, probably from an infection she contracted during childbirth. One baby died. The other, Jasper, faced a hard life. John Kendall denied he was the father. County officials agreed, but did not want taxpayers to foot the bill for raising Jasper, so they found Kendall legally responsible for his son's care. Kendall soon bound Jasper out to a friend who owned a nearby plantation. For the next 22 years, Jasper worked as an indentured servant. In 1686, he sued for his freedom, won, and then disappeared from local records.

Anne Orthwood's path to an early grave and Jasper's passage from servitude to freedom were a product of economic and social changes taking place in Virginia between the 1660s and 1680s. Anne was born into poverty and a fatherless home in Bristol, England. In 1662, she joined a torrent of nearly 30,000 English streaming to Virginia and Maryland during the 1650s and 1660s to work as servants. Their labor, and that of a slowly increasing population of enslaved Africans, more than doubled Virginia's tobacco exports during the 1660s. Meanwhile, masters tightened their grip on servants and slaves. In 1662, Virginia lawmakers empowered them to punish female servants like Anne who became pregnant and deprived masters of their services.

Had Anne survived, she would have faced the prospect of several lashes and at least two more years of servitude. Hard labor and harsh laws gave indentured servitude a bad image in

< Elsje (Rutgers) Schuyler Vas, 1723, attributed to Gerardus Duyckinck I.

England and fueled the resentment of servants and ex-servants in Virginia. In 1672, legislators addressed these concerns by enacting a law that emancipated male bastards at age 21, three years sooner than the standards set by English poor law. Jasper's lawsuit was a direct result. Despite his master's protests that English poor law entitled him to Jasper's services until he turned 24, Anne's son based his claim on the 1672 Virginia law that his mother's former master helped to write. But the change in the law did not improve Virginia's reputation overseas or calm sullen servants and ex-servants. Immigration from England slowed. Servants, ex-servants, and slaves joined a rebellion that nearly toppled the colony's government. Masters responded by buying more slaves and fewer indentured servants to tend their tobacco.

Increased reliance on slave labor was one of the many solutions to the conflicts and crises that North America's colonies and neighboring Indian societies weathered between 1640 and the 1690s. The resolution to these crises redrew the continent's political map, developed the economies of some English colonies, rooted African slavery in North American soil, checked Spanish power, and turned the English and French empires into North America's dominant European powers. Indians still controlled most of North America. But colonists, be they free, in servitude, or enslaved, claimed and held more of the continent, due largely to their tighter bonds to the world overseas.

◼ UNCIVIL WARS, 1640–1660

Death and violence gripped North America and the Anglo-Atlantic world in the 1640s and 1650s. Epidemics ravaged the Iroquois and Great Lakes peoples, fueling an increasingly destructive cycle of warfare between Indians. A civil war in England echoed in English North America, prompting religious, social, and economic upheaval that in turn led New England to diversify its economy and forge stronger ties to the Caribbean, where planters established English America's first society built on plantation slavery. Meanwhile, the Spanish expanded mission systems in Florida and New Mexico, brutally crushing Indian rebellions.

Smallpox and War Plague the Great Lakes

The arrival of thousands of Dutch and English colonists in the 1630s, many of whom carried the smallpox virus, enabled the disease to take root in northeastern North America. The first epidemic struck in 1633, followed by another six years later. The virus felled Indians of all ages but killed a disproportionate number of those between the ages of 15 and 40, those who usually did most of the farming, hunting, and caring for children, the sick, and the elderly. Traditional Indian remedies worsened the epidemics. Communal healing rituals spread the virus, and sweating and fasting, common Indian treatments for illness, made people sicker. By the early 1640s, epidemics had probably killed more than half the population of Iroquois, reducing it to around 10,000. They continued to ravage the Iroquois League and their Indian neighbors over the next 30 years.

Grief and rage at the toll that smallpox took set the Iroquois League and their neighbors on the warpath. The 1633 epidemic triggered a wave of Iroquois attacks on the Huron Confederacy. The epidemic of 1639–1640 launched a conflict between Iroquois and Huron that raged for 70 years. Some historians call it the "**Beaver Wars**" because control of hunting grounds was often the combatants' objective. Hunters had already emptied much of New England, New York, and Pennsylvania

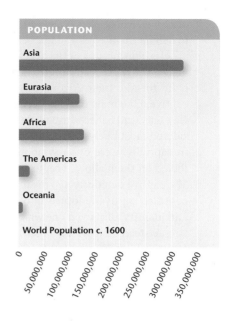

POPULATION

Asia

Eurasia

Africa

The Americas

Oceania

World Population c. 1600

0 / 50,000,000 / 100,000,000 / 150,000,000 / 200,000,000 / 250,000,000 / 300,000,000 / 350,000,000

IROQUOIS French drawing of an Iroquois (probably Seneca) tree bark carving depicting a mourning war raid. Each member of the war party drew the totem animal of his clan, each holding a weapon. The three upside down figures at center right indicate that the warriors killed two men and one woman. At bottom left one warrior carries two scalps, while the other watches over a captive.

of beaver, whose pelts bought firearms, hatchets, and other imports that enabled Indians to defend themselves and live better.

Indians needed better access to pelts, but replacing the kin claimed by disease and violence mattered far more to them. Indeed, the Iroquois waged "mourning wars" principally to take their Algonquian- or Iroquoian-speaking neighbors (such as Hurons) captive. Like most Indians in eastern North America, Mohawks, Oneidas, Onondagas, Cayugas, and Senecas usually targeted children, adolescents, and women—groups considered most likely to acculturate. Men taken prisoner, deemed least likely to accept life in captivity, were often symbolically incorporated in a different way. The torture inflicted on them allowed captors to assuage their grief and avenge the loss of loved ones. The captive demonstrated his manhood by meeting his excruciating death stoically. By contrast, captives adopted into a clan usually assumed the place, and often the name and identity, of a loved one who had died (Map 3.1).

A steady supply of Dutch firearms from New Netherland enabled the Iroquois League to outgun most of their Indian foes from the 1630s into the 1660s. The Huron, long allied with the French, and the Indians who sheltered them were perhaps the Beaver Wars' biggest losers. Iroquois ended the conflict by storming two Huron towns and a Jesuit mission and killing hundreds in 1649. Hurons who evaded captivity fled north and west, whereas Petuns, closely associated with Huron, sought shelter among other Iroquoian-speaking peoples—Neutrals and Eries. Iroquois warriors overwhelmed each as the refugees streamed west to Wisconsin. There they regrouped to form a new people, Huron-Petuns or Wyandot, in the 1650s and 1660s alongside thousands of Algonquians, also forced to flee their homelands by epidemics and Iroquois raids. Together the refugees plotted revenge against the Iroquois.

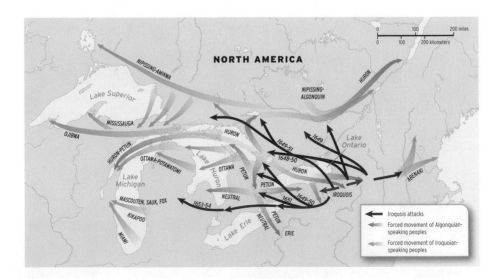

MAP 3.1 ▲ Iroquois Mourning Wars and the Dispersal of Great Lakes and New England Peoples, 1648–1653 The Iroquois League's mourning wars took their greatest toll on nearby Indian peoples between 1648 and 1653. This map shows peoples claimed or dispersed by Iroquois attacks and where those who escaped Iroquois raids sought refuge. Refugees who headed for Quebec were usually Christian converts.

In just one generation, the Great Lakes region and the Iroquois were transformed. Microbes and wars had depopulated a vast area that stretched from the Great Lakes south to the Ohio River and east to the Susquehanna River. The once-mighty Huron Confederacy had become a diaspora, with most of its people living in captivity within Iroquois's longhouse.

English Civil Wars and the Remaking of English America

Across the Atlantic, the English divided into those who believed that Charles I was their supreme leader and those who insisted that **Parliament** should have the ultimate political and religious authority. In 1642, the factions took up arms against each other, triggering the English Civil War. Most Puritans sided with Parliamentarians, who in 1649 tried Charles, beheaded him, and proclaimed that England had become a commonwealth. Four years later, the Puritan general **Oliver Cromwell**, commander of the New Model Army, staged a military coup and named himself Lord Protector. Cromwell died in 1658 after trying to appoint his son to succeed him. By then, the English had tired of political instability. Charles I's son and heir, **Charles II**, rose to the throne in 1660, an event that restored the English monarchy.

Leaders of six colonies, including Maryland and Virginia, responded to news of Charles's execution by declaring allegiance to his son. Barbados and Virginia, then the only colonies under direct royal rule, offered refuge to royalists fleeing England. In 1652, a Commonwealth fleet forced Virginia governor **William Berkeley** to accept England's new rulers before its commander removed him from office.

JOHN ELIOT, 1659   Eliot led the campaign to convert Indians in New England. He began to organize "praying towns," separate communities for Christian Indians, during the 1650s and later translated the Bible into the Massachusetts dialect of Algonquian. Eliot also lobbied vociferously against the Indian slave trade that arose during King Philip's War.

"THE QUAKERS MEETING"   The Society of Friends offended many English for several reasons, significant among them their willingness to permit women to speak during church services. This mezzotint, produced in the late 1600s, intended to satirize Quakers by showing them in a meeting as a woman stood on a box and preached to them.

In New England, England's Civil War brought religious, social, and economic upheaval. When the war began, New England's orthodox leaders rejoiced that their vision of a godly society might be transplanted to England. Reformers in England initially sought an alternative to Anglicanism. In the early 1640s, many thought that New England might offer one, a prospect that delighted Massachusetts Bay leaders. London printers published over 20 favorable works about New England between 1641 and 1643, most written by colonists. Virtually all recommended some aspect of New England's religious life to English readers. In 1644, Roger Williams and others published accounts in London that claimed that all New England colonies except Rhode Island regularly persecuted religious dissenters. In 1649, developments across the Atlantic dashed Puritan hopes when Cromwell formally recognized the Church of England as the official state religion.

The English Civil War also precipitated New England's first concerted effort to convert Indians, largely to improve the region's reputation overseas. Puritans in England founded the Society for the Propagation of the Gospel in New England, later the **New England Company**. The New Model Army was initially one of the society's largest benefactors. The missionary **John Eliot** led the campaign to evangelize Indians. He founded separate towns for baptized Indians in the 1650s and published a catechism and the Bible in Algonquian in the early 1660s.

Events in England also helped give rise to colonial North America's first witch scare. As many as 200,000 people in Europe, at least three-fourths of them women, were accused of witchcraft during the 1500s and 1600s. Approximately 60,000 people were executed. Witch hunts peaked in England in the mid-1640s, particularly in East Anglia, the birthplace of many New Englanders. Connecticut prosecuted and executed its first witch in 1647. Massachusetts Bay authorities convicted and hanged Margaret Jones, a midwife, a year later. In all, 79 New England colonists, 61 of them women, were accused of witchcraft; 33 were tried, and 15 were executed between 1647 and 1663. John Winthrop, Jr., son of Massachusetts Bay's first governor, was instrumental in ending New England's first witch hunt.

Some accused witches belonged to a new egalitarian sect that originated in England during the civil war. Its members called themselves the **Society of Friends**. Their enemies knew them as "**Quakers**" because their bodies "quaked" when they encountered God. Friends preached that people would find little of God's will in biblical verses, ministers' sermons, or formal services. Instead, God had given everyone an "inner light"—an innate ability to determine what God wanted for them and for the world. Friends preached and practiced pacifism, did not remove their hats on meeting someone who outranked them socially, and addressed superiors in familiar terms using "thee" or "thou" rather than the formal "you." They also created separate and autonomous governing structures for men and women and permitted women such as Mary Dyer to preach and serve as missionaries.

Such beliefs and practices brought Quakers persecution on both sides of the Atlantic, especially in most of New England. Their often confrontational tactics alienated ministers and magistrates. Massachusetts Bay officials executed four Quakers between 1659 and 1661, Mary Dyer among them. Quakers publicized such persecution as they lobbied English authorities to revoke New England colonies' charters.

The English Civil War created even bigger headaches for New England's leaders, slowing immigration to New England and thus provoking a full-blown economic depression. New England ran a large trade deficit with English merchants. The savings of thousands of English immigrants had streamed funds into the New England economy. The war halted the stream of immigrants into New England. When the immigrants stopped coming in the early 1640s, so did the money.

Colonists had to find other ways to earn income and produce some of what they could no longer afford to import. English immigrants to New England were among the Atlantic world's best-educated people and many had skills to process what the region's fields, forests, and seas offered. Massachusetts Bay boasted North America's first integrated ironworks, featuring one of only a dozen rolling and slitting mills in operation in the Atlantic world in the early 1650s. The ironworks soon expired in a flurry of bankruptcies and lawsuits. Other efforts to exploit New England's natural resources enjoyed more success. Axe-wielding men cut into massive forests, furnishing local and Caribbean carpenters with wood. The English Civil War sharply reduced the number of English vessels that fished off New England's coast, so crews of colonists filled the breach. They caught and salted cod, packing the fish in locally crafted barrels. New England-made ships ferried the fishermen into the sea and back.

The English Civil War also accelerated the development of New England's shipbuilding industry. By the early 1640s, New England-built ships, sailed by colonists, took salted fish, salt pork, horses, and timber to Spain, Portugal, and the West Indies. Three decades later, Massachusetts residents built and owned over 700 ships of at least six tons. New England shipyards soon employed thousands exporting vessels to England. Thousands more found work sailing the Atlantic or pulling cod from it.

Although New England colonies initially took actions against slavery, New England vessels eventually began to transport enslaved Africans. In 1646, a ship arrived in Boston from West Africa carrying the first enslaved Africans whom mainland English colonists brought across the Atlantic. Authorities charged the captain with kidnapping and repatriated his victims at public expense. Rhode Island responded to the Atlantic slave trade by outlawing lifelong slavery in 1652. The bill's authors noted that "there is a common course practiced among English men" to buy Africans so that "they may have them for service or slaves forever." Antislavery views, however, did not prevail. By the 1670s, Boston merchants were buying small numbers of enslaved people in Madagascar and selling them in the Caribbean and North America.

Necessity compelled New England to lay the foundation of a diverse economy. Heavy immigration was the region's economic lifeline in the 1630s. A generation later, colonists' trade with other North American colonies, Europe, and the West Indies sustained them. To John Winthrop, such ties seemed heaven sent. Just as Massachusetts Bay seemed about to go bankrupt, "it pleased the Lord to open to us a Trade with Barbados."

Planters and Slaves of the Caribbean

In 1627, English colonists splashed ashore on Barbados. Thirteen years later, Barbados, just 144 square miles, had as many English as Virginia. By 1680, it was England's wealthiest and most populous colony, with 60,000 people. The vast majority were enslaved Africans who toiled and died in the sugar cane fields that blanketed the island.

At first, it looked as if Barbados might become a smaller version of Virginia, a place where English grew tobacco on small farms staffed with white indentured servants. The island looked more alluring to young English men than New England or the Chesapeake. Two features soon distinguished Barbados from Virginia. First, in 1636, the governor declared that all Africans and Indians brought to the island were to be considered slaves unless they had a contract that said otherwise. Planters began to grow export crops other than tobacco and earn higher profits from them. These included cotton and indigo, source of a brilliant blue dye. The new crops enabled planters to buy more laborers, expand their estates, and experiment with cultivating sugar cane. Their success made them look like good credit risks to London merchants, who issued planters loans to purchase more land, enslaved Africans, and the expensive machinery that processed cane into sugar. Barbados soon replaced Brazil as the Americas' biggest supplier of sugar to Europe.

The sugar boom tied Barbados and New England together. Forests covered the island in the 1620s, partly because Spanish slavers had emptied it of people a century earlier. Cane fields and mills' need for lumber and fuel to boil cane juice down to sugar claimed most of the trees. New England forests provided wood to build and repair mills and barrels to hold molasses and sugar. New England's fields, meadows, and coasts fed Barbadian workers and allowed most of them to produce sugar and little else. The more land and labor devoted to cane, the less remained for growing food on Barbados.

The sugar boom of the 1640s accelerated the rise of African slavery and the decline of indentured servitude on Barbados. The more that planters demanded cane, the worse Barbados looked to English servants. Almost no one with better options would choose to work on a sugar plantation. Cane leaves cut skin, and cane fields are hot dirty places, full of rats and snakes. The rollers that squeezed juice from cane trapped and crushed fingers, arms, and heads. Servants, many of them Irish prisoners of war, rebelled in 1647, making enslaved African labor look more desirable to planters. In England, members of Parliament criticized the treatment of English servants in Barbados, increasing the planters' interest in and reliance on enslaved African labor (Table 3.1).

Barbados legislators sought tighter control of enslaved people by enacting English America's first slave code in 1661. The code prescribed different treatment and different levels of protection before the law for enslaved Africans and white servants. It deputized

Table 3.1 Estimated Number of Enslaved Africans Transported by Each Nation and/or Colony, 1601–1775

The Barbados sugar boom of the 1640s made England a major participant in the Atlantic slave trade. From 1651 until the American Revolution in 1775, ships registered to owners in England or Britain carried more Africans than those of any other European or American power.

	Spain	Portugal/ Brazil (c)	England/ Britain	Netherlands	British North America (c)	France	Denmark	Totals
1601–1625	83,496	267,519	0	1,829	0	0	0	352,843
1626–1650	44,313	201,609	33,695	31,729	824	1,827	1,053	315,050
1651–1675	12,601	244,793	122,367	100,526	0	7,125	653	488,064
1676–1700	5,860	297,272	272,200	85,847	3,327	29,484	25,685	719,674
1701–1725	0	474,447	410,597	73,816	3,277	120,939	5,833	1,088,909
1726–1750	0	536,696	554,042	83,095	34,004	259,095	4,793	1,471,725
1751–1775	4,239	528,693	832,047	132,330	84,580	325,918	17,508	1,925,314
Totals	150,509	2,551,028	2,224,947	509,172	126,012	744,387	55,525	6,361,580

Note: Places that were colonies between 1601 and 1775 are designated with (c).

free white men to police slaves' movements and encouraged them to whip those found without a pass from their masters. The **Barbados slave code** became one of the most influential pieces of legislation in the Anglo-Atlantic world. Many English colonies duplicated portions of it. Four copied it completely, including South Carolina and Georgia.

The sugar boom made England a major participant in the Atlantic slave trade and it created English America's first slave society. By 1684, enslaved Africans outnumbered whites more than two to one. Most Africans met an early grave. West Indian planters estimated that a young enslaved African male might survive only seven years. Few had families; planters preferred to buy young men because they considered them better workers. They also calculated that it was cheaper to import people than to ensure that those whom they already enslaved lived longer and healthier lives. Only the Atlantic slave trade sustained the black majority on Barbados and elsewhere in the English West Indies (Figure 3.1).

Church and Indians in the Southeast and Southwest

As the English colonies established roots in North America and the Caribbean, the Spanish mission spread in Florida and New Mexico. In 1633, Spanish friars added Apalachee Indians in the Florida Panhandle to their extensive network of missions. Their initiative answered a long-standing invitation from Apalachee chiefs who thought that better relations with the Spanish would bring them more power, prestige, and better access to imports. Fourteen years later, however, unconverted Apalachee and their

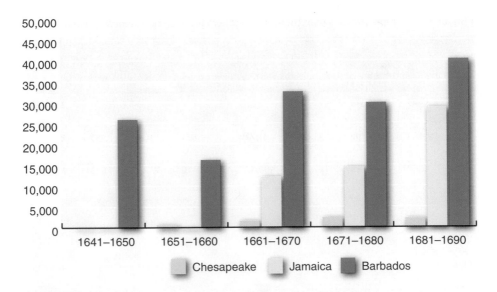

FIGURE 3.1 ▲ Enslaved Africans disembarked in the Chesapeake Colonies, Barbados, and Jamaica (estimated), 1641–1690 More enslaved Africans by far went to the English Caribbean than to English colonies in mainland North America. Over 20 times as many went to Barbados as to Virginia and Maryland between 1641 and 1690, partly because so many died young and were overworked in the island's cane fields.

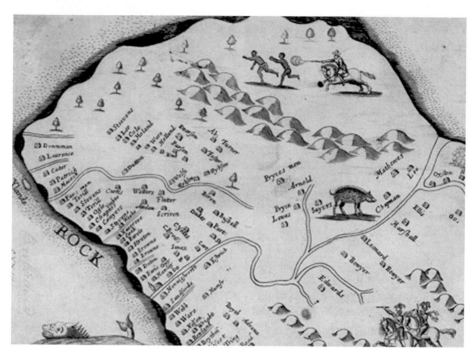

TWO ENSLAVED AFRICAN FUGITIVES FLEE A WHITE PURSUER   The image illustrates a map that accompanied a history of Barbados written by Richard Ligon, who visited there in the late 1640s. In 1661, Barbados enacted English America's first slave code, much of which addressed the capture and punishment of runaways.

Chisca allies set seven missions ablaze and drove the Spanish out. About 30 Spanish soldiers and 500 Timucua warriors recruited from missions retaliated, forcing Apalachee to surrender. They handed over those who the Spanish believed had led the rebellion. Some were hanged; the rest were sentenced to toil in St. Augustine. Florida's governor also demanded that Apalachee chiefs send laborers to the Spanish town, just as Timucua and Guales did.

The Apalachee integrated into Florida's economy with tragic results. In 1655, an epidemic followed the road that linked Apalachee, Timucua, and St. Augustine, spread largely by Indians forced to transport goods or work in the Spanish town. It devastated Apalachee towns already reeling from Spanish demands for tribute and labor. By mid-century, Apalachee's population plummeted from 30,000 to 10,000. Multiple villages of Guales and Timucua were consolidated into just one mission village for each people, neither of which could fill St. Augustine's appetite for labor any longer.

Many Timucua could take no more. In 1656, following rumors of an English raid, Timucua chiefs refused the governor's order to muster warriors and march to St. Augustine's defense. Lucas Menéndez, a Timucua chief who nursed grievances against the governor, refused to go. He persuaded some of his peers to attack Spanish colonists. They killed or drove off most colonists, but spared the friars who ran the missions. Unlike Guale insurgents in 1597 or the Apalachee in 1647, Timucua chiefs accepted missions as integral to their world. They communicated with letters written in a Timucuan alphabet that friars had taught them. Executions and sentences of forced labor in St. Augustine ended the **Timucua revolt**. The Timucua were forced to resettle into missions strewn along the road between Apalachee and St. Augustine, depopulating even more of north Florida.

The Timucua revolt gave friars the upper hand in their struggle with Florida governors. It rankled them that Governor Diego de Rebolledo ridiculed their efforts to reform Indian cultures. In 1658, friars had Rebolledo summoned to Spain to stand trial for using his office to abuse Indians. By 1675, 11,000 Indians lived in missions, most of them in Apalachee. Florida's mission system and the friars would never be more powerful.

Tensions between friars, officials, and Indians also roiled New Mexican politics. Small revolts in Taos in 1639 and in Tewa villages in 1650 temporarily allied church and state, as did rumors of a conspiracy between Pueblos and Indians of northern Mexico. However, cultural and linguistic differences made it hard for Pueblos to unite, and the revolts were soon suppressed. Rebels were hung or sold into slavery. Some sought refuge among Apaches and helped to organize raids on the colony.

The cease-fire between Franciscan friars and governors ended in the late 1650s. The new governor, Bernardo López de Mendizábal, thought the friars had too much power. He outlawed the use of involuntary Indian labor at missions. Friars charged that the governor undermined them by siding with village chiefs and medicine men and encouraging polygamy and ceremonial dances. Reacting to a drought that began in 1660, Pueblos revived **ritualistic** dances to make the rains return, rituals that friars labeled devil worship. Franciscans had Mendizábal arrested and taken in chains to Mexico City. They did the same to his successor, securing their dominance over New Mexico.

STUDY QUESTIONS FOR UNCIVIL WARS, 1640–1660

1. What impact did the English Civil War have on North America and the West Indies?
2. In what ways and for what reasons did Indian life change between 1640 and 1660?

■ NEW IMPERIAL ORDERS, 1660–1680

The 1660s heralded a new order for colonial English and French North America. New monarchs launched reforms and waged wars intended to forge integrated empires from scattered North American and Caribbean colonies. Conquest brought a large, diverse, and established population of colonists who were not English under English rule for the first time. Meanwhile, political and social changes in the Chesapeake and a new Barbadian colony in Carolina rooted plantation slavery in North America.

The English Colonial Empire and the Conquest of New Netherland

In 1660, English America learned that England again had a king. Charles II restored his father's ally William Berkeley to the governorship of Virginia. Massachusetts Bay feared retribution for having supported the defeated side in the English Civil War but still took months to proclaim the new monarch. Charles's reign brought enduring changes for colonists and Indians. By the time Charles II died in 1685, English entrepreneurs had founded four new colonies, and imperial officials had reorganized three others. New Netherland entered England's empire by conquest, making it the first Anglo-American society in which authorities governed large numbers of settled Europeans who were not English. All colonists faced an empire that sought to tighten oversight of their internal affairs and their commerce overseas (Figure 3.2).

Under Charles II, England established the **Navigation Acts** (Table 3.2), a series of laws that began to go into effect in 1651 that permitted free trade within England's colonial empire but restricted commerce with people outside it. English merchants applauded them, but the reaction among colonists was mixed. On the positive side, the laws guaranteed markets for their goods and services. Nevertheless, colonial planters and merchants chafed at the regulations. Planters thought the laws deprived them of markets by levying duties on tobacco and sugar and by requiring that those commodities be unloaded in England before proceeding to European markets. Merchants in the colonies objected that European imports destined for English North America also had to pass through England before being shipped across the Atlantic, an arrangement that they believed unfairly favored their English counterparts.

English officials looked to the Navigation Acts to sever English colonists' thickening ties with Dutch merchants. Massachusetts Bay grudgingly ceased trade with New Netherland during the **First Anglo-Dutch War** (1652–1654) but quickly resumed it when peace came, even though the first Navigation Act of 1651 clearly barred commerce

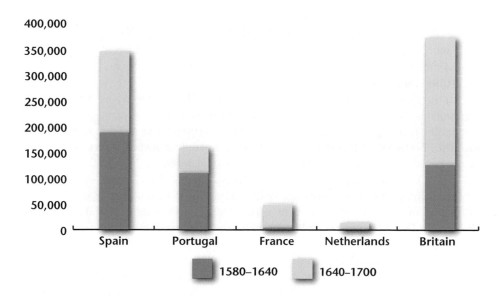

FIGURE 3.2 ▲ European emigration to the Americas, 1580–1700 Between 1580 and 1700, England sent more Europeans to the Americas than any of its rivals. Nearly half the European immigrants to the Americas between 1640 and 1700 were English. The majority of English went to mainland North America, where the populations of English colonies dwarfed those of European rivals.

Table 3.2 Navigation Acts

As English authorities began to see colonies as a key source of wealth, they began to regulate American colonists' commerce with Atlantic markets. Here are some of the most important laws, known as the Navigation Acts.

Year Legislation Passed	Key Provisions and Outcomes
1651	All goods sent to England from America, Africa, or Asia must be carried in vessels owned and staffed by Englishmen or English colonists Dutch merchants barred from English colonies Provokes First Anglo-Dutch War
1660	Only vessels owned by Englishmen and operated by crews that were at least three-quarters English may dock in colonial ports Stipulated list of "enumerated goods," including sugar and tobacco, which had to be shipped to England before they could be taken elsewhere
1663	Most non-English goods headed for English colonies must first be shipped through England and taxed there
1673	Colonists required to pay duties on enumerated goods shipped to England Customs agents appointed and stationed in every colony to collect duties
1696	Extends system of vice-admiralty courts from England to colonies to clamp down on smuggling and enforce Navigation Acts

with the Dutch. Dutch merchants also transported enslaved Africans to English colonies, especially when the English Civil War disrupted Anglo-Atlantic trade. In 1663, Charles II awarded the predecessor of the **Royal African Company** a monopoly on English trade with Africa, a concession that included the Atlantic slave trade. The company's attacks on Dutch shipping and forts in West Africa sparked the Second Anglo-Dutch War (1664–1667).

In North America, that war began when a small English fleet won New Amsterdam's surrender without firing a shot. The city and New Netherland became New York in August 1664, taking on the title of Charles's brother **James, Duke of York**. Commander Richard Nicolls knew that it would be difficult to control such a diverse colony, so he promised Dutch colonists a New York that would resemble New Netherland. The **Articles of Capitulation** granted Dutch residents religious liberty, freedom from military conscription, property rights, the ability to leave New York within 18 months, and free trade and freedom of movement within the English empire. The Articles also allowed the Dutch to continue following their inheritance customs.

England's grip on New York was tenuous. In 1673, a Dutch fleet delighted most Dutch and many English residents by conquering the colony. Dutch authorities seized property of English officials and merchants. A peace treaty returned the colony to England a year later, but the English were alarmed at New York's quick capitulation to the Dutch. Much of New York's "Dutch" majority, in fact, strove to become more "Dutch" in the wake of English conquest. The Dutch Reformed Church assumed a more prominent role in New York than it had in New Netherland. Another way for Dutch colonists to assert a Dutch identity was to continue to divide their estates in Dutch ways.

This gave Dutch women more power than English women had. Dutch inheritance law permitted women to keep property that they brought to a marriage, and divided estates equally between sons and daughters. These practices eroded gradually during the early 1700s.

Growing English domination of New York's public life during the 1680s alienated many Dutch and widened political divisions. An English minority seized the agenda in New York's first representative assembly in 1683. Three years later, all government bodies, including those of towns, followed English norms. Dutch who lived upriver resented the growing power of Manhattan's wealthy Anglo-Dutch merchants. So did most of the city's artisans, Dutch and English, who saw a small number of well-connected men conspiring with officials to issue regulations that threatened their livelihood. Dutch who considered the Dutch Reformed Church the bulwark of Dutch identity expressed dismay at English officials' growing influence over clergy. In 1689, this brew of class and ethnic tensions boiled over as political instability wracked the Anglo-Atlantic world and war erupted with France.

Quebec and the Expansion of French America

In 1665, as New Yorkers adjusted to their first year of English rule, a regiment of some 1,000 French troops landed in Quebec. The arrival of North America's first standing army doubled the number of men in New France. Louis XIV's minister **Jean-Baptiste Colbert** considered the regiment crucial to his plan to reform France's empire. He, like his English rivals, believed in **mercantilism**: an economic system in which colonies existed mainly to provide raw materials and to serve as protected markets for finished goods. To accomplish these goals, Colbert aimed to repopulate Canada, increase royal control over New France, diversify the colony's economy, and better integrate it into French-Atlantic trade networks.

First, the French had to curb Iroquois raids. Except for Mohawks, all Iroquois favored peace with New France, partly because England's conquest of New Netherland curtailed their supply of firearms. In 1666, the French launched their final invasion of Mohawk country, looting and torching dozens of longhouses and two years' worth of food stores.

After securing a tense peace, French officials focused on resettling New France. Colbert noted how colonization with families seemed to enhance English power and he wanted to emulate it. He directed officials to recruit male servants and young women, who would become wives in a society in which white men vastly outnumbered white women.

Wars in Europe and budgetary constraints stopped the flow of immigrants by the mid-1670s. However, New France's population had already reached 10,000 and continued to grow, mainly naturally. In New France, women gave birth to more children than women in France did, and more of their children survived to adulthood. France's population barely grew during the 1700s, whereas New France's practically doubled every generation.

Aside from more native-born French Canadians, New France attained few of Colbert's goals. He sought a New France that would serve the French economy as New England did the English. Instead, New France developed into a modest colony of landlords, tenants, and peasants that still depended on furs to pay for imports. Colbert envisioned that Canadian-built ships would ferry fish, provisions, and timber to

France's Caribbean colonies and return with sugar, rum, and molasses. However, New England outcompeted New France in the French West Indies. Its merchants provided more goods more cheaply as well as access to a far bigger colonial market.

As a consequence of its treaty with the Iroquois, New France gained greater access inland. Robert Cavalier de La Salle won approval to sail down the Mississippi and establish trading posts along the way. He reached the river's mouth in 1682, claimed the area for France, and named it Louisiana after **Louis XIV**. The **Hudson's Bay Company**, which had formed in England in 1670, competed with the French. The English, who offered more goods at better prices than the French, attracted Cree Indians who brought pelts to Hudson's Bay outposts. A struggle soon began between England and France for North America's interior. For decades, whoever best met Indian needs held the upper hand.

Chesapeake Servitude, Mainland Slavery

During the second half of the 1600s, Maryland and Virginia also experienced drastic changes. Both colonies originally relied on indentured servants as a source of labor. By the early 1680s, the Chesapeake resembled Barbados. It too had become a society dependent on slavery and founded on the principle of white supremacy.

Plantation slavery and racial consciousness emerged gradually and together in the Chesapeake. The legal status of people of African descent remained ambiguous into the 1660s. Many were considered indentured servants. A few gained freedom, owned land, and even held slaves. A 1668 law, however, compelled free black women to pay a tax, compounding the burden on struggling black families (Table 3.3).

Virginia lawmakers built most of the legal foundation for the perpetual enslavement of Africans during the 1660s. They laid one cornerstone in 1662 by declaring that a child's legal status should follow that of the mother. This broke with English law and gender norms, under which a child inherited legal status from the father. Worse, it made slavery heritable and in the masters' eyes, remade enslaved women into commodities valued for their production and reproduction. This encouraged masters to abuse enslaved women sexually and it emasculated enslaved fathers. Legislators laid another cornerstone in 1667 by resolving that slaves who had been baptized and had converted to Christianity did not have legal grounds to sue for freedom.

Although masters enjoyed new powers, they did not immediately purchase many more slaves. In 1670, the 2,000 enslaved Virginians formed 5 percent of the colony's population. Many did not come directly from Africa but rather from the West Indies, where planters traded slaves for grain and meat (Map 3.2) Still, around 6,000 Africans arrived in Chesapeake Bay between 1660 and 1690.

The gradual expansion of African slavery in the Chesapeake was tied to changes in indentured servitude and to the region's reputation in England. In the late 1650s and early 1660s, the number of servants who came to Virginia, three-quarters of them men, surged as their prospects declined in Barbados (Figure 3.3). But soon Chesapeake planters had trouble finding servants at a price that they were willing to pay. Improving job prospects in England kept many at home, as did reports of what awaited servants across the ocean. As with Barbados, news from the Chesapeake likened servitude to slavery. A critic in the 1670s insisted that masters tyrannized servants "as Turks do over Galley-slaves."

Table 3.3 Selected Key Legal Developments Concerning Slavery and Race in English America, 1635–1696

Slavery and racism emerged gradually and together in English America during the 17th century. Here are some of the key legal milestones in that process, one in which Barbados played a key role.

Year	Colony	Key Provisions
1635	Barbados	Governor declares that all Africans and Indians brought to the island to be considered slaves unless they have a contract that says otherwise
1641	Massachusetts Bay	Legalizes slavery within the colony
1643	Virginia	Women of African descent and all men made subject to tithe to support Church of England
1661	Barbados	First comprehensive slave code in English America, setting model for other colonies to follow
1661	Virginia	Indentured servants who run away with slaves to serve time that slave missed as well as time that they missed
1662	Virginia	Child's legal status to follow that of the mother rather than the father
1664	Maryland	Slavery defined as a lifelong legal condition
1665	New York	New English Assembly, composed largely of migrants from New England, recognizes slavery as lifelong condition
1667	Virginia	Denies that baptism provides legal grounds to sue for freedom
1670	Virginia	Indians taken captive outside colony and imported to serve for life; those captured within colony to serve 12 years (if children) or until age 30
1679	New York	Enslavement of Indians prohibited
1680	Virginia	Enslaved blacks barred from carrying arms, gathering (particularly for feasts and burials), or leaving plantations without a pass from their master
1691	Virginia	Whites barred from marrying blacks, mulattos, or Indians; children born of unions between English women and black men to become servants; mothers to pay fine, become servants, or have their servitude extended Masters owed compensation if their runaway slaves are killed while being captured Freed people ordered to leave colony
1692	Virginia	Special courts created for trying slaves accused of crimes
1696	South Carolina	Establishes first comprehensive slave code, modeled after that of Barbados, in English North America

Women and men experienced servitude differently. Recruiters told women in England weighing whether to cross the Atlantic that they would not have to work in the tobacco fields and that they could pick a husband in a society teeming with eligible bachelors. The first claim was usually a lie. "The Axe and Hoe have wrought my

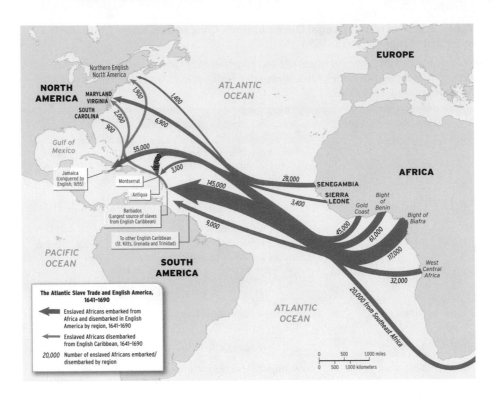

MAP 3.2 ▲ The Atlantic Slave Trade and English America, 1641–1690 Nearly one enslaved African in four died while crossing the Atlantic to English America between 1641 and 1690. Over half of those who survived the journey landed in Barbados. That island and others in the English Caribbean sent at least 5,000 enslaved Africans to England's mainland North American colonies.

overthrow," lamented singers of "The Trappan'd Maiden," a popular ballad that described what awaited women servants in Virginia. The second claim carried some truth. Female servants could find suitors, but they had to beware of men who might lure them to bed with promises of marriage and then leave them to deal with the consequences of pregnancy. Making matters worse, a 1662 Virginia law made female servants, frequent targets of sexual advances, solely responsible for compensating masters for time lost by pregnancy and labor. That could add at least two years to their servitude. If a servant mother died and the father dodged responsibility for paternity, her child had to become an indentured servant. This is the fate that befell Anne and Jasper Orthwood, whose story introduced this chapter.

Before the 1660s, young English men in the Chesapeake had reason to fear that they would not survive their servitude. But they also knew that they stood a good chance of owning land, even if it might not be the best land. By the mid-1670s, however, wealthy planters, many of them close associates of Governor Berkeley, had claimed most good land with easy access to Chesapeake Bay. Ex-servants and sons of small planters could either work as tenants or hired hands—or move to the colony's borders and risk Indian attacks.

FIGURE 3.3 ▲ **Migration of male and female indentured servants to English America, 1654–1686** These figures, based mainly on indentures recorded in Bristol, England, show that some two-thirds of indentured servants headed to Barbados in the 1650s. The Chesapeake colonies became the main destination for the next two decades for male servants and for the next three decades for female servants, including Anne Orthwood.

Other tensions roiled Virginia. Women's criticism of their neighbors often prompted their husbands to come to blows, so Virginia legislators tried to silence such women by sentencing them to a ducking, a centuries-old English punishment normally meted out to wives considered unruly. Offending women were marched to a pond or river, tied to a stool, and thrust underwater. In addition, small planters were angered by a tax hike that Governor Berkeley earmarked to bolster coastal defenses against Dutch attack. The small planters were already pressed by a long-term decline in tobacco prices.

Governor Berkeley also made powerful enemies, none more prominent than **Nathaniel Bacon**. The English aristocrat arrived in 1674, certain that his high birth entitled him to high office. Berkeley agreed, appointing Bacon to his council. Bacon believed that he had a more legitimate claim to power than did those who surrounded Berkeley. He took charge of a faction that opposed Berkeley, partly on grounds that Virginia voters had not elected representatives since 1662.

Bacon gained support as war erupted between colonists, most of whom wanted Indian land. In July 1675, Doeg Indians who lived in Maryland attempted to collect a debt from a Virginia colonist, a confrontation that claimed lives on both sides. Chesapeake militia leaders blamed Susquehannocks for sheltering Doegs. The Susquehannocks were themselves refugees, pushed south by Iroquois raids, who had resettled in Maryland at the invitation of its government. Virginia militiamen murdered Susquehannock chiefs and besieged their town. Susquehannocks retaliated by raiding Virginia in early 1676. Governor Berkeley responded in a measured way, condemning the militias while advocating punitive raids on Susquehannocks. The governor knew that war was engulfing New England and feared that an anti-English alliance of Indians from Massachusetts to Virginia might form.

Bacon's solution, however, was far more popular among white Virginians—target all Indians. In May, Governor Berkeley declared Bacon a rebel and organized elections. The governor's forces captured Bacon, but the newly elected burgesses asked that Berkeley pardon him. The governor did so, reseating Bacon on the council but refusing to authorize Bacon to attack the Indians. Bacon's followers took up arms and drove Berkeley from Jamestown, an event known as **Bacon's Rebellion**. The governor's supporters soon regained the upper hand. Bacon, desperate to save himself, promised freedom to the servants and slaves of Berkeley loyalists. About 250 slaves joined white servants and ex-servants to storm and torch Jamestown as Berkeley fled for his life. Charles II authorized Berkeley to offer freedom to servants and slaves who sided with him. The governor declined, calculating that it would alienate planters. Some of his allies thought otherwise. One persuaded hundreds of servants and slaves to surrender by promising them freedom, a ruse that effectively ended the rebellion.

Bacon's Rebellion remade Virginia's borders and its politics. Susquehannocks straggled north, where many submitted to Iroquois. Charles II appointed a commission to investigate matters in Virginia. It concluded that high taxes, vulnerability to Indian attack, official corruption, and concentration of land ownership sparked the uprising. The king, increasingly dependent on revenues raised from duties on tobacco, needed a stable Virginia, so he dismissed Berkeley. The war and growing English involvement in Indian diplomacy diminished the threat of Indian attacks. That made it easier for colonists to claim more Indian land. Meanwhile, a steep tax cut in 1686 stabilized provincial politics.

The rebellion accelerated the entrenchment of slavery and white supremacy. Planters fretted that a resentful white underclass might develop, so increasing numbers of planters opted to purchase enslaved Africans rather than indentured servants. Consequently, Virginia's black population grew to 5,000 by 1698 so that slaves comprised at least half the colony's unfree workers. New laws passed between 1680 and 1691 hardened racial distinctions and empowered masters and officials to exert more control over slaves and free blacks. In 1691, Virginia prohibited interracial marriage, punished white women for giving birth to interracial children, and required that anyone who was freed to leave the colony within six months or the person who freed them would be fined. Unlike Barbados, Maryland and Virginia retained a white majority. They formed the northern edge of a rim of societies based on African slavery that extended south to Carolina, the Caribbean, and Brazil.

The Creation of South Carolina

When Charles I was executed in the English Civil War, Sir John Colleton, one of his greatest supporters, fled England to become a Barbados planter. In 1663, Charles II rewarded his loyalty by granting the exclusive right to colonize land between Virginia and Florida to a group that Colleton headed. The planter and his partners named the colony "Carolina" to honor the king.

Carolina's proprietors envisioned that colonists would pay them to use their land and live peacefully alongside Indians. They promised land grants for each immigrant who paid for their passage as well as religious toleration and a representative assembly. Most colonists came from Barbados, and many took slaves with them. Barbados profoundly influenced the development of the new colony. Barbadians founded Carolina's first permanent colonial settlement in 1670 and comprised most of the 1,300 people of European descent who moved to South Carolina over the next two decades. Land drew most, whether they were sons of prominent planters who feared that their status would erode if they stayed on Barbados or young men, craftsmen, or small planters who decided that they would never succeed there. Barbadians helped to craft North America's first comprehensive slave code in 1696. They also oriented Carolina's economy toward the West Indies, which needed food and labor. White Carolinians or enslaved ones reared cattle and pigs and grew corn and peas, while a group whom colonists called Westo sent enslaved captives for export to the Caribbean.

Westo were probably Iroquoian speakers whom the Iroquois pushed south in the 1650s. By 1670, Westos had carved out a foothold along the Savannah River. Carolina needed secure borders and trade. Westos needed a convenient source of imported goods, especially weapons, without which Westos faced exodus or captivity. So began a lucrative English trade in enslaved Indians from southeastern North America. Westos raided what is today coastal Georgia to seize Yamasees, a newly formed people who had migrated there to seek refuge, and attacked other foes, including the Cherokee. Soon Carolina leaders decided that Westos had outlived their usefulness. Westo raids alienated too many other Indians, so colonists teamed up with the Savannah to kill or enslave most Westos. Ironically, Yamasees became allies to South Carolina in the 1680s and would remain so for three decades, supplying Indian slaves to the colony.

Carolina's growing dependence on trafficking in Indian slaves alarmed the colony's proprietors in England. In 1680, they ordered that no allied or friendly Indians within 200 miles of Carolina be enslaved. That left a huge loophole for colonists to exploit. Three years later, proprietors created a licensing system to ensure that only enslaved

Indians captured in "just wars" were exported, but their agents did not enforce it. Carolina profited handsomely from commerce with Indians and the West Indies. However, by the 1690s, the Indian slave trade exacerbated tensions between the English and Spanish, depopulated vast areas, and accelerated the transformation of the region's Indian politics.

Metacom and the Algonquian Battle for New England

Most New England colonists dreaded the news of Charles II's coronation. Their association with the losers of the English Civil War jeopardized their colonies' precarious legal standing. England revoked New Haven's charter and subjected its residents to Connecticut's authority in 1664. Although few Puritan dissidents fled England for Massachusetts Bay, the colony endured a wave of assaults on its legal right to exist. Quakers launched many of them, as did colonists in New Hampshire and Maine who did not want Massachusetts to govern them. Indians also petitioned Charles II as loyal subjects who deserved protection from disloyal colonists headquartered in Boston.

MEDALLION PRESENTED TO CHRISTIAN INDIAN SOLDIERS SERVING WITH MASSACHUSETTS FORCES DURING KING PHILIP'S WAR, 1676 Christian Indians helped New England win King Philip's War and secure release of captured colonists. Massachusetts Bay officials gave this medallion to Christian Indian soldiers for their service (to quote the inscription on the back of the medallion) "in the present Warr [sic] with the Heathen Natives of this Land."

Political uncertainty fed a growing sense of crisis in New England in the 1660s and 1670s. Some took defeat in the English Civil War as a sign that they had lost God's favor. Worse might befall them, they feared, as the generation that founded New England began to die off. Were they worthy, they wondered, of the founders' legacy? A growing number of ministers told them, in sermons called jeremiads, that they were not and never would be unless they changed their ways and honored God as their parents had.

Meanwhile, some New England colonists seized opportunities to forge new ties to England. In 1661, John Winthrop, Jr., became a charter member of the **Royal Society**, a group that advocated scientific inquiry. Its founders believed that people glorified God and bolstered faith by studying the natural world. Cotton Mather, a leading Boston minister, became a Royal Society fellow.

Colonists such as Winthrop and Mather sent specimens to London, corresponded with other fellows, and published in the society's journal. They subscribed to Royal Society journals and lent them to others. Winthrop donated New England's first telescope to Harvard, where others used it to observe comets in the 1680s. Their work informed the thought of Isaac Newton.

Colonists who joined scientific networks proclaimed themselves experts on Indians and used science to distinguish themselves from Indians and assert their Englishness. While in London, Winthrop reported to the Royal Society on how to grow and use corn. Winthrop and his American peers claimed that their engagement with science demonstrated their superiority to "superstitious" Indians who, they claimed, were incapable of such intellectual work. This reassured colonists who feared that life or birth in America made them seem inferior in the eyes of English across the Atlantic.

Algonquian peoples in southern New England were far more worried about their future. They had become the minority, forced to accommodate immigrants who had arrived only a generation earlier. As Miantonomi had warned in the early 1640s, Algonquians had to modify their ways to survive. Economic and environmental changes left them no choice. The more colonists traded overseas, the less they needed Indians. In 1661, a mint opened in Boston. Within a year, most New England colonists stopped using wampum as currency. Southern New England Indians increasingly found that they could only pay their debts with land. The more land they sold, the less they had for hunting and fishing. Multiplying herds of English-owned cattle and pigs threatened to overrun what land remained in Indian hands. The livestock trampled native vegetation; spread seeds of plants that colonists considered weeds; ate many of the same plants as deer; and devoured Indian plots of corn, beans, and squash. Indians who faced famine countered such invasions by filing suits in colonial courts or by killing and eating the invading animals.

Algonquians eventually decided to selectively adopt English ways and began keeping pigs. Colonists, however, refused to share public grazing lands with Indians. In 1669, Portsmouth, Rhode Island, officials forced Massasoit's son, the Wampanoag sachem **Metacom** (whom they called **Philip**), to remove his pigs from "Hog Island."

Metacom responded by organizing an Algonquian alliance to confront the English. The hanging of three Wampanoags, convicted in Plymouth of murdering a Christian Indian, ignited **King Philip's War** (1675–1676). It claimed thousands of lives and became the bloodiest conflict, on a per capita basis, in Anglo-American history. Indian attacks terrified colonists and destroyed 25 English towns. Massachusetts Bay leaders made plans to evacuate most of the colony and shelter colonists behind a ring of wooden ramparts a few miles from Boston.

Indians, regardless of which side they chose, suffered most from the war. English-led attacks compelled most to flee inland and keep moving, leaving them hungrier and more vulnerable to cold and disease. New York's governor persuaded Mohawks to side with the English, deny Metacom's pleas for help, and raid his allies. Both sides considered Christian Indians suspect. Massachusetts Bay soldiers rounded up and exiled most to a bleak island in Boston Harbor, where many died or were enslaved illegally. Other Christian Indians negotiated the release of English captives or fought alongside colonists. One shot Metacom, and another beheaded and quartered his corpse in August 1676. Metacom's head, stuck atop a post, remained on display in Plymouth for years. His wife and their nine-year-old son were jailed in Plymouth. She was not heard from again, but her son joined hundreds of Algonquians who were enslaved and put on a boat, most likely headed to the West Indies.

Metacom's death did not end the war. Algonquians in northern New England continued to raid boats and towns in New Hampshire and Maine. The attacks revived traumatic memories for colonists, who unleashed a torrent of published works about King

Global Catholicism, Indian Christianity, and Catherine/Kateri Tekakwitha

A young Mohawk woman died in April 1680. Father Claude Chauchetière called her Catherine, her baptismal name. His superior Pierre Cholenec gave Catherine last rites and claimed that he saw her pockmarked face clear after she died. Both men wrote a biography of Catherine. Chauchetière advised ill French colonists to pray for her help. Catherine soon won a regional following. Three hundred years later the "Mohawk saint" had an international one consisting largely of Catholic clergy and American Indians. Pope John Paul II beatified Catherine in 1980, the first step on the path toward sainthood.

In 1656, an Algonquin captive living in the Mohawk village Gandaouagué gave birth to Tekakwitha. Smallpox scarred the girl's face when she was six and killed her mother and brother. When war with New France broke out, the village residents fled. Peace required that they accept Jesuits. One baptized Tekakwitha on Easter Sunday in 1676, giving her the name of Catherine. She moved to Kahnawake, a village peopled mostly by Christian Mohawks located near Montreal. Kin awaited her there. Tekakwitha joined other devout women who practiced celibacy and inflicted pain on themselves. She became the group leader shortly before she died at the age of 24.

Jesuits viewed Catherine and her peers as women who had almost ceased to be Indian, but Catherine and her peers likely saw themselves as Catholic and Iroquoian. Baptism, a ritual in which one assumed a new identity to join a community, had Iroquoian analogs. So did abstaining from sex, burning or whipping oneself, and plunging into an icy pond. Jesuits interpreted these as acts of penance for sins. Tekakwitha and her circle could see them as preparation for possible torment, in this world or the next, and as a means to spiritual transcendence.

Chauchetière promoted Catherine's power to work miracles rather than her melding of Catholic and Indian beliefs. Tekakwitha's remains were exhumed in 1684 and buried in a mission chapel to accommodate pilgrims, almost all of whom were French Canadians. Chauchetière's biography of Catherine collected dust in France for nearly two centuries.

A campaign to beatify Catherine Tekakwitha began in the 1880s in the United States with strong support from Catholic bishops who believed that her beatification might counter rampant anti-Catholic prejudice by showing that Catholicism was "native" to American soil. The number of publications devoted to Tekakwitha's life surged over the

Philip's War that were read on both sides of the Atlantic. One, by **Mary Rowlandson**, a minister's wife whom Indians had captured, was published in Massachusetts and London in 1682. It became the second best-selling book in New England after the Bible. Rowlandson interpreted her ordeal and that of colonists as an act of God and an

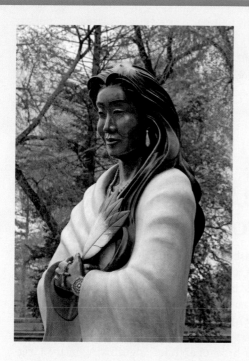

KATERI TEKAKWITHA   This bronze statue of Kateri Tekakwitha by Estella Loretto, a Jemez Pueblo sculptor, stands in front of the Cathedral Basilica of St. Francis of Assisi in Santa Fé. Unveiled in 2002 to mark the cathedral structure's 150th anniversary, it testifies to the devotion for Kateri Tekakwitha in New Mexico, particularly among Indians. A Vatican tribunal's investigation has found that her intercession miraculously saved the life of a hospitalized Lummi Indian boy in Washington State named Jake Finkbonner, prompting Pope Benedict XVI to declare Kateri eligible for canonization. She became a saint in 2012.

next century. In 1939, a group of white missionaries founded the Tekakwitha Conference in Montana to promote her beatification.

Meanwhile, Tekakwitha earned a following among Indian Catholics, who took control of the Tekakwitha Conference in the 1970s. Indian devotees revere Kateri Tekakwitha as someone who was fully Catholic and fully Indian. In 2012, Pope Benedict XVI officially declared her a saint. In life, Catherine/Kateri Tekakwitha in life journeyed between upstate New York and Quebec. In death, her example has circled the world.

- In what ways have Catholic clergy and Indians viewed the life of Tekakwitha since her death? In what ways have those portraits differed? What might account for such differences?
- Tekakwitha and Pocahontas chose to participate in colonial societies that profoundly altered their worlds. Are their lives, and the choices that they made, comparable? Explain.

example of His saving grace. English officials saw the war as they saw Bacon's Rebellion: both were proof that they needed tighter reins on colonists. Meanwhile, Algonquians who survived the war became captives, refugees, or struggled to remain autonomous peoples surrounded by colonists who increasingly pretended that they did not exist.

STUDY QUESTIONS FOR NEW IMPERIAL ORDERS, 1660–1680

1. Wars between colonists and Indians erupted across eastern North America in the 1660s and 1670s. Why? Did the conflicts share one underlying cause or did each have distinct origins? Explain.

2. How was slavery established in Virginia, Barbados, and South Carolina?

3. Why did royal power increase within the English and French colonial empires during the 1660s? What impact did royal reforms have on North America?

■ VICTORIOUS PUEBLOS, A NEW MID-ATLANTIC, AND "GLORIOUS" REVOLUTIONS, 1680 TO THE 1690s

The 1680s brought revolutions to the Spanish Southwest and the Anglo-Atlantic world that resulted in civil wars, social turmoil, and imperial conflicts throughout North America. Pueblo Indians began the decade by driving the Spanish from New Mexico but spent the next dozen years disputing what they should do with their independence. New English colonies emerged in the mid-Atlantic, each committed to religious freedom that attracted thousands of immigrants from other parts of English America, the British Isles, and western Europe. The overthrow of another English king in 1688 triggered revolts in three colonies and the first of many wars between England, France, and Indians for control of eastern North America.

The Pueblo War for Independence

On an August evening in 1680, Pueblo messengers departed Taos. **Popé**, a medicine man whom Spanish friars had recently whipped for practicing "idolatry," dispatched them to alert other towns that a planned uprising would begin in two days. New Mexico's diverse Indians united against Spanish rule. As their rebellion began, Indian warriors slaughtered horses and mules to constrict colonists' mobility before storming missions and Spanish towns. Within two weeks, 1,400 colonists, with 500 Indian slaves in tow, abandoned New Mexico, leaving behind hundreds of dead, including over 20 friars. Pueblos had waged the most successful war for independence in North American history to date (Map 3.3).

A number of factors prompted the war. Approximately 100,000 Indians lived in New Mexico when the Spanish conquered the region in 1598. By 1680, only 17,000 remained. The Southwest had endured a severe drought for two decades. Navajo and Apache raids in the 1670s worsened food shortages. Spanish demands for tribute and for sex from Pueblo women became even more onerous in such trying times. In 1675, the Spanish cracked down on Pueblo rituals, especially on those that beseeched **katsinas**— ancestral god spirits—to bring rain, fertility, and prosperity. That may well have been the final provocation.

Popé considered the Pueblo gods as the war's real leaders and himself as their instrument. Popé claimed the gods had punished Pueblos for having adopted the ways

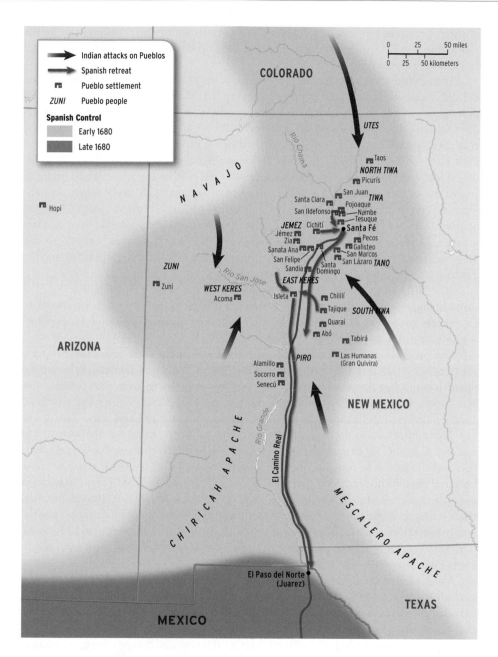

MAP 3.3 ▲ Pueblo War for Independence The Pueblo War for Independence, organized largely by Popé of Taos Pueblo, drove the Spanish out of New Mexico in 1680. Colonists sought refuge in El Paso del Norte (today's Ciudad Juárez, Mexico). They did not return for a dozen years.

of their foreign oppressors. Only when Pueblos returned to their preconquest beliefs would they regain the favor of katsinas and other gods who would restore an era of peace and prosperity.

That idyllic time, however, did not return. Most Pueblos wanted the Spanish gone but disagreed on what should happen once they left. Many men celebrated the end of monogamy, one of the friars' most hated impositions, by seeking a different or an additional wife. Pueblos restored kivas to reenact their creation, while many destroyed churches, crosses, and images of Jesus Christ and the Virgin Mary. Popé's allies rejected their Christian names for native ones and punished those who spoke Spanish or invoked Jesus or Mary. The most zealous sought to reject what the Spanish had brought, regardless of its usefulness. Spanish tools were to be cast aside and broken. Indians were to plant only corn and beans as their ancestors had and "burn the seeds which the Spaniards sowed." For many Pueblos, this went too far. Spanish tools had become integral to their lives. So had peaches, beef, and pork. All these they saw as "native" to their New Mexico. So were Jesus and the Virgin Mary, whom many had incorporated into the pantheon that created and sustained their ancestors.

Such differences fed conflicts that erupted almost as soon as the Spanish fled. The drought and Apache raids continued, as violence broke out within some towns between supporters and opponents of Popé's reforms. Warriors stormed granaries of neighboring communities, and nearly all Pueblo towns fell victim to Ute raids.

Popé died in 1692, just as the Spanish were launching their reconquest of New Mexico. They feared that growing French interest in Texas and Louisiana threatened Spanish control of northern Mexico and the silver that flowed from that region. New Mexico's new governor Diego de Vargas also believed that Pueblo victory had sustained a wave of Indian rebellions across northern Mexico and inspired new ones.

Many Pueblos had decided that they preferred a future under Spanish rule to one without it. According to some Pueblo accounts, a delegation representing several towns invited the Spanish to return. After Vargas reached Santa Fé, friars baptized over one hundred Pueblo children born after 1680. Many Pueblo leaders asked Vargas to stand as godfather to their children to gain his protection. Popé's successor Tupatú initiated peace talks and offered to join the Spanish against Pueblo holdouts. Vargas toured nearly two dozen towns, bullying most into submission. After returning to El Paso, he mustered several hundred men, most of them New Mexico refugees, and returned to Santa Fé in late 1693.

Vargas found the town in enemy hands. It took the Spanish and their Pueblo allies two days to take it. Vargas had dozens executed, enslaved 400 women and children, and parceled them out to colonists. It took nine more months to conquer most of the towns that refused to accept Spanish rule. In 1696, a Pueblo raid killed over 25 colonists and friars. Vargas forced Indian allies to attack holdout towns and compel those in hiding to surrender, finally bringing the **Pueblo War for Independence** to an end. Hundreds of Pueblos fled, seeking shelter among Hopis and Navajos.

Royal Charters for New Jersey and Pennsylvania

As Pueblos gained control of New Mexico, Indians whom the English called Delawares watched thousands of Europeans stream into their lands. England staked claim to the area by conquering New Netherland, which gave Charles II more opportunities to

WAMPUM BELT GIVEN TO WILLIAM PENN   It is believed that the Lenni Lenape (the Delawares) gave this wampum belt to Penn to represent, record, and commemorate their treaty with him at Shackamixon (located in today's Philadelphia) in the early 1680s. Delawares often invoked the memory of Penn when they negotiated with Pennsylvania authorities during the colonial era.

reward supporters. In 1664, he granted title to land between the Hudson and Delaware rivers to two Carolina proprietors, John Berkeley and George Carteret, who named their venture New Jersey. Twelve years later, Berkeley sold his share to a London-based group of Quakers, an act that split the colony into East and West Jersey. **William Penn**, one of England's most famous Quakers, was the son of an English admiral and a royal advisor. Charles repaid a debt to the deceased father and sought to rid England of the dissenting son by granting land west of the Delaware to Penn. He named it Pennsylvania. New Jersey and Pennsylvania roughly followed models set by New Netherland and Carolina, with proprietors promising European immigrants religious freedom. In 1665, New Jersey's original proprietors also promised them a representative assembly and free trade within the English Empire, all of which attracted English from New England and eastern Long Island. Quakers and Baptists saw New Jersey as a place to worship freely. So did the ultraorthodox Puritans who despised them. Migrants from New Haven, unable to live with its merger with Connecticut, founded Newark in 1666. Soon Barbadians came, some with as many as 30 enslaved Africans. East Jersey's proprietors recruited hundreds of Scots after taking on Scottish partners in 1683. Each group of free immigrants settled among their own, creating an ethnic and religious quilt that barely cohered politically. The only issue that united the 7,000 Europeans who lived in East Jersey in 1700 was hatred of **quitrents**, an annual fee that proprietors demanded for use of land that colonists had cleared, built on, and believed should be entirely theirs (Map 3.4).

The Quaker proprietors of West Jersey and Pennsylvania persistently recruited immigrants. In 1682, about 2,000 Quakers landed in Pennsylvania, followed by another 6,000 over the next three years. By 1700, Pennsylvania had 18,000 colonists who hailed from all over the British Isles and central Europe. Quakers lured fellow believers from Scotland, Ireland, Wales, and northern England. Penn had pamphlets printed in German and Dutch to advertise Pennsylvania's religious freedom, cheap land, and low taxes. Much of the colony's rapid population growth owed to American-born children, for many immigrants came as families. As in East Jersey, they usually settled near others who spoke and prayed as they did.

A new model city, Philadelphia, linked Pennsylvania to the Atlantic world. Founded in 1682, the town had 2,000 residents by 1700. Penn hoped that Philadelphia would avert the fate of London, where crowded dwellings let fire and plague spread easily.

MAP 3.4 ▲ **Eastern North America, 1660 and 1700** The English conquest of New Netherland in 1664 and the founding of colonies in New Jersey, Pennsylvania, Delaware, and the Carolinas, enabled the English to stake claim to and resettle most of the eastern coast of North America from Maine to South Carolina by 1700.

He oriented the city on a grid, with wide streets, room between low-rise homes to allow air to circulate and contain fires, and open space set aside for parks. The Philadelphia that emerged reflected little of his vision. Development sprawled along the Delaware River as merchants claimed valuable waterfront parcels. Land speculators and the artisans, shopkeepers, and indentured servants who streamed in made a dense urban environment of Penn's model city. So did merchants' ties to ports throughout the English Atlantic, which spurred more immigration and anchored a growing trade in flour and other provisions to the West Indies.

Links to the West Indies helped slavery take root in Pennsylvania, even as some there expressed opposition to slavery. In 1688, a group of four Germantown Quakers petitioned the local Quaker meeting to end the colony's participation in the Atlantic slave trade and bar slavery within it. Slavery, they insisted, made Pennsylvania Quakers look like hypocrites, handed ammunition to their critics overseas, and discouraged European immigration. Neither the Germantown Meeting, forced to consider North America's first antislavery statement, nor a superior meeting to which it forwarded the petition, decided the matter. By 1700, some 3,000 Pennsylvanians, one in six, were enslaved and of African descent.

Unlike in Carolina, Pennsylvania's leaders cultivated amicable relations with Indians. This owed partly to Quaker principles of pacifism and justice. Penn negotiated land concessions with Delaware leaders personally, learned their language, and bought land from them on terms that they found agreeable. The Delawares saw such transactions as a way to maintain ties to Pennsylvania's rulers, whose support they needed to counter Iroquois influence. Penn achieved mythic status for Indians. They invoked his memory as they negotiated with Penn's successors and tried to hold them to the lofty example that they claimed he had set.

English North America's "Glorious" Revolutions

In 1689, colonists in English North America hailed their new sovereigns William and Mary by taking up arms against their local leaders. When Charles II died in 1685, his brother James II became king of England. The next three years brought bitter disputes between James and Parliament over whose authority was supreme and over the king's embrace of Catholicism. When James suspended Parliament, his opponents feared the king would ally with France's Louis XIV to impose Catholicism and deprive them of liberty and property. Louis' persecution of Protestants fanned such fears. Over 100,000 Huguenots fled France. Many sought refuge in England, while over 2,000 journeyed to Massachusetts, New York, and South Carolina.

The Huguenots' ordeal incensed James's enemies in England. In 1688, they asked Prince William of Orange, Dutch husband of James's Protestant daughter Mary, to intervene. A few months later he did, backed by an army of 15,000. William invaded less to save English liberties than to save the Netherlands from an English–French alliance. Parliament declared the throne vacant after James fled to France and then invited William and Mary to occupy it. The victors trumpeted James's abdication as a peaceful and bloodless "**Glorious Revolution**" that preserved English liberty, even though mob attacks and pitched battles claimed thousands of lives in England, Scotland, and Ireland over the next two years.

Colonists had reasons to bid James good riddance. He had hit planters' pockets by raising duties on sugar and tobacco, which made those goods more expensive and decreased demand for them. He had created the **Dominion of New England** in 1685, modeling it on the Spanish system. The Dominion united eight contiguous colonies, from New England to New Jersey, under one governor, Edmond Andros, who dissolved representative assemblies; reduced town meetings to once a year; jailed dissidents; enforced the Navigation Acts; and barred Puritan congregations from using taxes to pay ministers. Most unsettling of all, the Dominion jeopardized land titles and required that their holders pay a quitrent on land that they had once owned outright.

Colonists in Massachusetts Bay, New York, and Maryland responded to news of the Glorious Revolution with violence. In April 1689, around 2,000 armed militiamen descended on Boston. Andros, guarded by 14 soldiers, surrendered. He and his closest advisors spent 10 months in prison before colonists sent them to England. In May, New York militias mutinied, forcing the lieutenant governor into exile. In Maryland, a group called the Protestant Associators demanded that the governor and his council proclaim William and Mary as monarchs of England. They refused, so the Associators overthrew the governor and council and put them under house arrest.

Ironically, colonists helped to strengthen royal authority. Maryland and Massachusetts both accepted governors appointed by the English monarch. Massachusetts's 1691 royal charter also curbed religion's influence over politics. Property holding replaced church

TIMELINE 1640–1700

AMERICA	YEAR	THE WORLD
Sugar boom begins on Barbados	**1640s**	
Puritan migration to New England halts	**1642**	English Civil War erupts
First colonial ship carrying enslaved Africans to North America docks in Boston	**1646**	
Apalachee rebellion in Florida	**1647**	
Iroquois attacks destroy Huron Confederacy Predecessor of New England Company founded to promote conversion of New England Algonquian	**1649**	Charles I beheaded; England becomes a commonwealth
First Navigation Act to regulate commerce of English colonies	**1651**	
First Anglo-Dutch War	**1652–1654**	
Rhode Island outlaws lifelong slavery for Europeans and Africans	**1652**	
Timucua rebel in Florida	**1656**	
	1660	Monarchy restored to England with crowning of Charles II
Barbados legislators create colonial English America's first comprehensive slave code Royal Society of London founded and colonists admitted as members	**1661**	
Virginia lawmakers decide that children should inherit their legal status from mothers rather than fathers	**1662**	
Proprietors receive English royal charter to Carolina Antecedent of Royal African Company granted monopoly to ship enslaved Africans	**1663**	
Second Anglo-Dutch War	**1664–1667**	
Aug English forces conquer New Netherland and rename it New York	**1664**	
Sep French raid on Mohawk Country	**1666**	**Sep** Great Fire of London destroys over 13,000 buildings and properties
Jun Mohawks join rest of Five Nations in peace treaty with New France	**1667**	
Fundamental Constitutions of Carolina written	**1669**	
First permanent English settlement in South Carolina Hudson's Bay Company Founded	**1670**	

membership as one key qualification to vote. The Glorious Revolution tightened the political bond between England and its colonies.

North America's Hundred Years' War Begins

William and Mary's coronation triggered war in Europe and North America. In 1690, rebels in New York and New England sought to demonstrate loyalty to their monarchs and defend Protestantism by planning an invasion of Canada, an initiative that ended in fiasco and mutual recrimination. Canadian Mohawks and Abenakis, backed by the

Third Anglo-Dutch War	**1672–1674**	
Jul New York captured by Dutch and renamed New Netherland	**1673**	
Oct Dutch return New York to English control	**1674**	
Jun King Philip's War begins in southern New England **Jul** Doeg Indian raid into Virginia sparks Bacon's Rebellion **Sep** King Philip's War spreads to northern New England	**1675**	
Aug King Philip's War ends in southern New England **Oct** Bacon's Rebellion ends	**1676**	Beginning of Russo-Turkish War
Apr English colonies and Iroquois League establish Covenant Chain **Aug** King Philip's War ends in northern New England	**1677**	
Aug Pueblo war for independence drives Spanish from New Mexico	**1680**	
Charles II grants Pennsylvania to William Penn	**1681**	
Mary Rowlandson's captivity narrative published Philadelphia founded Robert Cavalier de La Salle arrives at mouth of Mississippi River, claims watershed for France, and renames area Louisiana	**1682**	
James II crowned King of England Dominion of New England established	**1685**	
"Glorious Revolution" in England James II forced to abdicate throne	**1688**	William and Mary crowned King and Queen of England
Revolts inspired by "Glorious Revolution" overthrow governments of Massachusetts Bay, New York, and Maryland **Apr** Dominion of New England terminated	**1689**	
King William's War	**1689–1697**	
Massachusetts granted new royal charter	**1691**	
Jan Salem witch crisis begins **Aug** Spanish forces begin to reconquer New Mexico	**1692**	
May Salem witch crisis ends **Nov** Spanish complete reconquest of New Mexico and end Pueblo war for independence	**1693**	

French, raided New York and northern New England, torching English towns and taking captives as colonists barricaded themselves behind ramparts and heavy wooden doors. **King William's War** (1689–1697) marked New England's second devastating conflict in a generation. It struck when many were unsure of who had the right to govern them or on what terms. Massachusetts Bay still lacked a charter, so its rulers had no clear legal sanction to act.

The conflict sparked one of the last witch scares in the northern Atlantic world. In Salem, the terror of Abenaki attacks and uncertainty over who was in charge fed a panic that resulted in the execution of 20 and the accusation of nearly 200 on charges of witchcraft. The scare began in 1692 when Betty, the nine-year-old daughter of minister Samuel Parris, developed pains for which no doctor could find a physical cause. Tituba, an Arawak Indian from Guyana whom Parris purchased in Barbados and brought to New England, tried to end Betty's suffering by baking a cake that contained the girl's urine and feeding it to a dog. Popular belief held that the dog, whose form the witch had taken, would name the witch. Tituba was among the first women arrested. Her testimony convinced investigators that there were indeed witches in Salem who had made a pact with Satan. That, they thought, could explain the Abenaki raids and the symptoms that afflicted people, particularly young females, who implicated others, mostly women. Magistrates stopped prosecuting when a growing number of the accused were prominent figures rather than socially marginal ones—and when they began to doubt the evidence presented to them. Tituba eventually recanted her confession and was sold to someone who paid her jail fees.

King William's War had far bigger repercussions for Indians. It widened divisions within the Iroquois as anti-French Mohawks joined aborted English invasions of Canada. Most Iroquois were allied with the English. In 1693, French forces, guided by Canadian Mohawks, invaded Mohawk country, torched three towns, and headed north with 300 captives. Meanwhile, New France's governor encouraged Huron-Petuns and Algonquians to avenge the Iroquois raids that in the 1640s and 1650s had forced them from their homelands. Iroquois leaders concluded that the English would never honor their promises of assistance and looked to negotiate peace with New France. King William's War ended in 1697 for colonists. It raged four more years for most Indians and decimated Iroquois. Its diplomats thereafter strove for neutrality in the conflicts between the two European empires that claimed parts of the northeast.

For the Boston minister Cotton Mather, King William's War gave New England a new sense of purpose. He considered the region a shield that defended the English world and Protestantism against France and Catholicism. For English and French colonists, the war made their corner of the world seem more important. The war tightened bonds between North America and the European monarchs as the new world headed into the 18th century.

STUDY QUESTIONS FOR VICTORIOUS PUEBLOS, A NEW MID-ATLANTIC, AND "GLORIOUS" REVOLUTIONS, 1680 TO THE 1690s

1. What impact did the Glorious Revolution have on North America?
2. New York, New Jersey, Pennsylvania, and Carolina all became part of the English colonial empire as a result of Charles II's coronation. Did these colonies have anything else in common? Please support your answer with specific examples.

Summary
- Political instability gripped North America between 1640 and 1660 as Iroquois raids decimated their Indian foes; New England responded to civil war in England by diversifying its economy and forging ties to Barbados, English America's first slave society; and friars claimed more power in Florida and New Mexico.
- Between 1660 and 1680, the founding of South Carolina and war in Virginia entrenched slavery and white supremacy in an English North America enlarged by the conquest of New Netherland, scarred by warfare with Indians, threatened by expanding French claims, and governed by a new king who sought more control over colonial affairs.
- The 1680s and 1690s brought an Indian struggle for independence in New Mexico, the establishment of multicultural colonies in Pennsylvania and New Jersey, and more political instability in the English Atlantic world that sparked the first of many conflicts between the English and French colonial empires and posed new challenges for Indians.

Key Terms and People
Articles of Capitulation *86*
Bacon, Nathaniel *92*
Bacon's Rebellion *92*
Barbados slave code *82*
Beaver Wars *75*
Berkeley, William *77*
Catherine/Kateri Tekakwitha *96*
Charles II *77*
Colbert, Jean-Baptiste *87*
Cromwell, Oliver *77*
Dominion of New England *103*
Eliot, John *79*
Glorious Revolution *103*
Hudson's Bay Company *88*
James, Duke of York (James II) *86*
katsinas *98*

King Philip's War *95*
King William's War *105*
Louis XIV *88*
mercantilism *87*
Metacom/Philip *95*
Navigation Acts *85*
Parliament *77*
Penn, William *101*
Popé *98*
Pueblo War for Independence *100*
quitrents *101*
Rowlandson, Mary *96*
Royal African Company *86*
Royal Society *94*
Society of Friends/Quakers *79*

Reviewing Chapter 3
1. Environmental change played as big a role in shaping politics and economics in North America and the Caribbean between 1640 and the 1690s as disease or religion did. Does this chapter support this claim? Please use specific examples to support your answer.
2. Was the Pueblo War for Independence a unique event in the history of colonial North America up to the 1690s? If so, why? If not, why not?
3. In what ways did patterns of migration to, from, and within North America change between 1640 and the 1690s? What role did events in Europe play in the development of North American colonies and Indian societies?

Further Reading
Greer, Allan. *Mohawk Saint: Catherine Tekakwitha and the Jesuits*. New York: Oxford University Press, 2005. A superb account of Tekakwitha, Iroquois conversion to

Christianity, and the challenges that she and other Mohawks faced during the mid to late 17th century.

Gutiérrez, Ramón A. *When Jesus Came, the Corn Mothers Went Away: Marriage, Sexuality, and Power in New Mexico, 1500–1846*. Stanford, Calif.: Stanford University Press, 1991. Now more than 20 years old, but still the best account of Spanish colonization and Spanish-Pueblo relations in New Mexico.

Menard, Russell R. *Sweet Negotiations: Sugar, Slavery, and Plantation Agriculture in Early Barbados*. Charlottesville and London: University of Virginia Press, 2006. An excellent explanation of the causes and consequences of the Barbados sugar boom.

Pagan, John Ruston. *Anne Orthwood's Bastard: Sex and Law in Early Virginia*. New York: Oxford University Press, 2003. A carefully crafted study of gender, indentured servitude, and the rise of an "American" body of legal thought in mid-17th-century Virginia.

Pestana, Carla Gardina. *The English Atlantic in an Age of Revolution, 1640–1661*. Cambridge, Mass., and London: Harvard University Press, 2004. Presents the English Civil War as a transatlantic event that profoundly remade the English Empire.

Pulsipher, Jenny Hale. *Subjects Unto the Same King: Indians, English, and the Contest for Authority in Colonial New England*. Philadelphia: University of Pennsylvania Press, 2005. Explores English-Algonquian relations and their relationship to English imperial politics during the 17th century.

America In The World
PEOPLE, GOODS, IDEAS AND PRACTICES

EUROPE

AFRICA

ATLANTIC
OCEAN

ATLANTIC
OCEAN

Enslaved Africans

Fur

French colonists

Knowledge of New World species (such as corn)

Smallpox

Quakers

Navigation Acts trade regulations

Tobacco

Sugar

Barbados

English colonists

St. Augustine

Quebec

Smallpox

Fur

Huron fleeing
Iroquois attacks

Catholicism

Gulf of Mexico

NORTH
AMERICA

SOUTH
AMERICA

Spanish
colonists

PACIFIC
OCEAN

Goods	↑
Ideas	↑
People	↑

0   500   1,000 miles
0   500   1,000 kilometers

PRIMARY SOURCES FOR CHAPTER 3
FORGING TIGHTER BONDS, 1640 to 1700

SOURCE 3.1
"The Trappan'd Maiden" (c. 1600s)

For most of the 17th century, colonists of means in Virginia and Maryland depended on indentured servants from England to sustain and expand their enterprises. Although the majority of indentured servants were young men between the ages of 16 and 24, as many as one in three were women, most of them young. Word of the rigors of American servitude crossed the Atlantic, where such news helped give rise to popular ballads like the one below, entitled "The Trappan'd Maiden." Ordinary Englishmen and women coined the term "trappaned" in the mid-17th century to describe someone who had been tricked or deceived into a situation that resulted in ruin or loss.

Source: C. H. Firth, *An American Garland, Being a Collection of Ballads Relating to America, 1563–1759* (Oxford: B. H. Blackwell, 1915), 51–53.

This Girl was cunningly Trappan'd, sent to Virginny from England, Where she doth Hardship undergo, there is no Cure it must be so: But if she lives to cross the Main, she vows she'll ne'r go there again.

Tune of *Virginny*, or, *When that I was weary, weary, O.*
Give ear unto a Maid, that lately was betray'd,
And sent into Virginny, O:
In brief I shall declare, what I have suffer'd there,
When that I was weary, weary, weary, weary, O.

[Since] that first I came to this Land of Fame,
Which is called Virginny, O,
The Axe and the Hoe have wrought my overthrow,
When that I was weary, weary, weary, weary O.

Five years served I, under Master Guy,
In the land of Virginny, O,
Which made me for to know sorrow, grief and woe,
When that I was weary, weary, weary, weary O.

When my Dame says "Go" then I must do so,
In the land of Virginny, O;
When she sits at Meat, then I have none to eat,
When that I am weary, weary, weary, weary, O.

The Cloath[e]s that I brought in, they are
    worn very thin,
In the land of Virginny, O,
Which makes me for to say, "Alas, and
    Well-a-day!"
When that I am weary, weary, weary,
    weary, O.

Instead of Beds of Ease, to lye down when
    I please,
In the Land of Virginny, O;
Upon a bed of straw, I lye down full
    of woe,
When that I am weary, weary, weary,
    weary, O.

Then the Spider, she, daily waits on me,
In the Land of Virginny, O;
Round about my bed, she spins her web
    [of thread],
When that I am weary, weary, weary,
    weary, O.

So soon as it is day, to work I must
    away,
In the Land of Virginny, O;
Then my Dame she knocks, with her
    tinder-box,
When that I am weary, weary, weary,
    weary, O.

I have play'd my part both at Plow and
    Cart,
In the Land of Virginny, O;
Billets from the Wood upon my back they
    load,
When that I am weary, weary, weary,
    weary, O.

Instead of drinking Beer, I drink the
    water clear,
In the Land of Virginny, O;
Which makes me pale and wan, do all
    that e'er I can,
When that I am weary, weary, weary,
    weary, O.

If my Dame says "Go!" I dare not
    say no,
In the Land of Virginny, O;
The Water from the Spring, upon my
    head I bring,
When that I am weary, weary, weary,
    weary, O.

When the Mill doth stand, I'm ready
    at command,
In the Land of Virginny, O;
The Morter for to make, which makes
    my heart to ake,
When that I am weary, weary, weary,
    weary, O.

When the Child doth cry, I must sing
    "By-a-by!"
In the Land of Virginny, O;
No rest that I can have, whilst I am here
    a Slave,
When that I am weary, weary, weary,
    weary, O.

A thousand woes beside, that I do here
    abide,
In the Land of Virginny, O;
In misery I spend my time that hath
    no end,
When that I am weary, weary, weary,
    weary, O.

Then let Maids beware, all by my ill-fare,
In the Land of Virginny, O;
Be sure to stay at home, for if you do
    here come,
You all will be weary, weary, weary,
    weary, O.

But if it be my chance, Homewards to
    advance,
From the Land of Virginny, O;
If that I, once more, land on English
    Shore,
I'll no more be weary, weary, weary,
weary, O.

WORKING WITH SOURCES

1. What impressions of indentured servitude and Virginia does "The Trappan'd Maiden" convey, particularly to young women who might have contemplated journeying to North America? In what ways does the song contrast life in Virginia with life in England?

2. Does the song provide an accurate and representative portrait of indentured servitude, especially for women, in Virginia? Use what you have learned from reading Chapters 2 and 3 of the text to construct your answer.

3. Imagine that Anne Orthwood were to add some lyrics to "The Trappan'd Maiden" to reflect her ordeal in Virginia. What would she say? Write at least one additional stanza, consistent with the style and language of the ballad, that would express Orthwood's experience.

SOURCE 3.2

Committee of the Massachusetts Bay General Court, "A Memorandum of Indian Children Put Forth into Service to the English" (1676)

In the wake of King Philip's War, New England colonists forced many Indian captives to become bound laborers. Those deemed too dangerous to remain in New England—mostly men, but also some boys (likely including Metacom's son)—were enslaved and sold in the West Indies. Indian children, including many orphaned by their parents' death in conflict or by execution by colonial authorities, became indentured servants. Below is a memorandum prepared by a committee that Massachusetts Bay legislators charged to bind out Indian children to colonists. One committee member, Daniel Gookin Sr., openly sympathized with the plight of Christian Indians during and after the war.

Source: Proceedings of the Colonial Society of Massachusetts 19 (1918): 25–28.

Beeing of those indians that came in & submitted with John Sachem of Packachooge, with the names of the persons with whome they were placed & the names and age of the children & the names of their relations & the places they Did belong to, By Mr Daniel Gookin Sen[r], Thomas Prentis Capt' & M[r] Edward Oakes, who were a comittee appointed by the Counsel to mannage y[t1] affayr. The termes & conditions vpon w[ch] they are to serve is to be ordered by the Gen[ll] Court who are to provide y[t] the children bee religiously educated & taught to read the English tounge

2 Boy
A maid

To Samuel Simonds Esq. a boy named John his father named Alwitankus late of quantisit his father & mother p[r]ent[2] both consenting the boys age about 12 years

To him a girle named Hester her father & mother dead late of Nashaway her age ten years her onkel named John woosumpigin of Naticke

---

[1]That.

1 Boy   To Thomas Danforth esq a boy aged about 13 yeares his name John

1 Boy   To Leift Jonathan Danforth of [Billericay?] a boy aged twelve yeares, son to papamech alius David late of Warwick or Cowesit.

2 Boyes   To Mathew Bridge of CamBridge two Boyes the one named Jabez aged about ten yeares the other named Joseph aged six yeares their father named woompthe late of Packachooge ☞ one or both these boyes is away with his father 8 ber[3] 17th

1676

3 A boy & two Girls   To M[r] Jerimiah Shepard of Rowley a boy named Absolom his father of the same name late of Manehage aged about ten yeares.

To him a girle sister to the Lad named Sarah aged eleven yeares. These [illegible] of Naticke.

To him another girle aged about 8 yeares her named Jane her father & mother dead.

1 Mayd   To M[rs] Mitchell of Cambridg widdow a maid named Margaret aged about twelve yeares, her father named Suhunnick of quantisit her mother dead.

1 Boy   To Thomas Jacob of Ipswich a boy aged ten yeares, on wen-naputanan his guardian & on upacunt of quantisitt his grand mother was present. The Boy [illegible].

1 Boy   To on Goodman Read a Tanner of cambridge a Boy named John aged about thirteen yeares his father Dead.

1 Boy   To M[r] Jacob Green of Charel Towne a boy aged about seaven yeares his parrents Dead Late of quantisit but his mother of Narraganset.

1 Boy   To Thomas Woolson of Wattertowne a boy aged about 14 yeares his name John his father dead who was of Cowesit or warwick, his mother p[r]sent.

1 Boy   To Ciprian Steuens of Rumny Marsh but late of Lancaster a boy aged about six yeares son to nohanet of Chobnakonkonon. The Boy named Samuel.

1 Mayd   To Thomas Eliot of Boston a carpenter a maid aged about ten yeares her name Rebecka.

1 Boy   To Jacob Green Junior of Charles towne a Boy named Peter aged nine years his father dead his mother p[r]sent named nannantum of quantisit.

[2]An abbreviation for "present."
[3]October.

1 Boy	To on Goodman Greenland a carpenter of Charles towne on misticke side a boy named Tom aged twelve yeares his father named santeshe of Pakachooge.
1 Girle	To Mr Edmund Batter of Salem a maid named Abigal aged sixteen her mother a widow named quanshishe late of Shookannet Beyond mendon.
2 a Boy A girle	To Daniel Gookin Senr A Boy named Joshua aged about eight yeares son to William wunuko late of magunkoog; his father dead.
	To him a girle aged about six yeares daughter to the widdow quinshiske late of Shookanet beyond mendon
1 Girle	To Andrew Bordman Tayler of cambridge a girle named Anne sister to ye Last named.
1 Boy	To Thomas Prentis Junior son to Capt Prentis of Cambridge village a boy named John son to William Wunnako late of magnkoy that was executed for Thomas Burney, aged thirteen.
1 Boy	To Benjamin Mills of Dedham a boy aged about six years is [named?] Joseph Spoonans late of Marlboro.
1 Boy	To Mr Edward Jackson a Boy named Joseph aged about 12 yeares Late of magalygook cosen[4] to Pyambow of Naticke.

1 Mayd	To Widdow Jackson of Cambridge village a girle named Hope aged nine yeare her parents dead who wer of Narraganset.
1 Boy	To old Goodman Myles of Dedham a boy of [ ] yeares old. son to Annaweeken Decesed who was late of Hassanamesit his mother p^{r}sent.
1 Boy	To Capt. Thomas Prentis a Boy named Joseph son to Annaweken decesed Brother to the last named aged about 11 yeares ☞ this boy was after taken from Capt Prentice & sent up Mr Stoughton for [ ] Capt Prentis is to bee considered about it for hee has taken more care & paynes about those indians.
1 Boy	To John Smith of Dedham a boy aged about eight yeares his father dead late of Marlborow hee is Brother to James Printers wife
1 Mayd	To Mr John Flint [?] of Concord a mayd aged about [ ] yeares [illegible]
1 Boy	To Mr Jonathan Wade of mistick a Boy named Tom Aged about 11 yeares sonne to William Wunakhow of Magunkgog decesed
1 Mayd	To Mr Nathaniel Wade of mistick a maid aged about ten years daughter to Jame Natomet [?] late of Packachooge her father & mother dead

---

[4]Cousin.

It is humbly proposed to the Honble Generall Court, to set the time these children shall serve; & if not less y[n][5] till they come to 20 yeares of age. unto w[ch] those y[t] had relations seemed willing. and also that the Court lay som penalty upon them if they runne away before the time expire & on their parents or kindred y[t] shall entice or harborr & conceale y[m][6] if they should runne away.

Signed By the Comitee
Above named   Daniel Gookin Sen[r]
Edward Oakes.
Cambridge
8 ber 28 1676

WORKING WITH SOURCES

1. Under what terms were the Indian children bound out to colonists to serve?

2. What can you learn about the lives of Indian children from this memorandum? What does it tell you about the circumstances that brought them to be bound out and the lives that they might have lived once they became servants?

3. In what ways are the information contained and the values expressed in this memorandum similar to those in the *repartimiento* order for Indians on Española in 1514 (Document 1.2)? In what ways do they differ?

---

[5]Than.
[6]Them.

SOURCE 3.3

Germantown Quaker Meeting, "Reasons Why We Are Against the Traffic of Men-body" (1688)

As Pennsylvania's population and economy grew rapidly during the 1680s, so did the nascent colony's population of enslaved Africans and African Americans, a development that alarmed some. In 1688, four German colonists who belonged to the Germantown Quaker Meeting penned the petition below and requested that the monthly meeting consider it. Included as well are that meeting's response and the responses of the quarterly meeting in Philadelphia and the monthly meeting in Burlington, New Jersey. As Chapter 5 discusses, Pennsylvania Quakers did spearhead an antislavery initiative in the Anglo-Atlantic world, but not until the 1760s.

Source: George H. Moore, *Notes on the History of Slavery in Massachusetts* (New York, 1866), 75–78.

This is to the monthly meeting held at Richard Worrell's:

These are the reasons why we are against the traffic of men-body, as followeth: Is there any that would be done or handled at this manner? viz., to be sold or made a slave for all the time of his life? How fearful and faint-hearted are many at sea, when they see a strange vessel, being afraid it should be a Turk, and they should be taken, and sold for slaves into Turkey. Now, what is *this* better done, than Turks do? Yea, rather it is worse for them, which say they are Christians; for we hear that the most part of such negers are brought hither against their will and consent, and that many of them are stolen. Now, though they are black, we cannot conceive there is more liberty to have them slaves, as [than] it is to have other white ones. There is a saying, that we should do to all men like as we will be done ourselves; making no difference of what generation, descent, or colour they are. And those who steal or rob men, and those who buy or purchase them, are they not all alike? Here is liberty of conscience, which is right and reasonable; here ought to be likewise liberty of the body, except of evil-doers, which is another case. But to bring men hither, or to rob and sell them against their will, we stand against. In Europe, there are many oppressed for conscience-sake; and here there are those oppressed which are of a black colour. And we who know that men must not commit adultery—some do commit adultery *in* others, separating wives from their husbands, and giving them to others: and some sell the children of these poor creatures to other men. Ah! do consider well this thing, you who do it, if you would be done at this manner—and if it is done according to Christianity! You surpass Holland and Germany in this thing. This makes an ill report in all those countries of Europe, where they hear of [it,] that the Quakers do here handel men as they handel there the cattle. And for that reason some have no mind or inclination to come hither. And who shall maintain this your cause, or plead for it? Truly, we cannot do so, except you shall inform us better hereof, viz.: that Christians have liberty to practise these things. Pray, what thing in the world can be done worse towards us, than if men should rob or steal us away, and sell us for slaves to strange countries; separating husbands from their wives and children. Being now this is not done in the manner we would be done at, [by]; therefore, we contradict, and are against this traffic of men-body. And we who profess that it is not lawful to steal, must, likewise, avoid to purchase such things as are stolen, but rather help to stop this robbing and stealing, if possible. And such men ought to be delivered out of the hands of the robbers, and set free as in Europe. Then is Pennsylvania to have a good report, instead, it hath now a bad one, for this sake, in other countries: Especially whereas the Europeans are desirous to know in what manner *the Quakers* do rule in *their* province; and most of them do look upon us with an envious eye. But if this is done well, what shall we say is done evil?

If once these slaves (which they say are so wicked and stubborn men,) should join themselves—fight for their freedom, and handel their masters and mistresses, as they did handel them before; will these masters and mistresses take the sword at hand and war against these poor slaves, like, as we are able to believe, some will not refuse to do? Or, have these poor negroes not as much right to fight for their freedom, as you have to keep them slaves?

Now consider well this thing, if it is good or bad. And in case you find it to be good to handel these blacks in that manner, we desire and require you hereby lovingly, that you may inform us herein, which at this time never was done, viz., that Christians have such a liberty to do so. To the end we shall be satisfied on this point, and satisfy likewise our good friends and acquaintances in our native country, to whom it is a terror, or fearful thing, that men should be handelled so in Pennsylvania.

This is from our meeting at Germantown, held yᵉ 18th of the 2d month, 1688, to be delivered to the monthly meeting at Richard Worrell's.

Garret Henderich, Derick op de Graeff, Francis Daniel Pastorius, Abram op de Graeff.

At our monthly meeting, at Dublin, yᵉ 30th 2d mo., 1688, we having inspected yᵉ matter, above mentioned, and considered of it, we find it so weighty that we think it not expedient for us to meddle with it *here*, but do rather commit it to yᵉ consideration of yᵉ quarterly meeting; yᵉ tenor of it being related to yᵉ truth.

On behalf of yᵉ monthly meeting, Jo. Hart.

This above mentioned, was read in our quarterly meeting, at Philadelphia, the 4th of yᵉ 4th mo., '88, and was from thence recommended to the yearly meeting, and the above said Derrick, and the other two mentioned therein, to present the same to yᵉ above said meeting, it being a thing of too great weight for this meeting to determine.

Signed by order of yᵉ meeting. Anthony Morris.

The minutes of the Yearly Meeting, held at Burlington in the same year, record the result of this first effort among the Quakers.

At a Yearly Meeting, held at Burlington the 5th day of the 7th Month, 1688.

A paper being here presented by some German Friends Concerning the Lawfulness & Unlawfulness of Buying & Keeping of Negroes It was adjudged not to be so proper for this Meeting to give a Positive Judgment in the Case It having so general a Relation to many other Parts & therefore at present they Forbear It.

WORKING WITH SOURCES

1. On what grounds do Pastorius and his peers oppose slavery and the Atlantic slave trade? Keep in mind as you answer that they were Quaker men writing to other Quakers in 1688.

2. What became of the Germantown petition? In what manner did superior meetings respond to it?

3. Are there similarities in the ideas expressed in this petition, which opposes slavery, and the Barbados law (Document 3.1), which sought to strengthen it? If so, what are they and what explains those similarities? If not, why not?

SOURCE 3.4

Visual Document: Richard Ford, *A New Map of the Island of Barbadoes* (1674)

In 1674, Richard Ford made the map below of the island of Barbados. Published in England, it was the first economic map of an English American colony ever printed and soon became part of an atlas of maps that England's Office of Trade and Plantations compiled in the 1680s. Ford's map features the name of each plantation, usually named after its owner, as well as the sugar mills that produced the island's main export.

Source: Courtesy of the John Carter Brown Library at Brown University.

WORKING WITH SOURCES

1. What can you learn about Barbados in the 1670s from Ford's map? What impression of Barbados did Ford seek to give English users of his map?

2. After closely examining the map and reading the captions that accompany it, what features of life and society in Barbados did Ford choose to ignore or leave out?

Accelerating the Pace of Change

c. 1690–1730

In 1717, Philippe, the Duc d'Orléans and regent of France, handed control of trade between France and its North American colonies to John Law, a brilliant Scottish financier. D'Orléans hoped that Louisiana could produce tobacco, ending France's dependence on a supply imported from the Chesapeake via England, and he was confident that Law would deliver. Law devised a marketing scheme in which his firm, eventually named the Company of the Indies, sold shares to French investors to finance the colonization of Louisiana. He guaranteed that they would earn huge profits.

The price of company stock initially soared as the firm used the proceeds to send thousands of enslaved Africans, French convict servants, and Germans to the banks of the Lower Mississippi. Meanwhile, urban planners envisioned that New Orleans—founded in 1718, named after the Duc—would become a model French city. In 1720, however, the value of Company of the Indies stock plummeted and the "**Mississippi Bubble**" burst. A disgraced John Law fled France. The company that he abandoned abruptly halted shipments of food to Louisiana, leaving the colonists to starve. Some 13,000 Europeans and Africans, most of them brought in chains, had come to Louisiana since 1717. Only 6,000 remained 15 years later. Few people arrived over the next three decades. Largely cut off from direct contact with the Atlantic and virtually autonomous from the French Empire, a small group of American-born merchants made New Orleans the smuggling capital of the northern Gulf of Mexico. Meanwhile, Louisiana became a small

< *Tee Yee Neen Ho Ga Row (Hendrick Tejonihokarawa).*

and poor colony with an American-born black majority. Even so, it anchored French claims to North America's interior, extended European influence deep into Indian country, and accelerated the pace of changes already underway on the continent.

From the 1690s to 1730, European empires staked bigger claims to North America as colonial expansion, warfare, and wider dissemination of European goods eroded Indian power. Heavier immigration, a transatlantic Protestant movement that sought more pious believers and new converts around the world, and stronger political bonds overseas altered how colonists in British North America viewed each other, the British Empire, and the Atlantic world. A growing native-born elite empowered and informed by its ties to Atlantic networks led efforts to classify colonists by race, diversify British North America's economy, and distinguish themselves from newly arrived and poorer colonists.

A FRENCH VIEW OF LOUISIANA, c. 1720   This fanciful scene (the Gulf Coast has no mountains; few Mexican Indians visited Louisiana) shows what French officials and investors hoped Louisiana would become: a magnet to lure trade from Mexico to the French Empire. Instead, the colony's ports, especially New Orleans, became magnets for smugglers who dodged French regulations.

TURMOIL IN INDIAN NORTH AMERICA

In 1700, Indians comprised the vast majority of North Americans. One hundred years later, Europeans, Africans, and their descendants vastly outnumbered Indians, due largely to events that disrupted Indian life in North America between the 1690s and 1730. Diffusion of goods, especially horses and guns, promoted violence among Indians from the Rockies east to the Appalachians, stoking an Indian slave trade that moved captives across the continent and altered Indian politics, particularly in the Southeast. The founding of new colonies in Texas and Louisiana accelerated these developments, empowering some neighboring Indian peoples at the expense of others and extending European claims into the interior. Meanwhile, the power of Indians along the southeastern Atlantic coast and in the Northeast waned as wars sapped their strength and imports and colonists began to flood into their lands.

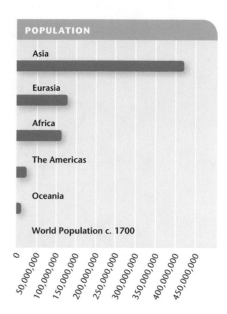

Horses and Violence on the Northern Plains

In the early 1700s, Indians of the northern Great Plains and Great Basin encountered new peoples and goods. From the North and East came French fur trappers and British traders bearing firearms. From the South and West came Indians mounted on horses.

Saukamappee, a young Cree adopted by Blackfeet, was a young man when Blackfeet people first saw horses. Sometime around 1730, Shoshone warriors wielding stone clubs and mounted on *Misstutin* (literally "big dogs" to the Blackfeet) slaughtered their stunned foes. Blackfeet soon acquired horses through trade or theft. Within a generation, they became a fully equestrian people who introduced horses to the Cree. In return, the Cree provided firearms that enabled Blackfeet to gain the upper hand over Shoshone (Map 4.1).

Crees and Shoshones played crucial roles in transforming the region. Cree men carried pelts to Hudson's Bay Company outposts, taking away firearms, knives, and twisted ropes of Brazilian-grown tobacco. The Cree traded the imports to Indians to their south and west. Shoshones occupied the northern end of an Indian network that funneled horses starting around 1700 to Indians who lived on the Columbia Plateau. These Indians incorporated the horses into their seasonal migration as they fished for salmon, hunted bison, and gathered berries and roots.

Indians' desire to acquire horses intensified trade in Indian slaves. Shoshones raided the Blackfeet partly to replace people who Utes had captured to sell to Spanish colonists in the Southwest. Pawnee villages in Nebraska served as way stations for captives from the Southwest and Northern Plains. Some ended up in the Great Lakes or South Carolina. Others went to New Mexico. French and Spanish colonists called

MAP 4.1 ▲ Horses and Guns Enter the Great Plains, c. 1600 to c. 1770 Horses spread more rapidly on Western trade routes along the Rockies than they did in the Great Plains. French traders, many of them from Louisiana, played a crucial role in introducing firearms to Plains peoples, as did the Hudson's Bay Company.

any enslaved Indian who came to them from the plains "Panis" (Pawnee) well into the 1700s.

The advent of the horse and growing commercial ties to colonists encouraged Plains peoples to further exploit captives. Comanches soon ranked among the most proficient captors. Marriage established a Comanche man's claim to independence, but he could not wed until he had acquired enough prestige through hunting, warfare, and capturing a foe's horses and people. By 1706, horses had carried Comanches from their Great Basin homeland to areas rich in bison herds on the southern plains. Their arrival on New Mexico's border recast relations between Indians, Hispanic colonists, and Spanish officials. So did the coming of French colonists to Texas in the 1680s.

Spanish Missions in Texas

In 1685, the French began to construct a fort near the Gulf coast. Spanish officials fretted that they might win over Indian customers and imperil Mexican silver mines and Spanish commerce in the Gulf. In the early 1690s, the French challenge and the Pueblo War for Independence spurred the Spanish to establish a mission and presidio (a fort) within the Hasinai Confederacy, a group of Caddoan-speaking towns in eastern Texas and western Louisiana. The Spanish knew the Hasinai as "the Kingdom of Tejas," the Caddo word for ally. They anticipated success, as "Tejas" people seemed to worship one God and were skillful farmers who had "civilization and government like the Mexican Indians."

By 1693, Hasinai forced the Spanish to leave, largely because the newcomers would not follow Hasinai gender norms. Hasinai delegations to other peoples normally included women and children to convey peaceful intentions. The Spanish party that founded Texas was composed entirely of men, but it marched under a banner that depicted the Virgin Mary, symbolic leader of the Spanish campaign to evangelize Texas. Hasinai interpreted the strangers' display of a woman's image as a sign of peace. But Spanish soldiers soon began to prey on Hasinai women, so they threw the Spanish out. The Spanish were unlike the French men who had arrived a decade earlier. The French had come alone rather than in heavily armed groups, and they had married Hasinai women who afforded them full membership in a society organized around matrilineal clans. Failure to obey Hasinai ways and an inability to meet Hasinai demand for imported goods curbed Spanish influence.

In 1716, however, the Hasinai permitted the Spanish to construct a presidio and missions at a new outpost, Los Adaes. Hasinai people welcomed the Spanish as long as they behaved well and provided an alternative source of goods. Spanish officials tried to honor Hasinai values by recruiting families to settle in Los Adaes, but found few takers. Celibate friars baffled Hasinai. They had no wives to feed them or offer hospitality to Hasinai men. For Hasinai, the priests were a drain on their resources. The Spanish abandoned the mission in the late 1720s. The colonists who stayed behind traded horses to the nearby French post at Natchitoches for food and firearms. The Hasinai prospered by supplying Louisiana with livestock and Indians with French goods, particularly firearms.

The Spanish also entered south Texas. In 1718, they founded missions and a presidio at San Antonio de Béjar, today's San Antonio. The small village attracted diverse bands of Indians from the lower Rio Grande Valley who, like the Spanish, sought protection from Plains Apaches. Apache raids on San Antonio were so frequent that local officials begged for more colonists to help defend it. Their pleas fell on deaf ears until 1731, when 55 colonists arrived, increasing San Antonio's Hispanic population to 300 and that of Texas to 500.

San Antonio remained a Hispanic island in an Indian ocean. Plains Apaches settled in river valleys where they could farm and pasture horses, making them tempting targets for Comanches and Utes. Apaches raided San Antonio to replace horses and to avenge colonists' enslavement of hundreds of their kin captured by Utes and Comanches or taken in Spanish-Pueblo raids.

Slaving raids also had a profound impact on Navajo. Navajo had offered refuge to hundreds of Pueblos who fled the Spanish. Pueblo refugees shared their weaving skills with Navajo. Soon, the Navajo economy depended on raising sheep and weaving wool into blankets and textiles. Navajos sometimes raided New Mexico for sheep. Spanish-Pueblo incursions between 1705 and 1709 took Navajo captives and forced Navajo to leave Spanish livestock alone.

Growing Navajo dependence on sheep had profound environmental and social consequences. By the 1720s, sheep had overgrazed canyons in northwestern New Mexico, which prompted Navajo people to move west in search of fresher pastures. Raising sheep also threatened to divide Navajo society into those who owned large flocks and those who did not. Rustling outsiders' flocks offered a way for poorer men to acquire sheep and ease tensions among the Navajo. So did new rituals. The Blessingway, which today forms the basis for Navajo ceremonialism, most likely emerged during the 1750s. It emphasizes reciprocity and gift giving, with the wealthier assuming responsibility for care of the less fortunate.

During this period, colonists and Pueblos in New Mexico found ways to compromise. After the reconquest, Pueblos accepted Spanish rule, helped to defend the colony, and joined in Spanish slaving raids in exchange for more autonomy and Spanish protection from Indian foes. Governors still required Pueblo men to construct public buildings, maintain irrigation systems, and work Spanish officials' fields, while Pueblo women performed domestic labor, ground wheat and corn, and baked bread. But Indian leaders of each town determined who should serve when. Pueblo dignitaries and medicine men, not missionaries, chose town leaders, and friars intervened less frequently in Pueblo society. Hispanics and Pueblos had settled into an uneasy alliance, largely as a consequence of the Pueblo War for Independence and Apache and Comanche raids.

Indians, the French, and the Making of Louisiana

In 1699, the French claimed the mouth of the Mississippi River by building a fort at Biloxi. They relied heavily on Indians. Indian farmers, hunters, and fishermen fed Louisiana well into the 1720s, even when Illinois colonists had begun to ship small quantities of wheat and large amounts of corn down the Mississippi. Colonists also needed Indians to defend them and trade with them. Indians noted that a disproportionate share of the first colonists of Louisiana and Illinois were French Canadians who knew Indian ways. Many became kin by marrying Indian women and settling in Indian towns.

The French arrived at a propitious moment for the Choctaw, who lived farther from English and Spanish sources of imported goods than most of their enemies did. By the 1690s, they were frequent targets of Chickasaw slaving raids who sold captives to South Carolina colonists. As a result, Choctaw looked to Louisiana's French colonists for support. In 1711, the colony's French governor strengthened the alliance. Fearful that the English might lure the Choctaw to their side, the governor declared Choctaw "the key to this country," which required that the French furnish them with "cloth to clothe them and weapons to defend themselves." Another measure of Choctaw influence on Louisiana survives in the word "bayou," a version of what Choctaw called *bayuk*—the lattice of rivers, creeks, and swamps found throughout the region.

The French alliance with the Choctaw proved vital to the survival of Louisiana. The area's last surviving Mississippian culture, Natchez, occupied a bluff with rich soils that offered protection from floods. For the French, it was an ideal place for establishing

INDIANS AND AFRICANS ON A NEW ORLEANS LEVEE, 1730s   An enslaved Fox woman, barrels of liquor, and bundles of deerskins occupy the foreground. An enslaved African boy and an Attakapas hunter stand to the right. He holds a calumet (peace pipe), used in Indian diplomatic rituals throughout the region. The scene indicates Louisiana's dependence on Indians and Africans.

tobacco plantations. Tensions flared between the Natchez and the French as colonists imported African slaves to begin growing tobacco in the 1720s. Natchez resented French incursions into their lands and their own growing dependence on French goods. According to Tattooed Serpent (also known as Stung Serpent), Natchez men had become too dependent on guns. Natchez women had been more industrious "and less vain" when they made blankets and mantles rather than buying them from the French. Before the French came, Tattooed Serpent asserted, "we lived like men who can be satisfied with what they have; whereas this day we are like slaves, who are not suffered to do as they please." Natchez warriors and African slaves joined together to strike back one morning in 1729. They killed over 200 colonists and captured nearly 300 African slaves and 50 white women and children. Choctaw warriors enabled French colonists to win the **Natchez War** and suppress Louisiana's enslaved Africans. French officials handed three Africans who had joined Natchez over to Choctaw, who burned them to death.

The war forced a Natchez diaspora and brought political change to Louisiana. Hundreds of Natchez were enslaved and sold to sugar planters in Saint Domingue. Hundreds more found sanctuary among Chickasaw people. Louisiana's governor, exasperated by his dependence on Indians, complained that "[t]he least little nation thinks itself our protector." He requested more troops so that he could compel Indians to respect him, but instead he lost his job. Louis XV, fed up with bad news from Louisiana, took control of the colony in 1731 and then mostly ignored it.

Slaving Raids, Expansion, and War in the Carolinas

To the east, people from Virginia and European immigrants moved deeper into Carolina, establishing small farms and new settlements. In 1710, the colony was divided into North Carolina and South Carolina. Although South Carolina did not depend on Indians as much as Louisiana did, the colony needed them to supply two exports: deerskins and slaves. Indian hunters provided deerskins, which Europeans often used instead of cowhides. Indian warriors captured people and traded them to the English colonists in Carolina, who shipped most of them to the West Indies. Some enslaved Indians had trudged from as far as the Northern Plains and the Southwest, but most came from southeastern peoples allied with France or Spain whom English-allied warriors had seized.

Slaving raids spread disease that killed thousands and fed violence that engulfed the Indian Southeast. Dozens of South Carolina soldiers accompanied thousands of Indians, most of them Creek, in a wave of attacks on Apalachee missions in northern Florida. They slaughtered hundreds, enslaved thousands, and reduced Florida's missions to ashes between 1702 and 1706 (Map 4.2). Five years later, Tuscarora people retaliated for slaving raids and colonists' encroachment on their lands by attacking farms and towns in North Carolina. South Carolina troops joined Catawba, Yamasee, and Cherokee forces that killed or enslaved about 1,000 Tuscaroras and won the **Tuscarora War** (1711–1713).

Peoples who suffered slaving raids often split apart. Some Tuscaroras stayed in North Carolina after the war ended. About 2,000 others found shelter alongside Iroquois. Some mission Apalachees relocated near St. Augustine for protection. Others sought refuge among other Indians in present-day Georgia and Alabama. Some Indians fled deep into Florida, with Indian slave raiders in hot pursuit. In 1711, nearly 300 Florida Indians boarded ships for Cuba, which offered them refuge.

The British Caribbean was the main destination for Indian slaves, although some remained in South Carolina where they comprised 15 percent of the population in 1708. Others were sold to New England, New York, and Virginia. Colonists in those regions bought them because they were cheaper than Africans, although they soon developed a reputation as "malacious, surly, and revengeful," according to Massachusetts legislators. In 1712, Massachusetts barred their entry. Other New England colonies followed suit.

Meanwhile, South Carolina had developed a bad reputation among its Indian neighbors. So many Indians left Charleston in chains that the port exported more slaves than it imported until 1715. Cherokees, Creeks, and Chickasaws felt cheated by traveling English traders licensed by the colony. Yamasee were particularly resentful. They had been allies to South Carolina for three decades, but by the early 1710s, Yamasees were deeply indebted to English merchants, mainly because they no longer had direct access to deerskins and Indian slaves. English planters coveted Yamasee lands and dreamed of growing rice on them.

In 1715, Indian grievances against South Carolina turned violent. Cherokees, Creeks, and Chickasaws killed English traders residing in their villages. Yamasees and Creeks burned and pillaged plantations. South Carolina's leaders begged for help from Virginia and Indian allies. Cherokee and Chickasaw dependence on English goods ultimately led them to side with colonists, a decision that brought Cherokees into conflict with Creeks. The English-Indian alliance won the **Yamasee War** (1715–1717) but not before it killed 1 in 16 colonists and took a far greater toll on Indians. Yamasee

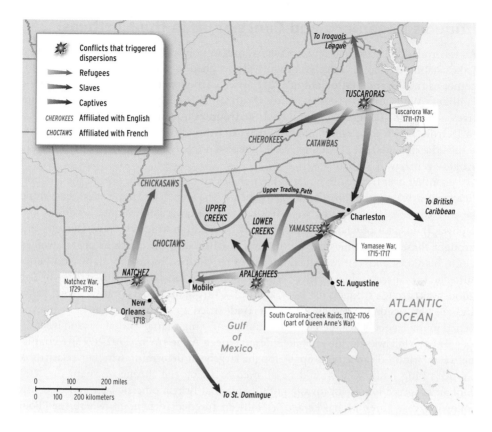

MAP 4.2 ▲ War, the Indian Slave Trade, and the Dispersal of Southeastern Indian Peoples, c. 1700–1730 Epidemics, demand for Indian slaves, and English and French invasions of Indian lands devastated the Southeast's Indian peoples. This map charts the movements of four peoples—Apalachee, Tuscarora, Yamasee, and Natchez—dispersed by conflicts with European colonists and Indians affiliated with them.

refugees fled to Florida. The war depopulated vast areas and led to hostilities between Creeks and Cherokees that lasted for decades.

Colonists and Indians struggled to stabilize relations in the wake of such devastation. South Carolina officials fixed prices on trade goods and copied the French practice of regularly exchanging gifts with Indian allies, who promised to capture and return runaway African slaves. Indians tried to remain autonomous by seeking multiple sources of imports, while Creeks used diplomacy to play the Spanish, French, and English against one another.

The Yamasee War transformed the Southeast. It slowed the Indian slave trade, as Indians refused to conduct more slaving raids for the English. The war also accelerated changes that had long been underway. By 1720, multiethnic and multilingual Indian communities, united by the need for common defense, had coalesced into new political entities: Catawba, Cherokee, and Chickasaw. The most diverse of these was the Creek Confederacy, which for most of the 1700s was the region's foremost Indian power.

Iroquois Hegemony and Concessions in the Northeast

As war roiled the Carolinas and Louisiana, Indian politics in the Northeast and Great Lakes stabilized, thanks largely to two treaties signed by Iroquois leaders, known together as the "**Grand Settlement of 1701**." In one, Iroquois people, decimated by King William's War, agreed to cease hostilities with Great Lakes peoples and exchange captives with them. The French guaranteed the Iroquois hunting and trading rights west to Detroit, which the French founded in 1701. Through the other treaty, Iroquois retained the right to trade at Albany. The league also promised to remain neutral in future Anglo-French wars.

Conflict over trade with Great Lakes peoples and factionalism within the Iroquois League nearly unraveled the "Grand Settlement." The French had hoped that they would be able to monitor relations between Iroquois and Ottawa, Potawatomi, Wyandot, and Ojibwa, thousands of whom accepted a French invitation to resettle near Detroit. This brought these French allies closer to sources of British goods, such as coarse woolen cloth, blankets, and kettles, which tended to be cheaper, more abundant, and better suited to Indian tastes than similar French imports. The most direct path to those British goods was through Iroquois territory, and in 1707 Iroquois leaders granted Great Lakes Indians permission to travel to Albany. As trade dried up at Montreal, the French intervened in the Iroquois League's internal affairs, enraging a large faction of Mohawks.

Those Mohawks decided to take sides in **Queen Anne's War** (1702–1713), a conflict between Britain, France, and Spain fought largely to determine whether relatives of France's king Louis XIV should be allowed to sit on the throne of Spain. In 1709, Mohawks agreed to join an invasion of Canada that British officials later canceled. The following year, three Mohawks and a Mahican traveled to London, where the "Four Indian Kings" (as the London press called them) met Queen Anne to lobby for a British invasion of Canada. Their efforts initially bore fruit. In 1711, Britain sent more than 5,000 troops across the Atlantic, the largest British military force yet to reach the Americas, to join New England and New York militiamen in an attack on New France. A storm off the coast of Canada ran nine ships aground, claiming over 700 lives and prompting the British to scuttle the mission.

By 1717, Iroquois agreed that neutrality was their best course. Tuscaroras driven north by British colonists helped to maintain that consensus, especially after Iroquois admitted them to their league in 1722. Iroquois forces directed their wars for captives at peoples such as Catawba and Cherokee and negotiated with British colonies to ensure that their warriors could travel freely to and from the Southeast.

Meanwhile, the French struggled to keep the Iroquois from taking sides in wars in the Great Lakes that involved their Indian allies. Peoples friendly to the French sought to drive a wedge between the Iroquois-allied Fox and the French, fearing that a French-Fox alliance would deprive them of trade goods. It helped their cause that New France had legalized Indian slavery in 1709 to meet colonists' growing demand for labor. Skillful diplomacy and "gifts" of Fox slaves persuaded the French to side against Fox in three wars (1712–1716, 1723–1725, and 1728–1735). Fox peoples numbered several thousand when **Fox Wars** began, but only a few hundred when the wars ended. The rest escaped to Iowa or were killed, adopted by their enemies, or enslaved by the French. Some Fox slaves deemed too dangerous were sent to the West Indies. The war chief Kiala and his wife (captors did not record her name) were auctioned in Martinique in 1734. No planter would bid on them for fear that they might incite a rebellion among African slaves, so the couple was deported to South America.

Peace between the Northeast's three main powers—British, French, and Iroquois—displaced weaker Indians. By 1722, Pennsylvania officials accepted Iroquois claims that they spoke for Delawares and Shawnees. The arrangement enhanced Iroquois power, partly because it provided the league's peoples an alternative source of British goods. But Delawares and Shawnees had their lands in eastern Pennsylvania sold out from under them. They headed west, where they began to upset the region's delicate balance of power in the 1740s.

The stability that Iroquois people enjoyed came at a high cost. The league's peoples could no longer mask their dependence on Europeans. In the 1720s, the Iroquois permitted the French and British to construct rival forts and trading posts near Lake Ontario. These diverted western Indians' trade and flooded Iroquois villages with cheap alcohol, eliciting requests that the sale of rum be banned west of Albany. "You may find graves upon graves along the Lake," said one protest in 1730, all "occasioned by Selling Rum to Our Brethren." Meanwhile, New York encroached on Mohawk country. The colonization of Iroquois, the Northeast's preeminent Indian power for generations, had begun.

STUDY QUESTIONS FOR TURMOIL IN INDIAN NORTH AMERICA

1. In what ways did horses and guns change life for Indians on the Northern Plains and in the Southwest?

2. What impact did the Indian slave trade have on North America?

3. What was the Great Settlement of 1701? By what means and at what cost did it bring political stability to northeastern North America?

◼ MIGRATION, RELIGION, AND EMPIRES

Indians' grip on eastern North America weakened in part because tens of thousands of enslaved Africans and European immigrants flooded in. The newcomers, particularly the Africans, provoked a backlash from white colonists that entrenched racism throughout colonial North America. Massive immigration, along with thickening transatlantic ties among Protestants who sought American converts and a more powerful British empire, bound North America more tightly to the Atlantic world.

The Africanization of North America

Colonial North America expanded rapidly in the early 1700s, largely as a result of its Africanization. More Africans landed in North America in the first decade of the eighteenth century than had done so between 1565 and 1690. They represented some of the nearly 70,000 enslaved Africans who together comprised the majority of immigrants to North America between 1691 and 1730.

The intensification of the Atlantic slave trade destabilized African politics and coincided with major economic changes in Africa. In 1704, a popular Christian

JAMAICAN DRUM   Sir Hans Sloane obtained this drum in Jamaica while visiting there in the early 1700s and noted that it had come from Virginia. Someone brought the drum from Africa to Virginia where enslaved Africans likely used it for funeral rites that helped them forge a sense of kinship and community.

movement erupted in West Central Africa that sought to end years of civil war between competitors for the throne of Kongo. The movement temporarily halted the flow of thousands of captives into the Atlantic slave trade. However, King Pedro eventually captured the throne five years later and sold most of the members of the movement into slavery. Meanwhile, gold production tailed off near the Gold Coast in the late 1600s. Warring states in the region needed to pay for firearms and gunpowder to equip armies, so the streams of captives were sent to the coast. The Gold Coast exported over 330,000 people between 1690 and 1730.

Most captives suffered alienation long before boarding a slave ship. Separated from kin and village, captives were viewed as disgraced outsiders as they traveled to the coast. Captives endured a long voyage across the Atlantic, shackled together and confined below deck. About one in five did not survive it. Merchants and captains, especially of British ships, gradually improved survival rates over time, earning bigger profits.

Enslaved people came to North America from all parts of Africa, but North American colonies remained a relatively small market for the Atlantic's vast and rapidly growing slave trade (Map 4.3). Most Africans brought to North America between 1691 and 1730 departed from Senegambia or the Bight of Biafra. North American colonists purchased only 5 percent of the Africans exported to the Americas and 10 percent of those carried in British ships.

Although more than two-thirds of the Africans shipped to North America between 1691 and 1730 arrived in Virginia or Maryland, the market for them extended to all the British and French colonies. South Carolina and Louisiana began to import Africans in large numbers in the 1720s. Over 3,000 enslaved Africans disembarked in northern British colonies between 1691 and 1730, including hundreds who arrived in New York from Madagascar in the 1690s. Another 6,000 arrived in New England, New York, and Pennsylvania via the West Indies (Figure 4.1).

Expanded cultivation of tobacco stoked North American demand for enslaved labor. Tobacco exports from Maryland and Virginia to Britain nearly tripled between 1705 and 1730. Louisiana imported thousands of Africans between 1717 and 1731, as planters tried and failed to make the colony a tobacco exporter that could compete with the Chesapeake and Brazil.

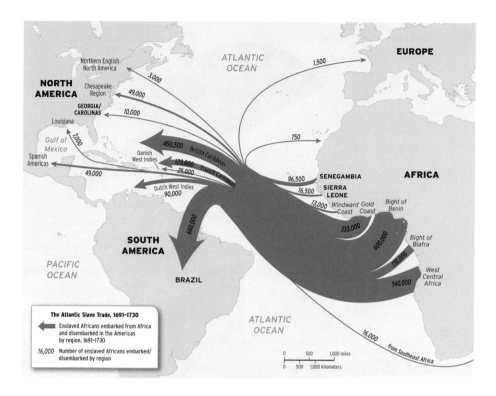

MAP 4.3 ▲ **The Atlantic Slave Trade, 1691–1730** This map provides a broad American perspective on the Atlantic slave trade. About 69,000 enslaved Africans landed in North America between 1691 and 1730, about two times as many as between 1641 and 1690. More than half arrived in the 1720s. But over 95 percent went elsewhere in the Americas, mostly to the Caribbean or Brazil.

Meanwhile, the expansion of rice cultivation made South Carolina a major destination for enslaved Africans. Carolina planters began to grow the crop in the 1690s, and by the 1720s, the knowledge, skill, and labor of thousands of recently arrived Africans enabled South Carolina to export millions of pounds of rice a year. African women pounded tons of rice a year to ready it for market.

Regional differences shaped Africans' lives in North America. Slaves did not comprise 20 percent of Virginians until 1710. Chesapeake planters bought so many Africans from different parts of the continent that it was hard for slaves to find a common language other than English. The presence of more American-born slaves meant that there were more enslaved black women in the Chesapeake than anywhere else in North America, so relatively more enslaved men could find partners and start families. By contrast, South Carolina and Louisiana had African majorities by the 1720s. Most who arrived in both colonies during that decade came from Senegambia, increasing the odds that they would meet someone who spoke their language or shared their memories of Africa.

For many Africans, North American slavery brought an early grave and profound social isolation. Colonists considered Africans dangerous and brutish, partly because they did not speak or understand English or French. As many as one in four succumbed

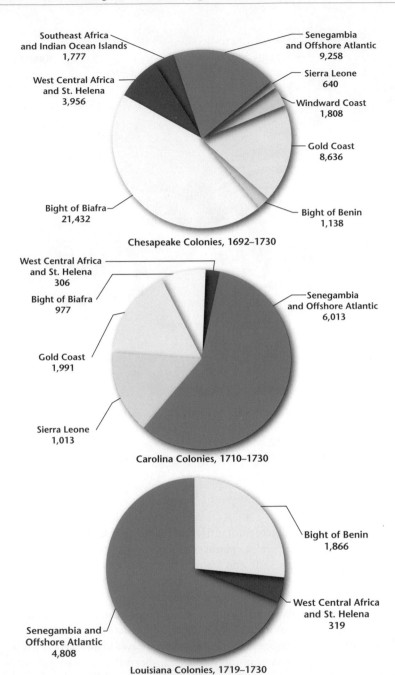

Southeast Africa and Indian Ocean Islands 1,777

Senegambia and Offshore Atlantic 9,258

West Central Africa and St. Helena 3,956

Sierra Leone 640

Windward Coast 1,808

Gold Coast 8,636

Bight of Biafra 21,432

Bight of Benin 1,138

Chesapeake Colonies, 1692–1730

West Central Africa and St. Helena 306

Bight of Biafra 977

Gold Coast 1,991

Sierra Leone 1,013

Senegambia and Offshore Atlantic 6,013

Carolina Colonies, 1710–1730

Bight of Benin 1,866

West Central Africa and St. Helena 319

Senegambia and Offshore Atlantic 4,808

Louisiana Colonies, 1719–1730

FIGURE 4.1 ▲ Regional origins of enslaved Africans disembarked in regions of North America (estimated), 1692–1730 Enslaved Africans sent from ports in the Bight of Biafra composed nearly half of those brought directly to the Chesapeake colonies between the 1690s and 1730, while those who left Africa from Senegambia comprised the majority of those sent directly from Africa to South Carolina and Louisiana.

to disease and died within a year of arrival. Africans combated alienation by adapting beliefs and practices of their homelands, many of which centered around honoring their dead. For most Africans, death initiated the soul's journey from the material world to the realm of spirits and ancestors. Those who died without kin risked becoming ghosts doomed to haunt the living. Only a proper funeral assured that the soul reached its proper destination and found peace, so friends and neighbors acted as kin to the deceased. They sponsored funeral processions—followed by singing, dancing, drumming, and feasting—to celebrate the soul's arrival to its resting place. These rituals alarmed colonists. Virginia officials feared that nighttime funerals would enable slaves to conspire and tried to ban them in the 1680s. In 1699, slaves in Philadelphia protested that their long days of work did not allow them to finish burials before sunset. Graves testify to how Africans honored their dead. Tobacco pipes often accompanied those buried in Virginia during the early 1700s, a practice common in West Africa.

Some Africans violently resisted enslavement. In 1712, some four dozen slaves set fire to a building in New York City and attacked the whites who came to extinguish the blaze, killing nine and injuring several more. Officials hanged 20 slaves, burned 3 at the stake, and hoisted 1 in chains until he starved to death. Investigators concluded that the rebels, many from the Gold Coast, sought "to destroy all the White[s] in order to obtain their freedom." The rebels prepared for battle as if they had been in Africa by binding one another to secrecy "by Sucking the blood of each Others hands," while some rubbed a powder on their clothing in the belief that it would make them invulnerable.

Meanwhile, Virginia masters had nightmares of slave conspiracies. They claimed to have uncovered six between 1709 and 1731. In 1729, a dozen runaways tried to create a sanctuary for themselves. Governor William Gooch ordered it destroyed to save Virginia from "a design which might have proved as dangerous" to whites "as is that of the Negroes in the Mountains of Jamaica." Gooch likened the runaways to Jamaican **Maroons**, participants in a form of resistance long common in the Caribbean and Brazil.

Many British colonists, alarmed by the rapidly growing numbers of Africans among them, tried to restrict the Atlantic slave trade. In Boston, Judge **Samuel Sewall** and merchant **John Saffin** debated the slave trade as the 18th century dawned. Sewall charged that the Atlantic slave trade was immoral and that it endangered whites because Africans took the place of "Men that might make Husbands for our Daughters" and would "remain in our Body Politick as a kind of extravasat [alien] Blood." Saffin countered with Anglo-America's first militant defense of the Atlantic slave trade and slavery. The Bible and the Atlantic world provided examples, he insisted, which indicated that God had decreed that some were to rule while others were "to be born Slaves, and so to remain during their lives." Pennsylvania lawmakers responded to the 1712 New York revolt by imposing a tax on each imported slave. Eleven years later, Virginia legislators imposed a duty on imported Africans to pay for a militia that would protect against possible slave rebellions.

The "Naturalization" of Slavery and Racism

The tens of thousands of enslaved people brought to North America between the 1690s and 1730 accelerated the growth of slavery in the British colonies and Louisiana. So did the births of thousands of children to enslaved women. Meanwhile, British colonists and French imperial officials, alarmed by a rapidly growing black population, enacted laws that codified slavery and enshrined racism throughout North America.

African and African American women in the Chesapeake raised the first large generation to be born into slavery in North America. In the early 1700s, an American-born slave woman usually conceived her first child by the time that she was 19. She could expect to give birth to nine children, six of whom might survive past age four. By the 1730s, the Chesapeake colonies were home to the first enslaved population composed mostly of native-born people of African descent.

Chesapeake masters' desire to cut costs helps to explain why they promoted the growth of slave families. Chesapeake Bay was farther from Africa than any other major market for enslaved Africans, which increased what Chesapeake masters paid for those brought directly from Africa. An enslaved African faced a high chance of dying soon after arrival and had to learn basic English to understand commands. Anglo-American masters also believed that American-born slaves were more intelligent, better suited for skilled labor, and less likely to rebel than Africans. In 1724, Hugh Jones, an Anglican clergyman in Virginia, contrasted Africans with American-born slaves who "talk good English, and affect our language, habits, and customs." Maryland and Virginia planters also encouraged the formation of slave families by buying more African women during the 1720s.

The growth of slavery spurred the creation of slave codes throughout colonial North America. In 1726, Pennsylvania became the last British colony founded during the 1600s to pass a comprehensive slave code. Meanwhile, Louisiana colonists mostly ignored North America's first imperially mandated slave code issued in 1685. In 1724, Louis XV explicitly extended the **Code Noir** to cover the French West Indies to Louisiana. The Louisiana Code Noir directed masters to provide slaves with a minimum amount of food and clothing as well as access to religious instruction. Slaves were to be baptized and married; married slaves had the right to stay together. Virtually all these provisions went unenforced. The Code Noir also afforded free people of color in Louisiana many rights that free whites enjoyed, among them to petition officials and testify in court. They quickly used such rights to get a discriminatory tax abolished. But the 1724 Code Noir discriminated against free people of color by banning interracial marriages and imposing fines on parents of mixed-race children. French officials hoped to ensure that Louisiana would not become like the French Caribbean, where a growing population of mixed-race people gave those islands a bad reputation in Europe.

The Code Noir was part of another wave that swept North America in the 1690s and early 1700s—the desire to draw a clear color line. Discouraging private **manumissions** was one way to limit the ranks of free blacks. By 1729, every northern British colony had made slaveholders financially responsible for freeing their slaves by requiring them to post bonds to ensure that freed people would not become a burden on taxpayers. Virginia, and South Carolina after 1722, required that freed people leave after manumission.

The new laws made life harder for free blacks. The slave codes of New York and New Jersey prohibited anyone freed after they took effect from owning real estate. Pennsylvania's slave code empowered local officials to sentence free black "loiterers" to at least one year's service and make indentured servants of children born to free black women. Virginia and South Carolina disenfranchised black men in the 1720s and Virginia reimposed a tax on free black women. The colony's governor thought that lawmakers should "fix a perpetual Brand" on free blacks, partly because they "adhere to and favor the slaves."

Prohibitions on interracial sex were crucial to guarding the color line. In 1705, Massachusetts outlawed marriage between people of African and European descent. Virginia's slave code of that year decreed that unwed white mothers of biracial children should pay a fine or serve a five-year indenture, whereas free whites who chose to wed a black partner were to be fined and spend six months in prison. North Carolina criminalized interracial sex for white women in 1715. A Pennsylvania law passed in 1700 made black male rape of a white woman a capital offense, but there was no penalty for raping a black woman.

The press reinforced the color line. In 1718, *The Boston News-Letter* published a story in which a white vigilante in Connecticut sliced off the genitalia of a black man who he claimed was about to rape a white woman. The paper's editors celebrated his deed, which they thought sent an unmistakable message to "all Negroes meddling with any White Woman."

European Immigrants and Imperial Expansion

Most Europeans who came to North America between 1690 and 1730 did so voluntarily, with the vast majority going to British colonies. Stronger commercial, personal, and institutional ties between British North America, Britain, and German-speaking Europe helped to determine who went where and when they arrived; so did political changes, including the **Act of Union**, which created the United Kingdom by merging the kingdoms and parliaments of England and Scotland in 1707.

The Act of Union opened a British empire fully to Scots. A Scot in New York, Samuel Vetch, touted the expansion of British North America as a way to knit the new United Kingdom together. He led a transatlantic campaign that advocated using British soldiers to conquer Canada and colonizing Nova Scotia with Scots. Soldiers from New England and Britain conquered Nova Scotia for the British Empire during Queen Anne's War, but most of it remained in the hands of French Acadians and Micmacs for decades. The 1,300 Scots who landed in North America between 1710 and 1730 mostly settled elsewhere, but they had a greater impact on British colonies than their numbers would suggest (Table 4.1). Many royal governors were Scots. Scottish doctors trained at the University of Edinburgh dominated the ranks of elite physicians in British North America and linked the colonies to scientific networks in Britain and Europe.

Immigrants from southern Ireland and Ulster (Northern Ireland) comprised a much larger stream of people to North America between 1690 and 1730. Most migrants from southern Ireland came as indentured servants and landed in the Chesapeake colonies or Pennsylvania. Ulsterite migration was largely a byproduct of that region's linen trade. The **Linen Act of 1705** encouraged the export of Irish linen to North America. In turn, linen manufacturing in northern Ireland boosted demand for flaxseed (the source of linen) that New England and Pennsylvania farmers grew. Overdependence on linen, rent increases, and crop failures between 1718 and 1729 prompted thousands of Ulsterites to set sail to North America (Table 4.1). The linen–flaxseed trade provided a way to get there. Emigrants boarded ships that had come to Ireland with bulky cargoes of flaxseed and were returning to the colonies with lighter and more compact linen. Passages were relatively inexpensive, so most Ulster migrants could pay their own way and travel as families. Most Ulsterites settled in Pennsylvania.

The State of the *Palatines*,

FOR

Fifty Years past to this present Time.

CONTAINING,

I. An Account of the Principality of the Palatinate; and of the Barbarities and Ravages committed by Order of the French King upon the Inhabitants; Burning to the Ground a great Number of their most Famous Cities, and throwing the Bones of Emperors, Princes and Prelates, out of their Tombs, &c.

II. The Case of the Palatines, Published by themselves, and Humbly Offered to the Tradesmen of England. With a List of them, and the Trades which the Men are brought up to.

III. The Humble Petition of the Justices of *Middlesex* to Her Majesty on their Behalf, with Her Majesties Order thereupon, and an Abstract of the Brief graciously Granted for their Subsistence.

IV. A Letter about Settling and Employing them in other Countries.

V. A Proclamation of the States-General for Naturalizing all Strangers, and receiving them into their Country.

VI. Lastly, Their present Encamping at Camberwell and Black-heath, in many Hundred Tents, by Her Majesties Grace and Favour, till they can be otherwise dispos'd of, and how they Employ themselves; with their Marriages, Burials, &c. Also the great Kindness their Ancestors shew'd to the English Protestants in the bloody Reign of Queen Mary.

PALATINE REFUGEE CAMP IN LONDON, 1709   Some 15,000 Germans fled war-torn areas of the Rhine Valley for London, lured by rumors that they would be resettled and granted land in North America. Many ended up in refugee camps like this one located near London from which they were transported to North Carolina and upstate New York.

Table 4.1 Estimated European Migration to British North America by Ethnic Group and Compared to Enslaved African Migration, 1700–1729

Over two-thirds of migrants who arrived in English/British North America between 1700 and the 1720s were enslaved Africans. The vast majority of European immigrants were not English, the first time that had happened in the history of English/British colonization of the Americas.

Decade	Germans	Ulster Irish	Southern Irish	Scots	English	Welsh	Other	Africans	Total
1700–1709	100	600	800	200	400	300	100	12,900	15,400
1710–1719	3,700	1,200	1,700	500	1,300	900	200	10,500	20,000
1720–1729	2,300	2,100	3,000	800	2,200	1,500	200	30,500	42,600
TOTALS	6,100	3,900	5,500	1,500	3,900	2,700	500	53,900	78,000

Note: "Germans" refers to German speakers, not to people who came from what is today Germany. "Africans" refers to people brought via the Atlantic slave trade from Africa who disembarked in British North America. "British North America" does not include Nova Scotia or the Caribbean.

Meanwhile, thousands of Germans headed for North America. They came in three waves. The first arrived between 1683 and 1709, mainly to escape religious persecution. They came from many parts of German-speaking northern and central Europe and sailed for Philadelphia, drawn by William Penn's promises of religious freedom, pamphlets published in German, or letters from kin or from fellow believers who had already emigrated. The second wave of German immigration occurred between 1709 and 1714 and hailed mainly from what is today southwest Germany, an area ravaged by Queen Anne's War. Most migrated to New York or North Carolina as participants in large planned colonization ventures. The third wave was the largest. Triggered primarily by overpopulation and land scarcity, it also originated mainly in southwest Germany and lasted from 1717 until 1775. Like Ulsterites, most Germans settled in Pennsylvania, while a small number went to Louisiana in the 1720s.

British colonists had mixed reactions to the Ulsterite and German immigrants. In New England, the minister **Cotton Mather** at first celebrated Ulsterite immigration as a way to bolster local defenses against French and Indian foes. He soon changed his mind, declaring that the Presbyterian newcomers had "most indecently and ingratefully given much disturbance to the peace of our churches." In Pennsylvania, James Logan, provincial secretary in the late 1720s, worried that the Irish might soon "make themselves Proprietors of the Province," whereas the Germans might ensure that "these colonies will in time be lost to the Crown." Sometimes such sentiments turned violent. In 1729, a Boston mob prevented a ship of Ulster immigrants from landing, charging that the "confounded Irish will eat us all up."

Although most Europeans chose to sail to North America, thousands came against their will. The Spanish, British, and French empires sent convicts to work in their colonies. Many of the hundreds who went to Florida in the early 1700s had been prisoners in Spanish and Mexican jails. They manned the fort that guarded St. Augustine. English officials sentenced Scottish and Irish rebels to servitude in North America or the West Indies on various occasions during the 1600s. A similar fate befell some 500 Scots who in 1715 participated in the **Jacobite Rebellion** against the crowning of **George I**. The governor of South Carolina purchased some and sent them to fight the Yamasee War.

Worries about surging crime led Parliament to make colonial servitude a tool of Britain's criminal justice system. The **Transportation Act of 1718** mandated exile to North America for seven years to life for those convicted of crimes ranging from theft to receipt of stolen goods to capital felonies. Most convicts sent to North America committed property crimes. A few were violent offenders. At least 3,000 had come from Britain and Ireland by 1730, the first of 50,000 to be transported to North America before 1775.

Convicts played a significant role in the colonization of Louisiana. Most Europeans who went to Louisiana before 1763 arrived between 1717 and 1721 and were prisoners or indentured servants, bound to serve the Company of the Indies for three years. In 1720, inmates at a Paris prison rioted and fifty destined for North American bondage escaped. Louis XV soon declared that there would be no more forced deportations to Louisiana. Few chose to go to Louisiana, partly because most who did died young en route or alongside a bayou. In 1726, Louisiana census takers counted 2,300 Europeans, including 300 indentured servants. Five years later, there were 2,000. Immigration to French Louisiana, like that to New France in the 1660s and 1670s, was brief and concentrated. Europeans did not return in significant numbers until Spain took charge of the colony in the 1760s.

European immigration left a profound mark on North America. It helped France cling to the middle of the continent. It pushed the boundaries of British North America outward, as Ulsterite and German immigrants settled new lands. It also reinforced British colonists' ties to an Atlantic Protestant network that had mobilized partly to counter what it perceived as a global Catholic threat.

Pietism and Atlantic Protestantism

In 1710, Cotton Mather, New England's most prominent minister, published *A Discourse Concerning Faith and Fervency*. It was one of his contributions to **Pietism**, a Protestant movement that linked North America, Britain, the Netherlands, and central Europe. Pietists promoted the personal piety of believers and the evangelization of all, including American Indians and enslaved Africans.

Pietism drew from many sources. These included English Puritanism, Anglicanism, and Dutch Calvinism. Pietists affiliated with Germany's University of Halle and the Church of England played crucial roles in spreading Pietism's principles overseas. Halle faculty influenced many German and Dutch pastors in New York, New Jersey, and Pennsylvania. Meanwhile, Anglican reformers in London founded the **Society for the Propagation of the Gospel in Foreign Parts** (SPG) in 1701. It focused on sending missionaries to North America and the West Indies.

The SPG devoted much of its attention to enslaved Africans. But SPG missionaries persuaded few masters that conversion would make for more obedient slaves. Pietists like Francis Le Jau in South Carolina usually blamed planters for their lack of success, claiming that they unduly limited access to slave audiences. But SPG advocates did not realize or did not acknowledge that their own message often discouraged Africans from converting. Le Jau required slaves seeking baptism to swear that they were not doing so to press masters to free them. African men had to promise to abandon **polygamy**. Missionaries also requested that enslaved converts devote part of each Sunday to attend services, the day they customarily had for themselves and one that they often spent trying to grow more food.

Some Anglicans confirmed masters' worries about the risks of evangelizing slaves. In 1729, James Blair, a Virginia clergyman, noted that some slaves converted because they believed that "Christianity will help them to their freedom." The following year, some slaves who were questioned concerning a rumored slave rebellion cited their conversion as justification. A few also claimed that George II had "ordered all those slaves free that were Christians." They linked conversion to Christianity and royal authority to their yearning for freedom.

Puritan and SPG missionaries evangelized Africans and African Americans in Northern cities. In 1693, Cotton Mather founded the Society of Negroes in Boston. Mather invited slaves, with masters' permission, to meet at his home every Sunday, where he preached against drunkenness, stealing, or disobedience. Mather further promoted evangelization of slaves by publishing *The Negro Christianized* in 1706. Meanwhile, Elias Neau, SPG missionary to New York City, operated a school that attracted as many as 1 in 10 black New Yorkers. Few attended more than three times, but many who never returned kept the catechism books that they had been given, hoping to learn to read.

The visit of the "Four Indian Kings" to London encouraged English Pietists to pay more attention to Indians. A mission to a Mohawk village enjoyed modest success before the SPG shut it down in 1719. Indian disinterest ensured that other SPG missions fared as poorly or worse. The same was true for most New England ministers who worked under the auspices of the New England Company.

Pietists were responding to French Jesuits' efforts among Abenaki groups in Maine. New England, they contended, was a key front in the battle to preserve British and Protestant liberty from French and Catholic tyranny. That struggle, British North Americans believed, also bound them more tightly to the British Empire and to the monarchs who headed it.

Imperial Authority and Colonial Resistance

Starting in the late 1600s, royal supervision of colonial British North America intensified, as did imperial efforts to regulate its economy. Colonists tried to skirt rules that they deemed contrary to their interests and promoted those that they thought served them well. In the process, their ties to their monarchs, the British Empire, and the Atlantic world grew stronger.

Royal authority played a bigger role in British colonists' lives in many ways. Monarchs began to appoint governors for New Jersey, Nova Scotia, South Carolina, and North Carolina between 1702 and 1729, bringing 9 of the 13 British mainland colonies under royal rule. By the 1720s, many colonists' homes contained mass-produced images of British royalty. Celebrations of royal holidays dotted the calendars of major port towns, which by 1740 staged at least six such events a year, including royal birthdays and coronation anniversaries. The most raucous was November 5th, Pope's or Guy Fawkes Day.

HANGING OF MAJOR STEDE BONNET Bonnet was a Barbadian planter who turned to piracy in 1717, preying on shipping along the Atlantic coast of North America and in the Caribbean. Captured along the North Carolina coast, he was convicted by Charleston's vice-admiralty courts and executed in 1718.

It commemorated the discovery of a Catholic plot to blow up Parliament. **Pope's Day** processions featuring the display (and sometimes burning) of papal effigies were common in port towns by the late 1690s. In 1702, Bostonians added an effigy of the **Pretender**—the Catholic Stuart who claimed the British throne during the 1715 Jacobite Rebellion—to the festivities. This practice spread throughout British North America. Colonists' enthusiasm for such rituals expressed their growing desire to be recognized as Britons who were loyal subjects and partners in a global battle against what they saw as a Catholic menace.

As British colonists celebrated their monarchs, imperial officials claimed more power over their commerce. In 1696, William III created the **Board of Trade**, an advisory council charged to oversee colonial matters. The act testified to the colonies' growing significance to England's economy. In 1700–1701, colonists in British North America and the West Indies comprised just over 10 percent of the market for goods England exported and produced almost 20 percent of the value of goods it imported. The Board of Trade implemented a series of **Navigation Acts** to tighten regulations on colonial trade and established **vice-admiralty courts** in the colonies to enforce the law.

Between 1700 and 1730, the Royal Navy and the vice-admiralty courts waged a war on piracy that colonists increasingly supported. Pirates had long found shelter in colonial ports as good customers who often paid in scarce silver or gold. However, the end of Queen Anne's War sparked a growth of piracy. As the Royal Navy was demobilized, mariners' wages were cut, and thousands lost their jobs. Many turned to piracy. As many as 5,000 pirates operated between 1716 and 1726. They increasingly targeted ships belonging to colonial merchants. Doing business with pirates also became less appealing after Parliament passed the first effective empire-wide law to combat piracy in 1700. It mandated the death penalty for those convicted of piracy or for aiding and abetting pirates.

Some pirates, driven from the Bahamas, sought sanctuary in North Carolina. Their leaders included Edward Teach, better known as Blackbeard. In 1718, a fleet of British, Virginia, and South Carolina vessels killed Teach and captured many of his associates, who were tried, convicted, and hanged. A similar fate befell hundreds more as colonial officials, naval officers, and vice-admiralty judges throughout North America tightened the noose on piracy, at times stringing up the condemned by the dozen. By the late 1720s, the British Empire had won the war on piracy, making the Atlantic safer for commerce that its leaders considered legitimate.

Securing raw materials for the Royal Navy that defeated the pirates also proved to be a challenge. As Britain's forests receded from overcutting, its shipbuilders became dependent on timber and naval stores (tar, pitch, and turpentine—used mainly to preserve and waterproof ships) from Sweden and Russia. The Navy especially needed timber for ship masts. Vast forests of white pine in Maine and New Hampshire seemed the solution to their problem. By 1717, North America made

GOSSIP MONGERS Putative portrait of Edward Hyde, Viscount Cornbury. Cornbury, governor of New York, acquired many enemies there. Some spread rumors in England that Cornbury wore women's clothing publicly. This portrait was painted in England, probably in the early 1700s, and is most likely of a woman. Decades later people in England began to claim that it was of Cornbury.

over half of England's tar and pitch. A series of laws enacted between 1691 and 1729 barred New England lumbermen and mill owners from cutting down and exporting mature white pines that the Royal Navy wanted to reserve for its masts. Colonists, often aided by corrupt officials, dodged the regulations. In 1734, gunshots and a mob turned away one official eager to uphold the law in New Hampshire. The Royal Navy had better luck at encouraging colonists to make naval stores by offering them financial incentives.

The challenges facing imperial officials illustrate key developments in the relationship between Britain and its North American colonies. Colonists could defy or ignore laws that they found onerous, often with the complicity of those charged to enforce them. Historians have called this arrangement "**salutary neglect**" and claim that it characterized the colonial-imperial relationship into the 1760s. Colonists also kept tabs on events in Britain and forged ties to prominent figures there. Although North Americans never wielded as much influence in London as their West Indian counterparts did, they often steered policies and politics to suit their purposes.

Factions of colonists enlisted contacts in London to fight local political battles, often targeting royal governors. One campaign centered around Edward Hyde, Viscount Cornbury, governor of New York and New Jersey. Cornbury's efforts to consolidate imperial authority and strengthen the Church of England won him enemies on both

New York, Madagascar, and Indian Ocean Piracy

Around 1680, pirates began to leave the Caribbean, their base for over a century, to dodge naval patrols. They set out in search of easier pickings. By 1690, a base in Madagascar gave them easy access to the Red Sea and Indian Ocean. Pirates often targeted a fleet that sailed between India and Mocha, an Arabian Peninsula port on the Red Sea that exported coffee.

New Yorkers helped to establish European piracy in the Indian Ocean. Like other North American port cities, New York welcomed pirates, who needed food, clothing, alcohol, and ship repairs and paid for them with scarce gold and silver. During the 1680s, New York merchants had learned that they could reap even bigger profits by shipping supplies to the Indian Ocean and charging pirates for the convenience.

Economic and political changes intensified New York's ties to the Indian Ocean piracy in the early 1690s. King William's War disrupted New York's economy, and the high unemployment that followed tempted some mariners to turn or return to piracy. After the colony's new governor, Benjamin Fletcher, took office in 1692, he granted pirates refuge, often using his official powers to designate them "privateers" and line his own pockets. Fletcher's Council consisted largely of merchants who traded with pirates. One councilor, Frederick Philipse, employed an agent in Madagascar who sold clothing, naval stores, firearms, ammunition, and liquor to pirates and local rulers. The local rulers handed war captives over to pirates, who sold them to Philipse's agent along with gold, silver, spices, and Indian textiles they had stolen. Rum sold in Madagascar for up to 30 times what it cost in New York, while slaves could be bought in Madagascar for

sides of the Atlantic: prominent colonists, members of the Whig Party in England, and English Protestants who were not Anglicans. Colonists accused Cornbury of corruption, charges that gained traction in London as the power of Cornbury's Tory (the party that opposed the Whigs) allies waned. Between 1707 and 1709, three colonists asserted, probably falsely, that Cornbury had often appeared in public in New York dressed in women's clothing. He was removed from office, his reputation in England in tatters.

Colonists' transatlantic lobbying undermined many royal governors. Royal governors faced obstacles that executives in Britain did not. Too many male colonists owned land and had the right to vote. They elected assemblies composed of wealthy men who jealously guarded their powers to tax and budget and frequently deprived governors of funds. Such bodies increasingly viewed themselves as mini-Parliaments obliged to defend and preserve what they understood to be British liberties against what they deemed arbitrary executive power. Colonists professed adoration for kings and queens, but they often showed contempt for those whom monarchs appointed to govern them.

a fraction of the price on Africa's Atlantic coast. Philipse shipped hundreds of Madagascar slaves to New York during the 1690s.

Events in the Indian Ocean, London, and New York severed New Yorkers' ties to Madagascar. Pirate attacks on ships belonging to subjects of India's Mughal Empire created a crisis for the **East India Company (EIC)** and England. Mughals imprisoned company employees and threatened to throw the EIC out. Meanwhile, Parliament passed the East India Act in 1698 to cement the firm's monopoly on English commerce in the Indian Ocean. London officials also cracked down on piracy by recalling Fletcher. His replacement, the Earl of Bellomont, denounced piracy as "not only injurious to the Honour of his Majesty, and the English Nation, but also highly prejudicial to the Trade of England." Bellomont ordered that illicit cargoes be confiscated. Some local officials defied him by helping to smuggle illegal goods into town. Philipse sent a ship to Delaware Bay to meet a vessel arriving from Madagascar. It offloaded most of the contraband and headed to Hamburg to sell it. Philipse tried to sneak East Indian cargo into New York, but officials confiscated it. He was removed from the Council. Philipse died in 1702, leaving over 90,000 acres of land, city real estate, slaves, and a small fleet, a fortune built largely on trade with pirates.

Two important precedents had been set. Ties between colonial merchants and pirates could be cut and imperial officials had demonstrated that they would act on the EIC's behalf against colonists' interests. In the 1770s, that became a major issue for colonists who drank tea provided by the EIC.

- Why did New Yorkers help to establish European piracy in the Indian Ocean? Why did English officials seek to sever their ties to Indian Ocean pirates in the 1690s?
- What relationship did the campaign to cut New York's ties to Indian Ocean pirates have to the British Empire's broader war on piracy during the 1700s?

STUDY QUESTIONS FOR MIGRATION, RELIGION, AND EMPIRES

1. In what ways and by what means did slavery and racism expand in North America during the early 1700s? In what ways did enslaved Africans adjust to their new lives in North America?
2. What impact did Pietism and growing royal authority have on British North America?

◼ LAYING FOUNDATIONS IN BRITISH NORTH AMERICA

Unprecedented levels of involuntary immigration and thickening ties to transatlantic networks transformed colonial North America. Colonial British North America's economy grew and diversified, financing the emergence of a native-born elite that could more easily imitate its English peers because a communications revolution kept colonists abreast of events across the Atlantic and within the colonies.

An Industrious Revolution

By 1730, colonists in British North America had laid a foundation for the economic development of what would become the United States in response to overseas and domestic markets. Households diversified the range of goods that they produced and services that they provided. Their Anglo-American version of a transatlantic "**industrious revolution**" enabled colonial British North America to take significant steps toward industrialization and created market-oriented societies that relied more heavily on enslaved labor and devalued the voices and skills of white women (Map 4.4).

The English Civil War had forced New England colonists to pursue a wider variety of ways to earn a living to narrow the region's trade deficit. Most continued to scratch out a living on small farms while others fished or cut timber for export. Migration to areas recently conquered from or ceded by Indians enabled New England to accommodate a growing and mostly native-born population—86,000 strong by 1690. Expansion also enabled the majority of households to be economically independent. By 1730, the region's population soared to over 200,000.

New Englanders responded by working harder and diversifying their labor. This was particularly true in coastal or densely populated areas. Fishermen journeyed further out to sea to catch more cod, which they processed on board rather than returning immediately to port. Whalers began to pursue their prey into the deep ocean. Meanwhile, more young men left home in hopes of becoming financially independent sooner. Some toiled on neighbors' farms, while others took up a trade such as blacksmithing, tanning, or shoemaking. Women and girls who churned butter, grew vegetables, and operated a growing number of spinning wheels in rural New England often secured a household's place in an expanding market economy.

Two developments marked the commercialization of New England's economy. One was use of paper money, introduced to ease the scarcity of coin. Massachusetts first issued paper money in 1690 as an emergency measure to finance wartime spending. By 1712, its government declared that paper could be used to pay private debts. Prominent Boston merchants and their creditors in England were incensed. They feared that debtors would repay loans, pegged to the value of silver or gold, with paper that would become worthless. Officials tried to blunt such objections by issuing paper money backed by mortgages on land. Paper money soon became one of the most controversial issues in colonial politics.

The other key development was the growth of manufacturing. Shipbuilding soared during the late 1600s and early 1700s in port cities and towns. The imperial wars that ravaged New England's borders fed demand for ships throughout the Anglo-Atlantic. Shipbuilding further diversified the region's economy and knit it more tightly. Shipyards created work for loggers and millworkers as well as for carpenters, joiners, and caulkers who crafted vessels and kept them seaworthy. Investors bought shares in ships, local firms insured them, and thousands of local men sailed them. By the early 1700s, New England shipbuilders competed with peers in New York and Philadelphia. Colonists built the vessels that plied the Atlantic seaboard, linking the mainland to the

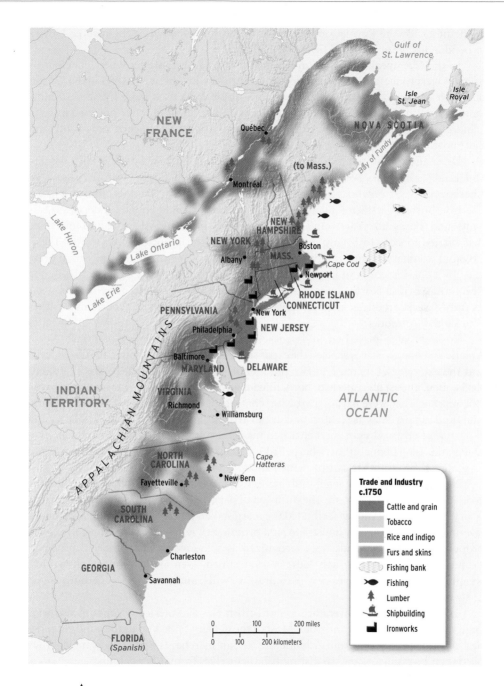

MAP 4.4 ▲ The Economy of British North America, c. 1750 The industrious revolution of the late 1600s and early 1700s made British North America a major supplier of ships, iron, rice, and naval stores to Atlantic markets and rapidly expanded grain and meat exports, much of which went to the Caribbean, Spain, or Portugal.

West Indies. By the Revolution, one-third of the ships known to the insurer Lloyd's of London had been launched from North America.

In the Chesapeake colonies, diversification was a response to dependence on tobacco. Overproduction and war kept tobacco prices low between 1680 and 1720, so plantations and small farms cultivated more wheat and raised more livestock. Abundant rivers and bigger grain harvests encouraged investment in water-powered mills to grind grain into flour. Clusters of mills gave rise to new towns such as Norfolk and Baltimore.

Diversification brought an early form of industrialization. By the 1720s, planters and English investors were operating iron furnaces and forges near the shores of Chesapeake Bay. Ironworks demanded enormous amounts of land, capital, and labor. The iron business attracted planters in part because it could employ indentured servants and slaves all year round. American-made iron served as ballast on ships that carried tobacco to Britain and could substitute for imported Swedish iron there. Colonial ironmasters soon discovered that they had a bigger market locally than overseas. By 1750, the center of iron manufacturing shifted north to Pennsylvania. By the Revolution, British North America made one-seventh of the world's raw iron and was its third-largest producer, an accomplishment that owed largely to thousands of slaves who staffed ironworks.

Enslaved labor played an indispensable role in the development of British North America's economy. Slaves enabled the expansion of tobacco production in the Chesapeake and the exponential increase in rice production in South Carolina. By the 1730s, enslaved men, almost all American born, filled many skilled positions in ironworks in the Chesapeake. They were part of a growing contingent of enslaved tradesmen on plantations and in port cities as planters and urban artisans looked to cut costs. The labor and expertise of enslaved craftsmen enriched masters, strengthened slavery, and helped it to expand. Such opportunities sharpened inequality among slaves, as trades remained virtually off-limits to African-born men and to women.

Meanwhile, white women found themselves increasingly cast to the sidelines of the economy and the legal system. The diffusion of paper money and growing use of promissory notes as paper money facilitated the marginalization of women. English common law only allowed property holders to sign promissory notes. Yet women rarely owned property, as their husbands were recognized as sole owners of all marital property. Women's participation in such court cases declined, even as their voices carried less weight in court. Fewer wives helped to draw up wills, and fewer widows administered husbands' estates.

The expansion and diversification of British North America's economy also widened the gap between rich and poor. Most of the benefits ended up in the hands of those best positioned to profit from Atlantic ties: urban merchants and large planters. They used their growing fortunes to distinguish themselves from other colonists.

A Creole Elite Pursues Gentility

Starting around 1660, England's merchants began to build stylish townhouses in cities, while its gentry, lesser aristocrats, remodeled country houses or built new ones according to the latest fashions. New standards of beauty, speech, dress, body carriage, and personal conduct arose. Three decades later, British North America's wealthiest strove to be genteel, modeling themselves on their English counterparts, and by the early 1700s, an American-born elite adopted and adapted transatlantic norms of gentility. By the Revolution, colonists who wished to be considered gentlemen and ladies— prominent merchants and planters, clergy, professionals, judges, and officials—were expected to follow the rules of "polite society."

Three developments heralded gentility's arrival in British North America and helped to disseminate it. One was the courtesy book. Intended principally for children and adolescents, courtesy books instructed readers on codes of conduct. These books admonished children to mind their table manners and stay clean when they played. They sought to inculcate deference to social rank, control over one's body, and regard for others' feelings. "Polite" people were gracious, elegant, and restrained individuals who did not offend or embarrass others.

Another sign of gentility was drinking tea, which the East India Company purchased in China and shipped to Britain. Around 1690, women of means in England began to gather in the parlors of urban townhouses and country estates to converse and drink tea. Etiquette required that hostesses buy a teapot, containers for sugar and cream, tongs, teaspoons, cups, and saucers as well as tea and sugar. By the 1720s, white women of means in the colonies had made "tea tables" the principal vehicle for spreading ideas about manners and taste.

The mansion house also hastened and symbolized the rise of gentility in North America. The Virginia mansions differed from the homes they replaced in many ways. They contained several rooms and were two stories rather than one. The first floor was principally for entertaining guests. It provided the stage for wealthy planters to host dinners and dances that displayed their gentility. The mansions were designed to conceal the labor that sustained their privileged inhabitants. Kitchens and laundries, operated mainly by enslaved women and supervised by planters' wives, were moved to separate buildings. Erected on bluffs and surrounded by landscaped gardens, the mansions trumpeted their owners' wealth and power.

The mansions reflected a more assertive and native-born Chesapeake elite. By the 1690s a clear majority of the region's prominent families were American born. They consolidated their power through intermarriage over the next few decades. Elites laid out new capitals at Annapolis in the 1690s and Williamsburg a decade later, housing the institutions of provincial government in stately brick buildings. In 1693, they chartered the College of William and Mary, British North America's second institution of higher education.

The Anglo-Atlantic's Communications Revolution

In 1690, a prominent English immigrant complained of Virginia, "We are here at the end of the World, and Europe may be turned topsy turvy ere we can hear a Word of it." Forty years later, fewer in British North America would have shared his frustration. A communications revolution had accelerated and broadened the flow of information across the Atlantic and throughout British North America.

The communications revolution had many intertwined components. The number of ships that traveled between England, North America, and the West Indies increased sharply, with the total number entering Boston harbor nearly tripling between 1688 and 1730. Intercolonial coastal trade grew even more spectacularly. The number of vessels

PRINTED AUTHORITY   This is the first issue of *The Boston News-Letter*, the first newspaper to be published continuously in British North America. The phrase "Published by Authority" indicates that the paper served as an official organ of the Massachusetts government. This issue was just two pages, one sheet printed on both sides.

docking in Boston from other British North American ports multiplied eight times between the late 1680s and the late 1720s. Heavier maritime traffic disseminated information more quickly and conveniently.

Mail began to move more rapidly overland after colonists launched a delivery service between Boston and New York in 1673. The service expanded in the 1690s to all of New England and Philadelphia, but it was so expensive that relatively few could afford to use it. Perhaps 1 person in 10 received one letter a year in colonies served by the expanded overland postal system during its first decade of operation.

Printed information reached more people as colonists began to publish their own newspapers. In 1704, *The Boston News-Letter* became British North America's first established newspaper. Its publisher, John Campbell, was Boston's postmaster, which

THE COFFEEHOUS MOB, FROM EDWARD WARD, *VULGUS BRITANNICUS*; OR, *THE BRITISH HUDIBRAS* (1710)   Coffeehouses were public spaces where men shared information, did business, and discussed politics. Note the newspapers and pamphlets on the table in the foreground. Some, including this image's creator, thought that coffeehouses enabled "vulgar" people like the patron who is hurling his coffee at another to spread gossip and disorder.

enabled him to get the paper to rural subscribers and boost demand for postal services. Campbell modeled his paper after *The London Gazette*, copying its format, publication schedule, and much of its content, while adding shipping lists, reports from meetings with provincial officials, and news gathered from mariners and correspondents in other colonies. *The News-Letter* provided little local coverage, focusing mainly on foreign news that interested merchants. Campbell soon had competitors in Boston, Philadelphia, New York, and other major cities.

Colonial newspapers became a forum for debating matters of local interest as publishers began to vie for readers. The *Courant* immediately took sides in the biggest controversy raging in Boston—whether residents should be inoculated against smallpox, after an epidemic had struck the city. Cotton Mather learned of inoculation, practiced in the Ottoman Empire and Africa, from his slave, who showed Mather his scar and described the procedure to him. Mather advocated inoculation to Boston's physicians, nearly all of whom countered that deliberately exposing people to smallpox would fan the epidemic. *The Courant* sided with them and poked fun at ministers like Mather, "Who like faithful *Shepherds* take care of their *Flocks*,/By teaching and practising what's Orthodox,/Pray hard against *Sickness*, yet preach up the POX!" The *Courant* persuaded Boston officials to halt inoculation, but *Courant* publisher James Franklin made powerful enemies who had him arrested in 1723 after he refused to obey an order to clear future issues of the paper with Massachusetts officials before publishing them.

TIMELINE 1676–1731

AMERICA	YEAR	THE WORLD
First coffeehouse in English North America opens in Boston	1676	
Hasinai Confederacy ejects Spanish soldiers and missionaries who staked claim to Texas	1690–1693	
Massachusetts Bay Colony issues paper money	1690	
College of William and Mary founded	1693	
	1694	University of Halle founded in Germany
England creates Board of Trade to monitor colonial affairs Vice-admiralty courts created to enforce England's Navigation Acts in American colonies	1696	
Anglicans found **Society for Promoting Christian Knowledge (SPCK)** Monopoly of Royal African Company on English Atlantic slave trade ends	1698	
French begin to colonize Louisiana by building fort at Biloxi	1699	
Bostonian Samuel Sewall condemns slave trade as immoral in *The Selling of Joseph* Parliament mandates death penalty for piracy or for aiding and abetting pirates	1700	
Church of England creates Society for the Propagation of the Gospel in Foreign Parts (SPG) Iroquois reach "Grand Settlement" with English and French empires and France's Indian allies **Jul** Detroit founded Boston merchant John Saffin responds to Sewall with militant defense of Atlantic slave trade and slavery	1701	
	1702–1713	Queen Anne's War erupts, pitting Austria, Holland, and Britain against France and Spain
English and Indian raids virtually destroy Spanish Florida's mission system	1702–1706	
Boston News-Letter becomes first continuously published newspaper in British North America	1704	
Linen Act permits export of Irish linen to English North America	1705	
Comanche complete migration from Great Basin to southern Plains	1706	
	1707	Act of Union joins kingdoms of England and Wales and Scotland to form United Kingdom
Indian slavery legalized in New France	1709	
German war refugees arrive in British North America	1709–1714	

Four Indian "kings" visit London to lobby for a British invasion of New France British forces capture Port Royal, Acadia	**1710**	
Tuscarora War in North Carolina	**1711–1713**	
British scuttle invasion of Quebec	**1711**	
First Fox War	**1712–1716**	
Slave rebellion in New York City North Carolina separates from South Carolina and becomes royal colony	**1712**	
Treaty of Utrecht ends Queen Anne's War; British Empire wins claim to Gibraltar, Hudson Bay, Nova Scotia, St. Kitts, and Newfoundland	**1713**	
	1714	George, Elector of Hanover, crowned George I of the United Kingdom
	1715	Jacobites in Scotland rebel against crowning of George I
Yamasee War in South Carolina, ending that colony's Indian slave trade	**1715–1716**	
Transportation Act approves exile of British convicts to North America as servants First wave of Ulster emigration to North America begins New Orleans founded San Antonio de Béjar founded, establishing a permanent Spanish settlement in Texas	**1718**	
Rice cultivation booms in South Carolina, increasing demand for enslaved Africans	**1720s**	
Tuscarora admitted to Iroquois League	**1722**	
Second Fox War	**1723–1725**	
Louis XV modifies Code Noir and extends it to Louisiana	**1724**	
Third Fox War	**1728–1735**	
First wave of Ulster immigration to North America ends	**1729**	
Natchez War in Louisiana	**1729–1730**	
Louis XV assumes control of Louisiana from Company of the Indies	**1731**	

James's younger brother Benjamin began to publish the *Courant* later that year. The paper folded in 1726, but not before demonstrating that there was a market for local political controversy and that newspapers could fill it.

Colonial newsprint connected colonists to one another. In 1706, *The Boston News-Letter* trumpeted that a servant and a slave who had fled Maine had been captured in South Carolina, thanks to an ad placed in the newspaper months earlier. After 1725, masters from as far away as Virginia advertised for runaways in *The Boston Gazette*. Newspapers became a common means by which masters tried to stop people whom they claimed as property from fleeing for their freedom. Newspapers also reported on events in other colonies. *The American Weekly Mercury* monitored Boston's smallpox controversy and alerted readers to efforts to shutter the *Courant*. Colonial newspapers still focused on news from Britain and Europe, gleaned mainly from London papers, but their attention to affairs elsewhere in British North America made colonists more aware of one another and set the stage for coverage of intercolonial events such as the religious revivals of the 1730s and 1740s.

The growth of social and commercial enterprises also helped to circulate ideas. The most common was the tavern, the number of which increased sharply during the late 1600s and early 1700s. By the 1720s, there was one licensed tavern for every 100 residents of Boston, New York, and Philadelphia. People gathered in taverns to share news as well as to drink and eat.

Meanwhile, coffeehouses sprang up in colonial cities. The first coffeehouse in the colonies opened in Boston in 1676, and by 1724, every major port city in British North America had at least one. Coffeehouses were places for men to do business and to get the latest information on local and global events. Leaders of Philadelphia's government began to meet in a coffeehouse in 1703, partly because its owner, unlike his peers elsewhere in the colonies, refused to sell wine or ale. Philadelphia also posted official municipal notices there. The Exchange Coffee House, opened in 1729, quickly became the hub of New York's real estate market. Others went to coffeehouses and taverns to read newspapers or listen to others read them aloud.

Coffeehouses were also places to receive mail from overseas, but security was a problem. In 1718, Boston's postmaster warned that letters deposited in coffeehouse mailbags might be "Opened, Imbezled or Detained." He requested that captains of ships headed for Britain collect mail at the post office. The communications revolution had brought the Atlantic world closer together and made British North American colonists more engaged participants in it.

STUDY QUESTIONS FOR LAYING FOUNDATIONS IN BRITISH NORTH AMERICA

1. How and why did British North Americans diversify their economies? What were the consequences of commercialization and diversification?
2. In what ways did ideas and practices in England influence society and culture in British North America?

Summary

- Horses, guns, and other imported goods diffused more widely among Indians, stoking conflict among Indians, expanding an Indian slave trade, and eroding Indian power in the Northeast and Southeast.
- Unprecedented levels of African and European immigration, a growing transatlantic Protestant network, and a mightier British empire expanded the borders of colonial North America, entrenched slavery and racism throughout eastern North America, and bound British colonists more tightly to the Atlantic world.
- British North America's economy grew and diversified, helping a native-born elite to form and encouraging the development of communication networks that accelerated and expanded the flow of ideas within the Anglo-Atlantic world.

Key Terms and People

Act of Union *127*

Board of Trade *132*

Code Noir *126*

East India Company (EIC) *135*

Fox Wars *120*

George I *130*

Grand Settlement of 1701 *120*

industrious revolution *136*

Linen Act of 1705 *127*

Louis XV *117*

manumission *126*

Maroons *125*

Mather, Cotton *129*

Mississippi Bubble *111*

Natchez War *117*

Navigation Acts *132*

Pietism *130*

polygamy *131*

Pretender, the *132*

Queen Anne's War *120*

Saffin, John *125*

salutary neglect *133*

Sewall, Samuel *125*

Society for Promoting Christian Knowledge (SPCK) *142*

Society for the Propagation of the Gospel in Foreign Parts (SPG) *130*

Transportation Act of 1718 *130*

Tuscarora War *118*

vice-admiralty courts *132*

Yamasee War *118*

Reviewing Chapter 4

1. "The circulation of people and goods between 1690 and 1730 eroded Indian power and increased that of colonists in North America." Does the evidence presented in this chapter support this statement conclusively? If so, how so? If not, why not?

2. In what ways did North Americans adjust to growing imperial influence between 1690 and 1730? What role did the flow of ideas across the Atlantic play in determining how colonists in British North America saw themselves and their relationship to the British colonial empire?

Further Reading

Barr, Juliana. *Peace Came in the Form of a Woman: Indians and Spaniards in the Texas Borderlands*. Chapel Hill and London: University of North Carolina Press, 2007. An excellent account of Spanish-Indian relations in 18th century Texas in which Indians compel colonists to conform to their ways of diplomacy.

Dawdy, Shannon Lee. *Building the Devil's Empire: French Colonial New Orleans*. Chicago and London: University of Chicago Press, 2008. Explains how New Orleans, through the actions of its residents and the ways that French officials perceived those actions, acquired its seedy reputation.

Gallay, Alan. *The Indian Slave Trade: The Rise of the English Empire in the American South, 1670–1717.* New Haven: Yale University Press, 2002. A prize-winning exploration of the Indian slave trade's impact on southeastern North America's Indians and on English colonization and imperial expansion.

McConville, Brendan. *The King's Three Faces: The Rise and Fall of Royal America, 1688–1776.* Chapel Hill and London: University of North Carolina Press, 2006. An iconoclastic view of British North American politics which argues that colonists regarded British monarchs highly until just before the American Revolution.

Richter, Daniel K. *The Ordeal of the Longhouse: The Peoples of the Iroquois League in the Era of European Colonization.* Chapel Hill: University of North Carolina Press, 1992. A masterful account of how the Iroquois resisted and adapted to colonization over the course of two centuries.

Smallwood, Stephanie E. *Saltwater Slavery: A Middle Passage from Africa to American Diaspora.* Cambridge, Mass.: Harvard University Press, 2007. A sensitive and haunting portrait of the Atlantic slave trade focused on trying to fathom its meaning and the meaning of enslavement to those who endured it.

America In The World
PEOPLE, GOODS, IDEAS AND PRACTICES

CHAPTER 4: Accelerating the Pace of Change c. 1690 to 1730

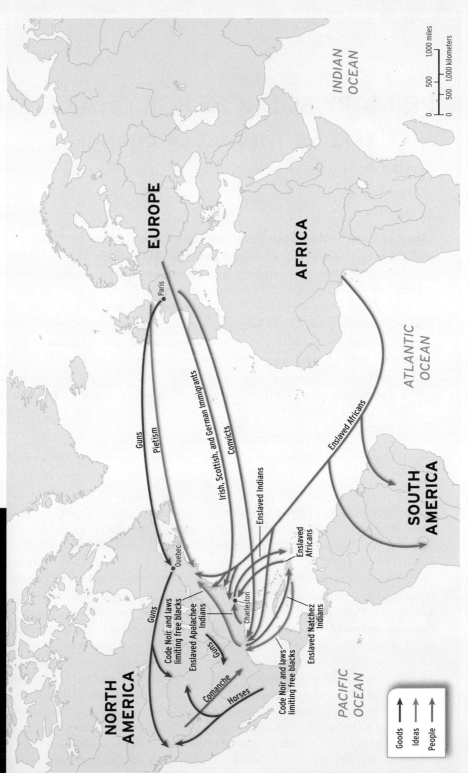

PRIMARY SOURCES FOR CHAPTER 4

ACCELERATING THE PACE OF CHANGE, c. 1690–1730

SOURCE 4.1

Excerpts from Saukamappee's Account of the Advent of Horses and Guns to the Blackfeet, as Told to David Thompson (1787–1788)

Fur trader David Thompson spent part of the winter of 1787–1788 living among the Piegans, who belonged to the Blackfoot Confederacy and lived in what is today Montana. While there, he met Saukamappee, a Cree whom the Piegans had adopted. Saukamappee, then probably in his late seventies, told Thompson about his youth and Piegan history. Here Saukamappee recalls a battle that took place around 1730 between the Piegans and their allies, who were armed with guns and metal weapons, and their longtime foes, the Shoshones (whom Saukamappee and his people called "Snakes"), who fought on horseback. He also recounts what the Piegans did after their victory.

Source: Richard Glover, ed., *David Thompson's Narrative, 1784–1812* (Toronto: Champlain Society, 1962), 241–43.

By this time the affairs of both parties had much changed; we had more guns and iron headed arrows than before; but our enemies the Snake Indians and their allies had Miss-tutim (Big Dogs, that is, Horses) on which they rode, swift as the Deer, on which they dashed at the Peeagans, and with their stone Pukamoggan knocked them on the head, and they had thus lost several of their best men. This news we did not well comprehend and it alarmed us, for we had no idea of Horses and could not make out what they were. Only three of us went and I should not have gone, had not my wife's relations frequently intimated, that her father's medicine bag would be honored by the scalp of a Snake Indian.

When we came to our allies, the great War Tent [was made] with speeches, feasting and dances as before; and when the War Chief had viewed us all it was found between us and the Stone Indians we had ten guns and each of us about thirty balls, and powder for the war, and we were considered the strength of the battle. After a few days march our scouts brought us word that the enemy was near in a large war party, but had no Horses with them, for at that time they had very few of them. When we came to meet each other, as usual, each displayed their numbers, weapons and shiel[d]s, in all which they were superior to us, except our guns which were not shown, but kept in their leathern cases, and if we had shown [them], they would have taken them for long clubs. For a long time they held us in suspense; a tall Chief was forming a strong party to make an attack on our centre, and the others to enter into combat with those opposite to them; We prepared for the battle the best we could. Those of us who had guns stood in the front line, and each of us [had] two balls in his mouth, and a load of powder in his left hand to reload.

We noticed they had a great many short stone clubs for close combat, which is a dangerous weapon, and had they made a bold attack on us, we must have been defeated as they were more numerous and better armed than we were, for we could have fired our guns no more than twice; and were at a loss what to do on the wide plain, and each Chief encouraged his men to stand firm. Our eyes were all on the tall Chief and his motions, which appeared to be contrary to the advice of several old Chiefs, all this time we were about the strong flight of an arrow from each other. At length the tall chief retired and they formed their long usual line by placing their shields on the ground to touch each other, the shield having a breadth of full three feet or more. We sat down opposite to them and most of us waited for the night to make a hasty retreat. The War Chief was close to us, anxious to see the effect of our guns. The lines were too far asunder for us to make a sure shot, and we requested him to close the line to about sixty yards, which was gradually done, and lying flat on the ground behind the shields, we watched our opportunity when they drew their bows to shoot at us, their bodies were then exposed and each of us, as opportunity offered, fired with deadly aim, and either killed, or severely wounded, every one we aimed at.

The War Chief was highly pleased, and the Snake Indians finding so many killed and wounded kept themselves behind their shields;

the War Chief then desired we would spread ourselves by two's throughout the line, which we did, and our shots caused consternation and dismay along their whole line. The battle had begun about Noon, and the Sun was not yet half down, when we perceived some of them had crawled away from their shields, and were taking to flight. The War Chief seeing this went along the line and spoke to every Chief to keep his Men ready for a charge of the whole line of the enemy, of which he would give the signal; this was done by himself stepping in front with his Spear, and calling on them to follow him as he rushed on their line, and in an instant the whole of us followed him, the greater part of the enemy took to flight, but some fought bravely and we lost more than ten killed and many wounded; Part of us pursued, and killed a few, but the chase had soon to be given over, for at the body of every Snake Indian killed, there were five or six of us trying to get his scalp, or part of his clothing, his weapons, or something as a trophy of the battle. As there were only three of us, and seven of our friends, the Stone Indians, we did not interfere, and got nothing.

The next morning the War Chief made a speech, praising their bravery, and telling them to make a large War Tent to commemorate their victory, to which they directly set to work and by noon it was finished.

The War Chief now called on all the other Chiefs to assemble their men and come to the Tent. In a short time they came, all those who had lost relations had their faces blackened; those who killed an enemy, or wished to be thought so, had their faces blackened with red streaks on the face, and those who had no pretensions to the one, or the other, had their faces red with ochre. We did not paint our faces until the War Chief told us to paint our foreheads and eyes black, and the rest of the face of dark red ochre, as having carried guns, and to distinguish us from all the rest. Those who had scalps now came forward with the scalps neatly stretched on a round willow with a handle to the frame; they appeared to be more than fifty, and excited loud shouts and the war whoop of victory. When this was over the War Chief told them that if any one had a right to the scalp of an enemy as a war trophy it ought to be us, who with our guns had gained the victory, when from the numbers of our enemies we were anxious to leave the field of battle; and that ten scalps must be given to us; this was soon collected, and he gave to each of us a Scalp.

WORKING WITH SOURCES

1. How, according to Saukamappee, did the Piegans initially react to Shoshone use of horses, and how did the Shoshones initially react to Piegan use of firearms?

2. How did their use of firearms influence the ways that Piegans regarded Saukamappee and other Crees?

SOURCE 4.2

Superior Council of Louisiana, Excerpts from Debates on Whether to Intervene in a Choctaw-Chickasaw War (1723)

In the early years of French Louisiana, the small colony needed to maintain good relations with Indians, and above all, Choctaws, who were often foes of Chickasaws, many of whom allied themselves with English colonists in South Carolina. In July and August 1723, the Superior Council of Louisiana, led by Governor Jean Baptiste Le Moyne, Sieur de Bienville, considered whether to intervene in an ongoing conflict between the two Indian nations. Below are excerpts from their deliberations. A few weeks later, the Council decided to endorse Bienville's recommendations.

Source: Dunbar Rowland and Albert Godfrey Sanders, eds., *Mississippi Provincial Archives, 1704–1743: French Dominion*, vol. 2 (Jackson, MS: Mississippi Department of Archives and History, 1932), 355–60.

Representation made by Mr. de Bienville to the Council, July 23, 1723.

By the letter of the Commissaries . . . it appears that these gentlemen are distressed because of the commerce of the Mississippi to see that we have war with the Chickasaws, and even seem to desire that we grant them peace. However on the representations that I have made them on this subject they are leaving the Council free to decide on war and peace.

That is the reason it is advisable that the Council deliberate seriously on this affair. My opinion is not at all that peace should be granted to this restless and faithless nation, for three reasons. The first is that the Choctaws who are our friends and our allies are pledged to declare war on the Chickasaws only on condition that we should listen to no sort of proposal of peace and [they have promised] that they would continue the war until the entire destruction of this nation, so it would be difficult not to say impossible, to make them change. I have even written to my brother de Chateaugué at Mobile in order to sound them, but they replied [asking] whether I had forgotten my promise and [saying] that now that they had avenged us they intended to avenge the deaths of several Honored Men whom they have lost in this war; that even if they were given three houses full of presents they would never consent to peace.

The second reason is not less essential than the first. It consists of the danger that there would be in seeing these two large and numerous nations agitated, and we should have to fear that they might combine against us and in that case the mischief would be beyond remedy.

The third reason is not less obvious. If the Chickasaws became our allies and our friends, they would have to renounce all commerce with the English to trade with the French. It is impossible for us to do this because, in addition to the fact that we never have enough merchandise, the English furthermore trade for their peltries at a rate far higher than that at which the French receive them. This would doubtless produce discontentment among these Indians and we should see ourselves every day on the verge of some rupture, and it is even to be feared that if we are still unable to establish at the Choctaws the small warehouse that the Commissaries order in order to supply that nation with the things it needs, they will abandon us. Even as early as last summer they sent some principal chiefs to Carolina to invite the English to come and establish some warehouses among them and this was promised to them, and recently my brother de Chateaugué informed me that the Emperor of the Kawitas who came to see me assured him that the English were preparing to go next September, six traders with sixty horses loaded with all sorts of merchandise that the Indians like.

When all these considerations have been well thought over and well examined I do not doubt that the Council will be of my opinion since that concerns the preservation of the colony which will always be uncertain and in continual alarms.

The Council is informed that four Chickasaw chiefs have been with me for more than two months who brought back to us one of the two French prisoners whom they had in the hope that that would induce us to grant peace to them more willingly. The other who was hunting when they departed from their village must now be at the Yazoos according to the information about him that has been given me by Mr. Delivilliers, the lieutenant who is in command there. These chiefs in return ask for one of their children eleven to twelve years of age and a woman who is related to them, who are here as slaves. The child still belongs to the Company and the woman has been sold on credit to a German. I do not think that the Council will refuse this exchange which appears to me so much the more just because two of these chiefs are known to all the French as being very fond of us. They made it known in 1720 when their nation declared war on us, [and] when they pillaged and undertook to kill all the Frenchmen who were trading among them. These [chiefs] by their influence saved them and themselves conducted them to the Choctaws. He thinks that such an indication of friendship deserves some compensation on our part, so much the more because it was these two chiefs who stripped themselves of all their goods in order to save the lives of the two Frenchmen when they were brought as prisoners to their village, and as a similar thing might happen in the future if the war with them continues, it is always to be desired that the unfortunate ones who fall into the hands of these barbarians may find a few good Indians who will snatch them from the fire.

At New Orleans, July 23, 1723.
Signed, Bienville.

On the representation above and from other sources, which was not communicated to me by the secretary of the Council until the first of the present month, . . . on the subject of the war that we have stirred up between the Choctaws and the Chickasaws in order to avenge the death of several Frenchmen killed by the said Chickasaws, my opinion is in the situation in which we are because of the few troops that there are in the colony and the posts so remote from each other that they cannot give each other mutual assistance, not one fort in a state of defence, the warehouses unprovided with all provisions and merchandise, a prevalent illness that has attacked everybody in general, to maintain this war between these two nations and to give the Choctaws, a nation that contains nearly eight thousand men, this bone to gnaw, [a nation] which since it is naturally warlike might with the assistance of the English disturb us in the future, and it is to be hoped for the welfare of the colony that all these strong nations may one after another become aroused against each other in order that their destruction may make it impossible for them to unite against us as might happen sooner or later. This opinion appears to me to be so much the more correct because Mr. de Chateaugué has said several times that he did not feel safe at Mobile against the Choctaws although at war with the Chickasaws. It is for this reason above all [others] that I decide to favor the continuation of this war in order to divert these two populous nations, until we are in a position to provide for it otherwise.

At New Orleans, August 3, 1723.
Signed, Le Blond de La Tour.
August 3, 1723.

After having maturely examined and considered the representation of Mr. de Bienville made to the Council on the twenty-third of last July concerning the Chickasaws for deliberation as to whether we ought to continue the war with the said nation or grant them peace as the Commissaries wish to do, the reasons that Mr. de Bienville presents are too strong with reference to the Choctaws who are our friends and allies for [me] not to be of his opinion until different orders are given by my said gentlemen the Commissaries, though I do not doubt that they will approve of it when they are informed of the consequences that are involved in supporting it, which force us to-day to keep our word to the Choctaws if we wish to avoid being at war with them. Nothing furthermore appears more just than to grant the four Chickasaw chiefs one of their children eleven or twelve years of age and a woman related to them, who are slaves here, and even a reward for their zeal for the French whom they have protected and caused to be saved by their influence; all in order to retain them constantly in our friendship and in order that if we continue the war with them the unfortunates who may fall into their hands may find the same favor that the others have had.

Signed, Fazende.
On August 3, 1723.

On the proposal to make war or peace with the Chickasaws I approve heartily Mr. de Bienville's reasons and my opinion is to leave the Choctaws free to make war on them. It appears to me that we owe this latter nation this satisfaction in consideration of the generous manner in which they have conducted themselves in avenging us and who besides it would be a great blessing if it were entirely destroyed. As for the four chiefs who are with Mr. de Bienville, as we have a peculiar obligation to them, my opinion is not to confuse them with the rest of their nation and to show the same consideration to them that they have shown to us. I approve that in gratitude for the Frenchmen whom they have saved or have brought to us they be granted their young boy and their woman relative; that they be escorted to a place of safety and even if it were possible that we should recommend to the Choctaws to spare them since it appears that it was without their consent that their nation attacked us.

Signed, Perry.
On August 3, 1723.

After having examined the representation of Mr. de Bienville on the subject of the war with the Chickasaws the reasons that he sets forth in it are very well calculated to make [us] decide to continue the war. It is to be feared that the Choctaws, a restless nation which is absolutely unwilling to hear any talk of peace and wishes to avenge its dead warriors, seeing itself unoccupied, may decide upon some other course which would be disadvantageous to us. There is only one thing to be observed, by no means to advance much to them. It will be necessary to give them powder and bullets, we cannot avoid it, but as for merchandise, it must not be paid until after the war or when they bring scalps and slaves; so my opinion is, with these observations, to continue the war.

In the matter of these Chickasaws who are here, the exchange that is requested is only too just and Mr. de Bienville has very prudently kept these slaves in order to return [them] to them. It will be necessary to recover from the German the woman whom he has and to promise the said Chickasaws to exchange with them every day their most noteworthy men and women prisoners for the Frenchmen who, having had the misfortune to fall into their hands, will be restored to us if that should happen in the future, without telling them that we wish to make war on them.

As for the two chiefs who were deprived of their merchandise and have always been inclined to the French [and] saved the life of some one and to whom it would be advisable to give some presents in gratitude, I do not know what is right for them. Mr. de Bienville who knows the taste and character of people of this sort perfectly will take the trouble, if he pleases, to have the memorandum drawn up and I will gladly sign it.

This is my opinion on the representation of Mr. de Bienville of the twenty-third of last July. I defer to the majority of the votes and to those that will be found to be better and in greater numbers.

Signed, Fleuriau.

WORKING WITH SOURCES

1. What do these deliberations reveal about French attitudes toward Indians?

2. What reasons do Bienville and other members of the council give to justify their decision? In what ways do their deliberations reflect concerns about Choctaw power and English influence in the region?

3. Why did the Chickasaw chiefs decide to intervene to save the lives of the French traders? What did they hope to gain by doing so? In what ways do the council's deliberations illustrate the importance of captives to the practice of diplomacy in southeastern North America?

SOURCE 4.3

Boston News-Letter, Editorial Favoring Indentured Servitude over Slavery (1706)

Although relatively few enslaved Africans and African Americans lived in Massachusetts in the early 18th century, the black population there was growing, largely because of Massachusetts merchants' engagement in the Atlantic slave trade. In 1706, an anonymous author composed and published an editorial on slavery in the *Boston News-Letter*, North America's first established newspaper. It was perhaps the first editorial to appear in a North American newspaper, and it is reprinted below in its entirety.

Source: Elizabeth Donnan, ed., *Documents Illustrative of the History of the Slave Trade to America*, vol. 3 (Washington, DC: Carnegie Institution of Washington, 1932), 21–23.

By last Years Bill of Mortality for the Town of Boston in Numb 100 *News Letter*,[1] we are furnished with a List of 44 Negroes dead last year, which being computed one with another at 30 *l.* per Head, amounts to the Sum of One Thousand three hundred and Twenty Pounds, of which we would make this Remark: That the Importing of Negroes into this or the Neighbouring Provinces is not so beneficial either to the Crown or Country, as White Servants would be.

For Negroes do not carry Arms to defend the Country as Whites do:

Negroes are generaly Eye-Servants[2], great Thieves, much addicted to stealing, Lying, and Purloining.

They do not People our Country as Whites would do whereby we should be strengthened against an Enemy.

By Encouraging the importing of White Men Servants, allowing somewhat to the importer, most Husbandmen in the Country might be furnished with Servants for 8, 9, or 10 *l.* a Head, who are not able to Launch out 40 or 50 *l.* for a Negro the now common Price.

A Man then might buy a White Man Servant we suppose for 10 *l.* to Serve 4 years, and Boys for the same price to Serve 6, 8 or 10 years: If a White Servant die, the Loss exceeds not 10 *l.* but if a Negro dies 'tis a very great Loss to the Husbandman. Three years Interest of the price of the Negro, will near upon if not altogether purchase a White Man Servant.

If Necessity call for it, that the Husbandman must fit out a man against the Enemy; if he has a Negro he cannot send him, but if he has a White Servant, 'twill answer the end, and perhaps save his Son at home.

Were Merchants and Masters Encouraged as already said to bring in Men Servants, there needed not be such complaint against Superiors Impressing our Children to the War, there would then be Men enough to be had without Impressing.

The bringing in of such servants would much enrich this Province, because Husbandmen would not only be able far better to manure what Lands are already under Improvement, but would also improve a great deal more that now lyes waste under Woods, and enable this Province to set about raising of Naval Stores, which would be greatly advantagious to the Crown of England, and this Province. . . .

---

[1] *Boston News Letter*, March 18, 1706.
[2] A servant whom one must supervise constantly.

Suppose the Government here should allow Forty Shillings per head for five years, to such as should Import every of those years 100 White Men Servants, and each to serve 4 Years, the cost would be but 200 *l.* a year, and a 1000 for the five years: the first 100 servants being free the 4th year, they serve the 5th for Wages, and the 6th there is 100 that goes out into the Woods, and settles a 100 Families to strengthen and Baracade us from the Indians, and so a 100 Families more every year successively.

And here you see that in one year the Town of Boston has lost 1320 *l.* by 44 Negroes, which is also a Loss to this Country in general, and for a less Loss, (if it may improperly be so called) for a 1000 *l.* the Country may have 500 Men in 5 years time for the 44 Negroes dead in one year.

A certain person within these 6 years had two Negroes dead computed both at 60 *l.* which would have procured him six white Servants at 10 *l.* per head to have Served 24 years, at 4 years a piece, without running such a great risque, and the Whites would have strengthened the Country, that Negroes do not. 'Twould do wel[l] that none of those Servants be liable to be Impressed during their Service of Agreement at their first Landing.

That such Servants being Sold or Transported out of this Province during the time of their Service, the person that buys them be liable to pay 3 *l.* into the Treasury.

WORKING WITH SOURCE

1. On what grounds does the author favor indentured servitude over slavery? In what ways did then-current events probably influence the content and tone of the editorial?

SOURCE 4.4

Reverend James McGregor, Petition to Samuel Shute, Governor of Massachusetts and New Hampshire (1720)

In the late 1710s, thousands of migrants left Ulster for North America. Many headed to New England, particularly to areas of southern New Hampshire that both New Hampshire and Massachusetts claimed. The Ulsterite Presbyterian founders of Nutfield suffered violent harassment from Massachusetts colonists and officials, which prompted the petition below from Rev. James McGregor to Samuel Shute, the governor of both Massachusetts and New Hampshire. Shute subsequently accorded Nutfield residents the right to choose their own leaders, and New Hampshire officials soon granted the town, which residents renamed Londonderry, legal recognition. Massachusetts officials and colonists disputed the Ulsterites' claims until 1740, when the British Empire confirmed that New Hampshire should govern the disputed area.

Source: Kerby A. Miller, Arnold Schrier, Bruce D. Boling, and David N. Doyle, eds., *Irish Immigrants in the Land of Canaan: Letters and Memoirs from Colonial and Revolutionary America, 1675–1815* (New York: Oxford University Press, 2003), 438–39.

Rev. James McGregor, Nutfield,
New Hampshire,
to Governor Samuel Shute, Boston,
Massachusetts, 27 February 1720

The Humble Apolegy of the People of Nutfeild
to His Exelency Sam^ll Shute Generall Govern^r.
and Commander in Cheife of his Majesties
Provinces of the Massachusetts Bay and New
Hampsh^r in New England—

May it Please Y^r Exelency

The Subscribers having Seen a copy of Y^r Exelencys Lettr. To Capt: White & Capt: Kembell, find themselves undr. a Nessessity of Vindicating themselves from the Charges given in against them; it being alowable by the Law of Nature & of Nations, to ye greatest Criminalls to Defend them selves when they Justly plead in their Own Vindication. We were Surprised to hear our Selves termed *Irish People* when we So frequently ventured our all for the Brittish Crown and Liberties against the Irish papists & gave all tests of our Loyalty wch the Government of Ireland Required and are always ready to do the Same here w^n demanded. Tho we Settled att Nutfeild yett we Used no Violence in the manr. of our Settlement, Seing no body in the Least offered to hinder us to Sett down in a desolate Wilderness; and we were So fare from hindering the English that Really had a mind to Plant wth. us, that, many of them are now incorporated wth. us. after our Settlement we found that two or three Different parties Claimed Nutfield, by virtue of Indian deeds, and we were Given to understand, that it was Nessesary for us to *hold the Soil by Some Right purchased from the Natives* accordingly we made applycation to the Honble. Coll. Wheelwright of Wells, and Obtained his Indian right; wch we have to Shew, his Deed being of Ninety Years Standing, and Conveyed from the Cheife Sagamores between the Rivers of Merimack and Piscattaqua, wth the

Consent of the whole Tribe of the Indian Nation, and well Executed, is the most authentic we have Seen; and the Subscribers Could not in reason think that a deed wch is not twenty years Old, of Land wch is not Sufficiently butted and bounded, from an Obscure Indian, Could Give any Right to Land wch had been Sold So many years before, by the Right owners. And the Subscribers hope they will be Excused, from Giving away So Good a Title, for Others that cannot pretend Rationally to be So well Supported; and wch they always refused to Warrantee and make Good, ag^st other Claimes. The Dutifull Applications wch we have made to both Courts, If we be inCorporated, in whatSoEver Province we fall to be, will Witness for our respect to his Majesty's gov^rmt. If Affidavits have been Given agst one of our Number as useing Some threttning Expressions, we hope it will not be Imputed to the Community. If our accusers be permitted to Come up in troops, as they have done, and violently demolish'd one of our houses, and destroyed part of our hay, and threttned and Insulted us wth impunity, to the Great terror of our wives and Children, when we Suffered patiently, and then accuse us to our Rulers of violence, Injustice, fraud, force, insolence, Cruelty, dishonour of his Majesties Governt, & disturbance of his Majesties Subjects, injuries, and Offences to the English, and the like, when we know our Selves to be Innocent, we think it hard measure; and must have Recourse to God, who forbideth to take up a bad report ag^st our Neighbour, and will, we hope, bring forth our Righteousness as the Light, and our Judgment as the Noon day. If we be Guilty of these disorders, we know we are Liable to a Legall Tryall and are not So weak as to Suppose our Selves to be out of the reach of Your Exelencys Government. The Subsscribers hope that If any other accusations come in ag^st them they will be allowed an Equall hearing before they be condemned; and as we Enjoy the liberty of the Gospell here, wch is So Great a mercy [we] Shall Improve it, for Gods Glory; and as he has taught us be Dutifull to his Majesties Govert, Sett over us, and If possible live peaceably wth all men, Shall be Desierous of Peaceable Neighbours, that want to Settle wth us, and to help us to Subdue a part of this vast and uncultivated Wilderness; and we Shall not Cease to pray for the Divine blessing on Yr Exelency's person and Govt.

Done at Nutfield Feb: 27: 1719/20 & Subscribed by——

James McGregore &c

WORKING WITH SOURCES

1. What do McGregor and the residents of Nutfield mean when they call their petition to Governor Shute a "humble apology?" In what ways does their petition reflect the influence of royalism in British North American politics in the early 18th century?

2. On what grounds do McGregor and his flock assert that they have a valid claim to the disputed lands? What is their response to assertions that they do not belong in Nutfield?

Battling for Souls, Minds, and the Heart of North America

5

In August 1763, 50 people boarded a ship in St. Augustine, Florida, heading to Havana, Cuba. Most had come to Spanish Florida after escaping slavery in South Carolina or Georgia or had parents who did. Now Britain claimed Florida as spoils of its victory over Spain and France in the Seven Years' War. Fearing enslavement if they stayed, Captain Francisco Menéndez and his neighbors in Gracia Real de Santa Teresa de Mose (the first free black town in what is today the United States) again sought liberty by fleeing south.

Few on board knew better than Menéndez how precarious freedom could be. Born in Africa in 1703 and later enslaved, he won his freedom at age 35 by serving in the Spanish military. In 1740, Menéndez commanded a contingent of free black soldiers who helped to save St. Augustine from British forces. Believing that his deeds in battle merited a royal commission and a salary from King Philip V, Menéndez resolved to go to Spain to make his case in person. He became a privateer to pay his way across the Atlantic, but never made it to Spain. In 1741, a Boston-based privateer captured and tortured Menéndez. The ship's captain renamed Menéndez "Don Blass" and took him to the Bahamas, where the British vice-admiralty court condemned him to slavery. Somehow Menéndez managed to get free, for by 1759 he again led the militia of Gracia Real de Santa Teresa de Mose.

Menéndez and his family tried to settle in San Agustín de la Nueva Florida, a new town created near Havana for 84 Florida families. Spanish authorities gave each household land, provisions, tools, and an enslaved African. Most Floridians soon abandoned the struggling town. Menéndez and his family returned to Havana.

< Portrait of George Whitefield by John Wollaston, oil on canvas, c. 1742.

Francisco Menéndez navigated many of the dramatic changes that profoundly altered North America and the Atlantic world between 1730 and 1763. Rapid expansion of British North America, largely through the immigration of enslaved Africans like Menéndez, fed conflicts with Indians and rival European empires. Menéndez won his freedom in one of these wars but lost it in the next. Meanwhile, as British colonists' demand for imported goods grew and their participation in transatlantic intellectual and religious networks became more active, a war for control of eastern North America broke out. Britain's resulting win of all of North America east of the Mississippi forced Menéndez and his neighbors to flee their homes to preserve their freedom.

◼ IMMIGRANTS AND INDIANS

African and European immigration to British North America surged between 1730 and 1775, elevating tensions within colonies that absorbed tens of thousands of newcomers. As immigrants and native-born colonists headed west, they displaced Indians, upsetting a precarious balance of power in eastern North America. Meanwhile, new Indian powers arose on the Great Plains, as imperial warfare and slave unrest convulsed the Southeast, New York, and the West Indies.

The Arrival of Immigrants in Chains

The population of colonial British North America soared from 900,000 in 1730 to 2.5 million 45 years later (Figure 5.1). Immigrants directly accounted for 40 percent of

POTTER FAMILY OF MATUNUCK, RHODE ISLAND, c. 1740   Here the Potter family of southern Rhode Island poses with an enslaved boy who is serving them tea, linking their aspirations to gentility with slavery. Rhode Island's enslaved population grew more than six times between 1720 and 1750, due partly to local merchants' growing participation in the Atlantic slave trade.

that growth. By the American Revolution, most people in British North America were immigrants or first-generation colonists.

Most who came to North America between 1730 and 1775 arrived in chains. Over 200,000 came from Africa (Figure 5.2). Enslaved Africans outnumbered European immigrants in every decade except the 1750s.

Most enslaved Africans entered North America through South Carolina or Virginia. "Negroes may be said to be the Bait proper for catching a Carolina planter, as certain as Beef to catch a shark," someone commented in 1738. Demand for enslaved labor in South Carolina plummeted during the 1740s as wars raged in the Atlantic and rice prices collapsed. It picked up again in the 1760s, when thousands landed in Charleston and were taken to Georgia, where slavery had been recently legalized.

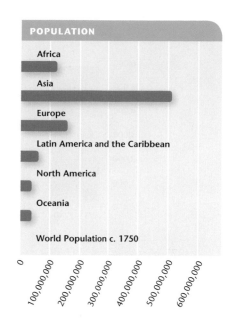

The number of slaves in northern British colonies increased sharply. The black population of New York, New Jersey, Pennsylvania, and Delaware tripled, and that of New England more than doubled between 1730 and 1770. Few enslaved northerners arrived directly from Africa prior to 1740, but instead had lived in the Caribbean or in another mainland colony (Map 5.1).

Slavery in northern colonies differed markedly from slavery in the South. Unlike slaves in the South, most of whom lived and worked on plantations, most northern slaves lived in or near a city, particularly Boston, New York, Philadelphia, or Newport. During the 1740s, one Bostonian in nine was enslaved, as was one New Yorker in five. In 1760, enslaved men, many of them owned by artisans, comprised 20% of Philadelphia workingmen. One Rhode Island household in seven owned at least one slave in 1774; some owned as many as 20. Most enslaved Northerners were men and lived with at most one other slave, making it harder to establish families or an autonomous culture. Still, black New Englanders, free and enslaved, staged annual Election Days to choose a "king" or "governor" by the 1750s. Their peers in New York and New Jersey did likewise. Whites in Salem, Massachusetts, complained in 1758 that "great disorder usually exists here on Election days by negroes assembling together, beating drums, using powder and having guns and swords." Africans in the Caribbean and Brazil had long staged similar events.

The growth of slavery in northern colonies owed partly to colonists' greater participation in the Atlantic slave trade. In the 1730s, Rhode Island merchants began to invest heavily in shipping and selling Africans (Figure 5.3). Four decades later, they controlled 70 percent of British North America's colonial slave trade, and their vessels had transported nearly 60,000 Africans across the Atlantic. Rhode Islanders' ability to supply New England rum to suit African tastes prompted Gold Coast merchants to seek their business. Once they had secured their human cargoes, more than two in three Rhode Island-based crews set sail for the Caribbean.

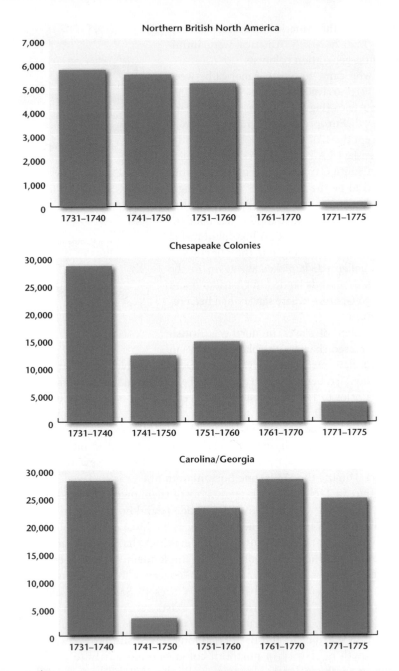

FIGURE 5.1 ▲ Estimated Numbers of Enslaved Africans Who Disembarked in North America by Region, 1731–1775 After 1750, South Carolina and Georgia became the main North American destinations for enslaved Africans, especially after Georgia legalized slavery. Declining demand for enslaved Africans in the Chesapeake owed largely to a natural increase in the region's enslaved population. Note the steady demand for enslaved people in northern colonies.

FIGURE 5.2 ▲ Rhode Island Participation in Atlantic Slave Trade, 1701–1807 Rhode Islanders' participation in the Atlantic slave trade increased sharply during the 1730s. It peaked in the 1760s and again in the two decades before the United States outlawed the Atlantic slave trade in 1808.

MAP 5.1 ▲ North America and the Atlantic Slave Trade, 1731–1775 Demand for enslaved Africans continued to surge throughout the Americas after 1730. Nearly three times as many enslaved Africans landed in mainland North America between 1731 and 1775 as in the previous 40 years, with most landing in South Carolina or Georgia rather than the Chesapeake colonies.

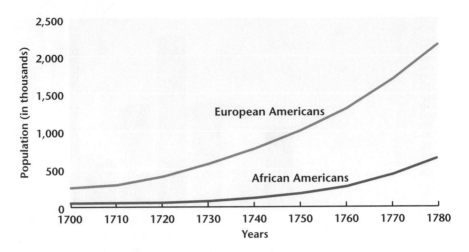

FIGURE 5.3 ▲ Population of Mainland British North American Colonies That Became Part of the United States, 1700–1780 Between 1700 and 1750, the population of British North America more than doubled, and it doubled again by the American Revolution, by which time one in five colonists was African or African American. Natural increase rather than immigration directly accounted for most of this rapid population growth.

Rhode Island dominated North American participation in the Atlantic slave trade until 1808, when the United States outlawed it.

Tens of thousands of British and Irish convicts also came to North America against their will after 1730. They made up the majority of English immigrants to North America between 1700 and 1776. Population growth and rising crime rates increased the number of convicts shipped to North America, as did more severe laws in England that mandated servitude in exile for crimes ranging from poaching to perjury. In 1731, a pamphlet published in London defended the convict trade as "Draining the Nation of its offensive Rubbish without taking away their Lives."

Over 90 percent of convicts did their time in the Chesapeake, where they toiled alongside slaves in tobacco fields, iron mines, and charcoal pits. They were cheap: a male convict could be bought for about one-third of what a young enslaved African man might cost in the 1760s. But, buying convicts was risky because they tended to run away more often than other servants or slaves.

Not all colonists welcomed the arrival of England's convicts. Among them was **Benjamin Franklin**, who campaigned vociferously against the transportation of convicted felons to the colonies. "What good mother," he wrote in the *London Chronicle* in 1759, "would introduce thieves and criminals into the company of her children, to corrupt and disgrace them?" Franklin's newspaper, *The Pennsylvania Gazette*, focused on convicts' crimes during the early 1750s. Franklin once suggested that colonists retaliate for the convict trade by exporting rattlesnakes to England, signing the essay "Americanus." He spoke to a British North America built largely on a transatlantic trade in people in chains.

The Impact of Irish and German Immigration

Ireland was the second largest source of immigrants to British North America between 1730 and 1775, with over half arriving after 1750 (Table 5.1). Most Irish who migrated between 1730 and 1763 were young, single, male indentured servants. Families from Ulster (Northern Ireland) who paid their own way across the Atlantic dominated Irish immigration from 1763 to the Revolution. Crop failures and slumping demand for linen in 1739 sparked a wave of immigration to North America over the next two years. The promise of better opportunities, particularly land ownership, led thousands more to follow (Map 5.2).

Most landed in Philadelphia or in New Castle, Delaware, where demand for indentured servants was high. Commercial ties linked those ports to Ireland. By 1750, Irish merchants in Philadelphia exported wheat and flour to Ireland and imported linens, flaxseed, and servants. Most ex-servants who concluded their terms headed for Pennsylvania's and New Jersey's frontiers, where land was cheaper. Ulsterites, later known in North America as Scots Irish, who had paid their own way went West immediately. After 1750,

(10)

gestrengen Herrn beliebt machen. Die Uebersetzung so im ersten Blat gedruckt, ist recht nach dem eigentlichen Sinn und Verstand der Worte und des gantzen Satzes von sechs Männern übersetzt, so beyde Sprachen verstehen. Um denen Lockvögeln unsere Unpartheylichkeit zu zeigen, folget hier der gantze Satz in englisch und teutsch.

And since Detachments of English from Britain sent to America will have their Places at home so soon supplied and increase so largely here; why should the Palatine Boors be suffered to swarm into our Settlements, and by Herding together, establish their Language and Manners to the Exclusion of ours.

Und weil die Schaaren von Engländern, welche man von Brittanien nach America abgeschickt hat, in ihrer eigenen Heimath so bald wieder aufgefült werden, nach dem sie hier gelandet sind, sich selbst so zahlreich fortpflanzen: warum seyden wirs, daß die teutschen Baurentölpel in denen Landschaften die wir angebauet haben, überall so lange herum streichen, bis sie endlich wie eine Heerde von ihrem eigenen Gezüchte sich zusammen lagern und ihre eigene Sprache und Sitten unter sich beybehalten, damit die unsren niemahls aufkommen mögen.

Nun mag es ein ieder nach belieben selbst übersetzen, so gut er kan, daß weiß ich gewiß, daß niemand einen Ehren Titel oder eine Lobrede daraus machen wird. Der Leser kan selbst urtheilen ob diese Lockvögel oder Verfälscher sind. Ich will ein wenig erklären, was das englische Wort Boor vor eine Bedeutung hat. Unter denen Engländern

"PALATINE BOORS" German printers in Pennsylvania made a point of broadcasting Benjamin Franklin's insulting "Palatine Boors" comment and translating it into German during charged elections in the mid-1760s. Here is an example from a German-language newspaper published in Philadelphia in 1764.

Table 5.1 Estimated European Migration to British North America by Ethnic Group and Compared to Atlantic Slave Trade, 1730–1775

Enslaved Africans comprised the majority of migrants to British North America during the 1730s, and they were the largest group of migrants entering the colonies in each decade thereafter. Most of the nearly 30,000 Germans to enter British North America during the 1750s arrived shortly before the Seven Years' War began.

Decade	Germans	Ulster Irish	Southern Irish	Scots	English	Welsh	Other	Africans	Total
1730–1739	13,000	4,400	7,400	2,000	4,900	3,200	800	60,700	96,400
1740–1749	16,600	9,200	9,100	3,100	7,500	4,900	1,100	21,600	73,100
1750–1759	29,100	14,200	8,100	3,700	8,800	5,800	1,200	38,200	109,100
1760–1769	14,500	21,200	8,500	10,000	11,900	7,800	1,600	51,600	127,100
1770–1775	5,200	13,200	3,900	15,000	7,100	4,600	700	31,000	80,700
Total	78,400	62,200	37,000	33,800	40,200	26,300	5,400	203,100	486,400

Note: "Germans" refers to German speakers, not to people who came from what is today Germany. "Africans" refers to people brought via the Atlantic slave trade who disembarked in British North America. "British North America" does not include Nova Scotia or the Caribbean.

more of them landed in Pennsylvania and trekked south to western Maryland, Virginia's Shenandoah Valley, piedmont North Carolina, and South Carolina's Upcountry. Thousands followed the Great Wagon Road, on which construction began in 1730, from Philadelphia to the southern backcountry.

Along the way, the Irish encountered thousands of Germans. Absolutist princes, high taxes, compulsory labor, and scarcity of land pushed over 70,000 Germans, mainly from the Palatinate (the region bordering the Rhine River), to North America between 1730 and 1775. The prospect of owning land, lower taxes, and religious freedom lured them across the Atlantic in numbers that alarmed German authorities. German archives contain many unfavorable letters and reports from North America because local officials preserved and used them to dissuade migrants from going there. In 1768, Joseph II, emperor of Austria, tried to curb emigration by ordering that no one from his empire could relocate there.

Most Germans landed in Philadelphia, where nearly 35,000 docked between 1749 and 1754. Before the 1750s, most German immigrants had come as families. Many had kin who wrote them about North America and helped them adjust to their new lives. After the 1750s, most German immigrants were single men who became "**redemptioners**," indentured servants who paid for their passage across the Atlantic by selling their services when they landed. In 1775, 1 in 10 colonists spoke German, as did 1 in 3 Pennsylvanians.

The influx of Germans alarmed many colonists, particularly Franklin. He referred to them as "Palatine Boors" who threatened to make Pennsylvania "become a Colony of *Aliens*, who will shortly be so numerous as to Germanize us instead of our Anglifying them, and will never adopt our Language or Customs, any more than they can acquire our Complexion." Such views, printed in London in 1755, came back to haunt Franklin.

That was partly because Germans comprised over 90 percent of naturalized British subjects in the mainland colonies. The **Plantation Act of 1740** allowed non-Catholic

Predominant Immigrant Groups 1775

- English
- Scots-Irish
- Highland Scots
- Dutch
- French
- German
- African
- **J** Jews
- **S** Swedes
- **W** Welsh
- **FH** French Huguenots

MAP 5.2 ▲ Race, Ethnicity, and the Colonization of British North America, c. 1775
European immigration and the Atlantic slave trade made an ethnic and racial mosaic of colonial British North America. The colonies were even more diverse than this map suggests, for it shows the largest group in each area, which often was not the majority. Most Scots arrived after the Seven Years' War.

aliens who resided for at least seven years in British North America, received communion in a Protestant church, swore allegiance to George II, and paid two shillings to become citizens. An average laborer could earn that in a day. The law also permitted Jews in the colonies to naturalize by excusing them from the religious requirement, a provision that in 1753 prompted Jews in England to lobby unsuccessfully for the same right.

Political controversies in Pennsylvania and the English- and German-language press spurred thousands of Germans to become naturalized British subjects. Most German voters traditionally supported the Assembly Party, which kept taxes low; did not demand military service of them or their sons; and opposed the colony's proprietor Thomas Penn, who sought to increase rents and land prices. In 1755, Christopher Saur published essays in his newspaper *Pennsylvanische Berichte* and in his annual almanac in which he likened Penn to the feudal lords who exploited Germans. Ten years later, over 2,600 Germans applied for naturalization just before an election that turned on whether Pennsylvania should be governed by the king or the Penns. The Penns had recently made it easier to own land. Many new German voters and a sizable number of more established Germans, appalled by what Franklin had written about Germans in the 1750s, sided with the Penns. Franklin and others in the Assembly Party lost their elections and left the colony's assembly.

Heavy immigration accelerated the expansion of British North America and sparked debates on who could be considered British and who belonged in the colonies. The labor of thousands of enslaved Africans accelerated the expansion of Virginia and Georgia and extended plantation agriculture to new areas. Meanwhile, thousands of German and Irish immigrants flooded into Pennsylvania and spilled into the southern backcountry. Resentful Indians, whom the new immigrants had pushed aside, watched from beyond the Appalachians, as did other Indians who feared that soon they might also lose their homelands.

Indian Displacement and the Rise of Sioux, Osage, and Comanche

The world of Indians who lived between the Rockies and the Appalachians changed even more rapidly as more people and imports flowed into North America after 1730. Massive European immigration meant exile for some eastern peoples. Wider diffusion of horses and guns enabled the rise of new Indian powers on the Great Plains, as Indians in the Southeast continued to adjust to life alongside three rival European empires.

Few Indians suffered more from displacement by immigrants than Delawares. A 1736 treaty between Pennsylvania and the Iroquois League awarded Iroquois the right to speak for all Indians who lived between them and Philadelphia. A year later, Pennsylvanians tricked Delaware leaders into the "Walking Purchase." Delawares thought they had agreed to sell no more land than what one man could walk in a day and a half through the woods. Delaware leaders believed that the backdated treaty was a forgery, and they probably accommodated the Pennsylvanians merely because they believed that the resulting land cession would not be extensive. Colonial officials sent runners along cleared and marked paths to claim 1,200 square miles of Delaware land. Iroquois brushed aside Delaware protests that Pennsylvania had tricked them. Many Delawares trudged to Ohio, where they settled alongside Shawnees, many of whom also

APACHE PICTOGRAPH, RATTLESNAKE CANYON, TEXAS   Comanche raids forced many Apaches to seek shelter in Spanish missions, where they came under friars' supervision. Resentful Apaches who fled the missions painted the mission church as a friar whose upraised arms suggest church towers and whose hands are crosses. Note the arrow piercing the friar's body.

had been exiled from Pennsylvania. The refugees, now beyond the reach of colonists and the Iroquois League, seethed as they pondered what they had lost (Map 5.3).

Meanwhile, horses and guns continued to transform life for Indians on the Great Plains. By 1760, virtually all Plains peoples had horses and most had firearms (see Map 4.1). Wider incorporation of horses encouraged more peoples to become nomadic and focus on hunting bison. This meant more work for women and for enslaved captives, who had to process the hides.

The dispersal of horses and guns encouraged more violence and led to the rise of three powers, the newest of which was the Sioux. Teton and Yanktonais Sioux gradually entered the Great Plains from Minnesota in the late 1600s, partly to hunt bison, but mainly to hunt beaver to trade to the French for firearms and other imports. As these Sioux depleted local stocks of beaver, they headed west, displacing less well-armed peoples such as Omaha, Cheyenne, Missouri, and Iowa. By the 1740s, agricultural peoples along the Missouri River impeded their expansion. The mobility that horses afforded Sioux enabled them to dodge smallpox epidemics that devastated agricultural villagers. By the time Lewis and Clark arrived in 1804, Sioux dominated the northern Great Plains.

Meanwhile, Osage Indians had become the main power on the east-central Plains. Their location between the Missouri and Arkansas Rivers enabled Osages to deny Indian peoples to their west and south access to supplies of trade goods from the French, including firearms. French colonists in Illinois had to maintain good relations with the more powerful and populous Osage, who sent them mules and Indian slaves.

The Comanches were the most powerful group of Indians to emerge in North America in the 1700s. Like Osages, Comanches played the Spanish and French against one another. Spanish law denied Comanches access to firearms in New Mexico, so they obtained them from the French. In return, Comanches offered bison hides, captives,

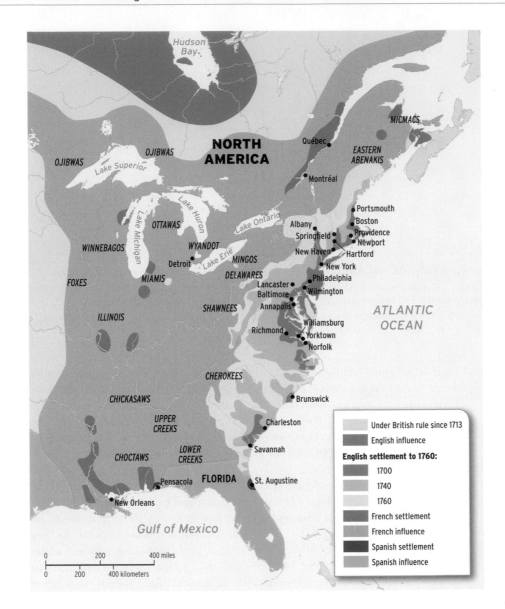

MAP 5.3 ▲ Political Map of Eastern North America, Mid-18th Century Most Indians in the Ohio Valley who chose to take sides between the French and British preferred the French. British colonization, focused on control of land and exclusion of Indian peoples, expanded rapidly between 1700 and 1740, particularly in Pennsylvania and Virginia. Note the westward exodus of Delawares and Shawnees from Pennsylvania.

mules, and horses. By the 1750s, Comanches dominated much of Oklahoma and Texas, forcing Spanish colonists and longtime Indian foes such as the Apache to patch over their differences. Apaches sought shelter within Spanish missions in Texas. Fear of Comanches also led Spanish colonists to ally with Utes to secure New Mexico's northwestern border, which extended violence and slaving raids well into the Great Basin as Utes funneled captives to New Mexico. Comanches brought Indian slaves and French guns to New Mexican trade fairs. Comanches' ability to limit Spanish power during the 1700s helped to make Anglo conquest of the region possible in the 1830s and 1840s.

Southeastern Indians confronted a different situation. Yamasee and Natchez wars left two principal Indian powers: Choctaws and the Creek confederacy. The conflicts also accelerated the depopulation of the region. This allowed the population of white-tailed deer to explode just as bovine epidemics struck Britain and western Europe. Creek and Choctaw men hunted deer and sent their skins to merchants in Louisiana, South Carolina, and Georgia to fill demand for hides in Europe. By the mid-1700s, as many as one million deerskins a year moved through South Carolina and Georgia. English traders lured Choctaw traders to supply more deerskins by selling them liquor and getting them into debt. Meanwhile, South Carolina officials attempted to persuade Choctaw people to abandon their long-standing alliance with the French and side instead with the British. Their efforts, and the concerted French response to them, led to a bloody civil war among Choctaw in the late 1740s. Environmental change, trade, and rivalries between European empires destabilized Indian societies and the Southeast.

Slave Resistance and the Creation of Georgia

In 1733, a group of English entrepreneurs led by **James Oglethorpe** founded Georgia. The colony's trustees hoped to offer sanctuary to Europe's persecuted Protestants and free British debtors from prison and redeem them through the hard work of establishing a new society. They also aspired to convert Indians, particularly those allied with the British. In addition, the trustees envisioned Georgia as a buffer between South Carolina, a slave state, and Florida, where hundreds who fled enslavement sought freedom among

MEDAL OF ST. CHRISTOPHER, FLORIDA Archeologists found this at the site of Gracia Real de Santa Teresa de Mose. St. Christopher, patron saint of travelers and of Havana, Cuba, is carrying Jesus over water. African beliefs that they would return to Africa after death may have encouraged Mose residents to identify with St. Christopher.

the Spanish and their Indian allies. That goal, and Oglethorpe's belief that slavery corrupted whites by encouraging them to be lazy, led the trustees to outlaw slavery in 1735.

Georgia's ban took shape as the Spanish encouraged slaves to flee South Carolina. In 1738, Florida's governor granted freedom to all fugitive Carolina slaves who reached the colony. A few months later, he licensed Gracia Real Santa Teresa de Mose, a town near St. Augustine, composed largely of people who had escaped slavery in South Carolina. The men of Mose, led by Francisco Menéndez, formed a militia to defend St. Augustine. The governor and Mose residents followed a precedent set in the Caribbean in the late 1500s in which Spanish officials allowed blacks who had escaped slavery to form towns in exchange for assurances that residents would defend the Spanish.

In 1739, offers of sanctuary in Florida helped to spark the **Stono Rebellion** in South Carolina, the largest and bloodiest slave revolt in colonial British North American history. The group of slaves who led the revolt had recently arrived from Kongo, were baptized Catholics, and likely had military experience in Africa. Rebels burned homes and killed over 20 whites as they headed for Florida. It took whites a month to restore order. In 1740, legislators passed a more draconian slave code in hopes of preventing further revolts and tried to limit how many Africans entered South Carolina by levying a duty on each slave imported.

The Stono Rebellion was part of a wave of slave revolts and conspiracies that rocked the West Indies and eastern North America between 1733 and 1741. The first revolt occurred in the Danish Virgin Islands. Akwamu slaves from Africa's Gold Coast took control of the island of St. John, where they hoped to establish a kingdom and enslave everyone who was not Akwamu. Three years later, Gold Coast slaves conspired to stage a similar revolt in Antigua. In 1739, Jamaica's **Maroons**, fugitives from slavery and their descendants, forced the British to sign peace treaties. Finally, rumors that slaves had plotted with foreign agents to commit arson, kill whites, and turn New York over to Spain convulsed the city in 1741. Officials interrogated nearly 200 people, banished more than 70, and executed 4 whites and 30 slaves.

War between the British and Spanish empires influenced events in South Carolina and New York. Parliament declared war on Spain in 1739, ostensibly to defend British commerce and mariners. The Spanish coast guard had boarded an English vessel and severed the ear of its captain Robert Jenkins, which was displayed in Parliament. The **War of Jenkins' Ear** (1739–1742) had two main American theaters—the Caribbean and southeastern North America—and was the first conflict in which large numbers of British colonists left North America to fight. British officers recruited 3,500 volunteers from New Hampshire south to North Carolina to help besiege Cartagena, Colombia, where hundreds died of disease. The survivors sailed to Guantánamo Bay, Cuba, to regroup and prepare to storm Santiago, where the British hoped to establish a colony. Disease claimed most. Few colonists returned from Cuba.

Meanwhile, British and Spanish forces, along with thousands of Indians, faced off in the Southeast. Troops under Oglethorpe's command failed to take St. Augustine, thanks partly to Mose's militia. The Spanish and their Indian allies invaded Georgia and were driven back to Florida. Georgia had shielded South Carolina from Florida, while Spain's policy of sheltering fugitives from British slavery had shored up Florida's defenses.

The War of Jenkins' Ear led to many changes. It cut South Carolina off from Spain and the Mediterranean, key markets for rice. This precipitated a recession that encouraged planters to diversify their crops. Many experimented with indigo, which yielded a blue dye that British textile firms imported from the Spanish and French Caribbean. An imperial bounty (bonus) on indigo initiated in 1749 helped to make it South Carolina's second most valuable export. After peace with the Spanish empire was restored, many South Carolina planters moved to Georgia. They argued strenuously that the region's climate and malarial swamps necessitated the exploitation of Africans, who, they claimed, were naturally suited to withstand both better than whites. In 1750, Georgia's trustees legalized slavery.

STUDY QUESTIONS FOR IMMIGRANTS AND INDIANS

1. In what ways did unfree and free immigration alter North America between 1730 and the 1760s?
2. In what ways did the movement of goods and people change Indian societies and Indian politics?
3. Was the impact of the movement of people different on southeastern North America than it was on North America as a whole? Please explain, using specific examples.

◼ MINDS, SOULS, AND WALLETS

In the 1730s, colonists in British North America began to participate in new ways in transatlantic intellectual, commercial, and religious networks. The most educated of them embraced and practiced science, while thousands flocked to sermons delivered by people who brought evangelical Christianity to both sides of the Atlantic and converted thousands of blacks and Indians. Nearly everyone in Eastern North America eagerly purchased British imports, as thickening ties to transatlantic and continental networks transformed how colonists and Indians thought of themselves and of their relationships to one another and to the world.

North Americans Engage the Enlightenment

After 1730, colonists became fully engaged in the ideas of the Enlightenment. This philosophical movement attracted intellectuals in Britain, continental Europe, and the Americas; celebrated the use of reason as the key to progress; and disseminated knowledge via international communication networks. Enlightenment participants saw themselves as part of a collective effort to improve humanity. They tried to determine a system of universal laws that governed nature and the development of human societies. Most viewed science as critical to discovering and understanding such laws, and most considered arbitrary authority, whether wielded by clergy or monarchs, an impediment to progress that must be challenged.

Expansion of the newspaper industry kept colonists informed on distant developments. The number of newspapers published in British North America rose from 5 to 22 between 1728 and 1760. By the early 1740s, a number of changes had occurred in the newspaper business. Printers began to produce them in Southern colonies, which

KING GEORGE'S WAR To British colonists, the most significant event of King George's War occurred when colonial soldiers besieged and captured the French fortress and town of Louisbourg in Canada. Newspapers like this issue of the *Pennsylvania Gazette* kept readers in the colonies abreast of developments at Louisbourg.

helped to reinforce their role as brokers for the purchase of servants and slaves as well as for the return of runaways. Colonists began to accept newspapers as legitimate vehicles for political dissent. Coverage of religious revivals and wars alerted readers to events in neighboring colonies and led many to identify more closely with one another and the British colonial empire.

The creation of more colonial colleges also facilitated the exchange of ideas. Clergy founded five between 1746 and 1766. They are today the University of Pennsylvania, Columbia, Princeton, Rutgers, and Brown. Most were established to train ministers, but all offered a secular and practical curriculum to students of all Christian denominations. The colleges trained a growing number of American-born doctors, lawyers, and merchants.

Beyond the walls of the colonies' colleges, libraries brought ideas swirling about the Atlantic world to colonists. In 1731, Franklin and other members of the Junto, a mutual aid society, formed the Library Company of Philadelphia, which lent books to members. By the 1750s, many towns had lending libraries. Many of the books patrons checked out offered self-improvement: advice on how to become a better farmer, public speaker, or bookkeeper. Histories filled library shelves. An increasing number of them addressed North America's past and were written by colonists. Like newspapers, such histories revealed and nurtured colonists' growing consciousness of ties that bound them to one another and to the British empire.

Novels, the most popular type of books borrowed from colonial libraries, also encouraged readers to think of themselves as part of an Anglo-Atlantic world. Relatively few colonists read them before 1740. Most early novels targeted an urban female audience, which was rather small in the colonies until the mid-1700s. Such works focused on women's marriage and career choices in an emerging commercial society in which families afforded daughters less guidance or protection, above all from grasping, lustful, or deceitful suitors. Some novelists, including Samuel Richardson, offered moral instruction. In 1742, his most popular work, *Pamela: Or, Virtue Rewarded*, was the first novel to be published in North America, two years after it appeared in Britain. It told the story of a servant girl who resists her employer's efforts to seduce her. Her virtue so impresses him that he asks her to marry him. *Pamela* evoked negative reactions from some female readers, but most seem to have identified with Pamela for having honored her parents' wishes and her principles while attracting a husband.

Meanwhile, more British North Americans became ambitious and noteworthy scientists. They continued the practice, begun in the 1660s, of providing firsthand accounts of local plants and animals and shipping specimens overseas. John Bartram and his son William toured eastern North America, gathered many of its plants into a botanical garden, and published accounts of their travels. Cadwallader Colden studied botany, maintained a horticultural garden, and furnished European contacts with seeds and seedlings. His daughter Jane inherited the garden, made hundreds of detailed observations of American plants, and became the Anglo-Atlantic's first widely acclaimed female botanist.

Benjamin Franklin was the 18th century's most famous American-born person in Europe, principally because of his scientific research. In 1747, Franklin left management of his print shop to others to concentrate on science and politics. He focused on electricity, long considered little more than a curiosity. Franklin had read Isaac Newton's works and attended a lecture in Boston given by an Edinburgh doctor who used demonstrations of electricity to wow audiences. Franklin designed experiments that led to inventions like the lightning rod, proving that scientific experiments could yield practical benefits. He also developed a set of general laws that seemed to govern how electricity worked and did so under controlled conditions resembling those in nature. His discovery prompted British philosopher Joseph Priestley to compare Franklin to Isaac Newton, which helped Franklin get elected to the Royal Society of London in 1756.

Franklin's reception overseas as a first-rate scientist who also was an American made him an exception. European scientists generally saw their American peers as suppliers of specimens and firsthand observations of North American nature, but did not think them capable of ascertaining laws that governed the universe. Such disdain led some colonial scholars to assert that as Americans, they were best qualified to explain and depict American flora and fauna. They began to speak of the emergence of a distinctly "American Philosophy," discussions that led Franklin and John Bartram to organize North America's first intercolonial scientific society in Philadelphia in 1743. Twenty-six years later, it merged with a rival to become the **American Philosophical Society** (APS), with Franklin as president. In 1771, the APS launched *Transactions*, a journal modeled on the Royal Society's most famous publication. Franklin sent copies of the first volume to Britain to trumpet British North America's latest and most erudite entry to the world of ideas.

Becoming a Consumer Society

Most British North Americans did not read *Transactions* or frequent libraries, but almost everyone bought the British goods that filled shops. By the 1750s, most white families proudly displayed British-made ceramic teapots and teacups, china, and silverware in their homes. "[O]ur Beds, our Tables and our Bodies are covered" with British-made cloth, commented one colonial pamphlet of that decade. In 1773, North Americans bought 26 percent of manufactured goods exported from Britain, almost five times as much as in 1700. British industry and Anglo-Atlantic shipping networks offered colonists an unprecedented number and variety of goods to choose from. Their expanding choices as consumers led colonists to redefine their relationships to one another and to the British empire (Map 5.4).

Drinking tea, a sign of refinement and gentility to British on both sides of the Atlantic, helped usher in the consumer revolution. One writer asserted in 1734 that New Yorkers had to "have their tea tho their families want bread." Indians drank tea, too. In 1750, a Seneca chief hosted two missionaries who were surprised to be served the beverage on a tea table.

In the 1740s, representatives (factors) of mercantile houses headquartered in Glasgow began to set up shop in Virginia to compete with large planters for the business of small farmers, producers of two-thirds of the colony's tobacco. Small planters sold tobacco at the "Scotch stores," selected from a wide variety of goods, and bought on long-term credit. This decreased the influence of planter elites who had long controlled their access to Atlantic markets. Colonial merchants and shopkeepers spurred demand by extending credit to customers. "Credit is to Trade, what the Blood is to the Body," a debtor wrote from a Newport jail in 1754. In the major port cities of New England and

SUSANNA TRUAX   Here Susanna Truax poses at ease with imported possessions. Her striped dress is made of British cloth. On the table behind her are a teapot, a full tea cup on a saucer, and a bowl with sugar cubes, all testament to her participation in colonial Anglo-America's consumer revolution.

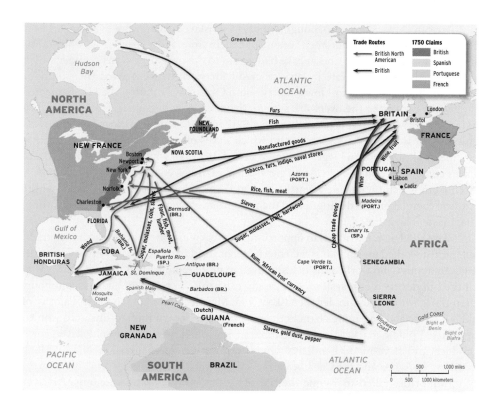

MAP 5.4 ▲ British-Atlantic Trade, c. 1750 By 1750, British North America was integral to British Atlantic commerce. Colonists' trade with Spain, Portugal, and the Caribbean helped them foot the bill for the manufactured goods that they imported from Britain.

the mid-Atlantic, wholesale merchants imported goods and shipped many of them to retailers in the countryside. The retailers bought on credit and sold the imported goods on credit to their rural customers, who paid their debts with what they made, grew, or raised. Retailers had those products hauled or shipped to wholesalers in the major port cities, who in turn sold many of them to the West Indies or southern Europe for specie or bills of exchange to pay creditors in Britain. Ships built by colonists and raw materials such as whale oil or naval stores such as tar or pitch also helped colonial merchants balance their accounts with British merchants.

Marketing via newsprint stimulated sales, as advertising featured more prominently in colonial newspapers. The 1750s saw a huge increase in the number of items advertised in newspapers as well as more detailed descriptions of goods that had recently reached warehouses in Boston, New York, Philadelphia, and Charleston. By the 1760s, newspapers devoted as much or more space to ads as they did to news.

Ads in newspapers indicate that British North America was becoming one interconnected market. Colonists could buy the same goods almost everywhere at the same time. Archeological studies reveal that colonists who shared a socioeconomic bracket bought virtually the same goods wherever they lived. A growing network of small coastal vessels carried imports from merchants in Northern cities to small ports in the South.

African Americans also bought imports. Enslaved men who lived in or near Charleston, especially tradesmen, often sold their time and expertise to whites. Enslaved ironworkers in the Chesapeake had access to the overwork system, under which they earned the market rate in cash or credit for work that exceeded their daily or weekly quotas. By 1750, most low country South Carolina plantations had implemented the **task system**. Like the overwork system, the task system assigned enslaved adults a daily or weekly work quota. Once they met it, they could tend their own gardens, raise chickens, or weave baskets. Gardens, in which slaves often grew African crops such as sesame or okra, offered a bigger and more varied diet than what masters provided, and slaves could sell what they made or grew. Their earnings enabled them to buy hats or cloth from which they made garments or had them tailored. Such attire displayed the fruits of their labor and distinguished them from slaves who wore the standard clothing that masters distributed.

Slaves had unequal access to opportunities to earn income. Those who had marketable skills, worked for an industrial enterprise, or lived in or near a city enjoyed advantages that most who worked the fields or lived in more remote areas did not. Slaves who labored under the **gang system**, commonly used to tend tobacco, had less autonomy than those who worked under the task system. Men accounted for the vast majority of skilled slaves and had more chances than women did to earn money. Enslaved women dominated public markets in Charleston and Savannah, where they sold slave-grown produce and slave-made handicrafts, replicating a gendered division of labor long common in Africa and the Caribbean.

Authorities failed to stymie the rise of an autonomous slave economy. Artisans feared that the hiring of enslaved men threatened their livelihood, and other whites insisted that hiring of slaves was a security risk. In 1740, just after the Stono Rebellion, such arguments prevailed as South Carolina legislators prohibited slaves from hiring themselves out and fined those who hired them. Eleven years later Charleston officials acknowledged how unrealistic such laws were by licensing enslaved men to work as porters, laborers, fishermen, or craftsmen and setting rates to eliminate bargaining between slaves and employers. This bothered some masters, one of whom complained in the *South Carolina Gazette* that his slave Cuffee often hired "himself out without my knowledge, whereby I am defrauded of his wages."

South Carolina authorities also worried about the role that slaves, particularly women, played in public markets. The slave code of 1740 permitted slaves to attend the Charleston public market on masters' behalf, provided that they carried tickets listing what they were to buy or sell. Slaves and masters soon agreed that slaves could hawk masters' produce and use part of the earnings to buy goods, resell them to other slaves when they returned home, and keep the profits. A market clerk claimed in 1741 that the "insolent abusive Manner" of slave marketers left him "afraid to say or do Anything in the Market." A petition submitted six years later complained that slaves who ran market stalls bought items that they resold to city residents, enabling them to evade "the government of their masters." Many masters fretted that economic autonomy afforded slaves too much power, but permitted it anyway. They enjoyed lower provisioning costs and encouraged slaves to be more industrious, while allowing few to earn enough to buy their or their children's freedom.

This anxiety about slaves' economic activities was part of a larger discussion in which wealthier colonists, mostly men, insisted that consumerism had led to moral and social decline. The poor (black or white), women, and youth no longer knew their place and no one could be sure who was who. A commentator complained in 1765 that one could no longer use clothing to distinguish between those "of great Fortune, and People of ordinary Rank." Conspicuous consumption, many charged, tempted all to live beyond their means.

Women took a disproportionate share of the blame for the ills of the consumer revolution. Two ironmasters complained in 1761 that they had to pay high wages and keep their ironworks' store well-stocked because ironworkers' wives required "a great deal of finery. They cannot do without tea, coffee, chocolate, and loaf sugar." Some women hurled the blame back at men. In 1746, one noted in a Boston newspaper that male readers had called tea "a Female Luxury." She retorted that her male friends were as "great *Tea-Sots* as any of us."

North America's growing significance to Britain led imperial officials to seek more control over the colonial economy. Between 1732 and 1764, Parliament enacted laws that tightened regulations on colonial manufacturing and restricted what British North Americans could export or import, particularly from the French and Dutch Caribbean (Table 5.2). Meanwhile, British lawmakers and imperial officials constricted colonists' ability to set their own monetary policies, measures that delighted merchants and other lenders in England.

Table 5.2 Key Laws Regulating British North America's Manufacturing, Trade, and Monetary Supply, 1732–1764

Imperial officials marked British North America's growing importance to Britain as a market for British goods and as a potential competitor for British manufacturers by crafting new regulations in the mid-1700s. Many colonists resented these laws, a sentiment that fed their resistance to imperial reforms in the wake of the Seven Years' War.

Name of Legislation	Year Passed	Key Provisions
Hat Act	1732	Barred colonists from producing beaver felt hats for export to other British colonies to protect British manufacturers
Molasses Act	1733	Imposed prohibitively high duty on sugar and molasses imported to British North America from French and Dutch Caribbean to protect British West Indies planters
Iron Act	1750	Barred colonists from building more rolling or slitting mills, which made hoops, tire iron, and nails that colonists usually imported from Britain
Currency Act	1751	Prohibited colonial governments from issuing more paper money, except in cases of emergency
Sugar Act	1764	Modified regulations issued under Molasses Act and bolstered their enforcement First overt tax raised by Parliament in British America Yielded more revenue than any imperial tax levied on British America prior to American Revolution
Currency Act	1764	Outlawed printing of paper money in colonies

Some colonists thought that such regulations signaled that Britain discounted their importance to the empire. In 1751, Franklin responded to the Iron Act by asserting that colonists' growing consumption of British goods should lead imperial officials to see them as fellow Britons who were partners in forging the empire's future. Seven years later, Franklin explicitly connected consumer choice and personal liberty. He asked, "Would you not say that you are free, have a Right to dress as you please, and that such an Edict . . . would be a Breach of your Privileges, and such a Government tyrannical?" In the 1760s and 1770s, thousands of colonists linked liberty and consumer choice by boycotting British imports to protest imperial reforms that they considered tyrannical.

Revivals and the Rise of Evangelical Christianity

In 1741, Hannah Heaton, a 20-year-old Connecticut woman, attended a sermon. Years later, she recalled how it had transformed her life: "It seemed to me I was a sinking down in to hell. I thot the floor I stood on gave way and I was just a going but then I began to resign and as I resigned my distress began to go off till I was perfectly easy quiet and calm . . . it seemed as if I had a new soul & body both." Heaton had participated in revivals that gripped most of British North America in the 1730s and 1740s and flared again in the South during the 1750s and 1760s.

Heaton remembered a time when religion became more important to residents of British North America. Church membership grew rapidly between 1730 and 1776. The number of church buildings tripled between 1740 and 1780. Ministers filled churches and preachers lured thousands to outdoors sermons with emotional messages of damnation and redemption delivered in simple and direct language that anyone could understand. The preachers brought evangelical Christianity to North America. They sought converts by stressing personal piety and the relative equality of all believers before God and one another. Most discounted adherence to ritual and reason and denied that formal education and theological training were the best claim to spiritual authority. Expression of such beliefs opened deep divisions within colonial Christianity and led colonists to identify more closely with fellow believers in other colonies and across the Atlantic.

In many ways, Hannah Heaton's spiritual awakening and that of thousands of other colonists was a legacy of Pietism, which celebrated the exchange of ideas and techniques across ethnic, national, and denominational lines and promoted the evangelization (the conversion to Christianity) of Africans and Indians. The United Brethren knitted these strands of Pietism together. Revived in Germany in 1727 on the estates of Count Nicolaus Ludwig von Zinzendorf, the Brethren, better known as **Moravians**, sought to create closed, economically autonomous, sex-segregated communities in which Christian liturgical rituals and piety infused daily life. In 1735, James Oglethorpe invited Moravians to Georgia, where they established a school to evangelize Indians. Five years later, the Moravians left after Georgia officials requested that they violate their pacifist beliefs by taking up arms in the War of Jenkins' Ear. They moved to Pennsylvania, founding Bethlehem and Nazareth. Persecution in Germany during the 1740s displaced thousands of Moravians, many of whom found refuge in 1753 in North Carolina. They played a key role in the development of Anglo-Atlantic Christianity by pioneering evangelizing techniques and sharing them with British and colonial **revivalists**.

Colonists filled leading roles in the transatlantic awakening, none more so than **Jonathan Edwards**, a Massachusetts minister. He merged Pietism with an emotional style of preaching and brought both to orthodox New England Puritanism. Edwards's charged sermons sparked a revival, an outpouring of religious enthusiasm, in the Connecticut River Valley in the 1730s. Edwards demanded that listeners repent and practice what they professed or face eternal damnation. Edwards broadcast news of his labors to an Anglo-Atlantic audience. Word of his deeds spread to Britain, prompting **George Whitefield**, an Anglican pastor, to tour British North America. Whitefield was probably the first transatlantic celebrity. He followed the Welsh model, a form of itinerant field preaching that drew huge socially mixed crowds, sometimes numbering in the tens of thousands. His tour itself garnered an unprecedented level of coverage of colonial events in North American newspapers (Map 5.5).

In part, public interest was so great because revivalists generated enormous controversy. Critics directed fire at the revivalists' enthusiasm and disdain for authority. Revivalists sparked conflicts between established ministers and itinerants, touring preachers who did not oversee a congregation. One faction within each denomination cast revivalism as irrational, too egalitarian, and too disrespectful of trained ministers. In 1738, North American Presbyterians divided after a ruling that required a university degree to become licensed as a minister. Defenders of the policy, mainly older clergymen born in Ulster, became known as the "Old Side." Their opponents, the "New Side" ministers were younger than Old Siders, and were mostly born in North America. Meanwhile, New England Congregationalists split into "Old Lights" and "New Lights." In 1742, Old Light supporters in Connecticut targeted itinerants by passing a law that declared that "any *Foreigner* or *Stranger*" who preached without permission from settled ministers was to be considered "a *vagrant*" and banished from the colony. In the 1740s and early 1750s, German Lutheran and Reformed ministers in Europe and North America targeted Moravians, largely because their preaching and attentive ministry attracted Germans in New Jersey and Pennsylvania who had no Lutheran or Reformed pastor to serve them. Such campaigns sometimes led to violence against Moravian missionaries.

Moravians also drew fire because they disobeyed gender norms. Hundreds of Moravian women in Germany and North America served as eldresses, teachers who instructed women and men, overseers, deaconesses, or itinerant missionaries. The "choir system" by which Moravian communities segregated the sexes, including some married couples, allowed women autonomy and challenged the model of the male-dominated nuclear family. Moravian hymns and imagery attributed some feminine characteristics to Christ. Moravian theology spoke of the Holy Spirit as "Mother."

Other revivalists also empowered women. Women's voices echoed loudly in New Light congregations that formed in New England during Baptist revivals in the 1730s and 1740s as well as in many Baptist churches in Pennsylvania. Women disciplined others for sexual misconduct, theft, and improper preaching. Women's votes helped to select some ministers, choose deacons, and admit new members, a practice last seen in England during the English Civil War. As evangelical congregations took root, however, women's influence within them ebbed. Male Baptists disenfranchised women as part of a broader retreat from sexual egalitarianism within their communities.

Even so, the ideals of the awakening and evangelical Christianity promoted egalitarianism and skepticism toward established authority. Baptists, **Methodists**, and

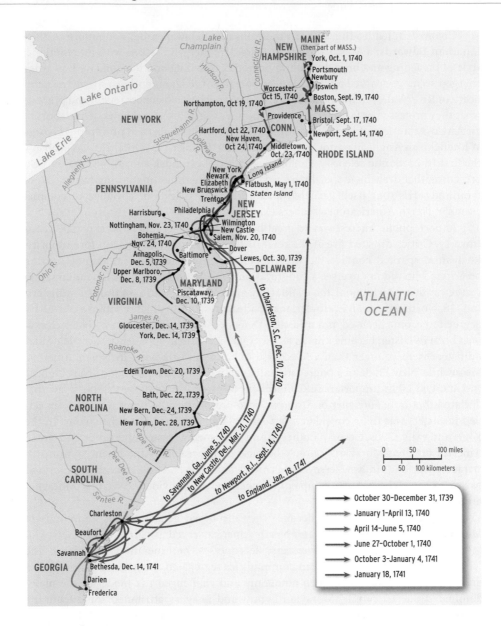

MAP 5.5 ▲ George Whitefield's First American Tour, 1739–1741 Whitefield preached to huge audiences in every English colony, some of which he visited multiple times. He died in 1770, having completed 15 preaching tours of Scotland, 3 of Ireland, and 7 of North America. But his first American tour was by far his most famous.

Presbyterians who evangelized Virginia in the 1760s and 1770s challenged the notion of a hierarchical, official, taxpayer-supported religion to which all must at least theoretically belong. Their efforts shaped James Madison's and Thomas Jefferson's views concerning the separation of church and state. Evangelicals helped to reconceive the relationship of the individual to the community and to society so that people could decide for themselves to which community they wished to belong. Finally, revivalists drew Africans, African Americans, and Indians to Christianity.

African, African American, and Indian Awakenings

Many blacks and Indians proved receptive to evangelical Protestantism, largely because preachers reached out to them with messages that they found attractive. Moravians were the first evangelicals in the Americas to target Africans and African Americans for conversion, establishing their first mission in the Danish Virgin Islands in 1732. Moravian outreach to Africans and African Americans spread from the Virgin Islands to the British West Indies, Pennsylvania, and New Jersey. Moravians were practically the only evangelicals permitted to proselytize among British West Indies slaves until the 1780s. They preached racial equality among believers but submission to masters, some of whom were Moravian church officials.

Like Moravians, George Whitefield considered enslaved Africans and African Americans his spiritual equals and he exhorted masters to practice what he preached. In 1740, Whitefield convinced the South Carolina planter Jonathan Bryan to build a school for black students. Bryan and his kin soon led a local movement to evangelize slaves. In 1743, they helped to found the Stoney Creek Independent Presbyterian Church where enslaved women were the majority of those admitted to full communion by the 1760s. Like Moravians, Whitefield reconciled himself to slavery. He advocated its legalization in Georgia and later became a slave owner. That did not diminish Whitefield's importance to some black converts. His death in 1770 moved **Phyllis Wheatley** to publish her first poem, which circulated through the colonies via newsprint.

A number of factors encouraged more slaves and free blacks to convert to Christianity. Charismatic sermons and services lured black audiences and kept them as congregants. So did the willingness of evangelicals, especially Baptists and Methodists, to permit blacks, be they enslaved or free, to preach and become leaders.

Demographic changes helped to spread evangelical Christianity among Africans and African Americans. The growing numbers of American born, English-speaking slaves lowered linguistic and cultural barriers to conversion. These slaves became the majority among blacks in Maryland and Virginia by 1730 and in South Carolina during the 1740s. By the American Revolution, just 1 in 3 enslaved people in South Carolina and fewer than 1 in 10 in Virginia was African. By the 1740s, cabins for families had replaced dormitory-style group or communal quarters, giving slaves more privacy to worship as they wished.

Similarities between evangelical and African rituals and worldviews attracted black converts. The beliefs and practices of Methodists and Separate Baptists resembled those of many West Africans. Baptism was akin to West and West Central African initiation rituals associated with the symbolic death and rebirth of initiates in which a ritual bath marked rebirth and preceded return to ordinary life. African beliefs that the world would return to an idyllic past found confirmation in Separate Baptists' and Methodists' acceptance of all converts as spiritual equals.

Separate Baptist preachers from New England, led by Shubal Stearns, arrived in Virginia in the 1750s. They preached redemption for all, welcomed blacks, and at first allowed women to serve as elders and deaconesses. This earned them the scorn of Regular

The Birth of Methodism

John Wesley, a missionary for the Society for the Propagation of the Gospel, arrived in Georgia in 1736. While at Oxford University, Wesley, his brother Charles, and George Whitefield belonged to a student group whose members called themselves "Methodists," due partly to their habit of rising early to plan how they would budget their time that day. Brought to Georgia by family friend James Oglethorpe, Wesley was to minister to Anglicans and convert Chickasaws, British allies against Choctaw and French. But he crossed the Atlantic with one main goal: to save his own soul, an outcome that he tied to work among Indians.

Wesley did not convert any Chickasaws, but the two years that he spent in Georgia shaped him and Christianity profoundly. He gathered two dozen Savannah parishioners into "a sort of little society" that met weekly "to instruct and exhort one another." Wesley also paid regular visits to colonists near Savannah who lacked a pastor; a prototype of the itinerant preaching and circuit system that later characterized Methodism. Wesley became familiar with Moravianism in Georgia, kept close ties to Moravians after he returned to London, and visited the Moravian settlement in Germany. He later adapted Moravian rituals that became Methodist hallmarks: watch nights (midnight vigils), love feasts (quasi-sacramental meals), and letter days on which believers communicated their spiritual accomplishments to peers far away. Wesley fused the Moravian concept that one could convert instantly and Anglicanism's belief that salvation was attainable to all who sought it. Enthusiastic preaching increased Methodism's

Baptists. Two Stearns followers founded North America's first African Baptist church, which was reconstituted in 1772 under four black ministers.

Meanwhile, Indians in eastern North America experienced two distinct forms of religious awakening. One owed mostly to the work of colonists and European missionaries. Moravians established five mission towns for Indians between the 1740s and 1760s, the most significant of them in Pennsylvania. They baptized hundreds of Mahicans and Delawares, particularly women and children. Moravian women's participation in evangelization encouraged such conversions, as did similarities between Moravian and Indian beliefs. Moravians and Indians believed that dreams offered revelation and required careful interpretation. Moravians associated the shedding of blood with spiritual power. Indians believed that menstruating women were powerful, had to be isolated from their families, and barred from preparing food or taking part in community ceremonies. Indian women were also attracted to Moravians' portrayal of the Holy Spirit as Mother. Mahican and Delaware Moravians afforded their male kin better access to colonial networks and served to bridge Christian and non-Christian Indian communities.

Meanwhile, missionaries and itinerants won Indian converts in New England. In 1753, Eleazar Wheelock, a New Light Congregational minister, founded a free school in Connecticut for Indian children who, he envisioned, would become agents of spiritual popularity, particularly among working people in Britain and North America. Wesley disliked the style until he read Jonathan Edwards' account of a revival in Massachusetts.

Like the Moravians, Wesley eagerly sought converts among slaves, but he later parted ways with the Moravians by becoming a militant opponent of slavery. Wesley visited Carolina plantations and soon conceived the outlines of what became the Methodist practice for evangelizing enslaved people: target "the planters who were most receptive to his message," learn which slaves "were best inclined and understood English," and travel between plantations. Organized Methodism came to the Americas in Antigua around 1760. Preachers targeted enslaved people for conversion. In 1766, Robert Strawbridge built North America's first Methodist preaching house in Maryland. He recruited Jacob Toogood, a slave, to preach. Wesley drew from the works of the Pennsylvania Quaker Anthony Benezet for "Thoughts Upon Slavery," an essay that he published in 1774. Wesley denounced colonial slavery as "the vilest that ever saw the sun." The following year, his disciple Thomas Rankin was probably the first Methodist in North America to oppose slavery publicly, telling a Maryland audience that "the sins of Great Britain and her colonies had called aloud for vengeance," including "the dreadful sin of buying and selling the souls and bodies of the poor Africans." Methodists were among the new nation's sharpest critics of slavery until southern Methodists reconciled themselves to slaveholding in the early 1800s.

- In what ways did movement of people and ideas shape the development of Methodism?
- What impact did John Wesley's visit to North America have on the course that Methodism took when adherents began to seek converts in North America?

and cultural transformation among their peoples. Another New Light minister, James Davenport, converted many Narragansetts in the 1740s. Narragansetts soon built a separate church in which they practiced a form of Christianity that resembled their traditional beliefs. It emphasized visions rather than Scripture, guided by ministers who lacked a formal education.

Narragansett Christians in part reacted to discrimination that Indians confronted in New England. By the mid-1700s, most Old Lights and Anglicans had black and Indian worshippers sit in separate pews or galleries. Within seven years of its founding, Dartmouth College's white students drove out Indian pupils.

Other Indians experienced a religious awakening in which converts rejected Europeans and their ways. Such "nativists" concluded that Indians could regain spiritual and political power only by rejecting most of what Europeans had brought, including Christianity, manufactured goods, and alcohol. In 1737, Shawnees and Onondagas spoke of a vision that God had "driven the wild animals out of the country" to punish Indians for killing game to trade it for alcohol. Some had come to believe that Indians were a race distinct from Europeans and Africans. Delawares told a missionary in 1751 that "God first made three men and three women, viz: the indians, the negro, and the white man." Europeans were made last, so they "ought not to think themselves better than the Indians." These views particularly resonated in Upper Susquehanna and Ohio valley towns composed largely of Delawares and Shawnees exiled from Pennsylvania.

The Delaware **Neolin** was the most influential figure in this Indian awakening. In 1761, he urged that Indians "learn to live without any Trade or Connections with the White people." Two years later, Delaware councils resolved to train boys in traditional ways of warfare and adopt a ritual diet that included an herbal tea that induced vomiting to cleanse them of the "White people's ways and Nature." Neolin's words found receptive ears, especially among Indians alienated by British traders and fearful that British colonists would soon invade their lands. By the early 1750s, Indians knew that the Ohio Valley, whether they had claimed it since time immemorial or had recently been forced to move there, had become the focal point of the struggle between the British and French for supremacy in North America.

STUDY QUESTIONS FOR MINDS, SOULS, AND WALLETS

1. What impact did the circulation of goods and ideas have on British North America? In what ways did the flow of goods and ideas shape how colonists related to one another and to the British Empire?

2. What was the relationship between spiritual awakening and the movement of goods and ideas in North America between 1730 and 1763? Did the relationship between such awakening and flows of goods and ideas change depending on whether one was white, black, or Indian? Explain.

■ NORTH AMERICA AND THE FRENCH AND INDIAN WAR, 1754–1763

In 1754, skirmishes between British colonists, the French, and Indians in western Pennsylvania erupted into a world war. North America became the focus of British and French aims and the cause of war between the two colonial empires. The conflict, often known as the **French and Indian War** in the United States and the Seven Years' War in Europe, transformed North America politically and socially. Victory made Britain eastern North America's dominant power and sparked new tensions between imperial officials, colonists, and Indians.

The Struggle for the Ohio Valley

In the 1740s, the delicate balance of power between the British and French, Iroquois, and Indians of the Great Lakes that had long kept the peace in the Ohio Valley tottered. Immigration to British North America and colonial expansion pushed Indians, mostly Delawares and Shawnees, into the Ohio Valley and beyond the reach of Iroquois. In 1744, the Iroquois League ceded claims to the Ohio Valley to Virginia with the Treaty of Lancaster. By early 1745, Virginia had granted over 300,000 acres to a group of land speculators composed mainly of well-connected planters who soon called themselves the **Ohio Company of Virginia**. After King George's War ended, the Ohio Company sent surveyors to map the area and traders to sell to Indians. They found plenty of takers; the British offered a wider array of goods at better prices than the French.

French officials responded by staking their claim to the Ohio Valley. The Ohio River and its northern tributaries linked Quebec, Illinois, and Louisiana, so British control of the region would effectively cut French North America in two. In 1749, a French expedition planted lead plates bearing the fleur-de-lis, the symbol of Louis XV, along the Ohio River, in a bid to stake claim to the area. The French also had more effective ways to assert influence. One was a staple of French and Indian diplomacy: distribute subsidized trade goods to recruit Indian allies from the Great Lakes to attack Indians with ties to traders bearing British goods. Another was new: build a chain of forts to halt British encroachment. Soldiers completed the last and most important of these, Fort Duquesne, the site of today's Pittsburgh, in 1754.

Construction of French forts provoked panic among British colonists and imperial officials. In June 1754, representatives of seven colonies and of the Iroquois League met at Albany in a bid to keep Iroquois from siding with the French. The **Albany Congress** dissuaded Iroquois from becoming French allies but did little to unite colonial governments that prized their autonomy. A few months earlier, Virginia's government had appointed the young planter and surveyor **George Washington** to command 200 men and build Fort Necessity. The fort was meant to shadow Fort Duquesne and block the way to Maryland and Virginia. Washington had little military experience and had been put in charge of poorly trained soldiers and an underfunded operation.

He also proved to be a poor diplomat to Indians, most of who were inclined to stay out of the conflict or side with the French because the British had thousands of land-hungry colonists and seemed to pose the greater threat. Washington had few Indian allies. Those he had refused to heed him. In May 1754, Indian warriors under his direction killed and scalped a French officer and a dozen French soldiers who had surrendered to Washington. Two months later, French and Indian forces overran Fort Necessity, killing 30. The humiliated survivors trudged east as French soldiers torched what remained of British claims in the Ohio Valley. The war for the heart of eastern North America had begun.

The War in North America and in Europe

For three years, the war went badly for Britain and its colonies. Word of Washington's defeat prompted officials in London to send two regiments of British soldiers under the command of Edward Braddock. Braddock and his army, accompanied by Washington and colonial militiamen, headed for Fort Duquesne. Braddock's incompetent diplomacy drove most Indians to the French. In July 1755, the British approached the Monongahela River, marching down a narrow road in orderly columns. Their French, French Canadian, and Indian foes, concealed behind trees or rocks, attacked from all sides. The British colonists sensibly aped their enemy's tactics or fled. Braddock and the British regulars did neither. Their European tactical training equated standing one's ground with valor and courage. It got nearly 1,000 of them killed or wounded at the Monongahela, including Braddock, whose body the survivors buried as they retreated. Only one

BENJAMIN WEST, *THE DEATH OF GENERAL WOLFE,* **1770** West, a Pennsylvanian, painted this 11 years after British forces captured Quebec. It is highly allegorical; only the officer clutching the flag could have been with Wolfe when he died. British colonists found West's work compelling. They purchased thousands of copies, an indication of their eagerness to identify as Britons.

field aide, Washington, escaped the battle unscathed. The debacle exposed Pennsylvania, Maryland, and Virginia to Indian raids, triggering political turmoil in Pennsylvania as victims and fearful colonists clamored for protection.

The battle at the Monongahela underscored Indians' importance to French strategy. So did subsequent defeats inflicted on British and provincial troops in New York, a key battleground. Only one British official, William Johnson, appointed in 1755 to the newly created post of Indian Superintendent for the Northern Colonies, managed to recruit Indian allies and persuade them to fight. Johnson was married to a Mohawk woman, so he could call on Mohawks for help. They answered his pleas once before following an Iroquois League recommendation to stay out of the war.

By 1758, three developments turned the tide in the British Empire's favor. First, the French lost most of their Indian allies. In 1757, nearly 2,000 Indians, including about

SKY OF ASH Thomas Davies, *View of the Plundering of and Burning of the City of Grymross.* Many Acadians who escaped removal at the hands of British and British North American soldiers sought refuge in present-day New Brunswick. From there some Acadians waged guerrilla warfare against the British. In 1758, British forces destroyed many Acadian settlements, including Grimrose ("Grymross" above), and deported their residents.

1,000 from the Great Lakes and further west, helped to besiege Fort William Henry. The commander of French forces, the **Marquis de Montcalm,** negotiated the surrender of the British and provincial garrison and promised it safe passage to a nearby British fort. Montcalm behaved as if he were fighting in Europe and dealing with a defeated foe. His Indian allies, denied even the weapons that their enemy had handed over, reminded him that he was in America by killing nearly 200 provincial soldiers and camp followers and taking away hundreds. Great Lakes warriors did not heed French requests for help in large numbers again, particularly as the French proved increasingly unable to supply them with the firearms and other goods that they needed (Map 5.6).

Meanwhile, new British leaders plotted a different course. In 1757, **William Pitt** assumed charge of war policy as anxiety gripped Britain. The war had recently spread to Europe. Pitt authorized large payments to Hanover and Prussia, financed by British taxpayers, which would enable them to continue fighting. The Royal Navy, the world's mightiest, would raid French ports; disrupt France's oceanic supply lines; and seize its outposts in Africa, India, and North America. Pitt hoped to tie down French forces in Europe and force France to sacrifice its colonies and the revenue they generated. By the time Pitt resigned in 1761, his plan had succeeded brilliantly. His successors, however, were left to determine how to pay for it.

Finally, British victory in North America came largely because tens of thousands of colonists took up arms. In 1758, they comprised almost half of the nearly 50,000 men whom British commanders sent into battle. Provincial leaders from the colonies recruited most in a matter of months.

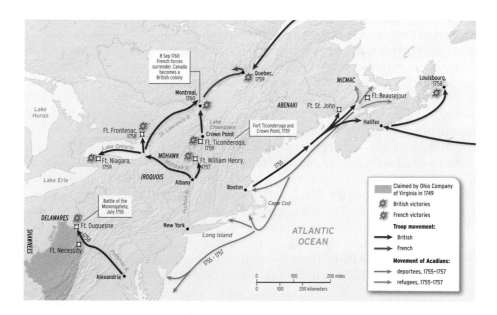

MAP 5.6 ▲ The Seven Years' War in Northeastern North America, 1754–1760
Together the Ohio Valley, upstate New York, and Canada comprised the bloodiest battleground of the Seven Years' War in North America. Shown here are the principal battles discussed in the text and when they occurred as well the routes that Acadian deportees and refugees took after the British invasion in 1755.

The British military advantage in North America arose from differences in how the English and French had colonized North America since the early 1600s. Massive immigration, high birthrates, and intensive resettlement of Indian lands gave the British a much larger potential fighting force in North America than the French. The French model of colonization—minimal and sporadic immigration, with extensive territorial claims backed by Indian alliances—could not match the British, who fielded twice as many troops in North America than the French. France counted on Indian allies to make up the difference. Once most Indians abandoned the war, British victory was a matter of time.

In 1758, Anglo-Americans won four key victories, three through combat and one through Indian diplomacy. The British took Louisbourg, key to France's naval defense of Canada, in July. A few weeks later, a force composed mainly of colonists captured Fort Frontenac, the key supply post to French forts and Indian allies to the west. An agreement concluded at the Treaty of Easton in October secured peace with Ohio Indians, above all the Delaware, in exchange for promises to bar colonization of their lands. With their supply lines cut and most Indian allies gone, French soldiers blew up Fort Duquesne. Anglo-Americans built a replacement and named it Fort Pitt.

French and Canadian forces retreated to Canada to await an Anglo-American invasion. It arrived in the summer of 1759, when troops commanded by **James Wolfe** besieged the city of Quebec. In September, they scaled the cliffs that guarded the city and engaged Montcalm's army. Within a day, the Anglo-Americans had won, although Wolfe and Montcalm died in battle. In April 1760, French forces surrounded Quebec, but British reinforcements soon broke the siege and effectively completed the conquest of Canada by taking Montreal in September. The war between European and Euro-American combatants in North America had ended.

The war between Britain, colonists, and Indians dragged on. In the Southeast, most Creeks chose to remain neutral. Abuse at the hands of British traders, British colonist violence, and incursions onto Cherokee lands had led Cherokee to side with the French in 1759. Colonists and British soldiers invaded Cherokee country two years later, burned 15 villages, and forced Cherokee leaders to cede land and acknowledge British sovereignty.

By then, the war outside Europe had shifted to the West Indies and Asia. The British captured Guadeloupe in 1759 and Martinique three years later. Only Saint-Domingue, the wealthiest plantation colony in the Americas, and Guyana remained of France's once-vast American empire. Between 1759 and 1761, the British East India Company won battles in India. In 1762, Spain entered the war on France's side. Britain retaliated by conquering Havana and Manila, capital of the Philippines.

In February 1763, Europeans agreed to end hostilities among themselves under the terms of the **Treaty of Paris**. The British emerged as the dominant European power in North America and the West Indies and seemed on their way to becoming the world's mightiest empire.

Britain Gains Control of Eastern North America

The French and Indian War opened new divisions in North America. The terms of the Treaty of Paris transformed eastern North America's political geography. France

EXILE OF THE ACADIANS FROM GRAND PRÉ.

EXILE OF THE ACADIANS FROM GRAND PRÉ This image depicts the mid 18th-century British expulsion of the Acadians from Grand Pré, their main settlement in Nova Scotia. Sympathy for the tragedy of the Acadians' forced migration out of British Canada was revived nearly one hundred years after it took place when Henry Wadsworth Longfellow published his poem "Evangeline," which depicted it. This British 19th-century engraving adopts Longfellow's view of the expulsion as a sentimental tragedy.

surrendered North America, swapping Canada for the return of Guadeloupe. France had lured the Spanish into the war by agreeing to cede Louisiana to them. The Treaty of Paris awarded control of that colony to Spain, which traded Florida to the British to regain control of Havana. The British Empire claimed almost all of North America east of the Mississippi.

For the vast majority of Indians west of the Mississippi, the new European division of North America changed little. In 1764, Spanish officials founded St. Louis to bolster their claim to the region, reap more profits from Indian trade, and clamp down on the Indian slave trade. Competition from British and French Canadian traders offered Indians of the upper Mississippi and Missouri river valleys better access to trade goods.

Most Indians who lived between the Mississippi and the Appalachians confronted a new challenge. They could no longer play two strong European rivals against one another as many had for decades. Worse, the more populous empire, the one that grew through intensive resettlement of Indian lands, had won, and its colonists wanted their land. Indians had two stark choices: accept British rule and gradually cede their lands or take up arms. Many opted to fight. Their success prompted the British to issue a decree in October 1763 that barred colonists from crossing the Appalachians, a decision that only widened divisions between imperial officials and colonists.

The French and Indian War elevated tensions between colonists and the empire for which they had proudly fought. To most British officials, the war's prosecution and steep costs demonstrated that they needed more control over colonial affairs, including tighter regulation of commerce. For colonists, particularly veterans, the war offered an often unsettling view of the British Empire. At least one-third of service-eligible men in Massachusetts fought in the French and Indian War. Their wartime experiences led many to think of themselves as a people distinct from the British officers who barked orders at them and the British regulars who marched alongside them. New England soldiers often saw British commanders as despots too eager to use the whip to maintain authority and British regulars as debauched sinners whose wickedness might cause New Englanders to lose God's favor in a war that they considered an epic struggle against Catholicism. This did not, however, make colonial veterans incipient revolutionaries. For years, their service made them identify more strongly as Britons and subjects of George III. But it also gave them perspectives and skills that some later drew on to resist imperial policies that they believed threatened their British liberties.

The war's prosecution also widened divisions among colonists. In 1756, many Quakers withdrew from Pennsylvania politics to protest the government's decision to support the war and dodge accusations that Quaker legislators had not budgeted enough to defend the colony adequately. Some left politics as part of a broader campaign for Quaker spiritual renewal, which required that Friends renounce activities that compromised core Quaker values.

A few Quaker reformers, particularly **John Woolman** and **Anthony Benezet**, targeted slavery. In 1753, Woolman denounced slaveholding as a violation of Quaker values. Benezet likened the Atlantic slave trade to Indians' taking of white captives during the French and Indian War. In 1758, the Philadelphia Yearly Meeting decided that Quaker monthly meetings should punish buyers and sellers of slaves. Meanwhile, Benezet lobbied against the Atlantic slave trade, recommending in 1771 that Britain outlaw it. Benezet's writings, and the relationships that he formed with activists in Britain, exported a campaign to abolish the Atlantic slave trade to the world's largest trafficker in enslaved Africans.

The French and Indian War permanently displaced tens of thousands of people. In 1755, New England and British soldiers stormed Nova Scotia. They aimed to secure what had for nearly 40 years been a British colony by deporting Acadians, who the British feared were a security risk because they were Catholic, spoke French, and often had kin ties to Micmac families. By year's end British soldiers had removed nearly 7,000 Acadians, torching their homes and fields and destroying the dikes that protected them from flooding during high tides. Some Acadians evaded British custody and sought shelter among Micmacs or Abenakis, while others moved to French Canada (Map 5.7).

British officials sent Acadians to 9 of the other 13 mainland colonies. Colonies that accepted Acadians scattered them across hundreds of townships, thinking that this would prevent them from aiding the French and compel them to assimilate. Most Acadians preferred to leave British America if they could not return to Nova Scotia.

MAP 5.7 ▲ Colonial Refugees and Exiles of the Seven Years' War, 1755–1765 British victories in the Seven Years' War forced thousands of colonists to leave their homes. This map shows the movement of Acadian deportees and refugees, thousands of whom began to relocate to Louisiana in 1765, as well as those of Hispanic, African, and Indian Floridians who fled British Florida for Cuba or Mexico.

TIMELINE 1727–1765

AMERICA	YEAR	THE WORLD
Junto founded in Philadelphia	**1727**	
First subscription library in British North America founded in Philadelphia	**1731**	**Mar** Treaty of Vienna signed, ending Anglo-French Alliance and beginning Anglo-Austrian Alliance
Parliament passes Hat Act	**1732**	
James Oglethorpe founds Georgia as colony to reform English debtors Parliament passes Molasses Act, placing duties on molasses imported to British colonies from French Caribbean **Nov** Gold Coast slaves rebel and seize most of St. John, Danish Virgin Islands	**1733**	
Jonathan Edwards leads religious revival in Massachusetts	**1734–1735**	
John Peter Zenger acquitted of seditious libel in New York, establishing precedent for press freedom	**1735**	
Slave conspiracy in Antigua results in execution of 88 slaves	**1736**	
Pennsylvania's proprietor makes "Walking Purchase" from Delawares	**1737**	**Sep** *The News Letter*, oldest English language newspaper still in publication, founded in Ireland
Gracia Real de Santa Teresa de Mose, a free black town, founded in Florida	**1738**	
Sep Stono Rebellion in South Carolina	**1739**	
War of Jenkins' Ear between British and Spanish Empire	**1739–1742**	
Evangelist George Whitefield completes first tour of British North America	**1739–1741**	
Parliament passes Plantation Act, streamlining naturalization in British American colonies South Carolina legislators enact new slave code	**1740**	
	1740–1741	Irish Famine kills 10% of population
Suspected slave conspirators tried and executed in New York City Moravians arrive in Pennsylvania and establish settlements at Bethlehem and Nazareth	**1741**	
Pamela, first novel published in British North America	**1742**	
Precursor to American Philosophical Society founded in Philadelphia	**1743**	
King George's War between British and French empires	**1744–1748**	
Massachusetts troops capture Louisbourg, Canada, from French	**1745**	

College of New Jersey (later Princeton) founded	**1746**	
End of King George's War spurs German emigrants from Rhineland to North America	**1749–1754**	
Parliament passes Iron Act Georgia's Trustees legalize slavery in colony	**1750**	Little Ice Age, a cool period covering several centuries, reaches its peak
Reverend Eleazar Wheelock admits Indians to Dartmouth College's Connecticut predecessor	**1753**	
Jun–Jul Albany Congress reaches treaty with Iroquois League and discusses potential union of British mainland colonies **Jul** French and Indian War begins, triggered by combat in western Pennsylvania between Virginia militia commanded by George Washington and French-Indian alliance	**1754**	
Jul British and provincial forces under command of General Edward Braddock defeated at Battle of Monongahela **Oct** 7,000 Acadians deported from Nova Scotia to British mainland colonies	**1755**	
	1756	Britain officially declares war on France
Prime Minister William Pitt revamps British war strategy **Aug** French forces capture Fort William Henry but alienate Indian allies	**1757**	British rule formally begins in India
May–Jul British and provincial forces besiege and capture Fort Louisbourg **Aug** British forces capture Fort Frontenac **Oct** Treaty of Easton makes peace between British authorities and Ohio Indians **Nov** French forces blow up Fort Duquesne to prevent British capture of it	**1758**	
Jun–Sep British forces under the command of Gen. James Wolfe besiege and conquer city of Quebec	**1759**	
Sep British forces capture Montreal, effectively ending war between British and French in North America	**1760**	**Oct** George II dies; his grandson George III becomes king of Britain
Spain declares war on British Empire; British forces capture Havana	**1762**	
Feb Treaty of Paris ends Seven Years' War: France cedes Louisiana to Spain; Spain cedes Florida to Britain; France cedes Canada, most of North America between Appalachians and Mississippi River, and four Caribbean islands to Britain **May** Pan-Indian alliance led by Pontiac (Ottawa) attacks Detroit to prevent British resettlement of Ohio Valley and Great Lakes region **Oct** George III issues Royal Proclamation barring colonists from settling west of Appalachians	**1763**	
Acadians begin to move to Louisiana	**1765**	

A few hundred Acadian men made it home, where they repaired dikes and reclaimed flooded lands for some of the thousands of New Englanders who moved to Nova Scotia during the 1760s. The next best option was to go to France or a French colony. Over 1,000 Acadians sailed to Saint-Domingue, resettled there by the French government. Nearly half of them left for Louisiana, where French officials remained in charge until 1766. There they began to call themselves Cajuns.

As Acadians dreamed of an American refuge, thousands of Floridians sailed away. British officials told free residents of Spanish Florida that they could stay and accept assurances of freedom of religion and respect for their property rights or sell what they owned and leave. Most left. Nearly 3,000 headed to Cuba between August 1763 and January 1764. They included Francisco Menéndez, his neighbors, and hundreds of Canary Islanders and Catalan soldiers who had recently arrived to defend Florida from the British. Hundreds of south Florida Indians also went to Cuba, whereas Floridians who fled Pensacola sought refuge in Mexico. Most were Spanish soldiers and their families. Others were Christian Yamasees, almost half of whom died en route before resettling in a separate town. Most refused to return when Spain regained control of Florida as a reward from the United States for supporting the American Revolution.

STUDY QUESTIONS FOR NORTH AMERICA AND THE FRENCH AND INDIAN WAR, 1754–1763

1. What explains French success early in the French and Indian War? What explains the British Empire's victory in the conflict?

2. What new divisions did the French and Indian War create in North America? Why did some of those divisions result in the movement of thousands from or within North America?

Summary

- Record levels of free and unfree immigration accelerated population growth in British North America and fostered political and cultural tensions within the colonies.
- British North American colonists, white and black, became vital consumers of imported goods and important participants in Atlantic intellectual and religious networks in ways that changed their understanding of who they were, while new Indian powers arose on the Great Plains and Indians in the Ohio Valley strove to reject the ways of the Euro-American world.
- The French and Indian War resulted in a British victory that altered North America's political map, creating new divisions within North America and forcing thousands to leave.

Key Terms and People

American Philosophical Society *165*
Benezet, Anthony *182*
Edwards, Jonathan *171*
Franklin, Benjamin *154*
gang system *168*
Maroons *162*
Marquis de Montcalm *179*
Methodists *171*
Moravians (United Brethren) *170*
Neolin *176*
Oglethorpe, James *161*
Ohio Company of Virginia *177*
Pitt, William *179*
Plantation Act of 1740 *156*

redemptioners *156*
revivalists *170*
French and Indian War
   (Seven Years' War) *176*
Stono Rebellion *162*
task system *168*
Treaty of Paris *180*
War of Jenkins' Ear *162*
Washington, George *177*
Wesley, John *174*
Wheatley, Phyllis *173*
Whitefield, George *171*
Wolfe, James *180*
Woolman, John *182*

Reviewing Chapter 5

1. Indians play a smaller role in this chapter than they did in previous chapters of *American Horizons*. Why?
2. "North America's relationship to the global circulation of people, goods, and ideas intensified between 1730 and 1763 but did not change fundamentally during that period." Do you agree? Explain, using specific examples from this chapter.
3. British North Americans considered themselves more British in 1763, even though they had never been more American. Why?

Further Reading

Breen, T. H. *The Marketplace of Revolution: How Consumer Politics Shaped American Independence*. New York: Oxford University Press, 2004. Details colonial Anglo-America's consumer revolution and links it to the American Revolution.

Faragher, John Mack. *A Great and Noble Scheme: The Tragic Story of the Expulsion of the French Acadians from Their American Homeland*. New York: W. W. Norton, 2005. An evocative overview of Acadian removal and of what happened to Acadians after they were expelled from their homeland.

Landers, Jane. *Black Society in Spanish Florida*. Urbana and Chicago: University of Illinois Press, 1999. Sharply contrasts slavery and freedom in Florida while under Spanish rule with slavery and freedom in the English colonies and in the states that bordered Florida.

Merritt, Jane T. *At the Crossroads: Indians and Empires on a Mid-Atlantic Frontier, 1700–1763*. Chapel Hill and London: University of North Carolina Press, 2003. Examines intercultural relations between Indians and European colonists in Pennsylvania in ways that are sensitive to gender as it explains why some Indians converted to Christianity while others rejected it.

Parrish, Susan Scott. *American Curiosity: Cultures of Natural History in the Colonial British Atlantic World*. Chapel Hill and London: University of North Carolina Press, 2006.

Explores and explains how British colonists' participation in scientific investigation of the natural world reinforced racist thought and helped to create an American identity.

Waldstreicher, David. *Runaway America: Benjamin Franklin, Slavery, and the American Revolution*. New York: Hill and Wang, 2004. A concise and engagingly written account of Franklin and the evolution of his views on slavery, focused on his activities as an entrepreneur and politician.

America In The World
PEOPLE, GOODS, IDEAS AND PRACTICES

CHAPTER 5: Battling for Souls, Minds, and the Heart of North America 1730–1763

PRIMARY SOURCES FOR CHAPTER 5

BATTLING FOR SOULS, MINDS, AND THE HEART OF NORTH AMERICA, 1730–1763

SOURCE 5.1

Future Residents of Gracia Real de Mose, Florida, Letter to Philip V, King of Spain (1738)

During the 18th and early 19th centuries, enslaved Africans and African Americans in South Carolina and Georgia sought freedom by fleeing south to Spanish-ruled Florida. Even though royal orders dating back to 1693 granted refuge and freedom to enslaved people who converted to Catholicism, Spanish colonists sometimes re-enslaved the fugitives. Francisco Menéndez, an African man who had escaped slavery in South Carolina, wrote petitions in Spanish that implored Philip V to intervene. In 1738, the royal governor recognized the freedom of all Carolina runaways, which prompted the letter of thanks to Philip V that appears below.

Source: Kathleen DuVal and John DuVal, eds., *Interpreting a Continent: Voices from Colonial America* (Lanham, MD: Rowman & Littlefield, 2009), 179–80. Translated from Audiencia de Santo Domingo 844, fol. 607, reel 15, P. K. Yonge Library, University of Florida, Gainesville.

My lord,

All the Black people who escaped from the English plantations, obedient and loyal slaves to Your Majesty, declare that Your Majesty has done us true charity in ordering us to be given freedom for having come to this country and for being Christian and following the true religion that saves us.

Disobeying a very high and sacred law, they bound us and made us slaves for many years, putting us through many miseries and much hunger. But obeying laws which Your Majesty decreed, the present Governor, Don Manuel de Montiano, has set us free, for which we greatly appreciate Your Majesty and thank him for this most royal kindness.

Likewise, the Governor has offered and assured us that he will establish a place for us, which is called Gracia Reál, where we may serve God and Your Majesty, cultivating the land so that there may be fruit in this country.

We promise Your Majesty that, whenever the opportunity arises, we will be the cruelest enemies to the English and will risk our lives in the service of Your Majesty, even to spilling the last drop of blood, in defense of the great crown of Spain and our holy faith.

Thus Your Majesty may order any amount of service from us because we are his faithful slaves all of our life and we will always pray Our Lord to guard Your Majesty's life and the life of all the Royal Family throughout the slow years that we poor people need.

Saint Augustine, Florida, 10 June 1738.

WORKING WITH SOURCE

1. What did the authors of this letter promise Philip V? Why did they make such a promise?

SOURCE 5.2

Canassatego (Onondaga), Excerpts from His Response to a Delaware Complaint Concerning the Walking Purchase (1742)

In 1736, the Iroquois League and Pennsylvania officials agreed that the Iroquois League would speak on behalf of all Indians who lived between the Iroquois homeland (in today's Upstate New York) and Philadelphia. The following year, Delaware Indians ceded about 1,200 square miles of land to Pennsylvania under the terms of the "Walking Purchase." Delawares issued a stream of protests concerning the "Walking Purchase" over the next few years, arguing that Pennsylvania officials had violated their agreement by dispatching runners along cleared and marked paths to claim as much territory as possible. In 1742, Onondaga chief and Iroquois spokesman Canassatego appeared at a treaty conference in Philadelphia and issued the following response to the Delaware delegation.

Source: Pennsylvania Colonial Records, vol. 4 (Harrisburg, PA: 1851), 578–80.

At a Council held at the Proprietors, July 12th.

PRESENT:

The Honble GEORGE THOMAS, Esqʳ, Lieutenant Governor.

James Logan,   Clement Plumsted,   ⎫
Thomas Laurence,   Abraham Taylor,   ⎬ *Esqrs.*
Robert Strettel,   ⎭

Mr. Richard Peters.

Canassatego,   ⎫
Skick Calamy, ⎬ *and sundry Chiefs of the six Nations.*

Sassonan and Delawares.

Nutimus and ffork Indians.

Pisquetoman,   ⎫
Cornelius Spring, ⎬ *Interpreters to the ffork Indians.*
Nicholas Scull,   ⎭

Canassatego said,

"Brethren, the Governor, and Council:

"The other Day you informed Us of the Misbehaviour of our Cousins the Delawares with respect to their continuing to Claim and refusing to remove from some Land on the River Delaware, notwithstanding their Ancestors had sold it by Deed under their Hands & Seals to the Proprietors for a valuable Consideration, upwards of fifty Years ago, and notwithstanding that they them[s]elves had about—Years ago, after a long and full Examination, ratified that Deed of their Ancestors, and given a fresh one under their Hands and Seals, and then you requested Us to remove them, enforcing your Request with a String of Wampum. Afterwards you laid on the Table by Conrad Weiser our own Letters, some of our Cousins' Letters, and the several Writings to prove the Charge against our Cousins, with a Draught of the Land in Dispute. We now tell You we have Perused all these several Papers. We see with our own Eyes that they have been a very unruly People, and are altogether in the wrong in their Dealings with You. We have concluded to remove them, and Oblige them to go over the River Delaware, and to quit all Claim to any Lands on this side for the future, since they have received Pay for them and it is gone through their Guts long ago. To confirm to You that we will see your Request Executed, we lay down this String of Wampum in return for your's."

Then turning to the Delawares, holding a Belt of Wampum in his Hand, he spoke to them as followeth:

"Cousins:

"Let this Belt of Wampum serve to Chastize You; You ought to be taken by the Hair of the Head and shak'd severely till you recover your Senses and become Sober; you don't know what Ground you stand on, nor what you are doing. Our Brother Onas'[1] Case is very just and plain, and his Intentions to preserve ffriendship; on the other Hand your Cause is bad, your Heart far from being upright, and you are maliciously bent to break the Chain of ffriendship with our Brother Onas. We have seen with our Eyes a Deed signed by nine of your Ancestors above fifty Years ago for this very Land, and a Release Sign'd not many Years since by some of your selves and Chiefs now living to the Number of 15 or Upwards. But how came you to take upon you to Sell Land at all? We conquer'd You, we made Women of you, you know you are Women, and can no more sell Land than Women. Nor is it fit you should have the Power of Selling Lands since you would abuse it. This Land that you Claim is gone through Your Guts. You have been furnished with Cloaths and Meat and Drink by the Goods paid you for it, and now You want it again like Children as you are. But what makes you sell Land in the Dark? Did you ever tell Us that you had sold this Land? did we ever receive any Part, even the Value of a Pipe Shank, from you for it? You have told Us a Blind story that you sent a Messenger to Us to inform Us of the Sale but he never came amongst Us, nor we never heard any thing about it. This is acting in the Dark, and very different from the Conduct our six Nations observe in their Sales of Land. On such Occasions they give Publick Notice and invite all the Indians of their united Nations, and give them a share of the Present they receive for their Lands. This is the behaviour of the wise United Nations, but we find you are none of our Blood. You Act a dishonest part not only in this but in other Matters. Your Ears are ever Open to slanderous Reports about our Brethren. You receive them with as much greediness as Lewd Woman receive the Embraces of Bad Men. And for all these reasons we charge You

---

[1]The Iroquois called William Penn "Onas" (which means "pen," a pun on his name) and also used the term to refer to subsequent leaders of Pennsylvania.

to remove instantly. We don't give you the liberty to think about it. You are Women; take the Advice of a Wise Man and remove imediately. You may return to the other side of Delaware where you came from, but we don't know whether, Considering how you have demean'd your selves, you will be permitted to live there, or whether you have not swallowed that Land down your Throats as well as the Land on this side. We, therefore, Assign you two Places to go—either to Wyomin or Shamokin. You may go to either of these Places, and then we shall have you more under our Eye, and shall see how You behave. Don't deliberate, but remove away and take this Belt of Wampum."

This being interpreted by Conrad Weiser into English, and by Cornelius Spring into the Delaware language, Canassatego taking a String of Wampum added further:

"After our just reproof and absolute Order to depart from the Land, you are now to take Notice of what we have further to say to you. This String of Wampum serves to forbid You, Your Children and Grand Children, to the latest Posterity, for ever medling in Land Affairs, neither you nor any who shall descend from You, are ever hereafter to presume to sell any Land, for which Purpose you are to Preserve this string in Memory of what your Uncles have this Day given You in Charge. We have some other Business to transact with our Brethren, and therefore depart the Council and consider what has been said to you."

WORKING WITH SOURCES

1. Why did Canassatego begin or end each statement by presenting wampum to the party he was addressing?

2. What did Canassatego want the Delawares to do? On what grounds did he support Pennsylvania's side in the Walking Purchase dispute and assert the Iroquois League's influence over the Delawares?

SOURCE 5.3

Benjamin Franklin, Excerpts from "Observations on the Increase of Mankind" (1751)

In 1751, Benjamin Franklin penned the essay "Observations on the Increase of Mankind," excerpts of which appear below. The passage of the Iron Act of 1750, which sought to restrict the development of colonial British North America's iron industry, seems to have prompted him to write it. Most of the essay focuses on population growth in the colonies, which, Franklin argued, made North America increasingly important to the economic development and strategic needs of the British Empire. The essay was first published in London in 1755. Franklin's political enemies capitalized on some of its contents a decade later, as Chapter 5 of the text discusses.

Source: Leonard W. Labaree, ed., *The Papers of Benjamin Franklin*, vol. 4 (New Haven, CT: Yale University Press, 1961), 225–34.

6. Land being thus plenty in America, and so cheap as that a labouring Man, that understands Husbandry, can in a short Time save Money enough to purchase a Piece of new Land sufficient for a Plantation, whereon he may subsist a Family; such are not afraid to marry; for if they even look far enough forward to consider how their Children when grown up are to be provided for, they see that more Land is to be had at Rates equally easy, all Circumstances considered.

7. Hence Marriages in America are more general, and more generally early, than in Europe. And if it is reckoned there, that there is but one Marriage per Annum among 100 Persons, perhaps we may here reckon two; and if in Europe they have but 4 Births to a Marriage (many of their Marriages being late) we may here reckon 8, of which if one half grow up, and our Marriages are made, reckoning one with another at 20 Years of Age, our People must at least be doubled every 20 Years.

8. But notwithstanding this Increase, so vast is the Territory of North-America, that it will require many Ages to settle it fully; and till it is fully settled, Labour will never be cheap here, where no Man continues long a Labourer for others, but gets a Plantation of his own, no Man continues long a Journeyman to a Trade, but goes among those new Settlers, and sets up for himself, &c. Hence Labour is no cheaper now, in Pennsylvania, than it was 30 Years ago, tho' so many Thousand labouring People have been imported.

9. The Danger therefore of these Colonies interfering with their Mother Country in Trades that depend on Labour, Manufactures, &c. is too remote to require the Attention of Great-Britain.

10. But in Proportion to the Increase of the Colonies, a vast Demand is growing for British Manufactures, a glorious Market wholly in the Power of Britain, in which Foreigners cannot interfere, which will increase in a short Time even beyond her Power of supplying, tho' her whole Trade should be to her Colonies: Therefore Britain should not too much restrain Manufactures in her Colonies. A wise and good Mother will not do it. To distress, is to weaken, and weakening the Children, weakens the whole Family. . . .

12. 'Tis an ill-grounded Opinion that by the Labour of Slaves, America may possibly vie in Cheapness of Manufactures with Britain. The Labour of Slaves can never be so cheap here as the Labour of working Men is in Britain. Any one may compute it. Interest of Money is in the Colonies from 6 to 10 per Cent. Slaves one with another cost £30 Sterling per Head. Reckon then the Interest of the first Purchase of a Slave, the Insurance or Risque on his Life, his Cloathing and Diet, Expences in his Sickness and Loss of Time, Loss by his Neglect of Business (Neglect is natural to the Man who is not to be benefited by his own Care or Diligence), Expence of a Driver to keep him at Work, and his Pilfering from Time to Time, almost every Slave being *by Nature* a Thief, and compare the whole Amount with the Wages of a Manufacturer of Iron or Wool in England, you will see that Labour is much cheaper there than it ever can be by Negroes here. Why then will Americans purchase Slaves? Because Slaves may be kept as long as a Man pleases, or has Occasion for their Labour; while hired Men are continually leaving their Master (often in the midst of his Business,) and setting up for themselves.

13. As the Increase of People depends on the Encouragement of Marriages, the following Things must diminish a Nation, viz. 1. The being conquered; for the Conquerors will engross as many Offices, and exact as much Tribute or Profit on the Labour of the conquered, as will maintain them in their new Establishment, and this diminishing the Subsistence of the Natives discourages their

Marriages, and so gradually diminishes them, while the Foreigners increase. 2. Loss of Territory. Thus the Britons being driven into Wales, and crowded together in a barren Country insufficient to support such great Numbers, diminished 'till the People bore a Proportion to the Produce, while the Saxons increas'd on their abandoned Lands; 'till the Island became full of English. And were the English now driven into Wales by some foreign Nation, there would in a few Years be no more Englishmen in Britain, than there are now People in Wales. 3. Loss of Trade. Manufactures exported, draw Subsistence from Foreign Countries for Numbers; who are thereby enabled to marry and raise Families. If the Nation be deprived of any Branch of Trade, and no new Employment is found for the People occupy'd in that Branch, it will also be soon deprived of so many People. 4. Loss of Food. Suppose a Nation has a Fishery, which not only employs great Numbers, but makes the Food and Subsistence of the People cheaper; If another Nation becomes Master of the Seas, and prevents the Fishery, the People will diminish in Proportion as the Loss of Employ, and Dearness of Provision, makes it more difficult to subsist a Family. 5. Bad Government and insecure Property. People not only leave such a Country, and settling Abroad incorporate with other Nations, lose their native Language, and become Foreigners; but the Industry of those that remain being discourag'd, the Quantity of Subsistence in the Country is lessen'd, and the Support of a Family becomes more difficult. So heavy Taxes tend to diminish a People. . . . 6. The Introduction of Slaves. The Negroes brought into the English Sugar Islands, have greatly diminish'd the Whites there; the Poor are by this Means depriv'd of Employment, while a few Families acquire vast Estates; which they spend on Foreign Luxuries, and educating their Children in the Habit of those Luxuries; the same Income is needed for the Support of one that might have maintain'd 100. The Whites who have Slaves, not labouring, are enfeebled, and therefore not so generally prolific; the Slaves being work'd too hard, and ill fed, their Constitutions are broken, and the Deaths among them are more than the Births; so that a continual Supply is needed from Africa. The Northern Colonies having few Slaves increase in Whites. Slaves also pejorate the Families that use them; the white Children become proud, disgusted with Labour, and being educated in Idleness, are rendered unfit to get a Living by Industry. . . .

21. The Importation of Foreigners into a Country that has as many Inhabitants as the present Employments and Provisions for Subsistence will bear; will be in the End no Increase of People; unless the New Comers have more Industry and Frugality than the Natives, and then they will provide more Subsistence, and increase in the Country; but they will gradually eat the Natives out. Nor is it necessary to bring in Foreigners to fill up any occasional Vacancy in a Country; for such Vacancy (if the Laws are good, § 14, 16) will soon be filled by natural Generation. Who can now find the Vacancy made in Sweden, France or other Warlike Nations, by the Plague of Heroism 40 Years ago; in France, by the Expulsion of the Protestants; in England, by the Settlement of her Colonies; or in Guinea, by 100 Years Exportation of Slaves, that has blacken'd half America? The thinness of Inhabitants in Spain is owing to National Pride and Idleness, and other Causes, rather than to the Expulsion of the Moors, or to the making of new Settlements.

22. There is in short, no Bound to the prolific Nature of Plants or Animals, but what is made by their crowding and interfering with each others Means of Subsistence. Was the Face of the Earth vacant of other Plants, it might be gradually sowed and overspread with one Kind only; as, for Instance, with

Fennel; and were it empty of other Inhabitants, it might in a few Ages be replenish'd from one Nation only; as, for Instance, with Englishmen. Thus there are suppos'd to be now upwards of One Million English Souls in North-America, (tho' 'tis thought scarce 80,000 have been brought over Sea) and yet perhaps there is not one the fewer in Britain, but rather many more, on Account of the Employment the Colonies afford to Manufacturers at Home. This Million doubling, suppose but once in 25 Years, will in another Century be more than the People of England, and the greatest Number of Englishmen will be on this Side the Water. What an Accession of Power to the British Empire by Sea as well as Land! What Increase of Trade and Navigation! What Numbers of Ships and Seamen! We have been here but little more than 100 Years, and yet the Force of our Privateers in the late War, united, was greater, both in Men and Guns, than that of the whole British Navy in Queen Elizabeth's Time. How important an Affair then to Britain, is the present Treaty for settling the Bounds between her Colonies and the French, and how careful should she be to secure Room enough, since on the Room depends so much the Increase of her People?

23. . . . And since Detachments of English from Britain sent to America, will have their Places at Home so soon supply'd and increase so largely here; why should the Palatine Boors be suffered to swarm into our Settlements, and by herding together establish their Language and Manners to the Exclusion of ours? Why should Pennsylvania, founded by the English, become a Colony of *Aliens,* who will shortly be so numerous as to Germanize us instead of our Anglifying them, and will never adopt our Language or Customs, any more than they can acquire our Complexion.

24. Which leads me to add one Remark: That the Number of purely white People in the World is proportionably very small. All Africa is black or tawny. Asia chiefly tawny. America (exclusive of the new Comers) wholly so. And in Europe, the Spaniards, Italians, French, Russians and Swedes, are generally of what we call a swarthy Complexion; as are the Germans also, the Saxons only excepted, who with the English, make the principal Body of White People on the Face of the Earth. I could wish their Numbers were increased. And while we are, as I may call it, *Scouring* our Planet, by clearing America of Woods, and so making this Side of our Globe reflect a brighter Light to the Eyes of Inhabitants in Mars or Venus, why should we in the Sight of Superior Beings, darken its People? why increase the Sons of Africa, by Planting them in America, where we have so fair an Opportunity, by excluding all Blacks and Tawneys, of increasing the lovely White and Red? But perhaps I am partial to the Complexion of my Country, for such Kind of Partiality is natural to Mankind.

WORKING WITH SOURCES

1. What were Franklin's views on slavery? In what ways do these views resemble those of the editors of the *Boston News-Letter*? In what ways do his views on slavery differ from those expressed in that document?

2. Why did Franklin take such a dim view of German immigration? How does his opposition to German immigration and slavery relate to his case for a more prominent role for colonists within the British Empire?

SOURCE 5.4

Diary of Hannah Heaton, Excerpts from Her Recollections of the Great Awakening (1750s)

Sometime in the 1750s, after she had married and resettled on a farm in North Haven, Connecticut, Hannah Heaton began to keep a diary in which she occasionally commented on her spiritual experiences and significant events such as the American Revolution. It seems that Heaton primarily saw the diary as a way to record and sustain her spiritual development. Later, she also came to view it as a way to instruct her children and have them remember her. Below are excerpts of Heaton's recollections of her conversion during the Great Awakening, when she was 20 years old.

Source: Barbara E. Lacey, ed., *The World of Hannah Heaton: The Diary of an Eighteenth-Century New England Farm Woman* (DeKalb, IL: Northern Illinois University Press, 2003), 6–9.

Now after a while i went over to new haven in the fall just before that great work of god began which was in the year 1741. There i heard mr tennant and mr whitefeild preach which awakened me much. Mr whitefeild laid down the marks of an unconverted person. O strange it was such preaching as i never heard before. Dont you said he when you are at the house of god long service should be over that your minds may be about your worldly conserns and pleasures. Is it not a wearines to you said he if one days serving god is so wearisom to you. How could you endure to be in heaven with him forever where nothing but praises are. He said if you was carried to heaven in this condition the first prayer you would make would be that yould might go into hell for that would be more agreeable to your natures. O thot i i have found it a wearines to me many a time over and over again. Then i began to think my nature must be changed but how to attain it i knew not. When i was coming from meeting to my quarters which was about 6 miles my company began to worry me to sing. I put them of till i feard they would be offended. . . . . I thot that was better than to sing a song but o they little thot how i felt. It was hard work for me to sing i felt in such distress in my mind but i went to frollicks all winter and stifeld the conviction i had of its being a soul ruining sin. I was much for fine cloaths and fashons. In the spring in may i went to middletown to keep election. One of the days while i was there i was at a tavern in a frolick. Then there come in a young man from long island belonging to the society that i did and told me how the work of god was carried on there and of several of my mates that was converted. My sister elisabeth also sent a letter. I trembled when i read it. She said her soul magnifyed the lord her spirit rejoysed in god her saviour. Her sighs was turned into songs the comforter is come. I had a strong impression upon my mind to go home which i did in a few days. As soon as i got into my fathers house young people come in and began to talk. Sister elisabeth began to cry over me because i had no intrest in christ. That i wonderd at but the next morning father examined me and i was forst to tell my experiences as wel as i could. He told me when i had done what a dreadful condition i was in. It took hold of my heart. I kept going to the meetings and was more and more concerned. And o what crying out there was among the people what shall i do to be saved. . . . O how i did invi toads or any creature that had no souls to perish eternally. Many a time i kneeled down to pray and my mouth was as it were stopt and i did vent out my anguish with tears and groans and a few broken speches. Now it cut me to think how i had spent my precious time in vanity and sin against god. My not regarding the sabbath no more was bitter to me now. . . . O how it cut me to think i could not get away from god but appear before him i must and i lived in daily expectation of it. Now sometimes it would be cast into my mind thus you need not be so conserned you are not so great a sinner as some are some have murdered and done dreadful things but you pray and go to meeting and god will not have a heart to send you to hell. This i thot was the devil trying to beat me of. . . .

I was such a loathsome sinner and he such a holy god sometimes i thot i was willing but he was not. I could hear of others finding mercy but o how it would strike me for i feard greatly that while others was taken i should be left. Now the promises in the scriptures was terror to me for i thot they belonged to the children of god. I had no part in them and i felt such an enmity against the way of salvation by christ. I could see no way to escape damnation. Now i began to feel like one lost in the woods. I knew not what to do nor what course to take for my heart began to grow hard. Now i could not cry and pray as before when i thot of hell. It did not terrify me as before it use to. Me thot i envied the very devils for they believed and trembled but i did not. Nothing now semd to help me. I grew worse and worse. . . . I thot it must be a gone case with me and i thot so the more because father never spoke one word to me about my soul in particular as i remember after he first examined me till after i had found comfort

which was about three weeaks after. It being in the year 1741 june 20 i was then i suppose in my twentieth year. It was the lord's day. I went to our separate meeting in the school house. . . .

Meeting being done i got away to go home. I thot i would not go to the night meeting which was to be at thomas sanfords for it would do me no good. I remember in the lot as i went i see strawberries and these thots past through my mind. I may as wel go to picking strawberries now as not its no matter what i do its a gone case with me. I fear i have committed the unpardonable sin and now herdned but as i was going home i considered at last. I turned and went to meeting. Soon after meeting began the power of god come down. Many were crying out the other side of the room what shall i do to be saved. I was immediately moved to pres through the multitude and went to them. A great melting of soul come up on me. I wept bitterly and pleaded hard for mercy mercy. Now i was brought to vew the justice of god due to me for my sin. It made me tremble my knees smote together then i thot of belshezer when he see the hand writing against him. It seemd to me i was a sinking down into hell. I thot the flor i stood on gave way and i was just a going but then i began to resign and as i resind my distres began to go of till i was perfectly easy quiet and calm. I could say lord it is just if i sink in to hell. I felt for a few moments like a creature dead. I was nothing i could do nothing nor i desired nothing. I had not so much as one desire for mercy left me but presently i heard one in the room say seek and you shall find come to me all you that are weary and heavy laden and i will give you rest. I began to feel a thirsting after christ and began to beg for mercy free mercy for jesus sake. Me thot i see jesus with the eyes of my soul stand up in heaven. A lovely god man with his arms open ready to receive me his face was full of smiles he lookt white and ruddy and was just such a saviour as my soul wanted every way suitable for me. O how it melted my heart to think he had been willing all this while to save me but i was not willing which i never believed before now. I cryed from the very heart to think what a tender herted savior i had been refusing how often i turned a deaf ear to his gracious calls and invitations. All that had kept me from him was my will. Jesus appeared altogether lovely to me now.

My heart went out with love and thankfulness and admiration. I cryed why me lord and leave so many. O what a fulnes was their in christ for others if they would come and give up their all to him. I went about the room and invited people to come to him.

WORKING WITH SOURCES

1. What, according to Heaton, prompted her conversion?
2. What did Heaton's conversion and the Great Awakening mean to her?

Empire and Resistance

On December 31, 1775, American Major General **Richard Montgomery** was killed while leading a failed invasion of Quebec by Continental Army soldiers. Montgomery attacked the Canadian capital city in a last-ditch effort to salvage the invasion that had stalled during a tough winter. The Continental Congress had hoped to force concessions from the British government by invading Canadian colonies. Instead, Montgomery died, and his fellow commander Benedict Arnold led a miserable retreat back to New England.

Montgomery was immediately hailed as a hero and martyr to the American cause of liberty. The Continental Congress authorized a huge public funeral in Philadelphia and built a monument to his memory. Ten years later Montgomery had become the subject of many other commemorations. American artist John Trumbull painted a heroic image of Montgomery's death that directly referenced a famous painting of the idolized British General James Wolfe, who had died in an attack on Quebec in the French and Indian War and was immortalized by painter Benjamin West. Even in fighting the British, Americans looked to British examples to define images of heroism.

Richard Montgomery was born into an aristocratic Dublin family, attended Trinity College, and joined the British army in time to fight against the French in Canada during the French and Indian War. He rose through the ranks from 1757 to 1763, serving in Canada, New York, Barbados, Martinique, and Cuba. By the end of the war, he was a respected captain in the British Army, one of the men who enforced the British empire with military power.

After the war, Montgomery befriended several members of Parliament in England who disagreed

< *The Death of General Montgomery in the Attack on Quebec, December 31, 1775* by John Trumbull, oil on canvas, 1786.

with their government's efforts to tax the American colonies. Growing disgruntled with the military hierarchy, Montgomery moved to New York in 1773, where he married Janet Livingston, a member of one of the colony's wealthiest families. Montgomery was elected to the New York legislature, where he voiced his opposition to British crackdowns on the colonies. Montgomery was a natural choice to be appointed a commander when the Continental Army formed in June 1775. When Montgomery was killed in Quebec, this time fighting *against* the British Army, he was one of the most experienced and promising military commanders in the American army.

As an American hero who until recently had been a British army officer, Richard Montgomery was in many ways the perfect symbol of how resistance began to undermine the British empire in North America between 1763 and 1775. Many American colonists had strong ties to Britain or had recently emigrated, and they mostly considered themselves obedient subjects of the British crown at the end of the French and Indian War. Yet the series of British taxes and government restrictions imposed on the colonies after the war convinced many Americans that the time had come to throw off imperial control. British military presence in North American heightened the tension.

Between 1763 and 1776, both the British and Spanish empires sought increased control over their North American subjects. North Americans, many of whom like Montgomery had cast off old identities to feel more "American," challenged European control. Spain was able to maintain control and spread its empire, but in the British case a cycle of protest and reaction would lead to a full-scale war and to the United States of America declaring its independence.

◼ ENGLISH AND SPANISH IMPERIAL REFORM

The French and Indian War ended in 1763, won by two newly crowned kings. George III became king of Britain in 1760, while Charles III was crowned in Spain in 1759. Both kings won substantial new colonial territory from France in the war and substantial financial burdens along with it. Besides an estimated £140,000,000 in war debt, it cost Britain about £300,000 per year to defend the North American territories. British and Spanish officials both began attempting to recover some costs from the profits of the colonies themselves as well as trying to calm internal conflicts. The new policies from new kings unleashed many unintended consequences in North America. Spanish royal officials consolidated their control over New Spain and managed to expand their territory despite some colonist resistance. Canadian and Caribbean colonists remained loyal to the British crown, in part because some were granted direct parliamentary representation, but many American colonists resisted imperial reforms and became rebellious.

Transatlantic Trade as an Engine of Conflict

Each region of the British colonies had its own economic character, but trade was central to all of them. New England shipbuilding and lumber equipped the navy that policed much of the rest of the British empire and provided barrels for the rum trade, and New England fishermen fed Europe with 240 million pounds of cod and mackerel each year. The Mid-Atlantic colonies added iron production, fur trading, and shipbuilding to their trade in agricultural products, and Quaker and Jewish merchants relying on transatlantic religious and kinship networks grew especially prosperous. Maryland and Virginia produced tobacco, a staple crop since the 17th century that made up more than 25 percent of all American exports by

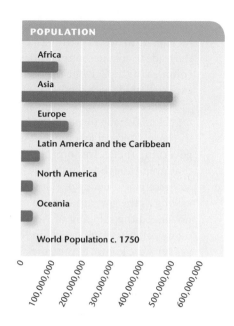

POPULATION

Africa

Asia

Europe

Latin America and the Caribbean

North America

Oceania

World Population c. 1750

0   100,000,000   200,000,000   300,000,000   400,000,000   500,000,000   600,000,000

PORTRAIT OF GEORGE III
George III assumed the throne of Great Britain in 1760, and he reigned as king longer than any previous British monarch, until 1820. The beginning of George III's reign was marked by the British defeat of the French in the Seven Years' War, but his keen regard for royal privilege was soon tested by the American Revolution.

the 1770s, whereas the Carolinas and Georgia contributed pine tar, indigo, and rice. Merchants in every colony also engaged in the slave trade. Britain sought to monopolize the trade of colonial commodities with Continental Europe and with Spanish and French colonies in the Caribbean. Because Americans imported 30 percent more than they exported, trade with the West Indies would help finance trade deficits elsewhere.

Since the 1660s, the British Parliament had imposed a series of controls and taxes on colonial trade through the **Navigation Acts**. But officials had not strictly enforced the laws. Colonial assemblies and merchants had by the 1760s become accustomed to governing themselves on trade matters. Trade in the British colonies was so lucrative that even though smuggling ran rampant, the government enjoyed sufficient revenue to encourage a policy of salutary neglect (ignoring infractions of the Navigation Acts as long as the government still made hefty profits). The British government largely monopolized the shipping of American trade goods to Europe and the West Indies, and many colonists were deeply indebted to English and Scottish wholesalers (or "factors" as they were known at the time). The colonial population doubled from 1 million in 1750 to 2 million in 1770, and Great Britain made good money both importing from and exporting to that growing population.

As transatlantic trade grew, so did North American cities. By 1775, Boston, New York, Newport, Philadelphia, and Charleston held more than 9,000 people, and each was a fast-growing commercial center. These cities, and a host of smaller ones, housed the legal, political, and financial institutions that facilitated imperial trade. In cities, colonists of different religions, income levels, and backgrounds lived close together. Boston, Philadelphia, and New York all experienced a sharp growth in poverty during the 1750s and 1760s. Urban trade and the close contact between people from different ends of the social spectrum (from slaves to artisans to merchants and imperial officials) would help to make colonial cities centers of political mobilization in the 1770s (Map 6.1).

The debts incurred by the British in the Seven Years' War caused British officials to renew their interest in North American trade when George Grenville became prime minister, first lord of the treasury, and chancellor of the exchequer in April 1763. Grenville enacted a series of policies that touched off colonial resistance. Grenville sought to lower the domestic tax burden in England by raising revenues from the colonies. He moved to enforce and expand trade regulations and invested new power in colonial customs officials, who were supposed to collect duties under the 1733 Molasses Act, which often went unpaid. By 1764, colonial exports to Britain reached £1.5 million annually, and Grenville hoped to increase the government's share.

Grenville's Program

Grenville moved the Sugar Act through Parliament in 1764. It was a clever piece of legislation designed to raise revenue through strict enforcement of trade taxes on the American colonies, even as it lowered many previous trade duties. The Sugar Act increased taxes not only on sugar but also on coffee, coconuts, whale fins, silk, and animal hides. The act also forbade American colonists from importing rum from any non-British source. Many colonists smuggled molasses from Spanish and French Caribbean islands to avoid paying taxes, and smuggled goods were often much cheaper than legal ones. Grenville established a new vice-admiralty court at Halifax, Nova Scotia, to seize

MAP 6.1 ▲ Ethnic Diversity The British colonies in North America were marked by an unusually high level of ethnic and racial diversity.

Table 6.1 Imperial Taxes in the 1760s and 1770s

Parliament passed a series of taxes on the North American colonies that sparked resistance and helped to propel the American Revolution.

Year	Legislation
1764	Sugar Act
1765	Stamp Act
1766	Declaratory Act
1767	Townshend Revenue Acts
1773	Tea Act
1774	Coercive or Intolerable Acts Boston Port Bill Massachusetts Government Act Quartering Act Quebec Act

any ships caught smuggling goods between the British American colonies and the French West Indies. Grenville also expanded restrictions on colonial paper money. The 1764 Currency Act required that both British trade merchants and trade taxes had to be paid in hard currency backed by precious metals. The colony of Virginia had tried to evade paying £250,000 in war debt by printing more paper money. These restrictions particularly affected tobacco farmers in the Chesapeake region who ran up huge debts with the Scottish trade firms (Table 6.1).

Grenville's legislation allowed for some expansion in colonial trade, including increases in rice exports from South Carolina to Latin America and New England timber exports to Ireland and Portugal. But stricter tax enforcement raised fears of overarching imperial control among many colonial residents. Elected assemblies in New York and North Carolina protested the Sugar Act on the basis that they had not been allowed to vote for taxes imposed on them by Parliament. But their protests were merely mild precursors of stiffer resistance yet to come.

Pontiac's Rebellion

As it tightened control on its colonial subjects, the British government took an even harder line in dealing with the Indian peoples who surrounded its colonies. Indians stretching from northern Canada to Florida were dismayed by the British triumph in 1763. Many had better trade, political, and personal relationships with the French than the British. They also feared that British officials and settlers would seize additional land. Sir Jeffrey Amherst, the commander-in-chief of the British forces in the imperial war who had a particularly bad reputation for subduing Indians, remained in charge as governor general of British North America after 1763. Amherst imposed new restrictions on Indian fur traders and aggressively seized Seneca lands. **Pontiac**, an Ottawa chief, interpreted Delaware prophet Neolin' s message of indigenous spiritual revival in military terms. He declared that the creator mandated resistance to "those who come to trouble your lands,—drive them out, make war upon them."

Pontiac did just that in the spring of 1763. He gathered forces from different groups of Ohio Valley and Great Lakes Indians who wished to keep British settlers from the land between the Allegheny Mountains and the Mississippi River and to drive British military forces back east of the Alleghenies. Beginning in May, Pontiac assaulted Detroit while his allied Potawatomie, Miami, Huron, Mingo, Ojibwa, and Shawnee forces attacked 11 different British forts and a number of settler communities. British superintendant of Indian affairs, Sir William Johnson, estimated the Indian population of the area to be as low as 50,000. Nonetheless the 3,500 warriors allied to Pontiac were well matched against a roughly equal number of British troops. Pontiac's forces captured most of the forts they attacked, but by fall their food and ammunition ran low—and many were afflicted with smallpox, in part spread by British troops who intentionally traded infected blankets.

In October 1763, London tried to deal with the rising violence by sending reinforcements. King George III issued the **Proclamation of 1763** that prohibited almost all settlement west of the Appalachian Mountains and restricted land sales to the east (Map 6.2). Britain also sought to license traders, who would be required to behave

MAP 6.2 ▲ North America in 1763 This map shows the line drawn in the Proclamation of 1763 and depicts the major clashes during Pontiac's Rebellion.

more favorably toward Indian suppliers and customers. But many British settlers simply ignored the Proclamation and continued to settle in Western territories occupied by Indians. Pontiac and many of his supporters concluded a peace agreement with the British in 1766, while thousands of settlers poured into their territories by the mid-1770s.

Bourbon Reforms

The Spanish government was more successful at centralizing control and reforming its empire in North America after 1763. In the peace of 1763 that settled the global war for empire, Spain acquired the French territory west of the Mississippi River and the city of New Orleans but traded possession of Florida to Britain in exchange for Havana, Cuba, which the British had occupied in 1762. Charles III (a member of the Bourbon dynasty that took control of the Spanish crown in the 1710s) and a group of reforming bureaucrats influenced by ideas of the Iberian Enlightenment sought to rebuild centralized control over North and South America. The Bourbon Reforms (as their actions came to be called) also aimed to increase Spanish revenues and control over institutions of the Catholic Church.

Charles III appointed José de Gálvez, after whom Galveston, Texas, is named, as Minister of the Indies, and Gálvez immediately sought to reduce the authority of Creole families who governed the mixed-race and indigenous populations in Spanish America. He claimed they were "too bound by ties of family and faction in the New World" to govern well. Gálvez and other officials tried to reform almost every area of imperial life: administrative, economic, and religious. Gálvez travelled to Cuba and Mexico to impose new regulations that raised greater revenue from trade customs, mining, and Indian tribute payments. In 1765, the Spanish crown broke up colonial trade monopolies long enjoyed by Seville and Cádiz merchants and increased taxes on merchants allowed into colonial markets. Gálvez installed Spanish salaried officials to collect taxes directly and imposed a state-sponsored monopoly on tobacco trading.

Several groups resisted the Bourbon Reforms. In addition to unrest among Indians, slaves, and mixed-race peasant farmers, imperial officials had to keep Creole elites from striking against royal authority. Jesuits, Catholic friars who had played a large role for hundreds of years in establishing the Spanish empire, now saw their economic and even their spiritual power challenged by Charles's royal decrees and colonial inspectors. When Jesuits resisted the Bourbon Reforms, Charles III expelled the 2,200 Jesuits from Spanish America in 1767. This expulsion set the stage for the reemergence of the Franciscan order in North America. The Franciscans would spread the Spanish empire further by building a system of missions in California and expanding their missions in Texas and New Mexico in decades to follow.

The Enlightenment and Colonial Identity

As the Spanish and English empires in North America underwent reforms in the 1760s, the European Enlightenment influenced both European leaders and their colonial opponents. The Enlightenment began in 17th-century France and Britain as an intellectual movement that emphasized the powers of reason, observation, and experience to explain the natural and social worlds. The ideas of Enlightenment thinkers influenced social and economic reform, science, philosophy, and social and political theory. Principles of human rights and individualism circulated in books, pamphlets, and newspapers throughout North America, especially in the British colonies. The works of English politician and philosopher **John Locke**, especially his *Two Treatises on Government* (1690), argued that governments must protect the rights of individuals to pursue life, liberty, and property. Scottish writers Francis Hutcheson and David Hume emphasized the potential of individuals to pursue moral progress, especially in a commercial age. The French writers who most influenced British North Americans were Voltaire and Montesquieu, whose *Spirit of the Laws* (1748) became a well-read guide on how to create a republic, a representative government with separation of powers.

Most British American colonists in 1763 saw themselves as part of the empire of British liberty, a view enhanced by Enlightenment principles. They believed that the British government was a bastion of liberty and property rights, and they revered the powerful check that Parliament could provide on royal authority in the British system of mixed government. But whereas Enlightenment ideals strengthened their allegiance to empire, they also exposed the colonies' economic and political dependence, leading some to oppose Great Britain. American colonists became fascinated with British writers who extolled more radical forms of republican government, such as Algernon Sidney, John Trenchard, and Thomas Gordon. Their republican ideas influenced colonists who viewed parliamentary and royal crackdowns as threats to liberty. Spanish Bourbon reformers were influenced by Montesquieu and by Spanish Enlightenment thinkers to apply rationalist principles to their reform efforts, but the Jesuits who opposed them cited more traditional Catholic doctrines in defense of church power.

Americans who opposed British taxes during the imperial crisis called themselves **Whigs** after the opposition political party in England that stood against excesses of centralized royal power. Learned Americans, interested in pursuing and promoting enlightened scientific knowledge, founded the American Philosophical Society in Philadelphia in 1769. **Benjamin Franklin**, David Rittenhouse, and John Bartram, three of its founders, were also internationally known scientists who belonged to the most important British scientific society, the Royal Society of London. But Franklin and several other founders of the American Philosophical Society would soon become leaders of colonial resistance to Britain.

STUDY QUESTIONS FOR ENGLISH AND SPANISH IMPERIAL REFORM

1. In what ways were British and Spanish colonial reforms similar or different?
2. Why did Pontiac's Rebellion help lead to the Proclamation of 1763?

◼ STAMP ACT AND RESISTANCE

When the British Parliament and Prime Minister Grenville imposed direct taxes on American colonists in 1764 and 1765, they galvanized colonial protest movements. Americans were used to taxing themselves, and they objected to change. The 1765

Stamp Act, which taxed paper products and documents, inaugurated a new era of resistance in the British colonies. Maryland lawyer Daniel Dulany urged fellow colonists during the Stamp Act crisis: "Instead of moping . . . and whining to excite compassion; in such a situation we ought with spirit, and vigour, and alacrity, to bid defiance to tyranny, by exposing its impotence." Men and women of various social classes across British North America heeded his call to defiance, and Parliament faced a resistance movement more widespread and coordinated than any they had seen before.

Parliamentary Action

In the months leading up to the Stamp Act's passage in March 1765, eight colonial assemblies sent petitions to Parliament in protest. But Grenville was determined to raise funds and to assert imperial authority. The bill assessed, for the first time, a unified tax that would fall on all British colonists across boundary lines. Grenville argued before Parliament that Americans were "virtually" represented in that body.

The Stamp Act taxed paper, shipping and legal documents, playing cards, dice, newspapers, pamphlets, almanacs, and calendars. Although the tax was approximately 30 percent lower than similar taxes within Great Britain, the amount mattered little to those who objected to what they saw as a change in Parliamentary authority, from the regulation of trade to direct taxation. To enforce the taxes, the British government appointed stamp "distributors" in each colony, chosen from among the colonial population to collect the taxes.

Protest and Repeal

When word of the Stamp Act reached the colonies, the Virginia House of Burgesses adopted resolutions of protest proposed by **Patrick Henry**. Virginia's Royal Governor, Francis Fauquier, dissolved the assembly rather than let protest grow. The stamp distributors provided a target for colonial resistance to the Stamp Act. In August 1765, after Andrew Oliver, the brother-in-law of Massachusetts Royal Lieutenant Governor Thomas Hutchinson, agreed to become the Stamp Distributor in that colony, a crowd in Boston hanged him in effigy from what became known as "liberty tree." A crowd led by a poor shoemaker, Seven Years' War veteran **Ebenezer MacIntosh**, then attacked Oliver's office and his house. The following day, Oliver resigned his post as stamp tax collector. Similar actions followed across the colonies over the next few months.

Crowd violence against British authority spread. In Boston, residents attacked officials of the royal admiralty courts and destroyed the house of Lieutenant Governor Hutchinson. Despite their traditional lack of shared political interests, both rich and poor people joined the protests, which worried colonial officials. A group of well-off Bostonian craftsmen calling themselves "The Loyal Nine" organized many actions in Massachusetts; while in Newport, Rhode Island, John Webber, a young transient, led the protests of local merchants. Groups of Stamp Act protesters soon began calling themselves "**Sons of Liberty**." The Sons of Liberty coordinated crowd actions, petitions, pamphlets, and consumer boycotts, and spread awareness of colonial protests between colonies. One of leaders of the Boston Sons of Liberty, **Samuel Adams**, claimed that British subjects would have pursued the same strategies if they saw "their essential Unalienable Rights . . . invaded by Parliament."

STAMP ACT Publisher William Bradford put this image on the front page of his *Pennsylvania Journal and Weekly Advertiser* newspaper on October 24, 1765 as part of the protest against the tax provisions of the Stamp Act. The Act required all printed material, including newspapers, to affix a "stamp" certifying that the proper taxes had been paid to British officials. Bradford's menacing skull-and-crossbones image reinforced the message that some colonists would be willing to resist the tax strenuously, even violently.

SAMUEL ADAMS Adams was a member of the Boston Town Meeting and the Massachusetts House of Representatives when he began to coordinate protests to increased British taxation and colonial control in the 1760s. Credited as one of the founders of the "Sons of Liberty," Adams circulated letters to other colonies calling for solidarity and protest against British authority. He became a member of the Continental Congress and later served as governor of Massachusetts in the 1790s.

In addition to popular protest, first the Virginia House of Burgesses and then other colonial assemblies passed legislation opposing the Stamp Act. The Massachusetts legislature called on other colonies to appoint delegates to a meeting in New York in October 1765. Twenty-seven delegates from nine colonies met for two weeks and passed a series of resolutions insisting that although colonial subjects owed allegiance to king and parliament, they were "entitled to all the inherent rights and liberties of his natural born subjects within the kingdom of Great-Britain." The Stamp Act Congress also protested in petitions to the British against taxation without representation while acknowledging obedience to the government. Ultimately, the actions of the Stamp Act Congress held no legal force, but they demonstrated an unprecedented level of cooperation among colonies and a strong resolution to resist taxation.

In the midst of the Stamp Act protests, George III replaced Grenville as prime minister, appointing the Marquis of Rockingham in July 1765. Rockingham, who aligned himself with the Whig party in Parliament, faced the immediate challenge of how to quell the unrest. The commander of British military forces in the colonies, General **Thomas Gage**, told the government that he lacked the time, resources, and troops to subdue the opposition, as such a wide range of the populace seemed to be involved. In addition to resisting the Stamp Act through crowd action and legislative protest, colonists in British America also began to organize boycotts of British trade goods. Their efforts increased fears among British merchants that an economic downturn might worsen. Rockingham faced a difficult choice in Parliament, especially after Whig leader **William Pitt** declared that Parliament had no right to tax the unrepresented colonists. Rockingham realized that enforcement of the tax had become impossible. On March 1, 1766, Parliament repealed the Stamp Act.

Empire and Authority

Although Parliament repealed the Stamp Act, Britain retained its authority to tax the colonies. The debate over repeal prompted discussion in both Parliament and in the colonies about the nature and limits of British sovereignty. But even parliamentarians friendly to the colonists' tax resistance, such as Pitt, were not willing to concede ultimate authority. Worried that Americans would take the wrong message from the repeal of the Stamp Act, Parliament passed the Declaratory Act. This new act reasserted the British right to control the colonies and pass laws "in all cases whatsoever," a phrase that echoed a declaratory act used to emphasize English control of Ireland in 1719. British commentators also stressed that the king's royal authority united all subjects of the crown throughout the empire, and most Americans agreed in 1766. Even protestor John Dickinson wrote that Americans admired their "excellent prince" in whose "good dispositions they could confide."

Apart from the Stamp Act, tensions inside the colonies provoked conflicts over imperial authority. In several colonies, conflict between eastern and western inhabitants over land rights, political representation, and Indian policy caused trouble for imperial officials. Pontiac's War had increased tensions, particularly in Pennsylvania. In 1763 and 1764, a group of armed men in western Pennsylvania calling themselves the "Paxton Boys" attacked Susquehannock Indians (also known as Conestoga) who had been guaranteed protection by the crown and by the royal government in Philadelphia. Benjamin Franklin negotiated a compromise when 600 armed westerners marched on the capital to protest the Paxton Boys' indictment. As a result, the Pennsylvania assembly granted the western part of the colony greater representation, which proved that armed protest could gain political representation. In the following years, groups of armed "regulators," farmers from western North Carolina, marched against imperial officials who tried to enforce taxes and legal judgments against them. Regulators destroyed the houses of North Carolina's royal governor William Tryon and Superior Court judge Richard Henderson.

This kind of unrest led Parliament to pass the first Quartering Act in 1765, authorizing British military forces to be permanently housed in the colonies—at the expense of colonists. In the midst of their resistance to the Stamp Act, many colonists refused to comply with the requirement to house and feed British troops. Colonists resented British troops. The Sons of Liberty in Charleston, South Carolina, argued in newspapers that they were willing and able to keep the peace themselves—even as they resisted imperial authority.

STUDY QUESTIONS FOR STAMP ACT AND RESISTANCE

1. Why did the colonial resistance movement continue, despite the Stamp Act's repeal?
2. In what ways did resistance to British taxation cause British North Americans to work together?

◼ CONSUMER RESISTANCE

Britain was expanding as a consumer society by the mid-18th century, and many American colonists wanted to emulate the British taste in clothing, furniture, and housing. Tied to the British empire through education, trade, and reverence for English liberty, Americans also found themselves enmeshed in a common world of goods and the credit relationships that enabled their circulation. Ironically, this developing consumer society in the colonies also provided a powerful new strategy of resistance during the rising tensions of imperial conflict after 1765. During the 1760s, the American population grew by an astonishing 40 percent; and, between 1700 and 1770, the per capita American expenditure on British goods grew by 20 percent. These growth trends meant that American consumers held enormous economic clout. When they began collectively to exercise that clout to protest British control and taxation, they helped accelerate an imperial crisis.

Townshend Duties

In June 1767, the British Parliament passed a new series of taxes that emphasized their resolve to legislate for the colonies "in all cases whatsoever," as the Declaratory Act stated. The annual cost of keeping troops in North America reached £700,000 (over $76 million today). Despite the fact that the Whig faction in charge of the British government was more sympathetic to American objections to "internal" taxation, they still sought to increase government revenue through a series of new taxes on trade. Chancellor of the Exchequer Charles Townshend ushered a series of taxes through Parliament known as the **Townshend Acts** or "Townshend Duties." These taxes hit a variety of commodities central to the transatlantic colonial trade: tea, paper, lead, glass, and paint. The acts also continued a previous tax on molasses, the essential product used to manufacture rum, although at a lower rate.

Along with the new taxes, Parliament continued to press for stricter enforcement of trade duties. The British treasury department created an American Board of Customs in Boston staffed by royal appointees. Vice-admiralty courts were established at Boston, Philadelphia, and Charleston and granted the authority to try smugglers without any local jury. The British government also centralized oversight of the colonies and instructed colonial governors to impose control over elected colonial assemblies. The presence of British troops in major American cities, under the terms of the 1765 Quartering Act, emphasized that military power might be used to enhance this new imperial control, and Parliament further authorized soldiers to be forcibly housed in private homes. When the New York assembly refused to enforce the Quartering Act, Parliament passed a restraining act that suspended its legislative authority until it complied. When considering the bill to discipline New York, Charles Townshend told Parliament that "The superiority of the mother country can at no time be better exerted than now."

The Non-Importation Movement

Colonists who opposed British taxation immediately responded to the Townshend Duties by renewing their collective action against the "superiority of the mother country." By October 1767, when news of the acts spread, men and women in Boston and elsewhere had started to discuss boycotting British imports. By the time the new taxes went into effect in November 1767, many American colonists had already pledged to avoid purchasing British goods and vowed to make do with their own homemade items and homespun cloth. By the spring of 1768, the non-importation movement had spread from Boston to New York, Philadelphia, Charleston, and other port cities. John Dickinson argued in his popular 1768 pamphlet series *Letters from a Farmer in Pennsylvania* that Parliament could regulate trade but that colonists would not submit to Parliamentary taxation of any kind. Samuel Adams drafted a petition to King George III, passed by the Massachusetts legislature in January 1768 and subsequently endorsed by Virginia and other colonial assemblies, that protested "taxation without representation" and called for colonies to coordinate their resistance.

Britain largely ignored the protests by colonial assemblies throughout 1768, and so the non-importation movement spread. In 1769, groups in several colonies signed formal non-importation agreements, called "associations," and the Sons of Liberty and other organizations who had protested the Stamp Act reemerged. In New England and the Middle Colonies, merchants led the non-importation movement, while in the Southern colonies associations of merchants, traders, politicians, and small farmers held meetings to endorse even broader boycotts. Several colonial governments—including the Boston Town Meeting and the Connecticut, New Jersey, and New York assemblies— passed resolutions supporting non-importation. Non-importation drastically reduced the trade of sugar into the North American colonies and increased hardship where sugar was produced in the West Indies, causing thousands of enslaved people to starve. But the British continued to ignore the boycotts.

Although broadly based, the non-importation movement fostered bitter disputes between those who supported Parliament and the boycotters. People caught selling or trying to buy British goods in major cities found themselves punished by angry crowds; several Boston newspapers even published violators' names on their front pages. Merchants who opposed the boycotts labeled the movement as the actions of "the deluded multitude." These merchants claimed that traders who subscribed to the non-importation agreements often violated them secretly to make higher profits.

Men and Women: Tea and Politics

The non-importation movement brought men and women together politically as they opposed imperial authority. Boycotts invested women's everyday activities of purchasing, preparing, and consuming commodities such as tea with political meaning. Tea drinking had become an important part of many white women's social rituals by the mid-1700s, linking American women to the British importers who traded tea from India and China to North America. From the upper classes who were drinking tea out of silver pots and china cups around polished mahogany tea tables established genteel social standards, to poor women who used pottery cups and prized only a few cups of the expensive beverage per week—white women were associated with tea. As one Boston newspaper predicted in November 1767, "The cost of consuming foreign tea is very expensive in this colony . . . to lay an extensive tax on its consumption, would be very disagreeable to the Ladies."

Male supporters of the non-importation movement appealed to women in speeches and newspaper articles to participate in the boycotts, and several women also wrote to newspapers appealing for the "Daughters of Liberty" to act. Female shopkeepers were among those who signed public pledges not to sell imported British goods, and city

TEA TABLES Polished mahogany tea tables like this one became the setting for genteel socializing in elite American homes where men and women drank tea, displayed their fine china and silver, and held conversations. Although the tea and china were imported, tables like this one were often made in the colonies by master furniture makers.

women made a show of drinking only coffee or herbal tea. Other women conspicuously wore only homespun fabric and held spinning bees to raise supplies of homemade textiles. New England shopkeeper Elizabeth Murray urged a relative that it was everyone's "duty to stand up for so valuable a country & not be tax'd" by Parliament or to keep soldiers in North America.

By the end of 1769, the British government realized that the Townshend duties had failed. The taxes had brought in less than £20,000, while British merchants had lost more than £700,000. Colonial merchants smuggled vast quantities of goods and traded

THE BOSTON MASSACRE   Paul Revere published this propagandistic engraving of the Boston Massacre in 1770. It shows British soldiers shooting down unarmed civilians in front of the Boston Custom House, which Revere relabeled as "Butcher's Hall." Revere was one of the best engravers in Massachusetts, and his work helped to spread outrage.

with Dutch merchants willing to sell illegal tea. The new British ministry, headed by Lord North, decided in 1770 to repeal all the Townshend duties except for the tax on tea, which would continue "as a mark of the supremacy of Parliament." The non-importation movement quickly faded with the repeal of the other Townshend duties, but the legacy of political mobilization would live on.

The Boston Massacre

While the Townshend duties were in place, harsh resistance to them in Boston particularly vexed the British government, which responded by sending British soldiers to keep order. Beginning on October 1, 1768, the first of 4,000 British soldiers arrived to police Boston, a city of just 15,000. The soldiers, stationed around the city in private residences, often clashed with local citizens—who feared the power of a standing army. Soldiers also competed for seasonal jobs with poor working people of Boston, many of whom were also active in the Whig resistance. Tensions heated up in February 1770 when a customs official killed 11-year-old Christopher Seider, sparking mob action and a skirmish between Boston rope workers and British soldiers on March 3.

Tensions boiled over on March 5, 1770, in the incident that became known as the **Boston Massacre**. A crowd began to harass a British sentry, and when eight soldiers came to his aid, the crowd threw rocks and snowballs at them. The soldiers fired into the crowd. Five working men were killed, including a runaway slave named Crispus Attucks. Following the skirmish, British soldiers and customs collectors withdrew to the fortress of Castle William on an island in Boston harbor. Public opinion against the British soldiers ran high, especially after silversmith **Paul Revere** published an inflammatory engraving of the incident depicting the British soldiers as cruel murderers. **John Adams** and **Josiah Quincy, Jr.**, Boston lawyers who were loyal to the Whig cause but believed in fair trials, helped to acquit the British commander, Captain Preston. Only two of the soldiers were found guilty of manslaughter, and they were lightly punished and released.

STUDY QUESTIONS FOR CONSUMER RESISTANCE

1. Why did North American colonists use non-importation as a resistance strategy against British taxation?
2. In what ways did protests mobilize elite white women and poorer men and women?

■ RESISTANCE BECOMES REVOLUTION

Between 1770 and 1776, resistance to imperial change turned into a full-on revolution. After a short cooling-off period at the beginning of the 1770s, colonial protests threatened to turn violent. Eventually, that violence would be channeled into organized revolutionary warfare. How could the colonists fight a war with Britain and still remain part of the British empire?

Boston Tea Party and Coercive Acts

Although the formal associations that organized boycotts during the non-importation movement faded away after 1770, the tax on tea remained, and many colonists continued to avoid drinking tea. Beginning in Boston, and then spreading to every colony, groups of elite and middling men formed Committees of Correspondence to provide networks of communication between Whigs in different colonies. The committees were in place when Parliament passed the Tea Act in March of 1773, granting the East India Company a monopoly on the North American tea trade. The monopoly lowered the price of tea, but it did not remove the tax, and it granted new powers to colonial customs officials and to the East India Company to appoint official tea merchants in each colony. This legislation reawakened popular protest, as Whigs quickly planned resistance against tea agents.

In several port cities, to avoid protests, government officials persuaded ship captains to leave port without unloading the East India Company tea. But in Boston in December 1773, Governor Thomas Hutchinson refused to allow the tea ships to leave Griffin's Wharf without unloading their cargo of tea. On December 16, Samuel Adams and other Sons of Liberty organized a huge mass meeting in Old South Meeting House where they denounced the tea shipments as instruments of British tyranny. That evening, 30 to 60 men disguised as Mohawk Indians stormed the tea ships and dumped 90,000 pounds of tea into Boston Harbor. The **Boston Tea Party** mobilized Bostonians and spread resistance to other colonies. Protestors burned a tea ship in Annapolis, Maryland; Princeton

"THE DESTRUCTION OF THE TEA"   This engraving shows the Boston Tea Party, or "The Destruction of the Tea" as it was sometimes known in the 19th century. The depiction of the incident shows how the Tea Party has been a subject of popular imagination since the end of the 18th century. Although the protesters did disguise themselves as "Mohawk Indians," the effect was likely not as complete as depicted here.

University students destroyed tea and effigies of Thomas Hutchinson; and new tea boycott associations formed—including one among the women of Edenton, North Carolina. One South Carolinian remarked that in Charleston, all ranks of individuals, "the gentleman and the mechanic, those of high and low life, the learned and illiterate," had been mobilized into political action.

The destruction of property in the tea protests shocked Parliament, which quickly sanctioned Massachusetts in a series of 1774 laws dubbed the **Coercive Acts** or the "Intolerable Acts" by Whig colonists. Lord North told the House of Commons that "We are now to establish our authority, or give it up entirely"—and not even Parliamentary representatives who favored the colonists' cause, such as Edmund Burke, would relent. The Coercive Acts closed the port of Boston and reorganized the Massachusetts government, altering its colonial charter to put more authority in the hands of royal appointees. The acts also imposed royal control over local courts; authorized troops to be forcibly billeted in private houses and buildings; and installed the British Army commander, Thomas Gage, as the new colonial governor. In addition to these Coercive Acts, Parliament also passed the Quebec Act in 1774—which further frightened Protestant New Englanders by expanding royal control in Canada and endorsing official Catholicism.

Empire, Control, and the Language of Slavery

The Coercive Acts galvanized political opposition inside Massachusetts, and Whigs soon organized a new boycott movement. The crackdown on Massachusetts also energized Whigs in many other colonies who feared similar repressive action. Virginia legislator **Thomas Jefferson** wrote in a pamphlet, *A Summary View of the Rights of British America*, that the colonies held natural rights to free international trade and that only the king, not Parliament, held limited sovereignty over the colonies. Philadelphians began to call for a meeting to issue colonial petitions to the king—the highest and last authority who might redress their grievances. After Virginia's royal governor dissolved the House of Burgesses, the legislative body met illegally at a tavern in Williamsburg to endorse a new boycott and to call for a continental congress to coordinate protests.

When Jefferson argued that Parliament sought to subdue the colonies through "a series of oppressions," he expressed a vision of the British engaged in "a deliberate systematical plan of reducing us to slavery." Jefferson's use of the word "slavery" signaled the extreme fear that many colonists had of being deprived of their liberties. The term was used by a range of Americans who shared that fear. During the boycott movement, **Abigail Adams** referred to tea as "this weed of Slavery." Her husband, Massachusetts lawyer John Adams, wrote that England, "once the land of liberty—the school of patriots—the nurse of heroes, has become the land of slavery." This language of slavery indicated how deeply many Whigs had come to fear the British government and the perceived corruption of the British system.

American colonists were not blind to the irony of calling themselves "slaves" to the British government while many colonists actually owned African American slaves. In fact, they intentionally used the term "slavery" to indicate a subordinate, degraded position with which they were intimately familiar. Many of the leaders of the Revolutionary movement, especially in colonies such as Virginia where the slavery was widespread, had social prestige because of inherited wealth based on slave ownership and labor.

Virginian **George Washington** wrote during the controversy over the Coercive Acts, "The crisis is arrived when we must assert our rights or submit to every imposition, that can be heaped upon us, till custom and use shall make us as tame and abject slaves, as the blacks we rule over with such arbitrary sway." In every colony, African American slaves lived beside free men and women, and that reality made political "slavery" all the more fearsome as the British asserted their power.

Mobilization

Parliament had intended the Coercive Acts to cut off Massachusetts from the other colonies, to isolate radicals and stop their rebellion. Instead, the acts aroused sympathy for Massachusetts and prompted Whigs in far-flung colonies to unite more than ever before. In September 1774, representatives of 12 colonies (the royal governor prevented Georgia from sending representatives) met in a Continental Congress at Philadelphia. Jamaica and other Caribbean colonies opposed the Coercive Acts, but their assemblies took no action to join the Continental Congress—since Caribbean planters served in and had more direct access to Parliament than did their neighbors to the north. Many colonists loyal to the British government questioned the authority of the **First Continental Congress** to speak for them. The Congress even discussed colonial independence, although very few delegates supported it. The First Continental Congress also charged committees in each colony to vigorously enforce boycotts; endorsed a declaration of rights and grievances on October 14, 1774; and then adjourned, hoping that their appeal to the king would check Parliamentary authority.

But an angry King George urged Parliament to impose even more control on the colonies to break what he deemed "disobedience to the law." Committees in all 13 British North American colonies organized for public defense. In Boston, Thomas Gage's troops had all but shut down the city. In the surrounding small towns and countryside, Whig men and women began to stockpile weapons, manufacture bullets, commandeer royal caches of gunpowder, and to practice military drill. Local militias in Massachusetts and Connecticut went on alert to respond quickly (as **minute men**) to possible British military action after Gage's forces captured a powder cache in Charlestown in September 1774. Virginia governor John Murray, Earl of Dunmore, told crown officials that committees in every township violently enforced boycotts and that Whig military companies organized to protect them. In the early months of 1775, Edmund Burke and other sympathetic members of Parliament tried unsuccessfully to get the North government to make concessions to the colonists.

War Begins

Early in 1775, General Gage decided to crack down on Concord, Massachusetts, where the dissolved colonial assembly met illegally and where he suspected colonists had a large stockpile of weapons and gunpowder. On the evening of April 18, 1775, Gage assembled 700 of his 3,500 red coats (as British soldiers were nicknamed) on Boston Common and readied them to be transported into the countryside. Whig activists Paul Revere and William Dawes rode out of Boston to warn the militiamen at Concord and nearby Lexington to ready themselves and to warn radical leaders Samuel Adams and John Hancock to leave Lexington, where they were hiding from arrest. In the early morning of April 19, Captain John Parker's company of militia skirmished with British soldiers led by Major John Pitcairn on Lexington green. Eight militia men were killed in the opening battle of the Revolutionary War.

Later that morning, five miles away in Concord, the local militia, now reinforced by other men from the surrounding countryside, engaged British regulars in a larger battle at the North Bridge. After the battle, the British soldiers made their way back to Boston along the winding 16-mile rural road. They came under fire from the woods, as hundreds of Massachusetts militia troops sniped at the regulars. Gage's troops holed up in Boston, awaiting reinforcements, as more than 10,000 colonial militia forces surrounded the city over the next month. Colonists up and down the eastern seaboard celebrated resistance to the British Army. Peter Timothy, the secretary of the Charleston, South Carolina, committee of correspondence, wrote in his newspaper that the "ever-memorable" battles on April 19, 1775, would mark "a grand epoch in the History of Mankind. . . . An Epoch, that in all Probability will mark the Declension of the British Empire!"

The Second Continental Congress convened on May 10, 1775, just one day after **Ethan Allen**, with assistance from men commanded by Benedict Arnold, had captured the British Fort Ticonderoga. As the British planned their next move, the Continental Congress set about organizing a Continental Army; and, on June 15 they chose as its commander George Washington, whose genteel Virginia heritage and military experience made him stand out among the delegates. Even before Washington could assume command, the **Battle of Bunker Hill** took place on June 17. Major General William Howe, who had arrived in Boston with reinforcements, ordered an attack on the heights at Charlestown, across the Charles River from Boston. The Americans fortified Breed's Hill, which they misidentified as Bunker Hill, and met the better-equipped regulars who streamed up the Hill in three waves of attack to try and capture the heights. Although the colonial forces retreated to end the battle, they claimed victory in proving they could hold up against greater numbers of well-trained soldiers. The British also suffered their heaviest casualty rate of the entire war: Of 2,500 soldiers, 228 died and 826 were wounded.

For the remainder of the year, the British remained in Boston plotting their next move, as Washington and the Continental Congress worked to organize and equip the Continental Army. American commanders planned an invasion of Canada, intended to rouse Canadians against the British, who had very few troops stationed there. Two expeditions, one led by Philip Schuyler and Richard Montgomery, the other by Benedict Arnold, set out for Canada late in the year, but both ended in disaster. By January 1776, Montgomery was killed and no groundswell of support emerged for the American cause in Canada. In Virginia, Governor Dunmore offered freedom to slaves and indentured servants who joined the British; and, in December, he led a force of British regulars, escaped slaves, and loyalists in a battle against a Virginia Continental Army regiment outside of Norfolk. Dunmore's force was defeated, he fled the colony, and many of the slaves who had joined his cause when he promised them freedom were sold back into bondage in the Caribbean.

STUDY QUESTIONS FOR RESISTANCE BECOMES REVOLUTION

1. How did Boston play a key role in the imperial crisis?
2. What British and North American actions caused colonial resistance to escalate into warfare?

Independence: Transatlantic Roots, Global Influence

The idea of political independence—that colonies could declare themselves to be a state separate from the colonial power—was an innovation in world politics in 1776. But the concept had roots in events and political philosophies that had taken shape in Europe in prior centuries. The Declaration of Independence would also have major global consequences, not the least in its influence on other independence movements, from 1776 until the present day.

The committee of the Continental Congress given the task of drafting the motion of independence in June 1776, led by Thomas Jefferson, was steeped in Western European political theory and history. Jefferson was able to draw on both theory and practice in drafting the Declaration. Statements of sovereignty and autonomy stretching back to the Scottish Declaration of Arbroath in 1320 made it clear that self-determination could be a major factor in international relations.

The idea that a people who held valid grievances against their ruler could declare independence was influenced by several Enlightenment theories about what constituted a legitimate government. Thomas Jefferson drew on the ideas in John Locke's *Second Treatise of Government*, published in 1689 during the Glorious Revolution, the culmination of almost a century of fighting over who should occupy the British throne. Jefferson employed especially Locke's notion that monarchs and legislative bodies derive at least some of their authority from the consent of those who are governed, and he paraphrased some of Locke's justifications for how tyranny might force the "dissolution" of an unjust government. Jefferson was also influenced by ideas about natural rights and the obligations of moral necessity in essays published by Scottish judge and philosopher Henry Home, Lord Kames, in the mid-18th century. Independence itself was a strong component of national sovereignty as defined by Swiss legal expert Emer de Vattel in his 1758 *The Law of Nations*. Jefferson may also have been influenced by 16th-century Spanish Jesuit writings on the limits of kingship.

News of the Declaration of Independence spread unusually fast throughout Europe, with copies appearing in newspapers and translated pamphlets in Britain, Ireland, Holland,

◼ DECLARING INDEPENDENCE

With the Revolutionary War well under way, the British Empire in North America reached its breaking point. As the first six months of the Revolutionary War unfolded, the Second Continental Congress began to consider the possibility of declaring independence from Great Britain, even though colonies had never before tried such a bold maneuver. How would the British colonies conceive of their separation from Parliament and the Crown? How would independent former colonies relate to the rest of the world? Would Spanish imperial reforms be met by similar resistance?

Austria, Denmark, Italy, Switzerland, and Poland by September 1776. Pamphlet copies also appeared in France, Spain, and Russia, whose rulers initially reacted cautiously even though they were supporting the American war effort against Britain. Translations of the Declaration also circulated around Latin America in the following decades, helping to influence Latin American independence movements from Mexico to Chile. Full translations did not appear in China, and several other Asian countries, until the 20th century, but English copies did circulate there.

As news of the Declaration spread, some Europeans resisted the notion that declaring independence was a legitimate political idea. This resistance intensified as Europe became embroiled in its own revolutionary conflicts by the end of the 18th century. As soon as news of the Declaration reached Britain, crown supporter John Lind wrote a scathing *Answer to the Declaration of the American Congress* that rejected the entire basis for the document. Some European translations of the Declaration, even in sympathetic countries such as Spain and Russia, downplayed the more radical implications of the document—toning down, for instance, the emphasis of the "pursuit of happiness" and the document's emphasis on natural and individual rights.

Even as the intellectual justifications of independence continued to be debated, the practical political strategy of declaring independence spread quickly in the decades after the American Revolution. By 1826, 20 other countries had declared their independence. Historian David Armitage, who has studied the global influence of the Declaration of Independence, notes that today "over half the countries of the world have their own declarations of independence." Armitage argues that countries as different as the Republic of Vietnam, Southern Rhodesia, Venezuela, and Liberia have all employed language similar to the U.S. Declaration in their own founding documents. Not all countries followed the U.S. model or justifications for independence, but the political tactic employed by the Continental Congress in 1776 has certainly influenced world history.

- Why was it so important for the Declaration of Independence to appeal to the broader world at large?
- In what ways do you think the Declaration of Independence has shaped global opinion of the United States?

The World's First Declaration of Independence

Through the first months of the Revolutionary War, many Whigs had continued to pledge allegiance to the king. They felt that royal authority would guard them against Parliament and that the empire need not be severed. In July 1775, the Continental Congress sent an **Olive Branch Petition** to George III asking him to settle the conflict; but, by spring 1776, Congress fielded petitions from colonial committees and assemblies calling for independence. In March 1776, British forces evacuated Boston and retreated to Halifax to strategize and reinforce before planning a full-out offensive

THE DECLARATION OF INDEPENDENCE   The Continental Congress took a huge risk by issuing the Declaration of Independence in July 1776. No colony in the history of the world had ever declared its independence and asserted its right to become a nation. Success depended on the reaction of the rest of the world and on the ability of the Americans to win their revolutionary war.

against the Americans. In May, the City of London petitioned George III to approach his colonies peacefully, but the king responded that the colonists had "brought upon themselves" the trouble "by an unjustifiable resistance to the constitutional authority of this Kingdom." When the king rejected peace, even moderates like Philadelphia's Robert Morris conceded that a "declaration of Independency" was probably inevitable.

Virginia's delegation to the Continental Congress, headed by Richard Henry Lee, proposed a motion to declare independence from Great Britain on June 7, 1776. After debate over whether independence would bring aid from France and Spain, Congress delayed voting on the resolution until the beginning of July to give colonial committees and assemblies time to endorse the idea. A Congressional subcommittee, which included John Adams and Thomas Jefferson, worked on the independence motion. Jefferson wrote the declaration, with some editing by Adams and Benjamin Franklin. The Continental Congress voted for independence on July 2, and the following day a large British fleet commanded by General William Howe bearing a rejuvenated British army force landed outside New York City.

The **Declaration of Independence**, issued by Congress on July 4, 1776, was the first document of its kind in world history. Many colonies, assemblies, and legislative bodies had in previous centuries put forth declarations concerning rights and privileges, and this document drew on historical precedents that defined the British rights and liberty. But never before had a group of colonies listed its grievances, declared itself to be an independent state, and asserted its own sovereignty. The Declaration began with a sweeping statement about rights that put a new twist on the Enlightenment ideas of John Locke: "We hold these truths to be self-evident, that all Men are created equal, that they are endowed by their Creator with certain unalienable Rights, that among these are Life, Liberty and the Pursuit of Happiness." The Declaration focused heavily on perceived violations of rights committed by the king and royal officials—perhaps because most Whigs already felt a separation from Parliament.

The Declaration appealed to "the rest of mankind" to recognize that the United States was free and independent of Britain. **Thomas Paine**, the radical British writer who had emigrated and taken up the colonial cause, urged Americans in his popular pamphlet *Common Sense* at the beginning of 1776 to declare their independence to guarantee political relations and trade with "foreign Courts." The Declaration of Independence itself, however, would not be sufficient to guarantee the success of the United States. The Revolutionary War intensified and offered a military test for the new nation that would last several more years.

Spanish Imperial Consolidation

By contrast to the British Empire, Spanish officials were able to bring more of North America under control through the Bourbon Reforms.

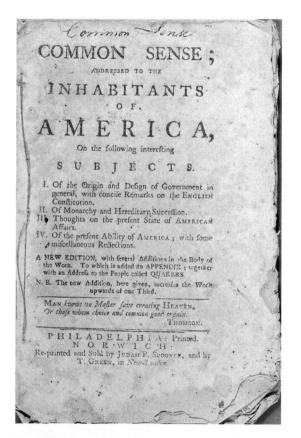

COMMON SENSE Paine was an English radical who had come to America in 1774, in part because he supported the American protests against Parliament. His immensely popular 1776 pamphlet *Common Sense* advocated independence and helped to gain public acceptance for that tactic among the patriot population. Paine also supported the American war effort with other pamphlets such as "The Crisis." Later in the 1780s, he moved to France and became an important figure in the French Revolution.

MISSION DOLORES   Father Junípero Serra founded the Misíon San Francisco de Asís (now known as Mission Dolores) in 1776 as part of the effort by the Franciscans to spread the Spanish mission system to the north in California from the 1760s to the 1780s.

S. F. 345.   Mission Dolores, Founded 1776, San Francisco, Cal.

José de Gálvez visited Mexico in the 1760s during his tour as inspector general of the Spanish colonies, and by the 1770s, many of his plans for California, New Mexico, and other areas of North America were bearing fruit. Franciscan friars Gaspar de Portolá, Father Junípero Serra, and Fernando de Rivera y Moncada established a string of missions and presidio forts stretching from southern to northern California by 1774. Juan Bautista de Anza (later the colonial governor of New Mexico) opened a new land route from Mexico and brought an infusion of colonists and livestock to Northern California. José de Gálvez put forth a plan in the 1760s to break the northern part of New Spain off from Mexico and bring it under direct crown control, and he got the chance to implement his plan when Charles III appointed him Secretary of the Indies in January 1776.

Charles III issued a royal order on August 22, 1776, that created the Comandancia General of the Interior Provinces. The Spanish colonies north of Mexico were formed into a semiautonomous territory for military defense, trade, and crown administration. Teodoro de Croix, a French-born Spanish official who later served as viceroy of Peru, was appointed as the first governor of the Interior Provinces. Croix was ordered to coordinate with the Spanish viceroy in Mexico City, but he exercised autonomous authority in many areas. Croix and Anza pursued aggressive policies against native peoples, for example, playing Comanche and Apache peoples against one another, and sought to control the increasing number of Russian settlers entering Spanish territory. The organization of the Comandancia of the Interior Provinces helped the California mission system to spread, which extended crown control over more Indian people and territory. The Comandancia set in motion the development of Northern Mexico as a semiautonomous region.

Spain had been slower to take control over Louisiana after the French ceded it in 1763, and the first Spanish governor, Don Antonio de Ulloa, did not assume office in New Orleans until 1766. No one in the city's mix of French, German, Indian, and free and enslaved African settlers wanted to submit to Spanish authority—especially the city's elites, whose extensive trade and smuggling Ulloa tried to control. Prominent citizens of New Orleans, led by several French settlers, revolted in October 1768, demanded that Ulloa leave the colony, and tried to rejoin the French empire. Spain sent a new governor, General Alexandre O'Reilly, with 2,000 troops to put down the revolt. O'Reilly swiftly seized the protest leaders, tried them, confiscated their property, imprisoned many, and executed 12 men by firing squad. The Louisiana revolt was the largest in

North America until that point, comprising the most aggressive imperial military crackdown in North America prior to 1774.

Spanish military force was effective at regaining civic control. Unlike the British, Spain maintained ultimate authority, and independence movements were postponed for several decades.

Ideology and Resistance

In the British colonies, the Independence movement helped to solidify ideological changes that had been underway since the imperial crisis first began in 1763. Elite colonists who supported the Whig cause invoked Enlightenment political ideas, but ordinary men and women who participated in collective protest also believed in the importance of "liberty" and "representation." Committees passing resolutions and crowds rioting against tax collectors or boycott violators found that their place as consumers in the markets of the Atlantic world empowered their political views. Preachers such as Boston minister Jonathan Mayhew, politicians such as Virginian Richard Henry Lee, writers such as Thomas Paine, and average people like Massachusetts shoemaker George Robert Twelves Hewes all concluded in their own ways that violations of American "liberty" demanded resistance against the British.

Techniques of resistance in the 1760s and early 1770s—pamphlet writing, riots, destruction of property, crowd actions to enforce community standards, burning enemies in effigy, petitions—were all familiar to the British. Crowds in England and Ireland regularly used these methods throughout the first three quarters of the 18th century to protest suppression of their political heroes, high food prices, taxes, and changes in foreign policy. Tens of thousands of people in England petitioned the government and took to the streets between 1763 and 1774 to protest the persecution of radical printer John Wilkes, who was denied his elected seat in Parliament. Cries of "Wilkes and Liberty!" could be heard in the streets of London and Middlesex but also in Charleston, New York, and Boston—where the Sons of Liberty and other American protestors linked their own movement to the Wilkesite cause, especially after seven people were killed and scores wounded in May 1768 in what became known as the St. George's Field Massacre in London.

British American colonists fit into a transatlantic tradition of protest, but only they turned their efforts into a full-blown movement for political independence and a revolutionary war. In the move for independence, Whig Americans rejected not just the actions of the British government but British control altogether. They moved from hoping that the king would protect them from Parliamentary control to rejecting the monarchy. They became Americans.

Taking Stock of Empire

In 1776, Spain was expanding its North American empire just as the British Empire in North America crumbled. New Spain stretched as far north as the presidio and Mission Dolores in San Francisco, and the Bourbon reforms increased crown control over extensive territory north of Mexico. British imperial reforms had achieved the opposite result. After successive attempts to raise revenue from the colonies, and successive resistance in return, 13 British colonies declared independence

TIMELINE 1763–1776

AMERICA	YEAR	THE WORLD
Feb Treaty of Paris ends Seven Years' War **May** Pontiac's Rebellion begins when Ottawa forces lay siege to Ft. Detroit **Oct** George III forbids settlement west of Appalachian mountains	**1763**	**Nov** Parliament accuses newspaper publisher John Wilkes of sedition **Nov** British reorganize governments of Quebec, Florida, and Grenada
James Otis publishes pamphlet denying British right to tax colonies **Apr** Parliament revises Navigation Acts and passes Sugar Act **Apr** Currency Act curtails colonial paper money	**1764**	**Nov** Jesuit order is expelled from France **Nov** Japanese peasants riot to protest high taxes
Mar Parliament passes Stamp Act, which taxes legal documents, printed matter, and other paper goods **May** Quartering Act requires colonists to house and pay for British troops **May** Virginia House of Burgesses protests Stamp Act and urges other colonies to join **Oct** Stamp Act Congress meets in Philadelphia, issues "Declaration of Rights and Grievances"	**1765**	Scotsman James Watt invents the steam engine **Aug** Joseph II becomes Holy Roman Emperor, rules alongside his mother Maria Theresa
Mar Stamp Act is repealed, but Declaratory Act stresses that Parliament can tax colonies in "all cases whatsoever" **Jul** Treaty ends Pontiac's Rebellion	**1766**	Ali Bey rules Egypt and declares independence from Ottoman Empire
Mar Charles III expels Jesuits from New Spain for opposing his Bourbon Reform program **Jul** Parliament suspends New York legislature for disobeying Quartering Act **Nov** John Dickinson's *Letters from a Farmer in Pennsylvania* begin to appear in newspapers **Nov** Townshend Duties tax a new range of colonial products	**1767**	**Mar** Charles III expels Jesuits from Spain, Parma, and Sicily
Jan Massachusetts legislature petitions George III to protest "taxation without representation"	**1768**	Ghurkas conquer Nepal *Encyclopedia Britannica* begins publication
May Virginia House of Burgesses resolves that parliament may not tax the colony **Jul** Father Junípero Serra founds his first mission church at San Diego de Alcala	**1769**	China forces Burma to submit to its rule **Aug** Napoleon Bonaparte is born
Mar Five men are killed by British soldiers in "Boston Massacre" **Apr** Parliament withdraws all Townshend Duties except for tax on tea	**1770**	*The London Evening Post* becomes first newspaper to reprint parliamentary business

from the British crown and formed the United States of America. Certainly not everyone in the British North American colonies supported independence, but the Whigs who supported the actions of the Continental Congress seemed to have the upper hand.

STUDY QUESTIONS FOR DECLARING INDEPENDENCE

1. On what grounds did the Declaration of Independence justify separation from Britain?

2. How did British colonial protests finally result in a revolutionary ideology by 1776?

3. How did the Spanish government consolidate control over increasing territory in North America in the mid-18th century?

Oct Boston Town Meeting urges Committees of Correspondence to form	**1772**	Russia and Prussia partition Poland
Apr Parliament passes Tea Act, seeking to bolster profits of the East India Company **Dec** 90,000 pounds of East India Company tea are thrown into Boston Harbor at Boston Tea Party	**1773**	British East India Company becomes a government agency Civil War commences in Annam (now Vietnam) Jesuits expelled from Holy Roman Empire **May** Muhammad Bey assumes power in Egypt, rejoins Ottoman Empire
Mar Parliament closes port of Boston and suspends Massachusetts legislature **Sep** First Continental Congress meets in Philadelphia **Oct** Continental Congress forms a Continental Association to coordinate non-importation **Oct** Parliament passes Quebec Act	**1774**	**May** Louis XVI assumes throne of France **Aug** Jesuit order expelled from Poland
Mar Patrick Henry delivers "Give me liberty or give me death" speech in Virginia House of Burgesses **Apr** Revolutionary War begins at Battles of Lexington and Concord **May** American forces capture Fort Ticonderoga **May** Second Continental Congress meets in Philadelphia **Jun** Congress forms Continental Army and appoints George Washington as commander **Jun** Battle of Bunker Hill **Oct** Congress forms the Continental Navy **Nov** Governor of Virginia offers freedom to slaves who join against rebellious colonists **Nov** Richard Montgomery captures Montreal **Dec** Richard Montgomery killed in the unsuccessful American attack on Quebec	**1775**	
Jan Thomas Paine's *Common Sense* is published **Mar** British forces evacuate Boston **Jul 4** Congress issues Declaration of Independence, creating United States of America	**1776**	Spain opens Buenos Aires to free trade

Summary

- Both the British and Spanish governments sought centralized control over their North American colonies following the Seven Years' War, in part to raise revenue.
- The 1765 Stamp Act inaugurated an opposition movement in the British North American colonies and touched off a debate over Parliament's authority to tax the colonies.
- Between 1767 and 1770, American men and women politicized consumerism by fighting British taxation with non-importation.
- Between 1770 and 1776, British authorities cracked down on colonial resistance, especially in Massachusetts, and touched off a revolutionary war.
- In 1776, Congress declared independence from Great Britain and created the United States of America, and the Spanish imperial government created the Comandancia General of the Interior Provinces.

Key Terms and People

Adams, Abigail *209*

Adams, John *207*

Adams, Samuel *200*

Allen, Ethan *211*

Battle of Bunker Hill *211*

Boston Massacre *207*

Boston Tea Party *208*

Coercive Acts (Intolerable Acts) *209*

Declaration of Independence *214*

First Continental Congress *210*

Franklin, Benjamin *199*

Gage, Thomas *202*

Henry, Patrick *200*

Jefferson, Thomas *209*

Locke, John *199*

MacIntosh, Ebenezer *200*

minute men *210*

Montgomery, Richard *191*

Navigation Acts *194*

Neolin *196*

Olive Branch Petition *213*

Paine, Thomas *215*

Pitt, William *202*

Pontiac *196*

Proclamation of 1763 *197*

Quincy, Josiah, Jr. *207*

Revere, Paul *207*

Sons of Liberty *200*

Stamp Act *200*

Townshend Acts *203*

Washington, George *210*

Whigs *199*

Reviewing Chapter 6

1. How did the circulation of people, goods, and ideas between Europe and North America help lead to the American Revolution?
2. Compare the consequences of British and Spanish imperial reforms in the mid-1700s.

Further Reading

Armitage, David. *The Declaration of Independence: A Global History.* Cambridge, Mass.: Harvard University Press, 2007. This excellent, short book examines the global influences on the Declaration of Independence and how the Declaration has influenced other countries' independence movements ever since. The volume also contains copies of various declarations of independence from around the world from 1776 to 1993.

Breen, T. H. *The Marketplace of Revolution: How Consumer Politics Shaped American Independence.* New York: Oxford University Press, 2004. Breen argues that American colonists forged a shared identity as consumers that empowered them and led to their political organization during the imperial crisis.

Elliott, J. H. *Empires of the Atlantic World: Britain and Spain in America, 1492–1830.* New Haven, Conn.: Yale University Press, 2006. This sweeping history contrasts the development of the British and Spanish colonies in North America over the course of more than 300 years. Elliott's book provides a good basis to compare how England and Spain dealt with resistance in the 1760s differently.

Fenn, Elizabeth. "Biological Warfare in Eighteenth-Century North America: Beyond Jeffrey Amherst." *Journal of American History* 86 (March 2000): 1552–1580. This important article examines the claims that British general Jeffrey Amherst intentionally traded smallpox-infected items with Pontiac's warriors and places the act in the context of other acts of germ warfare in the 18th century.

Young, Alfred F., Gary B. Nash and Ray Raphael, eds. *Revolutionary Founders: Rebels, Radicals, and Reformers in the Making of the Nation.* New York: Alfred A. Knopf, 2011. Twenty-two biographical essays discuss ordinary men and women in the American Revolution considered "radical" for their work on behalf of liberty and equality.

America In The World
PEOPLE, GOODS, IDEAS AND PRACTICES

CHAPTER 6: Empire and Resistance 1763–1776

EUROPE

AFRICA

London

British soldiers

Lumber

Ships

Demand for Independence

Tobacco

Tax laws

Rice, indigo, and pine tar

ATLANTIC OCEAN

Enslaved Africans

NORTH AMERICA

Boston

New York

Philadelphia

Non-importation Movement (1768)

Charleston

Enslaved Africans

Spanish missions

Gulf of Mexico

SOUTH AMERICA

PACIFIC OCEAN

0   500   1,000 miles
0   500 1,000 kilometers

Goods
Ideas
People

PRIMARY SOURCES FOR CHAPTER 6

EMPIRE AND RESISTANCE, 1763–1776

SOURCE 6.1

Charles III, King of Spain, Appointment of José de Gálvez as Visitor General to New Spain (1765)

In this appointment as Visitor General, Charles III gave great authority to José de Gálvez to inspect financial, judicial, and governmental matters in New Spain. Gálvez's main assignment was to improve the flow of revenues from the colonies to Spain, but these instructions also granted him enough power to accomplish other colonial goals, such as the expansion of settlement in North America and the expulsion of the Jesuits from New Spain.

Source: Herbert Ingram Priestley, *José De Gálvez, Visitor-General of New Spain (1765–1771)* (Berkeley: University of California Press, 1916), 404.

Instruction Reservada, March 14, 1765

The King: Don Joseph Galvez, of my Council, *Alcalde de mi Casa y Corte*, and honorary minister with seniority of the Council of the Indies; notwithstanding that I am well satisfied with the zeal, activity, prudence, and disinterest with which the branches and revenues of my royal patrimony are managed by my viceroy of New Spain and by the ministers of my real hacienda, the governors, and other subordinates who serve under their orders, it being necessary, on account of the large sums needed in attending to the obligations of my royal crown, to exhaust all means from the revenues to the end that the burden of imposing new contributions may be avoided, and to collect all legitimate duties as legally provided without altering established practice or dispensing voluntary favors, and to prevent abuses and all superfluous expenses not ab-solutely indispensable for the best administration of revenues:

I have deemed it convenient to my royal service to name you, Don Joseph Galvez—a minister in whom I have entire satisfaction and confidence, able, zealous, and skilled in the management of revenues—that you may, in the capacity of visitor-general to my real hacienda within the jurisdiction of the kingdom of New Spain, take cognizance of all of them, examine their proceeds, expenses, balances, and the whereabouts of their funds; demand any arrears in which the administrators, treasurers, lessees of revenues, or other persons who have managed rents, may be to my real hacienda; and regulate the system and management with which the revenues are to be administered in future, reducing expenses and salaries which can and ought to be lowered or abolished, so that the balances be not dissipated by unnecessary expense, but made more effective to their destined ends.

I grant you for all this, and for all that is to be expressed, the powers and jurisdiction which you need to give your commission entire fulfillment. To this end I desire that my viceroy and captain-general of New Spain shall take all measures which you ask and give you the assistance you need. . . .

WORKING WITH SOURCES

1. How did Charles III expect Galvez to raise royal revenues in New Spain?

2. What kind of power does this set of instructions grant to Galvez?

SOURCE 6.2

Thomas Hutchinson, Excerpts from Letters to Great Britain Describing Popular Unrest (1768, 1769)

Thomas Hutchinson, a native of Massachusetts who served as the colony's lieutenant governor and chief justice, found himself facing the wrath of protesters during the imperial crisis of the 1760s. His house was demolished by a mob protesting his proposed enforcement of the Stamp Act in 1765. In this letter from 1768, he describes riots in Boston to authorities in Great Britain and worries about resistance in the event that British troops were housed with Boston residents.

Source: Copy of Letters Sent to Great Britain, by His Excellency Thomas Hutchinson, the Hon. Andrew Oliver, and Several Other Persons, Born and Educated among Us (Boston: Edes and Gill, 1773), 9–12, 16.

Principles of government absurd enough spread thro' all the colonies; but I cannot think that in any colony, people of any consideration have ever been so mad as to think of a revolt. Many of the common people have been in a frenzy, and talk'd of dying in defence of their liberties, and have spoke and printed what is highly criminal, and too many of rank above the vulgar, and some *in public posts* have countenanced and encouraged them until they increased so much in their numbers and opinion of their importance as to submit to government no further than they have thought proper. The legislative powers have been influenced by them, and the executive powers intirely lost their force. . . . For four or five weeks past the distemper has been growing, and I confess I have been without

some apprehensions for myself, but my friends had more for me. . . .

The last spring there had been several riots, and a most infamous libel had been published in one of the papers. . . . Whilst we were in this state, news came of two regiments being ordered from Halifax, and soon after two more from Ireland. The minds of the people were more and more agitated, broad hints were given that the troops should never land, a barrel of tar was placed upon the beacon, in the night to be fired to bring in the country when the government troops appeared, and all the authority of the government was not strong enough to remove it. The town of Boston met and passed a number of weak but very criminal votes. . . .

In this confusion the troops from Halifax arrived. I never was much afraid of the people's taking arms, but I was apprehensive of violence from the mob, it being their last chance before the troops could land. As the prospect of revenge became more certain their courage abated in proportion. Two regiments are landed, but a new grievance is now rais'd. The troops are by act of parliament to be quartered no where else but in the barracks untill they are full. There are barracks enough at the castle to hold both regiments. . . .

The government has been so long in the hands of the populace that it must come out of them by degrees, at least it will be a work of time to bring the people back to just notions of the nature of government.

[In another letter from January 1769, Hutchinson appealed for more help to put down unrest in Boston. His letters were meant to be private, but copies were published in 1773, after Hutchinson had been appointed royal governor. They seriously damaged his reputation, and he fled to England after the American Revolution broke out.]

This is most certainly a crisis. I really wish that there may not have been the least degree of severity beyond what is absolutely necessary to maintain, I think I may say to you the *dependance [sic]* which a colony ought to have upon the parent state; but if no measures shall have been taken to secure this dependance, or nothing more than some declaratory acts or resolves, *it is all over with us. . . .*

There must be an abridgment of what are called English liberties. I relieve myself by considering that in a remove from the state of nature to the most perfect state of government there must be a great restraint of liberty. I doubt whether it is possible to project a system of government in which a colony 3000 miles distant from the parent state shall enjoy all the liberty of the parent state. . . . I wish the good of the colony when I wish to see some further restraint of liberty rather than the connexion with the parent state should be broken; for I am sure such a breach must prove the ruin of the colony.

WORKING WITH SOURCES

1. How does Hutchinson characterize the actions of people from different social classes?
2. How does Hutchinson think the colonial unrest should be controlled?
3. Why did the publication of these letters contribute to Hutchinson's disgrace and exile?

SOURCE 6.3

John Dickinson, "The Liberty Song" (1768)

John Dickinson published these song lyrics, meant to be sung to the British tune "Heart of Oak," in the *Boston Gazette* in July 1768 and then in the *Boston Chronicle* on August 29, 1768. This song was one of many that were sung in the colonies during popular protests against the British. The appearance song lyrics in newspapers could also cement allegiance to the cause, and printed lyrics could be posted in public places, such as taverns, to rouse public support. Protest songs were also used as drinking songs to accompany toasts at political gatherings. This song references a "bumper," a glass full of alcohol that is raised in a toast.

Source: Boston Chronicle, August 29–September 5, 1768.

The LIBERTY Song
COME join hand in hand brave
    AMERICANS all,
And rouse your bold hearts at fair
    LIBERTY's call;
No tyrannous acts shall suppress your
    just claim
Or stain with dishonor AMERICA'S name
        In FREEDOM we're born—Let's give
            them a cheer—
        Our purses are ready
        Steady, Friends, steady,
        Not as SLAVES, but as FREEMEN
            our Money we'll give . . .
Then join Hand in Hand brave
    AMERICANS all,
By uniting we stand, by dividing we fall;
In so RIGHTEOUS a Cause let us hope
    to succeed,
For Heaven approves of each generous
    Deed.
        In FREEDOM we're born, etc.

All Ages shall speak with Amaze and
    Applause,
Of the Courage we'll shew in support of
    our LAWS;
To die we can bear—but to serve we
    disdain.
For Shame is to FREEDOM more
    dreadful than pain
        In FREEDOM we're born, etc.
This Bumper I crown for our Sovereign's
    Health,
And this for Britannia's Glory and wealth;
That Wealth and that glory immortal
    may be,
If she is but JUST—and if we are
    but FREE
        IN FREEDOM we're born, and in
            FREEDOM we'll live
Our purses are ready,
Steady, Friends, steady
Not as SLAVES but as FREEMEN our
    Money we'll give.

WORKING WITH SOURCES

1. How does this song define freedom and slavery?

2. Why would protestors who sang this song be willing to toast to King George III and "Britainnia's Glory" while simultaneously resisting "tyrannous" Parliamentary taxes?

3. Do you think a song like this could convince anyone to join the Non-Importation Movement?

SOURCE 6.4

Abigail Adams, Excerpts from Letters to John Adams about the Battle of Bunker Hill and Conditions in Boston (1775)

Abigail Adams wrote several letters to her husband, John Adams, who was serving in the Continental Congress, to tell him about the Battle of Bunker Hill, which she had witnessed from across the Charles River. In the excerpts below, she reports on the death of Dr. Joseph Warren, a strong patriot who became known as the primary hero of Bunker Hill.

Source: Charles Francis Adams, ed., *Letters of Mrs. Adams* (Boston: Charles C. Little and James Brown, 1840), 39–40, 49, 52–53.

Sunday, 18 June, 1775

The day,—perhaps, the decisive day,—is come, on which the fate of America depends. My bursting heart must find vent at my pen. I have just heard, that our dear friend, Dr. Warren, is no more, but fell gloriously fighting for his country; saying, better to die honorably in the field, than ignominiously hang upon the gallows. Great is our loss. He has distinguished himself in every engagement, by his courage and fortitude, by animating the soldiers, and leading them on by his own example. A particular account of these dreadful, but I hope glorious days will be transmitted you, no doubt, in the exactest manner. . . .

Charlestown is laid in ashes. The battle began upon our intrenchments upon Bunker's Hill, Saturday morning about three o'clock, and has not cased yet, and it is now three o'clock Sabbath afternoon.

It is expected they will come out over the Neck to-night, and a dreadful battle must ensue. Almighty God, cover the heads of our countrymen, and be a shield to our dear friends! How many have fallen, we know not. The constant roar of the cannon is so distressing, that we cannot eat, drink, or sleep. May we be supported and sustained in the dreadful conflict. I shall tarry here till it is thought unsafe by my friends, and then I have secured myself a retreat at your brother's, who has kindly offered me part of his house. I cannot compose myself to write any further at present. I will add more as I hear further. . . .

5 July, 1775

I would not have you be distressed about me. Danger, they say, makes people valiant. I have been distressed, but not dismayed. I have felt for my country and her sons, and have bled with them and for them. Not all the havoc and devastation they have made, has wounded me like the death of Warren. We want him in the Senate; we want him in his profession; we want him in the field. We mourn for the citizen, the senator, the physician, and the warrior. May we have others raised up in his room.

16 July, 1775

The appointments of the generals Washington and Lee gives universal satisfaction. . . . I was struck with General Washington. You had prepared me to entertain a favorable opinion of him, but I thought the half was not told me. Dignity with ease and complacency, the gentleman and the soldier, look agreeably blended in him. . . .

As to intelligence from Boston . . . I heard yesterday, by one Mr. Roulstone, a goldsmith, who got out in a fishing schooner, that their distress increased upon them fast. Their beef is all spent; their malt and cider all gone. All the fresh provisions they can procure, they are obliged to give to the sick and wounded. . . . No man dared now to be seen talking to his friend in the street. They were obliged to be within, every evening, at ten o'clock, according to martial law; nor could any inhabitant walk any street in town after that time, without a pass from [British commander] Gage. He has ordered all the molasses to be distilled up into rum for the soldiers. . . .

Every article here in the West India way is very scarce and dear. In six weeks we shall not be able to purchase any article of the kind. I wish you would let Bass get me one pound of pepper, and two yards of black calamanco for shoes. . . . You can hardly imagine how much we want many common small articles, which are not manufactured amongst ourselves; but we will have them in time; not one pin to be purchased for love or money.

WORKING WITH SOURCES

1. What qualities does Adams admire in patriots and military leaders?

2. What evidence do these letters offer regarding women's roles in the American Revolution?

A Revolutionary Nation

1776–1789

When Benjamin Franklin arrived in Paris on December 21, 1776, thousands turned out to catch a glimpse of him. Franklin was visiting to court French military and diplomatic assistance for the American fight against Great Britain, France's traditional enemy. Franklin hoped to convince the French to support the American Revolution because, as he declared, "'Tis a Common observation here that our Cause is the *Cause of all Mankind*; and that we are fighting for their liberty in defending our own." French king Louis XVI was not sure that he wanted to support the Americans in their Revolution; nor was he, as Europe's most absolutist king, convinced that French "liberty" was at stake. But Franklin's personal popularity grew so quickly by the beginning of 1777 that the French government could not ignore American diplomacy.

Franklin was the most famous American in Europe. His scientific publications had endeared him to French aristocrats and intellectuals. The Comte de Chaumont invited Franklin to live at his estate outside Paris, and fashionable aristocrats sought Franklin as a party guest. Franklin dressed simply and often wore a fur hat to project a rugged American image, and the French became obsessed with his appearance. Franklin's face appeared on paintings, engravings, statues, jewelry, candy boxes, dishes, and handkerchiefs. Franklin wrote his daughter that "your father's face [is] as well known as that of the moon." Some fashionable Parisians even had their hair styled in a manner that imitated Franklin's. John Adams later wrote that "There was scarcely a peasant or a citizen, a valet de chambre, coachman or footman, a lady's chambermaid nor a scullion in the kitchen who was not familiar with Franklin's name."

< George Washington, by Charles Willson Peale, c. 1779–1781.

Franklin left the United States for France just a few months after signing the Declaration of Independence and with the experience of having lived for almost 20 years in Britain, representing colonial interests to the British crown. Franklin hoped to win foreign assistance for the Revolutionary War even as France and other European powers waited to see whether Americans could win. Between 1776 and 1789, the United States relied on foreign help as it secured its independence from Great Britain and struggled to form a government. But Americans, like Franklin, also believed that their Revolution offered a new vision of liberty to the rest of the world.

■ THE REVOLUTION TAKES ROOT

Following the Declaration of Independence in 1776, the United States became a sovereign nation, and each of the 13 states also established new forms of revolutionary government. The Declaration stated that it had become necessary for "one people to dissolve the political bands which have connected them with another"; but, in reality, many loyalists, Quakers, royal officials, and other American inhabitants did not cut ties to Britain or express allegiance to the new United States. The new nation would have to exert authority over these doubters, but it might never get that chance if it could not win the ongoing war with Great Britain. The United States faced five more years of warfare and the challenge of convincing the world that it was capable of governing itself and worthy of recognition. As the South Carolina legislator David Ramsay wrote, "Our enemies seemed confident of the impossibility of our union; our friends doubted it; and all indifferent persons … considered the expectation thereof as romantic." Against all this doubt, the American Revolution took deep root among most Americans.

BENJAMIN FRANKLIN   This portrait of Benjamin Franklin, commissioned by the American Philosophical Society in 1789, depicts him as a learned man of science. Documents about and pieces of his invention—the lightning rod—lie on the table before him, as a bolt of lightning strikes outside his window. Franklin's scientific knowledge was one of the bases of his great international reputation.

Ideology and Transatlantic Politics

The American revolutionaries expressed a set of political and social values that gave meaning to their actions. In their writings and in the state and national governments they established, patriots expressed an ideology of republicanism, which mixed classical Roman ideals with values from the European Enlightenment. The Declaration of Independence fused republican values with a Lockean emphasis on the property rights of free individuals when it termed "life, liberty, and the pursuit of happiness" as "unalienable rights."

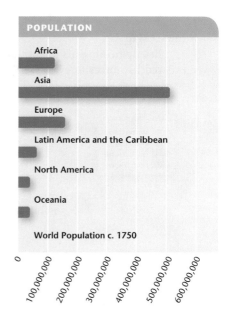

American Revolutionaries rejected monarchy and established themselves as citizens of a representative republic. Republicanism emphasized liberty and guarded against tyrannical exercise of governmental power—such as the colonists perceived in the conflict with Britain leading up to the Revolutionary War. James Madison wrote after the Revolutionary War that "we may define a republic to be . . . a government which derives all its powers directly or indirectly from the body of the people." But republicanism meant more than just a form of government because it also implied much about how citizens should relate to one another and to the forms of power in society. Revolutionaries believed that for a voluntary republic to flourish, its citizens must show civic virtue, a care for the common good. Ideally, instead of being governed by hereditary aristocracy and patronage, as one revolutionary put it, "all offices lie open to men of merit, of whatever rank or condition."

Because of their belief in republicanism, many American revolutionaries also believed that the future worldwide cause of liberty and the happiness of "the great family of mankind" rested on the success of their movement. This belief in their own role in world history put some revolutionaries in an awkward situation because they still had to gain European support for the war against Great Britain. John Adams, the Massachusetts politician who was sent to Europe as a diplomat and to negotiate foreign loans, firmly believed that America faced political danger in dealing with European monarchies. Adams desired good commercial and diplomatic relations with France, the Netherlands, and Spain, but he feared that "America has been the Sport of European Wars and Politicks long enough." Americans were in the paradoxical situation of needing help from European monarchs to win their own antimonarchical war—and thereby to guarantee the existence of their republic, which they believed could transform the world.

Trying Times: War Continues

Both British and American military commanders exercised caution in their approach to the Revolutionary War between 1776 and 1778. As a result, neither side gained a distinct strategic advantage. Each side won important battles, but neither was willing or able to inflict a crushing defeat on the other. As long as the revolutionary spirit and independence movement survived, it would take a monumental British effort to make the United States lose the war. The revolutionaries, although they enjoyed the support of about 70 percent of the white population in America, could not be assured of a victory either, especially if they could not convince other European nations to aid their cause (Map 7.1).

Briefly turning his attention south, British army commander **Sir William Howe** ordered his forces to evacuate Boston in March 1776. Nine British warships bearing

MAP 7.1 ▲ Major Revolutionary War Battles, 1775–1778 This map shows the locations of major battles in the first four years of the Revolutionary War and depicts areas of particular loyalist and patriot strength.

seven regiments of soldiers, commanded by General **Lord Cornwallis**, arrived off the coast of South Carolina. There they joined Sir Henry Clinton's forces in an attack on Charleston that revolutionaries narrowly rebuffed at the Battle of Sullivan's Island on June 28, 1776. British naval forces commanded by Admiral Sir Peter Parker sailed back north—headed for New York and Halifax.

In September 1776, William Howe and his brother Admiral **Sir Richard Howe** used their 32,000 British and German mercenary troops—dubbed "Hessians" by the Americans—to launch an attack against American commander General George Washington's forces at Long Island. The Howes' forces defeated the American army and militia troops in a series of battles stretching from Brooklyn Heights to White Plains, New York, through the fall. Although missing several chances to destroy the Americans, they managed to occupy New York City for the rest of the war. General Cornwallis's force chased Washington across New Jersey. Then, in the first week of December, Washington fled into Pennsylvania. Cornwallis left Hessian troops to watch the Americans across the Delaware, and returned to New York to go into winter quarters.

Thomas Paine correctly described the American military predicament when he declared in his pamphlet *The Crisis* on December 19, 1776, that "these are the times that try men's souls." Washington decided to cross the Delaware again and launch a surprise attack on the Hessian camp at Trenton, New Jersey, late on Christmas night. The unconventional attack was successful but also seemed to confirm that Washington was most successful when he avoided open European-style battles. Washington's victory at the Battle of Trenton, which he followed with a victory at the Battle of Princeton on January 3, 1777, represented two of his few early successes.

General Washington had trouble taking advantage of the successes at Princeton and Trenton. American forces were plagued by spotty militia performance, expiring enlistments, and conflict with loyalists, who took advantage of William Howe's offer to pardon any man who swore an oath to the crown or joined up with British military forces.

In the fall of 1777, Washington tried to defend the U.S. capital at Philadelphia, but Howe defeated him in a series of battles in and around Brandywine, Pennsylvania. Washington's force survived, but it was not clear whether American troops could beat the British in open battle. The British not only had the greater numbers of troops in most areas of the military conflict, they were also better trained and supplied. Congress fled Philadelphia, which Howe occupied in September. After losing a close contest at Germantown on October 4, Washington retreated and prepared to enter winter quarters at Valley Forge, Pennsylvania.

Further north, the British government sent Major General John Burgoyne in early 1777 to Canada with another plan to invade New England and recapture Fort Ticonderoga. His mixed force of British, Hessian, Canadian militia, Loyalist, and Indian troops made slow progress after capturing Fort Ticonderoga at the beginning of July. American commander Major General **Horatio Gates** dealt Burgoyne's troops a blow at Freeman's Farm on the Hudson River in September. Gates won an even bigger battle at Saratoga, New York, on October 7, forcing Burgoyne to surrender his entire 6,000-man army to Gates, who had proved that American forces could inflict decisive defeat. Although most of his troops were held prisoner for the remainder of the war, "Gentleman Johnny" Burgoyne was released on parole, as befit an officer of the day, and he returned to Britain in disgrace. Victory in the battle of Saratoga was one of the most significant moments in the entire Revolutionary War.

Alliance with France

The Battle of Saratoga was the turning point of the Revolutionary War because it helped to convince France to form an alliance with the United States. On December 4, 1777, Boston merchant Jonathan Loring Austin brought the news of Burgoyne's defeat at Saratoga to American diplomats Benjamin Franklin, Richard Henry Lee, and Silas Deane in France. The French foreign minister, the **Comte de Vergennes**, had authorized secret aid to the American revolutionaries since May 1776. Sympathetic aristocrats and merchants sent money and supplies. The playwright Caron de Beaumarchais, for example, set up the trade company Hortalez & Cie. to secretly funnel aid to the United States. From 1776 onward, the French supplied over 90 percent of the gunpowder used by the American military. Vergennes wanted to ally with the United States, but he had not been able to build political support for the move. Now, the news of the decisive American victory at Saratoga gave Vergennes all he needed to support the United States openly against France's enemy, Great Britain. Spain continued to drag its feet, but the French moved forward with an alliance.

The French government granted the United States diplomatic recognition at the end of 1777. In February 1778, France and the United States signed a Treaty of Amity and Commerce and a Treaty of Alliance in which France promised "not to lay down their arms until the Independence of the United States shall have been formally or tacitly assured." Congress ratified both treaties on May 4, 1778, creating the first diplomatic alliance in American history. Vergennes was preparing for a possible Austro-Prussian war on the Continent, so he hesitated to commit full French naval power to the fight in North America until 1780, but in April 1778, the Comte d'Estaing sailed for America with a fleet of 16 French warships and 4,000 troops. Early in 1778, George Washington despaired that the American military was in a "distressed, ruinous, and deplorable condition," and he feared defeat "if a remedy is not soon applied." Patriots hoped that French aid would bring just such a remedy.

STUDY QUESTIONS FOR THE REVOLUTION TAKES ROOT

1. In what ways did the Battle of Saratoga represent a turning point in the Revolutionary War?

2. Why did the American Revolutionaries seek and accept aid from European monarchies?

■ THE STRUCTURE OF AUTHORITY

One cause of George Washington's despair over future prospects was the unstable organization of the American government and military—which French aid could only partially address. While winning a war, the United States had to build an effective governmental structure. The Second Continental Congress had directed the early operations of the war and had declared independence from Great Britain, but by the time it ratified the treaty with France, it still operated under no formal constitutional authority.

It took the Congress more than 16 months to draft the **Articles of Confederation** and several more years for all the states to ratify it. In the meantime, Congress governed and states drafted constitutions. But questions of legitimacy remained. Although the Continental Army expressed clear allegiance to civilian Congressional authority, it had its own internal difficulties—especially regarding supply and the coordination of army and militia forces and enlistments. How could the United States build a government strong enough to reassure foreign powers of its legitimacy? If government failed, even foreign aid might not be sufficient to win the war or to solidify the American Revolution.

State Governments

In May 1776, even before the Continental Congress adopted the Declaration of Independence, it instructed individual colonies to begin drafting state constitutions. Whigs, who had been governing in practice without constitutional authority in many colonies, and who had been directing war operations, decided to focus their energies on written constitutions that would define state power. In many cases, state constitutions as written documents (different from the unwritten British constitution) grew out of royal charters and other colonial decrees. Everywhere they defined power counter to the colonial organization of government. By the end of 1776, 11 of 13 states had drafted state constitutions, and Georgia and New York completed theirs the following year. Each state pursued economic policies, contracted debts, and pursued land claims with minimum of coordination between them.

Every state established itself as a representative republic that derived sovereignty from the people, who would demonstrate their consent through voting. Each state established a balance between executive, legislative, and judicial powers, in keeping with the political idea of **separation of powers** articulated by the French Enlightenment philosopher the Baron de Montesquieu. Most states kept a judicial system similar to their colonial structures. Having cast off colonial governors who represented royal authority, however, most states limited the power of governors and established governor's councils appointed by the elected legislatures. Many states also implemented term limits for their governors. Almost every state established a two-house legislature, with a Roman-style senate that could brake any "excessively" democratic actions taken by the lower house. Some states enlarged their legislatures, to grant more representation to western areas that were filling up with settlers, and five states directly tied representation to population size, a very new concept. All but Massachusetts and Connecticut abolished established state religion, although most still required government officeholders to be Christian.

Despite similarities, some states were more democratic than others, varying the degrees of direct representation and restraint of government power in their constitutions. Pennsylvania had no governor at all and established a unicameral legislature with strict term limits that proportionally represented the population and was elected by all free men over 21 who paid taxes. By contrast, Maryland's revolutionary planter elites defined a government in which only the lower house of the legislature was popularly elected, with a powerful governor, and which had high property-holding qualifications for officeholders who served long terms. In all the states, even the least democratic, new ranks of men such as artisans began to assume offices and responsibilities that would never have fallen to them in the hierarchical days of colonial government.

Articles of Confederation

Soon after declaring independence, Congress realized the need to form a legitimate national government. A committee charged with the task of creating a national constitution drafted the Articles of Confederation in 1777, although deep disagreements among the states delayed full ratification. The Articles proposed a weak national government for "The United States of America." Most Americans closely identified with their separate states, and they were not ready for much in the way of national power, which they feared.

As North Carolina Congressman Thomas Burke wrote, "the United States ought to be as One Sovereign with respect to foreign Powers, in all things that relate to War or where the States have one Common Interest." The Articles limited centralized power and reserved decision making in most other areas to the states. Congress had no power to tax citizens of the states, which contributed to national financial problems. Congress controlled the military and the war-making power, but the Articles directly forbade sustaining a military force after the war. Each state exercised one vote under the Articles, and to change most national policies required 9 votes out of 13. Only a unanimous vote could change any provision of the actual Articles. Arguments over rival state claims to Western lands held up the ratification of the Articles of Confederation until 1781. By then, Congress was almost bankrupt.

Military Organization

In republican theories of government, it was important to restrain military power and subordinate it to civilian authority. When the first Continental Congress created the Continental Army in June of 1775, it built in several weaknesses to prevent the military from assuming too much power in society. Americans distrusted standing armies and viewed militias, in the words of the Virginia constitution, as "the proper, natural, and safe defense of a free state." But militias could never be effective enough to win a war against the British military, so the United States had to create an army and a navy and fill their ranks.

Congress initially restricted enlistments in the Continental Army to one year, but after severe problems recruiting new men became apparent by 1777, Congress authorized

VALLEY FORGE   Twelve thousand men were stationed at Valley Forge, where they faced near starvation, disease, and terribly cold weather. Thousands died of pneumonia and typhoid fever, and thousands more were listed as "unfit for service."

three-year terms, began to pay cash enlistment bounties, and promised land grants. By 1779, Congress allowed men to enlist for the duration of the war and paid bounties as high as $200. Continental officers at first recruited their own men, but after 1777, Congress imposed recruiting quotas on each state. Historians estimate the number of American men in arms during the Revolution at between 250,000 and 350,000, at least 10 percent of the total American population.

Volunteer state militias provided men to the Continental Army, but they also continued to fight in their own right throughout the war, partially as a republican restraint on excess military authority. Major General Charles Lee expressed a widespread republican belief when he declared that "a militia, animated by determination to preserve liberty, could become a formidable infantry." Although militia units were often less disciplined and organized in battle, they did contribute to troop strength and success, especially when the war turned South after 1778. Many men who enlisted in the revolutionary military, especially at the beginning of the war, expressed a strong allegiance to the revolutionary cause, but economic incentives also influenced the decision to join the Continental Army. The average soldier was in his late 20s. European officers serving with the Continental Army marveled at the success of common men, like shoemakers, who became American officers. But as a member of Congress, John Adams felt "wearied to Death with the Wrangles between military officers high and low. They Quarrell like Cats and Dogs."

The Continental Congress oversaw military affairs, but Congress also granted George Washington "full, ample, and complete" powers to direct the army as he saw fit. Both enlisted men and officers suffered from Congress' inability to guarantee adequate military supplies. Before Nathaniel Greene reorganized it in 1780, the Quartermaster General's office was overwhelmed trying to provide supplies and coordinate transportation. Congress lacked funds, struggled to provide food and shoes to troops, and did not provide consistent uniforms until 1781. During the brutal winter of 1777–1778, one-quarter of the 12,000 American soldiers who wintered at Valley Forge, Pennsylvania, died, partly because of poor food and shelter. Some judged the winter encampment of 1780 at Morristown, New Jersey, to be even worse. Hard conditions made it even more remarkable that the mutiny of the Pennsylvania line in January 1780 marked one of the only large-scale troop revolts of the war. Army surgeon James Thacher wrote during that winter that "both the resources and the credit of our Congress appear to be almost exhausted." Congress printed large quantities of paper money, which quickly lost much of its value.

Diplomacy and International Finance

Aside from paper currency, foreign credit was the main engine of war finance. The United States sent a series of envoys to European countries, particularly Britain's rivals, seeking recognition and funding. France, Spain, and the Netherlands extended aid with varying levels of enthusiasm. Prior to finalizing the treaties of Alliance and Amity and Commerce with the United States, French citizens were already supplying financial and material aid to the war effort. Their support increased markedly after the 1778 agreements. The United States could not have continued the war without French assistance. The French lent the United States approximately $7 million and gave more than $2 million in outright gifts.

GLOBAL PASSAGES

International Officers in the American Revolutionary Military

Many European military men volunteered to join the American military as officers in the Revolutionary War. These international volunteers brought with them connections to politicians and military establishments in Europe, personal financial resources, and military knowledge. Officers from Continental Europe enhanced the cachet of the American military forces and increased international approval for the American Revolution. As American diplomats in France, Benjamin Franklin and Silas Deane actively recruited aristocratic Europeans to join the Continental Army.

Tadeusz Kosciuszko, a graduate of the Polish Royal School and the French school of engineering and artillery, was commissioned as a colonel in the Continental Army in 1776 and played a key role in designing the fortifications at West Point and entrenchments at Saratoga. Kosciuszko ended the war as a brigadier general. The Chevalier Louis Duportail, sent to the United States even before the French joined the cause, served most of the war as a brigadier general and chief of army engineers. Benjamin Franklin recruited **Friedrich Wilhelm von Steuben**, an impoverished former Prussian staff officer who became inspector general of the Continental Army and an effective drill master during the winter at Valley Forge. He was one of Washington's most effective aides. Less effective was Casimir Pulaski, a Pole who commanded American cavalry and later his own elite corps (the Pulaski Legion) as a brigadier general in the Continental Army.

Other European countries also took an interest in the war, which German poet Christoph Wieland called "the greatest political event of the 1770s, and perhaps . . . of the entire century." The Spanish had sent some help but had largely held the United States at arm's length—in part because they did not wish to see colonial independence movements spread into Spanish America. Because of tensions in Europe, however, Spain declared war on Britain in April 1779. The Spanish governor of Louisiana and East Florida, Bernardo de Gálvez, captured several British forts along the Mississippi River and at Mobile and Pensacola, indirectly helping the American war effort. In January 1780, **John Jay** arrived in Madrid seeking diplomatic recognition, but the prediction by the French foreign minister that "Spain . . . will interest herself very little in the Americans" proved true. Despite promises to return West Florida to Spain after independence was secured, Spain never formally recognized American independence during the war—although the Spanish government did agree to open trade between the United States and Cuba and to loan the United States $170,000. The trade with Cuba was significant, given that it replaced much of the prohibited U.S. trade with the British West Indies and provided the United States access to hard currency. Cuba, whose large-scale sugar production was expanding under the Bourbon Reforms, also benefitted from the U.S. trade goods—especially food to feed the growing number of slaves on the island.

The most famous French volunteer, **Major General Marie-Joseph-Paul-Yves-Roch-Gilbert du Motier, Marquis de Lafayette**, joined the American cause in 1777 when he was only 19 years old along with his friend, the highly capable Johan de Kalb (who was also a French spy). Lafayette fought ably and played a major role in the defeat of Cornwallis at Yorktown in 1781.

Many of the foreign officers in the Continental Army who were not killed during the war (as de Kalb and Pulaski were) participated in revolutionary and independence movements in Europe in subsequent decades. Lafayette, Duportail, and other pro-American aristocrats joined the French Revolution when it began in 1789. Kosciuszko led several campaigns in the Polish independence movement against Russia during the 1790s. Lafayette and von Steuben were given American citizenship and land grants in thanks for their American service (Kosciuszko also received land). Several European officers, including von Steuben, retired in the United States. Both Kosciuszko and Lafayette returned to the United States after the War, and Lafayette's extended tour in 1824–1825 was one of the largest events commemorating the American Revolution during the first 50 years after the war.

- How might the willingness of these officers to serve in the American military have influenced opinion in Europe in favor of the United States?
- Does the service of men such as Lafayette and Kosciuszko in European revolutionary movements indicate that the American Revolution influenced Europe?

When the British captured neutral ships from several countries trading with the United States in 1780, Russian empress **Catherine the Great** responded by forming the League of Armed Neutrality to protect neutral shipping, although Russia never formally recognized the United States during the Revolution. Sweden, Denmark, Portugal, the Netherlands, and Sicily all joined the League—tying up British naval resources and attempting to open further U.S. trade. Of these countries, the Dutch were the friendliest to the American cause, allowing a smuggled arms trade to the Revolutionaries even before 1777. A few months after all of the Dutch provinces and Prince William V formally recognized the United States, American envoy John Adams convinced Dutch bankers to loan the United States $2 million in July 1782.

STUDY QUESTIONS FOR THE STRUCTURE OF AUTHORITY

1. What difference did foreign aid make to the American Revolution?
2. How did the ideology of republicanism affect U.S. government and military authority during the American Revolution?

■ SECURING INDEPENDENCE

With the French as allies, American revolutionaries had high expectations of winning the war, but the road ahead was not easy. The focus of the military conflict shifted to the seas and into the Southern states. Bitter social divisions there helped to intensify the fighting. Loyalists held onto their British identities, even as they were forced to fight their neighbors or leave their homes. African Americans assessed how to maximize their own potential for freedom in the midst of wartime chaos. Indian nations tried to decide whether their future interests lay with the British or the United States. Nothing seemed easy during the last years of the Revolutionary War, but one thing was certain—the United States would cease to exist if it did not win the war.

War at Sea

The most immediate impact of French assistance came in the naval war. As early as the first year of the war, the United States established a navy and an ambitious shipbuilding program, with several states also fielding their own naval forces. Although the U.S. Navy succeeded in several small attacks, such as when Commander Esek Hopkins captured the British fort at Nassau, Bahamas, in November 1776, Americans could not hope to defeat the British Navy—the strongest and best-equipped sea force in the world—that

USS *BON HOMME RICHARD* John Paul Jones commanded the USS *Bon Homme Richard*, a warship loaned to the United States by France and named in honor of Benjamin Franklin's *Poor Richard's Almanac*. Jones battled the British ship HMS *Serapis* off the coast of Yorkshire, England, in September 1779, and his capture of the British navy vessel helped to convince the French to increase their support for the naval war against Britain.

was blockading the northern U.S. coastline. Instead, the American navy and over 2,000 privateers harassed British war and commercial ships. Captain Nicholas Biddle, a former member of the Royal Navy, successfully raided British ships in the West Indies in 1777. Basing his U.S. naval operations in France, Captain John Paul Jones successfully raided the Scottish coastline and captured British prizes in the Irish Sea. Jones cemented his reputation in September 1779 when he defeated the British frigate *Serapis* in a thrilling battle, taking the ship as a prize after declaring "I have not yet begun to fight!"

French entry into the war diverted British attention away from the fight in America and forced them to commit ships to the English Channel, the Mediterranean, the Caribbean, and off the coast of India to defend their empire. Sir William Clinton partly abandoned Philadelphia and the blockade of the U.S. coast in 1778, diverting 5,000 men to the sugar-rich West Indies where he expected to engage the French. The French concentrated most of their force on the Caribbean islands that they had lost to the British in the Seven Years' War. The French admiral **Comte d'Estaing** arrived with his fleet in the summer of 1778; and, after botching an attack on British-controlled Newport, Rhode Island, he sailed for the West Indies. The British captured St. Lucia in December 1778, but the French captured and held the island of Grenada.

MAP 7.2 ▲ The Caribbean during the Revolutionary War Much of the hottest naval warfare in the Revolutionary War took place around the Caribbean where countries battled to control trade and tried to wrest control of islands away from one another.

D'Estaing failed to oust the British from Savannah in September 1779—in part because he followed a French pattern of failing to coordinate well with U.S. ground forces. In 1780 and 1781, French naval assistance proved more effective. Commodore Ternay carried 5,500 French army troops under the Comte de Rochambeau to reinforce the Continental Army in July 1780, and in October 1781, the French admiral **Comte de Grasse** added his fleet to the fight at Yorktown.

War in the South

Britain's cabinet war ministers, led by **Lord George Germain**, shifted the focus of their ground efforts to the South in 1778. On March 8, 1778, British officials replaced Commander Sir William Howe with **Sir Henry Clinton**, whom they ordered to abandon Philadelphia to attack the Carolinas and Georgia. As Clinton tried to evacuate his army from Philadelphia back to New York, he ran up against George Washington's army. In winter quarters at Valley Forge, Washington's troops had suffered, but they had also been strengthened by the training and drill offered by the new inspector general of the army, the Baron von Steuben. U.S. and British forces clashed at Monmouth, New Jersey, on June 28, 1778; and, although Clinton's army escaped, only a poor performance from Washington's second-in-command Charles Lee kept the Americans from crushing the British Army.

The South saw much of the worst fighting between patriots and loyalists of the entire war. The British invaded Georgia and easily captured Savannah in December 1778. Support from loyalists, thousands of runaway slaves, and some Cherokees helped subdue the patriot civilian population, and the British were able to recapture the Georgia state government. The patriot defeat in South Carolina was even more disastrous. The British sent forces over land to surround Charleston, and British Generals Clinton and Cornwallis fought "storm, rain, hail, snow, and ... waves" to sail to Charleston with additional troops. They bottled up American commander Major General Benjamin Lincoln in the City of Charleston, and after six weeks of siege and bitter fighting, Lincoln surrendered the city and his entire army on May 12, 1780. Clinton returned to New York, and he left Cornwallis in charge of putting down further resistance in South Carolina and pushing into North Carolina, with an eye toward eventually conquering Virginia. In the following months, the backcountry of South Carolina witnessed brutal clashes between loyalist/British detachments and patriot militias. In 1780 British lieutenant colonel **Banastre Tarleton** acquired a bloody reputation by moving quickly between skirmishes, destroying property, and killing prisoners.

Without consulting General Washington, and against his wishes, Congress appointed Horatio Gates to command the Continental Army's Southern Department. Cornwallis crushed Gates at Camden, South Carolina, and his troops retreated in disarray. Gates himself rode as fast as he could all the way to Hillsboro, North Carolina. But the bitter defeat did little to change the course of the war, as rural skirmishes persisted and Cornwallis waited for an uprising of loyalists. Instead, many white Southerners began to support the Americans out of anger when the British shielded runaway slaves.

After Camden, Congress removed Gates from command and replaced him with Nathanael Greene, who was probably the finest strategist in the American military. Although his army was in poor shape, Greene took heart from the victory of American militia forces at Kings Mountain, South Carolina, on October 7. Greene recognized that he was unlikely to defeat Cornwallis in open battle, so he divided his army into four parts and kept British and loyalist forces on the run through the Carolina backcountry. Greene, and his able subcommander **Daniel Morgan**, who bested Tarleton at Cowpens in January 1781, engaged Cornwallis in three open battles that year at Guilford Courthouse, Hobkirk's Hill, and Eutaw Springs. The Americans lost all three battles, but they inflicted terrible damage on Cornwallis's combined forces. Greene wrote of the campaign, "We fight, get beat, rise and fight again." Greene's strategy inflicted some of the heaviest casualties of the war on Cornwallis, who moved into Virginia and marched toward Yorktown.

Loyalists: Resistance and Migration

The loyalist population played a large role in the British war effort. Loyalists, dubbed "Tories" by the revolutionaries, made up almost 20 percent of the total population of the United States. Loyalists expressed different notions of "liberty" than those put forth by the revolutionaries, and they held onto British identity and obedience in the midst of conflict. Not all loyalists agreed with one another beyond opposing independence. Several ethnic or religious minority groups who relied on crown protection remained loyal, although they did not constitute a majority in any state: Germans in the Mid-Atlantic, Anglicans in New England, landholders in the Hudson Valley, Scotch-Irish immigrants in the southern backcountry, and Dutch settlers in New Jersey. Although they aided the British military by providing supplies and even taking up arms against their neighbors, loyalist opposition to the Revolution was not enough to enable the British to win the war.

Estimates of the number of loyalists who fled the United States for England, Canada, and the West Indies during and immediately after the war reach as high as 80,000, or 1 out of every 40 people in the United States. Many who emigrated were wealthy before the war, and Congress seized millions of dollars in loyalists' property. An estimated additional 20,000 African American slaves ran away from their masters and sought British protection during the war, including some who emigrated to Canada, Nova Scotia, and Sierra Leone after the war. White and black loyalists who resettled elsewhere in the British Empire sometimes helped to shore up imperial control, but some faced discrimination. Black emigrants to Canada achieved freedom, but many runaway slaves who joined the British were re-enslaved in the West Indies.

Loyalists who resettled in England found they sometimes experienced what Samuel Curwen called an "uneasy abode in this country of aliens," but most found it even more difficult to return to their former homes—even after the war ended. **Benedict Arnold**, the Continental general who defected to the British side in 1780, became a scorned British military officer. Even groups who were merely ambivalent about the war and tried to remain neutral, such as the Pennsylvania Quakers whose religion forbade fighting, found it difficult to reintegrate into American society.

Indian Warfare

Indian populations in North America were also torn apart by the Revolutionary War. Many groups had barely finished navigating the tension-filled terrain created by the French loss in the Seven Years' War when the Declaration of Independence again placed them between rival powers. The United States might be even less generous toward Indians than Great Britain had been, but not all Indian peoples aligned themselves with the British. Religion, trade, political calculations, and personal relationships influenced Indian decisions, and divisions existed, even within tight-knit kinship groups. Some native peoples also used the Revolution as an opportunity to try and advance their own regional interests, such as when **Joseph Brant** led Mohawk and other Iroquois troops against Pennsylvania and New York frontier settlers in the "Border War" of 1777–1779. Iroquois attacks, particularly in the Wyoming Valley, Pennsylvania, were long remembered for their brutal force.

Even Brant, who was a respected commander, could not unite the powerful Six Nations entirely in favor of the British. Some Oneida and Tuscarora peoples in New England joined the American army at Valley Forge. Oneida fighters played a decisive role in the American victory at the Battle of Oriskany in 1777, which destroyed their own village but set up the American victory at Saratoga. By the end of the war, most other Iroquois groups had joined Brant in his support for the British, especially after American Major General John Sullivan pursued a scorched-earth campaign against them in New York in the summer of 1779. After the war, the British resettled Brant and his Iroquois allies in Canada.

The United States was not as generous to its Indian allies, notably pushing Delaware people into the arms of the British after failing to follow the terms of an alliance signed at Pittsburgh in 1778. Other Delaware were forced to abandon their lands in Ohio. Delaware

BATTLE OF YORKTOWN   This painting depicts the British surrender at the Battle of Yorktown in 1781, the last major campaign of the Revolutionary War. In the image, American General Benjamin Lincoln accepts the sword of surrender from British General Cornwallis's subordinate officer. Artist John Trumbull painted a larger version of this image inside the rotunda of the U.S. Capitol building.

warrior Buckongahelas lamented in 1781 that his people had been drawn into the Revolutionary War, "a family quarrel, in which I was not interested." Many Shawnee tried to remain neutral, but many Shawnee warriors ended up fighting for the British in an attempt to hold onto Ohio lands. American troops attacked Cherokee in 1776, 1780, and 1781, and many Cherokee aligned themselves with loyalist militias in the brutal fighting in the Carolinas and Georgia. Overall, it is difficult to generalize about how the American Revolution affected the native peoples, but one fact stands out: the lives of most Indians did not improve as a result of the Revolutionary War or its outcome.

African Americans at War

Like Indians, not all African Americans adopted the same stance toward the Revolutionary War. But those who were able to fight—either on the American or the British side—often managed to change their social status as a result. African Americans constituted a small but significant percentage of Revolutionary fighters on land and water, and in some battles—such as the 1778 battle at Monmouth, New Jersey—black men fought on both sides.

African American men served in the British infantry and navy, and many runaway slaves worked as spies and laborers for British forces. Some African Americans who were re-enslaved in the West Indies continued their military service by becoming part of the British West Indian Regiments that fought in the Napoleonic Wars in the 1790s. Harry, a slave who was transported to the Dutch Island of St. Eustasius during the war, made a public reputation for himself as a Methodist preacher, although he continued to be enslaved.

Service in the American military presented a path to personal freedom, and many black men and women supported the patriot cause. Although George Washington initially banned blacks from the Continental Army, the need for troops forced him to abandon this policy within months; and in some areas, black men made up as much as 25 percent of American fighting forces. Many northern slaves enlisted, and their state governments sometimes purchased their freedom from their masters, whom they replaced in service. Some, such as the Concord, Massachusetts, slave Richard Hobby, joined the American military when their masters were absent. Even in Southern states, some slaves and many free black men enlisted in the American army and militias. Both Massachusetts and Rhode Island set up separate, black militia units, but for the most part, black and white men served together in integrated companies. Black men enhanced their personal freedom by joining the war effort, and their status as Revolutionary War veterans would also help the antislavery cause after the war.

Peace and Shifting Empires

The final phase of the Revolutionary War began when British general Cornwallis entrenched his troops in Yorktown, Virginia, in August 1781. General Washington learned of Cornwallis's move and realized that Yorktown's position on the Chesapeake Bay made it vulnerable. He also learned that de Grasse's French squadron would soon arrive. So Washington boldly marched almost his whole army, accompanied by French forces under the Comte de Rochambeau, from New York to Virginia to link up with Greene. By the end of September, the American forces surrounded Yorktown and laid siege to

Cornwallis's force. For almost two weeks, the American and French forces pounded Cornwallis's men with artillery fire and pushed them back toward the Chesapeake coast with carefully executed skirmishes. Under increasing pressure, Cornwallis realized he had no escape, and on October 19, 1781, he had a subordinate, General Charles O'Hara, surrender his entire army (Map 7.3).

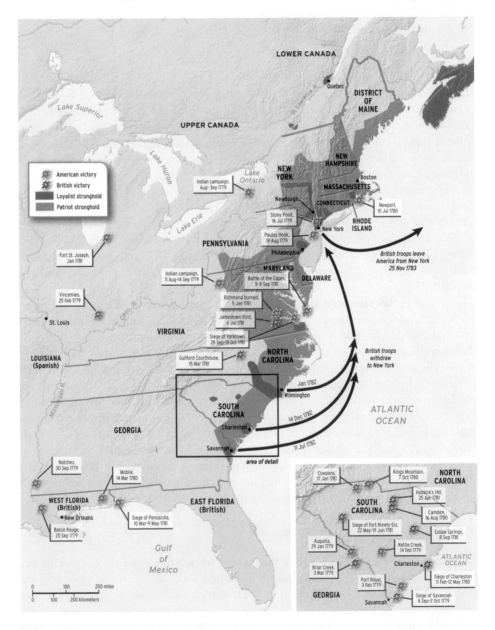

MAP 7.3 ▲ Major Revolutionary War Battles, 1779–1783 Although the Revolutionary War was mostly concluded after Cornwallis's surrender at Yorktown in 1781, skirmishing continued until the Treaty of Paris in 1783 ended the conflict.

When British prime minister Lord North heard the news of Yorktown, he reportedly exclaimed, "Oh God! It is all over!" The British government decided to pursue peace. The new British prime minister Lord Shelburne sent merchant Richard Oswald to Paris at the beginning of 1782 to negotiate with Benjamin Franklin. They concluded a preliminary peace agreement in November 1782 without any input from French officials. French foreign minister Vergennes was impressed with the Americans' diplomacy, and he negotiated a separate peace with Britain and convinced the Spanish to do the same. The Netherlands also concluded a separate treaty. American negotiators Franklin, John Jay, John Adams, and **Henry Laurens** successfully played French and British interests against one another when they concluded negotiations with Britain and signed the final Treaty of Paris on September 3, 1783.

The terms of the Treaty of Paris favored the United States, largely because the British had decided to cut their losses. The treaty recognized American independence and established borders stretching from the Great Lakes down the Mississippi River to the 31st parallel. Britain granted American fishing rights off Nova Scotia, and Congress agreed to honor war debts, to restore confiscated loyalist property, and to disallow retribution against British supporters. Britain's Native American allies were incensed that Britain had negotiated away land rights without consulting or involving them. The British and Americans agreed to free passage on the Mississippi, but the Spanish objected and blocked free trade on the river in 1784. In their separate negotiations, France, Spain, and Britain swapped possession of several Caribbean islands, and Britain traded control of East and West Florida to Spain in return for Gibraltar. Although the British dragged their feet enforcing parts of the Treaty of Paris, the agreement nonetheless concluded the first-ever successful colonial war of independence and guaranteed the existence of the United States of America.

STUDY QUESTIONS FOR SECURING INDEPENDENCE

1. How did divisions inside the United States shape the course of the Revolutionary War?
2. What were the immediate consequences of the Treaty of Paris?

■ RESTRUCTURING POLITICAL AND SOCIAL AUTHORITY

By winning the Revolutionary War, patriots gained the chance to make permanent their experiment with republican government. Now the national and state governments would have to solidify their efforts to govern for "the cause of all mankind." But Americans faced obstacles to the peaceful refashioning of society, and not everyone agreed on how to proceed. How could loyalists be reintegrated into society? What consequences did republican liberty hold for subordinate people in society? Could the states govern harmoniously and share power with Congress? How would Americans pay the crushing debts incurred during the war? Would economic changes brought on by the war continue as the United States struggled to become successful in trade? Social and economic changes accompanied the shift in politics in the new nation, but nothing went smoothly.

Power in the States

During demobilization from the Revolutionary War, Congress and the states were still negotiating their power relationships. Under the Articles of Confederation, Congress coordinated national policy, but states exercised great power directly over their citizens. Several states, including Massachusetts, ratified less democratic constitutions in the 1780s. States gradually repealed laws against loyalists, although many loyalists, especially in northern states, never regained all the property they had lost in the war.

The states had to deal with political tensions unleashed by what John Jay called the "rage for emigrating to the western country," which sometimes worsened clashes between states. Western inhabitants, many of whom were veterans lured by land bounties or by land investment companies, demanded increased representation of western areas in state legislatures, which tended to overrepresent eastern elites. South Carolina, North Carolina, Georgia, and Virginia all moved their state capitals to towns that lay further west, partly because of the shift in population. Hard-fought campaigns to separate Vermont, Kentucky, and Franklin (in modern-day Tennessee) into new states created political tensions, but none succeeded until after 1787. States also clashed with one another over rival land claims. Virginia peacefully ceded western territory to Congress in 1784, but border conflicts raged between Pennsylvania and Connecticut and between Pennsylvania and Virginia. New York and New Jersey engaged in an all-out trade war between 1783 and 1787.

The states' individual war debts and their shared national war debt made conflicts over land and representation even more difficult. Congress could not agree on how to finance these debts, but legislation in 1785 promised the states future repayment. Robert Morris, who directed national finances until 1785, and his political allies, wanted the states to grant Congress the power to tax, which would keep debt in national hands and enhance centralized power. But on a national level, the states could not even agree to grant Congress the power to impose a small impost tax. Southern states, especially Virginia, owed particularly large debts, which they might never be able to pay. By 1786, New York was the first of several states that began to assume national debts directly, which threatened to further weaken the national government.

Economic Change

A dizzying mix of economic opportunities and crises emerged in the postwar years. Devalued paper currency that Congress had printed during the war created inflation and conflicts between Congress and state governments who were required to pay war bills in hard currency after 1781. Congress had printed hundreds of millions of dollars' worth of bills of credit by 1778, but by 1781 they had lost 99 percent of their value. States also printed their own paper currency throughout the 1780s, causing further inflation. Prices declined after the war, but they did not return to their prewar level until 1789. State governments assessed property taxes and rival duties on trade goods. Congress defaulted on foreign and domestic loan payments after the war because it simply lacked funds.

The United States expanded foreign trade after the Revolution, but European powers still tried to restrict some international commerce. The war had opened new Caribbean and European trade routes. Now Britain closed its Caribbean island colonies to American trade, and both France and Spain left high duties in place on

PAPER CURRENCY These are just a few examples of the paper currency printed by various states during and after the Revolution. Widespread trade of state paper notes, and even paper certificates printed by banks or land companies, helped contribute to inflation and economic uncertainty during the period.

American-Caribbean trade. As a result, port cities such as Boston, Philadelphia, Newport, and Charleston faced slow recovery from the war, and their economies were depressed throughout the 1780s. The West Indies had become America's largest market for foodstuffs, and the crippling of that trade decreased farm income. Some U.S. exports to Europe and Latin America increased during these years, as the war settlement allowed Americans to trade directly with those areas legally for the first time. A few merchants who gained special Spanish permission enriched themselves by trading flour and other products to Cuba. Tobacco, lumber, iron, and shipbuilding supplies remained popular, and corn and wheat also became highly prized American goods in Europe. Although the Treaty of Paris had guaranteed American fishing rights, Britain embargoed American fish, and France imposed high taxes. Americans continued to import far more than they exported, a fact that further exacerbated the shortage of hard currency.

Women and Revolution

Many women had participated in the Revolutionary War. As many as 20,000 accompanied the Continental Army as camp followers. These women, many of whom were related to soldiers, played vital roles cooking, doing laundry, and giving medical care to the troops. Other camp followers probably served direct military roles: bringing water to cool artillery pieces or even occasionally themselves firing weapons. The most notable example of a fighting woman was **Deborah Sampson Gannett**, who disguised herself as a man and twice enlisted in the Continental Army. After the war, Gannett went on a speaking tour and published a memoir about her experience and her husband later received a federal widow's pension. Wealthier women organized by **Esther DeBerdt Reed** and **Sarah Franklin Bache** formed the Ladies' Association of Philadelphia, which raised funds and distributed clothing to needy soldiers in 1781.

Although American women had contributed mightily to the war effort, they had little direct political influence and no political power in the new republic. The Revolution did cause some shifts in white women's roles and gave them an important part to play in spreading republican values. Historians use the term "republican mother-hood" to describe the social expectation that women would contribute to the republic by raising their children—especially their sons—to be good citizens. In a society that was struggling to define itself according to the civic virtue demanded of a liberated citi-zenship, women could also exert broader influence over society and culture in a way that had political consequences. As Delaware politician James Tilton put it, "The men possess the more ostensible powers of making and executing the laws, but the women, in every free country, have an absolute control of manners, and . . . in a republic, man-ners are of equal importance with laws." As the patriot women who had participated in the boycott movements before the Revolution had learned, women could also exert some degree of influence through their consumer choices.

Women's support for the patriot cause and their special role in spreading republi-can ideology did not translate into their inclusion in American politics. New Jersey allowed a small number of independent, property-holding women to vote for a time, but formal political participation was largely a male privilege. Many states liberalized divorce laws following the Revolution to allow women to separate from abusive or run-away husbands, although **coverture** laws still meant that married women could not own property. Patriot women lost confiscated property if their husbands were loyalists be-cause state laws did not recognize that they could possess separate political identities. The impact of republicanism and women's actions in the Revolutionary War opened up the possibility of women's actions being seen as politically significant, but decades elapsed before their direct political participation widened significantly.

Racial Ideology and Questioning Slavery

The Revolutionary notion that "all men are created equal" pushed antislavery efforts forward in many northern states. But slavery thrived elsewhere, and African Americans still faced constant racism and resistance to their full participation in American society.

Some black veterans, such as New Hampshire's Prince Whipple, used their Revolu-tionary military experience to argue on behalf of African American freedom. Whipple and other African American men petitioned the state legislature in 1779 to end slavery "for the sake of justice, liberty, and the rights of mankind." In 1783, New Hampshire adopted a state constitution that ended slavery in the state.

Before the Revolution, some Quakers and Mennonites had argued against the in-stitution of slavery. After the war, Revolutionary ideology, black military heroism, and continued petitions by African Americans helped to expand the antislavery cause. Blacks generally lacked equal rights, but slavery was on the defensive. Vermont's state constitution became the first to outlaw slavery in 1777, and slaves who sued for their freedom under the Massachusetts 1780 constitution ended slavery there a few years later. Pennsylvania, and several other northern states, passed laws that gradually outlawed slavery by granting freedom to slaves once they reached a certain age. This gradual approach allowed the institution to linger into the 1820s in New York and New Jersey. In the states stretching south from Maryland, the institution of slavery survived and even intensified after the Revolution. Delaware, Maryland, and Virginia legislatures allowed individual slave owners to free their slaves for a time in the 1780s, but by the turn of the century, fear of slave rebellion ended that practice.

BROTHER PRINCE HALL
WARRANTEE WORSHIPFUL MASTER, AFRICAN LODGE 459 A. L. 5784. A. D. 1784
FOUNDER OF COLORED FRATERNITY OF FREE AND ACCEPTED MASONS.
BOSTON, MASS.
COPYRIGHT, 1924 BY W. H. CUSTON
RAISED TO MASTER MASON.

PRINCE HALL   Although early biographical details of Prince Hall are hard to authenticate, he most likely was a former slave who served in the Massachusetts militia during the Revolutionary War. After the war, he became one of the most prominent free black men in Boston, where he worked to end slavery in Massachusetts and to better the lives of African Americans. He is depicted here in his role as the founder of the first black Masonic lodge in the United States, African Lodge No. 1 in Boston, an organization that also worked for black emancipation and betterment.

STUDY QUESTIONS FOR RESTRUCTURING POLITICAL AND SOCIAL AUTHORITY

1. In what ways did the Revolutionary War change the social roles of some women and African Americans?
2. Why was the economy in the post-Revolutionary United States so unstable?

◼ A FEDERAL NATION

Many average Americans had fought for liberty in the Revolutionary War, but they were suffering in the postwar economic chaos. State and national governments faced troubles, but few people agreed on solutions: some favored a stronger central government, and others looked to the states for solutions. How could these two visions of government be satisfied by elite politicians who also wanted to control the democratic unrest that seemed to be bubbling up in the states? The creation of the U.S. Constitution was a victory for more centralized power, but the concept of **federalism** also insured that the states would remain powerful. A new politics arose based on the concept of **popular sovereignty**, the notion that the people could consent to granting power to both state and federal governments without giving up their rights as the true source of authority in American society.

Debt and Discontent

The uncertain economic system in the United States following the Revolutionary War caused hardship and unrest. While governmental leaders worried that the Articles of Confederation provided too little national tax power, poor men and women felt simultaneously squeezed by heavy state taxation—poll taxes, land taxes, and taxes on certain occupations such as tavern keeping. The poor faced a variety of other economic challenges, starting with inflated prices. Both taxes and private debt payment often required hard currency, but many poor people had little access to anything other than devalued paper money or the direct trade of farm goods. Although excess paper money hurt them by causing inflation, the poor relied on it.

By 1785, as the number of people imprisoned for the inability to repay debts rose above 1,000 in each state, debtors from New Hampshire to Massachusetts to Virginia began to organize themselves to oppose state and county enforcement of debts. Taking lessons from the pre-Revolutionary political protest movements, debtors petitioned state legislatures for the redress of their grievances and to demand the reinstatement of paper currency. Debtors, many of whom lived in western counties that were underrepresented in state legislatures, were angry that their hard currency payments often went to land speculators who held state war bonds.

Some groups took stronger action and resorted to armed protests to close down county courts. One Connecticut lawyer worried about "contentions and civil discord in almost every state in the union." Armed individuals and groups tangled with sheriffs seeking to seize property from debtors in Virginia, Pennsylvania, Delaware, New Jersey, New York, and Massachusetts. The largest insurrection came when Revolutionary veteran Daniel Shays organized protestors in Western Massachusetts at the end of 1786 into an armed resistance movement. Denied the right to assemble to protest creditors and tax collectors, the Shays threatened violence. In December 1786, the Shaysites shut down courts in Springfield, Massachusetts, and a month later they marched against the state arsenal in that city. Massachusetts governor Benjamin Lincoln called out the state militia to put down **Shays' Rebellion**, and Daniel Shays himself fled to Canada.

Lincoln also appealed to Congress for help in suppressing Shays' Rebellion. Although the rebellion ended before Congress responded, a number of national leaders seized the opportunity to call for enhancing the power of the national government. George Washington agreed with his friend John Jay in 1786 that "our affairs are drawing rapidly to a crisis." Elites and politicians worried that popular uprisings like Shays' Rebellion could spread or get out of control. A small meeting in Annapolis, Maryland, in September 1786 solidified conversations among nationalists like James Madison and Alexander Hamilton, who thought the time had come to change the Articles of Confederation. The Annapolis Convention issued a call for all the states to send delegates to a new convention in Philadelphia the following summer.

Constitutional Convention

Instead of merely changing the Articles of Confederation, the Philadelphia convention proposed an entirely new U.S. Constitution. It was, perhaps, not surprising that delegates to the Constitutional Convention moved beyond amending the Articles of Confederation because they largely came from the elite, creditor class of merchants, lawyers, and plantation owners who believed that the weakness of the national government and the popular unrest threatened social order. They also rose above those interests to create a political document that has become the longest-lasting written constitution for any government in the world. Every state but Rhode Island sent delegates to meet in Philadelphia in May 1787. Some of the most prominent leaders of the Revolution— George Washington, Benjamin Franklin, James Madison, and John Dickinson—came together to shape a new national government for the United States.

The convention elected George Washington presiding officer and agreed to meet in secret. Although the delegates tried hard to keep news of their deliberations from leaking out, we know much about what took place because of their written communications and the careful notes James Madison kept of their oral debates.

All of the proposals that the delegates debated fit within the conception of republicanism—the new national government would surely confirm the United States as a representative republic. They clashed over how to balance regional and economic interests within that representation, and though the delegates generally agreed that they needed to restrain volatile popular democracy, they did not agree on how to do that. In the first several days of debate, Edmund Randolph introduced James Madison's Virginia Plan, which proposed a two-house national legislature chosen according to proportional representation (based on population), a judicial branch, and a president elected by the legislature. Madison strongly advocated for the Enlightenment idea of **balance of powers** that would put authority in different branches of government, providing checks and balances against one another. Many states with small populations disliked Madison's plan, but it proved a useful starting point for debate—especially about the nature of Congress. William Paterson, a New Jersey delegate, proposed a rival New Jersey Plan that would keep more of the state power in the Articles of Confederation by retaining a unicameral legislature with equal state representation but which would have greater financial power. On July 16, the delegates adopted what became known as "The Great Compromise" between the Virginia and New Jersey plans and decided to form a bicameral legislature: A House of Representatives with proportional representation, and a Senate with equal state representation. Creating this form for Congress allowed the Convention to balance the interests of small and large states.

After the legislature was settled, other compromises followed. The delegates created the electoral college as a way to give power to the states and to restrain popular democracy. They also designated that the House of Representatives would stay quite small (as compared to the total population) in an effort to further insulate it from popular passions. Delegates to the convention largely tried to avoid the thorny issue of slavery, but they could not sidestep the institution altogether. After difficult debate, the delegates decided that three-fifths of slaves, or "other persons" as the final document phrased it, would be counted in the population for representation, although the convention never discussed direct citizenship rights or political status for the slaves themselves. The three-fifths compromise ensured that Southern states, where most enslaved people lived, would exercise strong political influence in the first decades of the republic. Delegates also agreed to restrict Congress from outlawing the international slave trade until 1808. Many of the political structures and compromises at the convention—including the electoral college—attempted to deal with the fact that some states had large slave populations whereas others had outlawed the institution altogether, but the delegates largely managed to avoid openly discussing the ties between their politics and slavery.

Near the end of the convention, Virginian George Mason proposed the inclusion of a bill of rights, a written guarantee of civil liberties, within the Constitution. Many delegates, despite their desire for a more powerful central government, still feared too much national power infringing the rights of individuals. Several state constitutions contained such guarantees, but most delegates did not think they were necessary. Even though they created a national government that was much more powerful—with the ability to tax and carry on foreign affairs—advocates believed that such power would only protect liberty, not threaten it. Several delegates, such as Marylander **Luther Martin**, were so upset by the exclusion of a bill of rights that they disavowed the work of the convention and opposed the Constitution. Three delegates refused to sign the final document. The Philadelphia Convention closed on September 17, 1787, and it remained to be seen whether such opposition would prevent the Constitution from being ratified.

Ratification

The new U.S. Constitution was ratified by specially elected conventions, not by the state legislatures, a majority of which would probably have rejected it. The Constitution was set to go into effect when nine of the 13 states ratified it. The Constitution's supporters, who dubbed themselves "Federalists," faced off against a very loose coalition of opponents, subsequently dubbed "Antifederalists." Federalist leaders, including Alexander Hamilton, John Jay, James Madison, and **John Marshall**, had impressive financing,

MERCY OTIS WARREN Warren was a sharp thinker and prominent resident of Boston who supported the revolutionary cause by publishing, anonymously, poetry and plays during the war. After the war, she opposed the U.S. Constitution on the grounds that it created too much centralized government power. She continued to broadcast her Antifederalist opinions in her 1805, three-volume, *History of the Rise, Progress, and Termination of the American Revolution*.

coordination, and access to newspaper and pamphlet publishers. They also counted among their ranks the most famous national and international Revolutionaries: George Washington and Benjamin Franklin. The Federalists won converts in commercial cities and seaports and from creditors who favored strong government power. The Antifederalists—including Samuel Adams, Elbridge Jerry, Patrick Henry, George Mason, Richard Henry Lee, George Clinton, and Mercy Otis Warren—were much less organized and much more wary of centralized power. Some Antifederalists objected to the lack of rights protection in the Constitution; others favored weak national power or direct democracy and agreed with Connecticut Antifederalist James Lincoln who warned that if the Constitution were ratified, "you are at once rushing into an aristocratic government."

Federalists displayed political skill as they easily won ratification in Delaware, Pennsylvania, and New Jersey by the end of 1787. Georgia and Connecticut each ratified the document in January 1788. In February, Massachusetts ratified the Constitution by a narrower margin but only after proposing amendments and making Federalists promise to add a bill of rights later.

As the ratifying conventions continued, the newspaper and pamphlet war between the Federalists and Antifederalists intensified. Madison, Hamilton, and Jay anonymously published the "Federalist" essays, sometimes called the "**Federalist Papers**," which offered wide-ranging arguments in favor of ratification. Their words, republished in books, pamphlets, and newspapers, helped to shape ratification politics and became some of the most enduring political commentaries in American history. Madison, Hamilton, and Jay applied Enlightenment political theories to the U.S. context and argued that the constitution was necessary. Madison, in particular, also took a new era of politics into account when he argued in Essays 10 and 51 that the Constitution could balance the behavior of self-interested Americans, who were not necessarily always guided by republican virtue.

By narrow margins, Maryland and South Carolina ratified the Constitution in the spring of 1788. When New Hampshire ratified it on June 21, 1788, the Constitution technically went into effect because nine states had completed the process. But it was unlikely that the new government would succeed without the support of the large and influential states of New York and Virginia. On June 23, Virginia gave its assent, delivering along with ratification 20 proposed amendments and support for a future bill of rights. On June 26, New York followed suit. North Carolina rejected ratification in August, only subsequently voting for ratification in November when it was clear the document would go into effect. Rhode Island, ever the dissenter, held out its ratification until May 1790 (Table 7.1).

At the conclusion of the Constitutional Convention in September 1787, Benjamin Franklin, less than a year away from his own death, rose to urge his fellow delegates to sign the new Constitution. He claimed that the document would "astonish our enemies, who are waiting with confidence to hear . . . that our states are on the point of separation." Franklin declared, "I consent, Sir, to this Constitution because I expect no better and because I am not sure that it is not the best. The opinions I have had of its errors, I sacrifice to the public good." That very notion of republican sacrifice for "the common good" had motivated many of those who fought in the Revolution. Conflicts during the war and developments in postwar society had proven that more struggle was necessary to find out whose version of "the public good" would reign in American government. And, as Franklin reminded the other convention delegates, much of the world would be watching to see if the United States of America could succeed.

TIMELINE 1776–1789

AMERICA	Year	THE WORLD
Jan Thomas Paine publishes *Common Sense* **Jun** Richard Henry Lee introduces first resolution of independence in Congress **Jul** Congress issues Declaration of Independence **Sep** British occupy New York City **Oct** Battle of White Plains, NY **Dec** Battle of Trenton, NJ	**1776**	Portugal unites South American colonies with Rio de Janeiro as capital
Aug Battle of Bennington **Sep** Battle of Brandywine, PA **Sep** Congress flees Philadelphia **Sep** The British occupy Philadelphia **Oct** Battle of Germantown, PA **Oct** John Burgoyne surrenders his British army to Horatio Gates after losing Battle of Saratoga **Nov** Congress submits Articles of Confederation to the states **Dec** Continental Army enters winter quarters at Valley Forge, PA	**1777**	British parliament suspends Habeas Corpus Act Chinese missionaries introduce Catholicism to Korea Portugal gains South American territory from Spain
Feb Treaty of Alliance and a Treaty of Amity and Commerce between France and United States **Mar** France formally recognizes the United States **Jun** Battle of Monmouth, NJ **Jun** British evacuate Philadelphia **Dec** British seize control of Savannah, GA	**1778**	**Jun** France declares war on Great Britain **Jul** War of Bavarian Succession begins
Aug American forces defeat Iroquois leader Joseph Brant	**1779**	British capture French African colony of Senegal and Gorée, key to slave trade Spain lays siege to Gibraltar **May** War of Bavarian Succession ends **Jun** Spain declares war on Great Britain but does not recognize the United States **Dec** Wars begin between Xhosa Bantu and Boers in southern Africa
Mar Spanish governor Gálvez captures Mobile from the British **May** British capture Charleston, SC **Aug** Battle of Camden, SC	**1780**	Peru rebels against Spain **Jul** Anti-Catholic Gordon riots in London **Nov** Britain declares war on the Netherlands
Jan Members of PA line mutiny **Jan** Battle of Cowpens, SC **Mar** Battle of Guilford Courthouse, NC **Sep** Battle of Eutaw Springs, SC **Oct** Cornwallis surrenders his army to the United States **Dec** City of Los Angeles founded	**1781**	British seize Dutch colonies in western Sumatra

Left	Year	Right
Apr The Netherlands recognizes the United States **May** Col. Lewis Nicola proposes George Washington become U.S. king	**1782**	Spain gains control of Florida
Jan France and Spain make peace with Britain Massachusetts Supreme Court declares slavery unconstitutional in that state **Mar** George Washington dispels Newburgh Conspiracy, rejects possible military coups **Sep** Treaty of Paris ends the Revolutionary War	**1783**	Spain reestablishes control of Peru **Jul** Britain forbids U.S. food exports to colonies in the West Indies France regains Senegal and Gorée
Jan Congress ratifies Treaty of Paris **Jun** Spain forbids American trade on Mississippi River **Aug** Russian permanent settlement in Alaska is founded	**1784**	**Aug** British Parliament passes India Act
Sep Annapolis Convention calls for amending the Articles of Confederation	**1786**	Lord Cornwallis becomes governor-general of India
Jan Shays' Rebellion is put down by Massachusetts militia **Feb** Congress calls for convention to amend Articles of Confederation **May** Constitutional Convention convenes in Philadelphia **Sep** Constitutional Convention closes **Oct** *The Federalist* papers first published **Dec** Delaware ratifies U.S. Constitution **Dec** Pennsylvania ratifies U.S. Constitution **Dec** New Jersey ratifies U.S. Constitution	**1787**	British assume control of Bahamas After Annam dynasty falls, France intervenes in central Vietnam
Jan Georgia ratifies U.S. Constitution **Jan** Connecticut ratifies U.S. Constitution **Feb** Massachusetts narrowly ratifies U.S. Constitution **Mar** Constitutional ratification fails in Rhode Island **Apr** Maryland ratifies U.S. Constitution **May** South Carolina ratifies U.S. Constitution **Jun** New Hampshire ratifies U.S. Constitution (technically fulfilling its ratification) **Jun** Virginia ratifies U.S. Constitution **Jun** New York ratifies U.S. Constitution (virtually guaranteeing it will succeed) **Aug** Constitutional ratification fails in North Carolina	**1788**	**Jan** Britain establishes penal settlements in Australia
Jan The U.S. Constitution takes effect	**1789**	

Table 7.1 When the States Ratified the U.S. Constitution

Date of Ratification	State
December 1787	Delaware New Jersey Pennsylvania
January 1788	Connecticut Georgia
February 1788	Massachusetts
April 1788	Maryland
May 1788	South Carolina
June 1788	New Hampshire Virginia
July 1788	New York
November 1789	North Carolina
May 1790	Rhode Island

STUDY QUESTIONS FOR A FEDERAL NATION

1. What factors led to the calling of the Constitutional Convention?
2. Why and how did Federalists and Antifederalists disagree so strongly over what form of government would protect liberty?

Summary

- The American Revolution centered around the best way to protect "liberty" and republican government, although not everyone in society agreed on how to do so.
- European help, especially from France, was essential to the American victory in the Revolutionary War, an international conflict.
- The ideology of republicanism built in some weaknesses to the American military, but forces performed surprisingly well against British troops and their allies.
- The Revolutionary War caused changes in the social roles and power of Native American groups, African Americans, and white women.
- During and after the Revolutionary War, finance and economic difficulties dramatized power struggles within the states and between the states and the U.S. national government.
- The U.S. Constitution created a new government based on ideas of federalism and popular sovereignty while at the same time seeking to restrain somewhat the forces of popular democracy.

Key Terms and People

Arnold, Benedict *237*

Articles of Confederation *229*

Bache, Sarah Franklin *243*

balance of powers *247*

Brant, Joseph *238*

Catherine the Great *233*

Clinton, Sir Henry *236*

Cornwallis, Lord *227*

coverture *244*

d'Estaing, Comte *235*

federalism *246*

Federalist Papers *249*

Gannett, Deborah Sampson *243*

Gates, Horatio *227*

Germain, Lord George *236*

Grasse, Comte de *236*

Howe, Sir Richard *237*

Howe, Sir William *226*

Jay, John *232*

Laurens, Henry *241*

Marshall, John *248*

Martin, Luther *248*

Morgan, Daniel *237*

Motier, Marie-Joseph-Paul-Yves-Roch-
    Gilbert du, Marquis de Lafayette *233*

popular sovereignty *246*

Reed, Esther DeBerdt *243*

separation of powers *229*

Shays' Rebellion *246*

Steuben, von, Friedrich Wilhelm *232*

Tarleton, Banastre *236*

Vergennes, Comte de *228*

Reviewing Chapter 7

1. How did the United States win independence from the world's most powerful empire?
2. Why did the United States win the Revolutionary War?
3. How did the circulation of people, goods, and ideas across the Atlantic Ocean complicate and contribute to the American victory in the Revolution?

Further Reading

Gould, Eliga H. and Peter S. Onuf, eds. *The American Revolution in the Atlantic World*. Baltimore: Johns Hopkins University Press, 2005. This volume of essays presents a look at the American Revolution in the context of Atlantic world history. It includes 15 essays on social, political, military, and cultural history stretching from the imperial crisis through the ratification of the Constitution.

Higginbotham, Don. *The War for American Independence*. Boston: Northeastern University Press, 1983. This book is the best one-volume military history of the American Revolution. It explains how the United States won the war, with European help, despite organizational and strategic disadvantages.

Holton, Woody. *Unruly Americans and the Origins of the American Constitution*. New York: Hill and Wang, 2007. Holton argues in this book that although the framers of the U.S. Constitution feared the middling and lower sort, the Constitution was nonetheless shaped by the desires and interests of people in the states who participated in the ratifying conventions. The conventions were much more democratic than the Constitutional Convention.

Jasanoff, Maya. *Liberty's Exiles: American Loyalists in the Revolutionary World*. New York: Alfred A. Knopf, 2011. Jasanoff's book traces the fate of white Loyalists, Indians, and African Americans who supported the British during the American Revolution as they were exiled to Britain and the British empire including Canada, Sierra Leone, India, and Australia.

Gray, Edward and Jane Kamensky, eds. *The Oxford Handbook of the American Revolution*. New York: Oxford University Press, 2013. This collection features comprehensive articles by leading scholars the convey the latest scholarly opinion on the social, political, cultural, and military history of the Revolution.

Kerber, Linda K. *Women of the Republic: Intellect and Ideology in Revolutionary America.* New York: Norton, 1986. Linda Kerber examines women's participation in the American Revolution and how the Revolution then changed gender roles, especially for women. Kerber coined the term "republican motherhood" to describe the political importance given to white women's family duties in the aftermath of the Revolution.

America In The World
PEOPLE, GOODS, IDEAS AND PRACTICES

CHAPTER 7: A Revolutionary Nation 1776–1789

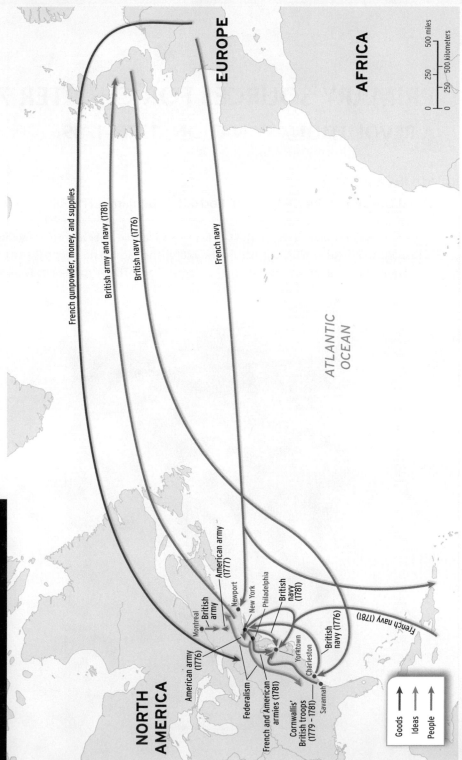

EUROPE

AFRICA

French gunpowder, money, and supplies

British army and navy (1781)

British navy (1776)

French navy

ATLANTIC
OCEAN

NORTH
AMERICA

American army
(1776)

Montreal

British
army

Newport

American army
(1777)

New York

Philadelphia

British
navy
(1781)

Federalism

French and American
armies (1781)

Cornwallis'
British troops
(1779 – 1781)

Yorktown

Charleston

British
navy (1776)

Savannah

French navy (1781)

0   250   500 miles
0   250   500 kilometers

Goods
Ideas
People

PRIMARY SOURCES FOR CHAPTER 7

A REVOLUTIONARY NATION, 1776–1789

SOURCE 7.1

Visual Document: Pierre Le Beau, Portrait of Benjamin Franklin (1780s)

Pierre Le Beau engraved this portrait of Benjamin Franklin after a portrait by Claude Desrais, and it was published in Paris in the 1780s. The caption notes that Franklin was "born in Boston in New England on 17 January 1706." The artist depicts Franklin in

BENJAMIN FRANKLIN
Né à Boston dans la Nouvelle Angleterre,
le 17 Janvier 1706.

the fur hat that he was fond of wearing in Paris to portray himself as a "rustic" American. He is not wearing his trademark spectacles in this portrait, but his famous face would have been very recognizable to Parisians nonetheless. This engraving is typical of the scores of Franklin portraits that Parisians reproduced on paper, candy boxes, ceramics, and other items in the 1780s.

Source: Courtesy of the Library of Congress Prints and Photographs Division, LC-USZ62-28230.

WORKING WITH SOURCES

1. Why would Parisians want to buy an engraving of Franklin like this one?
2. How does Franklin's appearance in this image communicate a message about his reputation?

SOURCE 7.2

Diary of Surgeon Albigence Waldo, Excerpts Describing the Continental Army's Encampment at Valley Forge (1777)

Albigence Waldo was a physician from Pomfret, Connecticut, who served as a surgeon with the First Connecticut Infantry Regiment, a militia unit that joined the Continental Army in Pennsylvania in September 1777. Waldo's diary entries about the Continental Army's winter quarters in Valley Forge, Pennsylvania, at the end of 1777 paint a harrowing picture of the conditions that soldiers there faced.

Source: "Diary of Surgeon Albigence Waldo, of the Connecticut Line," Pennsylvania Magazine of History and Biography 21 (1897): 305–09.

Dec. 12th [1777].—A Bridge of Waggons made across the Schuylkill last Night consisting of 36 waggons, with a bridge of Rails between each. . . . Militia and dragoons brought into Camp several Prisoners. Sun Set.—We are order'd to march over the River—It snows—I'm Sick—eat nothing—No Whiskey—No Forage—Lord—Lord—Lord. The Army were 'till Sun Rise crossing the River—some at the Waggon Bridge, & some at the Raft Bridge below. Cold & uncomfortable.

Dec. 13th—The army march'd three miles from the West side the River and encamp'd near a place call'd the Gulph and not an improper name neither, for this Gulph seems well adapted by its situation to keep us from the pleasure & enjoyments of this World, or being conversant with any body in it. . . .

Dec. 14th—Prisoners & Deserters are continually coming in. The Army which has been surprisingly healthy hitherto, now begin to grow sickly from the continued fatigues they have suffered this Campaign. Yet they still show spirit of Alacrity & Contentment not to be expected from so young Troops. I am Sick—discontented—out of humour. Poor food—hard lodging—Cold Water—fatigue—Nasty Cloaths—nasty Cookery—Vomit half my time—smoak'd out of my senses—the Devil's in't—I can't Endure it—Why are we sent here to starve and freeze—What sweet Felicities have I left at home; A charming

Wife—pretty Children—Good Beds—good food—good Cookery—all agreeable—all harmonious. Here all Confusion—smoke Cold—hunger & filthyness—A pox on my bad luck. There comes a bowl of beef soup—full of burnt leaves and dirt, sickish enough to make a hector spue,—away with it Boys—I'll live like a Chameleon upon Air. . . . See the poor Soldier, when in health—with what cheerfulness he meets his foes and encounters every hardship—if barefoot, he labours thro' the Mud & Cold with a Song in his mouth extolling War & Washington—if his food be bad, he eats it notwithstanding with seeming content—blesses God for a good Stomach and Whistles it into digestion. But harkee Patience, a moment—There comes a Soldier, his bare feet are seen thro' his worn out Shoes, his legs nearly naked from the tatter'd remains of an only pair of stockings, his Breeches not sufficient to cover his nakedness, his Shirt hanging in Strings, his hair dishevell'd, his face meager; his whole appearance pictures a person forsaken & discouraged. He comes, and crys with an air of wretchedness & despair, I am Sick, my feet lame, my legs are sore, my body cover'd with this tormenting Itch—my Cloaths are worn out, my Constitution is broken, my former Activity is exhausted by fatigue, hunger & Cold,

I fail fast I shall soon be no more! And all the reward I shall get will be—"Poor Will is dead!" People who live at home in Luxury and Ease, quietly possessing their habitations, Enjoying their Wives & families in peace, have but a very faint Idea of the unpleasing sensations, and continual Anxiety the Man endures who is in a Camp, and is the husband and parent of an agreeable family. These same People are willing we should suffer every thing for their Benefit & advantage, and yet are the first to Condemn us for not doing more!! . . .

Dec. 21st—Preparations made for hutts. Provision Scarce. Mr. Ellis went homeward—sent a Letter to my Wife. Heartily wish myself at home—my Skin & eyes are almost spoil'd with continual smoke.

A general cry thro' the camp this Evening among the Soldiers, "No Meat! No Meat!"—the Distant vales Echo'd back the melancholly sound—"No Meat! No Meat!" Immitating the noise of Crows & Owls, also, made a part of the confused Musick.

What have you for our Dinners Boys? "Nothing but Fire Cake & Water, Sir." At night, "Gentlemen the Supper is ready." What is your supper, Lads? "Fire Cake & Water, Sir." Very poor beef has been drawn in our Camp the greater part of this season.

WORKING WITH SOURCES

1. How did his experience at Valley Forge give Waldo a sense of how military men are separated from civilians?

2. What were the causes of suffering at Valley Forge?

SOURCE 7.3

Boston King, Excerpts from "Memoirs of the Life of Boston King: A Black Preacher" (1798)

In his memoir, Boston King describes escaping from slavery to fight with the British in 1780 and his subsequent attempts to keep his freedom. The British moved King to Canada after the war, and he later emigrated to Sierra Leone with his family.

Source: Boston King, "Memoirs of the Life of Boston King: A Black Preacher (1798)," in *If We Must Die: African American Voices on War and Peace*, ed. Karin L. Stanford (New York: Rowman & Littlefield, 2008), 21–23.

My master being apprehensive that Charles-Town was in danger on account of the war, removed into the country, about 38 miles off. Here we built a large house for Mr. Waters, during which time the English took Charles-Town. . . . To escape his cruelty, I determined to go to Charles-Town, and throw myself into the hands of the English. They received me readily, and I began to feel the happiness of liberty, of which I knew nothing before, altho' I was much grieved at first, to be obliged to leave my friends, and reside among strangers. In this situation I was seized with small-pox, and suffered great hardships; for all the Blacks affected with that disease, were ordered to be carried a mile from the camp, lest the soldiers should be infected, and disabled from marching. . . .

Being recovered, I marched with the army to Chamblem. . . . From thence I went to a place about 35 miles off, where we stayed two months: at the expiration of which, an express came to the Colonel to decamp in fifteen minutes. When these orders arrived I was at a distance from the camp, catching some fish for the captain that I waited upon; upon returning to the camp, to my great astonishment, I found all the English were gone, and had left only a few militia. I felt my mind greatly alarmed, but Captain Lewes, who commanded the militia, said, "You need not be uneasy, for you will see your regiment before 7 o'clock tonight." This satisfied me for the present, and in two hours we set off.

As [we] were on the march, the Captain asked, "How will you like me to be your master?"

I answered, that I was Captain Grey's servant. "Yes," said he; "but I expect that they are all taken prisoners before now; and I have been long enough in the English service, and am determined to leave them." These words roused my indignation, and I spoke some sharp words to him. But he calmly replied, "If you do not behave well, I will put you in irons, and give you a dozen stripes every morning." I now perceived that my case was desperate, and that I had nothing to trust to, but to wait the first opportunity for making my escape. . . .

I tarried with Captain Grey about a year, and then left him, and came to Nelson's-ferry. Here I entered into the service of the commanding officer of that place. But our situation was very precarious, and we expected to be made prisoners every day; for the Americans had 1600 men, not far off; whereas our whole number amounted only to 250: But there were 1200 English about 30 miles off; only we knew not how to inform him of our danger, as the Americans were in possession of the country. Our commander at length determined to send me with a letter, promising me great rewards, if I was successful in the business. . . .

Soon after I went to Charles-Town, and entered on board a man of war. As we were going to Chesapeak-bay, we were at the taking of a rich prize. We stayed in the bay two days, and then sailed for New-York, where we went on shore. Here I endeavored to follow my trade, but for want of tools was obliged to relinquish it, and enter service. . . . I then went out on a pilot-boat. We were at sea eight days, and had only provisions for five, so that we were in danger of starving. On the 9th day we were taken by an American whale-boat. I went on board them with a cheerful countenance, and asked for bread and water, and made very free with them . . . my mind was sorely distressed at the thought of being again reduced to slavery, and separated from my wife and family; and at the same time it was exceeding difficult to escape from my bondage. . . .

[In 1783] the horrors and devastation of war happily terminated, and peace was restored between America and Great Britain, which diffused universal joy among all parties, except us, who had escaped from slavery, and taken refuge in the English army; for a report prevailed at New-York, that all the slaves, in number 2000, were to be delivered up to their masters, altho' some of them had been three or four years among the English. . . . The English had compassion upon us in the day of distress, and issued out the Proclamation, importing, That all slaves should be free, who had taken refuge in the British lines. . . . Each of us received a certificate from the commanding officer at New-York, which dispelled all our fears, and filled us with joy and gratitude. Soon after, ships were fitted out, and furnished with every necessary for conveying us to Nova Scotia.

WORKING WITH SOURCES

1. King relates how he found "the happiness of liberty" for the first time after his escape from slavery. Of what did his sense of "liberty" consist?

2. How did King use different kinds of work and labor to maintain his freedom?

3. Why was King so happy to go to Canada at the end of the war?

SOURCE 7.4

James Madison, Excerpts from "Federalist No. 51" (1788)

James Madison published this essay in the *New York Packet* on February 8, 1788. He wrote anonymously as "Publius" as part of the effort to convince the New York convention to ratify the U.S. Constitution. In this essay, Madison sought to reassure New Yorkers that the federal government would not grow too powerful.

Source: The Federalist: A Commentary on The Constitution of the United States (New York: G. P. Putnam's Sons, 1888), 322–25.

To what expedient, then, shall we finally resort, for maintaining in practice the necessary partition of power among the several departments, as laid down in the Constitution? The only answer that can be given is . . . by so contriving the interior structure of the government as that its several constituent parts may, by their mutual relations, be the means of keeping each other in their proper places. . . . In order to lay a due foundation for that separate and distinct exercise of the different powers of government, which to a certain extent is admitted on all hands to be essential to the preservation of liberty, it is evident that each department should have a will of its own; and consequently should be so constituted that the members of each should have as little agency as possible in the appointment of the members of the others. Were this principle rigorously adhered to, it would require that all the appointments for the supreme executive, legislative, and judiciary magistracies should be drawn from the same fountain of authority, the people, through channels having no communication whatever with one another. . . .

It is equally evident, that the members of each department should be as little dependent as possible on those of the others, for the emoluments annexed to their offices. Were the executive magistrate, or the judges, not independent of the legislature in this particular, their independence in every other would be merely nominal.

But the great security against a gradual concentration of the several powers in the same department, consists in giving to those who administer each department the necessary constitutional means and personal motives to resist encroachments of the others. . . . Ambition must be made to counteract ambition. The interest of the man must be connected with the constitutional rights of the place. It may be a reflection on human nature, that such devices should be necessary to control the abuses of government. But what is government itself, but the greatest of all reflections on human nature? If men were angels, no government would be necessary. If angels were to govern men, neither external nor internal controls on government would be necessary. In framing a government which is to be administered by men over men, the great difficulty lies in this: you must first enable the government to control the governed; and in the next place oblige it to control itself. A dependence on the people is, no doubt, the primary control on the government; but experience has taught mankind the necessity of auxiliary precautions. . . .

But it is not possible to give each department an equal power of self-defense. In republican government, the legislative authority necessarily predominates. The remedy for this inconveniency is to divide the legislature into different branches; and to render them, by different modes of election and different principles of action, as little connected with each other as the nature of their common functions and their common dependence on society will admit. . . . The weakness of the executive may require, on the other hand, that it should be fortified.

WORKING WITH SOURCES

1. How would keeping the powers of the branches of government separate help in "the preservation of liberty," according to Madison?

2. Why was the independence of the judicial and executive branches from the legislative branch so important to Madison?

3. What roles do "interest" and "ambition" play in controlling government power, according to Madison?

A New Nation Facing a Revolutionary World

8

I n April 1793, the French Revolutionary government sent **Edmund Charles Genet** on a diplomatic mission to convince the United States "to assist in every way the extension of the empire of liberty." Genet was to cement the 1778 French alliance with the United States and seek help in France's newly declared war on Great Britain, Spain, Austria, and Prussia.

Genet hoped also to sign a new commercial treaty with the United States, to use the United States as a staging ground to outfit privateers, to expel Britain and Spain from Canada and Louisiana, and to recruit U.S. citizens for French military service. The Girondins—the political group that controlled Revolutionary France early in 1793—hoped that Genet would build the U.S. French financial relationship forged during the American Revolution. But they misunderstood U.S. politics and President Washington's desire to keep the nation neutral.

As Genet traveled from South Carolina to the U.S. capital at Philadelphia, he defied American officials who wished him to keep a low profile because they were not ready to support the French Girondist government. He received an enthusiastic welcome, however, from crowds of men and women who demonstrated their support for the French Revolution by cheering, displaying French symbols, and attending banquets and balls in his honor. Genet encouraged people to oppose Washington's Proclamation of Neutrality in the European war, issued two weeks after his arrival. He hatched a secret plan in Georgia to mobilize backcountry Americans against the East Florida Spanish government, which had angered American settlers by shielding runaway slaves. Genet also outfitted and launched several American ships as French privateers.

< Général Toussaint Louverture (1743–1803).

Genet's fortunes changed when his political faction fell from power in June 1793. By August 1793, Washington's politically divided cabinet unanimously agreed to request that the French recall Genet. Secretary of State Thomas Jefferson wrote diplomatic letters making the request while still trying to maintain the U.S. relationship with France that he and his political allies prized. The Girondins' rivals, the Jacobins, agreed to recall Genet, to help ensure that the United States would continue to export food to France. In the spring of 1794, the new French government threatened to arrest and execute Genet (as they had many other Girondins), but President Washington instead allowed the man who had threatened U.S. neutrality to avoid being sent home to the guillotine. Genet, despite threatening to drag the United States into the European wars, was given asylum. He settled in New York State, where he married Cornelia Clinton, one of his political supporters and the governor's daughter, and lived quietly until his death in 1834.

The controversy over Genet's actions demonstrated how connected the new American nation continued to be to events in Europe—where the French Revolution was dramatically changing the political and social landscape. Even as U.S. citizens accustomed themselves to living under the terms of their new federal constitution, revolutionary change in France meant that they would have to be careful not to become ensnared in global turmoil.

■ THE UNITED STATES IN THE AGE OF THE FRENCH REVOLUTION

As Americans tried to implement their own government, they faced a new world changed by revolutions in both France and Haiti. Many Americans believed that the French Revolution grew out of a concept of American Revolutionary liberty, a familiar republicanism. But French radicalism and political conflict quickly increased after 1793, and the French Revolutionary wars, especially with Great Britain, created a challenge for the new U.S. government. Against a backdrop of international turmoil, Americans fought their own ideological and political battles. As first president of the United States, George Washington wanted to remain neutral in the European wars, but such a position was not always easy. Conflicts in Europe helped to fuel the growth of the first U.S. political parties, which reflected deep disagreements among Americans about how their new government should work. In a revolutionary world, how would Americans manage their own political and social change?

The New Nation and the New Revolution

Initially, Americans believed that the 1789 French Revolution was linked to American Revolutionary ideals, especially as expressed in the Declaration of Independence. When the Estates General, the third estate of the French legislature, formed the National Assembly in June 1789 and street fighting escalated after the storming of the notorious Bastille prison in Paris in July, the American minister to France, Thomas Jefferson, looked on approvingly. At first, American friends such as the Marquis de Lafayette took a hand in shaping a new French government. King Louis XVI fled the capital, and in August, the Estates General issued the Declaration of the Rights of Man and of the Citizen, declaring "Men are born and remain free and equal in rights." As Jefferson left France to take up his post as the first U.S. Secretary of State, he thought that American liberty was taking root in Europe. Most Americans sup-

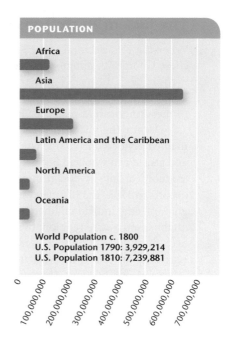

POPULATION

Africa

Asia

Europe

Latin America and the Caribbean

North America

Oceania

World Population c. 1800
U.S. Population 1790: 3,929,214
U.S. Population 1810: 7,239,881

0   100,000,000   200,000,000   300,000,000   400,000,000   500,000,000   600,000,000   700,000,000

ported the French Revolution in its early stages. In towns and cities around the United States, Americans showed their enthusiasm by wearing French clothing, imitating French public festivals in honor of "Reason" and "Liberty," and celebrating French military victories.

Although the United States responded positively when France declared itself a republic in 1792, events soon weakened U.S. support. The execution of the royal family in 1793; the execution or imprisonment of leaders beloved by Americans, such as Lafayette; and France's bid to spread revolutionary republicanism through warfare soon divided U.S. opinion. During "the Terror" in France, hundreds judged to be political enemies of "the people" were executed by guillotine—which many Americans, like John Adams, viewed as far too radical. To many members of the American elite, the French seemed to endorse a dangerous excess of equality and democracy. But others, such as Jefferson himself, continued to view France as a new beacon of liberty.

In an already contentious domestic political scene, Americans could not avoid conflict over the French Revolution and its social and political consequences. If the French based their revolution on American liberty, was the United States susceptible to the same kind of "Terror"? Would the French situation affirm or disrupt American politics? Would the French abolition of slavery in its Caribbean colonies in 1794 affect the United States? Attorney General Edmund Randolph wrote to President Washington that he worried about the "ardour of some, to transplant French politics, as fresh fuel for our politics." Not all American political developments directly related to the French Revolution, but the backdrop of European change and uncertainty influenced Americans who worked to implement their federal government and to arrange their domestic politics.

The Rise of Party Tensions

When the U.S. electoral college met for the first time in February 1789, it unanimously chose George Washington as president. His personal prestige and Revolutionary War heroism caused Americans to trust him with the expanded powers given to the federal government by the new Constitution. John Adams, the Massachusetts statesman and former American Minister to Great Britain, was elected the first vice president.

Despite the unanimity of support for Washington, the cabinet and Congress remained divided during his first term. Congress was dominated by merchants, lawyers, and gentlemen who had been strong supporters of the new Constitution. They soon introduced a slate of constitutional amendments as promised during the ratification debates in 1788. The 10 amendments, known as the **Bill of Rights**, focused primarily on guaranteeing individual liberties and restraining Congress from inhibiting the press or establishing a state religion; they were ratified by the states in 1791. The old divisions over the Constitution, however, were soon overtaken by a new set of disagreements regarding the proper uses of federal power and attitudes toward Britain and France.

Secretary of State Thomas Jefferson and Secretary of the Treasury Alexander Hamilton opposed one another at almost every turn. They headed rival political factions during the 1790s, creating the first political parties in American history—the Federalists and the Democratic Republicans—even though neither side believed in the legitimacy of parties. Federalists, led by the brilliant Hamilton, Washington's former aide-de-camp, favored the strong use of federal power, greater taxation, and keeping direct political power in the hand of educated elites. Federalists thought the United States should restore good relations with Great Britain, and Hamilton was among political leaders most critical of the antiaristocratic "excesses" of the French Revolution. Democratic Republicans, led by Jefferson and James Madison, favored the French and their democratic style. Jeffersonians argued that state governments should continue to check the power of the federal government. They rejected Hamilton's plans to encourage commerce and financial development. Jefferson believed farming to be the base of the ideal developing economy; in addition, he insisted, in contrast to Hamilton, that democratic politics should include the participation of nonelite white men, especially farmers and artisans (Table 8.1).

Federalists and Democratic Republicans possessed different interpretations of the consequences of the American Revolution, clashing over notions of how government power ought to be used. The Federalists envisioned a version of American "liberty" that

Table 8.1 Political Parties in the 1790s

Federalist Party	Democratic-Republican Party
• Favored strong federal government • Favored friendship with the British • Opposed the French Revolution • Power base among merchants, property owners, urban workers in commercial enterprises • Minority party after 1800 • Strongest region: New England	• Favored limited federal power • Hostile to Great Britain • Sympathetic to the French Revolution • Power base among Southern planters and Northern farmers • Majority party after 1800 • Supported by urban artisans and working men

rested on traditional republican values and elite leadership, whereas the Democratic Republicans generally favored a more personal notion of democratic "liberty." Each party also built up support among the populace, among voters and men and women unable to vote but who still participated in public rituals that demonstrated their support for one side or another. When Bostonians celebrated George Washington's birthday with parades, fireworks, and public celebrations, they attached themselves to the Federalist cause. When Philadelphians turned out for Independence Day celebrations that featured public readings of the Declaration of Independence and French-style festivals of "liberty," they openly supported Democratic-Republican politics.

One of the first issues that Hamilton's and Jefferson's supporters contended over—the assumption of state Revolutionary War debts by the federal government—also revealed the regional strength of each faction. Jefferson, James Madison, and other Southerners opposed the assumption of state debts because they wanted to restrict centralized power and because many Southern states had already paid back their creditors. Hamilton argued that the federal government had to pay the outstanding debts of large states such as Pennsylvania and New York to reassure foreign governments of the fiscal power of the United States. In the summer of 1790, the two sides compromised. Congress voted to assume the debts but pacified skeptical Southerners by voting to locate the new federal capital city on the Potomac River in the District of Columbia, south of the previous capital in Philadelphia.

In 1790 and 1791, Hamilton's financial proposals drove the two political factions further apart. Hamilton wanted to encourage economic development by wielding federal power that the Democratic Republicans opposed. He issued a report on Public Credit arguing for financing public debt and proposing excise taxes. Hamilton also proposed the creation of a National Bank, supported by federal funds and private shareholders. Although Jefferson and Madison argued that the bank was unconstitutional, Congress chartered it in February 1791. The Democratic Republicans also opposed Hamilton's efforts to encourage domestic production of goods by imposing international tariffs and funding American economic enterprise.

Although neither the Federalists nor the Democratic Republicans were yet organized as political parties, they were increasingly open about their mutual opposition. By 1792, each side patronized its own newspaper: **John Fenno** edited the Federalists' *Gazette of the United States* and **Philip Freneau** edited *The National Gazette* for the Democratic Republicans. Neither side nominated official candidates in elections, but voters could choose allegiances because local candidates' sympathies were usually widely known, and many smaller newspapers openly supported one side or another.

Neutrality and Jay's Treaty

Amid infighting and opposition, President Washington tried to remain neutral regarding the two developing political parties, just as he wanted neutrality for the United States between Britain and France. By February 1793, however, he grew increasingly concerned that the United States was getting too involved in France's new revolutionary wars. Even Jefferson wanted to keep the United States out of war, but he favored France and was keen to honor the 1778 alliance between the "sister republics." Hamilton, who Jefferson was convinced was a monarchist, believed that the alliance should be suspended. President Washington issued a Proclamation of Neutrality in the European wars on April 22, just weeks after he had been inaugurated for his second term. The Proclamation of Neutrality aimed to keep open U.S. ships' trading rights with Britain, France, and their Caribbean colonies. Washington also hoped a neutral stance would allow the United States to secure its borders and avoid further hostilities in North America with Spain and with Indians allied to European powers.

The United States wanted to maintain trade relations with Britain and France but risked becoming a pawn between the two bigger European powers. The British government ordered the Royal Navy to seize any U.S. ship trading with the French in the Caribbean, and they took hundreds of American merchant vessels as prizes and began to kidnap American sailors and impress them into Royal Navy service. To stop this, Washington sent Chief Justice John Jay to London to negotiate a treaty with the British government, the terms of which Washington kept secret from the public for months. Thomas Jefferson resigned as Secretary of State at the end of 1793, in part because he believed that Hamilton had influenced Washington to become pro-British.

When the Senate finally debated **Jay's Treaty**, which granted the United States trade rights on the Mississippi, in the British East Indies, and at western forts, French minister to the United States Pierre Adet, U.S. Secretary of State Edmund Randolph, and several state legislatures all opposed it. They saw the treaty as a repudiation of America's revolutionary commitment to France and a potential violation of neutrality. Opponents of the treaty charged that it was ragingly pro-British. Angry crowds of Americans with French and Democratic-Republican sympathies burned Jay in effigy. As the Senate narrowly ratified Jay's Treaty in June 1795, President Washington's popularity plummeted.

The Popular Politics of Rebellion

A series of events in 1794 also tested Washington's popularity and confirmed the intertwining of domestic politics and trade. Hamilton's 1791 excise taxes on distilled liquor threatened Westerners, who could gain more profits by shipping spirits to urban markets than by shipping bulky corn or wheat. Farmers in Virginia, Kentucky, Maryland, North Carolina, and South Carolina refused to pay the taxes. But Pennsylvanians mounted the hottest protest when, in July 1794, crowds attacked locally despised tax collector John Neville and burned his house. Within weeks, 6,000 protesters, including some members of the Pennsylvania militia, gathered outside Pittsburgh and threatened more widespread violence against the Whiskey Tax.

The **Whiskey Rebellion** in western Pennsylvania prompted Washington to assert federal power using military force. Hamilton, who was increasingly close to Washington, led 15,000 federalized militia troops from other states into Pennsylvania in September. Troops avoided widespread violence but arrested several leaders of the rebellion. The use of federal military power against domestic protesters outraged Democratic Republicans. President Washington, who blamed Democratic Republicans for the unrest, suggested that radical pro-Jefferson political clubs, called Democratic-Republican societies, had encouraged protesters. Although these societies did not conspire against the government, Federalists and Republicans disagreed about whether clubs that encouraged democratic politics and protest were dangerous or legitimate. The Whiskey Rebellion, and the controversy over Democratic-Republican societies, revealed deep disagreement over the proper exercise of federal power and the proper role of popular politics—especially against the backdrop of French popular upheaval. In 1794, some wondered if the

Whiskey Rebellion and its suppression might be the beginning of an American version of the French "Terror." Indeed, the Whiskey Rebellion was one of the largest domestic uprisings in North American history before the Civil War, and President Washington put it down using unprecedented executive power.

Indian Warfare and European Power

Federal power was also contested in Western conflicts between settlers and Indians who were trying to navigate between increasingly aggressive U.S. citizens and traditional European enemies and allies. After 1789, the British kept seven forts south of Upper Canada, and they actively traded and negotiated with Miami, Shawnee, and other tribes in the Ohio region who frequently clashed with U.S. settlers encroaching on their land. Settlers in Western lands granted to Revolutionary War veterans also pressured Ohio-region Indian peoples.

The Washington administration sent the small U.S. army, supplemented by Western militia troops, to pacify the Ohio country in 1790 and in 1791. General Josiah Harmar attacked Miami Town, an Indian-British trade hub, in October 1790. Miami warrior **Little Turtle** surprised Harmar's force with superior numbers and tactics and inflicted a crushing defeat that cost Harmar his job. The following November, Little Turtle organized Miami, Shawnee, and other allied tribal forces, with British logistical support, to resist when **Arthur St. Clair**, governor of the Northwest Territory, led another attack on Miami Town. At the Wabash River, Little Turtle's forces killed more than 600 American soldiers and delivered one of the greatest ever victories by Indians over the United States.

In 1794, Washington sent U.S. army forces—this time headed by former Revolutionary War general **"Mad" Anthony Wayne**—to fight against the Shawnee and Miami Confederacy. Wayne commanded almost 4,000 army and militia troops, he built strong forts, and he exploited Indian disagreements. In August 1794, Wayne destroyed Indian villages, and he defeated what he called "the grand emporium of the hostile Indians of the West" at the Battle of Fallen Timbers. The following year he signed the Treaty of Greenville with 12 Indian nations in the Northwest Territory, some of whom signed unwillingly because it granted U.S. settlers access to wide tracts of land. The Battle of Fallen Timbers was a watershed in Indian history, as it compelled many to accommodate U.S. demands and allowed the United States to launch an assimilation program. The British stayed out of the conflict temporarily but stood ready to exploit future tensions as settlement increased.

During the period of calm between the United States and Britain after Jay's Treaty and the Treaty of Greenville, the Spanish, weakened by their involvement in European wars, sought to reduce tensions with the United States. In 1795, they agreed to a new treaty. That summer in Madrid, U.S. diplomat Thomas Pinckney negotiated a highly favorable agreement with prime minister Don Manuel de Godoy, as Godoy sought to settle Spain's war with France. **Pinckney's Treaty**—also known as the Treaty of San Lorenzo— fully opened Mississippi River trade to the United States, provided tax-free markets in New Orleans, settled Florida border issues, and guaranteed Spanish help against Southwest Indians who wanted to block U.S. settlers from expanding west. The U.S. Senate unanimously ratified the new treaty in 1796, and it seemed for a moment that the United States might have stabilized threats from Indian and European powers.

■ PARTY CONFLICT INTENSIFIES

George Washington, battered by his critics but sure that he had successfully stabilized the new republic, decided not to serve a third term as president—setting a precedent that would stand for over 100 years. Despite controversies during his second term, Washington's personal prestige, reputation, and leadership had helped to ensure the smooth beginnings of the federal government. Many Americans worried about what would follow after his retirement. As he left office in 1796, Washington published a "Farewell Address" warning "Against the insidious wiles of foreign influence." He urged Americans to trade with Europe but to guard against overinvolvement in European politics and "to steer clear of permanent alliances with any portion of the foreign world." Washington wanted the United States to chart its own course in the world and avoid being pushed around by more powerful nations. Washington also warned against factionalism in U.S. politics, but it soon became clear that the United States could avoid neither international problems nor party politics.

Adams in Power

John Adams won the presidential election of 1796, despite opposition from fellow Federalist Alexander Hamilton, who thought him insufficiently conservative. States chose members of the electoral college in a patchwork of methods ranging from popular voting to selection by state legislatures, and the electors did not have to reflect popular opinion in their votes. Prior to the ratification of the Twelfth Amendment in 1804, the candidate who received the second highest number of votes in the electoral college was elected vice president. Neither the Federalists nor the Democratic Republicans yet formally nominated candidates for the presidency, and several electors split their votes for a variety of Federalist and Democratic-Republican candidates. As a result, Thomas Jefferson received the second-highest vote total and was elected vice president. The fact that the president and vice president led opposing political parties showed how the parties themselves were not yet solidly organized, disciplined entities.

President Adams had to navigate between Jefferson's democratic party on the one hand and Hamilton's conservative wing of his own party on the other. In 1796, Federalists also won a slim majority in Congress, and they moved quickly to fill the federal judiciary with their allies. Although Adams handled crises well, he was never able to match Washington's popularity nor to unite the country around Federalist politics.

GEORGE WASHINGTON'S RETIREMENT Sarah Montgomery Thompson embroidered this picture, based on a popular painting, to celebrate George Washington's retirement from the presidency in 1797. The woman in the picture represents liberty; she holds in her hand a pole topped by a cap, both symbols of liberty. Liberty commends George Washington as he points across the Potomac River back to his home at Mount Vernon.

Adams assumed that reverence for the presidency would continue during his service. George Washington's birthday had been celebrated widely as a holiday, but similar Adams celebrations never caught on outside his native New England. John Adams found constant personal and political support from his wife Abigail, who was particularly suspicious of French influence over Jefferson and the Democratic Republicans.

John and Abigail were the first presidential couple to take up residence in the White House, as the planned city of Washington, DC, became the new U.S. capital in 1799. John prayed in a letter to Abigail, "May none but honest and wise Men ever rule under this roof." French planner Pierre L'Enfant, English architects Benjamin Henry Latrobe and William Thornton, and a variety of Irish and African American surveyors and builders worked throughout the 1790s to build a capital city whose design reflected American reverence for Greek and Roman classical ideals. Americans also reflected their political ideas in their taste for neoclassical designs of furniture, silver, glassware, pottery, and china—much of it imported from England. French style also continued to be popular, even as the Anglo-French wars accelerated.

Quasi-War with France

As the United States got caught up in the war between Britain and France, President Adams faced pressure to declare war on France. Adams wrote in a 1796 letter, "I dread not a War, with France or England, if either forces it upon Us, but will make no Aggression upon either, with my free Will, without just and necessary Cause and Provocation." Adams pursued a balancing act of nonaggression throughout his term, despite diplomatic and military crises with France and the persistent urging of some other Federalists. In mid-1796, the French decreed that neutral trade ships would be subject to capture just as British ships were. The British also continued to harass U.S. traders. Tensions rose further during Adams's first few months in office when the French

JOHN AND ABIGAIL ADAMS   John Adams and Abigail Adams had a close relationship nurtured by frequent correspondence when they had to be apart. Abigail was one of John's strongest supporters when he was vice president and president, and she resented political criticism of her husband. Both John and Abigail remained strong supporters of Federalist causes for the remainder of their lives.

PATRIOTIC DECORATING   Mirrors like this, made from wood or plaster covered in gold leaf, became popular among wealthy, fashionable Americans in the 1790s. Decorating one's home with furniture featuring the bald eagle, a symbol of the United States, was a way to display patriotism and a taste for lavish material goods.

rejected American envoy Charles Cotesworth Pinckney, one of the negotiators of Jay's Treaty with Britain.

Over the objection of many fellow Federalists, and with little consultation with Vice President Jefferson or other Democratic Republicans, Adams decided to send Elbridge Gerry and John Marshall to join Pinckney in a new diplomatic delegation to France. Emboldened by Napoleon Bonaparte's military victories in western Europe, the French were openly hostile to the Americans when they arrived in October of 1797. In what became dubbed "The XYZ Affair," French officials, identified to Congress and in the American press only by those initials, humiliated the American diplomats by demanding bribes that insulted U.S. sovereignty. The chairman of the House Ways and Means Committee famously expressed American resistance to French demands when he declared "Millions for defense, but not one cent for tribute!" Henrietta Liston, the wife of the British Minister to the United States, commented that public opinion seemed suddenly to shift and flow "with violence against the French party" as anti-French petitions flooded into Washington.

Controversy raged throughout 1798, and the Federalist Congress verged on declaring war. Congress fortified the U.S. Navy, and Adams ordered Hamilton to strengthen the still-small U.S. Army. French and U.S. ships skirmished in the Caribbean. In early 1799, as French ships hovered off the coast of America, the two countries seemed to be involved in an undeclared Quasi-War. To deflate tensions, Adams decided to send a new team of diplomats to France in October. Although he managed to avoid all-out war, he faced criticism from political opponents and from fellow Federalists, who thought he was weak on France.

Alien and Sedition Acts

President Adams was less successful at balancing domestic political tensions during the Quasi-War with France. Believing that he had public support, Adams and his allies in Congress passed a series of **Alien and Sedition Acts** during the summer of 1798. These acts only aggravated political and social conflicts around the country. The three "Alien" acts severely restricted immigration into the United States and gave the president power to deport anyone thought to be dangerous—even for spreading radical political ideas. The Sedition Law imposed steep fines and prison sentences on anyone found guilty of conspiring to "oppose any measure or measures of the government of the United States" or anyone who spoke or wrote maliciously against the government or the president. Both sets of measures targeted Democratic Republicans, who found support among immigrants from Ireland, France, and the Caribbean as well as from radical newspaper editors. Many Federalists thought they were imitating successful measures the Pitt government in England had imposed to suppress opposition, but the Alien and Sedition Acts backfired.

Unlike many French revolutionaries, most Americans did not really wish to overthrow the social order, and the Sedition Act seemed like an unconstitutional overreaction to political opposition. Several high-profile newspaper editors, convicted of sedition and imprisoned for writing against the Adams administration, became martyrs who galvanized public support against the Sedition law. In August 1798, Vice President Jefferson secretly drafted resolutions, passed by the Democratic-Republican controlled Kentucky legislature, denouncing the laws as unconstitutional and arguing that states need not comply with them. James Madison drafted a similar set of resolutions for Virginia. Other state legislatures, including Massachusetts and Maryland, denounced the Kentucky and Virginia Resolutions as dangerous precedents for state nullification of federal law. Americans entered the election year of 1800 barely at peace with France and fraught with internal division over the practice of political opposition.

Slave Rebellions: Saint-Domingue and Virginia

Anxieties among American elites in the late 1790s also increased because of revolutionary upheaval close to home—especially in the form of slave revolts. In 1791, black slaves

PROPERTY PROTECTED, a la Françoise.

QUASI WAR WITH FRANCE   This cartoon, "Property Protected á la Françoise," lampoons the Quasi-War between the United States and France and the XYZ Affair. In the image, menacing French figures threaten America, represented by the woman dressed in fashionable clothing with a Native American feathered headdress. The "French Directors" demand private plunder to put in their sack at the point of a sword labeled "French Argument." Meanwhile, John Bull, a character representing Great Britain, sits atop a mountain in the background laughing at the conflict.

in the French colony of Saint-Domingue (now the nation of Haiti) on the Caribbean island of Hispaniola revolted against their masters, whom they drastically outnumbered. The rebel slaves joined forces with promonarchical Spanish army forces to fight the French colonial government on the island, the richest European colony in the Western hemisphere. Led by charismatic former slave **Toussaint Louverture**, the rebels switched to the French revolutionary cause in 1794 after the French government abolished slavery. Louverture, now the governor general of Saint-Domingue, bested Spanish and English forces and took over the entire island of Hispaniola for the French; he also pacified the large mixed-race population on the island. By the end of the decade, Toussaint ruled Saint-Domingue, and many white politicians in the United States were unsettled by the specter of a formerly enslaved black rebel ruling a major French colony near U.S. shores (Map 8.1).

Their fears seemed justified when a Virginia slave named **Gabriel**, emboldened by the Saint-Domingue revolt and the political divisions he witnessed in his state, planned a large-scale revolt to coincide with the 1800 presidential election. Gabriel's master, Thomas Prosser, hired him out, which enabled Gabriel to build a network of associates in Richmond that included other slaves and radical French émigrés. Gabriel believed that free blacks and white artisans would join his cause, and he planned to carry a banner reading "death or Liberty," a play on Patrick Henry's phrase from the American Revolution, when he marched on the capital at Richmond. Instead, Gabriel and his

MAP 8.1 ▲ Migration out of Saint-Domingue/Haiti, 1793–1809 Thousands of people fled or were forcibly removed from the island of Saint-Domingue during the Haitian Revolution. Many, including slave owners, slaves, and free people of color, ended up in U.S. cities.

compatriots were betrayed, and he was tried and executed in October 1800. Virginia legislators imposed harsher slave codes in the aftermath of the rebellion to crack down on any rebellious slaves who might be inspired by Saint-Domingue.

STUDY QUESTIONS FOR PARTY CONFLICT INTENSIFIES

1. What diplomatic challenges (both with Europe and with Indian nations) faced the United States during the 1790s?

2. How did the Alien and Sedition Acts expose fundamental differences between Democratic Republicans and Federalists?

■ THE "REVOLUTION" OF 1800 AND THE REVOLUTION OF 1804

Thomas Jefferson claimed, "The election of 1800 was as real a revolution in the principles of our government as that of 1776 was in its form." Jefferson referred to the shift in power from the Federalists to his own Democratic-Republican party and to his hopes that he might return the United States to the principles of the American Revolution as his supporters interpreted them. Because most Americans still believed that politicians should hold disinterested republican values, they did not openly accept party politics despite practicing them. It seemed remarkable that presidential power could change hands peacefully from one party to another. Jefferson's own power would be tested by the continued tensions from the Anglo-French Wars, now fueled by Napoleon Bonaparte's rise to power in France. Meanwhile, the radical social and political upheaval in Saint Domingue grew until the colony declared its independence as the Haitian republic in 1804. Thomas Jefferson brought his Democratic-Republican "revolution" to the American government as other revolutions continued to reverberate around the Atlantic. Both "revolutions" would change American politics.

Jefferson Elected

One Connecticut Federalist predicted that if Jefferson beat Adams for the presidency, "the soil will be soaked with blood, and the nation black with crimes." Although Jefferson served as vice president under Adams, the two men held truly opposite opinions, and Adams had largely ignored Jefferson. Adams also faced opposition from Alexander Hamilton and other conservative members of his own Federalist party. Neither Jefferson nor Adams openly campaigned for the presidency, but members of their party engaged in vitriolic battles on a state-by-state basis throughout 1800.

State campaigning and legislative elections leading up to the presidential race mattered enormously because the states controlled the electoral college. Voters exercised little direct choice in the presidential election. In 10 of 16 states, the presidential electors were chosen by the state legislature, and the remaining 6 used a patchwork system in which only some of the presidential electors were chosen by popular vote.

By the time each state had chosen its members of the electoral college, in early December, it was clear that the election would be deadlocked. When the electoral college votes were officially tallied, Adams was defeated for president, but neither Burr nor Jefferson could be declared the winner. Thomas Jefferson and Aaron Burr tied with 73 votes each, and John Adams received 65. The Constitution provided that the candidate with the most votes would become president, while the runner-up would assume the vice presidency, but the Democratic Republicans had failed to plan their electoral voting well enough to have their intended vice presidential candidate, Aaron Burr, come in second. With Burr and Jefferson tied, the Constitution stipulated that the House of Representatives, still ruled by a Federalist majority, would decide the election.

In February 1801 during a driving snowstorm, the House met in continuous session to decide the election. Although he had earlier agreed to take the vice presidency, Burr refused to concede, and he even considered striking a deal with Federalists to become president. Ultimately, however, after 36 rounds of balloting, Jefferson prevailed, and Burr was elected vice president. Constitutional crisis was averted as the Federalists ceded the presidency to the Democratic Republicans.

Democracy: Limits and Conflicts

As they transitioned into power, the Democratic Republicans wished to erase the Federalist influence in politics: the use of centralized federal power, the turn toward Britain, the public debt, the excise taxes. As the Democratic Republicans believed in a democracy built on the power of free, white, property-holding men, they limited the political voice of women and free African Americans, both of whom had made some limited advances under the Federalists. In 1807, for example, the New Jersey legislature disenfranchised property-holding women and free African Americans who had voted for decades, largely because they supported the Federalist party. The writer Judith Sargent Murray claimed that intelligent women of means should share some equality with men, but even such elite white women lost out to the "common" white man in Jeffersonian America.

The Democratic Republicans exercised power in Congress and the executive branch during the first decade of the 19th century, but they still had to battle the Federalists in state politics and in the federal judiciary. Among his last presidential acts, John Adams appointed Federalists to the federal courts and other offices and nominated moderate Virginia Federalist John Marshall as chief justice of the Supreme Court. Marshall became a strong opponent of the Democratic Republicans as he put his imprint on the Court. In the landmark 1803 case of *Marbury v. Madison*, Marshall's opinion established the principle of "judicial review," the right of the U.S. Supreme Court to rule on the constitutionality of legislation and executive actions—especially important because Marshall declared that "a law repugnant to the Constitution is void." The case concerned a battle between one of Adams's Federalist appointees and Democratic-Republican Secretary of State James Madison, but in the long run, the particulars mattered far less than Marshall's assertion of judicial authority. The Democratic Republicans tried to counter Federalist judicial power using their impeachment powers but with little effect.

The divide between the parties in the United States remained bitter, not the least because neither one was yet convinced of the legitimacy of party politics. In 1801, John Adams called the Democratic Republicans "a group of foreign liars, encouraged by a few ambitious native gentlemen," while most Democratic Republicans held Federalists in no higher regard. Unless personal honor became intertwined with electoral matters—as was the case in 1804 when Vice President Burr killed Alexander Hamilton in a duel over perceived personal insults during the New York governor's race—most battles took place in the realm of politics. Unlike the French or Haitians, Americans in the 1790s did not resort to widespread violence or turmoil to work out their ideological differences.

Haitian Revolution

Most white Americans were shocked as slave rebellion and colonial unrest in Saint-Domingue spread into a national revolution by 1804. Although the nation of Haiti declared its independence from France, and Haitians pledged to "live free and independent" in terms familiar to the American Revolution, the new republic did not receive U.S. government support. The 1805 Haitian constitution's permanent abolition of slavery and declaration that "No white man" would "ever be able to acquire any property" struck most white Americans as far too radical.

Revolutionary Migrations

Thousands of people moved around the Atlantic world as a result of the French and Haitian Revolutions—making migration one of the most important influences of the Atlantic revolutions. Free and slave migrants to the United States from France and Haiti brought with them food, clothing, language, and other traditions that influenced and changed American society.

Tens of thousands of people fled France during the early years of the Revolution there, many of whom were clergy and aristocrats, but the ranks of émigrés (as they were known) also included soldiers, peasants, and even workers and middle-class bourgeois radicals whose enemies expelled them. Among the thousands who spent time in the United States was the former British radical and American Revolutionary pamphleteer Thomas Paine, who assumed French citizenship in 1792 (the year he published *The Rights of Man*) only to flee Napoleon back to the United States in 1802. Most French émigrés did not have the choice to return home until at least the 1820s because the French government confiscated and sold their property and condemned many of them.

Philadelphia, the capital of the United States during the 1790s, became the center of French culture in America during that decade, as scores of French émigrés settled there. Louis Philippe, the future king of France, took part in Philadelphia high society and romanced several American women. One émigré, the Comte de Moré, referred to Philadelphia in the 1790s as "the Ark of Noah full of refugees." French émigrés in Philadelphia established political clubs, fraternal lodges, cultural societies, and businesses ranging from bakeries to wig shops to bookstores and newspapers.

The slave rebellion in Saint Domingue that became the Haitian Revolution prompted even more migration to the United States: between 1793 and 1809, at least 15,000 slaves,

Toussaint Louverture fought off a French invasion early in 1802. But later that year, French troops arrested him and deported him to France, where he died in prison. Napoleon Bonaparte, the recently declared Emperor of France, vowed to suppress Louverture because he was a rival political leader and because he represented, in Bonaparte's opinion, the "black barbarism that was on the rise" in the Caribbean. The French probably planned to reimpose slavery if they could control Saint Domingue. **Jean-Jacques Dessalines**, another former slave and a skilled military commander, took over leadership of the black revolt. In 1802, after a bloody campaign, Dessalines captured the French stronghold of Le Cap Français. He then expelled French troops and most of the remaining white residents who had not already fled or been executed. On January 1, 1804, Dessalines declared Haitian independence.

The new Haitian republic found little support with President Jefferson, the author of the Declaration of Independence. Napoleon correctly asserted that "the Spanish, the English, and the Americans . . . are dismayed by the existence of this black Republic." The 1805 Haitian Constitution defined all citizens of the Haitian Republic as "Black" white French colonists, and free people of color fled from the island to America. Most San Dominguan refugees, about two-thirds of them white and one-third of them black, ended up in American port cities (Philadelphia, New Orleans, New York, Boston, Baltimore, and Charleston) because they often escaped on French merchant ships.

The thousands of white slave masters who managed to force their slaves to accompany them from Saint Domingue presented a dilemma for the United States. Slave masters sought loopholes, for example, to the Pennsylvania manumission law that promised freedom after six months to any slave brought to the state. In 1809, Congress voted an exemption to the recent prohibition on international importation of slaves when it allowed white masters to bring more than 3,000 slaves with them to Louisiana from Cuba, where they had taken refuge after the Haitian Revolution. In 1811, Charles Deslondes, a slave brought to Louisiana, led one of the bloodiest and largest slave rebellions in American history.

The United States also influenced Saint Domingue. Haitian leader Jacques Dessalines was an admirer of the American Revolution, and future Haitian president and king Henri Christophe had very possibly served among hundreds of mixed-race Saint Dominguans alongside French troops at the Siege of Savannah during the American Revolution. In later decades, hundreds of African Americans would emigrate to Haiti, viewing the island as a bastion of black power and freedom. Their journey formed just part of the complex story of migration across the Caribbean.

- How do you think the migration of tens of thousands of people across the Atlantic and the Caribbean shaped the relationship between the United States and the revolutions in France and Saint Domingue?
- How significant was the decision by Congress to allow Saint Dominguan slaveholders to bring slaves into the United States after the international slave trade had been outlawed?

regardless of their origin, a radical notion to most Americans. White politicians were concerned that American slaves would be encouraged by the successful slave revolt and national revolution in Haiti. Moreover, Jefferson sought good relations with Napoleon. Several Southern states extended repressive laws they had passed in the aftermath of Gabriel's Rebellion. These laws further restricted the rights of free blacks, imposed harsher slave discipline, and forbade slave owners from freeing slaves and slaves from purchasing their own freedom. The Adams administration had encouraged Louverture's efforts against the French, but now Jefferson refused to recognize the independent Haitian republic.

The Louisiana Purchase

Although Thomas Jefferson supported the limitation of federal government power, as president he exercised great authority in expanding the territory of the United States. In the October 1800 Treaty of San Ildefonso, Spain secretly ceded the entire Louisiana territory, including New Orleans, back to France. More than one-half million Americans living west of the Appalachian Mountains relied on the Mississippi River for their growing agricultural trade, and they worried when Spain closed New Orleans as a precursor to the transfer of power. Jefferson was convinced that development of land by American small farmers held the key to the country's future, and he wanted to prevent Napoleon from pursuing an empire in North America. Although Jefferson had long favored France, he wrote to Robert Livingston in April 1802 that "The day that France takes possession of New Orleans, we must marry ourselves to the British fleet and nation."

Instead, Jefferson found a surprising solution to the crisis. Napoleon, preoccupied with troubles in Haiti and a recent military defeat in Egypt, sought to rebuild strength for the next round of war against Great Britain. As a result, when Jefferson sent Robert Livingston and James Monroe to France to attempt to purchase New Orleans and a portion of West Florida, Napoleon's foreign minister Talleyrand instead offered to sell the entire Louisiana territory.

The Constitution did not directly address whether the federal government could purchase new territory, but after some agonizing, Jefferson concluded that the "laws of necessity, of self-preservation, of saving our country when in danger" authorized the purchase. In April 1803, he paid $15 million to purchase the vast Louisiana Territory, which almost doubled the size of the United States. Jefferson argued that this strong use of federal power fit with his Democratic-Republican vision because it opened so much land for farming. The Louisiana Purchase was hailed as a glorious triumph when it was announced on July 4, 1803, but the reactions of Indian nations who would be brought into contact with the United States remained to be seen.

STUDY QUESTIONS FOR THE "REVOLUTION" OF 1800 AND THE REVOLUTION OF 1804

1. How "revolutionary" was Jefferson's election in the "Revolution" of 1800?
2. Why did slave revolts and the Haitian revolution scare Americans?

◼ TRADE, CONFLICT, WARFARE

Jefferson hoped the Louisiana territory could develop U.S. economic growth in agriculture and trade. Between the 1790s and 1807, the United States increasingly defined itself as a commercial nation with a role in the world economy. International trade energized the American economy, but it also led the nation into conflict and war in North Africa and Europe. Trade offered economic benefits, but they came with diplomatic entanglements and military conflict.

Transatlantic and Caribbean Trade

The Anglo-French wars and Caribbean upheaval presented both opportunities and obstacles. Following the Revolutionary War, France, Britain, and Spain all opened new avenues of trade to Americans, who in the 1790s sought to expand opportunities even further. During the first Anglo-French War (1793–1801), American neutral traders had caused international friction, but commerce nonetheless increased. Americans continued to try to expand trade during the European Peace of Amiens (1801–1803), although it proved difficult. When the Napoleonic Wars resumed in 1803, Americans continued their enterprise, but they also increasingly found themselves lured into naval conflict.

When the French Revolution first spread into European warfare, the United States benefited because the French and British allowed Americans limited neutral trading rights that undermined previous Spanish and Portuguese monopolies. American exports grew from $20.2 million in 1793 to $94 million in 1801. Much of that growth came as the United States became the main trade intermediary between European nations and their Caribbean colonies. Both France and Britain allowed U.S. traders to carry goods to their rival colonies in the Caribbean by way of the United States. The Caribbean also absorbed great quantities of American products such as lumber, fish, livestock, corn, and wheat. American shipowners steadily increased their share of European and Caribbean trade.

During the period of European peace from 1801 to 1803, American exports again declined to $54 million; at the same time, however, U.S. traders increased their percentage share of the Caribbean re-export trade. Once the Europeans resumed warfare in 1803, U.S. trade in the Caribbean and Latin America again skyrocketed to its highest level ever. Exports peaked at $108 million in 1807. Imports increased even more, from $33 million in 1793 to $146 million in 1807—an indication of the growing appetite for European goods. Americans were increasingly connected to Europe and Caribbean societies through the goods they exchanged (Figure 8.1).

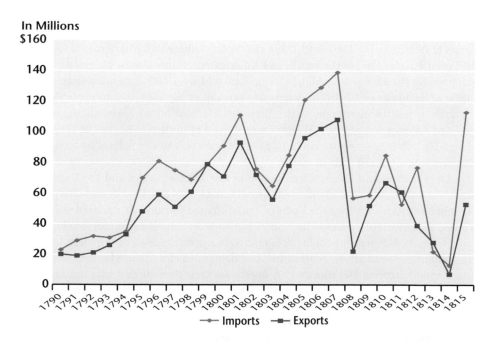

FIGURE 8.1 ▲ **Total U.S. imports and exports, 1790–1815** Use this graph to think about the causes and effects of the Barbary Conflicts and the War of 1812.

Americans curtailed one area of international exchange in this period—the international slave trade. Although the U.S. Constitution forbade Congress to outlaw the international trade before the year 1808, legislative debate on how to halt the international traffic in slaves began in 1806. Congressional representatives from slave and free states disagreed bitterly over the status of illegally imported slaves and punishments for slave smugglers. The British outlawed their slave trade in 1807, and the U.S. Congress followed by passing a law in March of that year banning the international slave trade as of January 1, 1808. The law was significant, although it did nothing to curtail the growing internal slave trade, and the U.S. population of slaves would skyrocket in coming decades even without legal international imports.

One contemporary economic commentator remarked that "the most adventurous became the most wealthy" during the rise in European trade, but those adventurers also exposed themselves and the United States to great risk. Although European states periodically recognized U.S. neutral trading rights, they also regularly interfered with U.S. shipping. After their 1805 victory over Napoleon at the Battle of Trafalgar, the British denied the United States right to engage in re-export trade with France and began seizing scores of U.S. ships and their cargo. Between 1803 and 1812, the British also detained an estimated 6,000 U.S. sailors and impressed them into the Royal Navy.

Mediterranean Trade: Barbary Wars

The United States also faced conflict in the Mediterranean. In the 17th and 18th centuries, ships from the Barbary states of Algeria, Morocco, Tunis, and Tripoli harassed traders in the Mediterranean and captured foreign hostages. Lacking European protection after the Revolutionary War, the United States sought to contain the Barbary privateers—or pirates, as Europeans and Americans called them—by concluding a series of treaties in the 1780s and 1790s and paying tribute to Barbary rulers. Congress had been reluctant to pay too much, and Americans continued to be harassed and kidnapped. By the mid-1790s, Algiers alone had sold over 100 American citizens into slavery. The image of Christian Americans serving as captive slaves in exotic Muslim settings, spread by newspaper articles, pamphlets, and books about their captivity, aroused American opposition. When Congress paid $1 million to Algiers in 1796 to free American captives—a figure equal to roughly one-sixth of the federal budget—other Barbary leaders raised their demands.

Despite President Jefferson's reduction of the defense budget and the Democratic Republicans' general skepticism of building U.S. naval power, Jefferson proved willing to fight in North Africa. When the Pasha of Tripoli, **Yusuf Qaramanli**, declared war on the United States in 1801, Jefferson imposed a blockade on Tripoli and endorsed shipbuilding. When the U.S. warship *Philadelphia* ran aground off the coast of Tripoli in 1803, the Tripolitans captured all 307 of its sailors and demanded more than $1.5 million in tribute. Captain **Stephen Decatur** and his *Enterprise* crew then slipped into the harbor of Tripoli and burned the *Philadelphia*. **William Eaton**, the U.S. consul to Tunis, invaded the Tripolitan city of Derna with the help of Yusuf Qaramanli's rival, his brother Ahmed. In June 1805, the United States and Tripoli reached a peace agreement that included a new U.S. payment of $60,000 in tribute to ransom the captured American sailors.

Later, Algiers declared war on the United States, but it agreed to a peace treaty after Capt. Decatur captured the flagship of the Algerian fleet in June 1815. Despite creative military action, the ongoing Barbary conflicts exposed how weak the United States remained in the world. Only after 1815, when the nation proved it could wage war against Great Britain, did the Barbary states agree to stop demanding tribute payments and allow freer Mediterranean trade.

Western Discontents

Although the Louisiana purchase had blunted the influence of France inside North America, many U.S. citizens still clashed with Spain, Britain, and Indian interests. Several Americans conspired to seize Spanish territory in East Florida and Mexico. After Vice President Burr was not reelected for a second term, he sought to aggrandize himself with a set of convoluted imperial maneuvers. By 1805, Burr organized Western settlers and planned an attack to wrest control of Mexico from Spain. One of his coconspirators, James Wilkinson, who was both the highest-ranking U.S. army general and a paid Spanish secret agent, revealed the plot to Thomas Jefferson. Burr was captured and tried for treason in 1807, but Chief Justice John Marshall's narrow constitutional interpretation led to Burr's acquittal. Burr fled to England in 1808.

After the 1795 Treaty of Greenville, white American settlers poured into the Northwest Territory, which occupied roughly the area of modern-day Ohio, Indiana, Michigan, and Wisconsin. Population increased so quickly that Ohio reached 60,000 residents and became a state in 1803. This status placed additional pressure on Shawnee and other Northwest Indians who had resisted American expansion and worked with the British after the Revolution. By 1810, there were 230,000 whites in Ohio, and Indian peoples felt constant pressure from this expansion. **Tecumseh**, who had helped lead Shawnee warriors against the United States in the 1790s, moved further west to the White River in Indiana where he established Prophetstown. Tecumseh's brother, **Tenskwatawa**, who was known as "The Prophet," preached a religious revitalization that urged Indian peoples to reject the adaptation embraced by tribes like the Cherokee and, instead, to return to traditional ways of life. According to Tenskwatawa, Indians could continue to deal diplomatically and trade with the Spanish, French, and English, but Americans should be avoided because a revelation told him that they were "the children of the Evil Spirit."

Tecumseh gathered a coalition of warriors from several Indian tribes, including Osage, Winnebago, Kickapoo, and Creek, as he used his personal magnetism to build a Pan-Indian movement among tribes who all faced American encroachment on their lands. Tecumseh rejected the notion of private land ownership, and he urged other leaders to repudiate past American treaties and to refuse new ones. While Tecumseh was away gathering allies, Indiana territorial governor **William Henry Harrison** attacked Prophetstown and defeated Shawnee warriors at the Battle of Tippecanoe on November 7, 1811. Tecumseh aligned with the British in Canada and awaited further confrontation.

European Wars and Commercial Sanctions

American tensions with Britain, and to a lesser degree France, built after 1805. Britain and France moved to restrict trade and to impose naval blockades on one another. The British agreed to new trade relations with the United States in the Monroe-Pinckney Treaty of 1806, but the Democratic-Republican controlled U.S. Senate refused to ratify the treaty. In the summer of 1807, the British ship *Leopard* fired on the U.S. warship

Chesapeake and impressed several of her sailors—an action that outraged the American public. Britain declared in the November 1807 Orders in Council that U.S. ships would have to stop in British ports for licensing and inspection before they could trade with France or French colonies or they would be seized. The French countered later that year with the Milan Decree, which stated ships would be seized if they complied with the British orders.

The Democratic Republicans controlled large majorities in both houses of Congress, and they tried to avoid war by imposing commercial sanctions on Britain and France. Thomas Jefferson claimed that instead of war, "our commerce . . . if properly managed, will be a better instrument for obliging the interested nations of Europe to treat us with justice." Congress approved the Embargo Act in December 1807, which cut off all foreign trade. The act hurt European economies, but it did far more damage to the United States where the gross domestic product fell by 8 percent. James Madison, Jefferson's Democratic-Republican successor as president, continued to support the notion of controlling international relations through trade sanctions, even though the embargo seemed largely ineffective. In the Non-Intercourse Act of 1809, Congress reopened trade with countries other than Britain and France. All restrictions were lifted in May 1810 because they were too difficult to enforce.

France exploited the terms of the legislation that replaced the Non-Intercourse Act, known as Macon's Bill No. 2, to shift American hostilities decisively toward Great Britain in 1811. Macon's Bill No. 2 reopened trade with France and Britain but promised to reimpose sanctions on one side if the other agreed to stop harassing ships and recognize U.S. neutral trading rights. In July, the French foreign minister, the duc de Cadore, agreed to withdraw sanctions against U.S. shipping, although Napoleon's government only slowly abided by the agreement. U.S. political opinion then turned against Britain.

STUDY QUESTIONS FOR TRADE, CONFLICT, WARFARE

1. How did American policies toward naval interference by the Barbary states differ from those they applied to Britain and France?
2. What were the effects of European warfare on American commerce?

◼ THE WAR OF 1812

More than a decade of trying to remain neutral in the wars between France and England had not worked for the United States, and trade sanctions had failed. By 1812, American political ire focused on Great Britain. Especially now that the French were set to allow Americans free trade, how could the British be allowed to continue interfering with American ships and kidnapping American sailors? If the United States refused to fight Britain, would that not compromise its independence won in the American Revolution? Perhaps only warfare would give the United States a chance to be taken seriously on the world stage.

War Declared

President Madison and the belligerent Democratic Republicans in control of Congress, known as the War Hawks, agitated for war against Britain. Kentuckian Henry Clay, the Speaker of the House, and South Carolinian John C. Calhoun led the charge for war. They faced stiff opposition from Federalists, who feared that their largely New England constituents would be hurt by war and a cessation of trade. The British continued to harass American ships, although they repealed the Orders in Council and pledged to stop impressment. Just two days before the repeal, unaware that Britain had acted, the U.S. Congress narrowly voted to declare war.

The United States entered the War of 1812 on June 18, despite the resistance of Federalists and many residents of New England and the Mid-Atlantic states. The War Hawks hoped to guarantee "free trade and sailors' rights," to expel Britain from North America, and to pacify Indian nations who they felt stood in the way of American expansion in the West. Shawnee and many other Indians aligned themselves with the British, who promised to halt U.S. expansionism. Democratic Republicans, who had long opposed the British, welcomed the chance to prove that the United States was a force to be reckoned with in the world.

Opposition

Federalist New Englanders, on the other hand, had friendlier relations with the British and saw the war as unnecessary, and they spearheaded opposition to the war. Washington, DC, resident Julia Hieronymous Tevis commented that during the war, "The political animosity existing between the two parties was bitter beyond expression." In the week after Congress declared war, the severity of internal conflict became apparent as rioting broke out in Baltimore, a politically divided city. Alexander Hanson, a Federalist newspaper editor, denounced the war in print as "unnecessary, inexpedient" and as driven by Democratic-Republican personal grudges. In return, a pro-war mob demolished his printing office and destroyed other Federalists' property. Hanson was taken into protective custody, but a mob rushed the jail, savagely beat Hanson, and killed former Revolutionary War officer James Lingan, who was trying to protect him. City officials did little to stop the violence.

Despite the chilling effect of the Baltimore riots and accusations of disloyalty, Federalists maintained political resistance throughout the war. Some Federalist ministers preached against the war, and wealthy Federalist merchants declined to finance war bonds. New England Federalists were free to push their opposition because they still held state majorities. Federalist governors in Rhode Island, Massachusetts, and Connecticut all initially refused to mobilize state militias or have them controlled by federal officers, but eventually most militias did participate. In 1814, delegates from New England states gathered in secret at the Hartford Convention, where they discussed seceding from the union and endorsed the idea that states could nullify federal laws.

U.S. Offensives in Canada

As during the Revolutionary War, Americans unsuccessfully invaded Canada in the War of 1812. Expelling the British from their largest North American colony would

MAP 8.2 ▲ The War of 1812 This map depicts the major battles and campaigns in the War of 1812.

surely grant new land to the United States and deny support to Indian enemies. Henry Clay said that "Canada was not the end but the means" by which to strike against the British.

In July of 1812, Michigan territorial governor William Hull and his troops crossed into Canada at the Detroit River, but their progress stalled, and British General Isaac Brock then laid siege against the American fort at Detroit. By August, the Americans had surrendered Fort Mackinac and had delivered both Detroit and Fort Dearborn, the present-day site of Chicago, to the British. In October of 1812, American forces outnumbered British, Canadian, and allied Indian forces at the Niagara River, but Stephen Van Rensselaer's plans to capture the Queenstown Heights failed because he could not figure out a way to cross the river. Van Rensselear, called "Van Bladder" by his men because he spewed so much hot air in useless speeches, also abandoned plans to attack Fort Erie in November. In addition, commanding army general Henry Dearborn's attack on Montreal failed. Coordinating army and militia troops proved difficult, and on several occasions, militia men refused to cross the border into Canada because they claimed their commissions were null on foreign soil.

Secretary of War John Armstrong focused on Canada again in 1813, as Britain and the United States battled for control of the Great Lakes. In April, an American force under Zebulon Pike inflicted a bloody defeat on the city of York, present-day Toronto. Pike's men looted houses and burned government buildings. In the West, British General Henry Proctor, bolstered by Tecumseh's Indian forces, pushed back the Americans by invading Ohio and attacking Fort Meigs. Proctor failed to stop Indian forces from slaughtering American prisoners along the River Raisin, and. "Remember the Raisin!" became a rallying cry among American troops.

Tecumseh and Pan-Indian Resistance

General Proctor's second attack into Ohio in July 1813 was planned by Tecumseh, the Shawnee leader who had continued building alliances with Indians and the British since his forces' defeat by the American military at Tippecanoe in 1811. Proctor and Tecumseh unsuccessfully attacked Fort Meigs a second time and then went after Fort Stephenson, a small fortification on the Sandusky River expertly defended by Kentucky sharpshooters. When Proctor's men lost the engagement, the general blamed Tecumseh and returned his force to Canada. Tecumseh urged the British to continue the offensive

TECUMSEH AT THE BATTLE OF THE THAMES This 1833 engraving by William Emmons shows how Americans continued to be fascinated by the death of Tecumseh at the Battle of the Thames long after the battle in 1813. Richard Mentor Johnson, who claimed to be the man who shot Tecumseh, was elected vice president in part because of that reputation. Tecumseh was revered as a brave enemy whose tragic death nonetheless proved American superiority to Indians.

against the United States, and he compared Proctor to "a fat animal" that puts its tail "between its legs and runs off." Some of Tecumseh's allies grew disillusioned with the British, and the great warrior fought to hold together his coalition.

An American army and militia force commanded by former Indiana territorial governor William Henry Harrison and **Richard Mentor Johnson**, a Kentucky congressman, pursued Proctor as he pulled his forces back into Canada. On October 5, 1813, they clashed with Proctor and Tecumseh at the Battle of the Thames near Moraviantown. The American troops routed the British, and although the Indian fighters held out longer, they lost heart when word spread that Tecumseh had been killed. Some of Johnson's militia troops claimed to have cut off pieces of Tecumseh's skin as souvenirs after the battle. It is more likely that Tecumseh's men removed him from the field. Mutilated or not, Tecumseh's death also meant the death of his Pan-Indian resistance movement against the United States.

Although some of Tecumseh's allies immediately ended their British alliance and began to make terms with the United States, others continued to resist. Among those who fought in Canada were Little Warrior and other members of the "Red Stick" faction of the Creek nation. Since the 1780s, Red Sticks had resisted the Creek government's moves toward accommodation and their grants of land rights to the United States in Georgia and Alabama. After returning from fighting with Tecumseh in the summer of 1812, the Red Sticks, assisted by the Spanish, ignited a Creek civil war. After Red Sticks destroyed Fort Mims in August, U.S. army troops joined the fight, and **General Andrew Jackson** pursued the hostile Creeks with a vengeance. In November 1813, Jackson defeated the Red Sticks at Tallushatchee and Talladega and then almost completely wiped them out at the Battle of Horseshoe Bend in March 1814. The United States used the opportunity of the War of 1812 to tamp down Indian resistance.

Naval War

When it entered the War of 1812, no one thought that the United States could match the Royal Navy, the world's most impressive naval fighting force. Both at sea and on the Great Lakes, the U.S. Navy did better than expected and initially outperformed U.S. ground troops. Britain's navy was absorbed in the final struggle against Napoleon, and the United States fielded some skilled commanders. The Democratic Republicans swallowed their long opposition to naval warfare and endorsed a quick program of shipbuilding. Two impressive early victories came when Captain Isaac Hull's fast USS *Constitution* bested the HMS *Guerriere* off the coast of Boston in August 1812 and when Captain Stephen Decatur's USS *United States* captured the British frigate HMS *Macedonian* as a prize near the Canary Islands in October. In December, the USS *Constitution* outmaneuvered the HMS *Java* near Brazil. American privateers also captured British ships to aid the cause.

Early in 1813, Americans controlled Lake Ontario and repelled a British attack on their naval base at Sackets Harbor. Even more impressive was the September 10, 1813, victory at the Battle of Lake Erie, where **Oliver Hazard Perry** first commanded the *Lawrence* and then, when it became incapacitated, took the helm of the *Niagara* to beat a British fleet of six ships. After the thrilling victory, Perry wrote to William Henry Harrison: "We have met the enemy, and they are ours." Perry felt that his victory partly

PERRY AND THE WAR OF 1812
Oliver Hazard Perry rose to fame as a naval commander in the War of 1812. His decisive victory over the British at the Battle of Lake Erie and his smart leadership of the naval campaigns in the Great Lakes made him into a popular hero. He went on to collect more accolades against Algeria in the Barbary Wars.

JACKSON'S VICTORY AT THE BATTLE OF NEW ORLEANS   Paintings like this one, which glorified Andrew Jackson's victory at the Battle of New Orleans, helped to propel him into politics and to enhance his reputation for heroism. The image also shows in the foreground Kentucky "hunters"—rustic backwoodsmen who fought with Jackson and were revered in popular culture for their deft use of rifles and noted for their buckskin clothing.

vindicated his friend Captain James Lawrence, who had been killed in a battle between the USS *Chesapeake* and the HMS *Shannon* off the coast of Boston the previous June. Later in 1813, U.S. naval victories slowed once the British imposed a stronger blockade on the United States.

TIMELINE 1789–1815

AMERICA	YEAR	THE WORLD
Apr George Washington inaugurated first U.S. president	1789	Jul 14 Crowds storm Bastille in Paris, beginning French Revolution
Dec Philadelphia becomes U.S. capital city as Washington, DC, is built Dec Bill of Rights ratified	1790	
	1791	Aug Saint Domingue slave rebellion begins
Apr Washington issues Neutrality Proclamation	1793	Jan French King Louis XVI executed Mar France declares war on Spain
Sep Washington orders federal military power to put down Whiskey Rebellion Nov U.S. and British diplomats secretly sign Jay's Treaty	1794	Feb France outlaws slavery in its colonies May Toussaint Louverture switches allegiance from Spanish to French
Jun U.S. Senate ratifies Jay's Treaty with Great Britain Aug United States signs Treaty of Greenville with representatives from 12 Northwest Indian nations Oct Pinckney's Treaty (Treaty of San Lorenzo) opens trade on the Mississippi to United States	1795	May France and Holland ally in Treaty of the Hague Jul France and Spain sign peace agreement Nov Napoleon Bonaparte and four other "Directors" take power in France
Nov John Adams elected President; Thomas Jefferson elected Vice President	1796	Feb France revokes all U.S. treaties Aug Spain secretly cedes Louisiana Territory to France
Apr President Adams publicizes "XYZ Affair" Jun–Jul Congress passes Alien and Sedition Acts Nov Kentucky legislature passes Thomas Jefferson's "Kentucky Resolutions" Dec Virginia legislature passes James Madison's "Virginia Resolutions"	1798	Jul Napoleon Bonaparte wins Battle of the Pyramids in Cairo, Egypt
Feb USS *Constellation* captures the French frigate *L'Insurgente* in Caribbean Oct President Adams sends new diplomatic mission to France to avoid open war	1799	Dec Napoleon Bonaparte named First Consul of France
Aug Gabriel's Rebellion betrayed in Richmond, Virginia Sep United States and France agree to end Quasi-War	1800	Aug Act of Union between Great Britain and Ireland
Jan President Adams appoints John Marshall Chief Justice of the Supreme Court	1801	Jul Toussaint Louverture appointed St. Domingue governor for life

British Offensive

After Napoleon's October 1813 defeat, the British turned attention and resources on the United States. The U.S. troops faced more experienced, better supplied, and better commanded British soldiers.

In the north, the British and Americans traded the advantage in 1814. The governor-general of Canada, Sir George Prevost, planned an offensive at Plattsburgh, New York, in September, but he retreated after American naval forces won a decisive victory on Lake Champlain and cut off his supply route. American General James Wilkinson

Feb Supreme Court establishes judicial review in *Marbury v. Madison* **May** United States and France agree on Louisiana Purchase	**1803**	**May** Britain declares war on France
Nov Thomas Jefferson reelected president	**1804**	**Jan** Jacques Dessalines declares Independence of Haiti **Dec** Napoleon crowned emperor of France
Jun United States negotiates end to Tripolitan War	**1805**	**Oct** British defeat combined French/Spanish fleet at Battle of Trafalgar
Feb Aaron Burr is arrested for plotting against Spain in American West	**1807**	**Nov** British Orders in Council mandate licensing for all neutral traders **Dec** France's Milan Decree extends blockades to neutral powers
Jan Legislation outlawing the international slave trade becomes U.S. law **Dec** James Madison elected president **Dec** President Jefferson signs Embargo Act	**1808**	Revolutionary movements begin in Mexico
Mar Congress replaces Embargo Act with Non-Intercourse Act	**1809**	Dominican Republic declares independence
May Congress replaces Non-Intercourse Act with Macon's Bill No. 2 **Nov** President Madison opens trade with France and imposes sanctions on Great Britain	**1810**	
Jan Charles Deslondes leads 150–500 slaves and runaways in a violent rebellion outside of New Orleans **Nov** William Henry Harrison defeats Shawnee troops at Battle of Tippecanoe	**1811**	
Jun United States declares war on Great Britain **Dec** James Madison reelected president; Elbridge Gerry elected vice president	**1812**	**Sep** Napoleon Bonaparte invades Russia
Aug The Red Sticks rebellion ignites Creek War	**1813**	**Aug** Austria breaks from France, declares war
Mar Andrew Jackson puts down Red Sticks Rebellion at Battle of Horseshoe Bend **Aug** Washington, DC, burned by British **Dec** Treaty of Ghent is signed, ending War of 1812	**1814**	**Apr** Napoleon abdicates power **May** Treaty of Paris ends European war, restores Louis XVIII as King of France
Jan New England Federalists meet in Hartford, Connecticut, to discuss their opposition to War of 1812 **Jan** British defeated at The Battle of New Orleans	**1815**	**Nov** Treaty of Paris ends Napoleonic wars

failed in his effort to attack Montreal in October 1813, but fighting continued on the Niagara the following year. American troops won impressive victories at Chippewa and Lundy's Lane and twice attacked Fort Erie before blowing it up on November 8. The British occupied northern Maine and found the American locals largely sympathetic.

The major British offensive on the Chesapeake was more successful. Congress was slow to fortify Washington while the British blockaded the coast and invaded Maryland in August. On August 24, British forces defeated U.S. troops at Bladensburg, across the Potomac from the capital. Most of the inhabitants of the capital had been evacuated, and congressional clerks and first lady **Dolley Madison** saved government property and records. The British entered Washington on the evening of August 24 and burned almost every government building, including the White House, before leaving the next day. Then they captured Alexandria, Virginia, without a fight.

The British were stopped when they reached Baltimore in early September. Francis Scott Key wrote the poem "The Star-Spangled Banner" after watching the battle of Fort McHenry on September 13. For 25 hours, the British fired over 1,500 rounds, including exploding shells and screaming Congreve rockets, at Fort McHenry. But American forces survived the bombardment with their arms intact, and they repelled the British, who retreated from Baltimore on September 15. When the British left Maryland, they took with them 2,000 runaway slaves who later resettled in Canada.

The War Ends

Despite the intense fighting around Washington, DC, the British were anxious to negotiate an end to the American war now that they were at peace with France. Negotiators for both sides met in Ghent, Belgium, in the summer of 1814, and talks proceeded through the fall as fighting continued. The United States and Britain signed the Treaty of Ghent, which ended the War of 1812, on Christmas Eve 1814. Britain agreed to evacuate American territory, both sides pledged to make peace with Indian nations, and each side agreed to settle Canadian border issues by future negotiation. Ironically, the treaty made no mention of the prewar naval or trade conflicts that had led to war.

Despite the fact that the Treaty restored things to a prewar status quo, the United States claimed victory. In part, the Americans' claim was based on their most glorious battle, fought at New Orleans just days after the peace treaty had been signed, but before anyone in North America had learned of it. On January 8, 1815, Andrew Jackson, helped by a group of international privateers known as the Baratarian pirates, foiled a British attack on New Orleans. British commander Sir Edward Packenham's assault dissolved in the swamps and fog of the Gulf coast, and Packenham himself was killed as Jackson skillfully defended the city. Jackson seemed to prove that Americans could best a well-formed European force: the combined British force suffered 2,450 casualties compared to the Americans' 350.

Although the War of 1812 changed little in international politics, the United States emerged with a new set of heroes, including Andrew Jackson and Oliver Hazard Perry. Despite the fact that many of their war plans had failed, the Democratic Republicans gained luster from the war, and the Federalist party was all but destroyed by its opposition to the war and by backlash against the Hartford Convention. Simultaneously, the Napoleonic wars were over, and the United States had proved to its citizens and to the world that it could stand up to Great Britain and survive. The world stage had changed with the defeat of Napoleon, and the United States was poised to try and assume a new role in future international dramas.

STUDY QUESTIONS FOR THE WAR OF 1812

1. What caused the War of 1812?
2. How were American politics between 1789 and 1815 influenced by other nations, including Indian nations?

Summary
• The federal government and the first clash between political parties in the United States took shape against a backdrop of transatlantic revolution and warfare.
• Americans supported the French Revolution at first, but its radicalization after 1793 worsened rifts in American politics.
• The United States was increasingly tied to other parts of the world through trade and migration, but these ties also brought conflict and war with North Africans (The Barbary Wars) and Europeans (the War of 1812).
• Slave revolt in Saint-Domingue, which became the Haitian Revolution, influenced U.S. politics, slave revolts, and legal crackdowns on African Americans.
• Indians, some who united in a Pan-Indian movement, posed stiff military resistance to the United States.
• As political parties developed, American politics in the 1790s were contentious. The Democratic Republicans had the political upper hand after 1800, but the Federalists opposed them until after the War of 1812.

Key Terms and People
Alien and Sedition Acts *267*
Bill of Rights *260*
Decatur, Stephen *276*
Dessalines, Jean-Jacques *272*
Eaton, William *276*
Fenno, John *261*
Freneau, Philip *261*
Gabriel *268*
Genet, Edmund Charles *257*
Harrison, William Henry *277*
Jackson, Andrew *282*
Jay's Treaty *262*
Johnson, Richard Mentor *282*

Little Turtle *263*
Louverture, Toussaint *268*
Madison, Dolley *286*
Marbury v. Madison *271*
Perry, Oliver Hazard *282*
Pinckney's Treaty *263*
Qaramanli, Yusuf *276*
St. Clair, Arthur *263*
Tecumseh *277*
Tenskwatawa *277*
Wayne, "Mad" Anthony *263*
Whiskey Rebellion *262*
The XYZ Affair *266*

Reviewing Chapter 8
1. How did the movement of people between France, Saint-Domingue, and the United States influence political events in the 1790s?
2. Did the United States successfully use warfare to increase its territory and/or clout in the world between 1789 and 1815?
3. What signs do you see that the citizens of the United States were developing a national identity between 1789 and 1815?

Further Reading
Cotlar, Seth. *Tom Paine's America: The Rise and Fall of Transatlantic Radicalism in the Early American Republic*. Charlottesville: University of Virginia Press, 2011. Cotlar explores how the movement of radical people and ideas between Europe and America in the 1790s influenced U.S. politics. The Democratic Republicans were less radically democratic than many Europeans.
Egerton, Douglas R. *Gabriel's Rebellion: The Virginia Slave Conspiracies of 1800 & 1802*. Chapel Hill: University of North Carolina Press, 1993. Egerton argues that the

Election of 1800 provided the political context and opportunity for slave rebellion in Virginia. Gabriel's rebellion was also influenced by the revolutions in France and Saint Domingue. Both slave revolts discussed in this work had a great impact on Virginia politics.

White, Ashli. *Encountering Revolution: Haiti and the Making of the Early Republic*. Baltimore: Johns Hopkins University Press, 2010. White's book examines how the Haitian Revolution affected U.S. politics and society during the formative years of party contest in the United States. White pays particular attention to how refugees from Saint Domingue affected the racial thinking of U.S. citizens.

Zagarri, Rosemarie. *Revolutionary Backlash: Women and Politics in the Early American Republic*. Philadelphia: University of Pennsylvania Press, 2007. Zagarri's book shows how white women participated in the political culture and partisanship of the early American republic and that debates about women's rights started in the late 1780s, even as society at large was moving to restrict women to a more "social" and less political role.

America In The World
PEOPLE, GOODS, IDEAS AND PRACTICES

CHAPTER 8: A New Nation Facing a Revolutionary World 1789–1815

NORTH AMERICA

EUROPE

AFRICA

SOUTH AMERICA

ATLANTIC OCEAN

ATLANTIC OCEAN

PACIFIC OCEAN

Tobacco and other exports

British army (1812-1814)

Émigrés fleeing Revolutionary France

Money

American sailors

British army (1812-1814)

British army (1812-1814)

Whiskey tax law

Philadelphia

Washington D.C.

Quebec

Slave rebellion

Refugees from Haitian revolution

American settlers

Lumber, wheat, corn, fish and other exports

U.S. army (1812-1814)

Toledo

American settlers

Indian nativist revival and pan-Indian resistance

Prophetstown

U.S. army (1812-1814)

0   500   1,000 miles
0   500   1,000 kilometers

Goods
Ideas
People

PRIMARY SOURCES FOR CHAPTER 8

A NEW NATION FACING A REVOLUTIONARY WORLD, 1789–1815

SOURCE 8.1

Greenleaf's New York Journal, Anonymous Letters Reporting on Crowd Protests Against the Jay Treaty in Philadelphia (1795)

On July 8, 1795, the editor of *Greenleaf's New York Journal* printed two conflicting accounts of a protest against the Jay Treaty, the highly controversial treaty stabilizing relations between the U.S. and Great Britain. In the summer of 1795, the terms of the treaty were kept secret while the Senate decided whether to ratify it. But the secrecy did nothing to stop popular opposition. The Federalists and Democratic Republicans battled not only over the treaty itself, but also over the specifics and meaning of protests like this one held by Philadelphia sailors.

Source: Greenleaf's New York Journal, July 8, 1795.

Extract of a Letter from a respectable Citizen of Philadelphia, to his friend in this city. I must inform you of a circumstance which took place here on Saturday evening last. At eleven o'clock the ship-carpenters of Kensington, and a number of other citizens, about 500 armed with clubs, paraded the streets with a transparent painting of *Mr. Jay*; the figure in the attitude of presenting "THE TREATY" to an expecting, admiring Senate, with the left hand, and in the right, a pair of scales suspended—In the elevated scale, "*Virtue, Liberty and Independence*," were inscribed in large capitals; in the preponderating one "*British Gold.*" After passing through several streets, they returned again to Kensington, where the painting was *committed to the flames*. A small party of the Light-Horse attempted to disperse them, but without effect; they were driven from the field amidst a shower of stones, by which some were severely hurt, but no lives lost. I was an eyewitness to the whole proceeding, you may therefore rely on this account.

[Extract of another letter of the same date.]

The 4th of July passed over in quietness, whatever you may have heard to the contrary.

On the fourth [of] July a number of ship carpenters from Kensington, and some of the Democratic Society, intended to burn Mr. Jay's effigy opposite the president's house. They were warned not to attempt it, and the militia officers, light horse, artillery, &c. waited for them in Market-street, till ten o'clock, but deterred them from their design, they came down Second to Market, from thence to Front, about one o'clock Sunday morning, as silent as a funeral procession, till they got above Vine street, and supposing themselves out of danger, when they gave three cheers. I mention this in case it becomes the subject of conversation. You may know how to speak of it. Not ten persons in all the streets they passed knew any thing of it.

WORKING WITH SOURCES

1. Judging from these two opposing accounts, what is it possible to discern regarding the attitude of Philadelphia sailors and shipbuilders toward the Jay Treaty?

2. Which letter was likely written by a person with Democratic-Republican sympathies and which one by a person with Federalist sympathies?

3. Why would the New York newspaper publish these two conflicting accounts?

SOURCE 8.2

Visual Document: Anonymous Cartoonist, The Providential Detection (c. 1797–1800)

In this, one of the earliest political cartoons published in the United States, an anonymous Federalist cartoonist uses a variety of images to paint a shocking picture of the Democratic-Republican frontrunner in the 1800 election, Thomas Jefferson. The cartoon portrays him as a willing traitor to the United States who worships at the altar of revolutionary France—the "Altar of Gallic Despotism."

Source: The Providential Detection. Courtesy American Antiquarian Society, Worcester, Massachusetts, USA/The Bridgeman Art Library.

The eagle with the shield represents the United States as it swoops down to snatch the U.S. Constitution from a kneeling Jefferson before he can add the Constitution to the fire of French despotism. The French altar (which is supposed to recall similar altars to "Reason" that were used in high-profile radical revolutionary rituals in France) is surrounded by moneybags labeled "American Spoliations," "Plunder," "Sardinia," "Flanders," and with the names of other parts of Europe that France had invaded. A fire atop the altar is fed by radical writings—Democratic-Republican newspapers, including the *Aurora;* works by the English radical William Godwin; and French philosophical works by Rousseau and Voltaire. Falling from Jefferson's right hand is a copy of his famous letter to Philip Mazzei, an Italian diplomat and supporter of the French Revolution. The letter, which was published in a Paris newspaper in 1797, had criticized Federalists as monarchists and implied that George Washington was among them. The cartoon also contains religious imagery, showing the eye of Providence (God) looking down from the clouds and the Devil lurking behind the French altar.

WORKING WITH SOURCES

1. How did the cartoonist communicate his belief that Jefferson was dangerous? Might any symbols or parts of the picture particularly move viewers?

2. Do you think the cartoon was effective? Could it have changed anyone's mind about the French Revolution? Did it probably appeal only to Federalists who already opposed Jefferson, or could it have had a broader appeal?

3. Why do you think the cartoonist decided to use a visual to make this argument about Jefferson, instead of writing a newspaper article or pamphlet?

SOURCE 8.3

James Bayard, Excerpts from a Letter to Alexander Hamilton Describing His Dilemma in the Disputed Presidential Election of 1800 (January 7, 1801)

Delaware Congressman James Bayard was a loyal member of the Federalist Party. In this letter, he speculates to one of his party's leaders, Alexander Hamilton, about what might resolve the deadlocked presidential election and whether the Federalists in the House of Representatives would vote for Aaron Burr or Thomas Jefferson. When the ballots were cast in March, it was Bayard's vote that decided the election in favor of Jefferson.

Source: Allen Johnson, ed., Readings in American Constitutional History, 1776–1876 (New York: Houghton Mifflin Company, 1913), 214–15.

I assure you, sir, there appears to be a strong inclination in a majority of the federal party to support Mr. Burr. The current has already acquired considerable force, and is manifestly increasing. The vote which the representation of a State enables me to give would decide the question in favor of Mr. Jefferson. At present I am by no means decided as to the object of preference. If the federal party should take up Mr. Burr, I ought certainly to be impressed with the most undoubting conviction before I separated myself from them. With respect to the personal qualities of the competitors, I should fear as much from the sincerity of Mr. Jefferson (if he is sincere), as from the want of probity in Mr. Burr. There would be really cause to fear that the government would not survive the course of moral and political experiments to which it would be subjected in the hands of Mr. Jefferson. But there is another view of the subject which gives me some inclination in favor of Burr. I consider the State ambition of Virginia as the source of present party. The faction who govern that State, aim to govern the United States. Virginia will never be satisfied but when this state of things exists. If Burr should be the President, they will not govern, and his acceptance of the office, which would disappoint their views, which depend upon Jefferson, would, I apprehend, immediately create a schism in the party which would soon rise into open opposition.

I cannot deny, however, that there are strong considerations, which give a preference to Mr. Jefferson. The subject admits of many doubtful views, and before I resolve on the part I shall take, I shall wait the approach of the crisis which may probably bring with it circumstances decisive of the event. The federal party meet on Friday, for the purpose of forming a resolution as to their line of conduct. I have not the least doubt of their agreeing to support Burr.

WORKING WITH SOURCES

1. What are Bayard's objections to Jefferson and Burr?

2. Does this document offer evidence that the Federalists had become a well-organized political party by 1801?

SOURCE 8.4

James Mather and William Claiborne, Excerpts from Letters Regarding Caribbean Migrants in New Orleans (1809)

On July 18, 1809, James Mather, the mayor of New Orleans, wrote to Louisiana's territorial governor, William Claiborne, about refugees from the Haitian revolution who had come to New Orleans from Cuba. The emigrants, a mix of whites, free people of color, and slaves, presented a challenge to the city. Congress eventually passed a special exemption to the prohibition on the international importation of slaves to allow these slaves to be brought into the United States from Cuba.

Source: Dunbar Rowland, ed., *Official Letter Books of W. C. C. Claiborne, 1801–1816*, reprinted. (New York: AMS Press, 1976), 4:387–88, 422–23; 5: 1–2.

In answer to your much esteemed [letter] of yesterday, I beg leave to enclose here in for the information of your Excellency, a general statement of the People brought here from the Island of Cuba by thirty four vessels. . . . It is hardly possible to form as yet a Judgement on the general character of the different classes.—It may however be inferred from their conduct since they have lived among us, as also from various other circumstances.

1stly In what regards the Blacks, they are trained up to the habits of strict discipline, and consist wholly of Africans bought up from guineamen in the island of Cuba, or of faithful slaves who have fled with their masters from St. Domingo as early as the year 1803.

2dly A few characters among the free People of Color have been represented to me as dangerous for the peace of this Territory; I must however own your Excellency that in every other Territory but this, the most part of them would not, I think, be viewed under the same light if due attention should be paid to the effects of the difference of language, and if it should be considered that these very men possess property, and have useful trades to live upon[1]. . . . In the mean time there has not been one single complaint that I know of;

against any of them concerning their conduct since their coming to this place.

3rdly The white persons, consisting chiefly of Planters, and merchants of St. Domingo who took refuge on the shores of Cuba about six years ago, appear to be an active, industrious People. . . . They have suffered a great deal from the want of Provisions both at sea, and in the River.—Several of them have died, and many are now yet a prey to diseases originating, as it appears, from the use of unwholesome food and from the foul air they have breathed, while heaped up together with their slaves, in the holds of small vessels during their passage from Cuba. . . .

I know of no provision established by our Laws, to prevent free white persons who have means for their living, to come and settle in the United States. . . .

[On November 5, 1809, William Claiborne wrote to Secretary of State Robert Smith to express his suspicion and concern about the refugees from Haiti who had come into New Orleans through Cuba and Jamaica.]

At all times, the *utmost vigilance* on the part of the officers of the Government in this

---

[1]The free people of color were required to post bond and leave the territory within a set amount of time.

Territory, is essential, but it is particularly so at the present period, when foreigners and *Strangers* are daily arriving among us; of *whom*, many are of doubtful character and desperate fortunes, and may (probably) become willing instruments in the hands of those unprincipled, intriguing individuals, who would wish to disturb the *peace, and Union* of the American States. . . .

You are already acquainted with the difficulty and anxiety which the Emigrants from Cuba occasioned me;—I anticipate like difficulties with the French Emigrants from Sto. Domingo and Jamaica, who I suspect will repair hither with their slaves.

> [Just days later, on November 12, 1809, Claiborne again wrote to Secretary Smith about refugees from Haiti who were entering New Orleans from Cuba and Jamaica and bringing slaves with them. He feared that the city could not handle the influx of people, and that the international slave trade would be reopened, despite its being outlawed by Congress the previous year.]

Two or three vessels from the City of Sto. Domingo via Jamaica have recently arrived in the Mississippi, with passengers and some slaves on board and others are expected.—

Already New Orleans and its vicinity are crowded with the unfortunate refugees from Cuba, and if the French of St. Domingo, Jamaica (& perhaps Guadeloupe, for I am told it is about to [be] attacked) should also seek an asylum here, I shall deem it alike unfortunate for them and for us;—for independent political considerations, this society will be totally unable to furnish conveniences for so numerous and sudden an emigration, or to supply the wants of the poor and distressed. I am particularly desirous to discourage the Emigrants from bringing slaves with them.—Motives of humanity induce me to permit the Refugees from Cuba to land their slaves, but this indulgence cannot be extended much farther, for already Sir, it is represented to me, that Negro's purchased from the Jails of Jamaica, have been smuggled into the Territory, and I suspect if it was understood, that Negro's brought by the French of St. Domingo were permitted to be landed, that a Negro trade hither would be immediately commenced.—These considerations Sir, induced me to write the Letters to our Consuls at Havanah and Jamaica, and I hope the same will be approved by the President.—

WORKING WITH SOURCES

1. What problems do the mayor and the governor anticipate that the Caribbeans will bring with them to New Orleans?

2. Why did government officials accept these refugees if they were so troublesome?

3. What evidence does this document present about the ways that Caribbean emigrants confused and challenged Americans' racial attitudes?

American Peoples on the Move

1789–1824

Magdelaine Marcot, a woman of mixed Odawa and French heritage, married Joseph La Framboise in 1804 in a Catholic ceremony at Michilimackinac (in present-day Michigan). Magdelaine, who became known as Madame La Framboise, had already lived with Joseph since she was 14, and she was raising their two children, also baptized Catholics, among her mother's Odawa kin at Grand Haven, just as she had been raised.

Joseph and Magdelaine La Framboise established a fur-trade business that exploited contacts among French traders and Indian kinship networks stretching from Montreal into present-day Michigan and Illinois in the land around Lakes Michigan and Huron. In 1806, when Joseph was killed while embarking on a trade voyage, Magdelaine took over the business. She built a fur-trading empire that made her one of the richest women in North America.

Madame La Framboise made annual journeys between the Grand River valley and the trading post at Fort Michilimacinac, exchanging thousands of pounds of fur for goods that she sold to Indian people and earning as much as 10,000 pounds per year, 10 times the average take of fur traders in that region. She successfully negotiated trade licenses from the British and U.S. governments before and during the War of 1812. La Framboise managed fur suppliers, voyageurs who transported her goods, and two African American slaves.

Her business was so profitable and she exercised so much independent power that La Framboise was seen as a threat by John Jacob Astor's American Fur Company when it moved into the Michilimacinac area by 1818. Eventually, she joined Astor's trade network, which expanded her business contacts as far as present-day Iowa

< This dance blanket was made in the mid-1800s by Ojibwe/Dakota Indians who were engaged in fur-trading networks.

and South Dakota. In 1822, she sold her trading post on the Grand River and entered a genteel retirement.

La Framboise honored the customs of her Indian relatives, dispensing food and supplies to their communities and maintaining native dress throughout her life. She also established Catholic schools for Indian and Metis children. La Framboise built a house on Mackinac Island, where she became a patron of St. Anne's Catholic Church and where she hosted Frenchman Alexis De Tocqueville in the 1830s during his visit to observe the United States. Her daughter married the commander at Fort Michilimackinac, Capt. Benjamin Pierce, the brother of future U.S. President Franklin Pierce.

Magdelaine La Framboise was an exceptional success; but her story of trade, family, travel, and political negotiation typifies the movement and energy that many people experienced around North America between 1789 and 1824.

◼ EXPLORATION AND ENCOUNTER

At the turn of the 19th century, people and goods moved across the spaces of North America at an ever-faster pace. Governments on the North American continent sized up natural resources and prospects for future expansion beyond their areas of permanent settlement. The United States and Spain sent out expeditions to probe the boundaries of North America, to establish ties with Indian peoples, and to survey the natural world. Traders and merchants also encouraged contacts between peoples on different parts of the continent. Competition emerged as explorers and traders crisscrossed the continent.

Lewis and Clark Expedition

Even before he finalized the Louisiana purchase in April 1803 (see Chapter 8), President Thomas Jefferson asked Congress to fund a mission to explore beyond the Missouri River to claim territory and to establish trade relations with Indian nations. Jefferson appointed his private secretary, **Meriwether Lewis**, commander of the expedition. Lewis chose as his fellow "captain" **William Clark**, a retired army officer who was an excellent backwoodsman and cartographer. Lewis and Clark spent almost a year preparing for their journey, and when they set off on May 14, 1804, they took with them 29 men in what they called their "Corps of Discovery." The Corps included Kentucky hunters, soldiers, French Canadian boatmen, an interpreter, and Clark's slave, African American York.

Jefferson charged Lewis and Clark to communicate to Indian nations that the United States was now in control of the Louisiana Territory, to observe plants and animals, to make maps, and to explore routes for future trade to the Pacific. In 1804, the Corps traveled up the Missouri River and met with powerful Indian groups: Teton Sioux (Lakota), Arikara, and Yankton Sioux. Much of the area the Corps surveyed beyond the Missouri River was as yet unexplored by Europeans and Americans, and Lewis and Clark relied on local Indian knowledge. They wintered at the Mandan villages—in present North Dakota— where they were joined by French Canadian trader Toussaint Charbonneau and his wife, the Shoshone war captive **Sacagawea**, whom Charbonneau had purchased from Minitari people. Sacagawea remained with the expedition, even after she gave birth to a son. Sacagawea added essential linguistic and geographic skills to the Corps.

Setting out from the Mandan villages in April 1805, the Corps traveled up the Missouri alternately by foot and by canoe until August, when they struggled across the Rockies and the Bitterroot

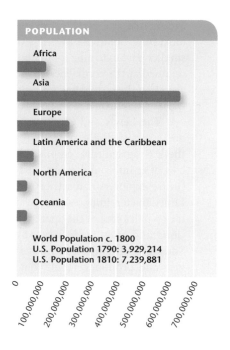

POPULATION

Africa

Asia

Europe

Latin America and the Caribbean

North America

Oceania

World Population c. 1800
U.S. Population 1790: 3,929,214
U.S. Population 1810: 7,239,881

0
100,000,000
200,000,000
300,000,000
400,000,000
500,000,000
600,000,000
700,000,000

Captains Lewis & Clark holding a Council with the Indians   *Page 17*

LEWIS AND CLARK   This idealized illustration of Lewis and Clark holding a council with some of the Indians they encountered on their journey of exploration appeared as an illustration in the 1810 edition of the journal of their travels, a very popular book. The image shows Lewis and Clark as carefully dressed orators who hold the attention of Indian men eager to hear what they say.

Mountains. The party reached the Pacific in November 1805 and established winter quarters at the Columbia River. Setting out again in the spring of 1806, the group split into smaller parties to attempt to find an easier crossing over the Rockies, but by the time they rejoined at the confluence of the Yellowstone and Missouri rivers on August 12, it was clear that they could find no easy overland Pacific trade route. The voyage concluded when the Corps returned to St. Louis on September 23, 1806.

The Lewis and Clark expedition succeeded in several ways, even though it did not establish the easy trade routes that Thomas Jefferson had hoped would expand the U.S. agricultural empire. The explorers observed and catalogued hundreds of species of animals and plants, and their maps and landscape descriptions were of use to future explorers and settlers. Lewis and Clark solidified U.S. claims over much of the Louisiana territory, and they claimed portions of Oregon—as they avoided several military parties sent by the Spanish to try to intercept them. They also established good relations and solid trade ties with several Indian groups, most notably Mandan and Shoshoni, although many other groups were skeptical of Lewis and Clark's flashy trinkets and pronouncements that Thomas Jefferson was their new "great father." Teton Sioux and Piegan were hostile to the Corps, and the expedition probably narrowly avoided all-out war with these Indian peoples who scorned the U.S. "Magnitude & power." The Lewis and Clark expedition would, nonetheless, feed decades of westward expansion by U.S. citizens.

Zebulon Pike

Spain, also skeptical of American power, contested the southwestern boundaries of the Louisiana Purchase. In 1786, the Spanish governor of New Mexico had concluded peace agreements with the powerful Comanche people and had sent explorer Pedro Vial across the southern plains to St. Louis. Although the Spanish government later ceded the Louisiana Territory to France, which sold it to the United States in 1803, neither treaty clearly defined the southwestern territorial border. Beyond New Orleans and St. Louis, as one historian has put it, the United States had merely bought "the right to enter the arena and compete for control of the Indian country stretching westward to the Rockies."

U.S. military commanders sent Captain **Zebulon Pike** to define the U.S. claim to the southwestern part of the Louisiana Territory. Between August 1805 and April 1806, Pike had journeyed up the Mississippi River to explore the source of the river and to form relationships with northern Indian groups. In 1806, General **James Wilkinson** sent Pike west from St. Louis to establish diplomatic ties with Osage and Comanche peoples; to try and negotiate peace between traditional enemies, the Kansas and Osage; and to explore the Arkansas and Red rivers without antagonizing Spain.

The task proved impossible. Pike survived intrigue and desertion by his Osage and Pawnee guides, but when he tried to negotiate with Pawnee near the Republican River, they revealed recent contacts with a large Spanish military force under Lieutenant Facundo Melgares. Abandoning most of his plans for Indian treaties, Pike followed Spanish and Indian trails across the Rockies. By January 1807, he was lost, and his expedition strayed all the way to the Rio Grande River—very near to Spanish settlement. The Spanish captured Pike and his men in February 1807. Pike was taken first to Santa Fe and then to Chihuahua for interrogation, and several of his men were imprisoned for two years. When Pike was allowed to return to St. Louis in July 1807, he published his journals, filled with his observations of the western territory and Mexico. They proved popular, although President Jefferson never considered Pike's military expedition as significant as Lewis and Clark's scientific and trade exploration. Pike's expedition proved that the United States could not take for granted expansion without resistance, even in the Louisiana Territory.

Plains Indian Peoples

Despite challenges, stories from the expeditions of Pike and Lewis and Clark made U.S. government officials and settlers increasingly interested in the Great Plains. The lives of Plains Indian peoples were changing quickly. By the 1790s, the use of horses for transportation, hunting, and war fighting had taken hold both west and east of the Rockies. Villages of Mandan, Hidatsa, and Arikara on the upper Missouri River acted as centers for trade networks that stretched from the Great Lakes to the Pacific Ocean. Western Comanche operated another trade center just northeast of the Rio Grande River. By the 1820s, Mandan and Arikara people found themselves squeezed between U.S. and British fur-trading companies.

Along with increased trade came diseases, including smallpox, measles, and whooping cough. All the Plains Indians were forced to try and maintain their societies as they faced downward population pressures. In some areas, mortality rates reached as high as 70 percent in the epidemic outbreaks in the first half of the 19th century.

Indian people contested for power. Fights between tribal rivals such as Apache and Comanche continued throughout the period. Nomadic Sioux people gained power over village-based groups such as Mandan and Arikara, whose population density caused epidemics to hit them harder. Factions within Osage tribes desired so badly to keep their advantage in the gun trade that they agreed in 1808 to cede "50,000 square miles of excellent country" (in latter-day Oklahoma, Arkansas, and Kansas) to the United States in return for trade goods. Osage lands became a depository for Indians forcibly removed from the East after the War of 1812. Plains peoples remained powerful until after 1824, but they were beginning to feel pressure from exploration across their lands and growth of the white population.

Astor and the Fur Trade

John Jacob Astor sought profit in western North America. After emigrating to the United States from Germany in 1784, Astor founded his North American Fur Company in New York City in 1785. Undaunted by British trade rules that required Canadian goods to travel to London before they could be sold to the United States, Astor began selling furs to New York and Europe. After Jay's Treaty (1794) allowed direct U.S.– Canadian trade, Astor built up his business and increased his inventory. Through the 1790s, most of the fur made into hats and outerwear in the United States still came from Canadian firms, including the Hudson Bay Company and the North West Company, which operated vast networks of semi-independent Indian and mixed-race trappers. Beaver hats became fashionable among all classes of American men by the 1790s as their prices dropped.

ANISHINABE/DAKOTA DANCE BLANKET   This dance blanket was made in the mid-1800s by Ojibwe/Dakota Indians who were engaged in fur-trading networks. The wool blanket, decorated with silk ribbon and glass beads and owned by relatives of Magdelaine La Framboise, shows a combination of Indian patterns and influences from U.S. quilting techniques.

By 1808, Astor had extended his business with a bold move into the newly expanding China trade. He wholesaled furs to China and received payment in trade goods such as tea and silks that he could sell in North America and Europe for a great profit. In 1808, hoping to take advantage of disruptions in the fur trade caused by the Napoleonic wars in Europe, Astor received a New York state charter and founded the American Fur Company. Astor planned a network of traders, like Magdelaine La Framboise, who would deal across North America directly with Indian hunters and enmesh themselves in Indian culture. He hoped to gain market share by expanding his operation through the Great Lakes and all the way to the Columbia River. In 1810, Astor formed a new joint-stock company, the Pacific Fur Company; and in 1811, he sent two expeditions to found a trading post on the Columbia River. From that post, Astoria, he hoped to challenge the Russian traders who dominated the Oregon territory.

Astor's plans, however, suffered during the War of 1812, when he failed to gain protection from the U.S. government. Under threat from the Royal Navy, Astor sold Astoria to the North West Company in October 1813. The American Fur Company survived, and Astor convinced Congress in 1816 to bar British citizens from fur trading in U.S. territory. Other smaller fur trading companies thrived in the United States—including the Missouri Fur Company, cofounded by William Clark—but Astor's business skill and the worldwide scale of his efforts made him one of the richest men in America. Later sensing a shift in tastes away from furs, Astor moved his fur fortune into New York real estate.

Asian Trade

Astor had been among the first Americans to engage in large-scale Chinese trade. In 1784, Philadelphia financier Robert Morris sent the first American vessel, *The Empress of China*, to Asia. Under the command of Captain John Green, it carried a load of ginseng (prized by Chinese men as an aphrodisiac) and other goods. The United States and China did not share diplomatic relations until 1844, but New York, Providence, Boston, Salem, and Philadelphia merchants quickly built up a significant trade, especially with the port of Canton. During the Napoleonic Wars, U.S. traders quickly expanded their exports to and imports from China. As merchant Thomas Hansyard Perkins remarked, "Embargoes and non-intercourse . . . crossed our path; but we kept our trade with China."

SALEM, MASSACHUSETTS This 18th-century engraving shows the port of Salem, Massachusetts, one of the busiest trading ports in New England. In the 18th century, Salem became a home to shipbuilding and cod fishing; and, by the turn of the 19th century, it had become a major hub for American trade with Europe, the West Indies, China, Africa, and Russia.

Uninhibited by European monopolies that sought to govern the tea trade, U.S. traders developed relationships with Canton's merchants, who controlled the Chinese tea market. After 1802, American merchants also became involved in the growing opium trade into China. Americans adeptly negotiated the complex system of taxes and bribes in Canton, although they had to follow rules that kept them confined to small areas of the country. The Chinese consumed great quantities of American trade products including ginseng, sea otter fur, and seal fur. But Americans bought even more Chinese products: silk, furniture, porcelain, silverware, wallpaper, hand-loomed cloth, and decorative objects of many varieties. Americans thought of China as an exotic and uncivilized "far eastern" place, but Chinese goods shaped their tastes and fashions. Many merchants viewed China as "the first for greatness, richness, and grandeur of any country ever known."

Many U.S. China merchants also spread into the burgeoning trade with India during the same period. As John Adams wrote in 1785, "There is no better advice to be given to the merchants of the United States, than to push their commerce to the East Indies as fast and as far as it will go." Before 1783, India had been closed to Americans because the British had allowed the East India Company a monopoly over trade. But the 1783 Treaty of Paris opened the way for American trade with India, and during the Napoleonic Wars in Europe, American merchants took advantage of trade disruptions to expand their Indian trade. American merchants focused mainly on Calcutta because the Bay of Bengal was the easiest entry point for small American ships, which had trouble risking the dangerous seas of the Indian Ocean.

By the 1820s, the trade between Calcutta and New England grew rich and included not only a huge variety of material but also cultural exchanges. Indian cloth, from cotton sheeting to printed chintzes and elaborate silks, was advertised widely in American newspapers as a luxury good. Americans also consumed saltpeter, indigo, ginger, animal hides, and shellac imported from Calcutta. Many Yankee traders paid cash for their goods purchased in India, but they also traded to India a smaller amount of American goods—rum, glassware, books, timber, and cigars. In 1793, Jacob Crowninshield imported a two-year-old live elephant from Bengal, and "Old Bet" was exhibited throughout the northeastern seaboard as a curiosity. In the 1830s, New England traders shifted into trading ice to Calcutta after Congress imposed high taxes on imported textiles and once Frederick Tudor perfected the insulated cargo holds necessary to transport ice all the way from the frozen lakes of New England to the Ganges River. From the 1830s to the 1850s, thousands of tons of ice were exported to India.

Unlike the fur trade in North America, American trade in China and India was rarely accompanied by significant exploration or scientific observation. U.S. merchants gained a foothold in the rich countries of Asia with pure profit in mind. Traders' and mariners' reports about the exotic-seeming East informed the American imagination. Asian trade helped fuel American interest in people, goods, and events far outside U.S. borders.

STUDY QUESTIONS FOR EXPLORATION AND ENCOUNTER

1. In what ways were North American trade and exploration interrelated in this period?
2. Describe the balance of power between the United States, Plains Indians peoples, and the Spanish between 1803 and 1815.

■ SHIFTING BORDERS

As nations expanded across North America, political tensions and clashes resulted. The United States expanded south and west as it created new states and struggled to integrate the territory of the Louisiana Purchase. The Spanish pushed north and east, extending the mission system in California and contesting U.S. expansion in the Louisiana territory. The British and Russians expanded their interests on the borders between the United States and Canada. Thousands of Indian groups sought to deal with these developments through both peaceful and warlike means. How could governments best organize efforts to expand as hundreds of thousands of people moved from place to place? Would expansion on the continent bring prosperity, political conflict, or both (Map 9.1)?

Jeffersonian Agrarianism

In the first quarter of the 19th century, an ideology that valued land and farming underlay much of the energetic movement within the United States. Thomas Jefferson called farmers "the chosen people of God" and referred to agriculture as "the most useful of the occupations of man." Jefferson believed that farmers made the most patriotic, hardworking

MAP 9.1 ▲ Exploration and Development in North America, 1803–1810 During the first decade of the 19th century, both Spain and the United States tried to spread their influence across North America.

citizens and thought that farming would undergird stable national development and wealth. In Jefferson's vision, independent, white farmers who prized liberty and community sustained the United States. As a prominent Virginian who owned a slave plantation, Jefferson also recognized the role that enslaved black labor would play in creating a class of free and independent white "farmer" plantation owners in slave-holding areas. Others embraced Jefferson's view of agriculture and its contribution to a distinctly American character. Almanacs praised farmers, books such as Hector St. John De Crevecoeur's *Letters from an American Farmer* and George Logan's *Letters Addressed to the Yeomanry of the United States* sold many copies, and agricultural fairs and competitions were popular.

Although Jeffersonians idolized farming, they also admitted that agriculture would have to be linked to trade and commerce. In the 1790s, Jefferson's Democratic Republicans did not wish the United States to become a commercial manufacturing country, in contrast to the beliefs of Alexander Hamilton's Federalist counterparts, but they knew that farmers would have to trade their products to provide a stable national economic base. **Yeomen** and plantation farmers needed at least two things to make this vision of the United States work—land and the ability to market their produce.

Both land and markets brought Jeffersonian farmers into contact with people and governments well beyond their national borders. Jefferson's purchase of the Louisiana Territory set the stage for his agrarian ambitions, but the mere purchase of the territory would not guarantee its smooth transition into American farmland. Jefferson himself never traveled west of the Blue Ridge Mountains, but his policies encouraged settlement far beyond them.

Northwest, Southwest, and New States

Between 1789 and 1824, new states joined the United States in waves, as the expanding population moved well beyond the eastern seaboard. For the first time, not all U.S. states bordered the Atlantic Ocean. Many settlers in frontier areas had already moved west one or more times in their lives. The first federal census in 1790 counted about 4,000,000 inhabitants of the United States, but by 1800 the number had increased to 5,300,000. So many people had moved west that population density barely increased, even though the population was increasing by almost one-third every 10 years. The first new admissions to the union came when western inhabitants broke away from already existing states to form their own political entities: Vermont in 1791, Kentucky in 1792, and Tennessee in 1796.

The 1787 Northwest Ordinance had set out procedures for the Northwest Territory to be surveyed and sold to settlers, who could then apply for statehood. The U.S. victory over Indian nations at the Battle of Fallen Timbers (1794), displacement of Indians during the War of 1812, and postwar treaties signed with Wendat and other northern Indian peoples, confining them to reservations, opened the way to white settlement. Congress accelerated the settlement process, for example, in the 1802 Ohio Enabling Act that set aside proceeds from land sales to build roads in the territory. Ohio became a state in 1803. Its population soared to over a half a million after 1810, and; emerged as the fourth most populous state by 1820. Indiana and Illinois became states in 1816 and 1818. Settlers tended to move more or less directly west into the Northwest Territory, and these new states reflected a mixture of regional cultures that sometimes conflicted. One U.S. official worried that politics were complicated by people's "attachment to local interests."

As migrants from Northeastern states flooded into the Northwest Territory—where slavery was prohibited—many Virginians moved into Kentucky and Tennessee, southern Ohio, Indiana, and Illinois. Other inhabitants of the original Southern states moved south and west into Alabama and along the Gulf coast to Louisiana, Mississippi, and Arkansas. After Massachusetts native Eli Whitney patented an innovative mechanized cotton gin in 1793, cotton processing became easier and more profitable, and settlers moved into many southern areas looking for new land for plantations. Land in Alabama and Georgia produced much better cotton than did land further north. U.S. cotton production increased 10-fold between 1800 and 1820. Parts of the Louisiana Territory also lured settlers who hoped to make their fortunes on plantations or in the fur trade.

The Missouri Compromise

In 1818, the territory of Missouri applied for admission to the union as a state, the first west of the Mississippi River. Because the number of free and slave states in the union was precariously balanced and because so many slaves lived in Missouri, controversy arose as soon as **Henry Clay** presented resolutions to the House of Representatives to admit Missouri to the union. In February 1819, New York congressman **James Tallmadge, Jr.**, amended the Missouri statehood legislation to ban further introduction of slaves there and to gradually emancipate slaves who already lived in the territory. After vigorous debate, the House of Representatives approved the amendments, but the Senate struck them down. The two houses of Congress could not agree on a Missouri statehood bill, and the matter had to be carried over to the next session of Congress.

Meanwhile, antislavery activists across the Mid-Atlantic and New England sent petitions denouncing slavery as an evil that could not be allowed to spread. Several state legislatures adopted competing resolutions for and against the admission of Missouri as a slave state. Congress reconsidered Missouri for statehood in December. Congressmen and President **James Monroe** debated constitutional issues such as whether Congress had the right to place restrictions on new states and whether slaves in the Missouri Territory should be immediately counted for representation under the Constitution's three-fifths clause. Some southern congressmen used the relatively uncommon argument that slavery was a positive institution instead of a shameful burden. The spread of cotton agri-culture seemed to raise the stakes on slavery's expansion.

Congress reached a complex compromise. Missouri would be admitted as a slave state and Maine would be admitted as a free state—thereby preserving the balance of slave and free states in Congress. Illinois Democratic-Republican Senator Jesse B. Thomas also proposed an amendment to define a line on the map to determine future free and slave states that he hoped would avoid future conflict. The line at 36°30' latitude across the Louisiana Purchase territory would permit slavery only to its south. Missouri would stand as the exception because it lay north of the line.

In March 1820, Congress approved the Missouri Compromise resolutions. After some additional wrangling when the new Missouri legislature prohibited free blacks from entering the state, Missouri was fully admitted to the union on February 26, 1821. The Missouri Compromise temporarily tamped down the political controversy over slavery, but Thomas Jefferson predicted future trouble when he wrote that the compro-mise filled him with "terror" because conflict "is hushed, indeed, for the moment. But this is a reprieve only, not a final sentence."

African American Migration and Colonization

The Missouri Compromise emphasized a basic fact of U.S. westward expansion between 1789 and 1824: as a group, black people were even more dramatically affected by demographic change and movement than whites. Both the slave population and the free African American population increased during that time. Over 100,000 slaves were imported into the United States between the end of the Revolution and the abolition of the slave trade in 1808. After 1808, the expansion of U.S. territory and demand for slaves in new plantation areas stimulated the internal market for slaves, and families were regularly broken apart by sales. One historian estimates that "a slave residing in the Upper South after 1815 would have a one-in-three chance of being traded out of state during the first forty years of his or her life." Slaves' living conditions usually deteriorated as they were moved into the Deep South. These conditions were symbolized by the coffle—the method of transportation used to move groups of people on what one slave called "that dreaded and despairing journey to Georgia." Groups of up to 30 people in pairs were chained or tied together by metal halters around their necks and then marched over long distances. Once they arrived at cotton or sugar plantations, most enslaved people faced brutal working conditions (Map 9.2).

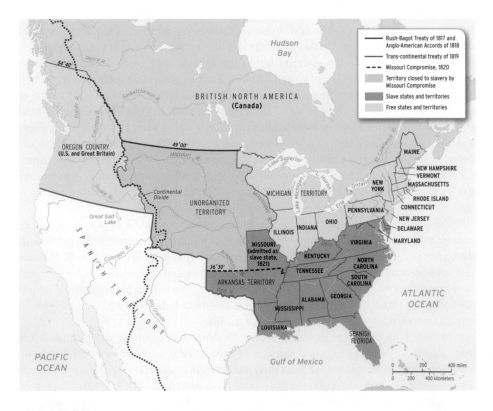

MAP 9.2 ▲ U.S. Expansion and Slavery, 1820 The expansion of U.S. territorial borders held great consequences for the development of the institution of slavery and for conflicts over slavery.

The Northwest Ordinance of 1787 had outlawed slavery in the Northwest Territory, but that prohibition did not mean the territories were hospitable to African Americans. Concerned that slaves might escape to freedom in the territories or to Canada, Congress passed the first federal Fugitive Slave Act in 1793. The act empowered local government officials to help recover runaways and imposed a fine on anyone who helped a "fugitive from justice." Some slave owners who migrated to Indiana and Illinois smuggled slaves with them, and many towns and states governed where and how free African Americans could live and work. In 1813, Illinois forbade free African Americans to settle there, and voters narrowly defeated a proposal to legalize slavery in Illinois in 1824.

Some free African Americans reacted against this kind of animosity by expressing an interest in migrating out of the United States altogether. In 1815, the Quaker sea captain Paul Cuffee, who was of African and Indian heritage, settled a shipload of free African Americans in the African colony of Sierra Leone. Sierra Leone was a British colony backed by private supporters where black British settlers, former American slaves who had fled to Canada, and maroons from Jamaica had all settled since the 1780s. In 1816, Presbyterian minister Robert Finley founded the **American Colonization Society** (ACS), which counted among its supporters Kentucky congressman Henry Clay, President James Monroe, and others who did not think the races could continue to coexist in North America. In 1821, the ACS transported its first free African American settlers to Liberia, the West African colony that the ACS would govern into the 1830s.

The colonization movement, as it was known, received most of its support from whites who hoped for the opportunity to gradually phase out the institution of slavery by transporting black people to Africa. Many free African Americans rejected the racism expressed by the ACS, even if they were interested in migration themselves. In its first two years, ACS convinced only 22 of the 10,000 free blacks in Philadelphia to embark for Africa. In 1824, some prominent free African Americans in New York and Philadelphia, including minister **Richard Allen** and sailmaker James Forten, founded the Haytian Emigration Society of Coloured People to help African Americans settle in Haiti, whose president Jean-Pierre Boyer offered to pay for their passage. Forten was a great supporter of the black republic in Haiti, although he utterly rejected the white vision of African colonization.

Spanish Expansion in California

The Spanish empire (independent Mexico after 1822) also pushed its boundaries outward between 1789 and 1824. Although the Spanish had traded with Indians in California since the 1500s, they did not establish colonies there until the 1760s. During the 1780s and 1790s, Spanish officials took steps to expand the colonized area in California to create a buffer between the silver mines in Mexico and Russian and British settlements in Oregon that were moving south.

The main vehicle for Spanish colonial expansion in California was the mission system, which extended government control over territory through a mixture of religious and military means. Franciscan friars, supported by Spanish soldiers, would establish a mission church, baptize nearby Indians, and employ them—sometimes by force—in farming and other trades. Between 1769 and 1821, friars baptized more than 70,000 Indians at the 20 missions that spread across the territory of Alta California. Many Indian people, including Ipai villagers, resisted being colonized, but their

SAN JUAN DE BAUTISTA, CALIFORNIA The mission of San Juan de Bautista was founded in 1797 by Fr Fermín de Lasuén, the successor to Junípero Serra, the Franciscan friar who spearheaded the spread of the Spanish mission system northward in California. This illustration pictures the church building at the mission that was begun in 1803.

defenses were weakened by the population collapse brought on by European diseases. Other Indians, like some Chumash, embraced baptism but retained a syncretic view of the world that maintained their native beliefs alongside Roman Catholicism. Some Christian Indians later rejected baptism, and Chumash rebelled against the Spanish in 1824.

Severe drought in the 1790s caused many Indians to seek refuge in the missions where Spanish friars provided food in exchange for labor and conversion. Hispanic settlers called *Californios*, many of them mixed-race Mexicans and descendents of earlier Spanish soldiers and southern Indians, claimed land, and their livestock threatened native land use. Spanish soldiers compelled Indian laborers to build the system of presidio forts that further consolidated control over California territory. The missions prospered, growing from crude chapels to elaborate adobe towns surrounded by farm fields and trading posts.

STUDY QUESTIONS FOR SHIFTING BORDERS

1. How did Spanish expansion in California compare to efforts of the United States to expand westward between 1789 and 1824?

2. How did the westward expansion of the United States revive and exacerbate conflicts over slavery?

◼ SOCIAL AND CULTURAL SHIFTS

The movement of goods, people, and ideas across and beyond North America at the beginning of the 19th century affected the creation of an "American" culture within the United States. The lawyer and future congressman Charles Jared Ingersoll wrote in 1810 that Americans were an "adolescent people . . . dispersed over an immense territory," both attracted to the old culture of Europe and seeking to establish their own identities. Ingersoll's use of the word "adolescent" captured the awkward nature of an American society seeking simultaneously to look backward and forward as it experienced rapid change.

Indian Acculturation

At the turn of the 19th century, native women and men adopted a variety of strategies ranging from acculturation to native cultural revival to deal with change and demographic pressure. Indian groups who lived within the United States continued to adapt after more than a hundred years of intensive contact with Europeans and Americans. During the same years in which Tecumseh and Tenskwatawa led movements for cultural revival and military resistance among Shawnee and their allies (see Chapter 8), some Indian people who lived further south used a different strategy—of acculturation and accommodation. Some Cherokee, Choctaw, Chickasaw, and Creek accepted U.S. Indian policies that encouraged them to "civilize" by adopting European-style agriculture, clothing, and culture. Creek warriors fought a civil war during the War of 1812 partly because of internal disagreements over assimilation, but the pro-acculturation forces triumphed with the backing of Andrew Jackson and U.S. military power.

Cherokee people pursued survival by ceding land in exchange for education and the promise of good U.S. relations. Henry Knox, George Washington, and Thomas Jefferson—along with other U.S. officials—believed that "civilizing" Indians would prevent their extinction. American government agents and missionaries lived within Cherokee society. Although they never adopted private land ownership, many Cherokee did adapt to other American customs: they changed their gender roles to match American family structure, some owned slaves, and they centralized their government under a National Council structure in 1808 that removed power from the traditional matrilineal clans. The council also extended citizenship to the biracial children of Cherokee men and white women (who could not belong to a clan), and mixed-race Cherokee became prominent leaders. **Sequoyah** standardized the Cherokee alphabet, which made printing possible, and more than 25 percent of Cherokee people could read by the 1820s—a high figure that gained international attention.

Cherokee leaders disagreed about the degree to which acculturation would solve their problems, and some agreed to move their families west to Arkansas territory to gain favor with the United States. Tensions rose after the War of 1812, and white population growth near Cherokee lands in Tennessee, Alabama, and Georgia accelerated the debate over survival and acculturation. As early as 1785, Cherokee leader Corn Tassel had warned that "when we entered into treaties with our brothers, the whites, their whole cry is more land!" Cherokee people continued to adopt new social roles to try and respond.

Gender in Early Republican Society

What it meant to be a white woman also changed in this period. Following on the heels of the revolutionary ideology of republican motherhood, women were expected to help create a better republican society through their ability to raise educated children to be

NEEDLEWORK SAMPLER This sampler was sewn by Catharine Ann Speel in Philadelphia when she was 12 or 13 years old, in 1805. Girls often sewed samplers like this to practice stitches and to show off needlework skill, which they learned from family members and at schools. Speel's sampler is typical in showing a house, the alphabet, animals, and a man, and it includes a typical moral poem. Speel identifies herself as her mother's daughter on the sampler, emphasizing female lineage.

good citizens. As it became clear that a successful republic would be shaped by a virtuous society as well as by correct politics, women also claimed the ability to augment male political virtue by leading benevolent and refined social activities.

White women's educational opportunities expanded dramatically during the early republic, in part as a reaction to the theories of British feminist **Mary Wollstonecraft**, who was read widely in the United States. Women's rights advocate **Judith Sargent Murray** wrote that "women have a talent" and "should be taught to depend on their own efforts." New schools for girls were founded in every region, and girls were included in the growth of, mostly Northern, public education. After 1789, women also began to find career opportunities as teachers, and many of the most important girls' academies were founded by women such as **Emma Willard** and Julia Tevis. Most girls were not offered the same education as boys—for example, classical languages were largely off limits. But academic subjects such as math and history joined girls' education in needlework and dancing. Educators differed on whether girls should be educated for their own intellectual fulfillment or more to serve the interests of family and society; but, in either case, greater education meant progress as female literacy rates soared.

Advances in women's legal status proved to be more modest, as state coverture laws continued to define married women as legally under their husbands' control. In the 1790s, however, it became easier for women to obtain divorces. Women petitioned both state and federal legislatures, they participated in political rituals such as Fourth of July celebrations and French Revolutionary festivals, and some wrote for newspapers and magazines. Single women and widows, who could own property, ran businesses such as the Brandywine Ironworks, the successful boilerplate manufactory controlled by Pennsylvania Quaker Rebecca Lukens. Prominent women in Washington, DC, such as congressional wife **Margaret Bayard Smith** and especially first lady **Dolley Madison**, directly influenced politics by organizing social events that fostered political party organization. The vast majority of poorer women and all black women led less public lives, and changing gender roles affected their daily lives more slowly.

Literature and Popular Culture

Women formed one of the quickest-growing audiences in the United States for the dramatic increase in books, magazines, newspapers, and other kinds of print culture. Historians estimate that by 1790, more than 90 percent of the white population in the United States could read—a figure estimated to be twice as large as in Britain. The availability of reading material greatly increased in the following decades. A much smaller percentage of African Americans were literate because many slaves were prohibited from learning. As the postal service expanded, subscription newspapers and magazines made up the majority of mail. By 1822, the United States had more newspaper readers than any other country, and hundreds of papers were printed in small towns in every state and territory. Religious magazines and literary journals, such as the *North American Review*, also attracted wide readership.

Until after 1825, when improvements in printing occurred, most books in the United States remained expensive and were imported from Britain. But publishers such as Philadelphia's Matthew Carey showed interest in producing a truly

CHARLOTTE TEMPLE "GRAVE" This photograph from the early 20th century shows the grave at Trinity Church, New York, constructed around 1804, for the fictional character Charlotte Temple. The fictional character created by Susannah Rowson was such a popular figure of tragic romance that after this grave was installed, visitors flocked to leave flowers, pieces of hair, and love letters as tributes to her. Alexander Hamilton is buried nearby.

"American" literature even before then. Many books relied on the American Revolution for plot, and authors such as Mason Locke Weems sought to inspire their readers with biographies such as his *Life of Washington* (1800). **Hugh Henry Brackenridge**'s *Modern Chivalry* (1804) satirized the social climbing of Americans on the move. **Susannah Rowson**'s best seller *Charlotte Temple* (1791) appealed to legions of middle-class female readers by transporting the English seduction novel to the United States—it emphasized the fragility of women's virtue in highly sentimentalized language. More writers—including Rowson, Washington Irving, and James Fenimore Cooper—began to earn their living by publishing. Alongside their fictional works inspired by America's past, histories were very popular. Many cheaper books were plagiarized because copyright enforcement remained quite lax. Transatlantic book culture also nourished American Christianity, as the American Bible Society (1816) and the American Tract Society (1823) grew out of English efforts to spread religious publications.

Americans also amused themselves with traditional sports such as horse racing, cock fighting, and foot races. City dwellers might visit neighbors in taverns or coffee houses, whereas their rural counterparts met at fairs, dances, or quilting bees. During the 1790s, most state legislatures lifted their colonial prohibitions on theater performances; and by the 1820s, professional companies performed dramas, comedies, and light operas in most cities. Famous English actors made money in the United States, as audiences continued to revere European high culture while also clamoring to watch "true-blue" American plays.

By the time Susannah Rowson died in 1824, young middle- and upper-class white women who avidly read *Charlotte Temple* and other novels had turned her into the first U.S. literary celebrity. They bought, passed around, and discussed her book, and some even made pilgrimages to a gravestone for the character Charlotte Temple in New York's Trinity churchyard. By consuming novels such as *Charlotte Temple*, women showed their influence in American culture, even as religious and literary critics warned that novel reading was a dangerously immoral activity. One critic warned in 1798 that as a young woman reads a novel, "evil steals imperceptibly into her heart."

African American Culture: Slaves and Free People

Even though the institution of slavery denied slaves control of their own lives, African American men and women strengthened black culture between 1789 and 1824. Black culture varied by region and among slave and free populations. The end of the legal slave trade in 1808 meant that blacks could establish their own fully native-born culture, influenced by many different regional African traditions in religion, food, clothing, funeral, and burial traditions. Black and white culture continued to be intertwined because many slaves lived with their masters on small farms.

Cultural traditions helped enslaved people to survive the violent reality of day-to-day life, especially on larger plantations. Josiah Henson remembered how he and his fellow slaves balanced misery with the pleasure of family life during his youth in the 1790s: "Along with memories of miry cabins, frosted feet, weary toil under the blazing sun, curses and blows, there flock in others, of jolly Christmas times . . . midnight visits to apple orchards, broiling stray chickens, and first-rate tricks to dodge work." Despite the wide variation in slave life caused by working conditions, the density of the black population, and even the personality of individual slave masters, black people maintained pieces of their own identities despite the institution that controlled them.

The free African American population experienced huge growth in the new republic, especially in the Northern states that had abolished or phased out slavery since the end of the American Revolution. The free black population in the United States grew from around 60,000 in 1790 to approximately 235,000 by 1820. Both Northern and Southern free African Americans tended to live in cities. In Boston, New York, Philadelphia, Richmond, Charleston, and New Orleans, distinct free African American cultures emerged. Even as the great majority of the African American population

MAP 9.3 ▲ African Americans as a Total Percentage of Population, 1790 What is significant about the geographic location of densely populated African American communities?

continued to live in slavery, both enslaved and free blacks built up family, church, work, and community networks that enriched their lives and fought slavery. As James Forten put it, "Though our faces are black, yet we are men" who seek to enjoy human rights and to help "our afflicted Brethren."

African Americans in cities, often excluded from white institutions, set about establishing their own mutual aid societies, black fraternal lodges, schools, and churches. Most urban black men and women were poor laborers, but a rising class of well-to-do shop owners, hairdressers, doctors, and ministers formed political and social organizations, especially in Philadelphia and Boston. Two former slaves, Richard Allen and **Absalom Jones**, founded the first independent black Protestant church, the Bethel Church, in Philadelphia in 1792. Allen wanted African Americans "to worship God under our own vine and fig tree," and similar congregations sprang up across the North. In 1816, the independent black churches banded together to form the African Methodist Episcopal (AME) denomination. Efforts to found AME churches in the South were blocked after the thwarted 1822 slave revolt plot attributed to Denmark Vesey. Vesey, who was a fervent Christian, was convicted of planning a violent rebellion in South Carolina, whose state legislature promptly forbade separate black churches. Wherever black churches could thrive, however, they nurtured African American cultural aspirations and efforts toward freedom.

Roots of the Second Great Awakening

Many African Americans belonged to Methodist, Baptist, and other Protestant churches that had dramatically increased their membership by the 1790s. The new denominations born in the 18th-century Great Awakening began to experience a new surge of growth, as the Methodists and Baptists quickly grew to be the largest two Protestant denominations by mid century. Even the more traditional Presbyterian church experienced growth that outpaced population increase during the early republic. The Roman Catholic Church went from installing John Carroll as its first American bishop in 1789 to administering nine separate dioceses in 1829.

A new wave of revivalism took hold across the United States at the turn of the century, and many different kinds of people were swept up in it. Popular preachers held outdoor camp meetings that attracted a mixed audience of whites and blacks, unchurched and church members. The 19th-century camp meeting revivals provided experiential, social occasions when people gathered to hear sermons, meet neighbors, and express religious enthusiasm by speaking in tongues, shouting, weeping, and declaring their salvation. Camp meetings proved most popular in the South and West. The largest and most famous meeting at Cane Ridge, Kentucky, in 1801 attracted as many as 20,000 people to the backwoods. Camp meetings bore some similarity to the informal, and often secret, outdoor gatherings that characterized the Christianity of American slaves, and they also adapted customs from Scots and Ulster revivals. Revivals such as Cane Ridge eventually led to the founding of even more new Protestant denominations such as the Church of Christ, which strayed away from the strict Calvinism of previous centuries. On the other end of the social spectrum, but nonetheless enthusiastic, were the throngs of students who flocked to the Yale College chapel in New Haven, Connecticut, to hear the inspiring sermons of moderate evangelical **Timothy Dwight**, the university president who was Jonathan Edwards's grandson. Dwight converted and educated a generation of ministers including **Lyman Beecher** and Nathaniel Taylor, who became leaders of the **Second Great Awakening** as it grew into a more defined religious movement in the later 1820s and 1830s.

STUDY QUESTIONS FOR SOCIAL AND CULTURAL SHIFTS

1. Did African American survival strategies differ from those of Indians? If so, how? If not, why not?

2. In what ways did printed materials influence the creation of "American" culture from the 1790s to the 1820s? How did print culture affect different groups in different ways?

◼ FINANCIAL EXPANSION

In the aftermath of the War of 1812, the United States had the chance to capitalize on new trade opportunities and the settlement of new territories brought on by population movement. Enterprising merchants such as John Jacob Astor proved that astronomical profits could be made by people who opened up new avenues of trade and finance, but debates persisted about how much the U.S. government should support business ventures. With the Federalist Party effectively dead in national politics following the War of 1812, leading Democratic-Republican politicians adopted some of the old Federalist embrace of high finance, but not without conflict. Financial expansion helped to contribute to President James Monroe's opinion that the United States was on a "high career of national happiness," but by 1819, good feelings soured as an economic depression took hold.

Banks and Panics

President James Madison had been convinced by the War of 1812 disruption of foreign trade that the United States must do more to encourage domestic manufacturing.

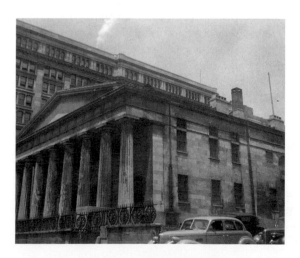

THE SECOND BANK OF THE UNITED STATES   This building in Philadelphia was designed in the Greek revival style by William Strickland and constructed between 1818 and 1824. Between its incorporation in 1816 and the bank war with the Jackson administration that caused it to fold in 1836, the Second Bank of the United States was the most important financial institution in the country.

Madison proposed to build roads and canals, to enact tariffs on foreign products, and to reauthorize the charter of the **Bank of the United States** (BUS). Madison had bitterly opposed the BUS on constitutional grounds when Alexander Hamilton proposed it in 1791, but he now believed that the "expediency and almost necessity" of wartime finance meant that the United States needed a federal bank. Although some "Old Republicans" like Virginian John Randolph opposed the bank and the encouragement of manufacturing, even Thomas Jefferson himself embraced Madison's vision by 1816 when he wrote that "We must now place the manufacturer by the side of the agriculturalist."

The BUS consisted of a partnership between federal government and private investors, and their intertwined interests became difficult to separate at the end of the War of 1812. Financial speculators, including John Jacob Astor and his fellow merchant Stephen Girard, bought up bonds and notes, and as their investments fluctuated, so did their commitment to central banking. In January 1815, President Madison vetoed Congress' proposed recharter of the BUS because the bill gave too much private advantage to merchants like Astor and Girard. True to his roots as a strict interpreter of the U.S. Constitution, Madison also vetoed the 1816 "Bonus Bill" that would have funded public transportation because the Constitution did not expressly grant Congress authority to pass such legislation.

Madison still hoped for a central bank, but Congress was contending over a variety of financial issues. Each of the more than 200 private and state banks issued its own bank notes, a practice that drove up inflation. Madison's supporters in Congress, including South Carolinian **John C. Calhoun** and Speaker of the House Henry Clay, proposed a charter for a Second Bank of the United States. The new federal bank; to be based in Philadelphia, would stabilize U.S. currency and would exert control over private investors. President Madison approved the new charter of the Second Bank of the United States in April 1816. In the same month, a 25 percent tariff on foreign wool cloth, cotton, and iron went into effect. Congress also passed legislation authorizing a National Road and other internal improvements advocated by Madison and Henry Clay. But when Congress also raised its own salary rate, voters turned out the majority of representatives in the 1816 election.

In the spring of 1817, newly elected president James Monroe toured the Northern states to reach out to disgruntled Federalists, but before he could depart, Monroe had to deal with more controversy over the Second Bank of the United States. A House of Representatives investigation uncovered what one member called "a system of fraud, stock-jobbing, and speculation" that enriched the bank's private directors and threatened public finance. The directors of the Baltimore branch of the BUS alone had embezzled over $1.5 million, an astronomical sum at the time. The public lost confidence in the bank, but a bill to revoke its charter failed in Congress in February 1819.

At the same time, a severe depression halted business expansion. Since the end of the War of 1812, U.S. exports had increased by over 100 percent and agricultural prices had soared. But by the end of 1818, rampant speculation in cotton and land, a shortage of gold and silver to back up U.S. currency, and the recovery of the British economy spelled trouble. The plummet of cotton prices in Europe and the United States demonstrated how that product had tightened the links in the transatlantic economy. In 1819, banks and businesses backed by inflated currency began to fail in droves, and the Second Bank of the United States reacted too slowly to prevent a collapse of the economy. The effects were traumatic. Personal bankruptcies soared, land prices plummeted, and the financial crisis even temporarily slowed down the tide of settlers who were willing to uproot and seek new farmland on the frontier.

Corporations and the Supreme Court

Less than two weeks after the Second Bank of the United States survived its challenge in the House of Representatives in 1819, the Supreme Court entered the political debate over federal economic power and issued one of its most important decisions ever. The court unanimously decided in the case of *McCulloch v. Maryland* that central banking was constitutional. Furthermore, Chief Justice John Marshall's opinion supported the idea that the federal government represented the people of one, unified United States. According to Marshall, even though the Constitution did not explicitly grant Congress the right to charter national banks, it implied that Congress could do so because it could exercise powers given by the people "for their benefit." The decision struck down a hefty tax that Maryland had imposed on the Baltimore branch of the BUS and declared that federal laws must supersede state action. In the future, the decision would hold power even beyond the issue of banking, as it declared that Congress could use broad powers implied by the Constitution so long as Congress avoided anything expressly forbidden in that document.

John Marshall, an old Federalist whose market ideas matched the new economic climate, led the Supreme Court to deliver several other opinions that buoyed American business and investment. In 1819, the court decided in *Dartmouth College v. Woodward* that New Hampshire could not alter the Dartmouth College charter because Dartmouth was a private corporation whose property the state should not violate. The decision

JAMES MONROE Samuel F. B. Morse painted this portrait of President James Monroe in 1819. Monroe's presidency was marked by the strong influence of cabinet ministers, especially Secretary of State John Quincy Adams, and by nationalist policies that encouraged territorial expansion. The Monroe Doctrine that bore his name warned European countries not to intervene in the affairs of the Western Hemisphere.

Francisco de Miranda, the United States, and Latin American Independence

At the end of the American Revolutionary War in 1783, Francisco de Miranda first came to the United States, where he toured cities and battlefields and befriended American military commanders, politicians, and figures from high society. A native of Caracas, Venezuela, Miranda had become a colonel in the Spanish army, but he fled to the United States to avoid charges of financial misuse. Convinced that Latin America should walk in the Revolutionary footsteps of the United States and declare independence from Spain, Miranda devoted the remainder of his colorful life to that cause.

After returning to Europe in 1785, Miranda spent four years trying to convince European courtiers and diplomats, including Russia's Catherine the Great, to support Latin America, gaining much attention but little success. He fought in the French Revolutionary military, but ran afoul of radicals after 1793 and fled to Britain, where he rallied support from Spanish exiles and sympathetic members of the British government for a plan to liberate all of Latin America and install an independent parliamentary monarchy ruled by what he called an "Inca." U.S. politician Alexander Hamilton was drawn to Miranda's plan during the Quasi-War with France in 1798 and hoped to lead U.S. army troops to support him, but Hamilton was not able to convince fellow Federalist President John Adams to fully endorse Miranda. Adams believed that trying to spread democracy in Latin America was "as absurd as similar plans would be to establish democracies among the birds, beasts and fishes."

Miranda returned to the United States in 1805 and gathered U.S. support for an invasion of Venezuela. Miranda told President Jefferson and Secretary of State Madison of his plans at a dinner party, and he later claimed that he had their "tacit approval," although Jefferson disavowed granting either implicit or explicit blessings to Miranda. Miranda did receive considerable help from New Yorkers William Stevens Smith (John Adams's son-in-law) and Samuel G. Ogden, who aided Miranda in outfitting the *Leander*, a small ship; purchasing weapons; and enlisting a crew composed mostly of New York City toughs and apprentices, some of whom thought they were enlisting to protect President Jefferson or to guard a mail ship to New Orleans. President Adams's grandson also enlisted with Miranda. Miranda failed to realize that Spanish officials were spying on him as he prepared for the expedition against their colony.

In February 1806, Miranda embarked from New York City and chartered two additional ships in Santo Domingo. Even though the British Navy afforded his vessels some

encouraged the development of business corporations, which were just beginning to emerge as a major factor in the U.S. economy and which provided a great advantage to entrepreneurs by limiting their personal liability for business failures. In 1824, the court ruled in a case concerning steamboat monopolies, *Gibbons v. Ogden*, that the protection, two of Miranda's ships were captured by the Spanish when the party first tried to land in Venezuela. Sixty of Miranda's men were captured and imprisoned in Puerto Cabello, and 10 were sentenced to death. Henry Ingersoll, a former printer's apprentice who had been taken on board to print Miranda's propaganda, wrote in his diary that he and the other prisoners were chained and "marched to the Gallows, where we beheld our companions hanged and beheaded." Ingersoll and the other Americans were imprisoned in Cartagena for years until public outcry and family appeals to European diplomats helped free them. Several resolutions in Congress for the U.S. government to come to their aid failed because federal officials disavowed any responsibility for Miranda's actions.

PORTRAIT OF FRANCISCO MIRANDA (1750–1816)

After the capture, Miranda regrouped at Barbados and invaded the Venezuelan city of Coro in August 1806. He found no support among local residents and clergy, and he eventually fled back to England. Later, when the Venezuelan independence movement began in 1811, Miranda returned, and for a time in 1812 he became the country's ruler. But he quickly lost the faith of Simón Bolívar and other independence leaders, who handed him over to the Spanish. He died in a Spanish prison in 1816, never having gained full support from the United States, a country whose revolution he felt Latin America should "prudently imitate."

- Compare Miranda's 1806 Venezuela invasion to Andrew Jackson's takeover of Florida in the First Seminole War.
- Why do you think neither President Adams nor President Jefferson wanted to support Miranda even though other Americans supported his plans?

Commerce Clause of the Constitution granted the federal government the sole right to regulate interstate commerce. Marshall and the Supreme Court cut through arguments that a "narrow construction" of the Constitution prohibited federal expansion of the economy, and they helped to fuel business development for decades to come.

STUDY QUESTIONS FOR FINANCIAL EXPANSION

1. In what ways did the three branches of the federal government each affect the economy during the 1810s?
2. In what ways did the Panic of 1819 reveal the strengths and weaknesses of U.S. economic development?

■ POLITICS AND HEMISPHERIC CHANGE

Although financial crisis slowed settlement for a time after 1819, a new wave of political and military engagements would soon again spark frontier movements. In the aftermath of the War of 1812, the United States showed a new confidence in foreign policy. The United States claimed to have no imperial ambitions, but aggressive military action by General Andrew Jackson and assertive diplomacy from Secretary of State **John Quincy Adams** added territory and enhanced the international stature of the nation. The United States linked itself firmly to the rest of the Western Hemisphere when it took an interest in revolutions in Latin America. But how could the United States solidify its new position without igniting more trouble with European nations?

First Seminole War

Since acquiring Louisiana in 1803, U.S. officials had tried various measures to gain Spain's territory in Florida. In 1818, conflict with Seminole Indians gave them new opportunity. Although it is not clear whether Secretary of War John C. Calhoun and Secretary of State John Quincy Adams intended to endorse belligerent action, they nonetheless capitalized on aggressive tactics employed by General Andrew Jackson to gain control of Florida. Seminoles, a mixed group of native peoples and former slaves, encouraged runaways from the United States to seek refuge in their territory in Spanish East Florida. Seminole groups also harbored Creek runaways who had fled south and west after Andrew Jackson crushed the Red Sticks rebellion in 1814. The United States refused to return Creek lands after the War of 1812 in spite of agreeing to do so in the Treaty of Ghent. In November 1817, U.S. general Edmund Gains burned the Creek village of Fowltown, Georgia, an action that caused reprisals from Florida Creek and Seminole against American settlers across the border. Calhoun sent Jackson to pacify the situation.

In March 1818, Jackson invaded Spanish territory with a force of Tennessee volunteers, regular army soldiers, and Creek allies hostile to the Red Sticks. Jackson had told President Monroe in January that he wanted to seize "the whole of East Florida," and when he received no reply, he took it as license to act freely. On April 6, Jackson captured the Spanish fort at St. Mark's, and he then attacked Seminole villages on the Suwannee River. In addition to burning property while fighting Indians and African Americans, Jackson also arrested and executed two British citizens whom he accused of helping the Seminole. On May 28, Jackson occupied the Spanish capitol of Pensacola, expelled governor **José Mascot**, appointed a U.S. territorial governor, and declared that Spain would have to give up Florida if it could not control Seminole people within Spanish territory.

Jackson's actions caused uproar in Washington, DC, where the French, British, and Spanish protested his aggression. Although most of Monroe's cabinet believed that Jackson had exceeded his orders, Secretary of State John Quincy Adams restrained the executive reaction against Jackson. Adams, who had entered treaty negotiations with Spanish diplomat **Luis de Onís**, used the Seminole war as leverage and stressed that Spain had to demonstrate mastery of Seminole people to be trusted. In November 1818, after Onís pulled out of talks, Adams returned control of Pensacola and St. Marks to the Spanish, but controversy over Jackson's actions continued. In January 1819, President Monroe's annual message to Congress disavowed intentions to take over Spanish Territory. Congress immediately began to investigate and to debate whether Jackson's actions had been correct. Henry Clay delivered a blistering speech denouncing Jackson, but resolutions to censure Jackson were roundly defeated. Mississippi representative George Poindexter declared that Jackson had "fulfilled the measure of his country's glory," and many Americans seemed to agree as they thronged to praise him on a February triumphal tour around the eastern seaboard. Early in 1821, Congress reduced the size of the army and removed Andrew Jackson from service.

Transcontinental (Adams–Onís) Treaty

President Monroe, who was quite indecisive, relied heavily on Secretary of State John Quincy Adams to guide him through many different policy decisions. Adams carefully balanced rivalries with other cabinet ministers including Treasury Secretary William H. Crawford and Vice President Daniel D. Tompkins. Adams put his stamp on a whole new era of U.S. foreign policy, and he did much to consolidate the status of the United States as a country to be taken seriously in the world. He had accompanied his father, John Adams, on several diplomatic missions as a young man, and he refined his negotiating skills during the War of 1812 as minister to Russia, where he befriended Czar Alexander I. On taking office, Adams immediately improved U.S. relations with Great Britain. He oversaw the Rush–Bagot Agreement in 1817 in which the British agreed to demilitarize the Great Lakes. In the midst of the diplomatic controversy over the Seminole War, Adams and U.S. Minister to Great Britain **Richard Rush** also cemented the Convention of 1818 in which the British agreed to set the border between the United States and Canada at the 49th parallel. After Adams sent a warship to the Oregon coast, the British also agreed to return Astoria to the United States and to recognize some U.S. territorial rights in Oregon.

Shocked by the lack of response from Great Britain to U.S. aggression in Florida and facing growing pressure from the independence movements in Latin America, Spanish officials decided to cut their losses and cede Florida when Luis de Onís returned to his negotiations with Adams in late 1818. Now confident that he could gain Florida, Adams made an even bolder proposal to acquire new territory from the Spanish, who still resisted U.S. claims on the southwestern border of the Louisiana Purchase territory. Adams proposed that Spain cede territory all the way to the Pacific Ocean north of California at the 42nd parallel. This was the first U.S. government bid to extend its territory across the entire continent of North America, a move that Adams wrote in his diary would form "a great epocha in our history." In exchange for Spanish recognition of U.S. rights in Oregon, Adams consented to forgo all claim to Texas. Adams and Onís agreed to these terms in the Transcontinental Treaty in February 1819.

The United States and Latin American Revolutions

The U.S. Senate ratified the Adams–Onís Treaty just two days after Adams presented it. But Madrid held up final agreement until 1821, in large part because of arguments over U.S. response to the revolutions that had spread across most of Latin America. The United States had proclaimed neutrality in Spain's wars with its colonies in September 1815, but many U.S. traders and private citizens sought to aid Latin American rebels. In August 1817, Washington diplomats turned away an envoy from independence leaders Juan Martín Pueyrredón, Bernardo O'Higgins, and José San Martín, who sought recognition for Argentina, Peru, and Chile. Monroe and Adams reinforced the official position of neutrality despite Henry Clay's legislative efforts and frequent speeches demanding U.S. help to cast off the "despotism" of Spain.

Spain demanded that the United States not aid the Latin American rebels, but public opinion was in the rebels' favor. Many were convinced that these independence movements emulated the American Revolution, and others hoped that the United States might extend its influence south. The successes of Simón Bolívar against Spanish forces in Colombia, Ecuador, and Venezuela between 1819 and 1821; Augustín de Iturbide's securing of Mexican independence in 1821; and San Martín's independence victory in Peru in 1821 helped to convince the Monroe administration to alter its course and propose recognition of the Latin American independence movements in March 1822. By 1826, Congress had agreed to recognize the Republic of Greater Colombia, Mexico, Chile, Argentina, Brazil, the Provinces of Central America, and Peru. Only the black republic of Haiti would have to wait until 1862 for U.S. recognition (Map 9.4).

The Monroe Doctrine

The U.S. recognition of Latin American independence did not end its wrangling with Spain, and, in 1822, other European powers also indicated that they might intervene in the region. Rebellions in Spain and Naples in 1820 had disturbed the Quintuple Alliance powers in Europe (Russia, Austria, Prussia, France, and Britain) who feared that monarchy itself might be threatened by liberal challenges. After the October 1822 Congress of Verona, France restored Spain's King Ferdinand VII to the throne; and the United States feared that France, Britain, or other powers might also move on Latin America. By April 1823, Spain retained only Cuba and Puerto Rico as colonies. Although John Quincy Adams agreed to let Spain maintain control there, he warned that the United States would not approve if Spain let any other European power intercede and that the United States might be prepared to invade Cuba if Spain disagreed. Adams also took a hard line in British trade negotiations and objected to a Russian claim on American territory in Oregon. British Foreign Minister **George Canning** opposed European intervention in Latin America, but American officials worried that he would be ignored by other Alliance powers. Canning told U.S. diplomat Richard

MAP 9.4 ▲ Latin America and the Caribbean, c. 1830 This map shows the dates that various Latin American and Caribbean countries attained their colonial independence.

Rush that he would be willing to issue a joint British-American statement warning Europeans against Latin American intervention. Secretary of State John Quincy Adams was suspicious of Canning's motives, however, and he decided the United States should respond alone.

Adams took a bold approach and decided to warn Europe in no uncertain terms. Adams drafted Monroe's seventh annual message to Congress, and in it he enunciated

TIMELINE 1789–1823

AMERICA	YEAR	THE WORLD
Mar Pennsylvania lifts ban on theater	1789	Jeremy Bentham publishes *Introduction to the Principles of Morals*
Apr Congress establishes patent office **May** First U.S. copyright law takes effect	1790	France grants Jews recognition of civil rights *The Bounty* mutineers settle on Pitcairn Island
Mar Vermont becomes 14th state	1791	William Wilberforce fails to get Parliament to outlaw slavery in British colonies **Sep** Mozart's *The Magic Flute* first performed in Vienna
May Robert Gray claims Columbia River and part of Oregon Territory for United States **Jun** Kentucky admitted to the union	1792	Bubonic plague kills over 750,000 in Egypt Denmark abolishes slavery Mary Wollstonecraft's *A Vindication of the Rights of Woman* is published in London and quickly spreads across Europe and the United States
Apr Scottish fur trader Sir Alexander Mackenzie explores across North America and reaches Pacific Ocean **Oct** Eli Whitney refines his cotton gin design	1793	
Susannah Rowson's novel *Charlotte Temple* is published **Jun** Richard Allen founds Bethel Church in Philadelphia	1794	**Mar** U.S. Revolutionary hero Tadeusz Kosciuszko begins unsuccessful uprising in Poland
Jun Tennessee becomes 16th state	1796	British doctor Edward Jenner invents smallpox vaccine
Eli Whitney contracted to manufacture 10,000 rifles for army using interchangeable parts	1798	Thomas Malthus publishes *Essay on the Principles of Population*
Library of Congress is established	1800	German Alexander von Humboldt maps the S. American Orinoco River Ludwig von Beethoven's first symphony first performed in Vienna
Mar Ohio becomes the 17th state in union	1803	Abortion outlawed in Great Britain
May Lewis and Clark expedition begins **Nov** Lewis and Clark take up winter quarters with Mandan Indians	1804	
Hugh Henry Brackenridge publishes *Modern Chivalry* **Apr** Lewis and Clark expedition reaches mouth of Yellowstone River **Aug** Zebulon Pike explores for source of Mississippi River **Nov** Lewis and Clark reach Pacific Ocean	1805	
Noah Webster publishes American dictionary **Jul** Lewis and Clark split Corps of Discovery into two parties **Jul** Zebulon Pike sets out to explore south western Louisiana Territory **Sep** Lewis and Clark expedition ends in St. Louis	1806	Construction of the Arc de Triomphe begins
	1807	Parliament forbids slave trade in British colonies

Left	Year	Right
Apr John Jacob Astor incorporates American Fur Company **Nov** Osage cede lands in Missouri and Arkansas to United States in treaty signed at Ft. Clark, KS	**1808**	Goethe publishes Part I of *Faust*
Campbellite Church of Christ splits from the Presbyterian Church **Jun** John Jacob Astor founds Pacific Fur Company **Oct** President Madison annexes part of West Florida to Louisiana	**1810**	
Jan Congress authorizes President Madison to acquire East Florida	**1811**	British capture Dutch colony of Java
Apr Louisiana becomes 18th state **Jun** Missouri Territory is organized	**1812**	**Aug** Swiss archaeologist John Lewis Burckhardt documents ancient city of Petra in current-day Jordan
Emma Willard opens her first school in Middlebury, VT	**1814**	Britain buys Cape Colony, South Africa, from Dutch for £20 million
Sep United States declares neutrality in Latin American wars of independence	**1815**	
Indiana admitted to the union **Apr** Congress passes 25 percent trade tariff **Dec** James Monroe elected President	**1816**	
Mar John Quincy Adams becomes Secretary of State **Apr** Rush–Bagot agreement improves relations between United States and Britain	**1817**	
Apr Gen. Andrew Jackson takes control of West Florida in the First Seminole War **Dec** Illinois admitted to the union	**1818**	**Feb** Bernardo O'Higgins and José de San Martín declare independence in Chile
Jan Cotton prices drop, touching off the Panic of 1819 **Feb** Adams–Onís Treaty signed **Feb** Motions of censure against Andrew Jackson fail in Congress	**1819**	**Aug** Manchester protests against Corn Laws result in violence
Mar Missouri Compromise—Missouri and Maine become U.S. states **Dec** President Monroe is reelected	**1820**	**Jan** George III dies; George IV becomes King of England
Adams–Onís Treaty ratified **Feb** Mexico declares independence **Jul** José de San Martín declares Peru's independence **Sep** Mexico cements its independence	**1821**	
Mar President Monroe suggests that United States should recognize Latin American countries	**1822**	First Ashanti War in West Africa begins
Dec Monroe Doctrine articulated in Monroe's annual message to Congress	**1823**	

what would become known as the **Monroe Doctrine**. In the December 1823 address, Monroe declared that the United States shared common interest with other states in the Western Hemisphere and that the political system in Europe was "essentially different" from that of the democratic republics in North and South America. Monroe maintained that the United States would not interfere in European politics or with existing European colonies in the Western Hemisphere, but neither should Europe insert itself any further in the West. Europe could not be allowed to extend its power or monarchical political system in North or South America without, in Monroe's words, "endangering our peace and happiness." European powers should not seek future colonies in the Western Hemisphere and should not seek to reconquer independent states. President Monroe later argued that only Haiti did not earn the right to self-determination because "the establishment of a Government of people of color in the island . . . evinces distinctly the idea of a separate interest and a distrust of other nations."

In later decades and centuries, the Monroe Doctrine would be used as a justification of U.S. intervention in Latin American countries, but for the time being it was mostly a bold statement of independence from European influence. Since 1789, the United States had more than tripled the area of its territory, and its growing population was settling larger areas every year. But the United States did not yet have the military power entirely to enforce its grand vision.

STUDY QUESTIONS FOR POLITICS AND HEMISPHERIC CHANGE

1. In what ways did the Monroe Doctrine indicate that the United States aspired to a new status in the world?
2. John Quincy Adams has been called one of the most talented Secretaries of State the United States has ever had. Why?

Summary

- Between 1789 and 1824, the United States, Spain, Great Britain, and Russia expanded on the North American continent through exploration, settlement, and trade.
- Different Indian peoples responded to pressures on their lives through various combinations of warfare, trade, diplomacy, and cultural assimilation.
- The physical expansion of the United States and the expansion of cotton farming led to conflicts over slavery.
- A new "American" culture reflected the changing social roles of women, African Americans, Christians, and others.
- The United States was increasingly connected to the rest of the world through trade even as new foreign policy following the War of 1812 defined a more assertive position for the country.

Key Terms and People

Reviewing Chapter 9

1. Both government policies and individual initiative were crucial to the expansion of the United States. Which was more important, and why?
2. How did the movement of people around North America influence political events between 1789 and 1824?
3. What were some of the most important ways that attitudes toward nature shaped actions of U.S. citizens between 1789 and 1824?

Further Reading

Chasteen, John Charles. *Americanos: Latin America's Struggle for Independence.* New York: Oxford University Press, 2008. This book traces Latin American wars for independence starting in 1808 and examines how various Latin American colonies became independent nations. Chasteen shows the interplay between the United States and many Latin American revolutionary nations.

Forbes, Robert Pierce. *The Missouri Compromise and Its Aftermath: Slavery and the Meaning of America.* Chapel Hill: University of North Carolina Press, 2007. Forbes analyzes the complex political history of American expansionism that led to the delicate Missouri Compromise and traces the consequences of the Compromise for U.S. politics and society.

Hackel, Stephen. *Children of Coyote, Missionaries of Saint Francis: Indian-Spanish Relations in Colonial California, 1769–1850.* Chapel Hill: University of North Carolina Press, 2005. In this book, Hackel examines how California Indians coped with and resisted Spanish religious and military colonial control, even as their populations were decimated by disease. The author presents a particularly in-depth case study of the Mission of San Carlos Borromeo.

Howe, Daniel Walker. *What Hath God Wrought: The Transformation of America, 1815–1848.* New York: Oxford University Press, 2007. Howe's sweeping overview of U.S. history from 1815–1848 integrates excellent discussion of territorial expansion, slavery, religious revival, and the development of American literature.

Nash, Gary B. *Forging Freedom: The Formation of Philadelphia's Black Community, 1720–1840*. Cambridge, Mass.: Harvard University Press, 1988. Nash's account of the free black community in Philadelphia shows how ties of kinship, economic activity, and religion provided the means to create the urban center of free-black society in the United States. Nash shows how many African Americans succeeded, despite racism and growing segregation.

America In The World
PEOPLE, GOODS, IDEAS AND PRACTICES

CHAPTER 9: American Peoples on the Move 1789–1824

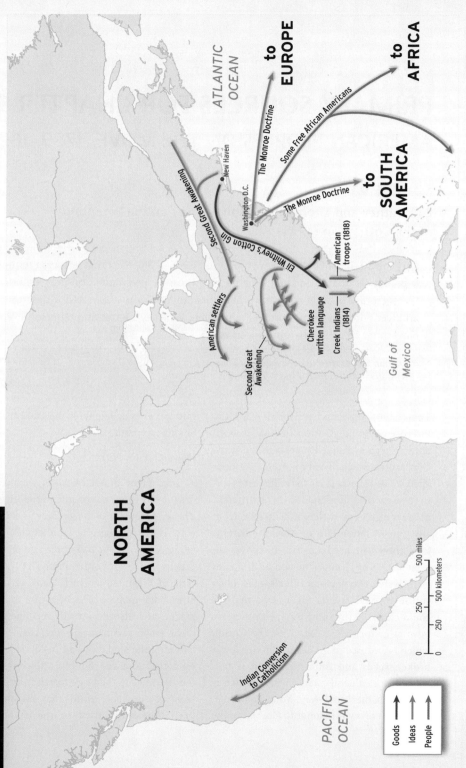

NORTH AMERICA

ATLANTIC OCEAN

to **EUROPE**

to **AFRICA**

to **SOUTH AMERICA**

The Monroe Doctrine

Some Free African Americans

The Monroe Doctrine

New Haven

Washington D.C.

Second Great Awakening

Eli Whitney's Cotton Gin

American settlers

Second Great Awakening

American troops (1818)

Cherokee written language

Creek Indians (1814)

Gulf of Mexico

Indian Conversion to Catholicism

PACIFIC OCEAN

Goods

Ideas

People

0   250   500 miles

0   250   500 kilometers

PRIMARY SOURCES FOR CHAPTER 9

AMERICAN PEOPLES ON THE MOVE, 1789–1824

SOURCE 9.1

Eli Whitney and Thomas Jefferson, Letters on the Patenting of the Cotton Gin (1793)

On June 20, 1793, Eli Whitney wrote to Secretary of State Thomas Jefferson requesting a patent for the cotton gin that he had recently invented. Congress empowered the secretary of state to grant a patent to anyone who submitted a description of an invention, drawings, a model, and a fee. Whitney's letter and Jefferson's reply of November 16, 1793 are reproduced below.

Sources: John Catanzariti, ed., *The Papers of Thomas Jefferson,* vol. 26 (Princeton, NJ: Princeton University Press, 1995); Eli Whitney Papers, Yale University Library.

That having invented a Machine for the Purpose of ginning Cotton, he is desirous of obtaining an exclusive Property in the same. Concerning which invention, your Petitioner alledges as follows (viz) first. That it is entirely new and constructed in a different manner and upon different principles from any, other Cotton Gin or Machine heretofore known or used for that purpose. 2d. That with this Ginn, if turned with horses or by water, two persons will clean as much cotton in one Day, as a Hundred persons could cleane in the same time with the gins now in common use. 3d. That the Cotton which is cleansed in his Ginn contains fewer broken seeds and impurities, and is said to be more valuable than Cotton, which is cleaned in the usual way. Your Petitioner, therefore Prays your Honor to Grant him the said Whitney, a Patent for the said Invention or Improvement. . . .

[November 16, 1793]

Your favor of October 18, including a drawing [of] your cotton gin, was received. . . . The only requisite of the law now uncomplied with is the forwarding of a model, which being received your patent may be made out & delivered to your order immediately. As the state of Virginia, of which I am, carries on household manufactures of cotton to a great extent, as I also do myself, and one of our great embarrassments in the cleaning the cotton of the seed, I feel a considerable interest in the success of your invention, for family use. Permit me therefore to ask information from you on these points, has the machine been thoroughly tried in the ginning of cotton, or is it as yet but a machine of theory? What quantity of cotton has it cleaned on an average of several days, & worked by hand, & by how many hands? What will be the cost of one of these made to be worked by hand? Favorable answers to these questions would induce me to engage one of them to be forwarded to Richmond for me.

WORKING WITH SOURCES

1. What claims for improvement in cotton gin design does Whitney make?
2. What aspects of the new gin most interest Jefferson?

SOURCE 9.2

Journal of Benjamin Carpenter, Reflections on the India Trade (1790)

Benjamin Carpenter captained his merchant ship, the *Ruby*, from Boston in 1789 hoping to trade at Port Louis in the Mauritius Islands, but when he arrived there, he found the French port in an upheaval caused by the French Revolution. He sailed to Ceylon (Sri Lanka) instead and then to India to continue trading first in Madras and then in Calcutta. Here, he comments in his ship journal about U.S. trade prospects in India.

Source: Benjamin Carpenter, "From the Journal of the *Ruby*, 1789–1790," in *Yankee India: American Commercial and Cultural Encounters with India in the Age of Sail, 1784–1860*, ed. Susan S. Bean, 61–63 (Salem, MA: Peabody Essex Museum, 2001).

On your arrival at Calcutta you will proceed as at Madras—the manner and customs are the same with this difference only—the inhabitants are more sociable and friendly. You will find them ready to assist you in everything. They are very liberal and deal on honorable terms. On my arrival at Bengal I was an utter stranger to every person there—and notwithstanding I was destitute of even a line of recommendation, I found the greatest hospitality and very soon became acquainted with the principal merchants there.

The produce and manufactories of Bengal are every way suited for the American market, but as the trade to this country is a very recent affair, they have not those goods on hand which we are most in want of. For this reason our ships are obliged to wait three or four months for a cargo. This inconvenience is easily remedied by a previous order. You may then be sure to have your goods in readiness on your arrival, and then your detention may not be more than three weeks or a month. . . .

A voyage from America may be performed in fourteen months—and a person well acquainted with a suitable cargo will seldom fail to make a good voyage. Their sugar and niter will ballast your ship, you can fill her with dry goods. The sugar is of a superior quality to West India sugar and is sold at six rupees per maund of eighty-two pounds English. The country abounds with a great variety of drugs of the first qualities. . . . They are sold astonishingly cheap, and if care is taken in choosing them they will turn to very good account in Europe. There is many articles in Bengal which would answer well in America that we are not yet acquainted with. There are also many things [that are] the produce of America that would net good profit and would be a sure remittance in India. . . .

America abounds with furs of different kinds, any quantity of the various species would very readily sell in Bengal at 100 percent profit. They purchase them to send to China, which is by far the best remittance they can make. It is a little surprising that [given] the number of ships we have sent to China that none of them should think of furs. They are certainly the best article they can carry. . . .

3000 barrels of whale oil would readily sell in Calcutta for 20 Rupees on the barrel which is double the price it sells at in America. . . .

After duly considering the advantage arising from this trade, there is no one can venture to affirm that the commerce with India is prejudicial to America. . . .

Having contracted for a quantity of chintz to be manufactured at Chandernagore (a French factory about 30 miles from Calcutta). In order to choose patterns and expedite matters, I this morning hired a buggerow and made an excursion up the river. . . .

The navigation to Chandernagore is perfectly safe and there is a sufficient depth of water for a vessel of 1,000 tons to anchor within a cable's length of the shore. If we can conquer the silly jealousies subsisting between the American merchants and persuade them to unite their property to establish a factory here, I am fully persuaded they would realize forty percent per annum on their stock. This is certainly a far greater profit than they can gain on their Europe, West India or any other trade whatever.

WORKING WITH SOURCES

1. What kinds of goods does this document show were involved in the U.S.–India trade?
2. Why would this description make the India trade sound attractive to prospective ship captains?

SOURCE 9.3
Susannah Rowson, Preface to Charlotte Temple (1794)

Novelist Susannah Rowson explained the purpose of her novel *Charlotte Temple* in the preface to the Philadelphia edition of the book. She argued that her novel should not be seen as dangerous for young women, as many novels were perceived to be at the turn of the 19th century. The publisher of this edition of the work, Matthew Carey, also preceded the novel with this review from a contemporary magazine:

"It may be a Tale of Truth, for it is not unnatural, and it is a tale of real distress— Charlotte, by the artifice of a teacher . . . is enticed from her governess, and accompanies a young officer to America.—The marriage ceremony, if not forgotten, is postponed, and Charlotte dies a martyr to the inconstancy of her lover and treachery of his friend.—The situations are artless and affecting—the descriptions natural and pathetic; we should feel for Charlotte, if such a person ever existed, who, for one error, scarcely, perhaps, deserved so severe a punishment. If it is a fiction, poetic justice is not, we think, properly distributed."

Source: Susannah Rowson, *Charlotte: A Tale of Truth*, vol. 1, 2nd ed. (Philadelphia: Matthew Carey, 1794).

For the perusal of the young and thoughtless of the fair sex, this Tale of Truth is designed; and I could wish my fair readers to consider it as not merely the effusion of Fancy, but as a reality. The circumstances on which I have founded this novel were related to me some little time since by an old lady who had personally known Charlotte, though she concealed the real names of the characters, and likewise the place where the unfortunate scenes were acted: yet as it was impossible to offer a relation to the public in such an imperfect state, I have thrown over the whole a slight veil of fiction, and substituted names and places according to my own fancy. The principal characters in this little tale are now consigned to the silent tomb: it can therefore hurt the feelings of no one; and may, I flatter myself, be of service to some who are so unfortunate as to have neither friends to advise, or understanding to direct them, through the various and unexpected evils that attend a young and unprotected woman in her first entrance into life.

While the tear of compassion still trembled in my eye for the fate of the unhappy Charlotte, I may have children of my own, said I, to whom this recital may be of use, and if to your own children, said Benevolence, why not to the many daughters of Misfortune who, deprived of natural friends, or spoilt by a mistaken education, are thrown on an unfeeling world without the least power to defend themselves from the snares not only of the other sex, but from the more dangerous arts of the profligate of their own.

Sensible as I am that a novel writer, at a time when such a variety of works are ushered into the world under that name, stands but a poor chance for fame in the annals of literature, but conscious that I wrote with a mind anxious for the happiness of that sex whose morals and conduct have so powerful an influence on mankind in general; and convinced that I have not wrote a line that conveys a wrong idea to the head or a corrupt wish to the heart, I shall rest satisfied in the purity of my own intentions, and if I merit not applause, I feel that I dread not censure.

If the following tale should save one hapless fair one from the errors which ruined poor Charlotte, or rescue from impending misery the heart of one anxious parent, I shall feel a much higher gratification in reflecting on this trifling performance, than could possibly result from the applause which might attend the most elegant finished piece of literature whose tendency might deprave the heart or mislead the understanding.

WORKING WITH SOURCES

1. How does Rowson argue that her novel can teach good morals to young women?

2. What does this document indicate about public opinion in the 1790s on the nature of women?

SOURCE 9.4

Anne Royall, Excerpts from Letters from Alabama (1818)

The writer Anne Royall's *Letters from Alabama*, originally written as a series of letters to her friend Matt and later published as a book, recounts her travels around that state in the years after the War of 1812. She noted economic developments in the area and expressed sympathy for several Cherokee families, who had been forced off their farms. She also commented on Andrew Jackson's plantation.

Source: Anne Royall, *Letters from Alabama on Various Subjects* (Washington, DC: 1830), 54–60.

Melton's Bluff, January 12th, 1818

Dear Matt,

It is unnecessary to state what you have learned from the newspapers, that this land was abandoned last Fall by the Indians. The fires were still smoking, when the white people took possession. Although I had travelled through a beautiful country, the two preceding days, and my mind had been raised to the highest pitch of expectation by repeated descriptions of this land; yet, it far exceeded all I anticipated. . . .

About ten o'clock we came in sight of the first Indian farm—but Indian farm no longer! The smoke was issuing slowly through the chimney. Why, these Indians have been like us!—could not be savage—cornfields—apple trees, and peach-trees. Fences like ours—but not so high—trusted to their neighbors' honesty—perhaps these being more civilized had more reason to fear their neighbor. . . . The house looked tight and comfortable; the fruit-trees are large, and show age—there the Indian sat under their shade, or stood up and plucked the apples—wonder he did not plant more—suppose he did not know how to make cider. . . .

Melton's Bluff, January 14th, 1818

Dear Matt,

Melton's Bluff is a town, and takes its name from John Melton, a white man . . . [who] became displeased with the white people; attached himself to the Cherokee Indians; married a squaw, and settled at this place many years ago. . . . He became immensely rich; owned a great number of slaves. . . .

When the Cherokee Indians abandoned this area last fall, some of them went up the river to the Cherokee nation, there to remain, till boats were provided for their removal to the west, by the government; others went directly down the river to Arkansas. . . . The order for their departure was sudden and unexpected. . . .

Here is a very large plantation of cotton and maize, worked by about sixty slaves, and owned by General Jackson, who bought the interest of Old Melton. . . . I took a walk with some ladies to-day, over the plantation, as we wished to hav[e] a nearer view of those snowy fields . . . together with orchards, gin houses, gardens, Melton's mansion, and a considerable negro town.

WORKING WITH SOURCES

1. What relationship does Royall observe as existing among the Cherokee, slaves, and white people?

2. In 1818, Alabama was one of the fastest-growing areas of the country, and it was viewed as a place filled with natural resources. How do Royall's observations show that attitude toward Alabama's bounty?

Market Revolutions and the Rise of Democracy

10

O n July 4, 1830, the residents of Portland, Maine, found themselves bitterly divided by politics. Instead of holding one celebration of Independence Day, Democrats who supported Andrew Jackson held their own separate event, as they no longer wished to celebrate alongside Jackson's opponents who controlled local government. The two factions were splitting into two parties—the Democrats and the Whigs. Rival newspapers, the Democratic *Eastern Argus* and the *Portland Gazette,* added fuel to the fire of political disagreement in Portland. Both sides used Fourth of July parades, ritual toasting, celebrations, and newspapers to celebrate the nation's birthday and to blast their opponents.

After the rival parades directly passed one another in the center of town, each side adjourned to separate locations where partygoers could enjoy the company of those who agreed with them. The Jacksonian Democrats met at Mr. Attwood's boarding house with elaborate decorations, including a live bald eagle and two miniature commercial sailing ships. The anti-Jacksonians repaired to the City Hall, which was also "handsomely decorated" for their celebration. The newspaper editors each accused the rival celebrants of being the tools of "vile" party politics instead of engaging in true patriotism, and each party claimed to have hundreds more participants than the other side.

The ritual toasts—long an Independence Day tradition—revealed the bitter partisan divide between Portlanders. The Jacksonians cast President Jackson as the "youngest political son of the late Thomas Jefferson"; "the sincere and untiring friend of the *simple* mechanic"; and a supporter "of the rights of the People, and worthy of their suffrages." Several toasters wished for Democratic

< Portrait of Andrew Jackson by Ralph Eleaser Whiteside Earl.

electoral success in the Fall elections, and Ebenezer Webster threatened the Democrats' electoral opponents: "We will toast them . . . and baste them with democratic butter." Meanwhile, back at City Hall, the anti-Jacksonians labeled their opponents "political skunks and other vermin."

Portland's role in the transatlantic economy helped drive political disagreements. Maine grew rapidly between its admission to the Union in 1820 and 1830, and its expanding population benefited from thriving agriculture, fishing, lumber, and shipbuilding industries. Maine served as an entry port for cotton, feeding the new textile mills sprouting up throughout New England. Advertisements in local newspapers announced regular commercial and passenger ship traffic between Portland, Boston, and European cities including Belfast and Frankfort. The Cumberland and Oxford canal opened in 1830 to connect the interior of southern Maine to the port of Portland.

Andrew Jackson's supporters in Portland made a clear distinction between their support of this state effort, financed by the locally chartered Canal Bank, and what they considered to be the unconstitutional "**American System**" of Henry Clay that promoted the use of federal government funds for infrastructure projects. The Portland Jacksonians toasted the defeat of the American System and Jackson's veto of the Maysville Road Bill, the most famous federal internal improvement project. The Jacksonian Democrats in Maine drew most of their support from poor fishermen, working men, and small merchants, whereas the anti-Jacksonian Whigs attracted wealthier business supporters.

The partisanship displayed in Portland, Maine, characterized the splits in national and local politics taking place all over the United States. Disagreements over how government should best manage the burgeoning capitalist and commercial enterprise in the developing nation would change the character of U.S. politics as the country entered the worldwide Industrial Revolution.

■ THE MARKET SYSTEM

Americans had grown used to buying and selling goods since the mid-1700s. The pace and scale of these economic exchanges accelerated, however, and between 1789 and 1832, a fuller market economy took shape in the United States. In a market economy, market forces influence the production, distribution, and consumption of goods. Before 1789, most rural Americans lived on interdependent family farms, although many, such as Southern tobacco planters, raised staple crops and participated in international trade. At the turn of the 19th century, more and more farmers began to produce surplus goods that they could sell locally, regionally, or internationally for cash. Although the vast majority of Americans remained in rural areas, a greater percentage of Americans were moving into towns and cities where manufacturing took place. The greater supply of foreign and domestic manufactured goods that fueled the market system allowed farm families to specialize because they could purchase goods instead of having to produce or trade for everything they needed. The market system intensified economic competition, changed business and labor patterns, and had a profound effect on the lives of everyone in the United States. Technological change, government action, and international exchanges all intensified the development of market capitalism.

Internal and External Markets

The U.S. market economy emerged from the connection of local, regional, national, and international networks of exchange—all of which grew between 1789 and 1832. Although the shifts took place unevenly, by 1800 it was clear that labor markets, capital investment, and prices converged to

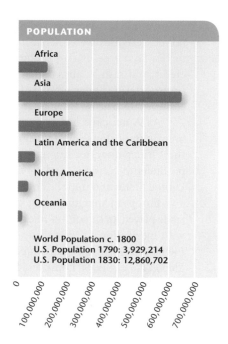

POPULATION

Africa

Asia

Europe

Latin America and the Caribbean

North America

Oceania

World Population c. 1800
U.S. Population 1790: 3,929,214
U.S. Population 1830: 12,860,702

0   100,000,000   200,000,000   300,000,000   400,000,000   500,000,000   600,000,000   700,000,000

BUTTER CHURNING   Making butter was a traditional part of women's work in the dairy producing Mid-Atlantic states and became an increasingly market-oriented economic activity in the early 19th century. Women could sell surplus butter for cash they could use to buy other household products. Eventually, butter became an international trade commodity.

create a market system based on currency exchange and commodities. Everyday economic activities were increasingly influenced by market prices and wider economic forces. In a free-market economy, open competition and the exchange of products, credit, and cash balance the optimum production and price of goods. As new kinds of transportation and machinery became available by 1820, many farmers made decisions about what to grow, when to grow it, and how to process it based on market forces.

As Americans had more opportunities to sell their goods, market connections grew in importance for both agricultural and manufactured products. After the turn of the 19th century, for example, cotton planters in Georgia and Alabama shipped their products to New England textile mills that manufactured and sold cloth across the United States and into the South and West.

European manufacturing could also affect prices and supplies, and international trade played an important role in the market process. Raw materials and trade fluctuated with international disturbances such as the Napoleonic Wars and the War of 1812. The towns and cities inside the United States that grew most rapidly were those—such as Providence, New York, St. Louis, and Philadelphia—that had links both to internal networks of agricultural trade and to external ports that could facilitate international exchange.

Examining one particular product, such as butter, can show how the market transformation worked. Butter went from a product that families produced for themselves to the stuff of international commerce. Mid-Atlantic farm women practiced dairying and butter making widely at the end of the 18th century, and by 1790, surplus butter was traded between farms and sold in Philadelphia. After the War of 1812, more and more women specialized in butter making and started to produce large quantities for sale as a commodity. The stable price for butter, between 17 and 25 cents per pound between the 1790s and 1830s, meant that women could provide income from butter when other farm products fluctuated because of wars or hard economic times. Martha Ogle Forman, a Maryland dairywoman, wrote in her diary in 1824, "We now make more butter than we know what to do with." In fact, she did know what to do with the surplus butter: she sold it for profit.

Women like Forman could spend more time making butter because they were able to purchase manufactured cloth instead of spinning and weaving at home. As supplies of store-bought cloth accelerated into the 1830s, so did the production of butter. Farms also adopted new milking methods and new breeds of cows that gave more milk. Butter could be preserved with salt for over a year, and Mid-Atlantic butter was sold in markets in Philadelphia, Providence, Annapolis, Charleston, Boston, and other port cities. The international market also grew. Between 1802 and 1835, Americans exported 67 million pounds of dairy products overseas to Europe, the Caribbean, and China. By 1851, men became more involved with butter making, which began to move into factory production.

The same kind of story could be repeated for scores of other commodities, including cheese, grain, whiskey, pork, and lumber. Homemade and farm goods spread through local, regional, national, and international markets. Individual farmers made decisions based on calculations of price, supply, and demand. The market economy grew through a million single decisions about what to buy, what to produce, and how to sell it.

Technology: Domestic Invention and Global Appropriation

The invention and adoption of new technologies also fueled market activity. Tench Coxe, aide to Treasury Secretary Alexander Hamilton and founder of the Society for

Establishing Useful Manufactures, recognized that "machines ingeniously constructed, will give us immense assistance" with economic growth. In the Patent Act of 1790, Congress granted inventors a 14-year monopoly on patented machinery and processes, and patents provided an economic incentive for invention. The federal government went from issuing three patents in 1790 to 573 in 1831. The new interest in manufacturing during the War of 1812, when foreign trade was severely restricted, especially spurred domestic invention. The U.S. government issued 244 patents for butter-making equipment alone between 1802 and 1849, and increased butter productivity occurred in part because women adopted more advanced tools and churns.

Americans invented new technologies to improve both agriculture and manufacturing. By 1792, Delaware inventor Oliver Evans licensed his designs for continuous-processing flour machinery to more than 100 mills. In 1819, Jethro Wood patented an iron plow constructed from interchangeable parts. After revolutionizing the production of cotton with his mechanized cotton mill in 1793, **Eli Whitney** turned his ingenuity to manufacturing muskets with interchangeable parts. Thomas Blanchard, a mechanic at the Springfield, Massachusetts, Armory, invented dozens of machines that allowed for accurate manufacturing of wooden and metal gun parts. In 1831, Illinois inventor **Cyrus McCormick** built his first mechanical reaper, a machine that would revolutionize harvesting in the decades to come.

Americans also appropriated some new technologies from abroad—especially from Great Britain. By the early 1780s, British textile mills used mechanized looms and carding machines, but textile workers were discouraged from leaving the country and could be fined if they gave up trade secrets. American agents in New York, Maryland, Pennsylvania, and Massachusetts tried to pay English mechanics to build machinery for them, and they openly advertised in newspapers for men willing to divulge the secrets of British textile inventor **Richard Arkwright**. Trying to stop the smuggling of British machinery into the United States, British consul Phineas Bond, Jr., even inspected cargo in the port of Philadelphia. **Samuel Slater**, a former British textile worker, immigrated to the United States in 1789 and parlayed his knowledge of both machinery and labor management practices into the first successful mechanized mill in the United States. Other British technologies, such as the first steam-powered train locomotives brought to the United States in 1829, were imported legally.

Water and Steam Power

Water power had been harnessed for centuries at saw mills, leather tanneries, and grist mills, but its application in manufacturing grew in the 1790s. The power created by waterfalls turned water wheels that powered machines with gears and belts. Because of favorable geography, by the early 19th century, Americans were global leaders in harnessing water power for manufacturing. Across the North water power contributed to the growth of textile mills that used machinery to card, spin, and weave cotton and woolen cloth. Thomas Keystone wrote in 1810 that water-powered carding machines "are everywhere established and are rapidly being extended." After the turn of the century, water-powered cotton gins, sugar mills, and rice mills proliferated in the South. Waterwheels drove furnaces and forges essential to ironworks. By 1830, there were an estimated 50,000 water mills in the United States, and the first industrial towns and cities all grew near bodies of water. Location near a water source was so important to all these industries that competition for land near waterways was fierce.

STEAMBOATS   Robert Fulton's ship *"Clermont"* was the first commercially viable steamboat in the world. Fulton and Robert Livingston received a monopoly on New York Hudson River steamboat travel and launched the *Clermont* in 1807.

Harnessing steam power from heated water was probably the most important technological innovation in the early market economy. Steam power allowed greater mobility because machinery did not have to be near a waterway. British inventor **James Watt** perfected the first modern steam engine in 1769, although it took several decades of innovation by engineers to make steam power efficient and easy to use. In the first decade of the 19th century, Oliver Evans, the successful American flour mill inventor, patented a high-pressure steam engine that would be used in the first railroad locomotive and in other industrial applications. Steamboats were probably the first significant American contribution to international technology. Steam-powered transportation had the ability to increase the speed of trade dramatically. Pennsylvanian **John Fitch** first used steam to power a boat in August 1787. After several decades of scrambling by various inventors to produce a commercially viable steamboat, **Robert Fulton** perfected a usable high-powered boat engine. Fulton worked with wealthy investor and politician **Robert Livingston** to obtain a monopoly on steamboat traffic in New York waters; and, in August 1807, he launched the *North River Steamboat*—also known as the *Clermont*— the world's first successful commercial steamboat.

Steamboats quickly spread throughout America's inland waterways, and by 1812 steamboats plied waters in the trans-Appalachian West. French engineer Jean Baptiste Marestier observed in 1819 that "America now possesses several hundred [commercial steamboats] and the people of the New World are already reaping immense benefits." He worried about American "superiority over other nations" in steamboat travel. That same year, the *Savannah*, the first American ship with auxiliary steam power, crossed the Atlantic Ocean. By 1830, hundreds of steamboats, traveling nearly twice as fast as in the 1810s, traded goods on oceans and rivers.

Transportation and Communication

Improvements in transportation—steamboats, roads, canals, and early railroads— played a crucial role in the spread of the market economy throughout the United States in the early decades of the 19th century. Both federal and state governments invested heavily to speed up and lower the cost of moving goods. Despite political controversy over use of too much federal power, federal government expenditures on transportation improvements went from less than $100,000 in 1789 to over $1.5 million in 1832. In 1804, **Albert Gallatin**, Thomas Jefferson's Treasury Secretary, initially proposed the first comprehensive plan for internal improvements.

Henry Clay—who served as a U.S. senator, Speaker of the House of Representatives, and Secretary of State between 1809 and 1832—became the leading advocate of publicly funded transportation. Subsidies for roads and canals, in particular, became one of the cornerstones of his "American System"—a group of laws intended to spur domestic economic development that also included **tariffs** and currency regulation. Clay's plans for public improvements, however, ran afoul of several presidents who opposed the overuse of federal power. In 1817, James Madison vetoed the "Bonus Bill" that would have used Bank of the United States funds to pay for roads and canals because he judged it to be unconstitutional. Road building increased exponentially in these decades and proved a key to increased market activity. In the 1790s, turnpikes— roads tailor made for wagons bearing goods—were constructed up and down the eastern seaboard; by the 1820s, they carried hundreds of thousands of tons of freight per year. Many roads, including turnpikes, were built by private companies, encouraged by state subsidies and charters. Congress also took action and authorized the Cumberland Road from Maryland to Ohio in 1806. Efforts to revive funding for a National Road after the War of 1812 were blocked by arguments that road building could not serve a truly "national" interest. In 1822, Congress authorized repairs to the Cumberland Road and extended it to Vandalia, Illinois, but President Monroe, calling the bill unconstitutional, vetoed it. Political controversies over whether roads concentrated too much federal power in one location repeatedly hamstrung a consistent program of federal funding for roads.

Following the War of 1812, several states supplemented road-building projects with early efforts at canal building. Although they would not come into wide use until the later 1820s, canals promised to expand market activity because they mainly aimed to connect inland waters to major avenues of river and oceanic trade. New York authorized construction of the Erie Canal in 1817, but it took almost a decade to be finished. Ohio and Virginia also began major canal projects.

Early railroads also promised to further economic development. In 1830, the Baltimore and Ohio Company founded the first railroad in the United States and opened 13 miles of passenger service between the Baltimore port and Sandy Hook, Maryland. Between 1830 and 1833, a rail line between Charleston and Hamburg, South Carolina, used steam-powered locomotives to transport hundreds of passengers along

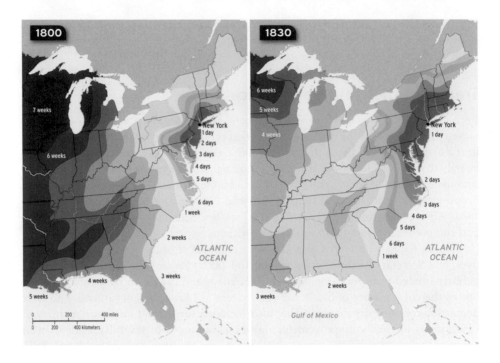

MAP 10.1 ▲ Transportation Times Inside the United States, 1800–1830 This map shows how long it took to travel from New York City to other points in the United States. Transportation improvements and technological developments dramatically improved travel time between 1800 and 1830.

the world's longest run of track. These relatively small beginnings would inspire a later era of growth in industry and transportation (Map 10.1).

Transportation advances also improved communication. Congress created the U.S. Postal System in 1789, and by the 1820s it delivered mail along nearly 2,500 postal routes. Increased business activity led to even faster growth: 5,000 post offices opened across the United States between 1819 and 1832. Although Americans used the postal service unevenly in different locations, the mail provided an important means for both private and public communication. A letter could cost as much as 25 cents to mail, but newspapers could be sent for only one and a half cents. The mails also carried political pamphlets, and advances in papermaking meant that they could be printed more cheaply. Business documents also traveled through the mail and made market connections across great distance possible.

STUDY QUESTIONS FOR THE MARKET SYSTEM

1. In what ways were the market changes in the U.S. economy between 1789 and 1832 revolutionary?

2. What role did transportation play in U.S. economic development in this period?

■ MARKETS AND SOCIAL RELATIONSHIPS

In addition to changes in technology, and transportation, the transition to a capitalist market economy in the United States also changed the ways that people related to one another in families, workplaces, and neighborhoods. When the magazine *The North American Review* considered in 1832 "the influence of machinery . . . and its effects on society" in the market economy, it had to pause to ask, "is this influence . . . good or evil?" As with any huge change in an economic system, individuals felt the effects unevenly and experienced them in ways that defy simple description. Journeymen or agricultural laborers, who might have once counted on advancing to shop or farm ownership, now often found themselves working permanently for wages. Patterns of labor on farms and in households changed the relationships between husbands and wives, children, and hired help. Slaves, who both provided labor and were defined as commodities, also saw themselves subject to market forces.

Manufacturing and the Factory System

The factory system of production, one of the biggest economic innovations, radically changed the ways that workers related to business owners and to one another. The factory system referred to the centralization of manufacturing under the ownership of one person or a corporation. Instead of manufacturing goods in homes or in small

SPINNING MILL   Samuel Slater founded the first successful mechanized spinning mill in North America in Pawtucket, Rhode Island, in 1790. Water-powered mills, such as Slater's, soon spread across southern New England, changing employment patterns in the region and fueling the industrial revolution.

WORK FLOOR OF A COTTON MILL   This engraving of the work floor of a cotton mill shows the power looms at work weaving cloth. Note the gendered division of labor: women operate the looms, while the sole visible man repairs the leather straps that used water power to run the looms. Working on a factory floor like this in the 1830s was a huge change in atmosphere from home textile production.

family-owned workshops, the factory system brought together many unrelated workers under one roof. Instead of working for master craftsmen in a hierarchical system, factory workers labored for wages in defined jobs—usually concentrating on one aspect of production. The factory system did not have to include the widespread use of machines; it was more about ownership and the organization of labor. But as U.S. factories developed, they also become mechanized.

British textile manufacturing firms instituted the factory system in the 1770s, and as Americans turned their attention to domestic production by the 1790s, they became interested in this system. The transition from home work to factory work took place slowly at first; but, several early New England industries, including textile mills, shoemaking, and clock making, began to centralize production as they also adopted mechanization. By the 1830s, the factory system had spread to other industries.

In 1790, British immigrant Samuel Slater and wealthy American merchant **Moses Brown** founded the first mechanized cotton mill in the United States in Pawtucket, Rhode Island. By 1793, Slater and Brown had expanded into a larger factory on the Blackstone River, where they housed 1,500 water-powered spindles under one roof. The women wageworkers at Slater's mills used spinning skills they had developed at home and applied them in an industrial setting. The operations also employed children as spinners and men as mechanics. Initially, Slater marketed cloth that was produced partially in workers' homes. Slater and his associates, spreading throughout New England in the 1790s and early 1800s, founded scores of additional mechanized mill operations. By 1810, 31 mechanized mills were operating in the United States, most in Rhode Island or near Philadelphia. The Boston Associates, a corporation formed by wealthy men, including Samuel Cabot Lowell and Nathaniel Appleton, raised the stakes in 1814 when they founded their mill operation in Waltham, Massachusetts. The Boston Associates started their mills with a capital investment of $400,000, almost 10 times Slater and Brown's first investment, and they centralized all aspects of cloth production under one roof. In an effort to manufacture mass-produced cloth and to capture market share, the Waltham mill owners introduced a labor system that was different from the British model adopted by Slater. They recruited young farm women, who provided the bulk of their mill work and lived in company-controlled boarding houses at the mill. The boarding houses enforced strict rules of conduct both on and off the factory floor. Most of these young "Mill Girls" viewed wage work as temporary, until they could marry and return to farming. The mills paid relatively high wages, but the work was difficult—with one woman in charge of 128 fast-moving spindles or two power looms. The Boston Associates mills were so profitable that they soon established company towns at Lowell, Chicopee, and Lawrence, Massachusetts, and Manchester, New Hampshire. By the mid-1830s, when the "Mill Girls" began to be replaced by a more permanent class of immigrant workers, the boardinghouses became less important and relative wages dropped. But the mills continued to influence the character of life in New England into the 20th century.

Whether in a mill town or in a town like Lynn, Massachusetts, where hundreds of families manufactured shoes, workers saw their lives changed by the advent of the factory system. Working conditions were generally better than they were in British textile cities such as Manchester and Barmen, where poverty, malnutrition, and disease were rampant. Even for people accustomed to hard work, however, labor in mechanized factories posed challenges. As mill worker Lucy Davis explained it, "The work was much harder than I expected and quite new to me." Factory work was often unsafe, and by the 1830s working conditions deteriorated as work sped up. It is no coincidence that the first widespread strikes and forms of labor resistance accompanied the rise of the factory system. Instead of being defined primarily by family relationships, workers began to see themselves in terms of their labor—now a marketplace commodity as much as butter, clocks, or cloth.

Slavery and Markets

The burgeoning capitalist market economy also held deep consequences for enslaved people who did not own their own labor and who were regarded as market commodities to be bought, sold, and traded. Slavery had for centuries played a vital role in the transatlantic market economy, and slaves provided the labor for many of the raw materials for factories in the United States and in Great Britain. As cotton agriculture intensified between 1789 and 1832, slaves played an increasing role in the market economy, although many historians argue that the Southern economy itself resisted a full integration into capitalism. As commodities, slaves were bought and traded in large open-air slave markets in most Southern cities. One master wrote in Louisiana in 1818 that "Negroes will yield a much larger income than any Bank dividends" (Map 10.2).

This market logic helped to intensify the racism that increasingly defined all African American lives. Newspapers across the country advertised slaves for sale alongside

SLAVE AUCTION ADVERTISEMENT   This advertisement for a slave auction was typical of ads that ran throughout the South up until the 1860s. Although slaves were advertised for sale and for rent as commodities alongside agricultural and trade goods, their humanity also mattered as evidenced by the note that Hannibal was "of good character."

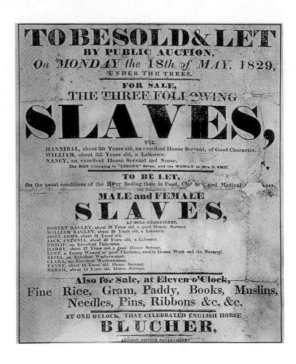

agricultural produce, manufactured items, luxury goods, and livestock. After the expansion of the cotton economy in Alabama, Mississippi, and Louisiana, the internal slave trade followed the demand for cotton, and in the 1820s, 155,000 slaves were sold into those areas from other states. Some estimates indicate that the domestic slave trade comprised as much as 15 percent of the Southern economy. Each sale of an enslaved person represented the rupture of a family and the misery of countless individuals who lived in the slave system. Charles Ball who escaped from slavery and became an antislavery activist, wrote in his autobiography of "the horrors" of being sold away from his family at the age of four. He described how many slaves never recovered from the "shock" of the "sudden and overwhelming ruin" of their families.

Class

Whereas slaves were characterized by race, free workers came to be defined as members of a working class. The concept of economic and social class includes a variety of different factors. The relationship of workers to capital helped to create the economic power structures that divided people by class. Social class also contributed to the feelings of affinity and connection that people in different strata of society developed with one another in opposition to those of lower or higher rank. But class never developed in a vacuum apart from race and gender, and people developed multiple identities simultaneously. These identities were shaped by daily activities and relationships.

As the breakdown of the artisan system relegated more Americans to the ranks of permanent wage earners, many workers felt an increasing identification with fellow workers across different trades and industries. Although the United States had a more

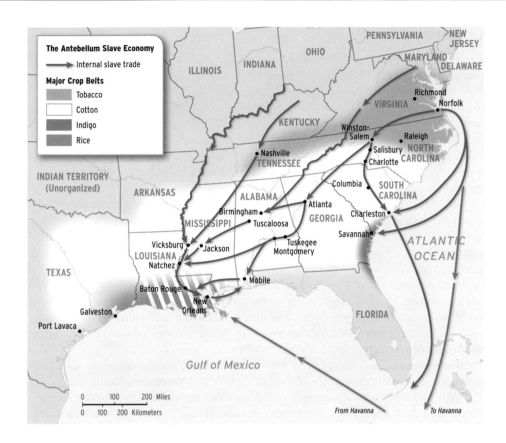

MAP 10.2 ▲ The Antebellum Slave Economy This map depicts the internal slave trade that continued after Congress outlawed the international trade in 1808 and also depicts some illegal trade that continued with Cuba. Note the location of staple crops that relied on slave labor.

equal income distribution than Europe, the divide between rich and poor grew significantly.

Wealthy planters, professionals, Western landowners, and industrialists all displayed their earnings in the consumption of luxury goods and housing. Emerging middle-class Americans—such as tradesmen, clerks, and housewives—also had access to a growing array of consumer goods such as clothing, furniture, and imported housewares that reinforced their sense of refinement. Middling Americans tended to live in modest-sized houses but to decorate them more elaborately than poorer workers could. If the factory did not provide housing, many factory workers rented rooms in boarding houses, where they might lodge with relatives or other workers.

One sign of working-class identification came when workers began to band together to strike against their employers. After journeyman shoemakers organized one of the first labor protests in American history in 1806, they were prosecuted for conspiracy, but nonetheless strikes became more common. Boardinghouse life at the Lowell textile mills bred a sense of "sisterhood" among the workers there that reinforced the women's decision to strike in the late 1820s for better working conditions, hours, and pay.

Urban and Rural Life

The differences among social classes were on display most clearly in the American cities that grew dramatically between 1789 and 1832. The U.S. Census recorded that just 201,655 people lived in cities in 1790—5.1 percent of the population. By 1830, however, the number had grown to 1,127,247—8.8 percent of the population. New York was the largest city in the country in 1830, with just over 200,000 residents, but the next largest city, Baltimore, was less than half that size. No American city was as grand or well developed as London, Amsterdam, Mexico City, Cairo, or Beijing, but American cities were growing fast and assuming a greater role in U.S. culture, politics, and the economy.

Just as in Europe, cities most connected to markets and manufacturing experienced the fastest growth. Cities energized by the market revolution—including New York, Philadelphia, Charleston, Cincinnati, Baltimore, New Orleans, and St. Louis—each developed a flavor of urban culture that mixed popular entertainment, vice, religion, and trade. Social reformers worried that young, unattached men caused upheaval in the city—especially in New York, where young men joined raucous street gangs and fire companies. Writer George Foster wrote that northern cities were "infested with a set of the most graceless vagabonds and unmitigated ruffians." Housing in U.S. cities grew increasingly segregated by class and race, but city streets constituted one of the major sites of social mixing on a day-to-day basis.

Rural economies also expanded, even as family remained the dominant social and economic unit in the experience of the vast majority of Americans. In the first half of the 19th century, economic growth relied on rural agricultural production in both Europe and the United States, and a high rate of rural mobility enhanced economic opportunity. The growth of larger towns also energized rural areas. The trading post and steamboat stop of Madison, Indiana, for example, grew from a few hundred residents in 1812 to well over a thousand by 1830. Towns like Madison housed the mills, markets, and shops that fueled the growth of both rural and urban capitalism. Networks of rural families engaged in trade and, with increasing frequency, market transactions.

STUDY QUESTIONS FOR MARKETS AND SOCIAL RELATIONSHIPS

1. Why did the shift to wage work change the relationship between workers and bosses?
2. How did the market economy affect urban and rural areas differently?

■ DEMOCRACY AND THE PUBLIC SPHERE

Alongside the rise in the market economy, by the 1820s, U.S. political life grew more democratic than ever before. Democratization spread political power to new groups, especially to poor white men who had never held much direct power in American public life. But political rights were also carefully proscribed, and, the consolidation of political power in the hands of white men that had begun in the 1790s and that excluded women,

African Americans, and Indians picked up speed. The spread of communications and expanded opportunities for participation in political rituals like Fourth of July parades—especially in growing cities—also meant that a wider group of men and women had a chance to influence public life, even if they had little direct power. The ability to debate, celebrate, and influence political life in this expanded "public sphere" developed in the United States just as voting gained importance and politicians had to place new emphasis on persuading the public to support them.

Voting and Politics

The U.S. Constitution had guaranteed a republican government, but it had left voting regulation to the states. After 1800, voting took on added importance in U.S. life, and participation in politics became one of the hallmarks of American democracy. At the turn of the 19th century, American leaders still expected deference from common people, and politicians could be criticized for campaigning too vigorously on their own behalf. During the 1800 presidential election, a New York Federalist newspaper sniped that Aaron Burr "stoop[ed] so low as to visit every corner in search of voters"—implying that his electioneering betrayed him as unworthy of political trust and power. The Democratic-Republican victory in that election simultaneously expanded efforts to widen voting rights for white men.

Once the Federalist party, associated with social elites, died out after the War of 1812, the expansion of white male suffrage took off. No new state admitted to the union after 1815 required property for white men to vote. Even though Congress in the 1780s had set high property-holding requirements for voting in Western territories, after the turn of the century Congress removed most impediments to white male voting. A revised Massachusetts state constitution ratified in 1820 removed a religious test and property requirements for white male voters, and New York followed suit in 1821. By 1824, virtually all white men in the United States were eligible to vote, although several states, notably South Carolina and Virginia, resisted removing property requirements until decades later.

Black men saw their voting rights constrict in the same era. The 1821 New York constitution, which expanded white male suffrage, retained property requirements for black male voters. Every state admitted to the union after 1819, with the exception of Maine, disenfranchised black men altogether. By 1830, the Jacksonian Democrats, the chief proponents of universal white male suffrage, lost the support of propertied African American men who could vote in Northern states.

Even though race proscribed voting rights, by 1828 vastly more American men possessed voting rights than in other countries worldwide. Even France and many countries in Latin America—which had undergone revolutions similar to that in the United States—did not spread the franchise as widely. Great Britain reserved voting for men who held large quantities of property, and even many middle-class white men could not cast ballots there. Even after the Reform Bill of 1832 liberalized British voting rights, far more U.S. men were eligible to vote. The focus on suffrage as a fundamental right and an important factor in U.S. politics also energized voter turnout, which soared to 57 percent in the 1828 presidential election. Voting now also more directly influenced presidential selection than it did previously. In 1800, only two states chose their members of the electoral college by popular vote, but by 1832, only South Carolina did not.

Election of 1824

The emphasis on white men's voting rights changed the character of the 1824 presidential election, as the old Democratic-Republican party came apart—the victim of its own success. Newly energized local participatory politics led state conventions to nominate presidential candidates—all of whom were Democrats but who differed in political outlook. By the fall of 1824, the four leading candidates were Treasury Secretary **William Crawford**, Secretary of State John Quincy Adams, Speaker of the House Henry Clay, and war hero Andrew Jackson. Crawford and Jackson, from Georgia and Tennessee, respectively, enjoyed strong Southern support, whereas Kentuckian Henry Clay drew support from the West. John Quincy Adams locked up New England. Jackson had long clashed with both Adams and Crawford, but he was an even stronger nemesis of Clay's—especially because Clay had criticized Jackson's actions in the Seminole War. Crawford, who had the support of **Martin Van Buren** and his highly organized faction of New York "Bucktail" Democrats, emerged as the early front-runner in the race, but a stroke left his health impaired and hurt his chances.

Andrew Jackson received 42 percent of the popular vote, which was recorded for the first time, as opposed to 33 percent for Adams and 13 percent for both Clay and Crawford. But when the electoral college met, no candidate emerged with the clear majority demanded by the Constitution: Jackson got 99 electoral votes, Adams got 84, Crawford earned 42, and Clay received 37. The Twelfth Amendment to the Constitution (1804) stipulated that the House of Representatives would decide the election from among the top three candidates—and as Crawford's health deteriorated, the race boiled down to Jackson and Adams.

HENRY CLAY   Clay, a longtime congressman, was Speaker of the House during the contested presidential election of 1824. Clay's support in the House helped John Quincy Adams win the election, and his rival Andrew Jackson claimed the two men had struck a "corrupt bargain" after Adams appointed Clay as secretary of state in 1825.

Each state delegation in the House received one vote, and Henry Clay—as Speaker of the House—exercised great influence over the election he had just lost. In January, Clay met with Adams. When Congress convened in February, Clay supported Adams, who was then elected president, even though Andrew Jackson had won more popular and more electoral college votes. Jacksonians accused Clay and Adams of striking a "corrupt bargain" to elect Adams. The election splintered the Democratic-Republican party and set the stage for a dramatic comeback by Jackson in 1828.

John Quincy Adams

John Quincy Adams, who had been a powerful and successful Secretary of State under President Monroe, served one largely unsuccessful term as president. In his inaugural address, he announced that "the will of the people" should be the guide "of all legitimate government upon earth," but throughout his term he fell prey to the very "collisions of party spirit" that he pledged to avoid. Adams championed many of Henry Clay's "American System" infrastructure and economic policies, but Congress blocked his proposals for a bankruptcy law and plans to bolster public credit through the Second Bank of the United States. Adams was ridiculed as elitist for proposing to fund scientific education and a national astronomical study. Adams appropriated federal funds for road and canal-building projects, but he had less success when promoting the program of high trade tariffs of Clay's "American System." The vote of Vice President **John C. Calhoun** defeated an 1827 bill to raise the trade tax on woolen cloth. Calhoun renounced his previous support of Clay and Adams when he decided trade taxes would hurt his native South Carolina. Calhoun's critique of a broad 1828 trade tax, dubbed "The Tariff of Abominations," helped to solidify his and Jackson's opposition to the "National Republicans" as the Adams–Clay wing of the Democratic party had become known. Adams even lost the upper hand in foreign policy. He was roundly criticized for his willingness to participate in a Panama conference on North and South American solidarity proposed by Simón Bolívar in 1826.

Andrew Jackson, "The People," and the Election of 1828

Andrew Jackson spent most of John Quincy Adams's term renewing his own campaign for the election of 1828, and Adams's own sitting vice president, John C. Calhoun, became Jackson's running mate. Losing the 1824 election, despite receiving the majority of popular votes, convinced Jackson that democratic suffrage was vital to the health of the republic. In the 1828 campaign, he took his appeal directly to the people. Martin Van Buren, the savvy New York politician who pioneered modern political electioneering, orchestrated a campaign to attract votes promoting Jackson as a war hero and dubbing him "old Hickory"—a strong leader who wouldn't break under pressure. The Democrats also organized conventions and public campaign events. Adams and the National Republicans largely rejected the new campaigning, although both sides viciously attacked one another in newspapers. Jackson won the election by a landslide; he got 56 percent of the popular vote and 68 percent of the electoral vote.

Jackson's ascendency benefitted from the tensions in society created by the market revolution. Jackson was a wealthy plantation owner by the time he was elected president, but he cultivated the image of a backwoods commoner and expressed commitment to democratic equality, at least among white men. Jackson did not endorse any of the labor-oriented workingmen's (or "Workey") third parties that sprang up in the 1820s and early 1830s, but he did oppose the use of government power to advance the interests of the moneyed few. Much of Jackson's democratic appeal was based on his personal presence, and when he threw open the White House to "the people" for his inauguration in March 1829, hundreds flooded in to greet him. One newspaper wrote that, "It was a proud day for the people . . . General Jackson is *their own* president." In his inaugural address, Jackson thanked the "free people" for choosing him as president and promised them "accountability" as he undertook the "task of reform" of American government.

Jackson and the Veto

Jackson had ample opportunity to put his beliefs in reform, limited government, and direct democracy into action during his first term as president. Many of Jackson's efforts centered around putting men loyal to him in power and alienating those who opposed him. By the middle of his first term, Jackson had gathered around him a "kitchen cabinet" of informal advisors composed of loyal politicians, including Secretary of State Martin Van Buren, Attorney General **Roger B. Taney**, and Senators **Thomas Hart Benton** and **James K. Polk**. Others, including Vice President Calhoun who secretly worked to bolster South Carolina's opposition to federal trade tariffs, found themselves alienated from Jackson and all but excluded from power. Jackson positioned himself as the protector of "the people" who would wield his presidential veto to protect them from Congress

As part of this reform program, Jackson challenged the American System both as it had been enacted during Adams's presidency and as it continued to be championed by Henry Clay. In Jackson's first annual message to Congress, he declared that "Every member of the Union . . . will be benefited by the improvement of inland navigation and the construction of highways in the several states," but he also warned that such projects should be funded by the states because federal action may not be "warranted by the Constitution." In the spring of 1830, Congress voted to invest $150,000 in a turnpike company that sought to improve 64 miles of road across Kentucky from Lexington to Maysville. Arguing that he could not allow federal expenditure on a road built within one state, Jackson vetoed the **"Maysville Road" Bill**. He subsequently vetoed other road-building projects. The Maysville Road and other vetoes hastened the division of national politics into pro- and anti-Jacksonian camps—even as Jackson won the support of an increasing number of average voters, who liked his antielitist tone.

Jackson took an even harder line against the Second Bank of the United States (BUS), the financial source for much of the investment in the American System. Jackson had long been suspicious of centralized banking—indeed, of most banking—and he viewed the BUS as a "hydra of corruption" that manipulated the paper currency market, benefited elites, and suppressed the financial hopes of common Americans. Jackson's position against the BUS gained him support from average people harmed by bank-induced inflation and from many state officials who supported local banks. Jackson feared that the BUS might have "power to control the Government" and that it benefitted "a few Monied Capitalists." The bank legitimately raised the credit of the U.S. government and the stability of the U.S. economy, but Jackson styled it as a political enemy.

Although the congressional charter of the BUS did not expire until 1836, the Bank's president, **Nicholas Biddle**, applied for renewal in January 1832, and Congress passed a new charter in June of that year. President Jackson quickly vetoed the charter and sent a message to Congress declaring that the BUS was unconstitutional (notwithstanding the Supreme Court's contrary decision decades earlier). Biddle fought back by opposing Jackson's reelection that fall. Jackson installed his staunch supporter Roger B. Taney as Treasury Secretary. Taney removed federal deposits from the BUS and chose to do federal banking with smaller state banks instead. Biddle continued to fight by contracting credit, but the bank was never rechartered, and it died after 1836. Jackson's strength in "the Bank War" effectively killed centralized federal banking in the United States until the 20th century. Jackson cemented his democratic reputation declaring that "it is to be regretted that the rich and powerful too often bend the acts of government to their selfish purposes."

STUDY QUESTIONS FOR DEMOCRACY AND THE PUBLIC SPHERE

1. What factors contributed to the expansion of white male suffrage by the 1820s?
2. In what ways and by what means did Andrew Jackson harness anxieties over the market economy to his political advantage?

▪ ECONOMIC OPPORTUNITY AND TERRITORIAL EXPANSION

The culture of economic growth pushed some U.S. citizens to expand further into Western territories during the era of the market revolution. One Western settler remembered that when she first came to St. Louis in 1817, "it was a small place, the population not exceeding fifteen hundred, and four brick buildings"; but after 1820, "emigrants began to pour in from all parts, . . . bringing with them wealth and enterprise." As U.S. citizens populated Western territories in the Louisiana Purchase and beyond, they constantly looked for new resources and new trade opportunities. Some, pushing beyond U.S. boundaries, even sought to establish colonies in Mexico or to conquer Indian territory, bringing greater conflict.

Texas Colonization

Moses Austin was typical of many Americans who saw booms and busts and moved west during the market revolution. In 1798, Austin established the first American settlement in Missouri at Potosi—named after a massive Bolivian silver mine—where he built up a substantial fortune in lead mining and smelting. After losing much of his fortune when the Bank of St. Louis, which he cofounded, failed during the Panic of 1819, Austin decided to seek a new fortune in Spanish territory. Looking for opportunity in Texas—a northern province of Mexico—Austin pushed his business horizons further than most entrepreneurs. Moses, and his son **Stephen Austin**, would become the most important among several founders of private colonies in Texas. Texas colonization set the stage for decades of conflict between the United States and Mexico and eventually led to the Mexican-American War.

Moses Austin died of pneumonia shortly after securing permission to found a settlement in Texas from Spain's royal governor in San Antonio in December 1820. Stephen Austin took up the plan to settle 300 families along the Brazos River. The Mexican government of Agustín de Iturbide decided that inviting settlers into sparsely populated Texas would strengthen frontier defenses and provide a bulwark against the United States. Such colonization efforts were common in Latin America during the 19th century, but Mexico's reliance on Anglo-Americans marked a different path.

Over the next several years Austin received additional grants, and he was the most successful of the *empresarios*, colonization agents who headed private colonies whom the Mexican government had granted permission to start Texas settlements. Austin wanted to integrate his territory into international markets. He attracted over 1,200 families to his lands, and many of them established profitable ranches and farms. Austin and the other *empresarios* remained largely independent throughout the late 1820s, as they appointed their own civil authorities and conducted raids against Krankawa and Tonkawa Indians.

Although Mexican authorities frowned on it, Austin allowed settlers to bring slaves into Texas as long as they were officially classified as indentured servants. When the Mexican government outlawed slavery in Texas in 1830, Austin garnered an exception for his own colonists. Slaves comprised 10 to 15 percent of the Texas population by 1835. Most of the 10,000 Anglo-American settlers in Texas in 1830 arrived from the Southern United States, and they held onto their Protestant religion despite mandatory pledges to become Catholic. Many prominent Tejanos who lived near the Anglo colonies engaged in ranching and trade with the colonists, even though Anglos outnumbered them by 1830. After 1831, when new Mexican governments began to raise taxes and to exert stronger control over Texas, tensions between Mexican officials and Anglo and Tejano settlers quickly rose.

Santa Fe Trail

Texas was not the only contact point between the United States and Mexico that touched the international market economy. Between the 1790s and 1830s, the Santa Fe Trail facilitated the growth of New Mexico as a major outpost of international trade (Map 10.3). By 1810, New Mexico emerged as an important trade site in northern New Spain after the Spanish subdued Comanche and Apache in the area and a network of Chihuahua merchants established commercial traffic. Following Mexican independence in 1821, Americans entered the New Mexico trade when **William Becknell** led a group of traders from Missouri across Plains Indian trails to Santa Fe. With little investment, Becknell's group realized a 2,000 percent profit by selling cotton cloth, iron hardware, and other manufactured goods to Indian and Spanish inhabitants. In 1822, Becknell began to lead wagon trains between Missouri and New Mexico.

The Santa Fe Trail quickly became a lucrative trade route between the United States and Mexico. By 1825, the U.S. government surveyed the Santa Fe Trail and secured treaties with Kansas and Osage people, allowing commercial traffic across their lands. Plains Indians disagreed about the validity of treaties allowing U.S. trade across their lands, and American traders complained that some Osage were still "lurking about the main pass way—seeking whom they may rob or murder." In 1829, President Jackson authorized U.S. infantry troops to escort shipments of U.S. goods. Despite Indian

MAP 10.3 ▲ Texas and the Santa Fe Trail, c. 1830 In the 1820s, greater numbers of Americans were drawn to the Southwest to trade along the Santa Fe Trail or to settle in the Mexican colonies of Texas. The Santa Fe Trail linked up major international trade networks.

conflicts and high Mexican trade tariffs, both Mexican and U.S. traders regularly earned 40–100 percent profits in the Santa Fe trade. Traders' reports published in U.S. newspapers, pamphlets, and magazines piqued American interest in New Mexico and California.

The Black Hawk War

In the Old Northwest, the competition between Indians and Americans for resources was even fiercer, and instead of establishing trade, the United States moved to push Indians off their land. Between 1800 and 1820, American settlers streamed into Illinois, which became a state in 1818. The white population grew to over 55,000. In northwestern Illinois, Sac and Fox Indians retained land where they farmed and mined lead, despite a probably invalid 1804 treaty in which some representatives agreed that their tribes would move west of the Mississippi River. In the decades following the War of 1812, they were pushed across the river into Iowa Indian Territory, as the federal government issued leases to lead miners, who then invaded Sac and Fox land in northwestern Illinois.

GLOBAL PASSAGES

Whaling

Americans hunted whales starting in the 17th century, but following the American Revolution, commercial whaling grew in scale. By the 1790s, U.S. vessels sailed all over the world in search of whales, which could be broken down into a variety of trade commodities: oil for lamps, bone stays for corsets and other clothing, and ivory. Between 1794 and 1803, U.S. whale ships harvested between 3,000 and 12,000 tons of whales per year.

After the War of 1812, the industry began another huge expansion, with more and larger American ships traveling record distances around the world in search of whales. After 1818, American whalers shifted from mainly fishing off the coast of Peru, New Zealand, and Chile to taking advantage of concentrations of sperm whales in the central Pacific Ocean off the coast of Japan and in the Indian Ocean. British whalers dominated the North Atlantic, but Americans controlled other waters, where ice was less of an impediment to profitable fishing. By 1830, American whaling ships went to sea for as long as five years at a time and often sailed halfway around the world.

The American whaling industry was based on Nantucket Island, Massachusetts, until the early 1820s, when New Bedford, Massachusetts, became dominant. New Bedford's deeper port accommodated larger ships, and its connection to inland markets helped speed the trade of whale products. Before 1825, most crew members on American ships were American citizens, but after that date more sailors from the areas where whaling occurred began to appear on ship crew lists. New Bedford's population was filled with people from around the world who came to the United States on whaling vessels. Herman Melville, the author of the whaling novel *Moby Dick*, demonstrated how these sailors could frighten 19th-century Americans when he wrote that "in New Bedford, actual cannibals stand chatting at street corners; savages outright . . . it makes a stranger stare." By 1835, 35 different U.S. port cities launched whaling ships.

Whaling captains, whose wives often ran family trade businesses in port cities, frequently became wealthy from the products of whaling. Average sailors, who performed difficult work breaking down and processing whales while they were still at sea, received wages commensurate to those of most textile workers, although skilled craftsmen might do well on an especially successful voyage.

Whaling provided raw materials for scores of trade products and introduced Americans to important parts of the world—including Japan and Hawaii. Whaling and

In May 1832, the Sac leader **Black Hawk**, who had fought with Tecumseh's Pan-Indian forces against the United States in the War of 1812, returned to Illinois with hundreds of Sac, Fox, and Kickapoo people. Black Hawk had clashed with **Keokuk** and other Sac and Fox leaders who favored accommodation to U.S. terms. The governor of Illinois, John Reynolds, called out the militia to drive Black Hawk's people out of the state.

WHALING   This engraving shows whalers trying to take a whale in the Arctic Ocean and dramatizes the danger, a common theme in visual depictions of whaling. Small parties set out from the main whaling ship to harpoon the whale, but one boat is overturned, plunging the sailors into the icy water. The upended boat flies the American flag.

its transoceanic reach also influenced American culture, as writers such as Herman Melville and popular-culture depictions of sailors made a mark on the public mind. Whales and their by-products became one of the most important engines of capitalist development—by the middle of the 19th century, whaling was the fifth-largest industry in the United States.

- Why do you think American culture was so fascinated with whaling if it was just another capitalist industry?
- Compare and contrast how whaling and butter making contributed to the growth of the market economy.

When Black Hawk tried to surrender, the militia fired on him, but Indian warriors fought them off. Secretary of War **Lewis Cass** ordered federal troops to reinforce the Illinois militia and some Sioux allies. The combined force, including future national leaders Zachary Taylor, Jefferson Davis, and Abraham Lincoln, pursued Black Hawk into Wisconsin territory. An August battle at the Bad Axe River ended with most of

BATTLE OF BAD AXE RIVER, 1832   This painting depicts the 1832 Battle of Bad Axe River, where Sac and Fox followers of Black Hawk were brutally defeated, ending the Black Hawk War. Black Hawk, a Sac leader who had fought with Tecumseh's Pan-Indian forces in the War of 1812, led a movement to reclaim land in Illinois in 1832; but the defeat and his subsequent capture ended the movement.

Black Hawk's band (including women and children) being shot, despite the display of a white surrender flag. Black Hawk himself sought refuge with Winnebago Indians, who subsequently turned him over to American authorities.

The treaties that ended the short Black Hawk War ceded additional Sac, Fox, and Winnebago land to the United States. After serving a year in prison, Black Hawk published a popular autobiography and toured the country, where most observers treated him as a symbol of what they believed to be a defeated and doomed Native American race. In the next decade, many Sac and Fox people would be removed further west, as their economic prospects diminished.

STUDY QUESTIONS FOR ECONOMIC OPPORTUNITY AND TERRITORIAL EXPANSION

1. What factors drove Anglo colonization of Texas?
2. How was the market economy different in the West than in the Northeast and the Southeast?

◼ EXPANDING MARKETS

In the 1820s and 1830s, market activity in the United States expanded even more rapidly than it had in the preceding decades, and the United States played an increasing role in the transoceanic world economy. The market economy that built up in the 1790s entered a new phase of development as it spread and enriched the United States. Although not yet on par with major world economic powers, the United States began to undergo its own version of the Industrial Revolution that was transforming western Europe. Although President Jackson and his opponents disagreed about funding for internal improvements, almost every U.S. politician supported economic development of some kind. Even organizations such as the New York Tract Society that argued against the evils of the market economy spread their message through mass-produced pamphlets and used the roads, mail systems, and technologies promoted by capitalist growth to get their message across. By 1830, the world of markets influenced the everyday lives of more and more Americans.

The Legal Structures of Capitalism

In the 1810s and early 1820s, the U.S. Supreme Court delivered several rulings that encouraged federal involvement in commerce and the rise of the business corporation—one of the major financial tools of capitalist development. John Marshall, a proponent of economic activity, guided decisions that encouraged capitalist development during the last years of his long tenure as Chief Justice. Between 1825 and 1835, however, Marshall's Supreme Court came under withering attacks by Jacksonian politicians who accused it of "judicial tyranny," claiming that the court encouraged the same kind of elitist economic power as the Second Bank of the United States. Jackson was able to appoint three associate justices, who took an active role as Chief Justice Marshall became increasingly infirm in his old age. Although on the defensive, Marshall managed to promote the federal control of commerce, which he had advocated in 1824 in *Gibbons v. Ogden*. Marshall also wrote the opinion in *Craig v. Missouri* (1834), which invalidated a law that had allowed Missouri to issue its own paper money.

When John Marshall died in 1835, Andrew Jackson seized the opportunity to put the Supreme Court firmly in the hands of his Democratic supporters. Jackson appointed his Maryland ally, Roger B. Taney, as Chief Justice in 1836, and, the following year, he was able to appoint two more justices, leaving the old Marshall nationalists in the minority. Although Taney supported economic development, he favored less federal intervention than Marshall had. Ruling in the 1837 case of *Charles River Bridge v. Warren Bridge*, Taney had the chance to make his legal mark early in his first term as Chief Justice. Writing for the majority, Taney ruled that the 1785 Massachusetts charter for the private Charles River Bridge had not guaranteed exclusive rights and that courts should not be overly involved in matters of economic development better left to state legislatures. Taney wrote that new technologies and transportation improvements should be allowed to take their course; as "the object and end of all government is to promote the happiness and prosperity of the community by which it is established," local governments would best know how to encourage growth. Taney's rival on the court, Justice Joseph Story, wrote a blistering dissent charging that the decision allowed the interference with sacred corporate rights. But Taney had deftly supported economic modernization while also preserving a narrow interpretation of federal power that pleased Democrats and helped to alienate the newly forming Whig party.

The Inland Empire

The completion of the Erie Canal indicated just how state governments could invest in the growth of the market economy. When the federal government refused to participate in the project to connect Lake Erie to the Atlantic, New York State funded it entirely. New York governor **DeWitt Clinton** ceremonially broke ground for the project in 1817.

Detractors, who doubted the value of the project, dubbed the canal "Clinton's Big Ditch." Defying critics, the canal was completed in less than 10 years. At the opening of the Erie Canal in 1825, Clinton poured a ceremonial cask of Lake Erie water into the Atlantic Ocean and declared, "May the God of Heavens and the Earth smile . . . and render it subservient to the best interests of the human race."

The Erie Canal was the world's largest canal at the time, and it contained several impressive feats of engineering—largely constructed by Irish immigrant laborers. The 363-mile-long, four-foot-deep canal contained aqueducts and locks that allowed traffic to flow smoothly over ravines and rivers, and it could carry boats each loaded with 50 tons of freight pulled by horses or mules walking alongside the canal. The canal also carried steamboats and passenger traffic. Each of the cities along the canal—Buffalo, Rochester, Syracuse, Utica, and Albany—experienced exponential growth and quickly became a commercial center. Moreover, the canal ensured that New York City would continue to grow as the major U.S. Atlantic trading port. One contemporary commentator noted that what "Europe already begins to admire, America can never forget to acknowledge, that they have built the longest canal in the world in the least time, with the least experience, for the least money, and to the greatest public benefit." The Erie Canal quickly became a symbol of American economic prosperity and ingenuity.

The Industrial Revolution

Americans declared the Erie Canal to be the greatest in the world because they were increasingly interested in their place in the world economy. Any accomplishment that

THE ERIE CANAL CELEBRATION   This painting by French artist Anthony Imbert shows the gathering of boats celebrating the completion of the Erie Canal, one of the most impressive engineering and transportation achievements in the world at the time. Note the range of international flags represented on the boats assembled to celebrate the connecting of Lake Erie to the Atlantic Ocean.

exceeded those of Europe seemed to be a special point of pride. As the Industrial Revolution in England rapidly expanded textile-producing towns, scores of agricultural workers moved from farm labor into factory work, and for the first time ever England became a net importer of food products—many of them grown in the United States. In 1830, American workers enjoyed 40 percent higher wages than their counterparts in England. The global labor market seemed to favor colonies and former colonies, with American and Canadian factory workers earning higher wages than many comparable workers in Europe. The total American economy remained smaller than most in Western Europe, even though the country expanded rapidly between 1789 and 1832.

As part of the early Industrial Revolution, Americans especially excelled at textile production because it combined their agricultural system, talent for mechanization, and the rapid adoption of new technologies. As one historian explained it, "The cotton industry . . . became in the process of development the great vehicle of a market economy." In 1831, the United States contained almost 700 textile firms that operated 1.2 million cotton spindles and 33,500 mechanized looms. The woolen industry was only one-quarter the size. Before 1830, France and England both consumed large quantities of American cotton, which fed European industrialization. Although working conditions in the United States were generally more comfortable than in England, the high level of child labor and the deteriorating conditions in some mills meant that greater labor woes would soon follow.

The Industrial Revolution in England helped to transform world markets and increase the importance of wage labor and technology—and as the United States began an Industrial Revolution of its own, it contributed to the first capitalist global transformation. Both Northern and Southern American industries were enmeshed in international trade like never before. Southerners, using slave labor, grew cotton that fed mills in the Northern United States and Britain, and they participated in systems of international credit, trade, and exchange. One historian has characterized Americans as playing a crucial role in the "pan-hemispheric plantation complex." Agriculture, fueled by market activity, continued to expand in all regions of the United States. Overall, U.S. exports grew from $20 million in 1790 to $82 million in 1832. Americans' role in the market economy also turned their attention to the wider world.

The simultaneous rise of democratic participation in politics by white men in the United States helped to divide political responses to the acceleration of the U.S. market economy. Even as the United States grew more democratic than ever before and was more democratic than most other nations, market forces intensified slavery, and many Americans were left out of democratic politics. Jacksonian Democrats, who walked a fine line between encouraging economic development, as they limited federal government while touting the rights of the common man, faced a particularly challenging set of political choices as the economy continued to grow after 1830.

STUDY QUESTIONS FOR EXPANDING MARKETS

1. Where and for what reasons did Jacksonian Democrats and their opponents agree and disagree about "internal improvements?

2. How were changes in the U.S. economy related to changes in U.S. politics between 1815 and 1832?

TIMELINE 1789–1832

AMERICA	YEAR	THE WORLD
Samuel Slater immigrates to United States from England **Jul** Congress passes first tariff in the United States **Sep** Congress creates U.S. Postal Service	**1789**	
Samuel Slater and Moses Brown found the first mechanized cotton mill in United States **Apr** Congress establishes U.S. Patent Office and 14-year monopolies on inventions **Aug** Congress votes to fund the U.S. national debt	**1790**	First rolling mill powered by steam in England
Alexander Hamilton sends report encouraging domestic manufacturing to Congress	**1791**	Paris Academy of Sciences standardizes metric system
Apr Congress establishes U.S. currency system	**1792**	
Jan Eli Whitney demonstrates interchangeable parts by assembling a musket from pieces selected from a pile by President Thomas Jefferson **May** Congress encourages U.S. settlement with favorable sales terms in Harrison Land Act	**1800**	Italian Alessandro Volta invents the electric storage battery
Treasury Secretary Albert Gallatin proposes a comprehensive plan of national canals and roads **Jul** 12th Amendment to Constitution is ratified	**1804**	
Frederic Tudor uses insulated ships to begin U.S. ice trade abroad	**1805**	
Aug Robert Fulton begins commercial steamboat service on the Hudson River	**1807**	British colonies of Sierra Leone and Gambia founded **Mar** British ejected from Alexandria, Egypt
Oliver Evans installs first steam-powered flour mill in Pittsburgh **Mar** Supreme Court decides in *Fletcher v. Peck* that contracts are sacred and that court can overrule state laws	**1810**	Hidalgo's "Grito de Dolores" launches Mexican independence war Frenchman François Appert invents canning process to preserve food
	1811	Workers in the Luddite movement riot and destroy textile machinery British suffrage activists found Hampden Clubs
Boston Associates incorporate their mill business in Waltham, MA	**1814**	Two-sided cylindrical printing press invented in Germany *London Times* begins publication using steam press
Jul Construction on Erie Canal begins	**1817**	British workers riot for higher wages in Derbyshire **Sep** Spain opens West Indies to British trade

Summary
- Between 1789 and 1832, the United States underwent what some historians call a "market revolution," and a capitalist economy took shape.
- Economic changes and mechanization altered American social relationships.
- By the 1820s, U.S. politics were becoming increasingly democratic by opening up suffrage and political participation to almost all white men.

May Vessel *Savannah* uses backup steam power to cross Atlantic	**1819**	British establish colony at Singapore Parliament passes maximum 12-hour work day for children in Britain
Congress sets minimum price of $1.25 for sale of public lands	**1820**	
William Becknell opens trade from Missouri to New Mexico on Santa Fe Trail **Sep** Russia claims exclusive settlement rights in AK	**1821**	Costa Rica wins independence **Mar** Greek war of independence begins
Mar Supreme court decides case of *Gibbons v. Ogden* **Dec** When electoral college reveals its votes, no presidential candidate receives a majority	**1824**	Joseph Aspdin patents Portland cement in England
Feb House of Representatives elects John Quincy Adams President **Mar** President Adams appoints Henry Clay as Secretary of State, part of what their enemies dub "the corrupt bargain" **Jun** Britain cuts off U.S. trade to its colonies in the West Indies **Oct** Erie Canal is opened with great ceremony	**1825**	**Sep** First ever passenger railroad opens in England
May Congress passes a trade tax, called by opponents the "Tariff of Abominations" **Dec** Andrew Jackson is elected President South Carolina legislature protests "Tariff of Abominations"	**1828**	**Sep** Shaka, Zulu king, is assassinated
	1829	**Sep** Mexico outlaws slavery in Texas, but exempts Stephen Austin's colony
Baltimore & Ohio Railroad becomes first U.S. railroad to carry passengers and freight Mexico forbids further colonization of Texas by American citizens	**1830**	English patent for push lawnmower issued
Cyrus McCormick builds first mechanical reaper, making crops much easier to harvest	**1831**	Scotswoman Jane Stewart invents hook-and-eye clothing fastener
Jan Second Bank of the United States president Nicholas begins "The Bank War" with President Jackson Sac and Fox Indians return to vacated lands in Illinois, touching off Black Hawk War **Aug** Black Hawk's Indians are destroyed in battle on Bad Axe River **Dec** Andrew Jackson reelected president	**1832**	First French passenger railroad opens

- U.S. citizens had economic interest in Western territories—which led to open trade, colonization of Texas, and warfare with several Indian groups.
- By the 1820s and 1830s, the United States was part of a new system of world markets, especially influenced by the early industrial revolution in Western Europe.

Key Terms and People

American System *328*

Arkwright, Richard *331*

Austin, Moses *345*

Austin, Stephen *345*

Becknell, William *346*

Benton, Thomas Hart *344*

Biddle, Nicholas *344*

Black Hawk *348*

Brown, Moses *336*

Calhoun, John C. *343*

Cass, Lewis *349*

Clinton, DeWitt *351*

Crawford, William *342*

Fitch, John *332*

Fulton, Robert *332*

Gallatin, Albert *333*

Keokuk *348*

Livingston, Robert *332*

Maysville Road Bill *344*

McCormick, Cyrus *331*

Polk, James K. *344*

Slater, Samuel *331*

Taney, Roger B. *344*

tariff *333*

Van Buren, Martin *342*

Watt, James *332*

Whitney, Eli *331*

Reviewing Chapter 10

1. How did the market changes in the United States after 1789 continue economic developments that had begun during the colonial period?
2. How did the transformation to a market economy increase tensions between equality and inequality in U.S. society?
3. What were the most important global influences on the U.S. economy?

Further Reading

Bernstein, Peter L. *Wedding the Waters: The Erie Canal and the Making of a Great Nation*. New York: W.W. Norton, 2005. This book offers an engaging narrative of the construction and success of the Erie Canal and argues that it was one of the most important achievements of the century, not only technically but because it helped to unite the East and West and to tie the United States to European trade.

Dolin, Eric Jay. *Leviathan: The History of Whaling in America*. New York: W.W. Norton, 2007. This book charts over three hundred years of the history of American whaling. In addition to presenting gripping tales of whaling voyages, Dolin shows how whaling led to New England's economic growth and helped to connect the United States to the rest of the world through an extensive trade network.

Deyle, Steven. *Carry Me Back: The Domestic Slave Trade in American Life*. New York: Oxford University Press, 2005. This book is an economic history of the domestic slave trade that developed after Congress outlawed the international slave trade in 1808. It shows how buying and selling slaves became an integral part of the U.S. domestic economy and involved thousands of individual slave owners in transactions that split up black families.

Jensen, Joan. *Loosening the Bonds: Mid-Atlantic Farm Women, 1750–1850*. New Haven, Conn.: Yale University Press, 1986. This is the classic account of how Mid-Atlantic farm women contributed to the growth of the U.S. market economy, especially through their dairying and butter-making activities.

Wilentz, Sean. *The Rise of American Democracy: Jefferson to Lincoln*. New York: W.W. Norton, 2005. Wilentz traces the rise of democracy in the United States in this narrative that covers the 1790s to the 1860s.

America In The World
PEOPLE, GOODS, IDEAS AND PRACTICES

CHAPTER 10: Market Revolutions and the Rise of Democracy 1789–1832

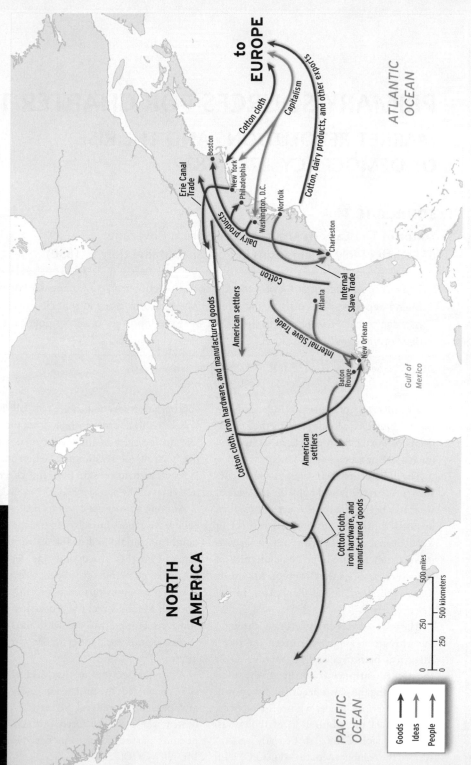

to
EUROPE

Cotton cloth

Capitalism

Cotton, dairy products, and other exports

ATLANTIC
OCEAN

Boston

Erie Canal
Trade

New York

Philadelphia

Washington, D.C.

Norfolk

Dairy products

Charleston

Cotton

American settlers

Internal
Slave Trade

Atlanta

Internal Slave Trade

New Orleans

Baton
Rouge

Gulf of
Mexico

Cotton cloth, iron hardware, and manufactured goods

American
settlers

Cotton cloth,
iron hardware, and
manufactured goods

NORTH
AMERICA

PACIFIC
OCEAN

Goods

Ideas

People

500 miles

500 kilometers

0   250

0   250

PRIMARY SOURCES FOR CHAPTER 10

MARKET REVOLUTIONS AND THE RISE OF DEMOCRACY, 1789–1832

SOURCE 10.1

Editor of The Eastern Argus, Excerpts from Coverage of Fourth of July Celebrations in Portland, Maine (July 9, 1830)

The editor of *The Eastern Argus,* the Democratic-Republican newspaper in Portland, Maine, reported on Fourth of July celebrations that took place in that city in 1830 in partisan terms. Newspapers in the 1830s were an important organ of political party development and organization.

Source: The Eastern Argus, July 9, 1830.

The Anniversary of American Independence was celebrated on Monday last, by the Republicans of Portland, in a style never equaled upon a like occasion in this State.

The illiberal and disingenuous course pursued in advance of the day, by the mangers of what has been called the *Town Celebration*, aroused a proper sense of self respect in Republicans, who resolved spontaneously, as it were, not to submit to the indignity of it. . . . Preparations were consequently made for a celebration among themselves, in self defence. . . .

The inside was tastefully decorated throughout with green boughs, evergreen and roses, historical paintings and engravings. Over the arched entrance from the street, stood erect, during the day, a beautiful, full grown, living American Eagle, whose fine appearance excited the admiration of thousands. Upon the face of the arch beneath, was inscribed the republican motto—VOX POPULI! On the inner side surrounded by other appropriate decorations, were two full rigged vessels in miniature suspended from the arch, and on the sides of the walk beneath were the portraits of Washington, Jefferson, and Jackson, as if to preside over and cheer the festivities of the occasion. . . .

At noon a procession was formed. . . . We believe we expose ourselves to the contradiction of no candid and disinterested man, in saying that this procession was decidedly the most numerous ever witnessed in this town, on any previous occasion. In passing through Middle Street the procession for the "town celebration" was met with, and the two parties passed each other under a military salute. . . .

After the services at the Meeting-house were concluded, the procession re-organized and passed up Federal Street . . . to the bower, where five hundred and sixty eight persons partook of a dinner, provided by Mr. ATWOOD. . . .

[Toasts were then given.]

By Gen. J. W. Smith, Vice President, *Those sacred Democratic principles of the party,* which in 1801 called forth the immortal Jefferson, and in 1829, the hero and illustrious patriot Jackson, to preside over this great and happy republic. . . .

By Doct. B. H. Mace. V. P. *The Democracy of New Hampshire*—Founded on a rock—Firm as the *Hills,* its pillars stand unmoved. . . .

By Mr. Daniel Robinson, V. P. *Andrew Jackson, President of the United States*—May he live to a good old age, for the benefit of the rising generation. . . .

By Hon. Wm. Chadwick. *The Hon'ble John Anderson, our Representative in Congress*—His untiring industry and successful exertions in behalf of our commercial interests, justly entitle him to the warmest gratitude of his constituents. . . .

By Hon. Luther Fitch. *The Fourth of July*—The anniversary of American Independence—the time to revert to the essential principles of the republic—to impress them upon the mind and the heart, that they may never be forgotten or abandoned.

WORKING WITH SOURCES

1. How did this celebration seek to link Portland's Democratic Republicans to the glory of America's past?

2. What were the partisan elements of the celebration? Which parts seemed to be purely patriotic?

SOURCE 10.2

William Sampson, Excerpts from People v. Melvin in Defense of the New York Journeymen Shoemakers (1809)

Attorney William Sampson, a Jacobin émigré from France, defended New York's journeyman shoemakers when they were prosecuted in 1809 for illegally colluding to go on strike and win a wage increase. In this case, called *People v. Melvin,* Sampson made an eloquent speech that argued that the journeymen deserved a fair chance in the changing market economy.

Source: John R. Commons, Ulrich B. Phillips, Eugene A. Gilmore, Helen L. Sumner, and John B. Andrews, eds., *Documentary History of American Industrial Society,* vol. 3 (Cleveland, OH: Arthur H. Clark Company, 1910), 279–80, 299–300.

Shall all others, except only the industrious mechanic, be allowed to meet and plot; merchants to determine their prices current, or settle the markets, politicians to electioneer, sportsmen for horseracing and games, ladies and gentlemen for balls, parties and bouquets; and yet those poor men be indicted for combining against starvation? I ask again, is this repugnant to the rights of man? If it be, is it not repugnant to our constitution? If it be repugnant to our constitution, is it law? And if it is not law, shall we be put to answer to it?

If it be said, they have wages enough, or too much already, I do not think any man a good witness to that point but one who has himself laboured. If either of the gentlemen opposed to us will take his station in the garret or cellar of one of these industrious men, get a leather apron and a strap, a last, a lap-stone and a hammer, and peg and stitch from five in the morning till eight in the evening, and feed and educate his family with what he so earns, then if he will come into court, and say upon his corporal oath that he was, during that probation too much pampered or indulged, I will consider whether these men may not be extortioners. . . .

Like most other societies of the same nature, the journeymen shoemakers' society is a charitable institution.

They raise a fund, which is sacred to the use of their helpless or unfortunate members, and to the relief of the widows and orphans of their departed brethren. . . . And to induce every one to join the society, while by his labour he may make something to spare for their fund, they refuse to work with any one who is so wanting in charity as not to join them. . . . Who will say that an association of this nature is illegal? . . . The masters were in the habit of crowding their shops with more apprentices than they could instruct. Two was thought as many as one man could do justice by. The journeymen shoemakers therefore determined to set their faces against the rapacity of the masters, and refused to work for those who were so unjust as to delude with the promise of instruction which it was impossible they could give. . . .

It is to be observed, that neither of these counts charge that the design of the defendants was to raise their wages. And though it should be admitted that a conspiracy to raise their wages would subject the defendants to an indictment, yet I doubt if any authority can be found to support an indictment for charges like these.

WORKING WITH SOURCES

1. What is the basis for Sampson's defense of the journeymen shoemakers?

2. Does this document show evidence that the journeymen were developing a sense of belonging to a working class that was separate from the master craftsmen for whom they worked?

SOURCE 10.3

Basil Hall, Excerpts from Travels in North America in the Years 1827 and 1828 (1829)

In 1829, Basil Hall, a British Naval officer from a Scottish aristocratic family, published a book recounting his travels in North America in the previous two years. In this selection, Hall describes parts of upstate New York and western Massachusetts, where he met people with many ideas about how to improve American transportation and trade.

Source: Basil Hall, *Travels in North America in the Years 1827 and 1828*, vol. 2 (Edinburgh: Cadell and Co., 1829), 93–94, 100–101.

On the 3d of October, 1827, we left Stockbridge, and proceeded across the country to Northampton, another of those beautiful New England villages, which it is impossible to overpraise. Our road was conducted through ravines, over mountain passes, and occasionally along the very summit of ridges, from whence we commanded a view of sufficient beauty to redeem, in the course of one morning, all the flatness and insipidity of our previous journey. The greater part, indeed, of the country which we had yet seen—always, of course, excepting the beautiful Lake George, and delightful Hudson—consisted either of ploughed fields, or impenetrable forests, or it was spotted over with new villages, as raw and unpicturesque as if they had just stepped out of a saw-pit. The towns of Massachusetts, on the contrary, were embellished with ornamental trees and flower gardens, while the larger features of the landscape owed their interest to the more vigorous accompaniments of rocks, mountains, waterfalls, and all the varied lights and shades of Alpine scenery.

In the course of this agreeable day's journey, we traversed a considerable portion of the route over which it has been seriously proposed, I was assured, to carry a rail-road between the cities of Boston and Albany. No single State, still less any Section of the Union, it seems, likes to be outdone by any other State; and this feeling of rivalry, stimulated by the success of the great Erie Canal—is an undertaking highly favoured by nature—has, I supposed suggested the visionary project in question. In answer to the appeals frequently made to my admiration of this scheme, I was compelled to admit, that there was much boldness in the conception; but I took the liberty of adding, that I conceived the boldness lay in the conception alone; for, if it were executed, its character would be changed into madness.

Albany and Boston lie nearly east and west of each other; while much of the intermediate space is so completely ribbed over by a series of high ridges running north and south, that the rail-way in question would have to pass along a sort of gigantic corduroy road, over a country altogether unsuited for such an undertaking. Besides which, several navigable rivers, and more than one canal, lying along the intermediate valleys, connect the interior with the sea, and thus afford far readier means of exporting or importing goods to or from New York, Albany, or Boston, than any rail-way can ever furnish.

The same reasoning might be applied to a hundred other projects in the United States, many of them not less impracticable, but which, although existing only on paper, are, nevertheless assumed completed, and cast into the balance of American greatness, till the imaginary scale, loaded with anticipated magnificence, makes the Old World kick the beam, to the great satisfaction of the inhabitants of this country, and the admiration of distant lands, who know nothing of the matter. . . .

At Worcester I met a remarkably intelligent person, with whom I fell into conversation on the subject of manufactures, and the measure which was then in agitation, and has since been carried, of protecting, as it is called, the domestic industry of that country by a new Tariff, or higher scale of duties on imported goods.

He contended that the manufactures of New England in particular, but also those of other parts of the Union, had grown up during the late war, when foreign goods were excluded, and had been enabled to flourish, more or less, ever since, in consequence of the protecting duties laid on foreign articles by the General Government.

WORKING WITH SOURCES

1. Hall claims that Europeans are overly awed by American transportation and manufacturing, yet he seems impressed himself. Why?

2. How do Hall's observations offer evidence both of states working together to implement internal improvements and of jealousies between states?

SOURCE 10.4

Andrew Jackson, Veto of the Bank of the United States (July 10, 1832)

When Andrew Jackson vetoed the reauthorization of the charter of the Second Bank of the United States in July 1832, he issued this message to explain his actions. Jackson later backed up his veto by withdrawing all federal funds from the bank and eventually triumphed in his political war with Nicholas Biddle, the bank's president.

Source: Francis Newton, ed., *The Statesmanship of Andrew Jackson as Told in His Writings and Speeches* (New York: Tandy-Thomas Company, 1909), 155–76.

A bank of the United States is in many respects convenient for the Government and useful to the people. . . . I sincerely regret that in the act before me I can perceive none of those modifications of the bank charter which are necessary, in my opinion, to make it compatible with justice, with sound policy, or with the Constitution of our country. . . .

Every monopoly and all exclusive privileges are granted at the expense of the public, which ought to receive a fair equivalent. The many millions which this act proposes to bestow on the stockholders of the existing bank must come directly or indirectly out of the earnings of the American people. . . .

It is to be regretted that the rich and powerful too often bend the acts of government to their selfish purposes. Distinctions in society will always exist under every just government. Equality of talents, of education, or of wealth can not be produced by human institutions. In the full enjoyment of the gifts of Heaven and the fruits of superior industry, economy, and virtue, every man is equally entitled to protection by law; but when the laws undertake to add to these natural and just advantages artificial distinctions, to grant titles, gratuities, and exclusive privileges, to make the rich richer and the potent more powerful, the humble members of society—the farmers, mechanics, and laborers—who have neither the time nor the means of securing like favors to themselves, have a right to complain of the injustice of Government. There are no necessary evils in government. Its evils exist only in its abuses. . . .

Nor is our Government to be maintained or our Union preserved by invasions of the rights and powers of the several States. In thus attempting to make our General Government strong we make it weak. Its true strength consists in leaving individuals and States as much as possible to themselves—in making itself felt, not in its power, but in its beneficence; not in its control, but in its protection; not in binding the States more closely to the center, but leaving each to move unobstructed in its proper orbit. . . .

I have now done my duty to my country. If sustained by my fellow-citizens, I shall be grateful and happy; if not, I shall find in the motives which impel me ample grounds for contentment and peace. In the difficulties which surround us and the dangers which threaten our institutions there is cause for neither dismay or alarm. For relief and deliverance let us firmly rely on that kind of Providence which I am sure watches with peculiar care over the destinies of our Republic, and on the intelligence and wisdom of our countrymen.

WORKING WITH SOURCES

1. What were Jackson's main objections to the bank charter?

2. What can you tell about Jackson's idea of democracy based upon his objections to the bank?

New Boundaries, New Roles

11

In early 1836, reports surfaced in the United States that a mixed band of American and Mexican separatists had been killed down to the last man in the defense of an old mission compound in San Antonio, Texas, called the "**Alamo**." Led by the Anglo Sam Houston and the Hispanic Lorenzo de Zavala, the Texas independence movement brought together a diverse group united by their opposition to receiving orders from remote Mexico City. Former Mississippi governor John A. Quitman led some of the many Americans who supported the independence movement. Quitman crossed the Sabine River into Mexico with 17 men and the confidence that he fought for freedom. "If I must die early, let me die with these brave fellows and for such a cause," he proclaimed. Quitman and his band joined Houston's army and helped Texas declare its independence from Mexico. U.S. president Andrew Jackson, serving out the last of his tumultuous eight years, did not interfere with Quitman or the other Americans who crossed the border to fight against Mexico, even though their actions clearly violated American neutrality laws.

Less than a year after Quitman helped separate Texas from Mexico, a different American invasion generated a much different presidential response. In the wake of "Patriot Uprisings" in Upper and Lower Canada (today's Ontario and Quebec), Canadian rebels retreated across the U.S. border into Northern cities such as Rochester, Buffalo, and Detroit. During 1837, thousands of Americans joined these Canadian separatists fighting the British, just as Americans had joined

< *Emigrants Crossing the Plains* by Albert Bierstadt, 1867.

Texans fighting the Mexicans. In December 1837, the U.S.-born Rennselaer Van Rennselaer led a small group of men across the Niagara river to establish a beachhead for the return of a well-known Canadian rebel; but Jackson's successor as president, Martin Van Buren, dealt aggressively with this group of American adventurers. Van Buren issued a proclamation denouncing the actions, alerted customs agents and U.S. marshals along the border, and eventually sent General Winfield Scott to manage relations in the region. Despite the heavy military presence, Canadian Patriots and their American supporters coordinated attacks along the border throughout the year. Pressed by armies on both sides, the men went underground in early 1838, but sporadic attacks occurred into 1841.

Neither the Texas nor the Canadian episodes received official government support, but Jackson's hands-off approach offered implicit support for the former. Mexico had only recently freed itself from Spanish control and many Americans viewed it as a weak neighbor, ripe for American conquest. Texas independence angered the Mexicans and America's harboring of Canadian rebels angered the British. In both situations, America negotiated solutions that demonstrated its rising status as a continental power but also one that remained loose at the seams.

◼ AN EXPANDING NATION

The three decades of peace following the War of 1812 gave Americans an opportunity to consolidate the territory that had been won permanently from the British. But even as settlers pushed west and traders sailed around the world, American control of the land within the boundaries of the original colonies remained incomplete, underscored by the extensive Cherokee and Creek landholdings in Georgia. Two substantial obstacles blocked American expansion west of the Mississippi River: Mexican control of most of today's Southwest and the presence of substantial numbers of Native Americans. West of the Mississippi, the United States claimed only a few military forts strung out across a vast expanse of plains and mountain territory controlled by a variety of Indian communities. Intermingled with the Western Indians lived tens of thousands of Spanish-speaking residents, most born while Spain still ruled the region. Anglo settlers who headed west into this landscape embodied the dynamism of the era. At the same time, many other Americans moved against their will, including enslaved people moved from Eastern states to the emerging cotton belt and Indians removed from the Southeast to Oklahoma. A growing population and a robust economy encouraged the United States to expand, but that expansion created new problems. Military difficulties arose as the settlers and explorers encountered people with existing claims to the land; political problems developed as leaders wrestled with whether the United States should follow the pattern of previous empires; and cultural conflicts grew as the country sought to incorporate people of widely different backgrounds into an already diverse nation.

Andrew Jackson and the Trail of Tears

Strong native communities stood opposed to the United States in the East as well. In the Southeast alone, the Cherokee, Choctaw, Chickasaw, Seminole, and Creek counted

75,000 members compared to 330,000 white people and 230,000 black people in the region in 1820. Illinois, Wisconsin, and Michigan likewise included large numbers of native peoples. The state and federal governments worked sometimes in cooperation and other times at odds with each other to push Indians farther to the west. Andrew Jackson came to the presidency strongly opposed to the presence of Indians in territory that could be profitably settled by whites and strongly opposed to the practice of the federal government negotiating with Indians as equals. As early as 1817, Jackson had described "treaties with the Indians as an absurdity." Born in the Carolina backcountry during the Revolutionary period, when native peoples contested U.S. borders, Jackson matured in Tennessee when that state was still inhabited by them. From his earliest encounters he developed a strong antagonism toward those he regarded as "blood thirsty barbarians." Jackson sought "to reclaim them [Indians] from their wandering habits and make them a happy, prosperous people," and

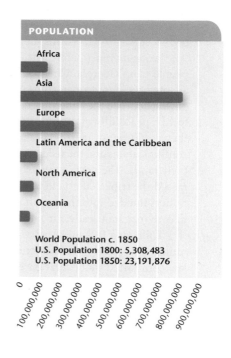

POPULATION

Africa

Asia

Europe

Latin America and the Caribbean

North America

Oceania

World Population c. 1850
U.S. Population 1800: 5,308,483
U.S. Population 1850: 23,191,876

THE CHEROKEE REMOVAL   The forced removal of Indians by the U.S. government created a demographic and historical catastrophe for Indian communities. Cherokee removal, represented here, began in the winter and imposed physical hardships as it alienated Indian people from their ancestral homelands.

as president he used the executive power to force this policy on Indians across the country. Most Anglo-Americans supported his policies.

Jackson's most public battle with Indians resulted from the expulsion of Cherokee people from Georgia. Cherokees, the largest native community in the Southeast, had adapted to American customs more than neighboring tribes. According to the treaties passed between the tribe and the federal government, the good faith efforts of Cherokees to live peacefully and productively alongside their American neighbors ensured that they could retain their land and their autonomy. But as new Anglo settlers generated conflicts, states and the federal government steadily increased pressure on Indians to sell their lands. The government of Georgia, where most Cherokee landholdings lay, harassed the tribe. After gold was discovered on Cherokee-controlled land in 1829, white miners flooded into the region. With their numbers nearing 10,000, they had the clout to convince state leaders to seek the complete expulsion of the tribe.

Following Jackson's lead, Congress passed the **Indian Removal Act of 1830**, which nullified 50 years' worth of treaties between the United States and many tribes. The law committed the federal government to creating an Indian Territory in present-day Oklahoma and to moving Indians by force into this new region. Cherokees, well-educated and protective of their treaty rights, vigorously resisted. Cherokee leaders sought legal protection against Georgia laws that asserted authority over the tribe. In a series of seminal cases, the Supreme Court, led by Chief Justice John Marshall, declared the Cherokee, like all recognized Indian tribes, "domestic dependent nations." Marshall intended this description to establish the sovereignty of tribes in relation to state governments, although not in relation to the federal government. In the 1832 *Worcester v. Georgia* decision, the court ruled against Georgia's claim that it held authority over the tribe, but the state and federal government ignored the ruling. Without recourse to the army, which could have protected Indian lands from settler encroachment, Marshall could not enforce the decision.

Under Georgia's protection, white settlers continued to move into Cherokee territory in the early 1830s. In 1835, the federal government negotiated a new treaty with a minority group of Cherokee. This new agreement exchanged all Cherokee claims to land in the East for claims in Indian Territory and a cash settlement. When U.S. forces arrived in early 1838, few Cherokee had prepared for the trip, and soldiers rounded up and confined people over the summer. Contaminated water, inadequate food, and disease killed many of those restricted in stockades; and many more perished on the 800-mile journey west. Estimates of fatalities connected with the "**Trail of Tears**," as Indians referred to the forced march, range from 4,000 to 8,000 (Map 11.1). The blatant violation of property rights backed by clear title to the land worried many white citizens, even those who disliked Indians. Davy Crockett, the legendary frontiersman, lost his congressional seat for opposing Jackson's policy. The violence and trauma of the forced march to the new Western lands created more political enemies for Jackson and a shameful legacy for the American government. Reformers, especially in New England, had protested the Indian Removal Act, and reports of the expulsion and death of so many Cherokees added new urgency to their calls for a more humane Indian policy.

While Jackson and white Georgians were expelling Cherokees from the northern reaches of the state, the Second Seminole War raged in the South. Instead of the Cherokee's legal maneuvering, Seminole fighters used their knowledge of the land and ecology to stymie American forces for years. In 1818, Jackson had led the U.S. Army

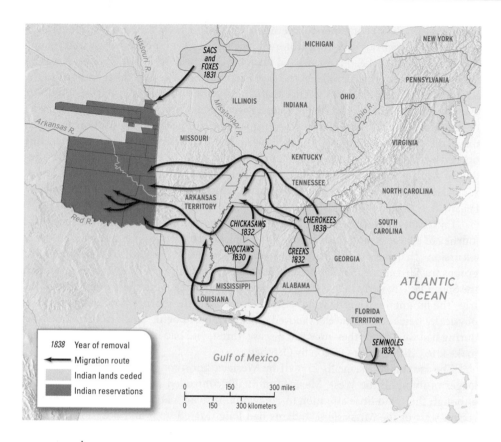

MAP 11.1 ▲ Indian Removals, 1830s This map shows the routes along which Indians were driven by the U.S. Army during the forced relocations of the 1830s. Jackson's policies moved the last large Indian communities living east of the Mississippi River into the frontier regions of the Oklahoma Territory.

during the First Seminole War, and he eagerly supported efforts to pacify the region at the end his presidency. Most of the fighting in the second conflict occurred within the Okefenokee Swamp and its hinterlands, a shifting maze of wet and dry ground that disoriented all but the most experienced soldiers. Led by Osceola, a skilled commander, Seminole fighters developed a pattern of attacking and retreating that frustrated and debilitated American troops, who also suffered disease and discomfort in the swamps. Despite the high cost to U.S. forces, the Army persevered; and by 1842, a staggering 90 percent of the Seminole community had been killed. The remaining 600 were permanently expelled into the wild region of southern Florida.

Re-Peopling the West

In the late 18th and early 19th century, settlers moved out of the Northeastern region— with a population density of 31 people per square mile—into the Midwestern territories (which held only 8 people per square mile) and farther west to the Great Plains. Few people needed to hear New York editor Horace Greeley's injunction to "go west, young man" to know that cheap land awaited them beyond the Mississippi. The result was an emigration stream that paralleled the expulsion of Cherokee and other Indians to the South, with the important difference that Anglo settlers moved voluntarily. Would-be Westerners first had to reach the Missouri River. From there, they traveled 2,000 miles to reach the Pacific shore. Between one-quarter and one-half of a million migrants made the trip between 1843 and 1870, when the first transcontinental railroad line opened and transformed the trip. Because wagons and the oxen that pulled them required a fairly easy grade and regular access to water, travelers could use only a few routes. Fur traders had pioneered these routes, which California and Oregon promoters began advertising in the mid-1830s (Map 11.2).

Emigrants moved in earnest after 1842 when news reports heralded the successful journey of a large wagon train of over 100 people. If the trip was not quite the "pleasure excursion" that the *Daily Missouri Republican* claimed, it was at least possible. Most groups traveled about 15 miles per day, leaving Missouri in early May, crossing through the South Pass in early July at 8,000 feet and only then reaching the hardest part of the trip. The mountains and the wide western rivers made the journey both dangerous and physically demanding; travelers moved quickly to avoid being stuck in the mountains during bad weather. If they survived disease, thirst, and bad weather, the settlers might make it to California or Oregon by October.

The rosy advertisements crafted by Western boosters rarely conveyed the challenges of living in the West. Mexico nominally controlled most of today's U.S. West, although they paid little attention to the region. Instead, native peoples dominated the region west of the Mississippi. Indians had long warred with and occasionally allied with the Spanish, but except for those Southwestern tribes who had to contend with a persistent Spanish presence, Plains Indians viewed each other as their most important threats. The few French traders who came through the area maintained amicable relations with native peoples to facilitate business deals. But the American settlers, who started arriving in the 1830s and then increasingly after 1841, posed a threat. Unlike the Spanish or French, these new inhabitants did not come to trade; they built farms and forts and intended to stay. Americans sometimes recognized differences within the larger native population and even established friendly relations; but generally, settlers' attitudes displayed their ignorance and fear.

In the deeper Southwest, many American settlers regarded the Mexican and Indian residents, whom they rarely distinguished, with a mix of loathing and disgust. At best, settlers treated them as obstacles to the expansion of American power in the region. An 1846 issue of the *Illinois State Register* described Mexicans in the region as "reptiles in the path of progressive democracy . . . they must either crawl or be crushed." The combination of biology and politics in the paper's explanation reflected contemporary American thinking that certain races might die out because they were "unfit" for the modern world. Few Americans demonstrated much sympathy for Indians or Mexicans displaced by settler encroachment. Ethnographers and scientists such as Harvard's Louis Agassiz added scientific weight to the biological explanation by using skull-size measurements to generate an intellectual hierarchy of the races. Agassiz's methods were hardly scientific—his data were faulty, and he failed to rigorously test and separate evidence from hypothesis—but white Americans accepted his results as natural, even inevitable.

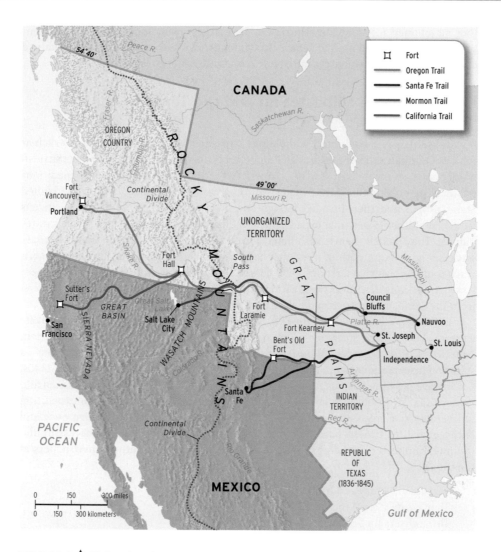

MAP 11.2 ▲ **Major Overland Trails** Western emigrants followed well-established routes across the continent. Starting at the Missouri River, the paths converged in the narrow passes through the Rocky Mountains and then diverged to head toward northern or southern towns on the Pacific Coast.

Spanish-speaking residents proved another obstacle to U.S. expansion. Mexican independence in 1821 barely affected the northern provinces of New Mexico and California. Living on Mexico's northern edge, far from the administrative center in Mexico City, these settlers maintained their largely pastoral and agricultural economy and Catholic beliefs. In 1834, Mexico had moved to reduce the power of the Catholic Church over the country by secularizing the mission lands, but this allowed elite landholders in many places to acquire still more property and social control. In some cases, especially the California territory, the ranchero elite allied themselves with Anglo settlers, but in others they maintained autonomy. In other cases, the villages created out of mission lands ensured local control and mutual dependency among the Hispanic residents, who retained control over land and resources into the 1870s despite Americans' efforts.

Latin American Filibustering and the Texas Independence Movement

As legal settlers ventured into U.S. holdings across the Mississippi, adventurers such as John A. Quitman and Rennselaer Van Rennselaer pushed south and west into the Spanish borderlands or north into Canada. Americans launched some of these expeditions while living outside the United States, but other groups organized within the United States proper and then invaded foreign soil. Between 1800 and 1860, U.S. citizens launched at least 19 separate expeditions into Spanish colonies or Latin American republics. The Spanish themselves offered mixed signals by periodically inviting Anglo settlers who took an oath of allegiance to the Spanish government into the northern reaches of their Mexico territory, even though few settlers seem to have respected these vows. Americans described these actions and the people who took them as filibusters, from the Spanish *filibustero* and before that, the Dutch term for "freebooter."

Filibusters clearly violated the U.S. Neutrality Act of 1818, which outlawed private warfare. Yet because so many people supported the cause of American expansion, Americans often regarded filibusters as heroes despite their frequent executions as spies and insurrectionaries in the countries they invaded. After tapering off in the 1840s, a new wave of filibusters pushed into Central America in the 1850s. John Quitman and Henry Maury—a southern lawyer and sea captain—recruited men for an expedition to liberate Cuba from the Spanish. William Walker—who invaded Mexico once and Nicaragua three times—became famous across America as the most successful and infamous filibuster of the age. The following poem ran in Southern newspapers at the time:

> Success to Maury and his men
> They'll safely cross the water
> Three cheers for Southern enterprise
> Hurrah for General Walker

Walker succeeded briefly in Nicaragua, occupying the post of "president" for several months in 1856, only to be expelled and later executed in Honduras. As the poem indicates, Southerners led most of the efforts in the 1850s, intending to add new slaveholding territory to the Union. As a result, filibustering in this decade became embroiled in the larger sectional conflicts over slavery.

Filibusters raised a set of questions related to American expansion and power, although few at the time considered the issue in such systematic detail. Who acted for the United States? Did privately organized ventures represent the interests of the nation? Would American expansion happen violently or peacefully? To what extent would the residents of a place be consulted before American acquisition? Did this style of expansion constitute imperialism? American leaders offered vague and shifting answers to these questions. As filibustering demonstrated, private ventures could sometimes serve as an advance guard for national expansion. Force and persuasion operated simultaneously as Americans expanded their borders.

Some historians argue that Texas should be counted as the grandest filibuster victory because so many Americans poured over the border in 1835–1836 to fight on behalf of the independence movement. But the roots of the Lone Star Republic were more complex. By 1835, two distinct groups in Texas, Tejanos (or Spanish-speaking Texans) and Texians (English-speaking Texans), both criticized Mexican misrule in its northernmost colony. Texians began the movement for Texas's independence, but many Tejanos supported it as well. By early 1836, a small group of English- and Spanish-speaking rebels retreated into an old Spanish mission in San Antonio called the Alamo. After a pitched battle lasting nearly two weeks, the Spanish forces, led by President and General **Antonio López de Santa Anna**, broke into the compound and killed all the defenders.

Despite this setback, independence forces, rallying to the cry "Remember the Alamo," defeated the main Spanish army and captured Santa Anna in fighting along the San Jacinto River a few months later. The victors issued a Texas Declaration of Independence signed by prominent Texians such as Sam Houston, a former Tennessee congressman, who became president of the new republic, and prominent Tejanos, such as Lorenzo de Zavala, who served as vice president. The success of the Texas independence movement built on widespread discontent among settlers over the failures of Spanish administration. Its most immediate changes reflected a desire to mimic its neighbor to the north. Mexico had abolished slavery in 1829, but Texas reinstated it and prohibited free blacks from residing in the new nation. The presence of a new slaveholding nation to the south worried those Northerners eager to stop the spread of slavery within the Union. Even with the exclusion of black men and women, Texas contained a diverse population. Spanish- and English-speaking communities contested for power over the next decade; and after the republic became part of the United States, Protestant Americans worried about the inclusion of so many new Catholics into the country.

Pacific Explorations

One of the hallmarks of the global ascendancy of western Europeans after 1500 was their use of the sea for warfare and trade. The Portuguese, who perfected a ship that could travel against the wind, used this new technology to begin exploring the West African coast in the mid-1400s. Spanish, English, French, and Dutch explorers soon followed, establishing direct trading links with African and then Asian peoples whose wares had only been accessible via the long overland routes across the Sahara or along the Silk Road, connecting China and the Middle East. Military expeditions often followed or accompanied the traders, although Europeans could rarely do more than provide protection to the traders who remained behind. The second wave of European exploration consisted of naturalists and ethnographers who took notes and gathered specimens on voyages across the oceans. The drafting of maps, the exhibition of plants and animals (and sometimes, of people), and the use of new ingredients in food and beverages offered evidence of European command of the globe. Americans emulated European powers by making similar expeditions.

In 1838, the U.S. Navy launched the South Seas Exploring Expedition. Lieutenant **Charles Wilkes**, a young but domineering sailor (he was court-martialed after the expedition for using excessive force against men under his command), commanded a six-ship flotilla that traveled 87,000 miles over four years of sailing (Map 11.3). Like European expeditions of earlier centuries, the American mission carried a bevy of scholars—including

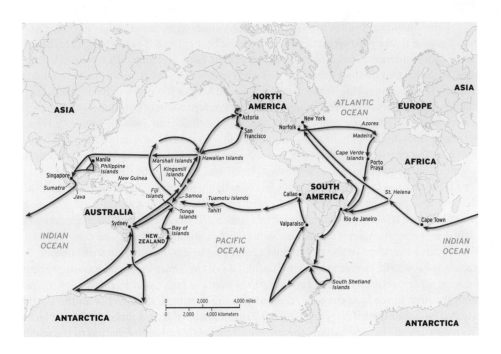

MAP 11.3 ▲ Path of the United States Exploring Expedition, 1838–1842 Navy Lieutenant Charles Wilkes led the first American circumnavigation of the globe. His flotilla included scientists who sought to map and identify places and products of interest to American traders and politicians.

naturalists, botanists, artists, and a linguistics expert—to gather information about parts of the world still quite foreign to most Americans. Wilkes traversed all the oceans except the Arctic, and naturalists collected samples everywhere the ship stopped. The 60,000 plant and bird specimens collected by scientists during the Wilkes Expedition formed the basis for the Smithsonian Institution when Congress created it a few years later.

Reflecting the growing curiosity among Americans about the rest of the world, Wilkes' reports of the trip detailed both the expedition's travels and also the history of the countries and people encountered along the way. Endorsing the common "civilizational" view, Wilkes described different countries at different levels of development depending on how closely they mirrored European attitudes and institutions. Despite his condescending attitude, especially toward people of the South Pacific, the reports contained a huge amount of descriptive material that helped U.S. residents situate themselves in the larger world. Wilkes's full circumnavigation of the globe also put the United States in a small group of modern nations whose explorers could claim to have traveled around the whole world. For Americans, the journey signaled their membership in the exclusive community of nations whose reach extended around the world. It also marked out for American businessmen and traders those places of potential interest for future investment and trade. A midshipman on Wilkes's expedition ominously anticipated the future course of interactions between Americans and those people they encountered in the Pacific: "I could not help thinking, how much better it would be to let them [the indigenes] go their own way, but No, No! We must have all the world like us, if we can."

STUDY QUESTIONS FOR AN EXPANDING NATION

1. Compare the various forms of expansion undertaken by Americans in the 1830s and 1840s. What are the similarities and differences among them?
2. What justifications did Americans offer for the dislocation of native and other long-settled peoples in areas within or adjacent to U.S. borders?

■ THE NEW CHALLENGE OF LABOR

Supporters of U.S. expansion drew a sharp distinction between the United States and Europe because they believed that the presence of "free land" ensured there could be no class system in the United States. Such boosters believed that new territory would provide space for future settlers and prevent the consolidation of land that sustained Europe's aristocracies. They worried about the social effects of the increasing economic transformations that threatened to create a working class dependent on the whims of factory owners. Nearly every American visitor to Europe's industrializing cities observed the problem. In 1845, American poet William Cullen Bryan described the poor in Edinburgh, Scotland, as "a throng of sickly-looking, dirty people . . . [a] wretched and squalid class" that according to his guide comprised more than half the city's population. The Jeffersonian ideal of a republic of free, self-sufficient farmers became even more compelling as Americans watched the changes wracking western Europe. There, industrialization produced an increasingly disaffected class of workers, and the influx of new workers and rapid technological and institutional changes in the United States in the 1830s and 1840s threatened to generate the same problems. Despite the vigorous efforts of filibusters and others, land acquisition alone did not solve the problem. The emerging industrial economy demanded workers who sold their labor as a commodity. For these men and women, the prospect of land ownership and self-sufficiency stayed forever out of reach. But laboring people in the United States, like those abroad, adopted new forms of politics and economic practice as a way to sustain the egalitarian promise of the country.

White Workers, Unions, and Class Consciousness

Building on an old European tradition, American artisans—such as bookbinders, wheelwrights, or cobblers—owned their own tools, supervised themselves (and often a team of apprentices), and enjoyed lives of respectability and modest comfort. The burgeoning use of steam power and mechanical reproduction in the early 1800s allowed factory owners to underprice and outproduce artisans. This process took several decades, but by 1830, the outlines of a new national economy had emerged. American consumers might have benefited from cheaper and more uniform goods, but skilled workers suffered. The rise of unskilled labor as a major category of work was the most

PATERSON IRON CO. PATERSON, N.J.

STEAMBOAT & RAILROAD FORGINGS.

NEW SCALE OF INDUSTRY The factories of the mid-19th century operated on a vastly larger scale than anything previously seen in early America. Industrial workers adjusted to laboring alongside a large and diverse array of individuals; but racial, ethnic, and gender differences inhibited worker organization.

visible symbol of this shift. Between 1820 and 1860, the number of factory workers in the United States increased nearly sevenfold, from 350,000 to 2 million. This transformation impacted the nation well beyond the economy, shaping politics, social relationships, and the very nature of American cities.

This period saw the rise of machine production; wherever possible, industrialists began substituting machines for the older system of handwork that had dominated production for centuries. In economic terms, artisans became wage laborers. In the process, they began selling their work to employers as they would any other good that could be bought and sold on the market. When workers struck bargains with honest employers who observed the rules of their contracts, the process of selling one's labor could appear normal and even beneficial. Some laborers maneuvered their way up the income ladder in this period, working, saving, and seizing opportunities when possible; but many more spent their lives as unskilled workers at jobs that did little more than keep them and their families barely alive. When employers did not respect contracts or used the glut of laborers as leverage to exploit the longest workday for the lowest salary, workers suffered terrible deprivation. In New York City, for instance, real wages among the city's major trades declined through the 1830s and 1840s, leaving workers' families earning only half of the $600 per year needed to support a family of four at the time. This decline hit unskilled workers hardest, who typically earned only 60 percent of a skilled workers' wages.

The first decades of the 19th century encompassed such a tangle of growth and decay, of success and failure, it resists easy summary. But most Americans at the time clearly saw the rise of a distinct American working class. For several decades after the Revolution, elites and even most artisans believed that America did not have distinct classes; but by the 1830s, few observers confused the absence of a titled aristocracy with the absence of social classes. The change had visible consequences in the Northeastern cities with the greatest industrial growth. New York, Philadelphia, and Boston all developed neighborhoods defined by class. As production moved out of the master's home or a home-based workshop, workers had less contact with the owner and his family and more contact with others in their same economic position. They lived in boarding houses and spent their leisure time with other working men in their own venues: bars, boxing arenas, and minstrel halls. In the mid-1830s, labor organizing reached a high point in many Northeastern cities, particularly among the skilled trades. New York artisans engaged in at least 35 strikes.

Skilled workers used strikes as measures of last resort, but protests over working conditions and wages pushed owners and workers further apart in the 1830s. Over the next two decades, male and female workers initiated more strikes, but usually with little effect, partly because the trade unions organizing among urban residents segregated themselves by gender, race, ethnicity, and craft. The ever-increasing pool of new workers provided a ready supply of strikebreakers for owners. In addition, the depression of 1837 made matters worse for workers. Union membership rolls dropped significantly, and pressure on workers to accept owners' demands—including lower wages—increased.

During the 1830s and 1840s, European workers and their intellectual allies urged increasingly radical solutions to their problems. Most famously, Karl Marx and Friedrich Engels issued the *Manifesto of the Communist Party*, which predicted the abolition of private property and the rise of the industrial working class to a position of political dominance. The *Manifesto*, published in 1848, expressed in print what Americans saw in the streets of Paris, Berlin, Vienna, and Budapest that year as Europe was seized by revolution. Although the 1848 Revolutions drew support from a wide range of reformers and sought political changes that Americans had already adopted (such as universal white male suffrage), most U.S. observers saw only violence and destruction. The June days, when French government forces violently suppressed a mixed force of workers and National Guard troops, epitomized the danger. One French conservative described the June days as not "a political struggle . . . but a class conflict, a sort of 'servile war,'" and this specter haunted American business and political leaders the way the Haitian Revolution haunted American slaveholders.

American workers, for their part, more closely followed the actions and the writings of English, German, and French reformers than revolutionaries. European writers and activists toured American cities in the 1830s, encouraging the formation of class-based political parties. These activists held other surprising ideas as well. Frances Wright, a Scotswoman, emerged as one of the most famous labor leaders of the day. Wright advocated free thought and women's rights, offering a vigorous critique of American inequality to thousands of rapt New Yorkers during her 1829 tour of the city. Her performance, one of the first public addresses on politics by a woman in the United States, scandalized and energized audiences in equal measure. Wright, like fellow activists Robert Dale Owen and George Henry Evans, called on American workers to use their voting power to alleviate the worst effects of industrialization. Born in England,

Evans came to the United States in 1820 and published his own papers: first the "Workingman's Advocate" and later "The Man." His papers, and the intellectual and organizational efforts of Wright, Owen, and others, inspired independent "Workingmen's Parties" in several Northeastern cities, but these parties achieved little change at the level of government policy.

Foreign-Born Workers

Some of the people who found their working lives unbearable in their home countries made their way to the United States. Between 1820 and 1860, just over five million immigrants entered the country, with nearly 95 percent coming from northwestern Europe (Figure 11.1). Although immigrants never comprised more than 2 percent of the total population in any given year, their cumulative impact grew considerably during this period. By the Civil War, the foreign born comprised 13.2 percent of the population.

Irish immigrants, mostly Catholic, composed at least a third of all those newcomers to American shores between 1820 and 1860. Many were driven by desperation produced by the "Great Hunger," as the Irish called the famine that plagued their country between 1845 and 1849. But many others came because Protestant English domination of the island's Catholic inhabitants ensured little chance for economic success. Although many immigrants found greater opportunities in the new world, American Protestants displayed strong prejudice against the Irish as well. An 1830 newspaper advertisement for domestic help in New York revealed the routine discrimination faced by many Irish immigrants: "Wanted. A Cook or Chambermaid ... must be American, Scotch, Swiss or African—no Irish." Irish immigrants tended to settle in the Northeast, and they typically came without the skills to help them succeed. As a result, the Irish

FIGURE 11.1 ▲ Immigrants, by Country or Region, 1820–1860 Northwestern Europe sent the most immigrants to the United States in the 19th century, especially during the Famine Years in Ireland. By midcentury, however, an increasingly diverse array of immigrants found their way to the United States.

took on mostly unskilled positions—in public works such as road building, in nascent factories, and in homes—and formed a substantial part of the poorest class by midcentury. Women comprised a majority of Irish immigrants at this time, which was unique for immigration patterns in the 19th century, and the lower wages paid for women's work further weakened their ability to earn enough to support themselves after the difficult and costly transatlantic journey. The influx of Irish workers allowed managers to push wages down. This economic pressure and the immigrants' Catholic faith stimulated anti-Irish riots led by native workers in the 1830s and, in the 1850s, the virulently anti-immigrant nativist movement.

German immigrants composed another 25 percent of the total immigrant flow between 1830 and 1860, but unlike the Irish, Germans emigrated in larger family groups. They tended to come from rural backgrounds and made the exodus with a strong faith in democracy and opportunity. The men who came tended to have labor skills that ensured they would not remain in unskilled positions for long, and this put them in starker competition with native-born Americans. The German women who emigrated tended to work within their homes or their own communities. Like the Germans, Scandinavian immigrants tended to move in family units; but they pushed even farther west, seeking out open land in the Midwest and Great Plains. Farming became the mainstay for these communities for the next several generations. In these sparsely settled areas in the mid-19th century, immigrants could recreate and maintain their home culture in ways that their families back in Europe could not. In an ironic twist, Scandinavian visitors to the United States in the late 19th century remarked on how traditional their American cousins appeared. America demanded national loyalty from the newcomers but little in the way of cultural assimilation. With each ethnic group free to practice its own traditions, the United States contained an increasingly diverse population as the 19th century progressed.

The New Middle Class

Even as the new immigrants struggled to secure employment, better established Americans seized opportunities to move up the income ladder. A new middle class emerged in the 1830s and 1840s, partly as a result of the rapid urban growth occurring across the nation (Figure 11.2). Members of this community lacked the wealth to live without working, but they did not perform the physical labor on which most Americans depended. What we now call "white collar" work emerged at this time. As industrial and other businesses grew larger and more complex, office workers, including clerks and accountants typically attired in cleaner "white" clothes than their working-class peers, were needed to manage the companies' information.

At 312,000 residents, New York City was the largest and wealthiest urban place in the United States in 1840, but the changes that occurred there reappeared in other cities over the next several decades. Cities provided the space for and stimulated the rise of a middle class. The anonymous nature of cities forced residents to identify and interact with one another as members of larger social or ethnic communities before they interacted as individuals. American cities, especially Northeastern ones, also generated a diversity of living conditions, from the squalid shacks of New York's Bowery to the opulent mansions along Fifth Avenue. Commercial establishments revealed the changes as well. New York, Philadelphia, and Boston soon teemed with retail establishments

BROADWAY, NEW YORK CITY   New York City led the nation in new retail districts and Broadway epitomized the allure and diversity of products and services that such areas promised the burgeoning consumer class.

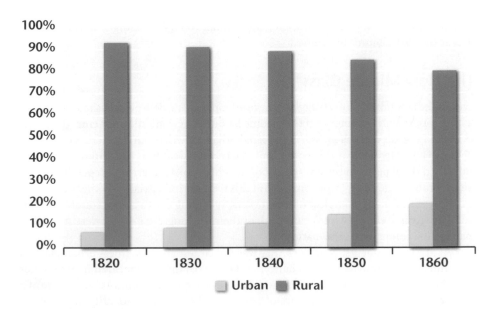

FIGURE 11.2 ▲ Urbanization, 1820–1860 Despite the increasing pace of urbanization in the United States, both the North and South remained overwhelmingly rural and agricultural at the time of the Civil War. Note: Urban areas were defined by the census as incorporated places of 2,500 or more residents.

selling a bewildering array of domestic- and foreign-produced goods. Mass-produced clothing sold best, followed by food, magazines, and books, all components of the increasingly commercialized, increasingly nationalized economy that defined the United States. The shops themselves, often several stories tall and outfitted with the latest light fixtures, paintings, and carpets, presented a new world of purchasing within which the burgeoning middle class could distinguish itself from those who bought their supplies in the small, single-room, family-run stores more common earlier in the century.

Another way rising middle-class families differentiated themselves from other Americans was by looking to Europe on questions of style in art, music, dress, and literature. Magazines from London and Paris circulated across the Atlantic, allowing Americans to associate themselves with the latest European trends. For the sons of American elites (and much more rarely, daughters), no education was complete without a "Grand Tour," an extended journey of travel and education in European cities. The necessity of anchoring themselves to the traditions of Europe revealed the anxieties that beset the middle classes in the period of transition and change in 1830s and 1840s America. At home, these concerns manifested themselves in the injunctions in advice manuals and books to avoid "confidence men and painted women"—the male and female scoundrels who exploited the anonymity and openness of the new urban places to cheat honest people out of their money and their reputations.

The Expansion of Slavery and Slaves as Workers

In contrast to the growing prominence and success of free labor in the North, white Southerners made increasingly effective use of slave labor. Thanks to **Eli Whitney**'s cotton gin, which processed picked cotton much faster than human hands could, Southern planters doubled the volume of cotton they grew each decade after 1800. As Britain and France increased their appetite for the cotton to produce the textiles that they traded around the globe, American investors saw new opportunities in the fertile lands of central Georgia, Alabama, and Mississippi. This region grew rapidly in the 1830s and 1840s, financed by the promise of high returns from cotton. But for African Americans, the cotton gin and the new Southwestern settlements promised only more generations of bondage. The high demand for labor in the region encouraged slave owners along the Atlantic seaboard to sell some of their slaves into an expanding internal slave trade. The route from Virginia and the Carolinas west and south became a Second Middle Passage, marked by the violence and hardship of forced marches and deprivation. In the 1810s, 120,000 slaves marched over the Alleghany Mountains and down the river valleys of the Deep South; by the 1830s, the number had increased to 300,000. Those who remained had to refashion their families, shorn of parents, siblings, or children, under the threat of being sold "down the river."

Many of the planters moving into the new Southwest were the sons of established slaveholders on the Eastern Seaboard. These young men typically moved ahead of their families. Slaves on the new cotton plantations worked under unusually brutal conditions. The young masters, eager to pay off debts incurred in travel and to prove themselves independent men, drove slaves through long hours of clearing land and planting crops. Without their families and the network of social institutions that occasionally checked such behavior, Southwestern masters subjected enslaved women to more sexual

Middlemen Abroad

Europe was not the only destination for interested travelers, and not all travelers toured for pleasure. A growing cadre of American merchants, missionaries, and officials began to circulate in the Pacific in the wake of Charles Wilkes's South Seas Expedition. These men joined a stream of European businessmen eager to trade for Chinese goods. Despite the linguistic and cultural differences within this group, they shared a common orientation as members of the commercial middle class—entrepreneurs from industrializing nations that sought opportunities to buy and sell in the massive and lucrative Chinese market. A marked feature of these new Western traders was their willingness to break the law to achieve high returns. One trader noted about his company's new ship that he hoped it would "make us some money . . . How, I don't care, so it is made." Because the Chinese had little interest in American goods, one of the few ways to accomplish this was through the illegal trade in opium. British merchants pioneered this practice, smuggling the drug from India or Turkey into China against the wishes of Chinese officials. American traders, such as Warren Delano (Franklin Delano Roosevelt's grandfather), entered the opium trade alongside them. The British, like the Americans, strongly discouraged the use of opium in their own countries but showed no reluctance to sell it to Asians; and both nations profited handsomely from the early global drug trade.

One of those new businessmen who enriched himself through the opium trade was Augustine Heard, born in 1795 to a prominent trading family in Ipswich, Massachusetts. By the time he was 45, Heard had made a dozen voyages to Indian and Chinese ports and many others in the Atlantic and Mediterranean. One of Heard's partners in China, George Dixwell, also drew on a distinguished New England lineage and counted doctors, businessmen, and teachers among his relatives. Dixwell's aunt cautioned him against the greed that characterized so many New England men who traveled to the Pacific. "I pray you not be over anxious about lucre," she warned him, "do not [make money] the object of your pursuit . . . it is unphilosophical, it is unchristian." No doubt Dixwell's aunt would have condemned the opium trade in even stronger terms, but the profits proved too attractive. Heard's firm, which became one of the largest American

exploitation and enslaved men to harsher punishments than in the East. Despite the higher mortality rates that accompanied relocation and life in the region, profits remained high, and so more planters flooded the area into the 1850s.

In the Upper South, most owners organized enslaved laborers as a "gang"—usually a squad of three or four men and women—and set them to work for a specified period of time (typically sunup to sundown). Under the task system, which flourished in regions dominated by staple-crop production (mostly cotton, sugar, and rice) and large landholdings, owners organized work around specific assignments. A group of workers trading enterprises in 19th-century China, gained a sure footing through trading opium in the 1840s. The results in China were devastating as addicts multiplied and drug-related crime destabilized the government.

Heard's company formed valuable relationships with opium producers and sellers in India. Kessressung Khooshalchund, a major Bombay trading firm, proved to be an important ally as the Americans contended with varieties in the quality of the drug, storage fees, competition among shippers, and Chinese anger over the drug's impact on its citizens. John Heard, Augustine's nephew, played an active role in soliciting Indian contacts and increasing the firm's commission profits. At the conclusion of a meeting with Kavaldass Luxmichund, an Indian manager for the Kessressung firm, Heard reported that Luxmichund "dipped his thumb into a dish of paint and gave me a mark on the forehead between the eyes, where . . . Hindoos wear the mark of their cast, so that I suppose I may now consider myself a baptized Hindoo. . . . He threw a heavy cashmere shawl over my shoulders, and put a diamond ring on my finger—true Oriental liberality and magnificence." This deep immersion in Asian cultures marked these rising businessmen as members of a cosmopolitan class. Their families bore the marks of their success as well. On his way home, John wondered what to do with Luxmichund's gifts because his mother and aunt already owned Indian cashmere shawls. Heard diversified his company's activities, supplying and selling tea, silk, and other Chinese goods to American companies. Most importantly, the firm established itself as a commission merchant acquiring information about the volume, quality, and price of Chinese goods and selling this information to American buyers. The shrewd diversification of Augustine Heard and Co., its willingness to engage in the drug market, and its appreciation for the global structure of modern capitalism produced real profit for its investors and an expanded sense of American commercial accomplishments for those who read about the firm in American papers.

- How does the importance of the early global drug trade challenge the traditional notion of market exchanges as benevolent or mutually beneficial?
- How would the cultural exchanges (such as the one described previously by John Heard) have shaped his or his family's perceptions of Indians?

might still function as a unit, but rather than simply laboring all day, they would be assigned a discrete unit of work to complete—so many acres of land to weed or so many pounds of cotton to pick. By allowing workers to use whatever time remained in the day after completing the task for their personal use, the task system built a small measure of incentive into slavery. Owners found the system advantageous for several reasons: slaves worked more efficiently; because slaves typically used extra time gathering or producing supplementary food for their families, owners could reduce the rations they provided; and because most slaves spent extra time with their families, it decreased the

EVOLVING HOME DESIGN   The layout of homes changed to accommodate the purchasing power of the rising middle class. "Parlors" started to appear—private but comfortable rooms in which families could display the furniture, carpets, and chandeliers that signaled their status.

likelihood that parents would run away. Even with these mercenary advantages for the owner, most enslaved people preferred the task system because it gave them at least some autonomy. Within the narrow space they carved out, slaves built stronger families and a more resilient and sustaining culture.

Another feature of the slave system provided a similar mix of dangers and opportunities for slaves: the growing rental market. As Southern cities and industries developed, urban residents rented slaves; and in other cases, corporations dominated the markets, usually because they needed labor but did not want to invest the capital to buy slaves outright (although corporate ownership of slaves also increased in the same period). Rented-out slaves sometimes lived with their temporary owners, in homes or barracks in the case of companies, but in many cases they found their own housing. Owners deducted some portion of a slave's total rental value to be applied to food and housing and gave this to the enslaved person who remained responsible for arranging for his or her own upkeep. This system benefited slaves by giving them a measure of daily autonomy from their owners although it also separated family members. It created new problems for city leaders responsible for policing slave behavior in place of absent masters. White workingmen also resented the competition from enslaved laborers.

STUDY QUESTIONS FOR THE NEW CHALLENGE OF LABOR

1. What were the effects of the increasing urbanization and industrialization in 1830s and 1840s America?

2. How did the rise of "free labor" and slavery both stabilize and unsettle the United States in this period?

■ MEN AND WOMEN IN ANTEBELLUM AMERICA

The economic changes confronting Americans in the decades before the Civil War produced and were shaped by changes in the size and nature of families and gender relations. Drawing on a burgeoning market in parenting advice literature, parents began rethinking how to raise and relate to their children. Love and the open expression of emotion received much more attention in the early 19th century than they had in previous generations. Rather than viewing households as little kingdoms—with a spouse, children, and other dependents recognizing the natural authority of the father as they would the king—parents began emphasizing the affectionate bonds that sustained families. Despite this new emphasis, the lines between men's and women's proper roles within both society and the family began to sharpen. Greater respect between spouses and the mutual obligations of all members of the "domestic" family did not necessarily lead to more liberal values with regard to women's place in the public world.

Gender and Economic Change

Nearly all women in the United States suffered under similar restrictions with regard to their public rights: women could not vote or hold office, could not sue or establish contracts, were barred from positions of leadership in their churches, and were rarely allowed access to higher education or divorce, even from abusive husbands. The law of **coverture** ensured that when a woman married, her property and any wages she might earn became her husband's. These legal constraints clashed with an increasing sense of women as unique individuals who deserved the same moral respect as men. As the nation developed, and especially as the American economy created new opportunities and new situations, states articulated the differences between men and women in law. Differences emerged most noticeably in the North, where the expanding economy drew upper- and middle-class men away from household-based production—principally farming—into paid employment at separate and dedicated work sites. Since the early colonial period, the household had been the basic social and economic unit, the site of both production and reproduction. As the new national and industrial economy took shape, paid work moved outside of the home. For the mostly urban upper classes, this meant that men left the home and women stayed inside it. Alexis de Tocqueville, the famous French visitor to the United States, observed of gender relations in the 1830s

NEW FAMILY PORTRAITURE   The new emphasis on domestic intimacy demanded new representations in family portraiture. The richness of the fabrics in this family portrait, the profusion of consumer items—tailored clothing, books, furniture, and furnishings—and the harmony with nature embodied by the open windows and doors all sought to demonstrate the virtue of this new model of family organization and presentation.

that "the inexorable opinion of the public carefully circumscribes [her] within the narrow circle of domestic interests and duties and forbids her to step beyond it."

Those families who experienced this transformation in work increasingly viewed the world outside the household as the "public" space and the domestic space of the home as "private." The men in these households believed that women ruled within the domestic world but should have little presence in the public one. Several factors converged to create this trend. The factories and offices that increasingly employed men outside of the home refused to hire women. Women had traditionally held greater authority in regard to childrearing and the daily household tasks. Finally, Americans regarded the public world of business and government as morally suspect if not corrupt. The market, they believed, functioned as a kind of free-for-all in which participants might engage in any noncriminal behavior in the pursuit of profit; and politics operated according to similar principles. In this world, women's perceived strengths—a highly developed moral sense and strong sympathies for others—became liabilities. As a result, men sought to exclude women from the public world for their own protection and because they would have been ineffective in the face of male aggression and ruthlessness.

This was not a uniquely American practice. Industrial revolutions in England, France, and other parts of western Europe split households as they did across America.

These changes did not occur uniformly across the country. Among families who moved West of the Mississippi River, the household continued to be the center of economic activity, as it was in the South. Men and women in these regions generally spent their days alongside one another. The shared responsibilities in these households appeared as soon as they started on the trek West. Women were responsible for feeding, clothing, child rearing, and doctoring the family if necessary. They also usually participated in the agricultural or pastoral work that sustained most Western families. Men were typically responsible for agricultural work, the animals, transportation, and protecting the family. The hardships of the journey ensured that men's and women's duties and needs often overlapped.

The middle-class women who staffed most of the nation's leading reform organizations rejected the intellectual assumptions that divided the genders. The leading female activists in the crusades for temperance, **abolition**, and women's rights drew scorn for their aggression rather than gentle treatment because of their natural sensitivity. Female volunteers performed much of the work done by a wide range of reform associations in the decades up to and through the Civil War. The **Grimké sisters**, Sarah and Angelina, ranked among the best-known abolitionists of the period, and a trio of women—**Susan B. Anthony**, **Lucretia Mott**, and **Elizabeth Cady Stanton**—led the fight for women's rights. Despite this, most men believed that women belonged in the home and not in the office, factory, or store. The separation of space by gender did little to advance modern notions of gender equality, but women could and did use the special protections owed to them under the ideology of separate spheres to educate themselves and to organize the broader movement for full equality. "We are a band of sisters—we must have sympathy for each other's woes," wrote one female activist.

Many Americans knew that the divisions of social and economic labor along gender lines varied within the nation. Class position determined, to a large degree, the extent to which men and women could rigidly separate their duties. Poor families needed the income of their female members and could not afford to remove them from paid work. Slavery, with its identical demands on the labor of black men and women, clearly violated the new norms, as did the many rural white households where production and reproduction remained rooted in the same physical place. Indians, who still controlled most of the western half of the continent, maintained their own gendered divisions of labor. Most importantly, women usually controlled the agriculture within native communities. Because early white observers routinely ignored women's work, they often overlooked the importance of farming to Indian economies and inaccurately criticized them for relying too heavily on hunting.

Ladies, Women, and Working Girls

At the same time that state legislatures and churches restricted women's options, women themselves seized new opportunities in the whirl of changes brought on by the market revolution. Some women, of course, pursued paid work out of necessity because their families required the active contributions of all members to survive. In New England, thousands of young women entered schoolhouses as teachers, and many more took employment in the textile mills dotting the region. The mills in Lowell, Massachusetts, in

SLAVE LABOR   Enslaved women worked alongside men performing long hours of fieldwork on tobacco, cotton, and rice plantations. The lack of gender distinctions in slave labor encouraged many whites to view black women as less feminine than their white counterparts.

particular, gained renown for their large labor force of young women, who ranged between the ages of 15 and 35. The Lowell Mill Girls, as observers called them regardless of age, worked in one of the first large-scale, steam-powered industries in the United States—and one of the most fully globalized. They wove cotton, grown by slaves working on plantations in the Southern United States, and shipped the finished products to consumers all across America and around the world. Less well known at the time were the female mill workers of the South. In Georgia, white women comprised a majority of the state's factory workers. In Macon, Columbus, Augusta, and the state capital of Milledgeville, textile factories employed thousands of young, mostly single, women. Like their peers in Massachusetts, these women remained part of their households and returned their often essential wages to the family.

Even in those places without the mechanized mills of Lowell or Augusta, women performed a wide variety of paid work. Most rural women already performed physically demanding and time-consuming household work, and many also engaged in small-scale domestic production. They sold most of the goods produced in town or city markets—from candles and clothing to butter, eggs, and small farm animals. For many of these women, the money they generated was the only cash income a farm family might possess.

Cities presented other working opportunities that women sometimes sought and sometimes were reduced to accepting. As American cities developed in the 1830s and 1840s, more city dwellers with money to spare paid for services that they would have done for themselves in a previous era or a more rural setting. Women filled most of the roles as cooks, cleaners, launderers, seamstresses, and all-purpose domestic help. More ominously, poor women sometimes resorted to prostitution. In the large cities, certain neighborhoods hosted a mix of bars, gambling dens, and brothels that ensured a steady flow of business while creating dangerous work conditions for women.

Enslaved women occupied the most ambiguous position within the prevailing visions of women's proper roles. Because of their enslavement, such women performed a range of tasks ordinarily undertaken by men. Female slaves in the field worked the same jobs as male slaves. Corporations sometimes owned or rented slave women, just like their male counterparts. In 1810, Virginia's Oxford Iron Works counted nearly one-third of its enslaved workforce as female, some of them cooking and cleaning for the male workers, but others performing regular foundry tasks alongside men. Slave women also contended with a high degree of sexual vulnerability that few free women ever experienced. Despite legal, religious, and social prohibitions, slave owners maintained sexual relationships with enslaved women. The increasing prevalence of **mulatto**, or mixed-race, people in the United States census offered physical proof of many of these relationships. Slave mothers educated their adolescent daughters in strategies to protect themselves from this omnipresent danger.

Masculinity on the Trail, in the Cities, and on the Farm

Despite men's dominance in American society in the 1830s and 1840s, notions of manhood changed as unpredictably as those of womanhood. Differences in region and ethnicity produced the sharpest distinctions. In the Northeast, with its concentration of urban areas and highly specialized economies, men found opportunities and incentives to build marriages and families on the basis of affection rather than the older model of hierarchy and authority. Although this transition promised more frequent demonstrations of love among spouses, it also

WORKING WOMEN This cover of a literary journal produced by Lowell Mill workers revealed the awkward position occupied by female workers, poised between the domestic worlds of home and the mercenary world of factories.

required men to abandon long-held notions of what constituted manly behavior. In earlier decades, affronts to a man's honor demanded an immediate physical, usually violent, response. As new norms of manhood took shape in the increasingly crowded and anonymous Northern cities, men placed a premium on self-control, a virtue that diminished conflict while allowing men to retain their honor. Another change was the open expression of emotion, particularly positive emotions, such as love, which took root especially among younger men and reformers. Male abolitionists, for instance, wrote and spoke with each other in extraordinarily intimate and emotional terms, a practice that mirrored the sympathy they strove to generate in the larger public on the issue of slavery. A letter from Charles Sumner, the antislavery Massachusetts senator to his friend, the poet Henry Wadsworth Longfellow, remarked of their correspondence: "Yr letters seem warm as a lover's heart. I can almost feel the heat when I break the seal."

New attitudes toward manhood took root more slowly in the South, where older and more traditional forms of masculine expression retained favor. The conflict surrounding statehood in the new territory of Florida, only brought within the Union in 1819, revealed the importance of expressions of masculinity to political and social authority. As residents built the case for statehood, two political factions coalesced around competing leaders. Men within the territory aligned themselves with one group or the other and zealously guarded the honor and positions of their peers. The Southern code of honor, heightened among white men because of the presence of slaves, demanded retaliation for any slight to one's own or one's group's public image or reputation. Floridians gouged eyes, bit off earlobes, and assaulted each other in ways calculated to produce shame by creating a public symbol of one's inferiority. The popular forms of ritualized violence among Southerners bonded white men in a shared ethos even as it alienated them from Northerners pursuing nonviolent expressions of masculinity. A similar atmosphere prevailed in the emerging Anglo West. The Hispanic West and those areas that received wagon trains included roughly equal numbers of men and women; but the mining towns, the newly formed ranches, and many of the large farms were overwhelmingly male. As a result, the region possessed fewer of the social institutions—churches, schools, and civic groups—that moderated the actions of young men and, consequently, a higher degree of violence and disruptive behavior than the East.

At the same time, the growing importance of evangelical Christian values, which stressed charity, humility, and compassion, rather than revenge, competed with the system of honor, especially in the South. The shift in emphasis from the public nature of honor, in which men most valued the way their peers viewed them, to Christianity, in which an individual's most important relationship was with God, represented a profound shift in Southern culture. As the *Religious Herald* boldly announced in 1837, "A public profession of Christianity is an avowal of our separation from the world, as regards it maxims, pursuits, and pleasures." This transformation happened slowly through the 1830s. As evangelical churches gained influence, the values they represented began to alter the tenor of Southern culture. Northern religious reformers sought similar opportunities to direct the energy and morality of American men. The increasing popularity of bare-knuckle fighting, a sport imported from England complete with foreign fighters, drew scorn from those who emphasized restraint and nonviolence. According to one commentator, boxing was "nothing but brutality, ferociousness, and cowardness," which tended to "debase the mind, deaden the feelings and extinguish every spark of benevolence." Despite such critiques, a wide swath of men from different classes watched, gambled on, and thrilled to matches that could last 50 rounds or two hours of fighting. The popularity of such spectacles revealed the tensions in American culture in the antebellum era—benevolence and sympathy existed alongside violence and aggression.

STUDY QUESTIONS FOR MEN AND WOMEN IN ANTEBELLUM AMERICA

1. How did men's and women's lives differ in the mid-19th century?

2. How did race, region, and class influence changes in masculinity and femininity in the period?

◼ FREEDOM FOR SOME

The dynamism that characterized gender relations in this period could be seen in the political system as well, where politics developed in two different directions simultaneously. On one hand, Americans broke away from European traditions by liberalizing democracy to include all white men. On the other, Americans increased their commitment to slavery, which created a society based on bonded labor that Western Europe had left behind with the end of feudalism in the 1500s. In Southern states, these two trends buttressed one another, whereas in the North, they began to generate concern about what kind of country America would become. The tension between liberty and slavery fueled several decades of conflict about the structure and the nature of American democracy. Did individual freedom include the right to enslave other people? Did the federal government have the authority to prohibit slavery? Rather than confront these polarizing issues directly, politicians clashed over apportionment, voting qualifications, and the regional balance of power in the country. The changes they made expanded access to electoral politics and retained an awkward sectional peace, but skeptics wondered whether even the robust American political system could contain the transformations coursing through the country in the 1830s and 1840s.

The Nature of Democracy in the Atlantic World

Americans drew inspiration from a wide variety of sources. The independence movements in Latin America—when various republics broke away from Spain's control between 1810 and 1825—fascinated and encouraged Americans in their own expansion of democracy. Americans found European democratic efforts equally compelling. **Louis Kossuth**, the journalist and political leader in Hungary, attained renown as a freedom fighter throughout the Americas. After his expulsion from Hungary in 1848 by the embattled Hapsburgs (the ruling family of the Austrian Empire), Kossuth toured the United States to great acclaim, receiving a 100-gun salute when his ship reached New Jersey and invitations to the White House and Congress.

The liberalization of politics in the United States dovetailed with the market liberalization that occurred at the same time. Despite the conservatism of most Jacksonian Democrats, a faction within the party—known as Young Democrats—began advocating the virtues of markets and global trade over the standard party line, which focused on self-sufficiency and agricultural development. Charles Wilkes's South Seas expedition alerted Americans to the opportunities waiting abroad. Likewise, Young Democrats applauded the British decision in 1846 to repeal its "Corn Laws," high tariffs on imported foodstuffs designed to protect Britain's agricultural sector. Pro–free-trade Americans hoped that the British move would spur the repeal of similar duties around the world and open foreign markets to American products. The same Young Democrats who applauded Wilkes's Pacific explorations and preached free trade celebrated European democratic movements. John O. Sullivan's *Democratic Review*, the unofficial organ of the movement, chronicled the fortunes of Italian, German, and Central European rebels, who themselves looked backward to the American rebels of 1776, against the old aristocracy of Europe.

Whether Americans took inspiration from Spanish- or Hungarian-speaking Democrats, they heard the same message: authority should reside in the common people.

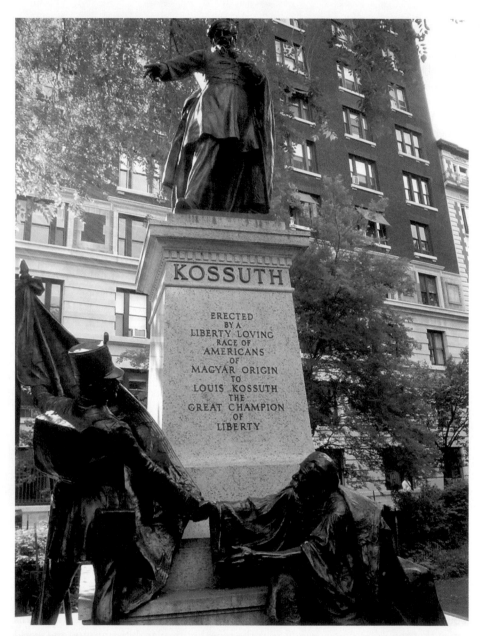

LOUIS KOSSUTH The lasting impression of the Hungarian Reformer Louis Kossuth can be seen in the monuments erected to honor his contribution to the global democracy movement. This one, in New York City, joined others in Cleveland, Washington, DC, and elsewhere across the United States.

The great accomplishment of the American Revolution had been to locate the government's sovereignty, not in the divine right of a king but collectively, in the people. "The people," in this sense, referred to participants in the political order. In Jacksonian America, this still meant native-born white men. The influx of Catholic immigrants, the increasing numbers of free blacks in the North, and the efforts by women to attain the vote challenged assumptions about who could participate in the political process; but white men protected their interests effectively until the Civil War. For several decades after the Revolution, reformers liberalized the political system while at the same time they obstructed efforts by women and racial minorities to gain access to the political system. Changes to the country's economic system followed a similar pattern. The era's prosperity seemed to prove that a decentralized government and open markets could accomplish what Europe's more centralized governments had failed to secure. Such an outlook ignored the active role that government (at all levels) played in stimulating economic development—whether it was the U.S. Army expelling Indians to make way for white farmers or the U.S. Navy establishing trading stations in the Pacific. It also ignored the fact that the profits of economic and political liberalization were not evenly distributed within the population. Enslaved people, Indians, and most women did not enjoy the benefits of limited government and free markets.

The Second Party System

The practical results of political changes in the United States in the 1830s and 1840s shocked many Europeans, particularly elite Britons who distrusted the wisdom of granting voting rights to, or enfranchising, all white men. While European politicians and thinkers watched, many gleefully anticipating the imminent collapse of the American

EARLY 19TH-CENTURY VOTING   Caleb Bingham's famous painting captured the social nature of voting in the first half of the 19th century. Men voted publicly, which created the possibility of coercion, intimidation, and fraud but also reinforced the collaborative process of democracy.

republic, Americans pushed ahead. In many states, reformers eliminated two requirements for voting and holding office that had kept the poor out of the political system:
property restrictions had required that officeholders and voters own real estate, and poll
taxes ensured that only men with disposable income could vote. Most of the millions of
immigrants to the country could naturalize themselves as citizens and assume full participation in the political system within a few years of arrival. From our modern perspective, a system in which only white males could vote seems a shallow democracy. But for
people at the time, who recalled the legacy of European governance that gave little power
to common people, the change was momentous. The addition of transforming previously
appointed positions into elected ones, including most local offices such as tax assessor,
sheriff, and local judges, produced the most democratic system in the Western world.

Another factor that broadened people's access to government was the rise of the
second party system, organized around Andrew Jackson. Jackson's bold leadership over
two terms in the White House generated a host of opposition. Reformers criticized the
callousness of his Indian removal, commercial interests condemned his destruction of
the bank, and state rights proponents had their own concerns about this slaveholding
son of the South who put down South Carolina's attempt to "nullify" the federal tariff.
During the 1830s, the **Whig Party** organized around a set of issues that enabled them to
build a national coalition; they captured the presidency in 1840 and again in 1848.
Whereas the Democrats encouraged the mass immigration of the 1830s and 1840s and
welcomed many of these voters into the party, Whig supporters tended to distrust the
largely Catholic and working-class migrants. Coming largely from the ranks of native-
born Protestants, Whigs espoused a vigorous nationalism; supported government investments in infrastructure to stimulate business; and, in some parts of the North,
endorsed moderate antislavery politics. In contrast, the Democratic Party preferred state
funding and control of development projects, which set them against the federal road,
bridge, and river improvements that Whigs promised would energize the American
economy. Sociocultural issues, such as closing all government services on the Christian
Sabbath and advocacy of temperance, also energized Whig voters.

Democracy in the South

To the surprise of many observers, Southern politicians actually liberalized their rules
regarding access to the vote and higher office earlier than many Northern ones. The
Southern slaveholders who filled most statehouses rarely initiated change, although
the most farsighted among them saw that incorporating nonslaveholding whites into the
political order on a more equal footing could ensure the security of the system. By allowing nonslaveholders to have more power in the political system, slaveholders hoped the
new voters would be less likely to challenge that system. Henry Wise, a Virginia Democrat who led the state as governor and played a pivotal role in the state's secession from
the Union, responded skillfully to challenges within the state for a more inclusive system.
Nonslaveholding men living in the western part of Virginia had long complained of unequal treatment by Eastern slaveholders—a lament heard throughout the Southern states
in the 1830s and 1840s. Although late by Southern standards, in 1851 Virginia abolished
the property requirement for voting and instituted universal white manhood suffrage.

The democracy that evolved in the presence of slavery assumed the mastery and autonomy of white men. The unique characteristics of a democracy based on race emerged
several decades before the Civil War. In the nation as a whole, politics knitted the country

together, connecting men and women across regions, classes, ethnicities, and religions. But because of the overwhelming endorsement of slavery within the South, neither party could risk being associated with any challenge to it. On this issue, the Southern wings of the two parties competed to outdo each other in protecting the South's peculiar institution. This weakness in the party system hastened the political collapse that produced secession and war. In addition, both Northern and Southern whites showed their preference for white rule. By 1840, free blacks could vote only in Maine, New Hampshire, Vermont, and Massachusetts. New York and Pennsylvania had recently repealed earlier grants of voting rights to black men.

The power of slavery to warp democracy appeared most ominously in South Carolina in 1832. Over the course of that year, politicians in the Palmetto State initiated a conflict with the federal government over the tariff. Beginning during the War of 1812, New Englanders had promoted a tariff—a federal tax on imported (usually finished) goods—as a way to stimulate domestic manufacturing and curb the importing of European products. If European goods became more expensive, tariff supporters argued, Americans would buy more goods made at home. New England manufacturers naturally favored the tariff. Southerners, with little industrial development

ADVANCING THE SOUTHERN ECONOMIC AND POLITICAL AGENDA Although South Carolina lost the nullification debate, its actions inflamed a sense of injured pride across the South. A decade later, James D. B. DeBow launched his eponymous magazine, *DeBow's Review*, as a platform for advancing the Southern economic and political agenda.

of their own, complained that the tariff helped the Northeast at their expense. They felt forced to buy either expensive Northern-made goods, which seemed to bolster the clout of a region many Southerners regarded as a rival, or pay the tariff-elevated prices for European merchandise. When George McDuffie, an upcountry South Carolina representative rose to speak about the issue, "his frame came alive with outrage. He shrieked. He kicked. He thumped. He spat. He seemed a revivalist in a death struggle with Satan." In 1828, President Adams supported a high tariff—known as the "tariff of abominations" by its enemies—that passed with strong Northern support. Southerners in and out of Congress complained vociferously about the legislation, which doubled the tax on many imported goods.

When Jackson came to the White House, many Southerners assumed he would push repeal of the tariff. But Jackson's home state of Tennessee benefited from a tariff on hemp imports, and despite his state rights philosophy, Jackson moved slowly against the law. Congress reduced the 1828 tariff in 1832, although it proved too late for the increasingly radical South Carolinians. South Carolina politicians saw only potential gain from denouncing the tariff in stronger and stronger language. By late 1832, John Calhoun—once Jackson's vice president and possible successor—had thrown himself fully against the tariff. He penned an "exposition" against the policy that condemned it as unconstitutional and destructive of the liberty that the Union was founded to protect. Building on Calhoun's theory, the South Carolina legislature passed an act "nullifying" the federal law and refusing to collect the tariff at its ports. Carolina politicians hoped to draw support from other Southern states, but none followed. President Jackson issued the most famous denunciation of the doctrine of nullification: "I consider, then, the power to annul a law of the United States, assumed by one State, incompatible with the existence of the Union, contradicted expressly by the letter of the Constitution, unauthorized by its spirit, inconsistent with every principle on which It was founded, and destructive of the great object for which it was formed." Congress passed a Force Act and Jackson appeared ready to lead U.S. troops into the South when a compromise was reached. Congress reduced the tariff further, and South Carolina repealed its nullification ordinance. The nation had come dangerously close to secession and war.

Conflicts over Slavery

Southern partisans lost the battle over nullification but this did not diminish their willingness to defend slavery. Because Southern politicians controlled most of the top committee chairmanships and other leadership positions within Congress, they blocked discussion of slavery at the national as well as the state level by imposing the "**gag rule**." On December 13, 1835, a Maine congressman introduced a petition from 172 "ladies" in his district who urged Congress to abolish slavery in the District of Columbia. Similar petitions had been printed in the records of Congressional debates, referred to committees, and never touched again. But with abolitionists' opposition to slavery growing more forceful each year, Southern representatives protested against the new petition from Maine and insisted that Congress reject it, an unprecedented request. James Henry Hammond of South Carolina, who made the original motion that produced what critics would call the gag rule, asserted that "he could not sit there and see the rights of the Southern people assaulted day after day, by the ignorant fanatics from whom these memorials proceeded." Hammond found support among his Southern colleagues, many Northern allies, and especially party leaders eager to see such a divisive issue removed from debate. For the next nine years, the U.S. Congress refused to consider or even print the memorials and petitions of citizens on the subject of abolition.

Partly owing to the dedicated efforts of former president John Quincy Adams, then representing Massachusetts in the House of Representatives, the House rescinded the rule in 1844. In the meantime, however, the rule underscored the power of pro-slavery Southern congressmen to control the institution and transformed the fight over abolition into a fight over free speech as well. Southern power, wielded arrogantly by men like Hammond, probably did more to stimulate antislavery sympathies among white Northerners than the work of dozens of dedicated abolitionists.

Only a tiny minority of Northerners counted themselves as abolitionists in the years before the Civil War, and even most abolitionists wanted only gradual and peaceful emancipation. The power of persuasion, however, could move millions; and given the North's advantage in population, Southerners needed to win—not just stifle—the debate over slavery. Reacting to abolitionist pressure, Southerners developed a robust defense of slavery, marshaling history, religion, morality, and economics to demonstrate why Americans had to protect and even extend racial slavery. Ministers such as Virginia's Thornton Stringfellow, political theorists such as George Fitzhugh, economists such as J. D. B. DeBow (publisher of the South's most important business magazine), and politicians such as Hammond and Calhoun together crafted a new defense of slavery that identified it as the one true foundation for white freedom.

The pro-slavery defense, as it has been called by historians, was built on the idea of racial supremacy espoused by prominent scientists of the day, such as Harvard's Agassiz and the Southern physician Josiah Nott. Both men articulated scientific explanations of white racial superiority based on an imputed link between skull size and intellectual ability. Slavery's defenders joined this modern argument to older endorsements of slavery, reaching back to the ancient Greeks and Romans and to the Bible. Many Protestant Christians at the time interpreted the biblical story of Ham as evidence that God had made black people to be the servants of white people. Pro-slavery theorists also built elaborate economic defenses of the institution, pointing to the remarkable wealth produced in Southern states through the use of slave labor. James Henry Hammond explained the political defense of slavery in another famous Congressional speech that alienated as many Northerners as his earlier fight for the gag rule had. According to Hammond, every society required workers who performed the brute labor on which all else rested. He referred to this class as the "mudsill" and flatly stated that members of such a class, owing to their constant low-wage labor, could not develop the intellectual capacities to contribute productively to the political life of their society. Hammond condemned Northerners for forcing white men—typically immigrants—into this role, whereas he lauded the South for using slaves in this capacity.

What could be called the "civilizational" aspect of the pro-slavery argument claimed that slaves could either be held in bondage in America or Africa. And, because America was a Christian nation and Africa was not, slavery in the United States must be better for the slaves. Over time, the argument went, slaves would adopt Christianity, ensuring eternal salvation for their souls. As Southerners knew, two awkward facts contradicted this part of the argument: after 1808, international law prohibited the importation of African slaves into the country, so all future slaves were native to the United States. Second, whereas Catholic Spain and Portugal made extensive efforts to convert their slaves to Christianity, Protestant England and later America made no similar effort. Before 1800, very few slaves had adopted Christianity. This failure became one of the chief criticisms of Northern opponents of slavery and eventually prompted a slavery reform movement within the South.

STUDY QUESTION FOR FREEDOM FOR SOME

1. Did the changes in American politics in the 1830s and 1840s serve a more liberal or a more conservative social order?

TIMELINE 1818–1856

AMERICA	YEAR	THE WORLD
Mar Congress passes Neutrality Act to suppress private warfare	**1818**	
	1821	Mexico secures independence from Spain Greeks win War of Independence against Ottoman Empire
	1825	Decembrist Revolt in Russia fails
Jul Cherokee Indians ratify tribal constitution modeled on U.S. Constitution	**1827**	
Frances Wright delivers first public address by an American woman to a mixed-gender audience **Aug** Discovery of gold on Cherokee land in Georgia	**1829**	
May Congress passes Indian Removal Act	**1830**	
Alexis de Tocqueville arrives in the United States for a two-year study of the country, resulting in 1835 publication of *Democracy in America*	**1831**	Polish Revolt against Russian Empire fails
Mar Supreme Court issues decision in *Worcester v. Georgia* holding that Congress has sole authority to regulate relations with Indian tribes **Nov** South Carolina legislature passes "Ordinance of Nullification" intending to nullify federal tariff	**1832**	
Mar Congress passes "Force Act" giving President Jackson power to suppress South Carolina's refusal to collect federal tariff	**1833**	
Dec Second Seminole War begins in southern Georgia/northern Florida	**1835**	
Mar Mexican forces led by General Santa Anna defeat and kill combined force of Texan and Tejano rebels at the Alamo **Apr** Mexican President and General Santa Anna defeated along San Jacinto River; Texas independence declared **May** U.S. House of Representatives imposes "gag rule" prohibiting introduction or discussion of petitions calling for abolition	**1836**	

Summary

- The 1830s and 1840s were a key phase in the expansion of the nation. Challenging Spain and Britain for dominance in North America, settlers flooded the landscape west of the Mississippi and dramatically changed the demography and the economy of the region.
- The economic growth spurred by new technology, especially the steam engine, helped drive the rise of a new middle class and of a more clearly defined and self-aware working class, mainly located in the cities.
- The new workplaces, distinguished from older household-based production, were almost entirely all-male places. This change helped generate the growing separation of men's and women's experiences in early America.
- In the South, the West, and among the variety of non-Anglo ethnic communities, men and women worked out different relationships with one another and different expectations of the future.

Dec Rensselaer Van Rensselaer leads American filibusters into Canada	**1837**	
Jan General Winfield Scott sent to Canadian border to suppress violence **May** General Winfield Scott arrives in Georgia and begins confining Cherokee people before their forced march to Indian Territory **Aug** Wilkes Expedition sets sail from Hampton Roads, Virginia	**1838**	
Mississippi passes first "Married Women's Property Act," granting married women independent rights to property brought into marriage	**1839**	First Anglo-Chinese War begins
Jun Wilkes Expedition returns **May** First successful large-scale wagon train departs Missouri for the Pacific Coast **Aug** Second Seminole War ends; 90 percent of the Seminole killed during conflict	**1842**	First Anglo-Chinese War ends
Dec Congress repeals "gag rule"	**1844**	Treaty of Wanghia between Qing Empire and U.S. enables first American ambassador to China
Irish famine begins	**1845**	
Jul "Declaration of Sentiments" passed at Seneca Falls, NY, by women's rights advocates calling for equality between men and women	**1848**	Democratic Revolutions in Italy, Hungary, Germany, and France
Dec Hungarian democracy activist Louis Kossuth tours United States	**1851**	
William Walker briefly holds office as president of Nicaragua before being executed	**1856**	

- Political elites imposed widespread progressive reforms, creating more democratic political systems across the country. Nevertheless, political power remained securely in the hands of wealthy white men.
- Partly because of the progressive reforms, outsiders of all sorts found ways to influence the political system. These groups, including Native Americans, women, new immigrants, and African Americans, also began using the language of American politics, especially the idea of an egalitarian democracy, to improve their own positions.

Key Terms and People

abolition *381*

Alamo *359*

Anthony, Susan B. *381*

coverture *379*

Grimké sisters *381*

Indian Removal Act of 1830 *362*

Kossuth, Louis *385*

Mott, Lucretia *381*

Reviewing Chapter 11

1. The most important boundary that changed in this period was the one between men and women. Do you agree with this statement? Why or why not?

Further Reading

Aron, Stephen. *How the West Was Lost: The Transformation of Kentucky from Daniel Boone to Henry Clay*. Baltimore, MD: Johns Hopkins University Press, 1996. An insightful study of land and development politics during the first half of the 19th century.

Berlin, Ira. *Generations of Captivity: A History of African-American Slaves*. Cambridge, MA: Belknap Press, 2003. The best and most concise history of slavery in North America from the early 17th century through emancipation.

Guttierez, Ramon A. *When Jesus Came, the Corn Mothers Went Away: Marriage, Sexuality, and Power in New Mexico, 1500–1846*. Stanford, CA: Stanford University Press, 1991. An analysis of the effects of Spanish invasion and settlement on gender roles and relations in the Southwest.

May, Robert E. *Manifest Destiny's Underworld: Filibustering in Antebellum America*. Chapel Hill: University of North Carolina Press, 2002. An engaging survey of the practice of filibustering in 19th-century America.

Stansell, Christine. *City of Women: Sex and Class in New York, 1789–1860*. Urbana: University of Illinois Press, 1987. An analysis of the changes in family, work, and gender patterns in industrializing America.

Wilentz, Sean. *Chants Democratic: New York City and the Rise of the American Working Class, 1788–1850*. New York: Oxford University Press, 1984. The seminal study of a pivotal moment in the development of a working class in the United States.

America In The World
PEOPLE, GOODS, IDEAS AND PRACTICES

CHAPTER 11: New Boundaries, New Roles 1820–1856

from
EUROPE

Labor unionism

Irish and German Migrants

Magazines, carpets, and manufactured products

ATLANTIC
OCEAN

Canadian
independence
fighters

Universal white male suffrage

**NORTH
AMERICA**

Cherokee

Creek and Seminoles

Choctaws

Chickasaws

Sac and Fox

Texas independence fighters

Gulf of
Mexico

American settlers

Santa Fe

to
NICARAGUA

Portland

Sutter's
Fort

PACIFIC
OCEAN

Knowledge of the Pacific

| 0 | 250 | 500 miles |
| 0 | 250 | 500 kilometers |

Goods
Ideas
People

PRIMARY SOURCES FOR CHAPTER 11

NEW BOUNDARIES, NEW ROLES, 1820–1856

SOURCE 11.1

John Ross, Excerpts from "Memorial and Protest of the Cherokee Nation" (June 21, 1836)

Since the 1820s, the state of Georgia had been working to eject the Cherokee, who occupied valuable lands where gold had been discovered. In 1835, a rump group within the Cherokee nation signed an agreement with the United States at New Echota to move to Oklahoma. John Ross, the principal chief, and the other elected Cherokee leadership did not sign or agree with the New Echota treaty, but the United States regarded the document as binding and sent the U.S. Army to forcibly evict the community in the summer of 1836.

Source: John Ross, speaking to the U.S. House of Representatives, on June 21, 1836, *S. Doc. No. 286,* 24th Cong., 1st sess.

Submitting the protest of the Cherokee nation against the ratification, execution, and enforcement of the treaty negotiated at New Echota, in December, 1835. . . .

Read and referred to the Committee of the Whole House to which is committed the bill (R. H. No. 695), *making further appropriations for carrying into effect certain Indian treaties.*

To the honorable the Senate and House of Representatives of the United States of North America in Congress assembled:

It is the expressed wish of the Government of the United States to remove the Cherokees to a place west of the Mississippi. That wish is said to be founded in humanity to the Indians. To make their situation more comfortable, and to preserve them as a distinct people. Let facts show how this *benevolent* design has been prosecuted, and how faithful

to the spirit and letter has the promise of the President of the United States to the Cherokees been fulfilled—that *"those who remain may be assured of our patronage, our aid, and good neighborhood."* The delegation are not deceived by empty professions, and fear their race is to be destroyed by the mercenary policy of the present day, and their lands wrested from them by physical force; as proof, they will refer to the preamble of an act of the General Assembly of Georgia, in reference to the Cherokees, passed the 2d of December, 1835, where it is said, "from a knowledge of the Indian character, and from the present feelings of these Indians, it is confidently believed, that the right of occupancy of the lands in their possession should be withdrawn, *that it would be a strong inducement to them to treat with the General Government, and consent to a removal to the west;*

and whereas, the present Legislature openly avow that their primary object in the measures intended to be pursued, *are founded on real humanity to these Indians*, and with a view, in a distant region, to perpetuate them with their old identity of character, *under the paternal care of the Government of the United States;* at the same time frankly disavowing *any selfish or sinister motives towards them in their present legislation.*" This is the profession. Let us turn to the practice of *humanity,* to the Cherokees, by the State of Georgia. In violation of the treaties between the United States and the Cherokee nation, that State passed a law requiring all white men, residing in that part of the Cherokee country, in her limits, to take an oath of allegiance to the State of Georgia. For a violation of this law some of the ministers of Christ, missionaries among the Cherokees, were tried, convicted, and sentenced to hard labor in the penitentiary. Their case may be seen by reference to the records of the Supreme Court of the United States.

Valuable gold mines were discovered upon Cherokee lands, within the chartered limits of Georgia, and the Cherokees commenced working them, and the Legislature of that State interfered by passing an act, making it penal for an Indian to dig for gold within Georgia, no doubt "*frankly disavowing any selfish or sinister motives towards them.*" Under this law many Cherokees were arrested, tried, imprisoned, and otherwise abused. Some were even shot in attempting to avoid an arrest; yet the Cherokee people used no violence, hut humbly petitioned the Government of the United States for a fulfilment of treaty engagements, to protect them, which was not done, and the answer given that the United States could not interfere. . . . The Cherokee delegation have thus considered it their duty to exhibit before your honorable body a brief view of the Cherokee case, by a

short statement of facts. A detailed narrative would form a history too voluminous to be presented, in a memorial and prof [*illeg*]. They have, therefore, contented themselves with a brief recital, and will add, that in reviewing the past, they have done it alone for the purpose of showing what glaring oppressions and sufferings the peaceful and unoffending Cherokees have been doomed to witness and endure. Also, to tell your honorable body, in sincerity, that owing to the intelligence of the Cherokee people, they have a correct knowledge of their own rights, and they well know the illegality of those oppressive measures which have been adopted for their expulsion, by State authority. Their devoted attachment to their native country has not been, nor ever can be, eradicated from their breast. This, together with the implicit confidence, they have been taught to cherish, in the *justice, good faith, and magnanimity of the United States*, also, their firm reliance on the generosity and friendship of the American people, have formed the anchor of their hope and upon which alone they have been induced and influenced to shape their peaceful and manly course, under some of the most trying circumstances any people ever have been called to witness and endure. For more than *seven long years* have the Cherokee people been driven into the necessity of contending for their just rights, and they have struggled against fearful odds. Their means of defence being altogether within the grasp and control of their competitors, they have at last been trampled under foot. Their resources and means of defence, have been seized and withheld. The treaties, laws, and constitution of the United States, their bulwark, and only citadel of refuge, put beyond their reach; unfortunately for them, the protecting arm of the commander-in-chief of these fortresses has been withdrawn from them. The judgments of the judiciary branch of the government, in support of their rights, have been disregarded and prostrated; and their petitions for relief, from time to time before Congress, been unheeded. Their annuities withheld; their printing press, affording the only clarion through which to proclaim their wrongs before the American people and the civilized world, has been seized and detained, at the instance of an agent of the United States. . . . The faith of the United States being solemnly pledged to the Cherokee nation for the guarantee of the quiet and uninterrupted protection of their territorial possessions forever; and it being an unquestionable fact, that the Cherokees love their country; that no amount of money could induce them voluntarily to yield their assent to a cession of the same. But, when under all the circumstances of their peculiar situation and unhappy condition, the nation see the necessity of negotiating a treaty for their security and future welfare, and having appointed a delegation with full powers for that purpose, is it liberal, humane, or just, that a fraudulent treaty, containing principles and stipulations altogether objectionable, and obnoxious to their own sense of propriety and justice, should be enforced upon them? The basis of the instrument, the sum fixed upon, the commutation of annuities, and the general provisions of the various articles it contains, are all objectionable. Justice and equity demand, that in any final treaty for the adjustment of the Cherokee difficulties, that their rights, interests, and wishes should be consulted; and that the individual rights of the Cherokee citizens, in their possessions and claims, should be amply secured; and as freemen, they should be left at liberty to stay or remove where they please. Also, that the territory to be ceded by the United States to the Cherokee nation west of the Mississippi, should be granted to them by a patent in fee simple, and not clogged with the conditions of the act of 1830; and the national funds of the Cherokees should be placed under the control of their national council.

The delegation must repeat, the instrument entered into at New Echota, purporting to be a treaty, is deceptive to the world, and a fraud upon the Cherokee people. If a doubt exist as to the truth of their statement, a committee of investigation can learn the facts, and it may also learn that if the Cherokees are removed under that instrument, it will be by force. This declaration they make in sincerity, with hearts sickening at the scenes they may be doomed to witness; they have toiled to avert such a calamity; it is now with Congress, and beyond their control; they hope they are mistaken, but it is hope against a sad and almost certain reality. It would be uncandid to conceal their opinions, and they have no motive for expressing them but a solemn sense of duty. The Cherokees cannot resist the power of the United States, and should they be driven from their native land, then will they look in melancholy sadness upon the golden chains presented by President Washington to the Cherokee people as emblematical of the brightness and purity of the friendship between the United States and the Cherokee nation.

JNO. ROSS,
JOHN MARTIN,
JAMES BROWN,
JOSEPH VANN,
JOHN BENGE,
LEWIS ROSS,
ELIJAH HICKS,
RICH'D FIELDS,

Representatives of the Cherokee nation.
Washington City, 21st June, 1836.

WORKING WITH SOURCES

1. Why do the Cherokee leaders use the language of treaties and law to make their case?

2. What do the Cherokee think is the cause of their expulsion?

3. What distinctions do the authors of this document draw between the conduct of Georgia and that of the United States?

SOURCE 11.2

The Phalanx, Excerpts from "The Strike for Wages" (November 4, 1843) and "The Ten Hour System" (May 18, 1844)

In the 1820s and 1830s, workers began going on strike to gain higher wages. When these efforts failed, labor leaders began advocating policy changes to protect laboring people. The *Phalanx* was one of many small workers' newspapers that flourished in northeastern cities.

Source: John R. Commons, Ulrich B. Phillips, Eugene A. Gilmore, Helen L. Sumner, and John B. Andrews, eds., *A Documentary History of American Industrial Society,* vol. 7 (Cleveland, OH: Arthur Clark, 1910), 231–33.

The Strike for Wages

There has been a very general "turn-out" in all the Atlantic cities among the working classes. In every trade almost there has been a strike for higher wages, and generally the demands of the workmen have been complied with by the "masters." The reaction in the commercial world has stimulated business a little, which has increased slightly the demand for labor, and as the population of this country has not yet become dense and excessive, the working classes by the subversive means of counter-coalitions to those which exist under our present false system of Industry and Commerce—leagues of wealth and industrial monopoly—are enabled to obtain a small advance of wages. But how trifling and pitiful an amount of benefit, after all, they receive, by such means, even when and for the time they do succeed; and how miserably inadequate to meet their wants and satisfy their rights, are such beggarly additions to their wages. Will not the working classes, the intelligent producers of this country, see what a miserable shift and expedient to better their condition is a "strike for wages?" Will they not see how uncertain the tenure by which they hold the little advantage they gain by it? Will they not see how degrading the position which forces them to appeal to and beg concessions of employers? Will they not see this and a thousand other evils connected with a false system of industry, and learn that the only remedy is a union among themselves to produce for themselves, to associate, and combine, and owning the land on which they live and the tools and machinery with which they work, enjoy the products of their own labor? We hope so, and then all such "civilized" false association, will be unnecessary. . . .

The Ten Hour System

The agitation of the subject of a reduction of the time of labor in factories is not, however, confined to England; in this country, the evils of the factory system in the exaction of an undue portion of the time of the laborer—twelve, fourteen, and even sixteen and eighteen hours out of the twenty-four, and in the excessive toil imposed on young children, have been severely felt. In a general way the subject has occupied the attention of politicians, from time to time, as elections were pending, and a vast deal of demagogism has been expended on it; but latterly it has been specially considered by the Legislature of Pennsylvania, and now in New England great feeling is manifested towards it in some of the manufacturing towns. An association of mechanics has been formed at Fall River, Massachusetts, for the special purpose of reducing the duration of labor to ten hours per day, and to effect this object, has started a spirited little sheet called the *Mechanic*. We wish, however, that we could impress upon our countrymen the degrading littleness and insufficiency of this attempt at a compromise of their rights, for it is neither more nor less than a demeaning compromise and dastardly sacrifice of their rights, for them to make terms which only modifies the condition but does not change the terms of dependence on masters. In wretched England, where the laborer is indeed a poor, degraded, helpless being, it is well that any amelioration can be obtained; but here, where the laboring classes are intelligent and generally possess the ability to do full justice to themselves, it does appear to us to be excessively weak and trifling, if not disgraceful, for them to talk about a reform which at the most can relieve them temporarily of a few hours' oppressive toil—can convert them from twelve and fourteen to ten hour slaves—but cannot elevate them to the dignity of true independence! What a farce is boasted American freedom, if free-men are reduced to such beggarly shifts! Do they not see that they exhibit the badge of slavery in the very effort to mitigate its oppression? Free-men would not talk about terms which involve only a question of time of subjection to the authority and will of another—they would consult and act for their own good in all things without let or hindrance!

WORKING WITH SOURCES

1. Why does the *Phalanx* argue against workers using strikes as a means of protest?

2. What is the newspaper's attitude toward a ten-hour workday?

3. What kind of solution does the paper recommend?

SOURCE 11.3

Visual Document: Fan with View of Foreign Factories at Canton (1790–1800)

In the late 18th century, European traders desperately tried to gain access to Chinese markets. The Chinese restricted their trading "factories" (or warehouses) to a confined section of Canton. This fan is one of many small consumer goods that would have been carried back to the United States.

Source: The Granger Collection, NYC. All rights reserved.

WORKING WITH SOURCES

1. What would American consumers have made of this object?

2. What does the array of European flags and facilities suggest about Chinese authority?

3. Why is the fence around the trading facility only present on the seaward side?

SOURCE 11.4

Amy Melenda Galusha, Letter to Aaron Leland Galusha (April 3, 1849)

The textile mills in Lowell, Massachusetts, housed one of the first large-scale industrial facilities in the United States. Many of the workers in the factory were young women.

Source: Galusha Family Collection, Lowell National Historical Park, Center for Lowell History, University of Massachusetts Lowell Libraries, http://library.uml.edu/clh/All/Gal.htm.

Lowell, April 3, 1849

Dear Brother,

I do not know but you will blame me for not answering youre kind letter sooner but I think you will excuse me when I tell you the reason which is this I have been very sick with the vere Loyd[1] I do not know as you will know what that is so I will tell you it is the same as the small pox only it does not go quite so hard on account of being evaxionated[2] I was at the Hospital one week and I was sick enough I can tell you my face was swolen so that if you had seen

[1] Varioloid.
[2] Vaccinated.

me you would not have known me from Adam but I am getting pretty smart again I am not sorry that I have had it now it is over for I shall not fear the small pox any more but I had a pretty hard time I think I shall go to work again next week I expect my sickness will cost me about 15 dollers time and all which is quite a sum as low as wages are now you wanted I should write about mens wages in the mill mens wages are good but boys wages very low I do not think it will be best for you to try to work in the mill you will have to work a good many years before you will be a capable over-seer and none but such can get good wages if you go into the mill now you will have to be very steady and I know that youre disposition will not admit of youre being confined from 5 in the morning till 7 at night in a noisey factory and luging around a great basket of bobbins you would soon get tired of that fun I will promise you and then you must put up with a great many things which you never had to put up with before you would probably get scolded sometimes and that you know that you would not bear very patiently which would make it all the worse for you you would soom get weary and discontented and then you would not be much better off for what you had done a boy canot get along so easy in the mill with their work as the girls do with theirs for it is harder to learn it the girls have nothing to do but tend the work after it is all fixed and set to going the men have to keep the looms and machinery in order and put in the webs [—] and fix them all in order for weaving before the girls have any-thing to do with it which makes the mens work more trying and more particular a great deal than the girls when I come home I will tell you all about it more than I can write I should be very glad to have you here whare I can see you but I know in all reason Lele[3] it will not be for your best interest I think the best thing that

you can do will be to go into some country town and learn a good trade get into some re-spectable shop and be steady and industrious and do what you think is perfectly right take youre bible keep it by you where you can get at it handy read a portion of it every day and follow its precepts every day be considerate in everything if any one asks you to do a thing stop and think if it is right you can easely tell whether a thing is right or wrong by stopping to to think if you think it is wrong tell them at once that it is not right and that you will not do it and let that be the last of it do not stop to argue the point at all for they may be better skilled in argument then you are and by that I means you may weaken a strong point if you think it is wrong say so and that will be enough be independent do not be persuaded by any one however smart or rich or influential to do a wrong action you have a good mind enough for anybody if you will be guided by that do not let the evil spirit get the uper hand at any time if you can—t decide upon any question yourself go to someone that you know to be good for advise do not associate with any whose character is the least doubtful of either sex especialy the oposite Lealand for heavens sake let no fancy get the uper hands of reason do not be too ardent an admirer of outside apearances if you are attracted by a beautiful form or face stop and consider watch the ac-tions and words with a jealous eye see if retir-ing modesty reigns there see if [torn area] place of all [torn area] of folly and frivalous ac-tions there is anything like common sense to guide the bark or if its frail and delicate form is left pilotless upon the vast ocean of time to be driven by the winds of pride and folly to the gulf of distruction Leland I think of you a great deal and tremble for youre welfare for many a boy has been ruined when young by keeping bad company but my sheet (is almost full or I

---

[3] A nickname for Aaron Leland Galusha.

might say quite full you must answer my letter as soon as you receive it give my love to [JC] and [—ll] write to them soon write soon).

(Write as soon as you receive this I heard from Canada last night Jane Westover come down and Mrs Stark).

Amy L. Galusha

(dear Lele be kind to pa an ma do not do any thing to greive or hurt their feelings for you do not know how much they feel for youre welfare Lele the world is cold pitiless and miserliy what I have suffered no one knows but I have lived to find a calm a blessed calm in a land of strangers I know that youre feelings are tender like as mine were and capable of believing the insinuations of heartless wretches who will deceive you and then expose every little word and action and egreavate it to the highest pitch put no confidence in any one however friendly they may appear until you have thoroughly proved them).

(give my love to [—] enquiring friends give my love to Aunt I and L and J and all uncle Bens folks).

(you must not show this letter to any body except ma or pa it is written from the fountain of an overflowing and affectionate heart and must not be exposed to the scorn of an unfeeling world).

WORKING WITH SOURCES

1. How does Amy compare the advantages and disadvantages of millwork for men and women?

2. What values does she believe a man should possess?

3. What kind of emotional relationship does Amy seem to have with her brother?

Religion and Reform

Tossing violently in a storm, a ship was driven ever closer to the shore of Fire Island, New York, on July 19, 1850. Out of the country for four years, Margaret Fuller was returning to the United States on that ship, with an Italian husband, a baby boy, and a new name, the Marchesa d'Ossoli. By the 1830s Fuller had become one of the best-known writers and thinkers in the United States. From 1846 to 1850 she worked, mostly in Italy, as one of America's first war correspondents, as she reported on the civil wars and nationalist movements wracking that country. A friend of Ralph Waldo Emerson and Henry David Thoreau, Fuller had edited the Transcendentalist magazine the *Dial*, offering insights into U.S. and European philosophy, literature, and art. She also wrote *Woman in the Nineteenth Century*, in which she argued for the full equality of men and women.

In 1844, Horace Greeley hired her as a full time critic for the *New York Tribune*. From that post she read and wrote widely. Like many Americans of the time she pursued a more Christian society. Her exposés took readers into the alms house, the asylum, and the prison, demanding reform and improvement. In addition to her religious faith, Fuller drew inspiration from classical and contemporary history and politics. She closely followed the nationalist movements in Germany, Italy, Poland, and Hungary, and Fuller chronicled these movements during her stay in Europe. Although she did not find "the genuine democracy to which the rights of all men are holy," her writings broadened Americans' horizons.

Tragically, in that July storm (described in the beginning of this chapter), Fuller's ship ran aground, and she and her husband and child drowned.

< Nat Turner, American slave leader, with his confederates in conference. Steel engraving, 1863, after Felix O. C. Darley.

The inscription on Fuller's tombstone encapsulated the reach of her vision: "By birth a child of New England; By adoption a citizen of Rome; By genius belonging to the world." Fuller served as a model, both intellectually and personally, for the first generation of women's rights activists. Susan B. Anthony said that Fuller "possessed more influence on the thought of American women than any woman previous to her time." Inspired by the global effort to achieve equality for women, Margaret Fuller embodied the possibilities and contradictions of the era of reform that defined the 1830s and 1840s. Although she was as deeply educated and as intellectually capable as any man, her family expected her to manage the household and attend to traditionally feminine duties. She demanded full equality, yet she reveled in the sensitivity of a "woman's heart" in her writings.

As Fuller's life demonstrated, Americans absorbed, transformed, and broadcast ideas that circulated around the globe in the 1830s and 1840s. Both Transcendentalists and evangelical Protestants created the transatlantic exchange networks. New theologies, new worship practices, and new reform movements spurred by these beliefs flowed back and forth across the Atlantic alongside the classical exchanges of philosophy and literature. The era proved to be one of the most tumultuous thanks to dynamic exchanges among Americans and their neighbors around the world.

◼ THE SECOND GREAT AWAKENING

In the early decades of the 19th century, a transatlantic revival movement spread from Britain to North America. This **Second Great Awakening**—following the similar religious dynamism of the 1730s—connected evangelical Christians on both sides of the Atlantic who exchanged ideas and strategies that inspired a broad set of social, cultural, and intellectual changes. Participants sought salvation and rebirth inside reenergized churches. The religious ferment of the 1820s and 1830s drew as much on the massive economic and social changes occurring in America as on theology. The increasingly rapid industrialization and urbanization of the country, the rise of a truly national commercial economy, and the surging middle class all spurred both celebration and anxiety (Map 12.1). Earlier generations of Americans engaged in mostly temporary and localized protest and reform. The evangelical reforms of the 1820s, 1830s, and 1840s, in contrast, drew on broad national support and lasted for decades. The issues they raised— the relationship between religious faith and politics, the responsibility of Christians to improve and uplift their society, and the tension between modernity and tradition— continue to engage us today.

Spreading the Word

In September 1830, **Charles Grandison Finney**, a young man trained in the law but fired with religious zeal, arrived in Rochester, New York. After his conversion, Finney rebuffed a legal client by saying, "I have a retainer from the Lord Jesus Christ to plead his cause, I cannot plead yours." Finney intended to unsettle the complacent and energize the believers. He succeeded magnificently. Preaching every day and three times on Sunday, meeting privately with individuals, and organizing prayer groups, Finney lit the spiritual fire that would consume western New York over the next several years. He spoke directly to people—men and women, rich and poor alike—in their own language. Without a formal pulpit, Finney addressed his listeners as equals. He beseeched them to accept the salvation that he had experienced. "A revival is nothing else than a new beginning of obedience to God," Finney proclaimed. "Just as in the case of a converted sinner, the first step is a deep repentance, a breaking down of heart, a getting down into the dust before God, with deep humility, and forsaking of sin."

As Finney explained, accepting one's sinfulness only began the work of reformed Christians: he exhorted the converted to live every day in accordance with the gospel. Here lay the socially transformative power of the Second Great Awakening. Ministers like Finney encouraged Americans to reform their society, to bring it more clearly into

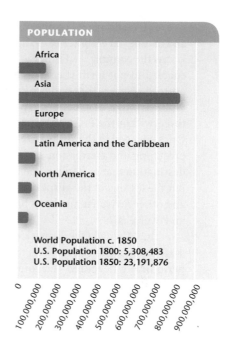

POPULATION

Africa
Asia
Europe
Latin America and the Caribbean
North America
Oceania

World Population c. 1850
U.S. Population 1800: 5,308,483
U.S. Population 1850: 23,191,876

0   100,000,000   200,000,000   300,000,000   400,000,000   500,000,000   600,000,000   700,000,000   800,000,000   900,000,000

MAP 12.1 ▲ New York State, 1830s The new transportation networks of turnpikes, canals, and railroads carried itinerant ministers as well as produce around the nation. The result was that the Second Great Awakening flourished in well-connected market towns and urban areas as well as more remote rural areas.

line with God's plan. Despite diverse interpretations of what that world should look like and an uneven embrace of evangelicalism, revivals encouraged massive social action all across the country. As Finney explained, "when mankind become religious, they are not enabled to put forth exertions which they were unable before to put forth. They only exert the powers they had before in a different way, and use them for the glory of God." Finney's religious experiences personified the journey that many converts took. He matured within the Presbyterian Church and studied law before turning to the ministry. Once engaged in the study of religion, Finney gravitated to the emotionalism of Baptist preaching and conversion. Convinced that the passive reception of scripture and predestination that he had learned as a boy had failed him, Finney implored his listeners to put the lessons of the gospel into practice in their lives. In the 1820s and 1830s, Finney and other revivalist ministers brought this message to listeners across the United States and overseas.

The "Burned Over" district of upstate New York earned its nickname because the scale and pace of conversions to the new evangelical faith suggested the wildfires that periodically devoured the countryside. Some converts had belonged to more established sects and others came from the ranks of unchurched Americans. Finney, and other itinerant ministers, who moved from community to community setting up congregations, borrowed from the Methodist practice of camp meetings, outdoor religious events, to develop a new style of open and accessible religion. Whereas their more conservative peers had eschewed public demonstrations of religion, evangelicals stressed the necessity of public revivals as a method of establishing and sustaining faith. Finney argued that "men are so sluggish, there are so many things to lead their minds off from religion . . . that it is necessary to raise an excitement among them, till the tide rises so high as to sweep away the opposing obstacles." This endorsement of public action and of the common sense of average people over the learned wisdom of trained ministers reinforced the accelerating democratization of American politics in the 1830s and 1840s.

Building a Christian Nation

Between 1820 and 1860, Americans built 40,000 new churches compared to the 10,000 they built in the 40 years before 1820. Although Protestant sects had dominated the religious life of the British colonies, a majority of citizens did not actively participate in organized religion. At the end of the revival period, probably one-third of all Americans attended church regularly. The evangelical movement spread from New York throughout New England, through Ohio, and through Kentucky into the South. Although many of the early revival preachers embraced a broadly Christian evangelicalism, the established sects sought to take advantage of the popular enthusiasm to build their particular denominations. Because of their resistance to the emotionalism of revivals, neither the Episcopalians (the American version of the Church of England) nor the Presbyterians benefited much from the movement. Instead, Methodists and the Baptists established themselves as leading American denominations as a result of the Second Great Awakening (Figure 12.1). The two faiths shared a close affinity with regard to doctrine, but the Baptists created a radically decentralized hierarchy that empowered local ministers and individual churches. In 1831, the year after Finney began his work

EXHORTATION AND PREACHING AT THE CAMP MEETING AT EASTHAM.

RELIGIOUS REVIVALS   Outdoor revivals served as one of the chief conduits of the new evangelical faiths. Their informality and the mixed audiences—men and women, blacks and whites, slave and free, rich and poor—contributed to the democratic feeling of the movement.

in Rochester, evangelicals reported over 600 revivals in New York State alone, with most organized by the Methodists and Baptists.

The power of churches in the colonial period came from their official sanction and the prominent role played by ministers and other religious leaders in local communities. The Revolution spurred American Christians to break with the Church of England, and the First Amendment to the constitution forbade the federal government from "establishing" religion. But the constitution did not prevent states from maintaining official religions, and several New England states did, with Massachusetts the last to break the connection in 1833. Under the leadership of Thomas Jefferson, Virginia disestablished its official religion just after the Revolution, eliminating the state's financial support for churches and ministers. The circulation of itinerant ministers further decentralized religion. Traveling preachers, often young, single men, adjusted to the physical rigors of long travel on horseback, rough accommodations, and long stretches away from home and family. The youth of most itinerants ensured they held less wealth and were less invested in established ways of thinking. These characteristics meant they might challenge the authority of propertied elites, especially when they did not belong to a specific community and did not suffer the social repercussions of criticizing those in power. Once a critical mass of conversions had occurred, people often organized themselves into a formal church. This process might take months or possibly years.

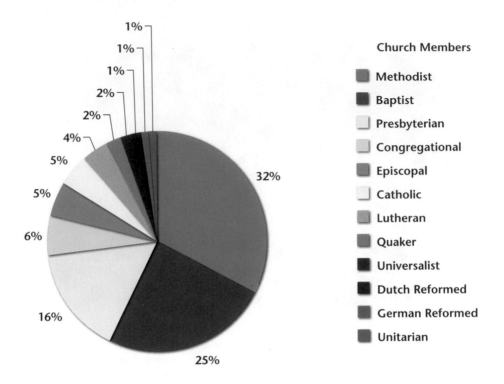

1% ┐
1% ┐
1% ┐
2% ┐
2% ┐
4% ┐
5%
5%
6%
16%
25%
32%

Church Members

- Methodist
- Baptist
- Presbyterian
- Congregational
- Episcopal
- Catholic
- Lutheran
- Quaker
- Universalist
- Dutch Reformed
- German Reformed
- Unitarian

FIGURE 12.1 ▲ Church Membership, 1850 The results of the Second Great Awakening were clearly visible by 1850, when Baptists and Methodists both counted millions of members, well ahead of other denominations. Note that the numbers are based on aggregate accommodations in churches as counted by the 1850 Census.

Mimicking the institutional traditions of the more established sects, evangelicals established colleges at which ministers could be trained. A raft of small colleges built across the Midwest served both denominational and public needs. Charles Grandison Finney assumed the presidency of Oberlin College in 1833, one of the earliest and most influential of these institutions, established by evangelical Presbyterians. Oberlin received support from an influx of students from Lane Theological Institute, another Midwestern evangelical institution whose administration had suppressed student activism against slavery. Southern evangelicals built as well; they founded Wake Forest, Richmond, Furman, Davidson, and Emory in the late 1830s and early 1840s. All told, evangelical reformers built 28 new denominational colleges between 1820 and 1850.

The Second Great Awakening spurred religious growth well beyond the established Protestant sects. The Catholic Church, a presence since the early colonial period, grew on the strength of the immigrant population to whom they ministered. Local, independent churches also sprang up across the nation. In some cases, charismatic charlatans swindled supporters out of money or into bed, while other devout ministers preached and brought their followers to new and meaningful relationships with their God.

Ann Lee, a former English Quaker who had moved to the United States, organized followers around a rigid doctrine of gender equality and millennial prophecy. Believers regarded Lee as a second incarnation of Christ and adopted her celibate lifestyle in pursuit of a "heaven on earth." Known as the Shakers for a ritual dance they performed, their asceticism and devotion to high-quality agricultural production and craftwork left a folk art legacy that lived on long beyond Lee.

The most successful of these new sects were the **Mormons**, founded by Joseph Smith in the same upstate New York district in which Finney preached. Smith composed *The Book of Mormon* after receiving what he regarded as divine visions. Preaching a conservative theology of patriarchal authority, Smith drew thousands of followers. But the sect generated fear and anger among other Americans. The Mormons' efforts to build a separate society, their willingness to live under a theocratic hierarchy, and, after 1852, their advocacy of plural marriage spurred mainline Protestant Christians to regard them as a threat. Persecutions followed as they moved from New York to Ohio and then to Missouri and Illinois. A confrontation in Illinois in 1844 left Smith dead and convinced **Brigham Young**, the new leader of the main community, that he must lead his people to a refuge. They chose as their destination the area around the Great Salt Lake, in today's Utah, then in largely ungoverned territory still belonging to Mexico. Young guided his community—more than 16,000 strong—over the mountains and out of the United States.

Interpreting the Message

Many of the changes proposed by Finney and other revival ministers angered and scared orthodox religious leaders. Traditionalists opposed measures that democratized the churches, especially the use of vernacular language, immediate church membership after conversion, and mixed-sex audiences where both men and women prayed publicly. Most problematic of all were the doctrinal revisions that Finney preached—revivalists abandoned the Calvinist belief in predestination and advocated a personal engagement with the Bible and their faith. Without denying that God held the power to save souls, Finney demanded that people use their free will to reject sin and pursue a more Christian life. Many of the new evangelicals also endorsed millennialism, a belief system organized around an imminent apocalypse, which made salvation all the more urgent.

The religious diversity of the old Middle Colonies (New York and Pennsylvania) ensured that evangelicals' calls, even those that elevated the power of individuals at the expense of institutions, resonated within an already pluralistic atmosphere (Figure 12.2). In New England, the Congregational Church, and to a lesser extent the Presbyterian Church, still reigned as the centers of power in local communities. There, reformers' demands challenged the authority of Congregational ministers and the hierarchy built on the partnership of the church and the Federalist Party. In Northern states generally, the call to act in a more Christian way evolved into an injunction to improve society. The Second Great Awakening targeted sin, both in the actions of individuals and in the effects these actions had on society. The pursuit of a Christian society propelled a host of reform movements including temperance; women's rights; prison, hospital, and asylum reform; better working conditions; and, most significantly, antislavery activism.

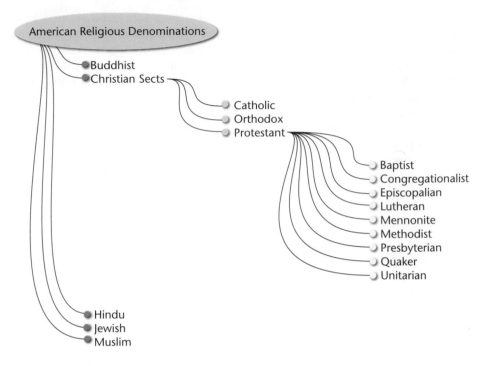

FIGURE 12.2 ▲ Subdivisions in American Religious Denominations The First Amendment's prohibition on state-supported churches and a great tolerance of religious diversity ensured that many sects flourished in the United States. Throughout the 19th century, immigrants brought new faiths to the United States that took root alongside the established denominations.

Religious reformers took advantage of two unique aspects of America's political system. In Britain, the tight connection between social position and political power ensured that reform efforts proceeded through Parliament. The U.S. system, by contrast, was more decentralized and the result was that in the early 19th century, American reformers more often went around government rather than through it. Reform movements also benefited from several changes in American law and society. Most importantly, the rapid growth of corporations and a variety of legal opinions establishing the autonomy of private institutions created a public sector and gave reformers the legal right and civic space within which to organize themselves. Reformers also took full advantage of the new print culture. Annual reports connected participants to a world beyond their own, and newspapers spread the language and goals of the movements.

At the same time the pursuit of perfection created tensions within American life about the role of religious institutions in democracy. Evangelical reform prompted people to ask doctrinal questions about the forces that could or should mediate the relationship between the individual and God and questions about the proper role for religious faith in politics and public policy. One abolitionist responded to fears of "mixing up" politics and religion with the call to "mix them, and mix them, and mix them, and keep mixing, until they cease to be mixed, and politics became religion and religion, politics." Other reformers and many outside the evangelical revival worried that the nation could not endorse particular religious values while ensuring personal liberty, too. Echoing Jefferson's concern, expressed in the Virginia Statute for Religious Freedom, they believed that "our civil rights have no dependence on our religious opinions any more than our opinions in physics or geometry."

STUDY QUESTIONS FOR THE SECOND GREAT AWAKENING

1. What strategies did evangelical ministers use to attract converts?
2. Why did so many people turn to evangelical Christianity in the 1830s and 1840s?

◼ NORTHERN REFORM

The most prominent and disruptive reforms concerned abolition of slavery, women's rights, and temperance. These three movements challenged America's political, economic, and social structure. Supporting them required believers to abandon deeply held beliefs about themselves, the natural world, society, and proper relations among each other. Because reform movements represented such a broad and fundamental challenge to American life, they drew on a wide variety of inspirations. In most cases, the Second Great Awakening and religious fervor energized reformers who organized within churches and drew explicitly on Christian doctrine to advocate particular changes. They often received funding from denominational institutions. But other reformers found their calling through secular channels, often by observing the plight of families broken by alcoholism, the slave trade, or domestic violence. Although reform movements appeared all across the country, Northern communities demonstrated greater sympathy for them. The rapid economic changes that characterized this era in the North provided reformers with more projects and weakened the natural opposition to reform that developed among entrenched elites.

Each of the major reform movements contained its own contradictions. Many antislavery activists, for example, worried about the negative effects of slavery on democracy without much regard for slaves as people. Some women's rights advocates used prevailing biological teachings about women's greater sensitivity to argue for their greater voice in public policy, while their opponents used that same information to argue for the exclusion of women from the public sphere. In certain cases, tensions between religious and secular reformers created friction, but generally they worked effectively together. The leadership of women in social reform movements created the greatest challenge. Women's active public role in reshaping American society in the 1830s, 1840s, and 1850s produced a backlash—even some friends of women's rights classified women's public protests as "out of place"—that curtailed many social movements, most noticeably the pursuit of equality between the sexes.

The Temperance Crusade

Most female reformers, and some men too, began their work with a focus on moral reform, especially prohibition of alcohol. In 1826, evangelical ministers formed the **American Temperance Society** (ATS), which initiated an enormously successful campaign. It was the first major reform effort to grow out of the revivals, and it drew support from ministers of all denominations. The movement did not end the consumption of alcohol in America, but it did help convince millions of people to rethink their relationship to drinking. Temperance also prompted numerous state legislatures to consider legal restrictions on alcohol, no easy feat given the important role alcohol played in American social rituals. Manual laborers, drawing on European traditions, drank alcohol during their morning and afternoon breaks. In 1825, the average American 15 years of age or older consumed seven gallons of alcohol per year, or the equivalent of 110 eight-ounce glasses. By 1850, the per capita consumption rate had fallen to less than two gallons per year. Evangelical clergy argued that alcohol represented a serious threat to the moral order and condemned the social effects of alcohol, mostly on the men who lost jobs, fell away from the church, and abused or abandoned their families. Lyman Beecher, probably the best known preacher in the country, regarded intemperance as "the sin of our land . . . that river of fire, which is rolling through the land, destroying the vital air, and extending an atmosphere of death" that would "defeat the hopes of the world."

Beecher founded the ATS, which called for a total prohibition of alcohol. Evangelicals succeeded in shifting public thinking about drinking by using statistics showing its deleterious effects. By connecting moral reform to scientific analysis and data, reformers broadened the appeal and the argument for their proposals. They needed strong arguments because their appeals demanded a high degree of sacrifice. They insisted that good Christians refrain from all alcoholic beverages, including those used in communion rites, and they even denied church membership to those who drank. These demands helped evangelicals to differentiate themselves clearly from Catholics, most of whom used wine in communion rites and came from cultures where alcohol played an important social role. As a result, temperance rarely had the support of immigrant communities or the Democratic Party, which welcomed them. Other Americans resented the campaign because they perceived it as an attack on individualism and basic freedom.

The desire to purify the body produced a variety of health-reform movements. The first sustained call for vegetarianism in the United States emerged at this time. Sylvester Graham, a pioneer in the field, devised an entire health system emphasizing the moderate intake of stimulants—including tea, coffee, and alcohol—as well as sex, which he advised should be restricted to once a month. His vegetarian diet relied on bread made from Graham flour, which included bran; the flour remains in use today in the United States in the crackers named after him.

The Rising Power of American Abolition

The campaign against slavery grew from humble origins within minority religious communities in England and America. In the 1850s, legislative debates over slavery—especially the 1850 Fugitive Slave Act and the 1854 Kansas–Nebraska Act—pushed

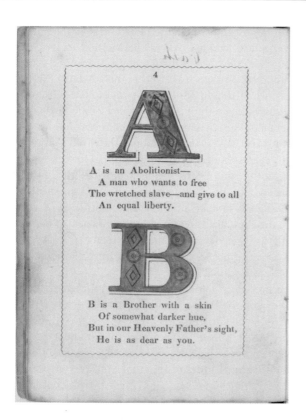

4

A is an Abolitionist—
A man who wants to free
The wretched slave—and give to all
An equal liberty.

B is a Brother with a skin
Of somewhat darker hue,
But in our Heavenly Father's sight,
He is as dear as you.

THE ABOLITION MESSAGE
Much to the horror of white Southerners, abolitionists printed grammar and spelling textbooks, such as this one, to carry their messages to young people.

THE DOUGLASS' MONTHLY
Douglass' Monthly was one of several papers that Douglass edited in his lifetime. All were widely read and all devoted themselves to the destruction of slavery and the advancement of racial equality.

many white Northerners into the antislavery camp; but in the 1830s and 1840s, supporters came mostly from within the evangelical world. Quakers and Methodists had his-
torically opposed the institution. John Wesley, Methodism's English founder, hated
slavery; and the early American Methodists Thomas Coke and Francis Asbury carried
on the fight in the late 18th century when they organized the Methodist Episcopal
Church of America. Slavery directly contradicted the egalitarian ethos of much Quaker
teaching; although Philadelphia merchants heavily invested in the institution in the
18th century, Pennsylvania hosted the first antislavery organization in the world. Granville
Sharp, the early English abolitionist, corresponded with Philadelphia Quakers when
he built the British movement. Even in the South, early evangelicals of all denominations often condemned chattel bondage as they pushed their congregants to pursue lives
more closely aligned with Jesus's message of universal brotherhood. Still, antislavery
work generally remained confined to the churches and schoolhouses of selected Northern hamlets. The key change within the movement came in the early 1830s as antislavery
activists transformed into abolitionists and began calling for an immediate end to
slavery.

The transition from conservative, gradualist reform to the call for immediate abolition can be seen in the shift of power from the Pennsylvania Abolition Society (PAS),
created in 1775 on Quaker principles of pacifism and antislavery, to the New England
Anti-Slavery Society (NEASS). The PAS, founded in the inspiring moment of the
American Revolution, had pursued a largely legalistic course seeking individual
emancipations of slaves within the state and gradual restrictions on slavery through
state law. The PAS reflected a conservative faith in elite action. Black people could not
join the organization and lawyers for the PAS made appeals strictly on the basis of
reason. By the 1830s, antislavery activists created a more vigorous and public campaign against the institution. Free African Americans in the North rejected gradual
emancipation, and their campaign educated and energized many white activists. In
1841, the black minister Samuel Ringgold Ward, for instance, assumed the pastorship
of the South Butler, New York, Congregational Church, and thanks to his efforts his
parishioners broke with the main denominational body and pursued independent
church reform centered on abolition. In Massachusetts, white activists joined their
black peers to create a new model of abolition society. Taking inspiration from the
ongoing political liberalization, activists abandoned the older legalistic strategies
and appealed directly to the people, often with stirringly emotional appeals. An 1831
edition of the *Abolitionist* included the following poem intended to shame white
Northerners into action:

> White Lady, happy, Proud, and Free, Lend awhile, thine ear to me;
> Let the Negro Mother's Wail Turn Thy cheek yet more pale.

Appeals such as these, and the sizeable black membership of the NEASS (nearly a
quarter of all members), signaled publicly that abolitionists had shifted both the nature
of their critique of slavery and the method by which they explained that critique to the
world. "Slavery is a crime," **William Lloyd Garrison** thundered, and "anything which
serves as a substitute for the immediate and absolute emancipation of slavery is delu-
sive, cruel, and dangerous." The NEASS became the model for the national **American
Anti-Slavery Society** (AASS), organized by Garrison in 1833 with immediate abolition as its core message. The AASS organized local chapters, sent speakers around the

country preaching against slavery, published narratives of slave life, and eventually appealed directly to Congress for national action on the subject. Garrison, in particular, pursued immediate emancipation with a unique vigor and effectiveness through his newspaper *The Liberator*—initiated in 1831—and his organizing and lecturing on behalf of the cause. By 1837, the AASS counted more than 1,000 chapters with 100,000 members, although abolitionists probably never comprised more than 5 percent of the Northern population. Between 1833 and 1838, Britain ended slavery in its Caribbean colonies, emancipating 800,000 people. Garrison and others drew courage from the British, and French, decision to abandon slavery, and they hoped that American leaders would soon follow course.

Garrison's stridency divided the abolition and reform communities as well as the country more broadly. His methods and his message, especially his pursuit of full racial equality for black Americans, frightened even some fellow antislavery activists. Theodore Dwight Weld, a convert to Garrisonian immediatism, initiated a series of discussions about slavery at Lane Theological Seminary in Cincinnati, Ohio, just across the river from Kentucky slavery. Emulating Garrison's racial egalitarianism, Weld and his students took up work in the city's black neighborhoods, where according to Weld, "if I ate in the City it was at *their* tables. If I attended parties it was *theirs—weddings—Funerals— theirs—Religious—meetings—theirs—*Sabbath schools—Bible classes—theirs." After the AASS began advocating immediate abolition, even other antislavery activists turned against them. Catherine Beecher, one of the most prominent reformers in the nation and sister of Henry Ward Beecher, condemned abolitionists as "neither peaceful nor Christian." Beecher, like many others in American society, saw immediate abolition as an attack on the right of property, perhaps the central ideological component of New World capitalism. Beecher argued that calls for immediate abolition increased racism and violence against blacks.

In fact, radical abolitionists more typically brought down a reign of social isolation, expulsion, and violence on themselves. Sarah and Angelina Grimké had been forced to relocate from South Carolina to Pennsylvania as they made their opposition to slavery publicly known, and opponents of abolition continually interrupted their meetings with force. The most notorious incident of violence, although hardly the only one, was the murder of **Elijah Lovejoy**, an abolitionist printer, who had relocated to Illinois in the mid-1830s. Despite warnings and attacks on his shop, Lovejoy continued his work until a mob killed him. Lovejoy's death and other acts like it radicalized many abolitionists. John Brown, whose attempted slave rebellion in Virginia in 1859 served as one of the catalysts to Civil War, said that Lovejoy's murder convinced him that abolition would not come without violence.

Garrison, Weld, and the Grimké sisters all represented the white face of abolition. Well known and well financed, they demonstrated the ability of 19th-century Americans to see beyond racial differences. But enslaved people themselves proved the most effective opponents of slavery, none more so than **Frederick Douglass**, the most famous and most rhetorically skillful of his generation. Born Frederick Bailey on a Maryland plantation, Douglass learned to read and in 1838, at the age of 20, he escaped and made his way to Rochester, New York, where he threw himself into the work of abolition. Articulate in print and speech with a commanding physical presence, Douglass traveled the country lecturing to abolition societies. In Rochester he started his own paper, which circulated across the North. Douglass's narratives of his life sold tens of thousands of copies in the

United States and abroad; and like other slave narratives at the time, it introduced readers firsthand to the horrors of slavery.

Black activists targeted the scheme, popular among whites around the country, that slaves should be freed and then deported from the country. This was the platform of the **American Colonization Society** (ACS), which, since its founding in 1817, continued to attract national leaders to its ranks. During the 1830s and 1840s, the ACS counted among its members the most influential politicians of both regions and parties. Colonization generated intense opposition from black Americans. James McCune Smith, a New York City physician with an interracial practice, led the campaign against the plan. Black opposition to colonization in the 1820s helped drive Garrison and other white abolitionists to support immediate abolition.

Women's Rights

Like the abolitionists and evangelical reformers more generally, advocates of women's rights drew inspiration and legitimacy by connecting their movement with predecessors in Europe. Lydia Maria Child, one of the most influential U.S. women's rights reformers, wrote biographies of an Englishwoman and two French women who provided models of active, virtuous womanhood. German reformers built on the democracy movement of 1848 to call for gender equality as well. In a sentiment with which many American reformers would have agreed, one German activist declared "the freedom of women is the greatest revolution . . . since it breaks fetters which are as old as the world." American women drew special inspiration from British author Mary Wollstonecraft's *A Vindication of the Rights of Woman* (1792). Wollstonecraft's manifesto rejected the

WOMEN'S RIGHTS   This statue, located today in the rotunda of the U.S. Capitol, immortalizes three leaders of the fight for women's rights in the United States—Elizabeth Cady Stanton, Susan B. Anthony, and Lucretia Mott—and conveys the as-yet unfinished nature of the struggle.

notion of natural differences between men and women and called for full gender equality. Women's efforts to challenge their second-tier status represented as profound a change as abolition. As one historian has noted, "to question sexual hierarchy and distinct spheres of gender was to question a pillar of traditional Christian society more basic and pervasive than the Sabbath."

The confidence to challenge that pillar came from women's success in other reform fields. According to a Boston minister in 1836, "it is to female influence and exertion that many of our best schemes of charity are due." Women played a crucial role in the abolition movement, perhaps the essential one. According to William Lloyd Garrison, "the Anti-Slavery cause cannot stop to estimate where the greatest indebtedness lies, but whenever the account is made up, there can be no doubt that the efforts and sacrifices of WOMEN, who helped it, will hold a most honorable and conspicuous position." Many female reformers toiled first in the abolition movement and then in the 1830s moved into women's rights. Beyond the reform movement women began playing a more public role in formal politics. Whigs capitalized on their connections with moderate reforms such as temperance and protection of the Sabbath to make explicit appeals for women's support. Although women could not vote, party leaders believed that wives influenced their husband's votes and that more public support would only help the party. In the 1844 and 1848 presidential campaigns, both Whigs and Democrats incorporated women into rallies and other events. This process revealed no essentially female politics; rather, women's beliefs appeared, like men's, to be most directly affected by their region and their class position. Southern women, for instance, supported slavery and helped steer both parties toward a stricter line against abolition.

Women themselves did not agree on reform. A famous debate between Catherine Beecher and Angelina Grimké clarified the challenges facing female reformers. In 1837, Beecher published her *Essay on Slavery and Abolitionism, with Reference to the Duty of American Females*, directed at Grimké's abolition work. In it she declared that "petitions to congress, in reference to the official duties of legislators, seem, IN ALL CASES, to fall entirely without the sphere of female duty." Grimké responded to Beecher by articulating a strict egalitarian creed: "Whatever it is morally right for man to do . . . it is morally right for women to do." Grimké boldly proclaimed that "I believe it is women's right to have a voice in all the laws and regulations by which she is to be *governed*, whether in Church or State." Beyond participation, she asserted women's right to rule as well, "just as much right to sit upon the throne of England, or in the Presidential chair of the United States." Even though a woman had just assumed the English throne—Queen Victoria was crowned in 1837—the active role played by the Grimkés, and other women, generated increasing criticism in the late 1830s and produced deep splits in the reform movement.

Frustrated by the conservative reaction of otherwise reform-minded men, a group of women in western New York organized a convention in 1848 to consider women's rights. The convention's "Declaration of Sentiments," modeled after the Declaration of Independence, listed infringements on women's rights and called for change, including the right to vote. Elizabeth Cady Stanton, one of the convention organizers and one of the most important leaders of the 19th-century women's movement, drafted the declaration. Stanton accepted the need to sacrifice women's exceptionalism to further the causes she advocated, writing in 1842 that "I am in favour of political action, & the organization of a third party as the most efficient way of calling forth & directing action." The participation of abolitionists at the convention demonstrated how many worked in both fields. Stanton declared that only Frederick Douglass, 1 of 32 men and the only person of color to attend the Seneca Falls Conference, could really understand what it meant to be disenfranchised. Douglass advocated strongly for women's full rights—his newspaper's masthead boldly declared "All Rights for All!"

Because many white and upper- or middle-class American women believed their responsibility was to raise moral children and preserve domestic space, they regarded female public activism on politically contentious topics as inappropriate. But for other women the belief that females possessed a stronger innate moral sense compelled them to advocate abolition. They believed that women's greater respect for moral behavior obligated them to address slavery, the chief sin in the nation, even if the act of doing so, which required organizing, fundraising, and petitioning, brought them into fuller participation in the public world of men. The female reformers of this period encountered contradictions that have challenged American women to this day. Embracing women's distinctiveness could both empower and isolate—women used their special position to make real reforms and helped blunt the worst side effects of early industrialization. However, by endorsing women's difference they also ensured that women remain separated from men, especially as more formal politics overtook reform efforts after the Civil War.

Activists' efforts to improve the position and condition of women usually entailed working from within existing institutions—the family, the church, and sometimes electoral politics. In some cases, however, reformers sought to remake society in radical ways, from the ground up. Building what historians now call "Utopian Communities," these men and women envisioned a new era built on the principles of equality, community engagement, and respect for all people. One of the guiding lights of the movement, Robert Dale Owen, left his native Scotland because the United States offered more promise for the sort of small-scale democratic life he supported. An advocate of abolition, a free school system, and an ardent defender of women's autonomy, Owen founded New Harmony, Indiana, in 1825. Owen took inspiration from socialism, as did other Utopian reformers who witnessed the destructive effects of early industrial capitalism. The community lasted only a few years, before lapsing into an individualism that Owen repudiated. He remained a vigorous advocate for progressive causes, writing one of the earliest books advocating birth control in the United States.

Making a Moral Society

A wide range of citizens participated in evangelical reforms, but the active support of a handful of wealthy elites ensured that the movement operated on a national, even global, basis. New York businessmen Arthur and Lewis Tappan occupied the pinnacle of this community. Arthur imported silk, and at its peak, his business grossed a million dollars per year. He made huge donations to reform organizations from 1825 to 1837, when the combination of a devastating fire and the national recession bankrupted him. During that period, he contributed more to evangelical causes than anyone else in the nation, as he helped found, fund, or manage the American Tract Society, the American Education Society, the American Bible Society, and the Home Missionary Society, among others. His brother Lewis showed equal enthusiasm to bring a new Christian ethos to business and used his financial success to bankroll new spiritual enterprises. Lewis, the creator of the Wall Street credit rating agency now known as Dun and Bradstreet, maintained extensive contacts with a broad range of both white and black abolitionists.

Although there is no doubt that the Tappans cherished their faith—both gave enormous sums of money, time, and energy to propagate a variety of reforms—it is also clear that the reforms they advocated made good business sense as well. Temperance offers the clearest example of how reforms often met the needs of both the new business elite and the evangelicals. As employers adopted new technologies, including clocks and steam-driven machinery, they expected workers to increase their own efficiency. Both owners and reformers targeted the old tradition of morning beer breaks, which artisans had retained from European cultures. Prohibition also ensured that workingmen did not arrive late or incapacitated because of late nights at the bar. Job seekers at the Rochester Woolen Mills, in upstate New York, were told that they "must be of moral and temperate habits." Because workers increasingly resided on their own, away from the residences of factory owners, increased church attendance and religious programs gave owners a way to monitor employees after hours. Still, even elites knew that religion resisted control. Although reforms probably spread faster because they buttressed the emerging industrial and commercial order, in other respects (particularly antislavery), reformers' actions generated political problems that elites preferred to suppress.

STUDY QUESTIONS FOR NORTHERN REFORM

1. What explains the militancy of abolitionists after 1831?
2. On what grounds did American women argue for greater freedom?
3. How did the various reform movements intersect with one another?

◼ SOUTHERN REFORM

Southern evangelicals faced a far greater challenge than their Northern coreligionists. Because slaveholders demanded absolute obedience from their slaves, they built a deeply conservative society. Any challenge to hierarchy and tradition threatened to undermine the foundation of that society. Despite this hurdle, Southern evangelical reformers confronted what they perceived as problems in Southern society. Most evangelicals strongly supported temperance and denounced the personal violence that characterized the system of Southern honor. A handful of brave reformers spoke out against slavery, but opponents often drove them from the region. Southern antislavery reformers were replaced by a new breed of thinkers who advocated for a more Christian slavery. Regardless of the measures they advocated, Southern reformers proceeded more cautiously than their Northern brethren. And, although Southern reformers often corresponded or met with their Northern or European peers, the emerging political culture of sectionalism curtailed cooperation across the regional divide.

Sin, Salvation, and Honor

The dominant value system in the white South prior to the Second Great Awakening emphasized an ethos of honor inherited from ancient models. Through the 1850s, Southerners consumed British Romantic fiction, particularly the courtly chivalry of Sir Walter Scott's novels. With little incentive to scrutinize their society, many white Southerners clung to this secular value system in the face of mounting tensions within their society. The evangelical movement in the South of the 1820s and 1830s expressly challenged prevailing values. Evangelicals sought to replace the standing system in which a person's wealth and status determined one's worth with a system in which one's piety and moral purity determined rank. Attracting followers proved difficult if people had something to lose, as revealed by the response of a Kentucky sheriff who treated his local Methodist preacher well but who refused to commit to the church because "his worldly prospects were good, and he would not give up all for Christ." Southern evangelicals advocated many of the same reforms as their Northern counterparts. Hundreds of Southern communities established local temperance societies, for example. Like Northerners, Southerners feared the effect of alcohol on families and society, but most of all, as one evangelical noted, because it was "one grand hindrance of the success of the gospel." Evangelicals supported Bible and tract societies, Sunday schools, home and foreign missions, and efforts to help prisoners and the disabled.

Southern women played a key role in the evangelical movement and reform, but they rarely extended their work into the broader public women's rights movement found in the North. Southern women tended to focus their efforts on the individual rather than societal level; they organized locally but not nationally; and increasingly by the 1840s, they sought reforms that promoted the stability of the slaveholding South. For example, in Petersburg, Virginia, a mill town south of Richmond, evangelical women organized Sunday schools, an Education Society, a Young Ladies' Missionary Society, a Married Ladies' Missionary Society, a Tract Distribution Society, and a Ladies' Benevolent Society. They also organized numerous ad hoc committees within the various churches and buttressed reform and benevolence with countless fairs and fundraisers. In addition to real benefits for the community, local and private relief systems allowed community elites to retain control over aid recipients. To receive aid, those in need had to pass the scrutiny of the "ladies." The insistence of Southern evangelicals to pursue reform while respecting the hierarchy of the conservative South reveals how religious revivals and the development of a distinct Southern political identity developed simultaneously throughout the 1830s, 1840s, and 1850s.

Pro-Slavery Reform

The antislavery attitude of early evangelicals in the late 18th and early 19th centuries inhibited the larger reform movement in the South. Early evangelicals sometimes criticized slaveholding, but more often they sought ways to accommodate their religious faith with their racial beliefs. Over time, articulating a pro-slavery Christianity provided one way to claim both piety and respectability. By the 1850s, the central evangelical reform project in the South became the Mission to the Slaves. Evangelical slaveholders came to regard the act of ministering to slaves as the purest expression of their faith.

Modeling their work on that of West Indian planters who pursued a similar movement in the 1810s, the Mission to the Slaves encouraged masters to improve the physical treatment of slaves with the threat of church or social sanctions for those who failed to do so. In addition, the mission advocated for laws to protect slaves from cruel treatment. As Robert Dabney, one of the foremost Presbyterian ministers of the period, declared, Christians "must be willing to recognize and grant in slaves those rights which are a part of our essential humanity." Owing to the power of slaveholders in Southern society, these reforms could only extend so far. Under Southern law, slaves could not legally marry—although they formed de facto marriages—and evangelicals regarded this as a gross violation of the proper relationship between adult men and women who bore and raised children together. Female evangelicals also advocated protection of female slaves from sexual exploitation. The other main reform of the Mission to the Slaves fulfilled a basic Protestant obligation—ensuring that every person could read the Gospel for himself or herself. Because of the circulation of abolitionist propaganda in the mails and the power of literacy, Southern states made it a crime to teach slaves to read. Evangelical reformers built Sunday schools and worked with individual masters to persuade them that limited literacy posed no threat.

As slaveholders increasingly found a home within evangelical churches, they articulated a more individualized and more paternalistic social order. They aimed especially to control those African Americans who converted to Christianity in large numbers for the first time and drew strength from their new faith. Southern evangelicals, by then firmly supporting the morality of slavery, used the occurrence of several major slave rebellions in the 1820s and 1830s to argue for the necessity of conversion. To pacify slaveholders' concerns that evangelical reforms would undermine control of their slaves, evangelicals emphasized that converted slaves would be more obedient. According to Basil Manly, "the dissemination of moral truth will always be found at once the cheapest & most effective support of law & order, the most certain check of incendiarism & turbulence."

Nat Turner and Afro-Christianity

Early Afro-Christianity drew on black folk traditions, many of them African practices. The results of this cultural fusion could be seen in the late 18th century, when Afro-Christians would gather in a circle to proclaim their faith and pray. The "ring" derived from West African traditions but blended easily with the evangelical tradition of small group, public ritual. Other similarities between West African practices and Christianity, including an emphasis on water as a conduit of spirituality, helped draw new worshippers to the faith; rivers, sacred places in African religions, became baptismal pools. The importance of burial practices and the belief that death brought a "homecoming," as well as a three-part hierarchy of gods that resembled the Christian trinity, made Christianity intelligible to West Africans. Muslim slaves brought to America in the colonial era by the French, Spanish, and the British provided another bridge between faiths.

AFRICAN AMERICAN RELIGIOUS PRACTICES The more informal and emotionally expressive religious practices adopted by African Americans alienated some white Christians but gave black Christians a distinctive and rich spiritual practice.

Malinke slaves in Spanish St. Augustine and Sengambians and northern Nigerians in Louisiana left ample evidence that they arrived in the New World already practicing Islam. The close kinship between the two faiths and the syncretic nature of Islam in West Africa ensured that New World Muslims could be expected to understand and perhaps absorb aspects of Christianity without much difficulty.

At least a quarter of all Southern blacks participated in churches by the end of the 1850s (mostly in biracial churches). Although blacks sat in segregated pews, they received egalitarian treatment in many respects. Records reveal that mixed-race churches held blacks to the same moral standards as whites and disciplined them for the same reasons—drunkenness, lying, adultery, and other breaches of the faith. But these same churches never overtly challenged white assumptions of racial superiority. In some cases, masters required slaves to worship with them because they feared the consequences of separate worship. But in other cases, the spiritual sustenance that enslaved people obtained may have outweighed the routine humiliation of separate seating and readings and homilies telling slaves to obey their masters. Certainly the body of Afro-Christian hymns and spirituals that emerged at this period shows a community asserting its solidarity and searching for ways to resist the dehumanization of slavery:

> O brothers, don't get weary
> O brothers, don't get weary
> O brothers, don't get weary
> We're waiting for the Lord
> We'll land on Canaan's shore
> We'll land on Canaan's shore,
> When we land on Canaan's shore,
> We'll meet forever more.

Effort by slaveholders to control African American belief generally failed. By the 1850s, Southern evangelical churches, particularly the Baptists and Methodists, had become major institutions in black American life. Instead of obedience, Afro-Christian theology stressed the equality of all people before God, the necessity of discipline for a people held in bondage, and the promise of eventual deliverance. In their creative use of Christianity, black evangelicals echoed the efforts of enslaved peoples in French and Portuguese colonies, particularly Haiti and Brazil, where a syncretic Afro Catholicism sustained generations of slaves in opposition to French, Portuguese, and later Brazilian slaveholders.

One commonality among all the leaders of slave rebellions in the 1820s and 1830s was their use of religion to radicalize their communities and their positions of religious leadership to mobilize those communities. Denmark Vesey, a free black man in Charleston, South Carolina, drew on these diverse traditions. According to the charges against him, Vesey organized a multiethnic band of slaves and free blacks in 1822 and planned a revolt. Captured before the plan could be sprung, investigators discovered religious leadership throughout the plot, including Morris Brown, an African Methodist Episcopal (AME) pastor. Vesey himself worked as a lay leader in the AME church and used scripture to draw supporters. According to one deposition against him, "his general conversation was about religion which he would apply to slavery, as for instance, he would speak of the creation of the world, in which he would say all men had equal rights, blacks as well as whites." "Gullah" Jack Pritchard surfaced as a leader in the Vesey conspiracy along with another AME member who also maintained a reputation in Charleston as a conjurer.

Evangelical religion's role in spurring resistance to slavery burst into public view with **Nat Turner**'s rebellion in Southampton County, Virginia (Map 12.2). Turner's skills and literacy earned him the respect of local whites who allowed him to preach to their slaves. Unbeknownst to whites, Turner had spent years praying and searching for

MAP 12.2 ▲ Nat Turner's Route in Southampton County, Virginia, 1831 Nat Turner and his band moved from house to house in an attempt to contain news of their rebellion. The violence of their actions marked a trail in blood through Southampton County and seared itself into the mind of the white South.

Celebrating the Black Atlantic

David Walker was not alone in his knowledge of global slavery or his faith in the resiliency of black people, nor was he alone in belonging to the maritime community. Black sailors possessed a unique mobility that exposed them to the diverse experiences and living conditions of people of African descent all around the Atlantic basin. The foremost among those experiences was the Haitian Revolution. Sailors who visited the island offered priceless knowledge about the reality of the hemisphere's only black republic. After watching a military procession, one noted, "they appeared to understand military tactics to perfection. They were elegantly dressed in red frocks and trousers, faced with blue and green. . . . On the whole they were first-rate soldiers." The idea of black soldiers parading would have been particularly impressive to African Americans, who could generally not own weapons and rarely marched in military formation. But Haiti represented more than physical power. Haitians' success at governing themselves proved to American activists that freedom was possible. Despite their pride in Haitians' accomplishments, black people in America (both enslaved and free) expressed great reluctance to speak openly about Haiti because they knew that even a mere mention could inspire panic and violence in whites. What they could and did celebrate openly, after 1838, was emancipation in the British West Indies. Black Americans, like West Indians themselves, enshrined August 1 as Freedom Day. By the 1850s, they held celebrations all across the Northern states, where speakers heralded the nonviolence of British emancipation. "Not by the sword and the bayonet," one Freedom Day participant argued,

the right way to fulfill his obligation to God, and he found it in a sacrifice that he likened to that of Jesus. In 1831, Turner built a network of loyal men and launched a bloody uprising that killed nearly 60 whites and sent the state into a panic. Although the militia dispersed the rebels and eventually apprehended and executed Turner, the widespread and disciplined organization among slaves on diverse plantations brought home to whites the deepest fears they had harbored since the Haitian Revolution at the end of the 18th century. To fearful whites, he seemed to portend the violence to come if they did not improve their treatment of slaves.

Southern Antislavery Reformers

Nat Turner's Rebellion occurred the same year that the abolitionist William Lloyd Garrison began publishing the *Liberator*, a confluence that most white Southerners did not regard as coincidental. Fearing additional slave rebellions, white Southerners quashed all criticism of slavery after 1831. James Henry Hammond's "gag rule" prevented congressional discussion of abolition from 1836 to 1844, and federal Postmasters "but by the force and power of truth." Freedom Day organizers used the ceremonies to unite African Americans with people of color around the hemisphere, but they also understood the political appeal of peaceful emancipation, especially when contrasted with Haiti's violent legacy.

Freedom Day celebrations offered elaborate festivals, with chartered trains to carry participants, parades hosted by civic and charitable groups, and banquets. These events gathered thousands of blacks and whites together, and speakers extolled both the virtue and wisdom of West Indian emancipation. They marshaled statistics to prove the economic superiority of free labor on the islands and celebrated the moral improvement of both free people and whites outside the confines of a slave society. These events offered community leaders an opportunity to combine a proud black identity with a universal uplift of humanity. Frederick Douglass, a frequent speaker at Freedom Day celebrations, asserted that August 1 "belongs . . . to the lovers of Liberty and of mankind the world over." "The sentiment," he noted, "that leads us to celebrate noble deeds . . . is nature and universal. . . . Neither geographical boundaries, nor national restrictions, ought, or shall prevent me from rejoicing over the triumphs of freedom." Like other African Americans, Douglass believed that commemorating West Indian emancipation would help the triumph of freedom in America as well.

- How did black Americans learn about the experiences of other enslaved people in the hemisphere?
- What lessons did they draw from these experiences and how did they shape the struggle against slavery in the United States?

before and after these dates prevented the circulation of abolitionist material in the Southern mails. Sarah and Angelina Grimké, born into a wealthy Charleston slaveholding family, earned fame as the most prominent Southern antislavery reformers. After a visit north and exposure to Quakers, Sarah embraced their faith, especially their opposition to slavery. Converting her sister, they challenged the very foundation of South Carolina society in their calls for emancipation. Isolated and silenced at home, they fled their family and their region, settling in Philadelphia, the leading Quaker city in the United States. After hearing Garrison speak, Angelina pushed beyond the staid boundaries of the Quaker world and entered antislavery work with a reformist zeal. Her *An Appeal to the Christian Women of the South* (1836) demanded emancipation on the grounds of Christianity and argued that the millennium would come only after slavery had been destroyed. The radicalism of her message combined with her personal background brought strong denunciations from conservative ministers in the North and howls of rage from Southerners who perceived her as a traitor.

David Walker, another exile from the South, proved even more dangerous than the Grimké sisters. Born to an enslaved father and free black mother in North Carolina,

Walker remained in the South until the mid-1820s, when he moved to Boston and immersed himself in the abolition movement. After writing briefly for a variety of journals, Walker penned and published *An Appeal to the Coloured Citizens of the World*. Electrifying in its language and vigorous in its argument, the document created a firestorm of criticism in both the North and the South; even many abolitionists found its frank call for resistance too vigorous. Walker, flatly denying the legitimacy of slavery, asserted the universal rights of all people to freedom. He called on the "candid and unprejudiced of the world, to search the pages of history diligently, and see if [any group of people] ever treated a set of human beings, as the white Christians of America do us, the blacks, or Africans."

Walker drafted a brief global history of slavery, running from biblical and classical examples to the role played by European colonizers of the New World who created plantation slavery. Walker's "appeal" sought an international audience. He compared the plight of African Americans to other subjugated peoples—Native Americans, the Greeks, the Irish, and the Jews. The range of his learning—from ancient Egypt to the modern Spanish empire—and his use of these examples proved that black Americans could and did educate themselves to a degree that would have surprised most whites at the time.

In Boston, Walker worked within the larger maritime community. Since the early days of European oceanic exploration, black men had worked as sailors; and they remained, in the 1830s and 1840s, among the most worldly and most important members of the African diasporic community in the Americas. Keen to rebut charges that blacks were incompetent to rule themselves, Walker argued that "the inhuman system of *slavery*, is the *source* from which most of our miseries proceed." Like most antislavery evangelicals, Walker condemned the hypocrisy of Christians holding fellow Christians in bondage. He cataloged the disasters that befell previous slave empires in the hopes of scaring white Southerners into action. Again and again he warned "white Christians" against their continuing sanction of this most diabolical of evils. He closed with the ominous warning that "Americans may be as vigilant as they please, but they cannot be vigilant enough for the Lord, neither can they hide themselves, where he will not find and bring them out." Walker himself was not vigilant enough, despite death threats against him; less than a year after publishing the *Appeal* he was found dead outside his office in Boston.

STUDY QUESTIONS FOR SOUTHERN REFORM

1. In what ways did Southern reform resemble Northern efforts? How were they different?
2. How did black Southerners conceptualize and experience evangelical Christianity?

◼ CHALLENGES TO THE SPIRIT OF THE AGE

In many respects, the era from the late 1820s to the early 1850s can be defined as much by the role of religion as by economic change, geographic growth, and political development. The growth of evangelical Protestantism preoccupied the lives of many Americans through this period, produced social reforms that changed the lives of millions, and helped propel the sectional divisions that produced the Civil War and emancipation. At the same time, however, the rise of an increasingly secular culture, expressed through novels, newspapers, and the work of mass political parties, matched the spiritual movements of the day. Some of this cultural work faced east, engaged with European questions expressed in largely British and continental idioms. In other cases, authors self-consciously rejected older models and sought to build a uniquely American culture. Much of it was condemned by religious figures because of what they regarded as vulgar content or expression. Most frustrating for the traditionalists was the persistent popularity and wide reach of these new forms of media and communication. Americans were building their first truly national culture.

Emerson, Thoreau, and the American Soul

Ralph Waldo Emerson began his professional life as a Unitarian clergyman but left the ministry in the midst of the tumult in the early 1830s. He wrote essays and criticism

THOREAU'S *WALDEN*
Thoreau's cabin and the image of man's relation to wildness articulated by *Walden* served for many readers as a counterbalance to the industrializing and urbanizing trends of the early 19th century.

over the next several decades, patronized younger authors such as Henry David Thoreau and Margaret Fuller, and pushed for broad changes in American life. Unlike most of the evangelicals, Emerson sought to reform the American mind. He celebrated a vigorous individualism, articulated most fully in his famous essay "Self-Reliance" in which he encouraged readers to reject tradition. "A foolish consistency is the hobgoblin of little minds, adored by statesmen and philosophers and divines," he wrote famously. Emerson's advice provided reassurance for the new classes that seized opportunities created by industrialization. His call to begin life anew mirrored what many entrepreneurs felt they were doing.

Henry David Thoreau attempted to live this philosophy when he retreated to a cabin outside Concord, Massachusetts, for two years. Unfortunately, he failed as a farmer and survived through the largesse of friends who stopped by with gifts of food. Although Thoreau could not remove himself entirely from the modernizing world he so distrusted, his volume chronicling the experience, *Walden*, pushed readers to think critically about the costs of the rampant materialism that sustained the dynamic economic growth of the era. *Walden* also represented a challenge to traditional Anglo-American ideas about land use. Thoreau did not seek to maximize the land and encouraged a respectful appreciation for man's dependence on the natural world.

Thoreau and Emerson became associated with the philosophy of transcendentalism, an American variant of European Romanticism. Turning away from the rationalism of the Enlightenment, transcendentalists desired to know the world through emotion and intuition. Although it was often expressed in obscure prose, this philosophy, like Emerson's writing in general, proved compatible with trends toward democratization in American society. Transcendentalists put little value on formal education and degrees. Instead, experience and intimate contact with the natural world earned their praise. As Thoreau's experience indicates, their philosophy called for action rather than talk. Both writers supported abolition and other social reforms, but neither appreciated the staid evangelical tone of the movement. Emerson denounced the hypocrisy that blinded would-be reformers from the full implications of their morality, demanding that "goodness must have some edge to it."

The First Mass Culture

Steam power and industrialization, in addition to improving the efficiency of American manufacturing, lowered the price of leisure and recreation items. Printers began producing newspapers in greater volume at a lower cost. In the early 1830s, thousands of "penny presses" sprouted in every city and many small towns throughout the country. These newspapers distinguished themselves from their predecessors because rather than relying on subsidies from political parties, they sought a mass readership. To accomplish this goal, reporters began writing "stories," largely human interest tales about murders, robberies, and assaults. James Gordon Bennett, the editor of the *New York Herald*, the most successful of the new breed of newspaper, realized that the average readers "were more ready to seek six columns of the details of a brutal murder, or the testimony of a divorce case, or the trial of a divine for improprieties of conduct, than the same amount of words poured forth by the genius of the noblest author of the times." Serialized fiction also began to appear, largely stories of romance and duplicity

MINSTREL SHOWS The degrading caricatures enacted in minstrel shows drew large white audiences and imprinted on many Northerners erroneous but lasting images of black life.

aimed at female readers. Reporters began investigating political news, particularly in Washington, DC, where they gained the scorn of politicians for their willingness to report on their foibles. Even as newspapers helped knit America together with a shared culture, through their focus on conflict they helped exacerbate the disagreements over slavery.

Alongside the theater, which continued to offer performances of Shakespeare and other European classics, arose a much rowdier and uniquely American form of popular entertainment: minstrelsy. Minstrel shows began in Northern cities where white male performers blackened their faces and imitated what they imagined to be black behavior. The shows became enormously popular in New York, Boston, and other major cities, with a repertoire of songs and stock characters. Stephen Foster, America's first major songwriter, gained his fame penning minstrel tunes such as "Camptown Races" and "Oh! Susanna," although Foster later wrote songs that celebrated more complex black characters. Minstrel shows succeeded partly because of the way they transgressed boundaries, with whites imitating, celebrating, and lampooning blacks all at once. The all-male audiences and the vigorous physicality of the performances transformed the theaters into showcases for masculine expression. **Walt Whitman**, the bard of the common man, regularly patronized the Bowery Theater, one of New York City's most famous minstrel venues. He described the crowd there as "a vast sea of upturned faces and red flannel shirt, extending its roaring and turbid waves close up to the foot-lights on either side, clipping in the orchestra and dashing furiously against the boxes."

WALT WHITMAN   Whitman's poetry celebrated the physical and emotional energy unleashed by American growth in the 1840s and 1850s.

The American Renaissance

The emergence of a group of American writers around midcentury—Emerson and Thoreau in essays, Nathaniel Hawthorne and Herman Melville in fiction, and Edgar Allan Poe, Walt Whitman, and Emily Dickinson in poetry—signaled for many Americans the maturation of their culture. In their settings, their language, and their themes, these authors made the United States a part of world literature. At the same time, however, they engaged in a dialogue with their peers across the Atlantic. They read and wrote with one eye on the European authors in whose traditions they worked—and European authors reciprocated the feeling. British novelist Anthony Trollope referred to Hawthorne as "a brother novelist very much greater than myself."

Hawthorne and Melville, in particular, wrote literature that reflected universal themes. Hawthorne went back in time, rather than far afield, to craft his most memorable work. In his *The Scarlet Letter*, he used New England's witchcraft trials of the late 17th century to explore contemporary morality. Melville first gained notoriety for a series of novels, *Typee*, *Omoo*, and *Redjacket*, drawn from his adventures as a young sailor in the Pacific Ocean. The novels blended travelogue and ethnography and provided detailed analyses of the lives of island inhabitants. Melville's most ambitious novel, *Moby Dick*, addressed universal questions of power, revenge, and madness. Nonetheless, Melville's work offers insights into mid-19th-century America. The ship that carries the whaling party in *Moby Dick*, the *Pequod*, carried a remarkably diverse crew; with Indian, African, and South Seas harpooners, white men and black, all bound together by their shared domicile and profession. Melville's imaginary ship mirrored the real-life diversity of America and the difficulty of reconciling so many competing interests and contradictory philosophies in one nation.

Melville's capacious imagination and welcome fictional embrace of diverse ethnic and racial types reflected a broad-mindedness common among this generation of writers. A number of writers, including Whitman, Dickinson, and Poe, took inspiration from what they called Oriental tales, which they read as a "symbol of the unfettered imagination." In many of his poems, Poe adopted the form and message of Asian literature—especially in his use of visionaries and visionary moments—including borrowing from the Koran and Islamic practices. At the same time, this trio of writers pioneered a distinct American poetry. Whitman advanced this project the furthest. His use of free verse, without either rhyme or meter, his frank sexuality, and his vigorous endorsement of the rough and authentic America distinguished his work. Rather than draw classical parallels or craft aspirational literature, Whitman celebrated the prosaic democracy of America, as in his most famous poem, "Song of Myself," where he writes

> I am of old and young, of the foolish as much as the wise,
> Regardless of others, even regardful of others,
> Maternal as well as paternal, a child as well as a man,
> Stuff'd with the stuff that is coarse and stuff'd with the stuff
> that is fine,
> One of the Nation of many nations, the smallest the same
> and the largest the same,
>
> . . .
>
> A learner with the simplest, a teacher of the thoughtfullest,
> A novice beginning yet experient of myriads of seasons,
> Of every hue and caste am I, of every rank and religion,
> A farmer, mechanic, artist, gentlemen, sailor, quaker,
> Prisoner, fancy-man, rowdy, lawyer, physician, priest.

Emily Dickinson, born in 1830, remained virtually unknown throughout her life. She remained in her parents' home in Amherst, Massachusetts, which she rarely left. She published only a handful of anonymous poems during her lifetime, but the posthumous discovery of her work has inspired fellow writers for the last century and a half. Moving beyond Whitman's experimentation with free verse, Dickinson unshackled every constraint, reimagining meter, rhyme, capitalization, grammar, and punctuation. Her work demonstrated new capacities in language that poets continue to explore. Dickinson professed her understanding of poetry in physical terms, ones that Whitman and Thoreau would well have understood: "If I read a book and it makes my whole body so cold no fire ever can warm me, I know *that* is poetry."

Politics as Gospel

The vitality and diversity of American culture in the 1830s and 1840s could be seen in the political system as well. Senators, congressmen, and presidents recognized the power and importance of the reform movements initiated by evangelicals, but they could not control it. The new issues of the 1830s and 1840s, especially the transformation of artisans into workers and the rapid commercialization of the national economy, spurred the rise of working men's parties in Northeastern cities, but these lasted only a few years and rarely influenced policy. As slavery began to assume greater national significance, antislavery reformers organized political parties under different names—the Liberty Party in 1840 and 1844 and the Free Soil Party in 1848—that likewise failed to take root. These failures, however, should not obscure the extent to which the nation's political culture reflected the larger dynamism and unpredictability of the era. The promise and the possibilities represented by these short-lived political parties and by the broader rise and fall of the Whig Party encouraged Americans to take politics seriously.

The Whig Party emerged as the main opposition to Democratic dominance. The Whigs coalesced around their shared antipathy for Andrew Jackson—they took their

TIMELINE 1801–1855

AMERICA	YEAR	THE WORLD
Aug Cane Ridge, Kentucky, evangelical revival held	1801	
Jan American Colonization Society founded	1817	
Feb Liberia is founded as a colony for freed American slaves	1820	
Jun Denmark Vesey arrested for organizing a slave conspiracy in Charleston, SC	1822	
Charles Grandison Finney leads his first revival Robert Dale Owen founds Utopian colony in New Harmony, IN	1825	
American Temperance Society founded	1826	
David Walker publishes *An Appeal to the Coloured Citizens of the World* Angelina Grimké joins her sister Sarah in Philadelphia where they become leading women's rights and antislavery activists	1829	
Apr Joseph Smith founds the Mormon Church	1830	
William Lloyd Garrison founds *The Liberator*, America's leading abolitionist newspaper Nat Tuner leads the deadliest slave rebellion in U.S. history in Southampton County, VA	1831	
Massachusetts is the last state to disestablish support of an official church Charles Grandison Finney assumes residency of Oberlin College American Anti-Slavery Society is organized under Garrisonian principles	1833	Britain ends slavery in the British West Indies Ottoman Empire recognizes independence of Egypt
Alexis de Tocqueville publishes Vol. 1 of *Democracy in America* James Gordon Bennett begins publishing the *New York Herald*	1835	
Abolitionist printer Elijah Lovejoy murdered in Alton, IL, by antiabolitionist mob Catherine Beecher and Angelina Grimké debate nature of women Severe recession strikes United States	1837	

name from the English political party that opposed absolutist kings. By 1840—the first year the Whigs won the White House—the party had emerged with both a guiding ideology and an official organization. The Richmond *Whig* defined their supporters as those who "prefer liberty to tyranny—who support privilege against prerogative—the rights and immunities of the people ... against the predominance of the Crown or Executive power." That ideology emphasized republican self-government and an active role for government at all levels to help foster economic development, although Whigs also criticized interference in markets. **Henry Clay** led the party during its two decades in existence, and his "American system" drew the support of Whig businessmen who wanted the federal and state governments to sponsor the construction of the infrastructure—roads, bridges, canals, and railroads—on which private enterprise could build American markets and cities.

The Whig Party also drew in reformers—from humanitarian groups protesting the treatment of Indians to some of the antislavery forces spread around the country. Whigs attracted primarily Protestant voters, often denouncing Catholic immigrants as "dupes" of the Democrats. They drew strength primarily in the North and the Upper South—Virginia, Kentucky, Tennessee, and North Carolina all saw strong Whig parties. Citizens' enthusiasm for the Democrats, the Whigs, and the smaller third parties made the 1830s, 1840s, and much of the 1850s a period of political dynamism and flux.

Frederick Douglass escapes slavery	1838	
Liberty Party nominates James G. Birney for president on an antislavery platform	1840	
Mormon founder Joseph Smith is killed in Illinois; Brigham Young leads Mormons to Utah First telegraph sent between Washington, DC, and Baltimore, MD Liberty Party again nominates James G. Birney for president on antislavery platform	1844	
Frederick Douglass publishes first edition of his "Narrative of the Life of Frederick Douglass"	1845	Irish Potato Famine begins, inaugurating a decade of disease that kills 750,000 Irish and drives two million into exile
Lewis Tappan helps found American Missionary Association, which joins antislavery churches	1846	
Nationalist movements occur in Italy, Germany, France, and Hungary Lucretia Mott and Elizabeth Cady Stanton lead Seneca Falls Convention, which produces "Declaration of Sentiments" calling for women's rights Free Soil Party nominates Martin Van Buren for president on platform opposing expansion of slavery in Western territories	1848	Karl Marx and Friedrich Engels publish *The Communist Manifesto*
Nathanial Hawthorne publishes *The Scarlet Letter* Margaret Fuller dies on her return to New York	1850	
Herman Melville publishes *Moby Dick*	1851	
Henry David Thoreau publishes *Walden*	1854	
Walt Whitman publishes first edition of *Leaves of Grass*	1855	

Men and women invested significant amounts of energy in organizing new parties and advocating new policies. "The spirit of the age," observed the English visitor Fanny Wright, was "to be a little fanatical" (Figure 12.3).

The willingness of people to spend time, money, and energy on politics demonstrates a commitment to American democracy that few other nations manifested. England, which saw the beginning of many of the working men's parties that inspired American workers of the 1830s, continued to maintain restrictions on voting and office holding that excluded a significant number of even white men from the polls. To international observers, Americans invested more of themselves in their public world. One of the most trenchant observers, the Frenchman Alexis de Tocqueville, expressed some skepticism about democratic forms of government. But de Tocqueville also drew inspiration from Americans' enthusiasm for politics and for their public world. He believed that Americans' willingness to create associations and parties would help restore the organic bonds that had once tied together the Old World's societies before the rise of capitalism and democracy. Whereas conservatives feared that the "tyranny of the majority" would overrule reason and liberty in open democracies, de Tocqueville predicted associations of "a thousand different types" would forestall the "tyranny of parties or the arbitrary rule of a prince."

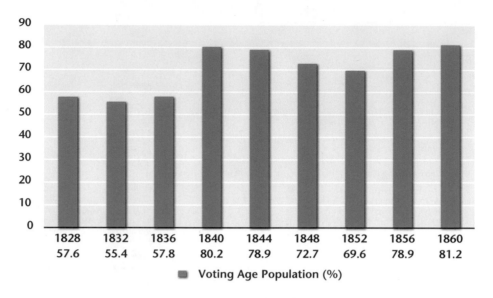

FIGURE 12.3 ▲ **Voter Turnout at Presidential Elections, 1828–1860** As states made more men eligible to vote, both Democrats and Whigs mobilized supporters in huge numbers. The political controversies of the 1850s further ensured that voting rates remained very high.

When de Tocqueville observed that Americans were insatiable "joiners," he testified to the emergence of a new civic space in the United States. European countries had official spheres and private spheres and—increasingly after the 16th century—marketplaces, but little room for organized public actions. The reform movements that flourished in America in the 1830s and 1840s did so because a strong evangelical impulse sustained them—many people understood their reform work as saving their own souls as well as those they helped—and because of changes in American law. Some of these latter changes—especially the rise of general incorporation laws as a part of the expansion of capitalism during Andrew Jackson's administration—created the opportunity for reformers to organize themselves in ways that would have been impossible in previous years. Social reformers also benefited from the larger process of democratization underway at the same time, which drew new participants into politics and empowered individual citizens to believe that they could solve problems in American life. However, this optimism waned somewhat in the 1850s, as reformers found that some problems resisted easy solution, especially slavery and the continuing growth of poverty among urban residents.

STUDY QUESTIONS FOR CHALLENGES TO THE SPIRIT OF THE AGE

1. How did transcendentalism relate to the evangelical reform efforts that defined the era?

2. Did the literature of Hawthorne, Melville, Whitman, and Dickinson create a more insular or more open America?

Summary
- Evangelical Christians on both sides of the Atlantic exchanged ideas and strategies during the Second Great Awakening and inspired a broad set of social, cultural, and intellectual changes in all parts of America.
- Northern women initiated reform efforts—including temperance, women's rights, and abolition—that targeted the same broad range of social ills as did their British counterparts.
- In the South, slaveholders harnessed the power of the Protestant churches to articulate a more individualized and more paternalistic social order, especially as a way to control those African Americans who converted to Christianity in large numbers for the first time and drew strength from their new faith.
- These spiritual movements were matched by the rise of an increasingly secular culture, expressed through novels, newspapers, and the work of mass political parties.

Key Terms and People
American Anti-Slavery Society (AASS) *408*
American Colonization Society (ACS) *410*
American Temperance Society (ATS) *406*
Clay, Henry *426*
Douglass, Frederick *409*
Finney, Charles Grandison *398*

Garrison, William Lloyd *408*
Lovejoy, Elijah *409*
Mormons *403*
Second Great Awakening *398*
Turner, Nat *417*
Walker, David *419*
Whitman, Walt *423*
Young, Brigham *403*

Reviewing Chapter 12
1. How were political democratization and religious awakening related during the antebellum era?
2. What distinguishes the evangelicalism of the 1830s and 1840s from the practice of Christianity in earlier periods?

Further Reading
Carwardine, Richard. *Transatlantic Revivalism: Popular Evangelicalism in Britain and America, 1790–1865*. Westport, CT: Greenwood Press, 1978. This book traces the intellectual and personal links that bound people together across the Atlantic.

Ginzberg, Lori D. *Women and the Work of Benevolence: Morality, Politics, and Class in the Nineteenth-Century United States*. New Haven, CT: Yale University Press, 1990. An analysis of how women's reform work both challenged and reinforced gender conventions in 19th-century America.

Heyrman, Christine Leigh. *Southern Cross: The Beginnings of the Bible Belt*. New York: Knopf, 1997. A study of the origins and maturation of evangelical denominations in the Southern United States through the Second Great Awakening.

Howe, Daniel Walker. *What Hath God Wrought: The Transformation of America, 1815–1848*. New York: Oxford University Press, 2007. A comprehensive history that reveals the intimate relationship between the emergence of new technologies, new ideologies, and new structures of politics in early 19th-century America.

Newman, Richard S. *The Transformation of American Abolitionism: Fighting Slavery in the Early Republic*. Chapel Hill: University of North Carolina Press, 2002. A clear analysis of the shift in strategy and goals from first-generation abolition in the 18th century to the more radical 19th-century activists.

Ryan, Mary. *Civic Wars: Democracy and Public Life in the American City During the Nineteenth Century*. Berkeley: University of California Press, 1997. A thoughtful study that chronicles how the development of American cities challenged public and political life.

America In The World
PEOPLE, GOODS, IDEAS AND PRACTICES

CHAPTER 12: Religion and Reform 1820–1850

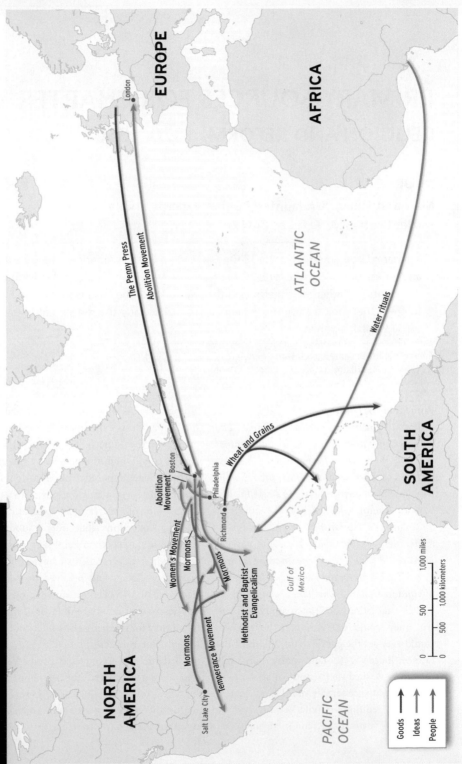

EUROPE

AFRICA

NORTH
AMERICA

SOUTH
AMERICA

ATLANTIC
OCEAN

PACIFIC
OCEAN

Gulf of
Mexico

London

Boston

Philadelphia

Richmond

Salt Lake City

The Penny Press

Abolition Movement

Water rituals

Wheat and Grains

Abolition
Movement

Women's Movement

Mormons

Mormons

Mormons

Methodist and Baptist
Evangelicalism

Temperance Movement

Mormons

Goods
Ideas
People

0   500   1,000 miles
0   500   1,000 kilometers

PRIMARY SOURCES FOR CHAPTER 12
RELIGION AND REFORM, 1820–1850

SOURCE 12.1
Margaret Fuller, "Undaunted Rome," Excerpt from a Letter to Her Brother, K. F. Fuller (1849)

Margaret Fuller emerged in the 1840s as a leading voice in American literary criticism and journalism. She wrote for both the *New York Tribune* and independently on women's rights and other reform efforts of the day. In 1846, the *Tribune* sent her to Europe to cover the revolutionary movements there, particularly the movement to create a unified Italian republic.

Source: Arthur B. Fuller, ed., *At Home and Abroad; Or, Things and Thoughts in America and Europe,* rev. ed. (New York: Tribune Association, 1869), 433–36.

Rome, May 6, 1849.

I write you from barricaded Rome. The "Mother of Nations" is now at bay against them all. Rome was suffering before. The misfortunes of other regions of Italy, the defeat at Novara, preconcerted in hope to strike the last blow at Italian independence, the surrender and painful condition of Genoa, the money-difficulties,—insuperable unless the government could secure confidence abroad as well as at home,—prevented her people from finding that foothold for which they were ready.

The vacillations of France agitated them; still they could not seriously believe she would ever act the part she has. We must say France, because, though many honorable men have washed their hands of all share in the perfidy, the Assembly voted funds to sustain the expedition to Civita Vecchia; and the nation, the army, have remained quiescent.

No one was, no one could be, deceived as to the scope of this expedition. It was intended to restore the Pope to the temporal sovereignty, from which the people, by the use of suffrage, had deposed him. No doubt the French, in case of success, proposed to temper the triumph of Austria and Naples, and stipulate for conditions that might soothe the Romans and make their act less odious. They were probably deceived, also, by the representations of Gaëta, and believed that a large party, which had been intimidated by the republicans, would declare in favor of the Pope when they found themselves likely to be sustained. But this last pretext can in noway avail them. They landed at Civita Vecchia, and no one declared for the Pope. They marched on Rome. Placards were affixed within the walls by hands unknown, calling upon the Papal party to rise within the town.

Not a soul stirred. The French had no excuse left for pretending to believe that the present government was not entirely acceptable to the people. Notwithstanding, they assail the gates; they fire upon St. Peter's, and their balls pierce the Vatican. They were repulsed, as they deserved, retired in quick and shameful defeat, as surely the brave French soldiery could not, if they had not been demoralized by the sense of what an infamous course they were pursuing.

France, eager to destroy the last hope of Italian emancipation,—France, the alguazil of Austria, the soldiers of republican France, firing upon republican Rome! If there be angel as well as demon powers that interfere in the affairs of men, those bullets could scarcely fail to be turned back against their own breasts. Yet Roman blood has flowed also; I saw how it stained the walls of the Vatican Gardens on the 30th of April—the first anniversary of the appearance of Pius IX.'s too famous encyclic letter. Shall he, shall any Pope, ever again walk peacefully in these gardens? It seems impossible! The temporal sovereignty of the Popes is virtually destroyed by their shameless, merciless measures taken to restore it. The spiritual dominion ultimately falls, too, into irrevocable ruin. What may be the issue at this moment, we cannot guess. The French have retired to Civita Vecchia, but whether to reëmbark or to await reinforcements, we know not. The Neapolitan force has halted within a few miles of the walls; it is not large, and they are undoubtedly surprised at the discomfiture of the French. Perhaps they wait for the Austrians, but we do not yet hear that these have entered the Romagna. Meanwhile, Rome is strongly barricaded, and, though she cannot stand always against a world in arms, she means at least to do so as long as possible. Mazzini is at her head; she has now a guide "who understands his faith," and all there is of a noble spirit will show itself. We all feel very sad, because the idea of bombs, barbarously thrown in, and street-fights in Rome, is peculiarly dreadful. Apart from all the blood and anguish inevitable at such times, the glories of Art may perish, and mankind be forever despoiled of the most beautiful inheritance. Yet I would defend Rome to the last moment. She must not be false to the higher hope that has dawned upon her. She must not fall back again into servility and corruption.

And no one is willing. The interference of the French has roused the weakest to resistance. "From the Austrians, from the Neapolitans," they cried, "we expected this; but from the French—it is too infamous; it cannot be borne;" and they all ran to arms and fought nobly.

The Americans here are not in a pleasant situation. Mr. Cass, the Chargé of the United States, stays here without recognizing the government. Of course, he holds no position at the present moment that can enable him to act for us. Beside, it gives us pain that our country, whose policy it justly is to avoid armed interference with the affairs of Europe, should not use a moral influence. Rome has, as we did, thrown off a government no longer tolerable; she has made use of the suffrage to form another; she stands on the same basis as ourselves. Mr. Rush did us great honor by his ready recognition of a principle as represented by the French Provisional Government; had Mr. Cass been empowered to do the same, our country would have acted nobly, and all that is most truly American in America would have spoken to sustain the sickened hopes of European democracy. But of this more when I write next. Who knows what I may have to tell another week?

WORKING WITH SOURCES

1. What does Fuller's position as a war correspondent (the first ever employed in this capacity) suggest about the relationship between events in Europe and the United States?

2. According to Fuller, why are other nations interfering in the effort to create an Italian republic?

3. What role did America play in this effort?

SOURCE 12.2

Charles G. Finney, Excerpts from "What a Revival of Religion Is" (1835)

Charles Finney was one of the leading ministers of the Second Great Awakening, a religious revival movement that occurred during the 1820s and 1830s. Originally a Presbyterian, Finney preached a widely accessible evangelical Christian message intended to create converts and energize believers to improve their own behavior and their society.

Source: Lectures on the Revivals of Religion Delivered by the Rev. Charles G. Finney, rev. ed. (Oberlin, OH: E. J. Goodrich, 1868). Also see http://www.gospeltruth.net/1868Lect_on_Rev_of_Rel/68revlec01.htm.

TEXT.—O Lord, revive thy work in the midst of the years, in the midst of the years make known; in wrath remember mercy. —HAB. iii. 2.

Religion is the work of man. It is something for man to do. It consists in obeying God with and from the heart. It is man's duty. It is true, God induces him to do it. He influences him by his Spirit, because of his great wickedness and reluctance to obey. If it were not necessary for God to influence men—if men were disposed to obey God, there would be no occasion to pray, "O Lord, revive thy work." The ground of necessity for such a prayer is, that men are wholly indisposed to obey; and unless God interpose the influence of his Spirit, not a man on earth will ever obey the commands of God.

A "Revival of Religion" presupposes a declension. Almost all the religion in the world has been produced by revivals. God has found it necessary to take advantage of the excitability there is in mankind, to produce powerful excitements among them, before he can lead them to obey. Men are so spiritually sluggish, there are so many things to lead their minds off from religion, and to oppose the influence of the Gospel, that it is necessary to raise an excitement among them, till the tide rises so high as to sweep away the opposing obstacles. They must be so excited that they will break over these counteracting influences, before they will obey God. Not that excited feeling is religion, for it is not; but it is excited desire, appetite and feeling that prevents religion. The will is, in a sense, enslaved by the carnal and worldly desires. Hence it is necessary to awaken men to a sense of guilt and danger, and thus produce an excitement of counter feeling and desire which will break the power of carnal and worldly desire and leave the will free to obey God. . . . There is so little principle in the church, so little firmness and stability of purpose, that unless the religious feelings are awakened and kept excited, counter worldly feeling and excitement will prevail, and men will not obey God. They have so little knowledge, and their principles are so weak, that unless they are excited, they will go back from the path of duty, and do nothing to promote the glory of God. The state of the world is still such, and probably will be till the millennium is fully come, that religion must be mainly promoted by means of revivals. How long and how often has the experiment been tried, to bring the church to act steadily for God, without these periodical excitements. Many good men have supposed, and still suppose, that the best way to promote religion, is to go along uniformly, and gather in the ungodly gradually, and without excitement. But however sound such reasoning may appear in the abstract, facts demonstrate its futility. If the church were far enough advanced in knowledge, and had stability of principle enough to keep awake, such a course would do; but the church is so little enlightened, and there are so many counteracting causes, that she will not go steadily to work without a special interest being awakened. As the millennium advances, it is probable that these periodical excitements will be unknown. Then the church will be enlightened, and the counteracting causes removed, and the entire church will be in a state of habitual and steady obedience to God. The entire church will stand and take the infant mind, and cultivate it for God. Children will be trained up in the way they should go, and there will be no such torrents of worldliness, and fashion, and covetousness, to bear away the piety of the church, as soon as the excitement of a revival is withdrawn. . . .

Backslidden Christians will be brought to repentance. A revival is nothing else than a new beginning of obedience to God. Just as in the case of a converted sinner, the first step is a deep repentance, a breaking down of heart, a getting down into the dust before God, with deep humility, and forsaking of sin. . . .

Christians will have their faith renewed. While they are in their backslidden state they are blind to the state of sinners. Their hearts are as hard as marble. The truths of the Bible only appear like a dream. They admit it to be all true; their conscience and their judgment assent to it; but their faith does not see it standing out in bold relief, in all the burning realities of eternity. But when they enter into a revival, they no longer see men as trees walking, but they see things in that strong light which will renew the love of God in their hearts. This will lead them to labor zealously to bring others to him. They will feel grieved that others do not love God, when they love him so much. And they will set themselves feelingly to persuade their neighbors to give him their hearts. So their love to men will be renewed. They will be filled with a tender and burning love for souls. They will have a longing desire for the salvation of the whole world. They will be in an agony for individuals whom they want to have saved—their friends, relations, enemies. They will not only be urging them to give their hearts to God, but they will carry them to God in the arms of faith, and with strong crying and tears beseech God to have mercy on them, and save their souls from endless burnings. . . .

FINALLY. —I have a proposal to make to you who are here present. I have not commenced this course of Lectures on Revivals to get up a curious theory of my own on the subject. I would not spend my time and strength merely to give you instructions, to gratify your curiosity, and furnish you something to talk about. I have no idea of preaching about revivals. It is not my design to preach so as to have you able to say at the close, "We understand all about revivals now," while you do nothing. But I wish to ask you a question. What do you hear lectures on revivals for? Do you mean that whenever you are convinced what your duty is in promoting a revival, you will go to work and practise it?

Will you follow the instructions I shall give you from the word of God, and put them in practise in your own lives? Will you bring them to bear upon your families, your acquaintance, neighbors, and through the city? Or will you spend the winter in learning about revivals, and do nothing for them? I want you, as fast as you learn any thing on the subject of revivals, to put it in practice, and go to work and see if you cannot promote a revival among sinners here. If you will not do this, I wish you to let me know at the beginning, so that I need not waste my strength. You ought to decide now whether you will do this or not. You know that we call sinners to decide on the spot whether they will obey the Gospel. And we have no more authority to let you take time to deliberate whether you will obey God, than we have to let sinners do so. We call on you to unite now in a solemn pledge to God, that you will do your duty as fast as you learn what it is, and to pray that He will pour out his Spirit upon this church and upon all the city this winter.

WORKING WITH SOURCES

1. What is Finney's critique of the established Christian churches?

2. What does Finney ask of his listeners?

3. How might people converted in this manner engage with public problems?

SOURCE 12.3
Elizabeth Cady Stanton, "Declaration of Sentiments" (1848)

This document was primarily written by Elizabeth Cady Stanton, a leading activist for the full citizenship of women. Passed at the Seneca Falls Convention in 1848, Stanton modeled her document after the Declaration of Independence.

Source: Elizabeth Cady Stanton, Susan B. Anthony, and Matilda Joslyn Gage, eds., *History of Woman Suffrage* (Rochester, NY: Charles Mann, 1887), 70–71.

When, in the course of human events, it becomes necessary for one portion of the family of man to assume among the people of the earth a position different from that which they have hitherto occupied, but one to which the laws of nature and of nature's God entitle them, a decent respect to the opinions of mankind requires that they should declare the causes that impel them to such a course.

We hold these truths to be self-evident: that all men and women are created equal; that they are endowed by their Creator with certain inalienable rights; that among these are life, liberty, and the pursuit of happiness; that to secure these rights governments are instituted, deriving their just powers from the consent of the governed. Whenever any form of government becomes destructive of these ends, it is the right of those who suffer from it to refuse allegiance to it, and to insist upon the institution of a new government, laying its foundation on such principles, and organizing its powers in such form, as to them shall seem most likely to effect their safety and happiness. Prudence, indeed, will dictate that governments long established should not be changed for light and transient causes; and accordingly all experience hath shown that mankind are more disposed to suffer, while evils are sufferable, than to right themselves by abolishing the forms to which they were accustomed. But when a long train of abuses and usurpations, pursuing invariably the same object evinces a design to reduce them under absolute despotism, it is their duty to throw off such government, and to provide new guards for their future security. Such has been the patient sufferance of the women under this government, and such is now the necessity which constrains them to demand the equal station to which they are entitled.

The history of mankind is a history of repeated injuries and usurpations on the part of man toward woman, having in direct object the establishment of an absolute tyranny over her. To prove this, let facts be submitted to a candid world.

He has never permitted her to exercise her inalienable right to the elective franchise.

He has compelled her to submit to laws, in the formation of which she had no voice.

He has withheld from her rights which are given to the most ignorant and degraded men—both natives and foreigners.

Having deprived her of this first right of a citizen, the elective franchise, thereby leaving her without representation in the halls of legislation, he has oppressed her on all sides.

He has made her, if married, in the eye of the law, civilly dead.

He has taken from her all right in property, even to the wages she earns.

He has made her, morally, an irresponsible being, as she can commit many crimes with impunity, provided they be done in the presence of her husband. In the covenant of marriage, she is compelled to promise obedience to her husband, he becoming, to all intents and purposes, her master—the law giving him power to deprive her of her liberty, and to administer chastisement.

He has so framed the laws of divorce, as to what shall be the proper causes, and in case of separation, to whom the guardianship of the children shall be given, as to be wholly regardless of the happiness of women—the law, in all cases, going upon a false supposition of the supremacy of man, and giving all power into his hands.

After depriving her of all rights as a married woman, if single, and the owner of property, he has taxed her to support a government which recognizes her only when her property can be made profitable to it.

He has monopolized nearly all the profitable employments, and from those she is permitted to follow, she receives but a scanty remuneration. He closes against her all the avenues to wealth and distinction which he considers most honorable to himself. As a teacher of theology, medicine, or law, she is not known.

He has denied her the facilities for obtaining a thorough education, all colleges being closed against her.

He allows her in Church, as well as State, but a subordinate position, claiming Apostolic authority for her exclusion from the ministry, and, with some exceptions, from any public participation in the affairs of the Church.

He has created a false public sentiment by giving to the world a different code of morals for men and women, by which moral delinquencies which exclude women from society, are not only tolerated, but deemed of little account in man.

He has usurped the prerogative of Jehovah himself, claiming it as his right to assign for her a sphere of action, when that belongs to her conscience and to her God.

He has endeavored, in every way that he could, to destroy her confidence in her own powers, to lessen her self-respect, and to make her willing to lead a dependent and abject life.

Now, in view of this entire disfranchisement of one-half the people of this country, their social and religious degradation—in view of the unjust laws above mentioned, and because women do feel themselves aggrieved, oppressed, and fraudulently deprived of their most sacred rights, we insist that they have immediate admission to all the rights and privileges which belong to them as citizens of the United States.

In entering upon the great work before us, we anticipate no small amount of misconception, misrepresentation, and ridicule; but we shall use every instrumentality within our power to effect our object. We shall employ agents, circulate tracts, petition the State and National legislatures, and endeavor to enlist the pulpit and the press in our behalf. We hope this Convention will be followed by a series of Conventions embracing every part of the country.

WORKING WITH SOURCES

1. What are the chief criticisms that this document makes regarding the treatment of women in 1840s America?

2. What is the effect of Stanton's decision to copy the language of the Declaration of Independence?

3. How would Americans in the 1840s have interpreted this comparison?

SOURCE 12.4
Visual Document: Woodcut, "A Horrid Massacre" (1831)

In 1831, an enslaved man, Nat Turner, led a slave revolt in Southampton County, Virginia. Turner used his experience as a preacher to the county's slaves to create a network of lieutenants and plan the attack. His group killed 56 white people but could not seize the county armory before the local militia counterattacked and dispersed them. Turner was later captured and executed. The woodcut shown here circulated widely in Virginia newspapers.

Source: F&A Archive/The Art Archive at Art Resource, NYImage.

HORRID MASSACRE IN VIRGINIA.

The Scenes which the above Plate is designed to represent, are—Fig. 1. a Mother intreating for the lives of her children.—2. Mr. Travis, cruelly murdered by his own Slaves.—3. Mr. Barrow, who bravely defended himself until his wife escaped.—4. A comp. of mounted Dragoons in pursuit of the Blacks.

WORKING WITH SOURCES

1. How does the author of this woodcut represent blacks and whites as individuals?

2. How does the difference in weapons suggest attitudes about the positions of black and white men in the society?

3. How does the bottom sequence present the organization and intent of the two sides in the struggle?

A House Dividing

13

1844–1860

I n November 1852, U.S. Commodore Matthew C. Perry left Norfolk, Virginia, with a fleet of "Black Ships"—new steam-powered warships. He sailed for the closed society of Japan, which Americans saw as a potential trading partner, a colonial target, and a port and refueling base for whaling ships. Only the Chinese, the Koreans, and the Dutch had limited access to Japan. Britain—which had defeated China in the First Opium War of 1839–1842—opened Western trade to the Pacific Rim, and their success encouraged the United States to approach China and Japan.

The U.S. government instructed Perry to be "courteous and conciliatory, but at the same time, firm and decided." The Japanese should be impressed with "a just sense of the power and greatness" of the Americans. After several months of negotiation, backed by threats that the steam-driven warships would shell the city of Tokyo, Perry secured a meeting with a high-ranking official. Coming ashore in early 1854, nearly 5,000 Japanese greeted the Americans. Cultural and gift exchanges complemented the official business. U.S. soldiers watched a demonstration of sumo wrestling, and U.S. Marines performed a close order drill exhibition. In one sailor's observation, "there was a curious mélange today here, a function of east and west, railroads and telegraph, boxers and educated athletes, epaulettes and uniforms, shaved pates and nightgowns, soldiers with muskets and drilling in close array, soldiers with petticoats, sandals . . . all these things, and many others, exhibiting the difference between our civilization and usages and

< *Storming of Chapultepec—Pillow's Attack* by Carl Nebel.

those of this secluded, pagan people." The condescension in this statement came mostly from ignorance. The Japanese had insulated themselves from the West, and, as a result, most Westerners knew little about Japanese life. The sailor's perspective also reflected common Anglo-American attitudes about racial and cultural differences that shaped debates in the United States and wherever Americans went abroad.

After he returned to the United States, Perry assured the country that commercial exchange with both Japan and China was imminent, either through diplomacy or force. Perry described the ascension of America to world power and the acquisition of colonies as inevitable and frankly admitted the likelihood of colonial acquisitions. "In the developments of the future, the destinies of our nation must assume conspicuous attitudes: we cannot expect to be free from the ambitious longings for increased power, which are the natural concomitants of national success." Although few politicians spoke this openly about American interventions overseas, Perry's vision of American power reflected the essence of what both Democrats and Whigs heralded in their campaigns and from the floors of Congress. Outgrowing its status as a recently freed colony, the United States was preparing to become a colonizing power itself.

DINNER GIVEN TO THE JAPANESE COMMISSIONERS ON BOARD U.S.S.F. POWHATAN.

PERRY IN JAPAN This image of Perry's dinner for Japanese commissioners on one of his fleet's ships emphasizes American power, but failed to capture the historical reality. In the 1850s, the United States was only emerging as a naval power and could do little more than ask that the Japanese open their markets to U.S. imports.

■ THE EXPANSION OF AMERICA

Expansion of trading opportunities in the Pacific was made possible by Western expansion during the 1840s. U.S. victory in the Mexican War brought the territory between the Louisiana Purchase line and the Pacific Ocean under U.S. control. Expansion intensified the conflict between Americans over whether new states should be organized with or without slavery, and political disputes over slavery in the territories generated increasing sectional animosities. These clashes spurred Northerners to fashion a new political coalition based around opposition to the expansion of slavery, a conservative approach to immigration and naturalization, and federal support for economic development. Concerned about the threat a sectional party in U.S. politics posed to slavery, Southerners reacted angrily and raised the possibility of leaving the Union.

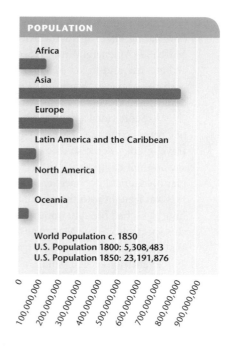

In addition to their predictable differences over economic development, immigration, and slavery, expansion became one of the key issues in the presidential campaign of 1844. In particular, the Democratic candidate James K. Polk advocated the annexation, or territorial incorporation, of Texas. Independent since 1836, the Lone Star Republic had grown from 30,000 residents to 135,000, and its leaders hoped to bring it into the United States as a state. Polk won the election and entered office six days after the United States annexed Texas.

The American Invasion and Conquest of Mexico

The open belligerence of the Polk administration inspired the war party inside Mexico, which took Texas annexation as an affront to the nation's honor. Throughout the period from 1836 to 1847, Mexican officials had contended with rebellions in a host of its states. These weakened the Mexican national government at the moment that it entered into war with a more unified and militarily proficient foe. Even as the United States ostensibly pursued diplomatic negotiations in late 1845 and early 1846, Polk created the pretext for war by ordering troops into contested territory south of the Texas border along the Nueces River. When Mexican forces attacked U.S. troops in April, Polk asserted that "American blood has been shed on American soil" and galvanized the country to support war. Most citizens eagerly endorsed the war. Proclaiming "Ho, for the Halls of Montezuma," volunteers flocked to the service. Early Whig opposition to the war crumbled as politicians recalled that the opposition of the Federalists to the War of 1812 had destroyed the party.

The United States launched a three-pronged invasion of Mexico. As General Zachary Taylor and Colonel A. W. Doniphan invaded Mexico's northern territories, Stephen Kearny led an expedition across New Mexico and into California. The Americans possessed a significant technological advantage with moveable artillery, which they used to devastating effect against Mexican forces. But with no sign of Mexican capitulation, in March 1847, General Winfield Scott, the highest ranking officer in the United States, landed at Veracruz and marched westward toward the capital (Map 13.1). After several clashes with the Mexican Army, Scott reached the outskirts of Mexico City in August. Despite determined and bloody resistance, the city fell to the United States on September 14.

As Scott's men advanced through the country, many read a recently published history of Cortés's conquest of Mexico by William Prescott. Prescott's account served as a kind of travel guide—some soldiers read the Spanish version to learn the language. Americans saw in their campaign a historic parallel to the first great clash of civilizations in Mexico. Navy lieutenant Raphael Semmes read the book and observed that "every step of our progress was fraught with the associations of three hundred years . . . Time, with his scythe and hourglass, had brought another and a newer race . . . Nothing could exceed the beauty of this spectacle." Some Mexicans too drew the same analogy, as one politician commented that "the soldiers are telling terrible tales that bring to mind the Conquest."

Even though U.S. soldiers prided themselves on liberating the country from the thrall of centuries of Catholic and Spanish tyranny, many chroniclers reflected the

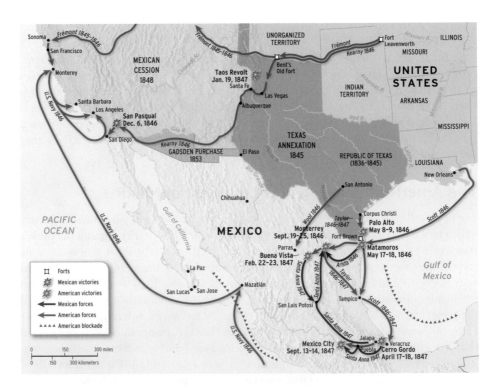

MAP 13.1 ▲ Mexican War The United States launched a three-pronged invasion of Mexico—with Stephen Kearny going into New Mexico, Zachary Taylor securing the southern border of Texas, and Winfield Scott leading the main army on its successful attack on Mexico City. The war added half a million square miles to the United States, more than a third of its prewar territory.

long-standing attitudes that had shaped Western settlement for decades. Characterizations of Mexican soldiers as "degraded," "hideous," and possessing minds "rather animal than intellectual" flowed back home in letters and newspaper reports. In some cases, the racial differences described by these soldiers were used to justify atrocities committed against Mexican soldiers and civilians. General Taylor, in particular, exercised little restraint over his soldiers. General Scott, by contrast, deplored the violence against civilians and managed to occupy Mexico City relatively peacefully. For most of these soldiers, victory in the war demonstrated the superiority of Anglo institutions and provided an opportunity for Mexicans to reform their fractious nation. In describing the conflict, one soldier wrote that "the American eagle seemed to spread his broad pinions and westward bar the principles of Republican government."

The war retained its popularity in the United States partly because American forces defeated Mexican forces in every major engagement in the 16-month conflict. Nonetheless, many Whigs and their supporters opposed the war and expansion because they feared it would lead America onto the imperial path that had ruined so many European nations. Whig politicians, such as Illinois Representative Abraham Lincoln, who maintained their opposition to the war, paid a high political price. But enthusiasm from battlefield victories overwhelmed debates over the war's initial legitimacy, and Lincoln lost his reelection to the House to a Democrat. Despite the tactical success that U.S. forces enjoyed during the war, the conflict turned out to be the bloodiest in U.S. history when measured on a per capita basis. The death rate for U.S. servicemen—110 out of every 1,000—remains the highest for any American war. More than 10 times as many U.S. soldiers died of disease during the war as died in combat, with 10,970 deaths from illness and 1,548 in battle. Yet the victory in the war concluded a 20-year history of Mexican–U.S. relations marked by conflict, mistrust, and violence.

The Emergence of the New American West

Once the war officially began, President Polk explained his goals: "I declared my purpose to be to acquire for the United States, California, New Mexico, and perhaps some of the Northern Provinces of Mexico." Mr. Polk's War, as critics called it, succeeded spectacularly in this regard. The Treaty of Guadalupe Hidalgo, approved by both sides, ceded Texas north of the Rio Grande, California, and New Mexico to the United States for $15 million. It brought 500,000 square miles, nearly 55 percent of prewar Mexico, into U.S. possession and expanded the continental United States by over 40 percent.

Americans coveted California because of its resources and coastal access to the Pacific Ocean and Asian markets. Just as U.S. settlers had poured into in Texas in the 1830s, they began streaming into California in the early 1840s. Like the early Texas colonists, these residents pledged nominal allegiance to Mexico but desired independence and annexation to the United States. In 1846, Lieutenant John Frémont, already famous as the "Pathfinder of the West" for his role in exploring the Southwest, reached Northern California on a mapping expedition for the U.S. Topographical Engineers. One month after Frémont supported a settler uprising that declared the "Bear Flag Republic" independent of Mexico, the U.S. Navy arrived off the coast of San Francisco. Although fighting in Southern California stretched later into the year, it involved small numbers and relatively few casualties. In January 1847, the Californios, Spanish-speaking Californians, capitulated to the U.S. Navy.

Global Gold

In Polk's 1848 speech he revealed yet more evidence for America's most "favored" status: the discovery of gold in California. Previous finds in Georgia, Alabama, and Colorado had drawn thousands of miners, but California's discovery suggested more potential than all these combined. Tens of thousands of men abandoned jobs and families and hurried West. As one East Coast clerk noted, "the thirst for California gold appears to be unabated and young men are enticed away from their business haunts, and daily occupations, for the sake of acquiring the filthy lucre." In 1849, 80,000 men came to California, where, as Mark Twain observed, they "fairly reveled in gold, whiskey, fights, and fandangos." Migrants were overwhelmingly male, from a wide variety of ethnic and racial backgrounds.

The influx of foreigners created a bewilderingly diverse culture among the camps. Entering them, one would have first noticed the pungent aroma of five-spice powder and the fermented complexity of soy sauce competing with roasting chilies and smoky corn carried along with the heady aroma of beef stewed with vegetables. Then, the breeze would have carried a cacophony of voices, accents, and languages: Mandarin, Portuguese, perhaps a smattering of Gaelic. Entering a gold mining camp in 1849 would have disoriented even someone with a global background. One of those who came was Edward Hargraves. Born and educated in England, he moved to Australia when he was 16. In 1833, Hargraves embarked as a crew member on a ship that became infested with fever. Rescued in the Torres Straits, he recovered in England and then returned to Australia. After a decade and a half of unpromising work in Australia, Hargraves

Farther up the coast, Americans were already consolidating new territorial gains. Starting in the late 18th century, British, Spanish, and Russian adventurers had clashed over the right to trade with the Indians along the coast of today's Oregon and Washington. U.S. traders joined the fray in the early 19th century, and by the 1820s, Spain and Russia abandoned the region. After the American Revolution, the United States and Britain struggled for supremacy in the region.

With the exception of the extreme Pacific Northwest and sections along the eastern front of the Rocky Mountain range, the Western regions annexed to the United States in the 1840s possessed a markedly different climate and topography than that of the Eastern United States. Early travelers reported on the aridity, giving rise to the label "Great American Desert." Lured by travel pamphlets promising fertile lands and their own experience in the East, settlers moving west brought expectations of profitable farming; but the dry western ecology forced them to modify their plans.

The 1859 discovery of gold in Colorado initiated the settlement of mid-America, which included ranching, freight hauling, and support services for the burgeoning towns in eastern Colorado and western Kansas. The consolidation of the broad middle seized on the opportunity presented by the discovery of gold in California. As one man described San Francisco in 1849, "the very air [is] pregnant with the magnetism of bold, spirited, unwearied action."

The Australian *Sydney Herald* had broken news of the rush in December 1848, just as many East Coast Americans heard the news from President Polk, and Hargraves set sail from Australia for California. Arriving in mid-1849, Hargraves learned the craft of excavating but found little gold. The fields had already become crowded and competitive. Some men abandoned prospecting and made money provisioning the men who were toiling for gold. Levi Strauss was one of these. A 24-year-old German immigrant, Strauss intended to open a dry goods business but responded to the necessity of miners for durable pants. Using a French fabric, denim, Strauss designed a rugged but comfortable pair that became the foundation of his company, and the origin of blue jeans in America.

The mining adventures that drew men from all over the world to California also drew global financial backing. Investors in New York, Philadelphia, London, and Berlin underwrote the hard labor provided by men from all over North America and from many European nations. Both the large-scale immigration and international investment underscored the growing importance of the Pacific and the interconnectedness of global economies. California gold spread around the world—miners dug out more gold in the first decade of California production than had appeared on world markets in the previous 150 years.

- Why did the California gold rush inspire foreign immigration?
- What did the gold rush reveal about the nature of global information and economies in the mid-19th century?

of North America under U.S. control alleviated security concerns that had troubled Americans since the early 19th century, when a host of European powers remained ensconced on the continent. Even if they did not know what to do with the land and even if, as some Americans feared, organizing the new territories would precipitate political conflicts, most celebrated the accomplishment. Many citizens probably agreed with President Polk when he announced in his 1848 state of the Union, "we are the most favored people on the face of the earth."

Conestogas, Comanches, and Californios

The greatest social conflict in the newly configured American West came from Anglo migrants who regarded Catholic superstition and sin, combined with "cowardly, ignorant, lazy" habits inherited from the Spanish, as the main impediment to fruitful use and development of the region. "If the one half be true that is told of the abomination of the priesthood," one American wrote of the Franciscans, "that order there must be a perfect embodiment of every wicked attribute that darkens the character of corrupt

SEEKING GOLD   Gold captured the imagination of Americans east and west. Although the popular image of a "gold seeker" was a young, single, white man, the allure of the precious metal drew men and women from all around the globe.

human nature." Anglo settlers believed every outrageous tale of Catholic corruption and depravity. By displacing the native Mexican elite and developing California, Anglos could make money, purify the "American" character, and fulfill their Christian duty.

Not every American shared these views. A long tradition of open trading brought early American travelers together with Mexicans, French, British, and Native peoples. The earliest permanent settlers usually trapped and hunted, intermarried with locals, and spoke both Spanish and English. For these men, and for later emigrants, California represented an escape from the pressures of the East: from dirty cities, tired land, and debts. Americans dreamed of reaching the fantastic new world in the Pacific. Even Henry David Thoreau, the poet of the eastern woods, felt that "my needle always settles between west and southwest. The future lies that way to me." Realizing those dreams, in California and the new Western territories more generally, proved harder than most settlers imagined.

Controlling the new territory proved nearly as great a challenge as acquiring it. The Conestoga wagons that had already begun carrying Anglo settlers across the Great Plains began heading south in greater numbers, but doing so brought them into the orbit of two powerful Indian nations—Apache and Comanche. Generations of Spanish and then Mexican settlers had tried and failed to pacify these two nations. In 1850, the Apache community probably numbered only 5,000, but their attacks on settler communities had inspired the Mexican government to offer bounties for the scalps of Apache men, women, and children. Comanche represented a more serious threat. More numerous and better organized than Apache, they had lived along the northwestern edges of Texas and in the New Mexico Territory since the early 18th century. The Comanche dominated the region well into the second half of the 19th century. They established their authority through military raids on neighbors—native, Mexican, and American—and sustained their empire through control of markets and regional trade.

Comanche controlled parts of northern Mexico, known as Comanchería, through their ability to reinvent themselves as the Spanish began to push north. Seizing new weapons and tools—especially horses—they wedded these technologies to existing practices such as raiding and slave taking. They created extended networks of kin and dependency across the Southwest. The result was a native power that existed independently although in connection to the Europeans and later Americans. At almost the same time Anglo settlers began arriving, Comanche society entered a period of internal conflict and decline that weakened them substantially due to the collapse of the bison population. Years of overhunting and a decade-long drought beginning in the mid-1840s destroyed the main source of food, a key commodity, and an essential part of the Comanche spiritual world. These events paved the way for U.S. forces to displace them. In 1852, weakened by starvation, Comanche chiefs appealed to a U.S. Indian agent for "a country we can call our own, where we might bury our people in quiet." The Comanche people did not all die—and although some conceded to U.S. policies that placed Indians on reservations, others resisted and defended their autonomy into the 1870s.

Despite the threats posed by Comanches and others, the prospect of gold drew immigrants to California. Creating a chaotic mix of languages, cultures, and values, Anglo settlers, European travelers, and Asian migrants all poured into California in 1849. Chinese and Irish migrants ranked at the top of the foreign-born contingent, followed by Germans, English, Welsh, Scottish, French, Chileans, Brazilians, Mexicans, and Canadians. Of these 70,000 new residents, probably 15 percent were from Central or South America, and they all labored alongside 6,000–7,000 Miwok Indians. All these new Californians also lived alongside 75,000 Mexican Americans who remained in California after the Mexican War. The Treaty of Guadalupe Hidalgo promised them the right to citizenship and respect for their land claims. Even with citizenship, land rights proved hard to maintain, and many Californios lost both status and property to the new arrivals.

Chinese, especially Cantonese, migrants came in pursuit of "Gum Shan" or "Gold Mountain," as the Cantonese referred to California. The Chinese came largely as contract laborers, usually relegated to the service industries that supported mines, and later worked in railroads and construction work. Like the thousands of African American men who came west, Chinese immigrants were segregated in their housing and were offered low-wage jobs with little chance for upward mobility. These men were especially prized by American miners as cooks and cleaners because without them the dramatically unbalanced sex ratios of the gold rush required that men do work that traditionally fell to women.

Despite being neither "North" nor "South," California could not escape the sectional controversies that roiled the country throughout the 1850s. Some Southern migrants to the state brought their slaves. Others waited until they received assurances that their property would be safe. Democrats dominated the state, but the party split into pro-slavery and antislavery factions. The violent conflict between these groups in California revealed how deeply the sectional conflict had impressed itself into the fabric of the nation.

STUDY QUESTIONS FOR THE EXPANSION OF AMERICA

1. What were the challenges facing U.S. control of the new Western territory?
2. Why did the United States enter war with Mexico, and how did the results transform the nation?
3. What did the gold rush reveal about the nature of global information and economies in the mid-19th century?

■ CONTESTED CITIZENSHIP

As the United States extended its power across the West and over the Pacific, the influx of an increasingly diverse stream of immigrants sparked debate over who could be an American. Native-born Americans, especially Protestants, reacted to the growing diversity by trying to narrowly define citizenship and the rights that came with it. Political and cultural conflicts wrought a massive transformation on the American electorate and partisan alignments. The failure of American politics as a result of these crises eventually helped bring the nation to war in 1861. The first phase of this process saw the collapse of the Whig Party in the face of a challenge from the nativist **Know-Nothing Party**.

The Patterns of Migration

After the conclusion of the Mexican War, immigrants flooded the Pacific Coast both from the eastern United States and from around the globe. Chinese laborers comprised the largest group of Asian immigrants into America at this time. Between 1840 and 1920, 2.5 million people left China for Hawaii, the United States, Canada, Australia, New Zealand, Southeast Asia, South America, and Africa. Although domestic disturbances and economic hardship compelled these moves, the vast majority of migrants to North America chose their destination. The high cost of travel ensured that many of the Chinese immigrants had to sign contracts agreeing to work for five years at a set wage

ARRIVING IN AMERICA   Immigrants entered the United States through coastal port cities. Many remained in the region where they landed, but others followed transportation corridors into the heart of the country, often tracing the routes laid down by earlier immigrants from their home countries.

once they arrived. Despite the potential for exploitation in this scenario, many young men saw it as an opportunity. Especially after the Gold Rush, news of fortunes circulated widely. One resident in China reported on the effect of the news: "Letters from Chinese in San Francisco and further in the country have been circulated . . . the accounts of the successful adventurers who have returned would, had the inhabitants possessed the means of paying their own way across, have gone far to depopulate considerable towns." They faced a hard life once they arrived. The California legal system established in 1849 created a rigid binary system of classifying its residents. Laws grouped Chinese, African Americans, and Indians together as "nonwhite" and denied them access to the vote, the state court system, and the schools.

In contrast to California, the New Mexico territory remained as fluid as it had been under Mexican control, largely because the United States imposed little military control. Instead, the Indian communities—Comanche, Apache, Navajo, Cheyenne, and Kiowa— continued to practice older forms of war making, diplomacy, and trade. But the rapid decline of buffalo herds on the southern Plains, the continued spread of diseases like smallpox, and expansion of the Anglo commercial economy increased U.S. authority in the region. American officials worried about the raiding and slave taking among Southwest Indians, a practice Anglos compared to the racial slavery of the Deep South. In 1850, the U.S. territorial governor of the region appealed to the federal government for funds with which he could redeem captives under the old system. "Trading in captives had been so long tolerated in this Territory that it has ceased to be regarded as a wrong; and purchasers are not prepared willingly to release captives without an adequate ransom." The prospect of using federal money to emancipate Indian slaves might well have unsettled Southern Democrats, who would certainly have seen a dangerous precedent in the practice. In any event, the governor received no response, and Native practices only ended with the full military intervention of the United States in the decade after the Civil War.

Although California and the West drew migrants from Mexico and the Pacific, the countries around the Atlantic basin remained the main source of immigrants bound for the United States in this period. As in earlier decades, most immigrants came from German states and Ireland, although the numbers of central and southern Europeans increased. The rate of immigration rose with each passing year, but the destination of most immigrants remained consistent: the North. The ports of Boston, Philadelphia, and New York attracted a majority of the nation's shipping traffic, both for people and for goods. Many immigrants remained in these ports, whereas many others moved westward along the lines laid down—in steel rail, macadamized turnpike, or narrow canal—during the great era of transportation and infrastructural development of the 1840s and 1850s. The combination of free labor policies and a booming economy drew most immigrants to the North. Cities such as Pittsburgh, Cleveland, Detroit, Cincinnati, and Chicago saw their populations explode. These second-tier cities grew at remarkable rates—Chicago increased from 5,000 residents in 1840 to 109,000 in 1860—and achieved a size that the leading coastal ports had required centuries to reach.

But not all of the immigrants went west or north. Some immigrants went south, to such ports as Baltimore, Richmond, Charleston, Mobile, New Orleans, and Galveston. Immigrants who entered Southern ports were more likely to remain in those cities or the surrounding area. Irish migrants established large expatriate communities in many of the southern Atlantic seaboard cities. These newcomers joined native Southerners, both black and white, who helped develop the urban South. Urban boosters promoted railroads, canals, and banks with the same fervor as their northern peers. Despite their eagerness to accumulate new technology, however, few white Southerners wanted to replicate the massive urban centers of the Northeast. They anticipated that the anonymity and size of large cities would weaken the ability of masters to control their slaves. Many also resisted the rise of a large community of working class whites, who might someday see little reason to support slavery. Because Southerners invested most of their capital in land and slaves, they had little left for the bond-driven commercial development that promoted urban growth in other parts of the country.

New Immigrants and the Invention of Americanism

Among Southern ports, New Orleans was unique for its size, its cultural diversity, and its centrality to dynamic new trade patterns. Occupied by the French and Spanish before entry into the United States through the Louisiana Purchase, the polyglot population consisted of the descendants of various European ethnic groups, an equally wide array of African ethnicities, and a large population of people of mixed descent that Louisianans referred to generally as "Creole." After the expulsion of French settlers from the Canadian province of Acadia during the Seven Years' War, many relocated to France's colony in southern Louisiana. Here they came to be called "Cajuns" in a corruption of the name of the area from which they came. New Orleans, in particular, invited fusion and cultural mixing. Protestant Americans regarded the city as an exotic and dangerous locale.

The French and Spanish built cathedrals and other public symbols of Catholicism in the city, and most Anglo-Americans continued to regard the faith as both foreign and hostile to democratic life. The entry of millions of new Catholics into the country over the 1840s and 1850s only increased fears about their presence in the country. In addition, the Catholic community was divided. A substantial body of English Catholics and French Catholics had migrated south from Canada and established themselves during the colonial era. The influx of Irish Catholics alarmed many native-born Catholics who feared that the Irish rejection of Anglo practices and values would further fuel anti-Catholic sentiment (Figure 13.1).

The political conflicts between old Protestants and new Catholic immigrants in the Eastern states propelled much of the public policy toward immigration, but Western territories possessed their own share of ethnic conflict. The movement of Chinese workers into the West after the Mexican War generated opposition from native-born workers. Many of the charges leveled at Chinese and other Asian immigrants were similar to the ones used against African Americans: Anglo-Americans accused Chinese men of "lusting" after white women and regarded them as childlike and savage, incapable of functioning as citizens in a republic. According to the *San Francisco Chronicle*, "When the [Chinese] worker arrives here he is as rigidly under the control of the contractor who brought him as ever an African slave was under his master in South Carolina or Louisiana." In 1851, **Hinton Helper**, a leading critic of slavery, told Californians that "I should not wonder at all, if the copper of the Pacific yet becomes as great a subject of discord and dissension as the ebony of the Atlantic." Like his recommendations for freeing the South from slavery—which in his view involved removing African Americans along with slavery—Helper thought Asian immigrants had no role to play in settling the West.

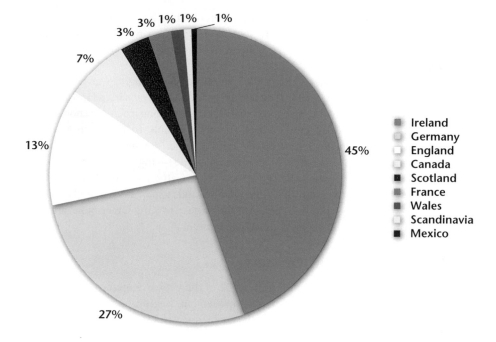

3% 1% 1%   1%

3%

7%

13%

45%

27%

- Ireland
- Germany
- England
- Canada
- Scotland
- France
- Wales
- Scandinavia
- Mexico

FIGURE 13.1 ▲ Foreign-born population subdivided by nationality, 1850 The high numbers of Irish immigrants, many of whom were Catholic, entangled public discussions of immigration policy with questions of religion. Note that the figure includes only the 10 largest emigrant countries, which collectively accounted for 96% of all immigrants.

The conclusion that Hinton Helper reached reflected one of the most pernicious aspects of mid-19th-century U.S. culture. Helper's advice—that black people should be removed from the South and Asian people removed from the West—drew on older traditions, such as those maintained by the American Colonization Society, and the newer science of race. Increasingly, white people in America expressed a harsher and more absolute conception of race and racial difference. Most white members of the Revolutionary generation believed implicitly in the intellectual, physical, and moral superiority of white people over darker-skinned people, but they rarely articulated this idea in their writings. What distinguished the antebellum generation was the centrality of racial thinking. The more diverse America became, the more its white residents emphasized racism as a central aspect of their worldview.

By this time, however, most states had endorsed universal white manhood suffrage; thus, following a short period of residence, new immigrants could participate in the political system. The high numbers of urban immigrants, especially in northeastern cities, raised concerns that these men would corrupt the political system. As one wealthy New York merchant worried, "these Irishmen, strangers among us, without a feeling of patriotism or affection in common with American citizens, decide the elections in the City of New York. They make Presidents and Governors, and they send men to represent us in the councils of the nation." The men who expressed such sentiments supported an increasingly aggressive response to what they perceived as a Catholic disruption of American civic life. A weekly New York journal emerged in the 1830s entitled the *American Protestant Vindicator and Defender of Civil and Religious Liberty against the Inroads of Papacy.*

Public schools became one of the key battlegrounds in the fight over religion and public life. The strong Protestant bias of "nondenominational" schools in Ireland left many Irish Catholics who emigrated with a profound distrust of nonparochial schools. Even native Catholics feared the conforming effects of public schools. In 1843, one American Catholic organization warned parents to guard their heritage: "you must, therefore, use all diligence that your child be instructed at an early age in the saving truths of religion, and be preserved from the contagion of error." Accordingly, Catholics requested that public schools respect Catholic beliefs or simply divert public funds to parochial schools. In 1844, when a Philadelphia bishop criticized the use of the Protestant King James Bible, it incited anti-Catholic riots that left 40 people dead and 60 injured.

The Know-Nothing Movement

New York, long the center of Irish immigrant life in the United States, experienced the most severe and most well-organized nativist movement. Beginning in the mid-1840s, different political organizations calling themselves some variant of the American Party formed. They shared general goals: to restrict office holding to native-born Americans, to retain the Bible in schools, and to extend the naturalization process from 5 to 21 years. Although these groups had little electoral success, they established the basis for the network of secret fraternal associations known collectively as the Know Nothings that emerged in the 1850s. Nativists feared that the mainstream political parties would not sanction their policies for fear of alienating the immigrant vote. If asked about the organization, members answered that they "knew nothing." Outgrowing this fear, however, the organization gradually became more openly political.

Nativists quickly created an opposition party that rivaled and drew strength from the Whigs. The Know-Nothing Party flourished and then disappeared, absorbed by the Republican Party, undone by conflict over slavery just like the Whigs. The brief existence of the party and the fact that it was mostly confined to the North suggests that its appeal was temporary and limited. But the movement tapped into long-standing fears, and nativism did not end with the collapse of the official movement. At the party's height, in the election of 1854, eight governors, more than 100 Congressmen, thousands of local officials, and nearly a million citizens proclaimed themselves Know Nothings. In some states, Know Nothings succeeded in restricting public funds for parochial schools, disbanding immigrant militias, imposing literacy tests for voting, and reforming church property ownership rules.

STUDY QUESTIONS FOR CONTESTED CITIZENSHIP

1. How did the entry of new immigrants into the United States in the 1840s and 1850s alter American life?

2. What were the political responses by native-born Americans to this movement?

3. How did the Know-Nothing Party put nativist beliefs into public policy?

SLAVERY AND ANTEBELLUM LIFE

The persistent efforts of enslaved people to escape bondage, to alter the conditions of their slavery, and to assert their own humanity destabilized the system and forced slave-holders to constantly adjust. The increasing defensiveness of slaveholders in the 1840s and 1850s stemmed as much from this internal pressure as from the external pressure applied by abolitionists. The basis of mid-19th-century slavery remained the physical domination that whites could and did exercise over slaves, the monopoly on weapons and state power, and the social network supporting slavery that manifested itself in slave patrols and a legal system that oppressed black people at the expense of whites. At the same time, slaves and masters struggled over the psychological, cultural, and social conditions of bondage. The complexity of these relationships, their continuous evolution over time, and the profoundly uneven distribution of power within the system of antebellum slavery taxes the empathetic sensibilities of modern readers; but the importance of understanding the perspectives of the different participants in the system demands that we make the effort.

The Paradox of Slavery and Modernity

The persistence of slavery into the 1850s surprised many Americans. Members of the Revolutionary generation expected that slavery would disappear over time. Most philosophical thought in late 18th- and 19th-century western Europe favored freedom and condemned slavery as inefficient and inhumane. But the United States proved a curious exception within the larger Western world. Defenders of the institution offered increasingly elaborate intellectual and religious justifications, as slavery in North America

SCENE ON THE LEVEE, AT NEW ORLEANS.

SLAVE LABOR   The dynamism of the Southern economy thrived on slave labor, applied to all sorts of farm, urban, and industrial work. Slavery's supporters understood this and fashioned an intellectual defense of the practice to sustain their lifestyle.

proved to be a remarkably adaptable economic strategy. When the Scottish thinker Adam Smith denounced slavery in his manifesto of capitalism, *An Inquiry into the Nature and Causes of The Wealth of Nations* (published in 1776), he argued for the greater efficiency of free workers and the necessity of free labor markets within a capitalist system. Smith did not anticipate the ability of slaveholders to adapt their system to an increasingly industrial and urban South. Because Southern cities did not receive the same surge of foreign immigrants as Northern ones, the growth of urban slavery proved vital to Southern cities.

Enslaved workers, often hired by companies from their rural masters, labored alongside white men in a host of occupations in antebellum cities. The tobacco factories of the Upper South used this system extensively. By 1860, hired slaves constituted fully one-half of the tobacco workers in Virginia. Richmond's Tredegar Iron Works, the largest industrial facility in the South, with over 1,000 workers, employed hundreds of enslaved men and women. Masters regarded slave hiring as advantageous because they could sign a contract, receive guaranteed compensation, and dispense with the day-to-day management of slaves. Many of the urban slaves, especially those hired in the 1850s, lived in rented rooms or boarding houses. Masters required them to deduct rent and food expenses from their wages, but enterprising slaves could work overtime or scrimp on necessities and actually set aside money for themselves.

Urban slavery produced other complications as well. With masters absent, enslaved people supervised themselves after working hours. If they congregated in noisy bars and gambling saloons as white workers did, who would oversee them? If they committed crimes, who would be held responsible? The anonymity of growing Southern cities gave slaves a chance to seize an autonomy that few could find on plantations. These problems generated tensions between masters and city officials. The latter understood the necessity of black labor to the operation of their communities but resented having to stand in as masters to supervise and punish enslaved people.

Urban slavery also generated class tensions within the white community and threatened its stability at a time when sectional politics demanded solidarity. In the 1850s, Tredegar's white workers, for instance, went on strike repeatedly over the use of enslaved workers in the factory. Joseph Anderson, the plant's owner, responded aggressively, but most white elites treaded carefully. Worse yet, a handful of Southern advocates of free labor framed a critique of slavery that drew on the class divisions among white Southerners. Hinton Helper, a North Carolinian, issued the most famous attack on slavery from within the South in his book *The Impending Crisis* (1857). Helper called on non-slaveholding whites to overthrow the planter class, destroy slavery, and exile black people from the country. "The lords of the lash are not only absolute masters of the blacks . . . they are also the oracles and arbiters of all nonslaveholding whites, whose freedom is merely nominal, and whose unparalleled illiteracy and degradation is purposely and fiendishly perpetuated," Helper wrote, setting off a firestorm among Southern elites.

Helper and the white strikers at Tredegar raised the central dilemma of protecting white labor inside a slave society. In the North, free labor theorists and politicians argued that white laborers could never be fairly treated in a slave society; whereas in the South, defenders of slavery sought a middle ground. Their precarious position rejected the natural equality of rights that lay at the heart of the American polity and advanced a hierarchical model in its place. South Carolina Senator and former Vice President **John C. Calhoun** framed the argument clearly: "all men are not created equal.

According to the Bible, only two—a man and a woman—ever were—and of those one was pronounced subordinate to the other. All others have come into the world by being born, and in no sense . . . either free or equal."

The West Indies, Brazil, and the Future of Slavery

Slaveholders knew from recent history that a false step could collapse the edifice of their power. By 1838, the British government had abolished slavery in its empire, most importantly on the sugar islands of the West Indies. Southerners carefully studied the events that followed British abolition. What they saw alarmed them. Although British emancipation granted compensation to owners, gave no land to ex-slaves, required a transition period of bonded labor by former slaves, and did not inspire the racial war that many whites had predicted, U.S. slaveholders regarded it as a dramatically unsuccessful act. Their evidence for the failure of emancipation rested on the decline in West Indian sugar production, which plummeted after the end of the apprenticeship period. Abolitionists, by contrast, hailed the "mighty experiment" as a success. Less concerned with staple crop production, they celebrated the rise of free labor and the self-sufficiency that ex-slaves pursued.

Some Southern slaveholders concluded that the real motive must have been an effort to weaken the United States by undermining slavery. As one South Carolina planter explained, Britain had abolished West Indian slavery to "kindle a flame of fanatical discontent" that would divide the North from the South. This theory gained ground during the debate on Texas annexation, when Southern congressmen alleged that the United States had to incorporate the state before the British assumed control and emancipated the slaves. At the World Anti-Slavery Convention of 1843, the assembled abolitionists encouraged Britain to underwrite the Texans' debt and use that aid as leverage to push for emancipation. When this news reached the United States, it bolstered U.S. support for annexation.

If the West Indies gave white Southerners doubts about the long-term security of slavery, looking farther south buoyed their hopes. Brazilian planters, independent of Portuguese rule since 1822, remained as committed to slavery as did their U.S. peers. Long after the United States outlawed the the Atlantic slave trade, Brazil continued to flout international sanctions; between 1835 and 1855 alone, over half a million Africans were smuggled into Brazil, many of them on ships captained by Americans. From shipbuilding to sailing to the commerce itself, Americans played a key role in the importation of Africans into Brazil long after the trade had been closed. The fervent dedication to slavery displayed by Brazilians encouraged John C. Calhoun to remark that "between her [Brazil] and us there is a strict identity of interest on almost all subjects, without conflict, or even competition." Reflecting American concerns about British antislavery work, which included patrolling the waters off the African and Brazilian coasts with the intention of returning illegally captured Africans, Calhoun supported "our mutual interest in resisting [London's] interference with the relation in either country."

Inside the Quarter

By 1860, four million black people were held in bondage in the American South. Viewed in financial terms, they represented the single largest investment of any kind in the

SLAVE HOUSING   Owners never spent more than the bare minimum to house slaves, but despite their rough surroundings, enslaved men and women built strong and loving families and protective communities whenever they could.

United States, with a total aggregate value of roughly three billion dollars. During the 1830s, 1840s, and 1850s, slave ownership contracted even as the slave population expanded: fewer white people owned more and more black people. By 1860, 25 percent of Southern households owned slaves, and of these, 10 percent owned more than 12 individuals.

Most slaveholders owned only one or a few slaves. In these situations, slaves worked alongside family members, slept under the same roof, and remained in close contact with white people throughout their lives. Those slaves who lived on large plantations enjoyed a small measure of distance between themselves and their owners. Slaves on plantations lived in their own "quarter," a collection of small cabins usually apportioned one to a family. Within this space, enslaved people fashioned families, communities, and their culture. Each quarter generated its own musicians, historians, storytellers, and healers. Links—of love, friendship, trade, or rivalry—connected slaves from one plantation to another. Despite the best efforts of whites, news and rumor always traveled faster from quarter to quarter than from big house to big house.

Slaveholders alternated between the stark choices laid out by one master who professed "the surest and best method of managing negroes, is to love them" and another who advised that "we have to rely more and more on the power of fear." Some adopted both these routines. Bennet Barrow, a notoriously harsh Louisiana master, ordered periodic whippings of all his slaves but also gave frequent holidays and brought Christmas presents back to his slaves from New Orleans. Owners had a strong economic incentive to keep slaves healthy and satisfied enough with their material conditions that they did not see flight or revenge as a better option. It did not require a humanitarian slaveholder to see that better treatment could return more profits in the long run.

Without denying the violence and brutality that underlay American slavery, the evidence also reveals that enslaved people used every opportunity to seek small measures of freedom within the system. These actions did not signal acceptance of slavery nor were they incompatible with the more public and physical acts of resistance that marked so much of the relationship between masters and slaves in the antebellum South. But these measures gave enslaved African Americans the chance to carve out space for spouses, for children, sometimes for literacy or advanced skills, and most importantly for themselves. Each small victory required enormous sacrifice and discipline to achieve, but the body of evidence that scholars have recovered from all aspects of slaves' lives demonstrates the vitality and richness of that life even within bondage.

Because enslaved people could not legally marry, some slaveholders regarded slave marriages as unions of convenience that they could sunder with a sale. Because of the overwhelming importance of family, the sale of enslaved people represented the greatest tragedy they could face. Sales may have disrupted one-third to one-half of enslaved families nationwide. Sales revealed the truly mercenary quality of American slavery.

One of the largest and most dynamic of such markets was located in New Orleans, where slaves arrived by ship, rail, and on foot before being sold and parceled out to the brutal sugar plantations in the region. The high walls of the slave market, built according to city code, kept these inhumane transactions out of sight.

The Creation of African America

The tremendous diversity of African backgrounds inherited by enslaved people in America complicated and enriched the efforts of African Americans to identify themselves as one people. By the early 19th century, free African Americans felt secure enough to claim Africa as a proud ancestral homeland, a practice that went back at least to the founding of the African Methodist Episcopal (AME) Church in Philadelphia in the 1790s. The standard historical and cultural assessments of Africa by whites at the time regarded the continent as uncivilized and dangerously backward. To assert a positive affiliation with Africa, as increasing numbers of free blacks did in the early 19th century, represented a fundamental challenge to the racist attitudes held by white Americans. Martin Delaney, a free black man from Virginia who moved to Pennsylvania and later worked with Frederick Douglass, built on earlier efforts to connect black Americans with Africa in historical, emotional, and physical terms. Before the Civil War, Delaney advocated the necessity of a separate black nation in Africa composed of émigrés from the United States where they could show their superiority in "the true principles of morals, correctness of thought, religion, and law or civil government." Delaney remained in the United States, serving as a major in the U.S. Army during the Civil War, the first black field officer in the United States; but the black nationalist idea of a return to Africa that persisted into the 20th century owed much to the decades of work done by men like Delaney.

Positive images of Africa played a central role in the music and folklore of the enslaved people. By the mid-19th century, black Americans had blended these images and ideas with European and Native American traditions to create a uniquely African American culture. Slave spirituals and songs expressed common goals and a shared identity.

> Hail! all hail! ye Afric clan,
> Hail! ye oppressed, ye Afric band,
> Who toil and sweat in slavery bound
> And when your health and strength are gone
> Are left to hunger and to mourn,
> Let independence be your aim,
> Ever mindful what 'tis worth.
> Pledge your bodies for the prize,
> Pile them even to the skies!

Alongside the folk traditions that have formed a basis for much of the investigation into the lives of American slaves grew a burgeoning Afro-Christianity. Careful studies have documented varying rates of African American participation in the different Protestant denominations, which suggests that enslaved people may have been able to chose the denomination to which they belonged. In Virginia, roughly 40 percent of enslaved Christians joined the Baptist church. Before Nat Turner's Rebellion in 1831, black ministers had played a key role in the leadership of enslaved evangelicals; however, following that event, Southern communities policed such activities more closely. Even without their own ministers, Afro-Christians continued to join churches and profess their faith.

The Afro-Christian faith differed in important ways from white evangelicalism. The nature of African American religion in the post-Civil War period offers some insights into the beliefs of enslaved people before the war. Whereas pro-slavery evangelicals focused on submission to God and to masters, Afro-Christians celebrated the day of jubilee, deliverance from evil, and the salvation that awaited those who believed. As one slave noted, "the idea of a revolution in the condition of whites and blacks, is the corner-stone of the religion of the latter." The prophetic tradition offered enslaved Christians an explanation of their world that recognized suffering but promised redemption. David Walker, author of the incendiary pamphlet *An Appeal to the Coloured Citizens of the World* (1829), took solace from God's omnipotence by quoting the Book of Common Prayer:

The wicked swell'd with lawless pride,
Have made the poor their prey;
O, let them fall by those designs
Which they for others lay

STUDY QUESTIONS FOR SLAVERY AND ANTEBELLUM LIFE

1. In what ways did enslaved men and women challenge the system of slavery?
2. How did they create families and lives even while still enslaved?
3. How did slaveholders respond to this challenge?

◼ THE RISE OF THE REPUBLICANS

The dispute over slavery that consumed Northerners and Southerners in the 1850s rarely recognized the humanity or the suffering of enslaved people that emerged so clearly from their music, stories, and actions. White Northerners opposed slavery—principally the expansion of slavery in the Western territories—because it corrupted and weakened the American political and economic system. Abolitionists appreciated the true horror of slavery—mostly as a result of the role played by black people in the movement after 1830—but they remained a tiny minority. Unlike the social and cultural issues that gave rise to the Know-Nothing Party, this dispute mapped itself along

Table 13.1 Political Parties, 1830–1860

The mid-19th century was one of the most vibrant and fluid periods in American politics. Different groups formed and dissolved a variety of partisan organizations before the emergence of the Republican Party in the 1850s.

Majority Party
Democrats (1800–): supported state rights, slavery, and immigration

Primary Opposition Parties
Whigs (1830–1850s): supported federal investment in infrastructure and social reforms stemming from Second Great Awakening American Know Nothing (early to mid-1850s): supported strong nativist platform Republican (mid-1850s–): supported antislavery policies in Western territories and federal investment in development

Issue-Specific Parties
Workingmen's (1830s): locally organized parties supporting workers' rights Liberty Party (1840s): abolition party Free Soil Party (1848 to early 1850s): opposed expansion of slavery into Western territories Anti-Masons (1828 to mid-1830s): opposed Freemasonry Southern Rights (1850s): supported Southern interests, especially protection of slavery Union (early 1850s): Southern offshoot of the Whig Party Constitutional Union (1860): conservative compromise party dedicated to preserving the Union

sectional lines and so held the potential to fracture the nation (Table 13.1). Northerners emerged from the political turmoil of the second half of the 1850s with a new Republican Party, which brought stability to Northern politics but whose sectional posture ultimately inspired white Southerners to abandon the Union.

Free Soil and Free Labor

Disputes over the expansion of slavery into the Western territories stretched back to the Confederation Congress, which adopted the Northwest Ordinance banning slavery in the Upper Midwest region. Because the legal restrictions applied only to existing territory and because slavery continued to be profitable, the expansion of U.S. territory forced this problem on each succeeding generation. The 1820 Missouri Compromise settled the conflict that arose regarding the incorporation of the Louisiana Purchase lands by establishing a boundary between slave and free territory along Missouri's southern border. The acquisitions after the Mexican War precipitated a new round of conflict when Pennsylvania Democrat David Wilmot proposed that slavery be excluded from any new territory gained during the war. Congress voted repeatedly on the Wilmot Proviso but never passed it. Each vote exacerbated sectional rather than partisan differences. As the *Boston Whig* explained of the Wilmot Proviso, "As if by magic, it brought to a head the great question which is about to divide the American people."

The men who organized the Republican Party in the early 1850s possessed the foresight to wed free soil—territories organized without slavery—to the emerging philosophy of free labor. Building on midcentury discussions about capitalism and labor that were taking place all across the Atlantic world, free labor theorists sought to incorporate propertyless men into the electorate without jeopardizing the stability of law and government. European nations had long restricted voting because they believed that propertyless men embittered by their failures might call for land redistribution if given the right to vote. The vast majority of unskilled (and even many skilled) workers in the United States owned no property. But rather than defining these workers negatively by the land they did not own, free-labor theorists identified them by what they possessed— their labor to sell. This new understanding of labor prompted a shift in emphasis in the legal foundations of American capitalism from the sanctity of property to the sanctity of contract. This view ensured that workers accepted certain responsibilities when they signed a contract—such as assuming liability for personal harm or death in hazardous jobs. It also meant that employers had to respect contracts as well and could not arbitrarily fire or lower the wages of an employee without risking legal retribution. With this change, laboring men now had an investment in the legal and political status quo. Free labor also relied on continuous upward mobility. Men who entered the workforce laboring for others would save their money, succeed to independence, and employ younger men. This process enriched families and society. This Republican ideology juxtaposed the virtue and efficiency of the North's autonomous workers with the immorality and inefficiency of the South's slave economy.

Whig—and later, Republican—economic policies promoted the expansion of a commercial economy into the new regions of the West. Before companies, creditors, and cash could reach the region, however, the West needed laws and governments. Only with the area securely organized, including the all-important court system to resolve conflicts over land deals, would investors commit resources. Because Northerners and Southerners clashed over whether the territory should be organized as free or slave land, territorial development stalled. As a result, one of the most important legislative initiatives of the era—the Transcontinental Railroad—only passed Congress during the Civil War when the exit of Southern Democrats from Congress gave Republicans the votes to organize the territories and pass the bill. Conflict over slavery's expansion effectively deadlocked Congress on major legislation for over a decade.

The Politics of Slave Catching

Outside Congress, problems manifested themselves along the border between slavery and freedom where slaveholders complained about the lack of cooperation they received from Northern state and local governments when their slaves escaped. The southern boundaries of Ohio and Pennsylvania emerged as the key battlegrounds. The 1842 Supreme Court case of *Prigg v. Pennsylvania* established federal policy on the issue. Edward Prigg, acting for a Maryland slaveholder, entered Pennsylvania to reclaim a woman and her children who had escaped from bondage five years earlier. Prigg carried them off, and Pennsylvania officials convicted him of kidnapping. A pro-slavery, Southern majority on the Supreme Court, which ruled that no state law could "in any way qualify, regulate, control, or restrain" actions taken by slaveholders to reclaim their property, established a broad right of recapture. Accordingly, the Court set Prigg free and voided the Pennsylvania statute under which he was arrested. Although the decision contradicted the Southern preference for state action on slavery by locating the protection of slave catchers at the federal level, Southerners strongly backed the decision.

Sectional disputes over slave and free territory manifested themselves in religious institutions. The subject had created controversy at national religious conventions for years, with antislavery forces from Northern churches sponsoring resolutions to prohibit ministers from owning slaves and churches from using slave labor. At the same time, Southern ministers crafted the biblical defense of slavery. After a decade of controversy over whether Christianity sanctioned slaveholding, the Baptist and Methodist Churches divided over the issue of slavery in 1845.

The tangled problems of slavery, territories, and economic expansion reached a critical point in 1850. Congress had been under pressure to admit California to statehood. Deadlocked over the question of whether California would be free or slave, Congress extended its session into the summer of 1850, and a mood of apprehension and fear gripped the capitol. Democrats and Whigs finally agreed to a series of bills that were collectively regarded as the **Compromise of 1850**. The final legislation admitted California as a free state, organized the remainder of the New Mexico Territory, banned the slave trade in the District of Columbia, empowered the Treasury to assume Texas's debts from its independence struggle, and gave the South a much stronger federal Fugitive Slave Act. This last provision proved to be the most controversial. It nationalized the process of slave capture and return by requiring federal judges to appoint "commissioners" to overhear cases of accused fugitives and by requiring the active complicity of state officers. Northerners, who assumed that most "slave catchers" simply kidnapped free blacks from the North, were appalled by the legislation, which assumed the guilt of the charged party, refused to allow blacks to testify, obviated the standard rules for evidence that would have been present in a court of law, and provided financial incentives for commissioners to find fugitives guilty ($10 as opposed to $5 for those found innocent).

All across the North, individuals protested passage of the legislation, which they believed made them complicit in slavery: "A filthy law," "an outrage to humanity," proclaimed Northern papers. Anyone who obeyed it ought to be "marked and treated as a moral leper," wrote one, while another advised those who did to "repent before God and ask His forgiveness." Bostonians made the most vigorous response, with abolitionists protesting and blocking the removal of accused fugitives through legal and illegal means. The 1854 rendition of the Virginia fugitive Anthony Burns, which precipitated an attack on federal marshals that left one dead, required President Pierce to mobilize the U.S. Marines to escort Burns from the city, as tens of thousands of Bostonians went out into the streets to protest. Burns, marched to the wharf past buildings hung with black bunting to symbolize residents' shame, was the last fugitive slave returned from Boston.

In the context of the fight over the return of fugitive slaves, Harriet Beecher Stowe published *Uncle Tom's Cabin*, which quickly became the most popular novel of the 19th century. It characterized the central crime of slavery as the destruction of slave families through sale and violence. Stowe, the daughter, sister, and wife of prominent Northern ministers, drew inspiration from her involvement with the evangelical movement. She later explained that the novel came to her in a flash, as though a vision granted by God. Stowe's frank depiction of the hypocrisy, the sexual exploitation of enslaved women, and the cruelty inherent in the system aroused violent opposition in the South, where book burnings and mass protests greeted the novel. Spurred by Stowe's novel, which was read around the world, a half-million women in England, Ireland, and Scotland sent a petition calling for emancipation to the U.S. Congress.

The reality of federal protection for slave catchers rather than fugitive slaves, dramatized so effectively by Stowe, inspired several Northern state legislatures to pass Personal Liberty laws designed to hinder the implementation of the **Fugitive Slave Act**. Southerners denounced these statutes as unconstitutional nullifications of federal law. When the federal government opposed slavery, Southerners increasingly used the language of state rights to criticize the actions; but when the federal government supported slavery, most white Southerners stood firmly behind its protection.

Western Expansion and the Kansas–Nebraska Act

The sundering of religious ties, the widening cultural differences, and the continuing political conflicts revealed internal tensions that contrasted sharply with the international optimism that the United States projected. As Commodore Perry launched his expedition to Japan, the author James Fenimore Cooper noted that Americans had "a longing to see distant lands" to determine the "differences which exist between the stranger and ourselves." Those global aspirations grew from a rapidly expanding economy and the new continental reach of the country itself even as some Americans worried that western expansion could initiate an internal collapse like those that had beset previous empires.

SACKING OF LAWRENCE.

SACKING OF LAWRENCE, KANSAS   As the status of slavery in the territories consumed the attention of politicians and citizens in the East, pro-slavery and antislavery factions engaged in personal and communal violence on the ground in Kansas. For Northerners, the infamous attack on the free-state capital of Lawrence represented slavery's chaotic and violent influence on American life.

If that collapse came, it would be on the Great Plains. As disputes over slavery increased in the early 1850s, pro-slavery settlers from Missouri pushed to make Kansas a test. They entered the Kansas territory with slaves or in support of slaveholding to dominate the territorial government so that when it presented Congress with a plan for admission, the state constitution would include slavery. Equally motivated to "win" Kansas, free-state settlers mobilized in the East and headed to the territory to combat the pro-slavery "ruffians." Organized by entities such as the New England Emigrant Aid society, free-state settlers understood themselves as the advance guard in a growing war over slavery within the United States. Armed with "Beecher's Bibles," local slang for the Springfield rifles carried by emigrants and named for abolitionist minister Lyman Ward Beecher, antislavery and pro-slavery forces knew this would not be a war of words.

Stephen Douglas, the Northern leader of the Democratic Party and champion of the Transcontinental Railroad, sought to pacify the conflict by organizing the territory under the banner of what he called "**popular sovereignty**." This would have left the decision for or against slavery up to the people present in a territory when it voted for organization. To allow popular sovereignty, Douglas had to engineer the removal of the Missouri Compromise, which, with its prohibition on slavery in territory north of 36°30′, prohibited a slaveholding Kansas. This policy change came in the **Kansas–Nebraska Act**, which Douglas hoped would resolve sectional conflict. Southerners supported the legislation, but the Northern response—overwhelming in its dissatisfaction—ruined Douglas's political prospects toward higher office. Tens of thousands of Northerners protested the act's removal of a 30-year-old policy that had, they argued, successfully curtailed the more violent sectional disagreements that were sure to appear without it. The most well-publicized critique, "The Appeal of the Independent Democrats," arraigned "this bill as a gross violation of a sacred pledge; as a criminal betrayal of precious rights; as part and parcel of an atrocious plot to exclude from a vast unoccupied region immigrants from the Old World and free laborers from our own States, and convert it into a dreary region of despotism, inhabited by masters and slaves." The bill undermined support among Northerners for the Democratic Party and inspired the formation of the Republicans. Concerned about what he regarded as an unwarranted acquiescence to pro-slavery forces, Abraham Lincoln reentered politics in 1854. The repeal of the Missouri Compromise was "wrong in its direct effect, letting slavery into Kansas and Nebraska—and wrong in its prospective principle, allowing it to spread to every other part of the wide world," Lincoln said.

Rather than stemming the bloodshed, the Kansas–Nebraska Act seemed to exacerbate it (Map 13.2). Newspapers carried weekly reports about bloody attacks and reprisals between free- and slave-state settlers. **John Brown**, an evangelical abolitionist from the East, perpetrated one of the most infamous such episodes when he and his sons attacked a family of pro-slavery settlers along Pottawatomie Creek, hacking them to death with broad swords. Possibly influenced by revolutionary activists from Europe with whom he collaborated, Brown had abandoned the pacifism and moderate approach of his eastern counterparts. This group included two Britons energized by the Chartist movement, a Polish revolutionary, a Bavarian, and a Vienna-born Jew who fought under Hungary's Kossuth. After the failures of 1848 to produce liberal states, European radicals may well have seen America as a more hospitable climate. Brown's actions reflected a frustration with slow pace of change. He and his sons escaped punishment for the massacre, but his infamy preceded him as he headed back East. The violence reached a head with the

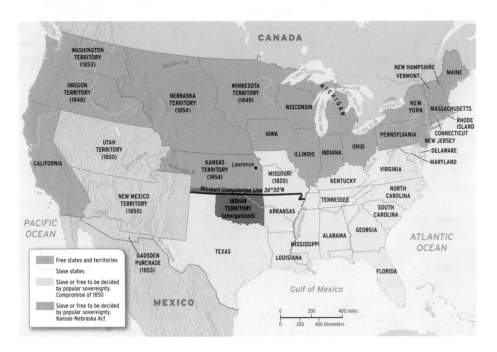

MAP 13.2 ▲ Territorial Organization, 1840s–1850s After the Mexican War, Americans fought, first rhetorically and then physically, over whether the new territory should be opened to slavery. The 1854 Kansas–Nebraska Act, intended to settle the controversy, only stoked more anger among Northerners who condemned its repeal of the Missouri Compromise line.

"Sack of Lawrence" in 1856, when a pro-slavery posse entered the Nebraska capital, destroyed two printing presses, and burned down the Free State Hotel.

In response to the attack on Lawrence, Massachusetts Republican **Charles Sumner**, the first abolitionist senator, took to the Senate floor for a two-day speech titled "The Crime Against Kansas." Because the speech mocked one of South Carolina's senators, Democratic Congressman Preston Brooks, the senator's cousin, attacked Sumner in the Senate and beat him into unconsciousness with his walking stick. For Northerners, Sumner was a martyr to the unchecked violence and incapacity for rational actions that typified the slaveholding South. Was it any surprise, said Northerners, that men who grow up beating their slaves should turn their whip on those with whom they disagreed? Brooks resigned his seat after a modest censure by the House, and his constituents immediately reelected him. Sumner earned the drubbing he received, Southerners said, and to replace the lost cane, thousands of them sent Brooks new ones, with inscriptions such as "Bully for Brooks!"

Rising Sectionalism

The rise of the Republican Party challenged the Democratic supremacy that had reigned since Andrew Jackson's day. Because of the population disparity between the sections, the North possessed more electoral votes and more seats in the House

DRED SCOTT   Scott's lawsuit made him perhaps the most famous enslaved person in the United States. The decision inflamed sectional tensions still more rather than extinguishing them as Chief Justice Roger Taney had hoped.

of Representatives. To stay viable at the national level, Democrats had to retain their bisectional coalition; and to accomplish this, the party had to respect the wishes of their Southern colleagues. Stephen Douglas observed this rule when he pushed for the repeal of the Missouri Compromise. But doing too much endangered the standing of Northern Democrats with their constituents. Those who sacrificed all to retain the support of Southern slaveholders were called "doughfaces." President Franklin Pierce, who had signed the Kansas–Nebraska Act and then supported an aggressively pro-slavery constitution when the territory petitioned for confirmation as a state, was a doughface. So was **James Buchanan**, a Pennsylvania Democrat elected president in 1856.

Despite the public scorn for men like Buchanan, the Democratic Party remained one of the last truly national institutions in the late 1850s. Gone were the churches, the voluntary associations, and the businessmen's alliances that had operated at the national level. Gone too was the Whig Party, a casualty of the sectional disputes over slavery.

Hoping to finally quell the violence and controversy in Kansas, Presidents Pierce and Buchanan had sided with pro-slavery forces in the state, including forcing through Congress a pro-slavery constitution that a clear majority of Kansas residents opposed. But problems and violence persisted, leading some to argue that the Civil War began on the plains of Kansas long before it started in the East.

Sectional tempers flared higher with the Supreme Court's *Dred Scott* decision in 1857. Widely regarded as one of the worst decisions of the High Court, it was yet another attempt to settle the pressing questions of the day that instead intensified them. Scott had been enslaved to an army surgeon who spent years posted to the Illinois and Wisconsin territory when those areas were under the Northwest Ordinance. Scott's lawyers claimed that he had been illegally held as a slave in free territory. Justice **Roger B. Taney**

TIMELINE 1829–1860

AMERICA	YEAR	THE WORLD
David Walker publishes *An Appeal to the Coloured Citizens of the World*	1829	
	1830	Colombia, Ecuador, and Venezuela established as independent nations
Britain ends slavery in British West Indies	1833	
Britain begins First Opium War in China (ends 1842)	1839	Dutch recognize Belgium independence
William Henry Harrison elected first Whig President but dies after a month in office, succeeded by John Tyler First World Antislavery Convention held	1840	"Act of Union" unites Upper and Lower Canada
	1841	Guatemala, El Salvador, Honduras, Nicaragua, and Costa Rica established as independent nations
Prigg v. Pennsylvania establishes national authority for reclaiming fugitive slaves	1842	
Methodist Episcopal Church forms in dispute over slavery Anti-Catholic riots in Philadelphia **Feb** U.S. Congress passes Texas Annexation Act	1844	Santo Domingo wins independence from Spain
Dec United States formally annexes Texas Baptists divide over slavery	1845	
Apr United States declares war on Mexico **Jun** "Bear Flag" Revolt initiates collapse of Mexican authority in California **Aug** Pennsylvania Democrat David Wilmot proposes amendment to Mexican War Appropriations Bill outlawing slavery in lands acquired from the war	1846	
Mar General Winfield Scott lands at Veracruz, Mexico, defeats Mexican forces, and begins march toward Mexico City **Sep** U.S. Army captures Mexico City	1847	
Feb Treaty of Guadalupe Hidalgo ends the Mexican War and cedes 500,000 square miles of Mexican territory to United States **Jul** Last U.S. troops leave Mexico **Nov** Whig Zachary Taylor elected president **Dec** Gold discovered near Sutter's Mill in California	1848	

wrote the majority opinion, ruling that Scott lacked the standing to bring the case and consequently dismissed it. His opinion also included the infamous line that the black man "had no rights which the white man was bound to respect." In direct contravention of the case law on the subject, Taney ruled that black people could not be citizens. On the question of where slaveholders could take their property in safety, Taney issued a broad federal protection of slavery.

This sweeping abolishment of a right that Northerners had exercised for the past 70 years shocked and outraged them. Republicans made the decision a key rhetorical weapon in their arsenal, evidence of a grand conspiracy among slaveholders and their allies in Washington to foist a fully nationalized protection of slavery on Northern states.

Compromise of 1850 passes, which includes provisions admitting California as a free state; opening New Mexico territory to organization under popular sovereignty; banning slave trade in Washington, DC; and creating strong federal Fugitive Slave Act	**1850**	China's Taiping Rebellion begins
Harriet Beecher Stowe publishes *Uncle Tom's Cabin*, giving expression to Northern antislavery sentiment Election of Democrat Franklin Pierce to presidency	**1852**	Establishment of the Second Empire in France under Napoleon III
Commodore Perry arrives in Tokyo Bay, Japan	**1853**	Gold Rush in Australia
Kansas–Nebraska Act passed abolishing Missouri Compromise Line of 1820 Rendition of fugitive slave Anthony Burns from Boston inflames Northern opposition to Fugitive Slave Act First Republican Party convention held in Jackson, MI	**1854**	Crimean War begins—Britain and France oppose Russian expansion into Ottoman Territory
American Party formally organizes, linking various nativist parties across the country	**1855**	Henry Bessemer patents more efficient process for steelmaking
May Charles Sumner delivers "Crime Against Kansas" speech in U.S. Senate **May** Preston Brooks beats Charles Sumner in Senate chamber Pro-slavery guerrillas from Missouri lead "Sack of Lawrence" in Kansas Territory **Nov** Democrat James Buchanan elected President Whig party collapses in most states	**1856**	Crimean War ends Second Anglo-Chinese War begins
Dred Scott ruling denies citizenship to African Americans Hinton Helper publishes *The Impending Crisis*, denouncing slavery's effect on the political and economic freedom of poor white men in the South	**1857**	Britain suppresses "Sepoy Mutiny" in India
Gold discovered near Pike's Peak in Colorado **Dec** John Brown leads failed slave insurrection at Harpers Ferry, VA	**1859**	**Nov** Charles Darwin publishes *On the Origin of Species*
Black population in the United States reaches four million	**1860**	Second Anglo-Chinese War ends

The *Dred Scott* decision fulfilled Southerners' highest hopes for protecting slavery in the territories, although in doing so through federal rather than state power, it undercut Southern arguments that state rights provided the surest foundation for slavery.

Abraham Lincoln reflected moderate Northern antislavery opinion on the decision, which he condemned strongly as wrong in legal, political, and moral terms, but pledged to obey while it stood. Other Americans were not so willing to acquiesce. John Brown, of Kansas fame, came east after the Pottawatomie massacre and planned a more direct response to the problem of slavery. Brown, along with his sons and a handful of black and white supporters, attacked the U.S. arsenal at **Harpers Ferry**, Virginia, in late 1859. Funded secretly by six prominent abolitionists, Brown had organized and drilled his men in a small southern Pennsylvania town not far from Harpers Ferry. The plan to seize the town and the arsenal misfired. The first victim was a free black man, a night watchman for the Baltimore & Ohio Railroad. News of the attack reached Washington, DC, and a squadron of U.S. Marines, led by Colonel Robert E. Lee, arrived in Harpers Ferry the next morning. Lee's forces penned Brown's men in a barn and killed several and captured the rest, including Brown. Brown was charged with attempting to incite a slave insurrection, and as expected was found guilty and executed.

Brown retained his composure in jail and on the scaffold. His famous pronouncement at his trial recognized that he could do more as a martyr than as a man: "Now, if it is deemed necessary that I should forfeit my life for the furtherance of the ends of justice, and mingle my blood further with the blood of my children and with the blood of millions in this slave country whose rights are disregarded by wicked, cruel, and unjust enactments, I submit; so let it be done!"

The public reaction in each section to John Brown's raid, like reactions to the caning of Charles Sumner three years before, reflected the yawning chasm between the people of the North and South. For Southerners, Brown was the predictable conclusion of the increasingly radical rhetoric of abolitionists bent on exterminating the Southern people. "Every village bell which tolled its solemn note at the execution of Brown proclaims to the South the approbation of that village of insurrection and servile war," wrote one prominent Southerner. Radicals in the North lionized Brown. Henry David Thoreau eulogized him, saying "some eighteen hundred years ago Christ was crucified; this morning, perchance, Captain Brown was hung. These are the two ends of a chain which is not without its links. He is not Old Brown any longer; he is an angel of light."

Most Northerners were less effusive. Democrats and conservatives denounced him in no uncertain terms, and Republicans like Lincoln condemned Brown's method while trying to respect his motive. Any sympathy, no matter how mild, proved too much for Southerners. The fire-eaters of the South used Brown's raid, ineffectual as it was, to spur Southerners on to support secession. Brown's plan and timing may have failed at Harpers Ferry, but he could scarcely have chosen a better time. A perfect storm of politics and sectionalism had gathered force throughout the 1850s, before Brown's raid concluded the decade, and sent Americans into the most contentious and important presidential election in U.S. history.

STUDY QUESTIONS FOR THE RISE OF THE REPUBLICANS

1. Why did Northerners and Southerners fight over Kansas and in what ways did such violence reshape national politics?

2. How did the dispute over slavery (in all parts of the country) escalate in the 1850s?

Summary

- American expansionists pushed the nation into conflict with Mexico and in the process dramatically changed the ethnic profile of the nation, as they drew within its borders Spanish-speaking residents of California and the Far West.
- Combined with the continuing influx of Irish and German immigrants, this demographic transformation scared Anglo-Americans into a repressive movement, known as nativism, designed to guarantee political control by Protestant elites.
- The acquisition of new territory inspired an escalating battle in Congress among pro-slavery and antislavery forces and mirrored the tensions within the South itself.
- As slaves fought against the system from within, and pro-slavery and pro-free-soil citizens fought each other in Kansas, Republicans coalesced around a policy opposing the expansion of slavery.

Key Terms and People

Brown, John *457*

Buchanan, James *459*

Calhoun, John C. *448*

Compromise of 1850 *455*

Douglas, Stephen *457*

Fugitive Slave Act *456*

Harpers Ferry *461*

Helper, Hinton *444*

Kansas–Nebraska Act *457*

Know-Nothing Party *442*

popular sovereignty *457*

Prigg v. Pennsylvania *454*

Dred Scott decision *459*

Sumner, Charles *458*

Taney, Roger B. *459*

Reviewing Chapter 13

1. How did the movement of people into and around the United States affect political developments of the period?
2. What was the relationship between slavery and the sectional politics of the 1850s?

Further Reading

Davis, David Brion. *Inhuman Bondage: The Rise and Fall of Slavery in the New World.* New York: Oxford University Press, 2006. A global history of commercial slavery that dominated the Western Hemisphere during the 17th, 18th, and 19th centuries.

Foner, Eric. *Free Soil, Free Labor, Free Men: The Ideology of the Republican Party Before the Civil War,* 2nd ed. New York: Oxford University Press, 1995. The clearest analysis of the various forces that shaped the early Republican Party.

Holt, Michael. *The Political Crisis of the 1850s.* New York: Norton, 1978. A concise history of the partisan collapse that prefigured the sectional crisis.

Johnson, Walter. *Soul By Soul: Life inside the Antebellum Slave Market.* Cambridge, MA: Harvard University Press, 1999. An insightful cultural and economic analysis of the operation of slave markets.

Rugemer, Edward Bartlett. *The Problem of Emancipation: The Caribbean Roots of the American Civil War*. Baton Rouge: Louisiana State University, 2008. A hemispheric history of the relationship between British emancipation and secession and war.

West, Elliott. *The Contested Plains: Indians, Goldseekers, and the Rush to Colorado*. Lawrence: University Press of Kansas, 1998. A fascinating history of the 1859 Colorado gold rush and the competing forces over development and settlement in the middle of the continent.

America In The World
PEOPLE, GOODS, IDEAS AND PRACTICES

CHAPTER 13: A House Dividing 1844–1860

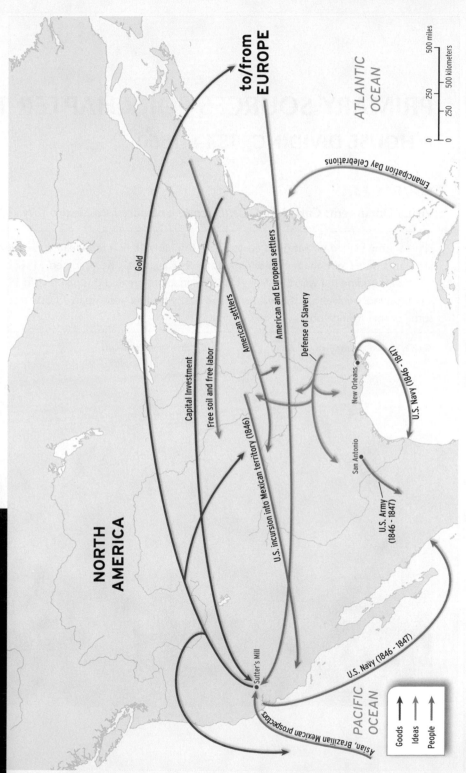

NORTH AMERICA

to/from EUROPE

ATLANTIC OCEAN

PACIFIC OCEAN

Gold

Capital Investment

Free soil and free labor

American settlers

American and European settlers

Defense of Slavery

U.S. incursion into Mexican territory (1846)

Emancipation Day Celebrations

New Orleans

San Antonio

U.S. Navy (1846 - 1847)

U.S. Army (1846 - 1847)

U.S. Navy (1846 - 1847)

Sutter's Mill

Asian, Brazilian Mexican prospectors

Goods
Ideas
People

0   250   500 miles
0   250   500 kilometers

PRIMARY SOURCES FOR CHAPTER 13

A HOUSE DIVIDING, 1844–1860

SOURCE 13.1

Visual Document: Carl Nebel, *Genl. Scott's Entrance into Mexico City* (1847)

Scott's army landed on Mexico's eastern coast in early 1847 and defeated the Mexican army in a series of engagements. On September 14, 1847, he occupied Mexico City, effectively ending the war. Carl Nebel, a German artist, created this painting in 1851 for inclusion in a book about the war by a journalist who had accompanied U.S. troops on some of their campaigns.

Source: The Art Archive/National History Museum Mexico City/Gianni Dagli Orti.

WORKING WITH SOURCES

1. Based on Nebel's portrait, what kind of city is Mexico City?

2. What does the representation of cavalry suggest about the U.S. military and its presence in Mexico?

3. What are the figures in the left foreground intended to signal about the Mexicans encountered by the army?

SOURCE 13.2

Governor James Henry Hammond, Excerpts from A Letter to Thomas Clarkson (1845)

Hammond served as governor and senator for South Carolina in the 1840s and 1850s. He emerged as one of the most vigorous defenders of slavery and the Southern social order. The document here, a response to the English abolitionist Thomas Clarkson's critique of Southern slavery, circulated widely in the United States and Britain.

Source: *Gov. Hammond's Letters on Southern Slavery: Addressed to Thomas Clarkson, the English Abolitionist* (Charleston: Walker and Burke, 1845).

Let us . . . turn to American slavery, to which you have now directed your attention, and against which a crusade has been preached as enthusiastic and ferocious as that of Peter the Hermit—destined, I believe, to be about as successful. And here let me say, there is not a vast difference between the two, though you may not acknowledge it. The wisdom of ages has concurred in the justice and expediency of establishing rights by prescriptive use, however tortious in their origin they may have been. You would deem a man insane whose keen sense of equity would lead him to denounce your right to the lands you hold, and which perhaps you inherited from a long line of ancestry, because your title was derived from a Saxon or Norman conqueror, and your lands were originally wrested by violence from the vanquished Britons. And so would the New England Abolitionist regard any one who would insist that he should restore his farm to the descendants of the slaughtered Red men, to whom, God has

as clearly given it, as he gave life and freedom to the kidnapped African. That time does not consecrate wrong, is a fallacy which all history exposes; and which the best and wisest men of all ages and professions of religious faith, have practically denied. The means, therefore, whatever they may have been, by which the African race now in this country, have been reduced to slavery, cannot affect us, since they are our property, as your land is yours, by inheritance or purchase and prescriptive right. You will say that man cannot hold *property in man*. The answer is, that he can, and *actually does* hold property in his fellow all the world over, in a variety of forms, and *has always done so*. I will show presently his authority for doing it.

If you were to ask me whether I was an advocate of slavery in the abstract, I should probably answer, that I am not, according to my understanding of the question. I do not like to deal in abstractions; it seldom leads to any useful ends. There are few universal truths. I do not now remember any single moral truth universally acknowledged. We have no assurance that it is given to our finite understanding to comprehend abstract moral truth. Apart from Revelation and the Inspired writings, what ideas should we have even of God, Salvation and Immortality? Let the Heathen answer. Justice itself is impalpable as an abstraction, and abstract liberty the merest phantasy that ever amused the imagination. This world was made for man, and man for the world as it is. Ourselves, our relations with one another, and with all matter, are real, not ideal. I might say that I am no more in favor of slavery in the abstract, than I am of pover[t]y, disease, deformity, idiocy or any other inequality in the condition of the human family; that I love perfection, and think I should enjoy a Millenium such as God has promised. But what would it amount to? A pledge that I would join you to set about eradicating those apparently inevitable evils of our nature, in equalizing the condition of all mankind, consummating the perfection of our race, and introducing the Millenium? By no means. To effect these things belongs exclusively to a higher power, and would be well for us to leave the Almighty to perfect His own works and fulfil His own covenants. Especially, as the history of all the past shows how entirely futile all human efforts have proved, when made for the purpose of aiding Him in carrying out even His revealed designs, and how invarially he has accomplished them by unconscious instruments, and in the face of human expectation. Nay more, that every attempt which has been made by fallible man to extort from the world obedience to his "abstract" notions of right and wrong, has been invariably attended with calamities, dire and extended, just in proportion to the breadth and vigor of the movement. On slavery in the abstract then, it would not be amiss to have as little as possible to say. Let us contemplate it as it is. And thus

contemplating it, the first question we have to ask ourselves is, whether it is contrary to the Will of God, as revealed to us in His holy scriptures—the only certain means given us to ascertain His will. If it is, then slavery is a sin; and I admit at once that every man is bound to set his face against it, and to emancipate his slaves, should he hold any. . . .

I think, then, I may safely conclude, and I firmly believe, that American slavery is not only not a sin, but especially commanded by God through Moses, and approved by Christ through his apostles. And here I might close its defence; for what God ordained and Christ sanctifies, should surely command the respect and toleration of man. But I fear there has grown up in our time a Transcendental Religion which is throwing even Transcendental Philosophy into the shade; a religion too pure and elevated for the Bible; which seeks to erect among men a higher standard of morals than the Almighty has revealed or our Saviour preached, and which is probably destined to do more to impede the extension of God's Kingdom on earth than all the Infidels who have ever lived. Error is error. It is as dangerous to deviate to the right hand as to the left. And when men professing to be holy men, and who are by numbers so regarded, declare those things to be sinful which our Creator has expressly authorized and instituted, they do more to destroy his authority among mankind than the most wicked can affect by proclaiming that to be innocent which He has forbidden. To this self-righteous and self-exalted class belong all the Abolitionists whose writings I have read. With them it is no end of the argument to prove your propositions by the test of the Bible, interpreted according to its plain and palpable meaning, and as understood by all mankind for three thousand years before their time. They are more ingenious in construing and interpolating to accommodate it to their new-fangled and etherial code of morals, than ever were Voltaire or Hume in picking it to pieces to free the world from what they considered a delusion. When the Abolitionists proclaim "man-stealing" to be a sin, and show me that it is so written down by God, I admit them to be right, and shudder at the idea of such a crime. But when I show them that to hold "bond-men forever" is ordained by God, *they deny the Bible, and set up in its place a Law of their own making.* I must then cease to reason with them on this branch of the question. Our religion differs as widely as our manners. The Great Judge in our day of final account must decide between us. . . . I indorse without reserve, the much abused sentiment of Gov. M'Duffie, that "slavery is the corner stone of our republican edifice;" while I repudiate, as ridiculously absurd, that much lauded but no where accredited dogma, of Mr. Jefferson, that "all men are born equal." No Society has ever yet existed, and I have already incidentally quoted the highest authority to show that none ever will exist, without a natural variety of classes. The most marked of these must in a country like ours, be the rich and the poor, the educated and the ignorant. It will scarcely be disputed that the very poor have less leisure to prepare themselves for the proper discharge of public duties than the rich; and that the ignorant are wholly unfit for them at all. In all countries save ours, these two classes, or the poor rather, who are presumed to be necessarily ignorant, are by law expressly excluded from all participation in the management of public affairs. In a repudlican [*sic*] Government this cannot be done. Universal suffrage, though not essential in theory, seems to be in fact, a necessary appendage to a republican system. Where universal suffrage obtains, it is obvious that the Government is in the hands of a numerical majority: and it is hardly necessary to say, that in every part of the world more than half the people are ignorant and poor. Though no one can look upon poverty

as a crime, and we do not generally here regard it as any objection to a man in his individual capacity, still it must be admitted that it is a wretched and insecure government which is administered by its most ignorant citizens, and those who have the least at stake under it. Though intelligence and wealth have great influence here as everywhere, in keeping in check reckless and unenlightened numbers, yet it is evident to close observers, if not to all, that these are rapidly usurping all power in the non-slave-holding States, and threaten a fearful crisis in Republican Institutious [*sic*] there at no remote period. In the slave-holding States, however, nearly one half of the whole population, and those the poorest and most ignorant, have no political influence whatever, because they are slaves. Of the other half, a large proportion are both educated and independent in their circumstances, while those who unfortunately are not so, being still elevated far above the mass, are higher toned and more deeply interested in preserving a stable and well ordered government, than the same class in any other country. Hence, slavery is truly the "corner stone" and foundation of every well designed and durable "Republican edifice." . . . I have yet to reply to the main ground on which you and your coadjutors rely for the overthrow of our system of slavery. Failing in all your attempts to prove that it is sinful in its nature, immoral in its effects, a political evil, and profitless to those who maintain it, you appeal to the sympathies of mankind, and attempt to arouse the world against us by the most shocking charges of tyranny and cruelty. You begin by a vehement denunciation of "the irresponsible power of one man over his fellowmen." The question of the responsibility of power is a vast one. It is the great political question of modern times. Whole nations divide off upon it and establish different fundamental systems of government. That "responsibility," which to one set of millions seems amply sufficient to check the government, to the support of which they devote their lives and fortunes, appears to another set of millions a mere mockery of restraint. And accordingly as the opinions of these millions differ, they honor each other with the epithets of "Serfs" or "Anarchists." It is ridiculous to introduce such an idea as this into the discussion of a mere Domestic Institution. But since you have introduced it, I deny that the power of the slaveholder in America is "irresponsible." He is responsible to God. He is responsible to the world—a responsibility which Abolitionists do not intend to allow him to evade—and in acknowledgment of which I write you this letter. He is responsible to the community in which he lives, and to the laws under which he enjoys his civil rights. Those laws do not permit him to kill, to maim, or to punish beyond certain limits, or to overtask or to refuse to feed and clothe his slave. In short, they forbid him to be tyrannical or cruel. If any of those laws have grown obsolete, it is because they are so seldom violated that they are forgotten. You have disinterred one of them from a compilation by some Judge STROUD, of Philapelphia [*sic*], to stigmatize its inadequate penalties for killing, maiming, &c. Your objects appears to be—you can have no other—to produce the impression that it must be often violated on account of its insufficiency. You say as much, and that it marks our estimate of the slave. You forget to state that this law was enacted by *Englishmen*, and only indicates *their* opinion of the reparation due for these offences. Ours is proved by the fact, though perhaps unknown to Judge STROUD or yourself, that we have essentially altered this law; and the murder of a slave has for many years been punishable with death in this State. And so it is, I believe, in most or all the slave States. You seem well aware, however, that laws have been recently passed in all these States making it penal to teach slaves

to read. Do you know what occasioned their passage, and renders their stringent enforcement necessary. I can tell you: it was the abolition agitation. If the slave is not allowed to read his Bible, the sin rests upon the Abolitionists; for they stand prepared to furnish him with a key to it, which would make it, not a book of hope and love and peace, but of despair, hatred and blood; which would convert the reader, not into a Christian, but a Demon. To preserve him from such a horrid destiny, it is a sacred duty which we owe to slaves, not less than to ourselves, to interpose the most decisive means. If the Catholics deem it wrong to trust the Bible to the hands of ignorance, shall we be excommunicated because we will not give and with it the corrupt and fatal commentaries of the Abolitionists, to our slaves? Allow our slaves to read your pamphlets, stimulating them to cut our throats! Can you believe us to be such unspeakable fools. . . . Is timely preparation and gradual emancipation suggested to avert these horrible consequences? I thought your experience in the West Indies had at least done so much as to explode that idea. If it failed there, much more would it fail here, where the two races, approximating to equality in numbers, are daily and hourly in the closest contact. Give room for but a single spark of real jealousy to be kindled between them, and the explosion would be instantaneous and universal. It is the most fatal of all fallacies to suppose that these two races can exist together, after any length of time or any process of preparation, on terms at all approaching to equality. Of this, both of them are finally and fixedly convinced. They differ essentially, in all the leading traits that characterise the varieties of the human species, and color draws an indellible and insuperable line of separation between them. Every scheme founded upon the idea that they can remain together on the same soil, beyond the briefest period, in any other relation than precisely that which now subsists between them, is not only preposterous, but fraught with deepest danger. If there was no alternative but to try the "experiment" here, reason and humanity dictate that the suffering of "gradualism" should be saved, and the catastrophe of "immediate abolition," enacted as rapidly as possible. Are you impatient for the performance to commence? Do you long to gloat over the scenes I have suggested, but could not hold the pen to portray? In your long life many such have passed under your review. You know that *they* are not "*impossible*." Can they be to your taste? Do you believe that in laboring to bring them about the Abolitionists are doing the will of God? No! God is not there. It is the work of Satan. The Archfiend, under specious guise, has found his way into your souls, and with false appeals to philanthropy, and foul insinuations to ambition, instigates them to rush headlong to the accomplishment of his diabolical designs.

WORKING WITH SOURCES

1. How does Hammond distinguish between slavery in the abstract and slavery in practice?
2. What is Hammond's political argument for slavery, and why does he believe that slavery is necessary in order for democracy to function?

SOURCE 13.3
Republican Party Platform (1856)

The Republican Party emerged from the collapse of the Whig Party in the mid-1850s. It combined some of the Whig's economic development policies (and, in some cases, parts of the American Party's nativism platform) with a significant opposition to the expansion of slavery in the western territories. 1856 was the first year that the party ran a presidential candidate, and although he lost, Republican congressional candidates won seats all across the North.

Source: http://www.ushistory.org/gop/convention_1856republicanplatform.htm.

This Convention of Delegates, assembled in pursuance of a call addressed to the people of the United States, without regard to past political differences or divisions, who are opposed to the repeal of the Missouri Compromise; to the policy of the present Administration; to the extension [of] Slavery into Free Territory; in favor of the admission of Kansas as a Free State; of restoring the action of the Federal Government to the principles of Washington and Jefferson; and for the purpose of presenting candidates for the offices of President and Vice-President, do . . . Resolved: That, with our Republican fathers, we hold it to be a self-evident truth, that all men are endowed with the inalienable right to life, liberty, and the pursuit of happiness, and that the primary object and ulterior design of our Federal Government were to secure these rights to all persons under its exclusive jurisdiction; that, as our Republican fathers, when they had abolished Slavery in all our National Territory, ordained that no person shall be deprived of life, liberty, or property, without due process of law, it becomes our duty to maintain this provision of the Constitution against all attempts to violate it for the purpose of establishing Slavery in the Territories of the United States by positive legislation, prohibiting its existence or extension therein. That we deny the authority of Congress, of a Territorial Legislation, of any individual, or association of individuals, to give legal existence to Slavery in any Territory of the United States, while the present Constitution shall be maintained.

Resolved: That the Constitution confers upon Congress sovereign powers over the Territories of the United States for their government; and that in the exercise of this power, it is both the right and the imperative duty of Congress to prohibit in the Territories those twin relics of barbarism—Polygamy, and Slavery.

Resolved: That while the Constitution of the United States was ordained and established by the people, in order to "form a more perfect union, establish justice, insure domestic tranquility, provide for the common defense, promote the general welfare, and secure the blessings of liberty," and contain ample provision for the protection of the life, liberty, and property of every citizen, the dearest Constitutional rights of the people of Kansas have been fraudulently and violently taken from them.

Their Territory has been invaded by an armed force;

Spurious and pretended legislative, judicial, and executive officers have been set over them, by whose usurped authority, sustained by the military power of the government, tyrannical and unconstitutional laws have been enacted and enforced;

The right of the people to keep and bear arms has been infringed.

Test oaths of an extraordinary and entangling nature have been imposed as a condition of exercising the right of suffrage and holding office.

The right of an accused person to a speedy and public trial by an impartial jury has been denied;

The right of the people to be secure in their persons, houses, papers, and effects, against unreasonable searches and seizures, has been violated;

They have been deprived of life, liberty, and property without due process of law;

That the freedom of speech and of the press has been abridged;

The right to choose their representatives has been made of no effect;

Murders, robberies, and arsons have been instigated and encouraged, and the offenders have been allowed to go unpunished;

That all these things have been done with the knowledge, sanction, and procurement of the present National Administration; and that for this high crime against the Constitution, the Union, and humanity, we arraign that Administration, the President, his advisers, agents, supporters, apologists, and accessories, either before or after the fact, before the country and before the world; and that it is our fixed purpose to bring the actual perpetrators of these atrocious outrages and their accomplices to a sure and condign punishment thereafter.

Resolved, That Kansas should be immediately admitted as a state of this Union, with her present Free Constitution, as at once the most effectual way of securing to her citizens the enjoyment of the rights and privileges to which they are entitled, and of ending the civil strife now raging in her territory.... Resolved, That a railroad to the Pacific Ocean by the most central and practicable route is imperatively demanded by the interests of the whole country, and that the Federal Government ought to render immediate and efficient aid in its construction, and as an auxiliary thereto, to the immediate construction of an emigrant road on the line of the railroad.

Resolved, That appropriations by Congress for the improvement of rivers and harbors, of a national character, required for the accommodation and security of our existing commerce, are authorized by the Constitution, and justified by the obligation of the Government to protect the lives and property of its citizens.

Resolved, That we invite the affiliation and cooperation of the men of all parties, however differing from us in other respects, in support of the principles herein declared; and believing that the spirit of our institutions as well as the Constitution of our country, guarantees liberty of conscience and equality of rights among citizens, we oppose all legislation impairing their security.

WORKING WITH SOURCES

1. How do the Republicans root their opposition to slavery in the Constitution?

2. How does this argument differ from that of more traditional abolitionists such as Douglass?

3. Why was the condition of Kansas, where few slaves lived, so important to the Republican Party?

SOURCE 13.4

Victor Hugo, Excerpts from A Letter to the *London News* Regarding John Brown (December 2, 1859)

In 1859, John Brown, a white abolitionist, attacked the U.S. armory at Harpers Ferry, Virginia, in a failed slave revolt. Brown was executed for attempting to incite an insurrection. Victor Hugo was one of the most well-known French writers of the 19th century. He worked in a variety of forms and gained fame for his poetry, novels, and plays. Hugo evolved into an ardent republican and championed democratic movements around the world.

Source: http://en.wikisource.org/wiki/Victor_Hugo%27s_letter_to_the_London_News_regarding_John_Brown.

To the Editor of the London News:

Sir: When our thoughts dwell upon the United States of America, a majestic form rises before the eye of imagination. It is a Washington!

Look, then, to what is taking place in that country of Washington at this present moment.

In the Southern States of the Union there are slaves; and this circumstance is regarded with indignation, as the most monstrous of inconsistencies, by the pure and logical conscience of the Northern States. A white man, a free man, John Brown, sought to deliver these negro slaves from bondage. Assuredly, if insurrection is ever a sacred duty, it must be when it is directed against Slavery. John Brown endeavored to commence the work of emancipation by the liberation of slaves in Virginia. Pious, austere, animated with the old Puritan spirit, inspired by the spirit of the Gospel, he sounded to these men, these oppressed brothers, the rallying cry of Freedom. The slaves, enervated by servitude, made no response to the appeal. Slavery afflicts the soul with weakness. Brown, though deserted, still fought at the head of a handful of heroic men; he was riddled with balls; his two young sons, sacred martyrs, fell dead at his side, and he himself was taken. This is what they call the affair at Harper's Ferry.

John Brown has been tried, with four of his comrades, Stephens, Coppic, Gree and Copeland.

What has been the character of his trial? Let us sum it up in a few words:—

John Brown, upon a wretched pallet, with six half gaping wounds, a gun-shot wound in his arm, another in his loins, and two in his head, scarcely conscious of surrounding sounds, bathing his mattress in blood, and with the ghastly presence [of] his two dead sons ever beside him; his four fellow-sufferers wounded, dragging themselves along by his side; Stephens bleeding from saber wounds; justice in a hurry, and overleaping all obstacles; an attorney, Hunter, who wishes to proceed hastily, and a judge, Parker, who suffers him to have his way; the hearing cut short, almost every application for delay refused, forged and mutilated documents produced, the witnesses for the defence kidnapped, every obstacle thrown in the way of the prisoner's counsel, two cannon loaded with canister stationed in the Court, orders given to the jailers to shoot the prisoners if they sought to escape, forty minutes of deliberation, and three men sentenced to die! I declare on my honor that all this took place, not in Turkey, but in America!

Such things cannot be done with impunity in the face of the civilized world. The universal conscience of humanity is an ever-watchful eye. Let the judges of Charlestown, and Hunter and Parker, and the slaveholding jurors, and the whole population of Virginia, ponder it well: they are watched! They are not alone in the world. At this moment, America attracts the eyes of the whole of Europe.

John Brown, condemned to die. . . . The more one loves, the more one admires, the more one venerates that Republic, the more heart-sick one feels at the contemplation of such a catastrophe. A single State ought not to have the power to dishonor all the rest, and in this case there is an obvious justification for a federal intervention. Otherwise, by hesitating to interfere when it might prevent a crime, the Union becomes a participator in its guilt. No matter how intense may be the indignation of the generous Northern States, the Southern States force them to share the opprobrium of this murder. All of us, no matter who we may be, who are bound together as compatriots by the common tie of a democratic creed, feel ourselves in some measure compromised. If the scaffold should be erected on the 16th of December, the incorruptible voice of history would thenceforward testify that the august Confederation of the New World, had added to all its rites of holy brotherhood a brotherhood of blood, and the fasces of that splendid Republic would be bound together with the running noose that hung from the gibbet of Brown!

This is a bond that kills.

When we reflect on what Brown, the liberator, the champion of Christ, has striven to effect, and when we remember that he is about to die, slaughtered by the American Republic, that crime assumes an importance co-extensive with that of the nation which commits it—and when we say to ourselves that this nation is one of the glories of the human race; that, like France, like England, like Germany, she is one of the great agents of civilization; that she sometimes even leaves Europe in the rear by the sublime audacity of some of her progressive movements; that she is the Queen of an entire world, and that her brow is irradiated with a glorious halo of freedom, we declare our conviction that John Brown will not die; for we recoil horror-struck from the idea of so great a crime committed by so great a people.

Viewed in a political light, the murder of Brown would be an irreparable fault. It would penetrate the Union with a gaping fissure which would lead in the end to its entire disruption. It is possible that the execution of Brown might establish slavery on a firm basis in Virginia, but it is certain that it would shake to its centre the entire fabric of American democracy. You preserve your infamy, but you sacrifice your glory. Viewed in a moral light, it seems to me that a portion of the enlightenment of humanity would be eclipsed, that even the ideas of justice and injustice would be obscured on the day which should witness the assassination of Emancipation by Liberty.

As for myself, though I am but a mere atom, yet being, as I am, in common with all other men, inspired with the conscience of humanity, I fall on my knees, weeping before the great starry banner of the New World; and with clasped hands, and with profound and filial respect, I implore the illustrious American Republic, sister of the French Republic, to see to the safety of the universal moral law, to save John Brown, to demolish the threatening scaffold of the 16th of December, and not to suffer that beneath its eyes, and I add, with a shudder, almost by its fault, a crime should be perpetrated surpassing the first fratricide in iniquity.

For—yes, let America know it, and ponder on it well—there is something more terrible than Cain slaying Abel: It is Washington slaying Spartacus!

Victor Hugo

Hautville House, Dec. 2d, 1859.

WORKING WITH SOURCES

1. How does Hugo characterize the actions of John Brown?

2. How might Americans have responded to Hugo's engagement with the event?

3. What role does he envision for Europe in the fight against American slavery?

The Civil War

14

A single cotton boll weighs less than one-quarter of an ounce. Individual fibers can be carried away by an exhaled breath. But the value of woven cotton to the global powers of the 19th century empowered white Southerners to enslave millions of people and helped convince them that they could win a war of **secession** against the North. Cotton's bonds proved stronger than iron or blood. How did this humble plant wind up implicated in the deadliest episode in American history?

Profits from cotton drove the great expansion of the slave regimes of Alabama, Mississippi, and northern Louisiana, and much of that profit came from overseas buyers. By 1860, British and French mills bought 70 percent of their cotton from the American South. The British textile industry employed nearly one-quarter of the country's workers. Southerners assumed that this dependency guaranteed foreign support in the event of a civil war. Robert Bunch, the British consul at Charleston, explained to London in 1860 that there existed an "almost universal conviction entertained by the South that Great Britain will make any sacrifice, even of principle or of honor to prevent the stoppage of the supply of cotton." Although Britain bought more raw cotton than anyone else, Southerners saw the same trend around the globe. Georgians were cheered by what one noted as the "progressive increase of the consumption of cotton in France, Belgium, Holland, Germany, and Spain."

To explain why wars happen, we need to understand both the underlying causes and those factors that enable people to initiate or wage war.

< Jefferson Davis and Cabinet with General Lee in the council chamber in Richmond, c. 1866.

Cotton performs double duty for the Civil War. Profits from the South's staple crops (cotton especially but also sugar and rice) reinforced the importance of slavery and encouraged Southerners to pursue economic and diplomatic strategies at odds with those that Northerners supported. Second, the global connections that cotton created gave Southerners the confidence to secede. As South Carolina's James Henry Hammond noted, "You dare not make war on cotton . . . Cotton is King!" Their control of this most important crop emboldened Southerners to perceive themselves as a world power even as their authority within the national community diminished. This paradox was hard to see in 1860, but the Civil War would soon test the durability of King Cotton's throne.

◼ SECESSION, 1860–1861

In 1860, widespread violence still lay in the future and adversaries sparred through politics. From the perspective of white Southerners, the rapid growth of the Northern states threatened the balance of power within the United States. Fearful about the future of slavery under a Republican administration, a majority of slaveholding states seceded from the Union. Few anticipated anything more than a short war, if that. Many Southerners assumed that their central place as cotton supplier to French and British textile manufacturers would bring recognition of their new nation before any real war began. For their part, Northerners interpreted secession as a repudiation of self-government, a threat to both America and the future of democracy around the world. Northerners went to war in 1861 to reunify the nation. Determined Southern resistance compelled increasingly severe measures from the North. Over time, a war for union evolved into a war for emancipation, with a twisted legacy of violence, anger, hope, and joy.

The Secession of the Lower South

The battle began with the election of 1860. Democrats convened their party in Charleston, South Carolina, home to the most rabid pro-secession wing of the party. The convention deadlocked over federal protection for slavery in the Western territories. Fire-eaters, advocates of immediate secession from Deep South states, abandoned the meeting rather than accept defeat on this measure. Northern Democrats reconvened in Baltimore several weeks later and nominated Douglas, whereas Southern Democrats nominated Senator John Breckinridge of Kentucky. Republicans likewise entered their convention in Chicago divided over who should lead the party. Most regarded party leaders William Henry Seward and Samuel Chase as too radical on the question of slavery. Local favorite **Abraham Lincoln** won the nomination partly because of his strong national showing in the 1858 senatorial campaign against Stephen Douglas and partly because he did not have a long track record. His moderate stance appealed to Republican Party managers keen to win conservative voters in the North. Lincoln made his personal opposition to slavery clear; but as a strict constitutionalist, he also recognized that neither Congress nor the president had authority over slavery where it already existed. Another group organized itself out of the remnants of the southern Whigs and nominated Kentuckian John Bell. Calling themselves the Constitutional Union Party, they advocated little beyond a moderate appeal to Union in their campaign platform. The four-way contest thus presented voters with the most complex ballot since the election of 1824 (Map 14.1).

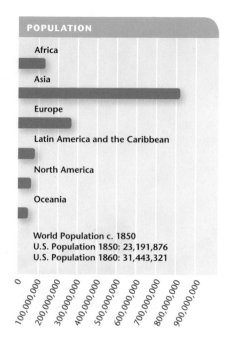

POPULATION

Africa

Asia

Europe

Latin America and the Caribbean

North America

Oceania

World Population c. 1850
U.S. Population 1850: 23,191,876
U.S. Population 1860: 31,443,321

The campaign mirrored the deep sectional divisions in the country. Lincoln appeared only before Northern audiences, and many Southern registrars refused to even print his name on ballots. Breckinridge campaigned in the South, and Bell toured mostly the middle of the country. Only Douglas campaigned nationally, reprimanding both Southern and Northern extremists who he believed threatened the Union. Breckinridge never advocated secession, although he was clearly the candidate most sympathetic to the cause of Southern rights. Although Lincoln was not an abolitionist, his firm opposition to the expansion of slavery into the Western territories alarmed pro-slavery Southerners. They regarded slavery's expansion as essential to their survival and perceived any restriction as a violation of constitutionally protected property rights. Although he captured only 40 percent of the popular vote, Lincoln won the election by securing a majority in the electoral college.

South Carolina was the first state to respond to Lincoln's election. On December 20, 1860, the state "dissolved" its relationship to the Union. The "Declaration of Causes" issued by the convention began with a stark explanation of slavery's centrality to secession: "our position is thoroughly identified with the institution of slavery—the greatest material interest of the world." Although Lincoln had not yet assumed office, the Republican presidential victory convinced white South Carolinians that Lincoln's administration would try to abolish slavery. Fire-eaters in Mississippi stated the case in equally stark language: "There was no choice left us but submission to the mandates of abolition, or a dissolution of the Union, whose principles had been subverted to work out our ruin." Other slaveholding states shared this sentiment. Alabama—and over the next six weeks, Florida, Georgia, Louisiana, and Texas—followed suit, although none demonstrated as much unity as South Carolina. In each of these states, substantial minorities opposed immediate secession. Pro-secession Georgians captured a bare 51 percent in voting for the state's secession convention, whereas in Texas, Governor Sam Houston (the hero of Texas Independence) tried to block the legislature from calling for a convention. Like many conservative Southerners, Houston hoped to avoid "the perils of revolution . . . with its attendant horrors of bloodshed, rapine, and devastation."

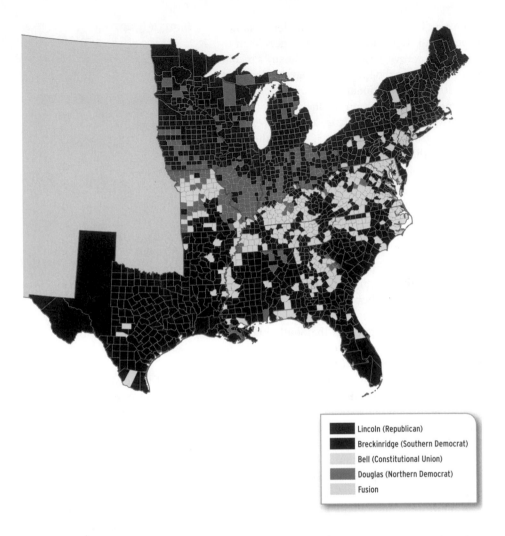

MAP 14.1 ▲ 1860 Presidential Election, by County The four-way contest exacerbated sectional discontent. Abraham Lincoln won the Northern states and enough electoral votes to secure the office, whereas John Breckinridge won the South, and John Bell and Stephen Douglas shared states in the country's middle.

Despite Houston's experience and stature, pro-secession forces in Texas and other states won the day and led their states out of the Union. On February 4, 1861, representatives of the seven Deep South states assembled in Montgomery, Alabama, and created the Confederate States of America.

Fort Sumter and the Secession of the Upper South

During the long interim between the election and Lincoln's inauguration in March 1861, President James Buchanan did little to address the crisis. Buchanan believed that

"Whew! That Old Hen, JEFF DAVIS, has been trying to hatch a Rotten Egg."

SECESSION This cartoon reveals Northern scorn for secession and the easy assumption among Northerners that curtailing the process would be quick and painless.

secession was unconstitutional but that he was powerless to intervene. Buchanan's "hands-off" policy gave seceding states the false impression that the U.S. government would do nothing to impede their exit. Lincoln waited out the lame-duck period at his home in Springfield, Illinois, where he reiterated his oft-stated position that the president had no power over slavery in the states where it already existed but that Congress could regulate or ban slavery in the territories.

Lincoln's inauguration on March 4, 1861, was a solemn affair; it occurred under the cloud of uncertainty about the Union's future that he had pledged to preserve. In his inaugural speech, Lincoln appealed to Southerners to remain loyal—"we are not enemies, but friends"—and to respect the shared history ("the mystic chords of memory") that bound them to the United States. Lincoln's supporters regarded the speech as moderate and conciliatory, but opponents considered his declaration that the Union would "hold, occupy, and possess the property and places belonging to the government" a threat to their peace and security. Both Lincoln and Mississippian **Jefferson Davis**, who resigned from Congress and accepted the presidency of the Confederacy, moved cautiously. Both faced similar challenges—needing to bolster their standing among their own anxious and angry citizens while avoiding war—and for both the momentum of events initiated by others pushed them along. Northerners demanded that Lincoln restore control over federal property—principally, coastal forts and armories in the South—while Southerners pushed Davis to assert Confederate control over the same places.

Even as both sides considered the possibility of war, Upper South representatives continued to embrace negotiation. Pro-secession forces knew they represented a minority view in the region, so they inflamed fear of Lincoln. Pro-Union forces sought conciliatory agreements from Lincoln and Congress that would reassure Southerners that slavery would be protected. Congress passed and two states ratified a new amendment that would have guaranteed slavery in the states where it existed. But these measures were too little too late. Republicans refused to compromise on the extension of slavery into Western territories, recognizing this as a core issue for their supporters. To entice their slaveholding brethren in the Upper South to join them, several Deep South states sent commissioners to the region to argue for the necessity of a unified slaveholding South. The Alabama Commissioner, Stephen Hale, told Kentuckians that Northerners "had been waging an unrelenting and fanatical war" against slavery since the 1830s. Under a Lincoln administration, whites would "be degraded to a position of equality with free negroes ... or else there will be an eternal war of races, desolating the land with blood, and utterly wasting and destroying all the resources of the country." Hale's conclusion was clear: "Disunion is inevitable."

The crisis peaked at Fort Sumter, an unfinished earthen fort located in Charleston Harbor. The U.S. commander, Kentuckian Robert Anderson, notified Washington that he could not continue to hold the fort without provisions. Lincoln sent an unarmed ship to restock the food supplies for the small garrison. On April 12, 1861, before the ship reached the harbor, Confederate batteries on neighboring islands opened fire on Fort Sumter. After a lengthy artillery duel, Anderson surrendered the fort. Northerners treated this attack on U.S. property as a declaration of war.

Mobilization for War

In the wake of the battle at Fort Sumter, Lincoln called up the militia, requesting 75,000 men enlisted for 90 days to help restore obedience to the law of the United States. This action forced Upper South states to choose sides. Upper South politicians who had resisted secession regarded Lincoln's decision to mobilize an army as an act of betrayal after the months of quiet negotiation. Four more slave states—Virginia, North Carolina, Tennessee, and Arkansas—left the Union for the Confederacy, whereas four others (Missouri, Kentucky, Maryland, and Delaware) remained loyal. A wave of martial enthusiasm swept both the North and the South. George Templeton Strong detailed changes in New York City: "The Northern backbone is much stiffened already. Many who stood up for 'Southern rights' and complained of wrongs done the South now say that, since the South has fired the first gun, they are ready to go to all lengths in supporting the government." At county courthouses, town squares, and city centers, hundreds of thousands of men volunteered for the Union and Confederate armies.

In retrospect, the North's military advantages seem so significant that Southern enthusiasm looks arrogant or rash. At the time, however, most Southerners and many Northerners identified differences more important than manpower and supplies. On paper, the North was much better equipped to fight. It possessed a 5:2 advantage in terms of eligible soldiers, over twice as many draft animals, and a vastly greater industrial capacity. Most importantly, the North had a more commercialized economic system (Figure 14.1). Southerners invested their money in land and slaves, and neither could easily be sold to pay for the war. But the South held both geographic and psychological advantages. The land mass of the Confederacy was three-quarters of a million square miles—larger than the size of continental Europe—with a 3,000 mile coastline; thus, it seemed too large to be conquered by Union forces. Southerners also fought

ENLISTING SOLDIERS   The local nature of enlistment and mobilization in the Civil War generated enthusiasm among soldiers and civilians alike. Both groups anticipated a short, relatively bloodless affair.

a defensive war—they knew the terrain and took pride and strength in the fact that they were defending their homes against invasion. William Russell, the British journalist traveling through the United States, observed that if Confederate nationalism took root, "it will be difficult indeed for the North to restore the Union. These pieces of bunting [national flags] seem to twine themselves through heart and brain."

The U.S. Army contained only 15,000 men in 1860, and nearly one-third of the officers and enlisted men resigned to join the Confederacy. The navy had only three functional vessels in U.S. waters ready for duty. As a result, Northern advantages, especially its larger population and greater economic resources, would matter only in a long war. Both sides anticipated a brief struggle—perhaps lasting no longer than the fall of 1861. South Carolina Senator James Chesnut famously predicted he could soak up all the blood spilled as a result of secession with his handkerchief, so confident was he that no war would erupt. Washington was unprepared for the influx of men who arrived in the late spring—tens of thousands more than Lincoln's initial call—and without proper facilities, they slept in the Patent Office, the hallways of the capitol, and any other federal facility that had space. The Confederacy established a training camp outside Richmond to accommodate the influx of troops from around the South.

Even more pressing for the North than space to house soldiers was a vision of the war's purpose. Frederick Douglass and other abolitionists saw the war as an opportunity to destroy slavery. In the May 1861 issue of *Douglass' Monthly*, Douglass began his campaign to forge the link between Union and emancipation. "Fire must be met with

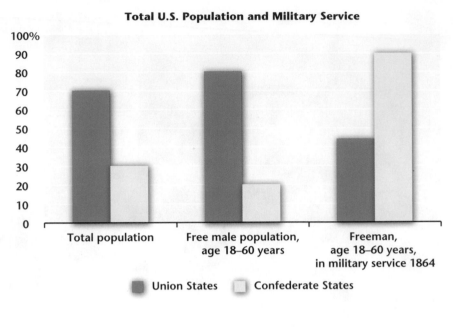

Total U.S. Population and Military Service

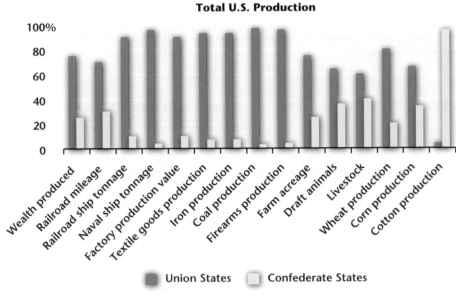

Total U.S. Production

FIGURE 14.1 ▲ Resource comparison, USA and CSA The North possessed significant advantages in industrial and agricultural resource production (except cotton), but this only became a factor over time. Confederates entered the conflict aware of their material deficiencies but confident that the war would not last long enough for them to greatly matter.

water, darkness with light," Douglass wrote, "and war for the destruction of liberty must be met with war for the destruction of slavery. *The simple way then, to put an end to the savage and desolating war now waged by the slaveholders, is to strike down slavery itself,* the primal cause of the war." Democrats and conservative Republicans condemned bloodshed and the destruction of property from other Americans. Lincoln seemed personally aligned with the broad middle of the country. A passionate defender of the Union, he insisted that the first and only goal for the North was the restoration of the rule of law and the obedience of Southern state governments to national law. White Southerners claimed they were defending their autonomy, their independence, as free people. They openly acknowledged that their freedom depended on the preservation of racial slavery. The vice president of the Confederacy, **Alexander Stephens**, famously proclaimed black slavery "the cornerstone" of the new republic.

From the Ballot to the Bullet

An outside observer coming to the United States in 1860 might have had a hard time understanding the source of differences between North and South. Both derived their values from the same historical and religious foundations—western Europe and Protestant Christianity. Both conceived of themselves as democratic and capitalistic. They spoke the same language, shared foodways, fashion, literature, and a developing popular culture of theater, music, and stage entertainment. Both used the American Revolution to justify their way of life. How could two people so similar conceptualize themselves as so different and fight such a catastrophic war? Most people at the time identified slavery as the key difference between the two sections. Despite the absence of the institution in the North, white citizens held racial views similar to those of their Southern peers. Nonetheless, the presence, durability, and dynamism of slavery in the American South produced, over time, sharply different understandings of freedom, citizenship, and the natural rights accorded to all human beings. Lincoln saw his challenge as proving that in democracies, there could be "no appeal from the ballot to the bullet."

The challenge for the North was to compel Southerners back into the Union without alienating them any further. Lincoln believed in the loyalty of most white Southerners who, he thought, had only been swayed temporarily by fire-eater rhetoric. His optimism proved misplaced; most white Southerners supported the Confederacy in 1861 and still did at the end of the war. The North began the war by treating Southern civilians as American citizens. Union armies were ordered not to confiscate or destroy Southern property. This policy aimed to placate Southerners and their conservative allies in the North and to prove that reunion posed no threat. Radicals in the North lambasted the policy as the "rosewater" strategy and argued that no war could be won by sprinkling perfume on one's opponent. General-in-Chief Winfield Scott, a hero of the War of 1812 and the Mexican War, proposed a more vigorous strategy to encircle the Confederacy along the rivers and coastlines and slowly constrict their ability to wage war. Critics who forecast an easy and quick victory lampooned the idea as the "Anaconda plan," arguing that it required too many men and too much time.

Just as public demand for action drove Jefferson Davis to attack Fort Sumter, by midsummer Northern public opinion drove Lincoln to attack the Confederate forces assembled near the railroad junction of Manassas, Virginia, about 20 miles southwest of Washington, DC. The battle attracted curious onlookers hoping to see the rebels retreat. The Battle of Bull Run, named by the North for the creek that flowed through the area, turned out to be far bloodier than anyone on either side had imagined. Although Union forces pushed Confederates back through the morning's fighting, a pause at midday allowed Southern troops to regroup and counterattack. The untrained Union soldiers broke and abandoned the field, scattering the tourists in a hasty retreat back to Washington. By the end of the day, Confederate forces had lost close to 2,000 men and Union forces close to 3,000. Although the Confederate victory embarrassed the North, it inspired greater mobilization and a stronger training regimen through the fall and winter of 1861. Confident that it represented their true superiority, Confederates basked in the victory.

STUDY QUESTIONS FOR SECESSION, 1860–1861

1. Why did the Civil War start in 1861?
2. Which played a greater role in the coming of the war: reason or emotion?

◼ WAR IN EARNEST, 1862–1863

In many respects, 1862 proved to be the most important year of the Civil War. As the war continued, it imposed increasing burdens on the populations of both sections. All of these costs—physical, ideological, and psychological—became clear during 1862, yet both sides fought on. As the bloodshed increased, soldiers and civilians on both sides longed for peace. As they moved further from peace, however, they increasingly came to view the other side as a mortal enemy. This prospect worried Abraham Lincoln, who understood the devastating nature of civil wars—the more energetically his commanders pursued Confederate defeat, the harder it became to achieve his goal of rebuilding the Union.

The North Advances

Although Northerners, Southerners, and European observers focused on fighting in the East, the war's center of gravity in early 1862 was in the West. There, Lincoln found the commander who developed a strategy that would eventually bring victory to the Union. The general was **Ulysses S. Grant**, a 40-year-old former army officer. Grant first achieved fame by conquering Forts Henry and Donelson, located on the Tennessee and the Cumberland rivers, respectively. Rivers were the one geographic weakness faced by the Confederacy—all the major ones flowed into or through the South and were used as avenues of invasion by Union forces. The capture of the two forts gave federal forces access to all of Tennessee, where they took 14,000 Confederate prisoners and provided a much-needed hero for Northern newspapers. Grant's new nickname—"Unconditional Surrender Grant"—reflected his vigorous prosecution of the war.

By early April 1862, Grant's soldiers had marched to the southern boundary of Tennessee, where they clashed with Confederate forces in a cataclysmic battle around

UNION NAVY EXPANSION   Grant effectively coordinated his movement into Tennessee with naval commanders. The North's rapidly expanding "brown water navy" allowed the Union to bring heavy guns into the range of forts along the Mississippi and Tennessee Rivers.

Shiloh Church. Although the battle was a stalemate—with Confederate forces winning the first day and Union forces the next—Northern soldiers retained their position on the battlefield while Confederates retreated into northern Mississippi. The scale of the battle garnered the most attention, with nearly 24,000 total casualties over the two days of fighting. Shiloh was several times worse than anything seen before in North America. Grant grimly noted that "I saw an open field . . . so covered with dead that it would have been possible to walk across the clearing, in any direction, stepping on dead bodies, without a foot touching the ground."

The horrific nature of Civil War battles resulted from the new, more accurate rifled musket with greater range and more powerful and accurate artillery. Officers on both sides failed to adjust the tactics they used in battle despite these new technologies. Trained in grand frontal and flanking (side) attacks, both armies continued to launch assaults against entrenched opponents despite the considerable advantage that the new weapons gave to the defensive side. With a few rare exceptions, attacking armies always suffered higher casualties and rarely emerged victorious.

As regular forces engaged in more deadly conflict, civilians experienced the terror and chaos of **guerrilla** conflict. In central Virginia, central Tennessee, Missouri, Arkansas, and much of Kentucky, pro-Confederate civilians spied on, sabotaged, and attacked Union soldiers as they advanced into the region. Pro-Confederate women, many with fathers or husbands in military service, often assisted guerrillas with food and information. U.S. soldiers grew increasingly wary of Southern white women. By war's end, some believed their defiance explained why the war lasted so long. Increasingly vigorous methods to curtail guerilla actions adopted by both governments failed to solve the problem.

The worst violence occurred in those places with the lightest presence of regular troops. Western Virginia, western North Carolina, and nearly all of Missouri were exposed to continuous guerrilla conflict. In these areas, noncombatants—including men, women, and children—used violence to settle old grudges, political resentments, and economic opportunity. Civilians recognized early on that armies ensured their safety; and as a result, increasing numbers of people fled to occupied towns over the course of the war. Cities such as Nashville, Little Rock, and Memphis saw their populations double or triple during the war as a result of the influx of refugees seeking security.

Stalemate in the East

Union forces moved decisively into Confederate strongholds in the West, but they remained stalemated in the East (Map 14.2). After the battle of Bull Run, Lincoln appointed General **George B. McClellan** the new commander of the Army of the Potomac. McClellan spent the winter reorganizing, outfitting, and training his men. The profusion of supplies and the lack of battles endeared him to the soldiers. When the spring weather improved enough to initiate a campaign, McClellan ferried his soldiers down the Chesapeake Bay to Fort Monroe—a Union outpost on the tip of the peninsula between Virginia's York and James Rivers. McClellan then squandered his advantage by moving with agonizing slowness up the Peninsula toward the Confederate capital of Richmond. From Washington, President Lincoln urged McClellan forward and paced the halls of the telegraph office set up across the street from the White House waiting for news. Unlike Jefferson Davis, Lincoln entered the war with no real knowledge of warfare or the military; but, reading tactical and strategy manuals late into the night, he learned rapidly on the job. Because of his lack of expertise and because of the complexities of Northern politics, Lincoln deferred to his generals early in the war. But as they continued to disappoint him, Lincoln assumed an increasingly active role in crafting the overall strategy that led to Union victory. On May 31, after a climactic battle within earshot of Richmond, McClellan pulled his forces back to a base on the York River and gave the Confederates a chance to regroup.

This pause coincided with the elevation of General **Robert E. Lee** to command of Confederate forces in Virginia. Whereas Lee's predecessors had been prone to retreat and delay, Lee favored the offense. His approach to war generated both enormously high casualties for Confederate forces and victories for the South. For many, Lee embodied the spirit of the Confederate nation. Paeans to his religiosity, gentility, and fierceness in battle circulated during the war and long after. Although Lee never became a political figure on the order of Napoleon, his stature helped convince the public to continue fighting. In late June, Lee succeeded in pushing McClellan's troops back to the James River. The campaign, known as the Seven Days, immortalized Lee for saving Richmond and for defeating a much larger Union force. For the North, the Peninsula campaign was a costly and humiliating defeat.

Another seminal feature of the Peninsula campaign was the erosion of slavery. Officially, the United States still protected slavery, but the army's disruption of civilian

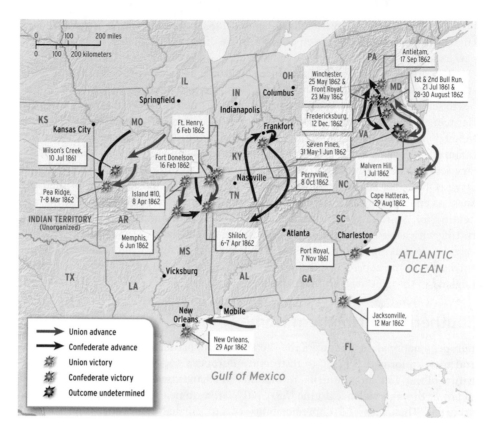

MAP 14.2 ▲ Major Battles and Campaigns, 1861–1862 Early in the war, Confederate forces established a de facto boundary along the Rapidan-Rappahannock River corridor in Virginia that they maintained through 1862. In the West, the Union experienced more military success, principally along the major rivers leading into the southern interior.

life inevitably weakened the system. With most white men in military service, communities could not muster slave patrols to catch runaways and stop slave conspiracies. As the Union army lumbered up the Peninsula, enslaved people seized opportunities to flee. Thus far in the conflict, however, Lincoln insisted the war was about union, not the end of slavery. He hoped to retain the support of the slaveholding border states—Missouri, Kentucky, Maryland, and Delaware—even at the expense of alienating abolitionists in the North. Regardless of official policy or political pronouncements, enslaved people fled by the thousands as the Union army moved through the region.

If Confederates drew dire lessons from the ancillary effects of the Peninsula campaign, they received great sustenance from the success of their armies in Virginia's Shenandoah Valley. In Spring 1862, a new hero joined Lee in the pantheon of Confederate history—Thomas Jonathan "Stonewall" Jackson—widely praised for his effective leadership and aggressive approach to warfare. In the Valley, Jackson outmaneuvered several Union armies. In a sequence of battles lasting through May, Jackson eluded larger Union forces and prevented them from reinforcing McClellan on the Peninsula.

When Jackson was killed by friendly fire in mid-1863, he became the Confederacy's best known martyr and part of the emerging culture of patriotic sacrifice that defined the new nation.

The Union worked to build a culture of national unity as well. Seeking to turn the ethnic diversity of the region into a strength, military recruiters encouraged communities to send regiments with specific ethnic identities into the northern armies. Irish and German groups led the way in 1861, as they enlisted in the "Irish Rifles" (39th New York Infantry), the "Fighting Irish" (69th New York State Militia), and "Die Neuner" (9th Ohio Infantry). Many of the men who enlisted in these units had been born abroad, and military service offered one way to establish their claim to full citizenship in the United States. Others felt an obligation to defend their new home and the honor of their old ones. As an Irish-American sergeant explained to his relatives in Ireland, "when we are fighting for America we are fighting in the interest of Irland striking a double blow cutting with a two edged sword For while we strike in defence of the rights of Irishmen here we are striking a blow at Irland's enemy and oppressor England." Many Irishmen enlisted with the hope of acquiring military training that could be put to use against England in the fight for Irish Independence.

Southern and Northern Home Fronts

European national revolutions of the late 1840s demonstrated the tension between liberal social reformers seeking to restructure European society and the unpredictable nature of war. In many countries, revolutions failed and conservative regimes returned to power through violence. In the U.S. Civil War, to some extent, the opposite process occurred. The chaos and unpredictability of war created unintended social consequences that white Southerners who initiated secession did not foresee. Paramount among these was class conflict: some poor and middle-class whites rejected secession partly because they saw it as a policy designed to protect the interests of the wealthy. Every Confederate state witnessed this tension. One of the most articulate spokespersons for this group was Tennessee's William G. "Parson" Brownlow. A journalist and politician, Brownlow made clear the extent and the nature of his opposition to the Confederacy in 1861: "We can never live in a Southern Confederacy, and be made hewers of wood and drawers of water for a set of aristocrats."

The process of military mobilization altered the gender dynamic of Southern society profoundly. Because Southern communities sent such a high proportion of white men to fight, white women had to assume new duties. Beyond the emotional costs for women left alone—one mother wrote to her daughter that she could "hardly endure the sadness of the change, the diminished family circle"—the most problematic new burden was managing slaves, especially the adult male slaves whose labor remained essential. Although women had long directed household slaves, they rarely disciplined male slaves. In Southern cities, women moved into new occupations as well. In Macon and Augusta, Georgia, they staffed textile mills; while in Richmond, they worked in munitions factories, and a sizeable number served as clerks in various Confederate Departments. Rural women took over virtually all the tasks that were necessary on farms, including making decisions about which crops to raise, how to grow them, and when to sell. By 1863, Michael Raysor, a Floridian serving in Mississippi, finally admitted to his wife that she had bested him as a farmer. "You said that you thought we would have near a hundred head of hogs to fatten this fall. This is doing well, aint it. I think you are a better farmer than I am you have done exceedingly well since I left."

The main push for social change in the North came not in the area of class or gender equality but in racial justice. Abolitionists, long derided as outcasts and denied access to political power, seized opportunities to press their agenda. Frederick Douglass and William Lloyd Garrison remained the leading spokesmen for the movement. From the beginning of the conflict, Douglass worked to frame the conflict as a war of liberty versus slavery. Even as they succeeded in turning the U.S. government away from its cozy relationship with slavery, abolitionists had little luck improving the attitudes of white Northerners toward black people. Discrimination remained commonplace across the North, and whites manifested a much greater passion for punishing slaveholders than they did for helping slaves. The conflict over slavery broke roughly along partisan lines. The Republican Party had already established its opposition to the institution and the Democratic Party had long harbored slavery's staunchest defenders. The result was that each party, using the issue to press for partisan advantage, complicated an already bloody political landscape.

As the war dragged on, the Democratic Party split into two wings: a pro-war faction that supported the Union while distancing itself from the Lincoln administration, and an antiwar wing known as the "**Copperheads**." Even those Democrats who functioned as a loyal opposition condemned and lampooned Lincoln in the harshest possible language, asserting that Lincoln was "willing to destroy his country, his party, himself, if he can destroy his opponents." The party gained support from this approach in the congressional elections of 1862, when Democrats reclaimed 28 seats. The Northern war effort was badly stalled in late 1862, and this delay played an important role in Democratic victories. Republican electoral fortunes rose and fell with the successes and failures of the Union army.

Despite popular sympathy for the president personally, many elites in the country, including prominent Republicans, regarded Lincoln as an uncouth backwoodsman not fit for higher office. Lincoln enjoyed the coarse popular humor of the day—he often read aloud from his favorite humorists while waiting in the telegraph office for battle reports—but his stories revealed a keen mind. Lincoln's use of language—both grand and commonplace—proved one of the North's greatest assets during the conflict. Democrats responded with fear mongering and openly racist rhetoric. They condemned emancipation and Lincoln for adopting it. "The only true policy for the American government," a Democrat wrote, was "the Constitution as it is, the Union as it was, and the Negroes where they are." This tactic reached a crescendo in the 1864 presidential election, when Democrats argued that Lincoln's policies promoted blacks at the expense of whites and that Lincoln supported interracial sexual relations.

The political landscape of the South was less partisan but no less complex or destructive. One of the Confederate government's first acts was to ban political parties. In the utopian vision of the Confederacy's founders, parties created social conflict where none existed; therefore, by abolishing parties, they could eliminate an important source of friction. This approach ignored the very real divisions—by class, region, religion, and ethnicity—that already existed within Southern communities, and it did little to quell social conflict. Instead of organizing a policy-based critique of Jefferson Davis and other leading officeholders, dissenting politicians targeted their venom directly at Davis. Alexander Stephens, Davis's vice president, became one of the administration's harshest critics, calling Davis "weak and vacillating, timid, petulant, peevish, obstinate, but not firm."

The Struggle for European Support

From the outset of the war, both Lincoln and Davis courted European support for their side—primarily from Europe's two great powers, Great Britain and France. Although Confederate emissaries traveled east, they had little luck, especially in Russia, which maintained a steadfast dedication to the North. France leaned toward the Confederacy but refused to act without Britain; so the two sides primarily struggled to capture British support. Whereas the British aristocracy sympathized with the Confederacy, based on a cultural and intellectual familiarity, the laboring classes seem to have supported the Union because of the Republican Party's devotion to the workingman and its opposition to slavery.

The first major international crisis in the Civil War revolved around the seizure of a British ship, the *Trent*, by the U.S. Navy in the Caribbean in late 1861. The U.S. commander, Charles Wilkes, arrested two Confederate commissioners sailing to London and France. The complexities of admiralty law during war clouded the legality of Wilkes's actions, but Britain—responding defiantly—came close to declaring war on the United States. Lincoln quietly sought a peaceful resolution, dashing Confederate hopes for a permanent break between the Union and Britain.

Confederate leaders' overconfidence in the persuasive power of cotton produced two deadly blind spots. Pinning their hopes on King Cotton diplomacy, Confederates initiated an embargo on cotton sales to Britain and France in May 1861, as they believed that economic pressure would force them to recognize the Confederacy. But Britain and France both held substantial stockpiles of cotton, which postponed the embargo's impact for well over a year; and for Britain, the volume and substance of Northern trade—especially food—was just as important as the Southern trade in cotton. During the Crimean War of the mid-1850s, U.S. wheat exports to Britain and France had skyrocketed, and these continued after the war. Confederates also failed to recognize the moral values of English textile workers, who derived their livelihood from Southern cotton but supported the Union because of its advocacy of free labor.

Nonetheless, influential members of the British Cabinet viewed the U.S. conflict as a net gain for Europe and the division of the country as inevitable given Southern military prowess. Momentum to recognize the Confederacy as a fully independent nation in the eyes of the world peaked in 1862. William Gladstone, the liberal statesman and later prime minister, asserted that "there is no doubt that Jefferson Davis and other leaders of the South have made an Army; they are making, it appears, a Navy; and they have made—what is more than either—they have made a Nation. We may anticipate with certainty the success of the Southern States so far as regards their separation from the North." Gladstone and others nearly succeeded in convincing Prime Minister Palmerston to recognize the Confederacy when Union forces rebuffed Robert E. Lee's September 1862 invasion of Maryland at Antietam.

After this Confederate defeat, and especially after Lincoln issued the preliminary **Emancipation Proclamation** in its wake, Britain never again came close to recognizing the Confederacy. Emancipation proved to be one of the most useful tools in Lincoln's diplomatic arsenal. In line with his increasingly progressive shift on emancipation, Lincoln initiated diplomatic recognition of Haiti in 1862, a first for the United States since the black republic established its independence from France in 1804. Emancipation also put the United States in synchrony with other global movements toward liberty. In 1861, Tsar Alexander II signed the "Emancipation Manifesto," freeing Russia's serfs. Like Lincoln's emancipation of slaves, Russia's change reflected an emerging liberal consensus around the supremacy of individual freedom and of freedom as a precondition for modern economic growth. Karl Marx, who traveled to the United States during the war as a correspondent for the Vienna *Presse*, conflated these events as well, noting that "the biggest things that are happening in the world today are on the one hand the movement of the slaves in America started by the death of John Brown, and on the other the movement of the serfs in Russia."

STUDY QUESTIONS FOR WAR IN EARNEST, 1862–1863

1. How was the war changing in 1862 in ways that people did not anticipate in 1861?
2. Who was winning the war in 1862?
3. How did international trends and events shape the war's diplomatic struggle?

◼ A NEW BIRTH OF FREEDOM

The centrality of emancipation as a global concern appears obvious in retrospect, but the most revolutionary change of the war came gradually and against the wishes of both Northern and Southern leaders. Although Lincoln had clearly expressed his personal antipathy toward slavery, as president he believed he had little constitutional authority to affect the institution. The action of enslaved people who seized opportunities to escape forced the North to endorse emancipation and destroyed the world's largest and most influential slave society.

Slaves Take Flight

Over the course of the war, at least 500,000 slaves fled to the safety of Union lines. Running away was an especially risky decision before the United States had officially committed itself to emancipation. The United States maintained a contradictory policy. At the top, Lincoln denied any interest in emancipation, largely to ensure the continued loyalty of the border states. In a famous exchange with New York newspaper editor Horace Greeley in August 1862, Lincoln proclaimed, "If there be those who would not save the Union, unless they could at the same time save slavery, I do not agree with them. If there be those who would not save the Union unless they could at the same time destroy slavery, I do not agree with them. My paramount object in this struggle is to save the Union, and is not either to save or to destroy slavery."

Politically conservative generals followed Lincoln's lead and returned slaves to masters who came to Union camps to reclaim runaways. A handful of liberal generals adopted more aggressive policies and refused to return escapees. Abolitionists celebrated two events in particular. In August 1861, General John Frémont, the 1856 Republican presidential candidate, ordered all property of all rebels in Missouri subject to confiscation. Recognizing the damage this action would do to Unionist sympathy in the slaveholding border states, Lincoln immediately revoked the order. In May 1862, General David Hunter, commander of the occupied territories of low country South Carolina, Georgia, and Florida, issued an order freeing all the slaves in his department. Again to the great dismay of abolitionists, Lincoln rescinded the order.

Despite the government's resistance, enslaved people continued to flee. Like Northern abolitionists, they recognized that the war grew out of a conflict over slavery. By actively supporting the Union, they could both achieve their own freedom and establish a claim to American citizenship. Once the United States sanctioned emancipation, it faced the challenge of how to handle and where to put the hundreds of thousands of refugees. To facilitate the continued movement of Union armies into the South, those who fled to Union lines lived in supervised facilities know as **contraband** camps. Falling between civilian and military control, the camps were unsanitary and overcrowded. The military also exploited refugees' labor and generally treated them only marginally better than they had been as slaves.

If contraband camps represented the worst of the Union's response to emancipation, the actions of many Union soldiers in the field represented the best. Only a small minority of soldiers came into the army as abolitionists; but over the course of the war, a great number changed their attitudes toward the practice. Exposure to slaves themselves, which few Northerners had experienced before the war, inspired sympathy for their suffering and anger at the abuse they received from masters. Some Northern soldiers used their power to rescue enslaved people and to alleviate the suffering of those who had run away. Sergeant E. C. Hubbard of Illinois entered the war angry that white men were killing one another "all for a detestable black man"; but, as he explained to his brother, after seeing how slavery worked in practice, he was "*forced* to change my opinion." In early 1864, he wrote home to his staunchly Democratic family that "*Slavery is gone*. Peace propositions to Richmond won't save it. . . . The war could never be ended without [slavery's] destruction." African Americans knew this intuitively, and they made vigorous efforts to join the army so they could participate. At the war's start, the U.S. Army excluded black men from service. However, by 1862, black units had been organized in Louisiana and along the South Carolina, Georgia, and Florida Sea Islands. These early regiments were incorporated into the U.S. Army when official black enlistment began in 1863.

From Confiscation to Emancipation

On the issue of emancipation, soldiers were often ahead of both their families at home and politicians across the North. While soldiers grappled with the reality of slavery, most Northerners continued to discuss it in the abstract, as only a piece of the larger political conflict. In 1861, Congress issued the First Confiscation Act, which provided the army with the authority to retain runaway slaves when their labor was being used directly for the Confederate war effort. They expanded this policy in 1862 by declaring

BATTLE OF ANTIETAM Photographer Matthew Brady captured the devastation of the Battle of Antietam when he arrived two days after the fighting. The exhibition of his photos, "The Dead of Antietam," traveled to Northern cities where horrified civilians saw photographic representations of war's costs.

FLIGHT FROM SLAVERY Eastman Johnson's painting captured the risk and drama of the flight undertaken by over 500,000 enslaved people who sought their freedom in the moments of change produced by the war.

free any slave belonging to a rebel owner living in those areas controlled by the Union army. As the war extended into 1862, Northern leaders recognized that by relying on slave labor to produce food supplies and other essentials, the Confederacy could mobilize an enormously high percentage of its military-age men; in most counties, the enlistment rate was well above 60 percent, nearly double that of Northern counties. By attacking slavery directly, the Union weakened the South's ability to fight.

Lincoln came to this conclusion well before he announced it publicly. After watching the hapless retreat of McClellan's army from the gates of Richmond in mid-1862 and the subsequent march of Lee's Confederates through Virginia and into Maryland in the fall of 1862, Lincoln endorsed the use of emancipation as a war policy. Although he risked alienating border state conservatives, Lincoln had given them ample time to see how the war destroyed the institution regardless of policy, and he knew the advantages that would accrue in foreign policy and Confederate manpower.

In August 1862, Lee's Army crashed through a Union force under General John Pope on the fields of Manassas, Virginia, the exact site where they had fought almost a year earlier. The outcome was eerily similar. Despite Pope's loudly proclaimed intention to rid Virginia of Lee, the retreat of Pope's army to Washington allowed Lee to march freely into the North in early September. On September 18, the armies fought again outside the small town of Sharpsburg along the banks of Antietam Creek. The battle proved to be bloodiest single day of the war, with nearly 23,000 casualties between the two sides. Despite a nearly 2:1 advantage in numbers, the North failed to break Lee's army, and the Confederates retreated safely back across the Potomac River. Although far from the clear-cut victory he had hoped for, Lincoln issued the Emancipation Proclamation on September 22.

Jefferson Davis believed the measure encouraged slaves to murder their masters and condemned the authors of emancipation as "those who have attempted the most execrable measure recorded in the history of guilty man." Lincoln offered a more noble interpretation when he commemorated a national cemetery at Gettysburg. The war heralded a "new birth of freedom," Lincoln said, not just by preserving the Union but by expanding the meaning of freedom to include black Americans as well. For black Americans, the day of jubilee arrived when the proclamation took effect on January 1, 1863. Henry Tuner, a free black minister in Washington, DC, recalled the celebration that evening: "Men squealed, women fainted, dogs barked, white and colored people shook hands, songs were sung, and by this time cannons began to fire at the navy-yard, and follow in the wake of the roar that had for some time been going on behind the White House. . . . Great processions of colored and white men marched to and fro and passed in front of the White House and congratulated President Lincoln on his proclamation. The president came to the window and made responsive bows, and thousands told him, if he would come out of that palace, they would hug him to death. . . . It was indeed a time of times, and a half time, nothing like it will ever be seen again in this life."

Government Centralization in Wartime

Emancipation emerged as the "crown jewel" in the Union's **hard war** policy, which targeted the ability of Confederates to fight by destroying infrastructure, transportation

WAR BONDS The Union's war bond campaign tied Americans to the war effort both patriotically and economically through the promise of interest on the notes that citizens bought.

networks, and food supplies for the army. In addition to being a moral act, emancipation allowed the North to seize a vital war resource from the Confederacy. But emancipation also generated criticism in the North because it altered the balance of power between the federal government and the states. Slavery had always been a "domestic institution," that is, one controlled by state law. Before the Civil War, emancipation in the North happened through the mechanism of state constitutional changes. By abolishing slavery through executive order—even in the midst of war—Lincoln reshaped the nature of American federalism. U.S. emancipation also stood out as unique among other slaveholding nations, which generally adopted gradual and compensated strategies to end slavery.

Confederate leaders claimed that they had seceded from the Union to protect state rights. In one of the many ironies of the Civil War, the first challenge to state rights came not in the North but from those same Confederate leaders. Most Confederate soldiers had enlisted in mid-1861 for one year; thus, their service was slated to end at the start of the 1862 campaign season. With reenlistments stalled, Jefferson Davis deployed both a carrot and a stick. The government offered furloughs and bounties for men who reenlisted; and for those who refused, Davis signed into law a national draft. American authorities had never resorted to a draft before, and Southern soldiers were galled by the policy, especially because the law automatically reenlisted men currently in uniform for an additional three years. Many soldiers believed that exemptions to the law—for certain categories of industrial workers, for state government employees, and for the clergy—amounted to class privilege. Letters of complaint filled newspapers and desertion reached a wartime high. Confederate leaders gradually adopted progressive policies to address concern about unequal sacrifice. Although dissent remained a persistent problem within the Confederacy, civilians and soldiers alike accepted the draft and other policies as necessary measures to help win their independence. The Union also adopted a draft, and it spurred similar resentment and anger among Northern men.

Still, the Confederacy led the way in centralizing measures during wartime. In 1863, the Confederacy adopted two new policies—impressment and a tax-in-kind—that gave significant power to Richmond at the expense of the states. Impressment allowed army quartermasters to seize necessary supplies in exchange for Confederate script. With no gold reserves, Confederate economic policy relied on printed money, rather than on metallic coin, and bonds. The new currency devalued so quickly that most civilians regarded impressment as little more than theft (Figure 14.2). The Confederacy also relied on new taxes. Because these failed to generate the necessary revenue, the Richmond government created a tax-in-kind, which levied 10 percent of all major foodstuffs. Southern civilians complained bitterly about the tax-in-kind and dodged it whenever they could; but the resources gained by the Confederacy were redistributed to needy families, often the widows of soldiers, in an attempt to equalize the suffering on the Confederate home front. The North imposed its own taxes and its more dynamic commercial economy produced more revenue.

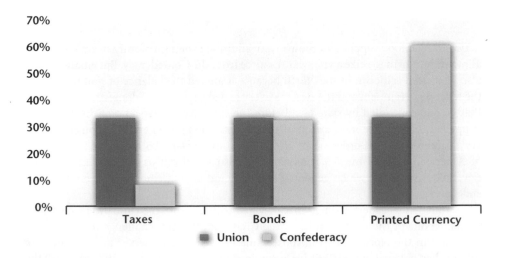

FIGURE 14.2 ▲ War financing, 1861–1865 The Union maintained a balanced assortment of funding devices throughout the war. Because most Southerners invested their wealth in land and slaves, they had less capital to shift into war production. Instead, the Confederacy relied more heavily on printed currency, which depreciated rapidly and contributed to a very high inflation rate.

STUDY QUESTIONS FOR A NEW BIRTH OF FREEDOM

1. Why did the North endorse emancipation in 1862?
2. What role did African Americans play in shaping that change?

■ THE HARD WAR, 1863–1864

The North's economic vitality played a substantial role in helping it wage the war. The Southern economy, although enormously profitable in the antebellum era, was not well suited to financing a capital-intensive modern war. Yet military success eluded the North partly because some northern commanders were reluctant to engage with the full weight of the region's strength. But that stance changed in late 1863, when Lincoln promoted Ulysses S. Grant, the victor in many Western theater battles, to general-in-chief of all Union forces and transferred him to Washington. Grant's approach, implemented by his lieutenants **William T. Sherman** and Philip Sheridan, exploited the North's manpower advantage and aimed directly at the Confederacy's ability to wage war. Grant, however, did not advocate unrestrained warfare. Despite popular memories of the burning of Georgia by Sherman, U.S. troops primarily targeted the public resources and facilities that sustained Confederate troops.

Invasion and Occupation

Southerners received their first tastes of the North's hard war policy during the battle of Fredericksburg, Virginia, in December 1862. After the battle of Antietam, Lee moved his troops east and Union troops followed. They reached the town of Fredericksburg, a major tobacco port, but needed to cross the Rappahannock River to establish a position in town. Confederate sharpshooters posted in buildings on the south bank fired on Northern engineers trying to build pontoon bridges. Union General Edwin V. Sumner demanded "the surrender of the city . . . at or before 5 o'clock this afternoon." Should the town's mayor refuse, Sumner would allow 16 hours for the removal of "women and children, the sick and wounded and aged, &c., which period having expired, I shall proceed to shell the town." The mayor evacuated the town and the Union besieged it. After the Confederates pulled back to a high ridge south of town, Union soldiers entered and, in their frustration, opened private residences and destroyed furniture and household materials. Although Union policy never sanctioned the wanton destruction of private property, the tenacity of Confederate resistance forced a shift in Union policy toward more destructiveness.

Military leaders formulated new strategies as Union armies advanced slowly through the Southern countryside. The Union seized New Orleans and other coastal spots in late 1861 and early 1862, victories that allowed Union troops to move into Louisiana and the Carolinas. In Tennessee and Virginia, the contest between Union and Confederate troops consumed scarce resources and left little for civilians. Southern women were often left to confront Union troops. In some cases they acquiesced; but in many others, they maintained a defiance that landed some in jail.

Despite its manpower advantage, the Union did not have the resources to hold all the territory they seized from Confederates permanently. Instead, they created garrisons in major towns that controlled, to the best of their ability, the regions around them. The result was a three-tiered system, with garrison towns at the center providing the highest degree of security and normal economic and social life. Beyond these were "frontier" regions, where armies provided a looser degree of control. Most dangerous of all were the "no-man's land" regions, places that neither army held but that they frequently raided.

Black Soldiers, Black Flags

In addition to adopting a new hard war policy, after the Emancipation Proclamation took effect on January 1, 1863, the Union began enrolling and organizing units of black soldiers, known as the **U.S. Colored Troops (USCT)**. Some were free black men from the North—Frederick Douglass's sons enlisted early—but many others were former slaves. Enlistment generated controversy in the North, most infamously as one of the causes of the New York City Draft Riots, five days of brutal violence waged by New York's white workingmen against the city's black residents. The riot started at draft offices but quickly turned into an attack on Republican leaders and black New Yorkers. Over 50 deaths, many of them brutal lynchings, shocked the nation and required the services of regular U.S. troops to suppress. Many white soldiers initially had mixed feelings about black recruits, but they were generally accepted once the new troops proved themselves in battle.

The proving grounds came in mid-1863 on the South Carolina coast and along the Mississippi River. At Fort Wagner, in Charleston Harbor, and at Port Hudson, north of Baton Rouge, black units participated valiantly in bloody attacks on Confederate positions. Northern newspapers reported both battles as evidence that black soldiers could perform as well as white troops. Although discrimination within the army

BLACK SAILORS   Although black sailors did not receive full equality, they often earned fairer treatment than their land-bound peers. Since the colonial era, trading and military ships had contained racially and ethnically diverse crews, and U.S. naval warships carried on this tradition with black and white seamen working alongside one another throughout the war.

remained—virtually no black men served above the level of sergeant, and black soldiers were paid less than white ones—prejudice against black troops gradually subsided in the North. By war's end, over 180,000 black men had donned the Union blue, and their participation late in the war proved a crucial source of manpower. For black soldiers and their families, military service provided a path to citizenship. As Frederick Douglass made clear, "once let the black man get upon his person the brass letters US, let him get an eagle on his button, and a musket on his shoulder, and bullets in his pocket, and there is no power on earth or under the earth which can deny that he has earned the right of citizenship in the United States."

For Confederates, however, black soldiers represented the worst threat that could be imagined. For decades, white Southerners had lived in fear of slave rebellions. Confederates initially responded by classifying black soldiers as slaves in a state of insurrection. State law prescribed death for this action and for the white officers who commanded them. Confederates also threatened to sell black soldiers captured by the South as slaves. The public nature of this debate put U.S. soldiers and their officers on notice, and President Lincoln threatened retaliation against Confederate soldiers if any Northern ones were killed indiscriminately. Although the Confederate policy remained vague, several racial atrocities shocked the Northern public. At Fort Pillow, Tennessee, on the banks of the Mississippi, Confederates under the command of cavalry general Nathan Bedford Forrest killed 300 members of the garrison, many of them black soldiers murdered after they had surrendered. The U.S. House of Representatives formally investigated what came to be known as the Fort Pillow Massacre. Although that event received the most notoriety, similar atrocities occurred in Virginia, Arkansas, Florida, North Carolina, and elsewhere.

The Campaigns of Grant and Sherman

Even without the complicating factor of racial difference, by 1863 the fighting had grown in scale and in violence. The two most important battles of the year concluded on the same day—July 4, 1863. At Gettysburg, Pennsylvania, Union forces defeated Robert E. Lee's Confederates in a three-day battle that produced nearly 50,000 casualties. It marked the first clear defeat of Lee by a Union general. The more strategically significant victory came at Vicksburg, Mississippi, the last major Confederate position on the Mississippi River (Map 14.3). Grant had tried to take the city for six months, and his inability to do so drove some Northerners to question his competence. When the city finally fell, Grant captured a 40,000-man army and the Union won full control of the river. "The father of waters flows unvexed to the sea," Lincoln remarked. The Union had cut the Confederacy in half. Control of water, whether the rivers or the Confederate coastline through the **blockade** imposed by the Union navy, proved essential to the North's eventual victory.

In late 1863, Grant and his lieutenants, pushing back Confederate forces at Chattanooga, Tennessee, effectively reduced the western Confederacy to the Deep South states of Mississippi and Alabama. After Lincoln called Grant east, he made Sherman commander in the region and gave him instructions to take Atlanta, the second most important Confederate city after Richmond. After several months of hard fighting, the Confederate Army abandoned the city to Sherman and moved north. Sherman

Learning from The War

Starting in the 18th century, European military practice began to emphasize a professional staff instead of the traditional patronage system, with officers appointed to curry favor with wealthy or well-connected elites. The change encouraged officers to educate themselves in military science, and the best way of doing that was through personal observation. Through the Napoleonic Era, many of these men attached themselves to foreign armies as retainers; but their primary purpose was to learn from and evaluate new technologies and tactics. The U.S. Civil War drew a host of foreign visitors to observe and learn from the conflict. Throughout the war, British observers circulated through the armies of both sides. The Frenchman Prince de Joinville traveled with McClellan during the Peninsula Campaign and later wrote up an assessment of the tactical blunders committed by the Union staff. Separately, two representatives of the French Artillery Corps—François de Chanal and Pierre Guzman—traveled around the North, inspecting hospitals, munitions factories, and forts. Their goal was to assess the new technologies being developed by Union engineers and scientists. Several Prussians also visited, including the cavalry commander Heros von Borcke, who joined J. E. B. Stuart's command for much of the war and used his insights to shape German cavalry tactics in the 1870s. For all these men, the U.S. Civil War promised new insights into communication, tactics, weapons, defensive fortifications, and training.

The Prussian General Staff sent Captain Justus Scheibert to observe the conflict, and he compiled his evaluation in a series of articles and books. The practice of warfare changed rapidly as a result of industrialization and the increasing professionalization of the military in Europe. The U.S. Civil War thus offered observers an especially important point from which to assess the directions that combat was likely to take in coming years. Scheibert's main assignment was to evaluate artillery and

reorganized his forces, destroyed the industrial base of the city, and left late in the fall. Sherman instructed his army to live off the land, taking what they needed. Divided into four columns, his men marched to Savannah with little opposition. Soldiers damaged Georgia's infrastructure, liberated thousands of slaves, and terrified the populace. Most of the personal violence and property destruction in the state came at the hand of "Bummers"—deserters from both armies—who followed Sherman's troops and took advantage of the chaotic conditions left behind. Sherman reached Savannah in late December—he presented the city "as a Christmas gift" to Lincoln—and then turned north into the Carolinas, intending to enter Virginia from the south and trap Lee's army between his force and Grant's in the north.

Emma LeConte, a college student living in Columbia, South Carolina, witnessed firsthand Sherman's invasion of that city. Although Confederates set the fires that fortifications. The technological breakthroughs on both sides of the Atlantic in artillery rendered the traditional European masonry fort infeasible, although Scheibert was surprised at the durability of earthen forts such as Fort Sumter, in Charleston Harbor. Later, Scheibert recognized the value of building on the advances made by Americans during the war, as he noted that "we Europeans have excelled because of what the Americans did."

Rifled muskets and rifled artillery attracted special interest as well. A British field officer who had traveled 3,000 miles across the North to evaluate gun foundries, factories, and the front lines predicted that before "this struggle closes there will be so great a development and improvement in all kinds of arms, both for military and naval warfare, that the world will act wisely in leaving itself open to profit by American ingenuity." Nearly all of the European observers, however, shared a scorn for the amateur nature of American armies, the "armed mobs from which nothing could be learned" according to a comment supposedly made by Helmuth von Moltke, the famed Chief of the Prussian General Staff. Ardant du Picq, a French military theorist, condemned the "lack of discipline and organization" in both armies that had made the war longer and bloodier than necessary. Nonetheless, European writers could hardly fail to appreciate the sustained power that armies on both sides exhibited over the course of the conflict. Only a nonspecialist, the German novelist Karl Bleibtreu, grasped the success of the American approach. He regarded the armies on both sides as having obtained "the highest grade of martial perfection" and anticipated that European nations would eventually adopt more democratic methods of staffing their armies.

- Why did Europeans observe the Civil War?
- What lessons did they take from it?

consumed much of Columbia, LeConte laid the blame squarely on Sherman. "There is not a house, I believe, in Columbia that has not been pillaged," she wrote, and "those that the flames spared were entered by brutal soldiery and everything wantonly destroyed. The streets were filled with terrified women and children who were offered every insult and indignity short of personal outrage—they were allowed to save nothing but what clothes they wore, and there is now great suffering for food." She concluded, "It would be impossible to describe or even to conceive of the pandemonium and horror." The destruction of Sherman's raid, although confined mostly to public property, caused enormous suffering and hardship for a people already wracked by several years of war.

In early 1864, when Grant assumed command, his aim was the defeat of Lee's army. Rather than following McClellan's 1862 water route, the Army of the Potomac headed

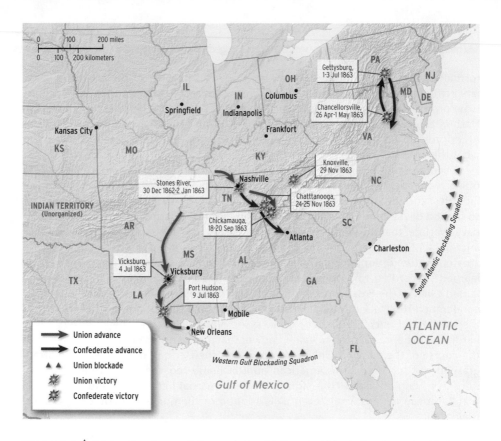

MAP 14.3 ▲ Major Battles and Campaigns, 1863 As in 1862, Union forces had little success against Confederates in the East in 1863, although the repulse of Robert E. Lee's army at Gettysburg inspired jubilation. In the West, Union successes were striking. They reclaimed all of Tennessee, took full control of the Mississippi River, and pressed into the northern tier of Deep South states.

directly to Richmond, and the spring campaign was the bloodiest yet. In six weeks of fighting, Grant lost over 55,000 soldiers and Lee over 30,000, the equivalent of fighting a battle of Bull Run every day for a month and a half. Grant trapped Lee's army outside Petersburg, a railroad town that served as the conduit for all supplies entering Richmond. The two armies entrenched along ever-lengthening lines stretched between the two cities.

STUDY QUESTIONS FOR THE HARD WAR, 1863–1864

1. Why did the level of violence and destruction increase in 1863 and 1864?
2. What role did race play in this process?

■ VICTORY AND DEFEAT, 1865

By late 1864, even staunch Confederates recognized that they were losing the war. Still, the Davis government refused to concede to the two essential terms that Lincoln demanded—reunion and emancipation. As a result, the war stretched into the spring of 1865, with increasing hardship for Confederate civilians facing scarcity imposed by the war and the blockade.

American Nationalism, Southern Nationalism

Given his increasingly untenable position around Petersburg, Lee's main hope in the fall of 1864 was that Lincoln would be defeated by the Democratic candidate, former Union General George McClellan, who had been nominated on a platform committed to ending the war immediately. As late as August, Lincoln himself assumed he would lose, so unpopular was his administration and the course of the war effort, which once again had bogged down. But Sherman's victory in Atlanta, Sheridan's in the Shenandoah Valley, and the capture of Mobile Bay reversed his fortunes and Lincoln was reelected. In his Second Inaugural Address, Lincoln set out a beneficent vision for postwar America—"with malice toward none and charity toward all"—but also offered a sobering assessment of responsibility for the war and American slavery. He argued that both the North and the South bore blame for the war's enormous human cost—over 750,000 dead. He did not claim to know God's will but believed the nation's punishment—in which "every drop of blood drawn with the lash shall be paid with one drawn by the sword"—revealed God's displeasure for the wrongs done to generations of enslaved Africans and African Americans.

In late March, as Sherman's men tramped through North Carolina, Lee realized that he would have to abandon Petersburg and Richmond. His men's rations had dwindled to virtually nothing, soldiers had left for home in the face of imminent defeat, and Grant nearly surrounded his army (Map 14.4). Lee hoped to move west, resupply his troops, and connect with the small Confederate force in North Carolina, but Union cavalry cut off his retreat. On April 9, 1865, Lee surrendered at the small crossroads town of Appomattox Courthouse. Joseph Johnston's army surrendered to Sherman on April 26 at Durham Station, North Carolina. As cannons tolled across the North, citizens took stock of their victory.

For most white Americans, the reestablishment of the Union was the war's principal accomplishment. When Lincoln issued his "Gettysburg Address," he explained democracy to the world in a way that both ruled out secession and enshrined the truly popular nature of the American experiment. The soldiers buried at Gettysburg, said Lincoln, sacrificed themselves to protect "government of the people, by the people, for the people."

Most Northerners also took pride in emancipation, even if few had supported it at the war's start. Northerners regarded emancipation as further ennobling an already noble victory. John Wesley Powell, who later became the first head of the U.S. Geologic Survey, fought in an Illinois unit during the war. His sweeping vision of victory reflected the thinking of many Northerners; "It was a great thing to destroy slavery, but the integrity of the Union was of no less importance." In Northern victory, Powell foresaw "the ultimate spread of Anglo-Saxon civilisation over the globe." Victory confirmed

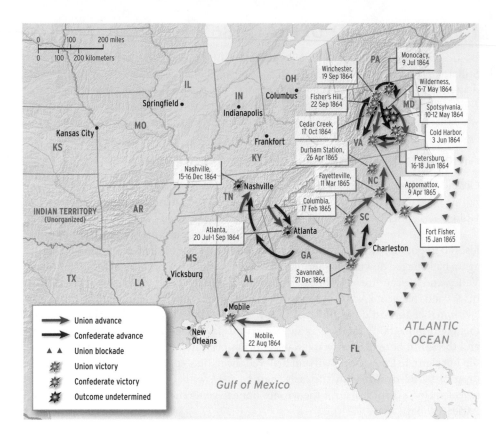

MAP 14.4 ▲ Major Battles and Campaigns, 1864–1865 William Sherman's capture of Atlanta and his ensuing march to the coast demonstrated the ability of Union forces to move through the center of the Confederacy. His army eventually moved north to join Ulysses S. Grant to trap the two remaining Confederate armies.

the sense of a unique destiny that most 19th-century white Americans regarded as theirs alone.

South of the Mason-Dixon Line, Southerners now shared with most of the world's people the experience of having been invaded, occupied, and defeated in a war. The result was a profound rupture in the historical experience of the United States. Despite the Confederacy's internal divisions, the sacrifices of war and the humiliation of defeat provided a common basis for white Southern identity in the postwar era. Rather than solving the problem of sectionalism, in many respects the Civil War created a more distinct and coherent "South" than had ever existed in American history.

The New Challenge of Race

Another central cause of the war that remained unresolved at its conclusion was the problem of race. The active role played by African Americans on behalf of the Union gave them a claim on the meaning of the conflict. Southern blacks provided crucial military intelligence to Union forces as they entered the region, ranging from basic information such as the location of roads, bridges, and mountain gaps to more detailed intelligence about the movement and size of Confederate forces. The military service performed by black men gave them an even stronger claim to citizenship. In a letter to the Democratic Congressman Roscoe Conkling, Lincoln explained the impact of blacks' willingness to fight. After the war, he wrote, "there will be some black men who can remember that, with silent tongue, and clenched teeth, and steady eye, and well-poised bayonet, they have helped mankind on to this great consummation; while, I fear, there will be some white ones, unable to forget that, with malignant heart, and deceitful speech, they strove to hinder it." In many ways, Lincoln's attitudes toward emancipation and black Americans reflected the average white Northerner. He came reluctantly to emancipation and he never adopted a modern conception of full racial equality, but he stood resolutely behind emancipation once it was Union policy; and by the war's end, he advocated limited political rights for black men.

Environmental and Economic Scars of War

As the war rearranged human relations, it also forced a reevaluation of the relationship between people and the environment. Since before the Revolution Americans had envisioned themselves as developing and enhancing nature. The environmental costs of industrialization and urbanization were already visible in the mid-19th century; and although some citizens felt the costs were too high, most Americans believed that they had a productive and responsible relationship to the land. For four years Federals and Confederates did little but destroy and consume. Sherman's marches through Georgia and the Carolinas left significant environmental devastation. In this region,

LASTING EFFECT OF WAR   The war's physical impact on the South marked the region as distinctive. Although the detritus of conflict was soon removed or repaired, the psychological impact and memories of the conflict lasted for generations.

TIMELINE 1861–1865

AMERICA	YEAR	THE WORLD
Dec 1860 to Feb 1861 Secession of Lower South (TX, LA, MS, AL, FL, GA, SC) **Apr 12** Confederates open fire on Fort Sumter in Charleston Harbor **Apr** Lincoln calls up 75,000 militia; precipitates secession of Upper South (VA, NC, AR, TN) **May** Benjamin Butler, Union commander at Fortress Monroe on York Peninsula, declares 3 slaves who entered his camp "contraband" and refuses to return them to their owners **Jul** Confederates win Battle of Bull Run (VA) and drive Union Army back to Washington, DC **Aug** U.S. Congress passes First Confiscation Act, which provides U.S. Army with authority to confiscate slaves whose owners employ them in direct support of Confederate military	**1861**	Kingdom of Italy proclaimed at Turin Tsar Alexander II abolishes serfdom in Russia
Feb Union forces capture Forts Henry and Donelson (TN), giving the North control of the Tennessee and Cumberland Rivers **Apr** Union wins Battle of Shiloh (TN), forcing Confederates back to Corinth, MS **Apr** President Lincoln signs legislation abolishing slavery in DC, with compensation for the owners **Jun** U.S. Congress outlaws slavery in U.S. Territories **Jul** U.S. Congress passes Second Confiscation Act that frees the slaves of any rebel in areas of the Confederacy controlled by Union army and giving Lincoln authority to use contrabands as soldiers **Jun–Jul** Lee repulses McClellan's advance on Richmond during Seven Days' Battles (VA) **Aug** Confederates win Second Battle of Bull Run (VA) and drive Union forces back toward Washington, DC **Sep** McClellan claims victory in Battle of Antietam (MD) after forcing retreat of Lee's army back across the Potomac **Sep** Lincoln issues Preliminary Emancipation Proclamation **Oct** Battle of Perryville (KY) forces Braxton Bragg to abandon Confederate invasion of Kentucky **Dec** Confederates win Battle of Fredericksburg (VA) with heavy Union casualties	**1862**	

a conservative estimate puts his destruction at 18,600 mules and horses, 13,300 head of cattle, 19 million pounds of fodder, 22 million pounds of grain and corn, and another 7 million pounds of foodstuffs. Millions of animals were killed and abandoned on the spot. Union General Jacob Cox noted that "from barn, from granary and smoke-house, and from the kitchen gardens of the plantations, isolated foragers would hasten by converging lines, driving before them the laden mule heaped high with vegetables, smoked bacon, fresh meat, and poultry." The wanton slaughter of animals produced a continuous track of rotting flesh and facilitated the spread of disease across the countryside.

The Union's targeting of Southern industrial resources (especially railroad lines) did considerable damage to the landscape as well. After the war, Georgians and South Carolinians, in particular, were confronted with a deeply scarred and damaged land. They also confronted a deeply depressed regional economy. The infrastructural and environmental damage, the destruction of fencing, the inability to tend farmland

Jan Lincoln signs Final Emancipation Proclamation, freeing all slaves held in Confederate-controlled territory **May** Confederates win Battle of Chancellorsville (VA) **Jul** Union wins Battle of Gettysburg (PA) **Jul** Union captures Vicksburg, MS, and gains control of the Mississippi River **Sep** Confederates win Battle of Chickamauga (TN), forcing Union troops back into Chattanooga **Nov** Union wins Battle of Chattanooga (TN), forcing Confederates back into Georgia	**1863**	"January Uprising" of Poles against Russia begins
May Battle of Spotsylvania (VA) **May** Battle of the Wilderness (VA) **Jun** Confederates win Battle of Cold Harbor (VA) but Union forces push south toward Petersburg **Mid-Jun** Siege of Petersburg, VA, begins **Sep** Fall of Atlanta, GA **Nov** Sherman's forces leave Atlanta for Savannah **Late Sep–Oct** Union wins decisive victories in Battles of Winchester, Fisher's Hill, and Cedar Creek, VA, giving Federals control of lower Shenandoah Valley **Nov–Dec** Union wins decisive victories in Battles of Franklin and Nashville, completing Union control of Western theater **Dec** Sherman occupies Savannah, GA	**1864**	First Geneva Convention established to regulate treatment of injured soldiers End of Taiping Rebellion in China, which leaves 20 million dead over 14 years of fighting War of the Triple Alliance— Paraguay against Argentina, Brazil, and Uruguay—begins
Feb Fall of Columbia, SC **Mar** Confederate Congress passes legislation providing for the enlistment of black men into Confederate military units **Apr** Petersburg and Richmond evacuated **Apr** Lee surrenders to Grant at Appomattox Courthouse, VA **Apr** Joseph Johnston surrenders to William T. Sherman at Durham Station, NC **Dec** 13th Amendment ratified, abolishing slavery in United States	**1865**	

during the war, the loss of capital as a result of emancipation, and the disorganization of the labor market ensured a slow road to recovery in the South.

In the North the experience was nearly the opposite. Although the North experienced substantial inflation, the war stimulated a boom in many Northern industries. Meat production, oil extraction, and all manner of military supplies, from clothing and tents to weapons and ships, saw rapid technological growth. The war hastened the use of mechanization and standardization in production, especially with regard to shoes and clothes, which had to be supplied to the army in huge volumes and standard sizes. The meat-packing plants of Chicago devised a "disassembly" line along which beef and hog carcasses were taken apart so that the constituent parts could be packaged—usually canned—and sold to the army. The techniques devised by Armour and Swift later became the foundation for Henry Ford's assembly line that revolutionized American manufacturing at the turn of the century.

The Last Best Hope of Man?

Like sectionalism and race, the third of the great causes of the Civil War—the dispute over the proper balance of federal and state authority—was not solved by the war. To be sure, the war established the supremacy of the Union and of the federal government. Congressional Republicans, with Lincoln's support, carved out new areas of federal power—especially with regard to banking and currency, Western lands, and development—although these were all initiatives that Republicans had supported before the war. On the larger question of ideology, the war did little to resolve the historical tensions between states and the central government. Northern Democrats maintained a steady criticism of the Lincoln administration for the measures it adopted, especially those that altered the traditional balance of American federalism.

At the same time, the war demonstrated that political movements inspired by a strong sense of nationalism could sustain liberal politics. In western Europe, in the years after 1848, nationalist movements often aligned themselves with conservative or reactionary politics, most famously in Germany. Lincoln's frequent exhortations for Americans to identify themselves with the nation—the "mystic chords of memory"—and his rhetorical efforts to place equality and justice at the center of American national identity, a "new birth of freedom," tied American nationalism to a liberalizing political agenda that sundered the government's long embrace of slavery and advocated development policies designed to support the homesteader as well as the speculator. Observers outside the United States affirmed Lincoln's sense of the liberal progress as a consequence of the war and saw how the Union's triumph could help them in their own reforms. The British statesman John Morley drew the connection: "The triumph of the North . . . was the force that made English liberalism powerful enough to enfranchise the workmen, depose official Christianity in Ireland, and deal the first blow at the landlords."

STUDY QUESTIONS FOR VICTORY AND DEFEAT, 1865

1. How did Americans (of all sorts) understand the meaning of the Civil War when it ended?

2. How does the history of the Civil War portrayed here compare to popular and/or family stories about the war?

Summary
- The rapid growth of the northern states, built on immigration from northwestern Europe and increasingly extensive economic ties with that part of the globe, threatened the balance of power within the United States.
- Conflicts over the future of slavery in the West propelled a majority of slaveholding states to secede, a decision buttressed by Southerners' assumption that their

central place as cotton supplier to the burgeoning French and British empires would bring recognition of their new nation before any real war began.

- The North interpreted secession as a repudiation of the essence of self-government, a threat to both America and the future of democracy around the world.

- The most revolutionary change of the war came as enslaved peoples seized opportunities to escape, forced the North to endorse emancipation, and destroyed the world's largest and most influential slave society.

- The war spurred the development of new military technologies and new rules about the relationship between soldiers and noncombatants in wartime that circulated within the Western world; raised concerns about America's emboldened and expansionist spirit; and alerted the globe to a new world power.

- Like similar nationalist struggles in Europe at the same time, the U.S. Civil War strengthened the central government but also created new problems of sectionalism and race, as an embittered white South sought to subjugate and control the 3.5 million African Americans freed during the war.

Key Terms and People

blockade *491*

contraband *484*

Copperheads *481*

Davis, Jefferson *471*

Emancipation Proclamation *482*

guerrilla *477*

Grant, Ulysses S. *476*

hard war *486*

Lee, Robert E. *478*

Lincoln, Abraham *468*

McClellan, George B. *478*

secession *467*

Sherman, William T. *489*

Stephens, Alexander *475*

U.S. Colored Troops (USCT) *490*

Reviewing Chapter 14

1. Why did the North win the Civil War?
2. How does the U.S. Civil War compare to other civil conflicts in the 19th and 20th centuries?

Further Reading

Ash, Stephen V. *When the Yankees Came: Conflict and Chaos in the Occupied South.* Chapel Hill: University of North Carolina Press, 1995. The clearest analysis of the nature and experience of occupation for both Southern civilians and Northern soldiers.

Gallagher, Gary W. *The Confederate War.* Cambridge, MA: Harvard University Press, 1997. A probing book that argues for the durability and resiliency of Confederate nationalism.

Grimsley, Mark. *The Hard Hand of War: Union Military Policy Toward Southern Civilians, 1861–1865.* Cambridge, UK: Cambridge University Press, 1995. The most compelling explanation of the shift in Union policy toward a more destructive conflict.

McCurry, Stephanie. *Confederate Reckoning: Power and Politics in the Civil War South.* Cambridge, MA: Harvard University Press, 2010. A vigorous reinterpretation of the Confederate political experience, focusing on the challenges presented by white women and enslaved people.

Rable, George C. *The Confederate Republic: A Revolution against Politics*. Chapel Hill: University of North Carolina Press, 1994. The best analysis of the political tension between nationalists and libertarians in the Confederacy.

Whites, LeeAnn. *The Civil War as a Crisis in Gender: Augusta, Georgia, 1860–1890*. Athens: University of Georgia Press, 1995. An insightful study of the dynamic relationship between gender conventions and war in the South.

America In The World
PEOPLE, GOODS, IDEAS AND PRACTICES

CHAPTER 14: The Civil War 1860–1865

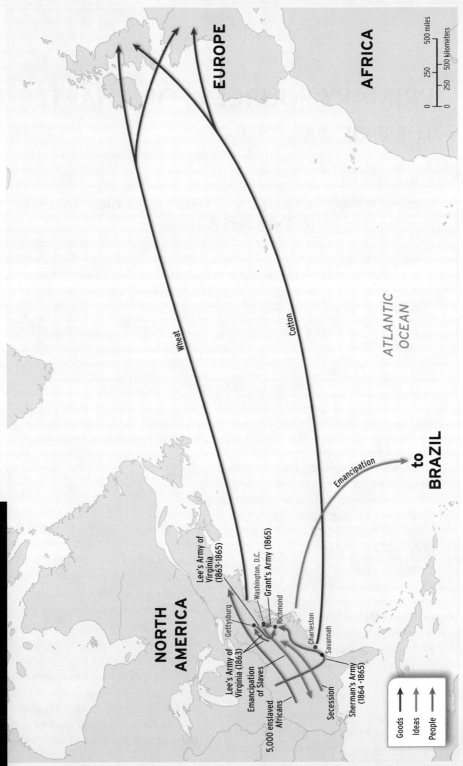

EUROPE

AFRICA

500 miles

0   250   500 kilometers

0   250   500 miles

ATLANTIC
OCEAN

Wheat

Cotton

Emancipation

to
BRAZIL

NORTH
AMERICA

Lee's Army of
Virginia
(1863-1865)

Washington, D.C.

Grant's Army (1865)

Richmond

Gettysburg

Charleston

Savannah

Lee's Army of
Virginia (1863)

Emancipation
of Slaves

5,000 enslaved
Africans

Secession

Sherman's Army
(1864-1865)

Goods

Ideas

People

PRIMARY SOURCES FOR CHAPTER 14

THE CIVIL WAR, 1860–1865

SOURCE 14.1

Corporal Wilbur Fisk, Excerpts from Letters to the Green Mountain Freeman (May 20, 1862, and April 7, 1864)

Wilbur Fisk, born and raised in Vermont, enlisted in Company E of the 2nd Vermont Volunteers in 1861. Over the course of the war, Fisk wrote over 100 letters to the Montpelier *Green Mountain Freeman*, his community's newspaper. The first letter below was written in the midst of the failed Union effort to seize Richmond. The second was written at a later point in the war, when the North was experiencing more success.

Source: Emil and Ruth Rosenblatt, eds., *Hard Marching Every Day: The Civil War Letters of Private Wilbur Fisk, 1861–1865* (Lawrence: University Press of Kansas, 1983).

May 20, 1862

The inevitable negro question would of course be the subject of the most animated conversation of anything we could bring up, for that inexhaustible subject claims preeminence in camp as well as court, and there are almost as many opinions expressed in regard to it in a tent's company as there are in Congress. The boys think it *their* duty to put down rebellion and nothing more, and they view the abolition of slavery in the present time as saddling so much additional labor upon them before the present great work is accomplished. Negro prejudice is as strong here as anywhere and most of the boys would think it a humiliating compromise to the dignity of their work to have it declared that the object of their services was to free the repulsive creatures from slavery, and raise the negro to an equality with themselves. I verily believe if such a declaration was made to-day a majority would be inclined to lay down their arms and quit the service in disgust. The most cordial reception by far that we have received since we left the free states, was tendered us by this sable species of human property. As we were passing by the premises of one of the more wealthy farmers on our way here, a group of negroes, a score or more composed of men, women and children of all ages, climbed upon the fence by the roadside and greeted us in in their earnest simple way "God bress you," "I's glad to see you," "I's glad you's come," "God bress you," and many similar exclamations as they bowed, and courtesied, and waved their hands to us, attesting their childish glee at seeing so many Union soldiers. They were dirty and ragged and probably as a perfectly natural result were ignorant and degraded, but they seemed to understand, as nearly all the negroes here do, that somehow all this commotion has a connection with them and will bring about their freedom in the end. They seem conscious of being at the the bottom of all this trouble, and all the deceptions their masters could invent have failed to rob them of this knowledge. . . .

April 7, 1864

Great confidence is felt in the plans that General Grant will adopt, and the means that he will have to use in crushing the last vestige of this Heaven accursed rebellion. Having authority that extends from the Atlantic to the Mississippi from Mobile to Washington, we may reasonably expect a concert of action in the coming campaigns that will ensure us success and victory. God grant that we may not be disappointed.

Success and victory! whose heart does not beat quicker at the thought? What consequences will have been achieved when this great rebellion shall have been forever humbled. It is not merely that this terrible war may be ended, and we safely at liberty again, that we hope to conquer our enemies and be once more at peace, but that the great principles of a free government, whose worth no mind short of Infinite Wisdom can estimate, and which even after the world has stood so long is still considered an experiment, may not be overthrown, and the progress of civilization and freedom may not be rolled back for ages, or receive a blow from which they may never recover. We are anxious of course to get out of this war, for we long most earnestly to return to the almost sacred hills and valleys of old Vermont, but we are not so anxious for this, as we are that the faith of the world in the intelligence and virtue of the common people, and their ability to govern themselves and maintain national unity without being rent asunder by internal strife and discord—a faith that despots the world over profess to

sneer at, and hold to be a delusion, and which stimulates the noblest energies of the masses of mankind—that this may be maintained, increased and perpetuated. If these principles succeed, Slavery must fall, and fall forever. The two are so antagonistical that, even if both are right, or neither of them, men embracing each could not possibly live together in peace, unless we are to suppose that God has given them a larger spirit of forbearance than is vouchsafed to humanity in general. There never was a real unity between them, and there never can be. Slavery is a relic of the darkest ages, and the poorest government on earth is better in principle than that. If we are going to have a free government at all, let us have it all free, or else we had better give up the name. Slavery has fostered an aristocracy of the rankest kind, and this aristocracy is the bitterest foe that a really free government can have. Slavery and despotism have challenged war with us, and by it she must abide. Slavery was jealous of the comelier strength that Freedom possessed; and maliciously envied her irresistible march onward to a higher destiny. Slavery drew the sword, and would have stabbed Freedom to the heart, had not God denied her the strength. She could not bear that her more righteous neighbor should be prospered, while she herself was accursed, and in her foolish madness she has tried to rend the Union in twain. With that institution it is success or death. Compromise with Slavery, and restore the Union with Slavery in it still! As well might Jehovah compromise with Satan and give him back part of Heaven.

There never before was a rebellion like this one. Generally a rebellion has been the outbreak of the people against the tyranny of a few. Their cause has usually been the cause of liberty, and more or less just. Knit together by the idea of freeing themselves from an odious despotism, and armed with justice, and backed by numbers, they have often succeeded, and history has applauded their bravery. In this war it has been different. The people have not rebelled against the few, but the few have rebelled against the people. Our government is the people's, and against this government the proud slaveholder has rebelled. With Slavery for a corner stone they hope to rob our government of her honor, and erect within our borders a rival government, which every attribute of the Almighty must detest. Can they succeed? Is the glory of our nation to be destroyed forever? Is the great experiment which our forefathers have made, and which has been our pride and boast so long, to be a failure after all? If the North will do her duty, we answer, Never! And the North *will* do her duty. She knows what it is, and she does not fear it. Never in a war before did the rank and file feel a more resolute earnestness for a just cause, and a more invincible determination to succeed, than in this war; and what the rank and file are determined to do everybody knows will surely be done. We mean to be thorough about it too. We are not going to destroy the military power of the dragon Confederacy and not destroy its fangs also. We have as a nation yielded to their rapacious demands times enough. We have cringed before Slavery as long as we will.

"Far better die in such a strife,
Than still to Slavery's claims concede,
Than crouch beneath her frown for life,
Far better in the field to bleed:

To live thus wage a life-long shame,
To die is victory and fame."

I almost lose my temper sometimes (what little I have got) when I hear men that really ought to know better, call this war a mere crusade to free the negroes, "a nigger war" and nothing more. But even if I was fighting to free the negroes simply, I don't know why I should be acting from a motive that I need be ashamed of. I verily believe that He who when He was on the earth healed foul leprosy, gave sight to the blind beggars, and preached the gospel to the poor, would not be ashamed to act from such a motive. And if he would not, why should I? Fighting to free the "niggers!" Why yes, my dear fellow, we are doing just that and a great deal more. But, sir, I am going to tell you, you would not speak of that so contemptuously, if you had not all your life long fed your soul upon motives so small, so mean, and so selfish, that the sublimer motives of sacrificing blood and treasure to elevate a degraded and downtrodden race, is entirely beyond your comprehension. Should such an event, however, rather help than hinder the success of this war, we trust that you will acquiesce in the result, and when the future of this country shall have become by this means more glorious than the past has ever been, we shall hope that you will find that your own liberty and happiness has not been at all infringed upon by giving the same liberty and happiness to a few ignorant and despised sons of Africa.

WORKING WITH SOURCES

1. How does Fisk characterize the attitudes of his fellow soldiers toward blacks and slavery?

2. How does he explain the relationship between slavery and democracy?

3. Why is Fisk fighting the war?

SOURCE 14.2

Kate Stone, Excerpts from Journal (April 21, 1863)

Kate Stone's mother owned a large cotton plantation 30 miles northwest of Vicksburg, Mississippi, the main target of the Union army in 1862 and 1863 because of its commanding position on the Mississippi River. "Brokenburn," the Stone plantation, encompassed 1,260 acres and was tended by 150 slaves, making it one of the largest estates in both the region and the United States. Rather than greet the Union forces at their home, Kate and her family fled south, eventually settling as refugees in east Texas.

Source: John Q. Anderson, ed., *Brokenburn: The Journal of Kate Stone, 1861–1865* (Baton Rouge: Louisiana State University Press, 1995), 190–93.

Friday we came down to Delhi in an immense dugout, a trip of six hours. All seven of us, Mamma, Aunt Laura, Sister, Beverly, I, and the two boys, with an assorted cargo of corn, bacon, hams, Negroes, their baggage, dogs and cats, two or three men, and our scant baggage. It was a dreadful trip. We were very crowded, the hot sun beaming on us as we were creeping down the bayou, hungry and tired. There was a very strong reflection from the water, and one of our poor Negroes was sick, groaning most of the way, and could not be made comfortable. We were glad enough to get out at the railroad bridge and walk the mile to reach Delhi.

The scene there beggars description: such crowds of Negroes of all ages and sizes, wagons, mules, horses, dogs, baggage, and furniture of every description, very little of it packed. It was just thrown in promiscuous heaps—pianos, tables, chairs, rosewood sofas, wardrobes, parlor sets, with pots, kettles, stoves, beds and bedding, bowls and pitchers, and everything of the kind just thrown pell-mell here and there, with soldiers, drunk and sober, combing over it all, shouting and laughing. While thronging everywhere were refugees—men, women, and children—everybody and everything trying to get on the cars, all fleeing from the Yankees or worse still, the Negroes.

All have lost heavily, some with princely estates and hundreds of Negroes, escaping with ten or twenty of their hands and only the clothes they have on. Others brought out clothes and household effects but no Negroes, and still others sacrificed everything to run their Negroes to a place of safety.

Everybody was animated and excited. All had their own tales to tell of the Yankee insolence and oppression and their hairbreadth escapes. All were eager to tell their own stories of hardship and contrivance, and everybody sympathized with everybody else. All were willing to lend a helping hand and to give advice to anybody on any subject. Nearly everybody took his trials cheerfully, making a joke of them, and nearly all are bound for Texas. Nobody "crying over spilled milk." Not a tear all day, though one knows there were heavy hearts bravely borne.

We got off from Delhi about sunset and reached Monroe after twelve. Nearly all remained on the cars until daylight, as it was impossible to get accommodations in town. It was amusing to watch the people wake up in the morning, wash their faces, smooth at their hair, and go to eating breakfast as leisurely and with as much *sang-froid* as though in their breakfast rooms at home. Everyone traveling on the cars now carries his own provisions, as you can get nothing if you do not, and no room if you get off.

We and the Lowry family were the last to leave the cars. Jimmy arranged his affairs, and about eleven when we were all thoroughly worn out we set off in a four-horse stage. We drove through Monroe, which seems to be a beautiful little town, but I was suffering with fever too much to like anything. The road up the Ouachita was lovely. It is a clear bright stream with forest shaded banks. The hard dry road was appreciated after the mud and water of the last months. The profusion of catalpa trees, all in full bloom, lining the streets of Monroe was indescribably fair in the early morning light. The deep green leaves seemed heaped with pyramids of snow. We never thought the catalpa could be so pretty.

We crossed the river at Trenton on a flat and came out two miles in the hills to this place, Mr. Deane's, but we hope to be here only a few days. The woods around here are beautiful with quantities of wild flowers and fruits. I have been sick in bed until today.

Yesterday Mamma and Jimmy went back to Delhi to get a party of soldiers to go back home with Jimmy and bring out the Negroes left there. All our and Aunt Laura's house servants, the most valuable we own, were left. She returned today, having succeeded in getting the soldiers, and the party with Jimmy as guide will leave this morning. We shall be very anxious until Jimmy returns as it is a most hazardous undertaking. Mamma did not realize the great danger until her return on the train. Some of the gentlemen were speaking of its hardihood, and fear if those of the party are captured they may be hanged as spies. She is very much alarmed.

We hear that the Negroes are still on the place, but the furniture and all movables have been carried out to camp by the Yankees. The Negroes quarreled over the division of our clothes. I have barely a change and the others have but little more. Our beds are all in the quarters. Webster, our most trusted servant, claims the plantation as his own and is renowned as the greatest villain in the country.

If we succeed in getting the Negroes we may say farewell to the buildings as no doubt they will be burned, but that may happen at any time. Mrs. Barr's and Maj. Haywood's homes have gone up in smoke.

WORKING WITH SOURCES

1. How does Stone describe the experience of being a refugee?

2. How did white Southerners perceive the Union army's intentions?

3. What happened to slavery as the Union army advanced into the South?

SOURCE 14.3

Spotswood Rice, Letters Written from Hospital (September 3, 1864)

Spotswood Rice, an enslaved man, worked as a tobacco roller before the Civil War. During the war, he enlisted in the 67th U.S. Colored Infantry. When he wrote the following letters, the first to his children and the second to his daughter's owner, Rice was confined to the hospital with chronic rheumatism.

Source: Ira Berlin, Joseph P. Reidy, and Leslie S. Rowland, eds., *Freedom: A Documentary History of Emancipation, 1861–1867, Series II: The Black Military Experience* (Cambridge: Cambridge University Press, 1982), 689.

[Benton Barracks Hospital, St. Louis, Mo., September 3, 1864]

My Children   I take my pen in hand to rite you A few lines to let you know that I have not forgot you and that I want to see you as bad as ever   now my Dear Children I want you to be contented with whatever may be your lots   be assured that I will have you if it cost me my life   on the 28th of the mounth. 8 hundred White and 8 hundred blacke solders expects to start up the rivore to Glasgow and above there thats to be jeneraled by a jeneral that will give me both of you   when they Come I expect to be with, them and expect to get you both in return.   Dont be uneasy my children   I expect to have you. If Diggs dont give you up this Government will and I feel confident that I will get you   Your Miss Kaitty said that I tried to steal you   But I'll let her know that god never intended for man to steal his own flesh and blood.   If I had no confidence in God I could have confidence in her   But as it is If I ever had any Confidence in her I have none now and never expect to have   And I want her to remember if she meets me with ten thousand soldiers she [will?] meet her enemy   I once [thought] that I had some respect for them but now my respects is worn out and have no sympathy for Slaveholders.   And as for her cristiananitty I expect the Devil has Such in hell   You tell her from me that She is the frist Christian that I ever hard say that aman could Steal his own child especially out of human bondage

You can tell her that She can hold to you as long as she can   I never would expect to ask her again to let you come to me because I know that the devil has got her hot set againsts that that is write   now my Dear children I am a going to close my letter to you   Give my love to all enquiring friends   tell them all that we are well and want to see them very much and Corra and Mary receive the greater part of it you sefves   and dont think hard of us not sending you any thing   I you father have a plenty for you when I see you   Spott & Noah sends their love to both of you   Oh! My Dear children how I do want to see you

HL   [Spotswood Rice]

[Benton Barracks Hospital, St. Louis, Mo., September 3, 1864]

I received a leteter from Cariline telling me that you say I tried to steal to plunder my child away from you   now I want you to understand that mary is my Child and she is a God given rite of my own and you may hold on to hear as long as you can but I want you to remembor this one thing that the longor you keep my Child from me the longor you will have to burn in hell and the qwicer youll get their   for we are now makeing up a bout one thoughsand blacke troops to Come up thar-ough and wont to come through Glasgow and when we come wo be to Copperhood rab-bels and to the Slaveholding rebbels for we dont expect to leave them there root neor branch   but we thinke how ever that we that have Children in the hands of you devels we will trie your [vertues?] the day that we enter Glasgow   I want you to understand kittey diggs that where ever you and I meets we are enmays to each orthere   I offered once to pay you forty dollers for my own Child but I am glad now that you did not accept it   Just hold on now as long as you can and the worse it will be for you you never in you life befor I came down hear did you give Children any thing not eny thing whatever not even a dollers

worth of expencs   now you call my children your pro[per]ty   not so with me   my Chil-dren is my own and I expect to get them and when I get ready to come after mary I will have bout a powrer and autherity to bring hear away and to exacute vengencens on them that holds my Child   you will then know how to talke to me   I will assure that and you will know how to talk rite too   I want you now to just hold on to hear if you want to   iff your conchosence tells that's the road go that road and   what it will brig you to kittey diggs   I have no fears about getting mary out of your hands   this whole Government gives chear to me and you cannot helps your self

ALS   Spotswood Rice

WORKING WITH SOURCES

1. How does Christianity inform Rice's commentary on slavery?
2. How would "Miss Kaitty" have responded to the reversal of power to which Rice refers when he says that he will come to her with ten thousand soldiers?
3. What does Rice's letter tell us about slave families and the relationship between parents and children?

SOURCE 14.4

Visual Document: Albany Evening Journal, "General Lee and His Army Have Surrendered" (April 10, 1865)

After abandoning Richmond, Robert E. Lee's army retreated west until Grant's troops cut them off at Appomattox Courthouse, a small village about 100 miles west of the city. Although one major Confederate army remained in the field (in North Carolina), many Northerners interpreted Lee's defeat as the end of the war.

Source: Courtesy University of Virginia Periodicals Collections.

WORKING WITH SOURCES

1. How does the newspaper explain the purpose and accomplishments of the war?

2. What is the relationship between emancipation and reunion in the announcement?

3. What does the word "treason" suggest about how Confederates might be treated after the war?

Reconstructing America

15

C ato, Stepney, Jane, Porter, Patience, and Peggy were among many enslaved black Southerners who lived on plantations in Liberty County, Georgia. In early 1865, they watched as the first wave of deserters from Sherman's Union army came through the county. The Union "Bummers" raided plantation houses and slave cabins alike, taking everything edible (and much that was not) and shooting animals they could not carry away. One Confederate described the raiders as "lost in the world of eternal woe. Their throats were open sepulchers, their mouths filled with cursing and bitterness and lies." Despite the hardship that ensued, enslaved people living in the region did nothing to obstruct the Union Army. Cato and Stepney, who both worked as drivers organizing and managing slave labor under the eye of a white overseer, effectively supported the Union by their inaction. Their stature in the community surely influenced others. They behaved, in the bitter but accurate words of a local slaveholder, as though they "now believe themselves perfectly free." In Liberty County, and throughout the rural South, whites and blacks shared a world based in the hierarchy of slavery and racial dominance and organized around the production schedules of staple crops. As Cato and the others observed the Yankee conquest of Georgia, they saw the dawning of a new era and began to work out what freedom meant. A wide range of choices, opportunities, and perils awaited black Southerners across the region.

Cato and his wife Jane, who lived on a nearby plantation, bided their time through the collapse of the Confederacy. Cato's long experience working the land and managing workers led him to reject the authority of a new overseer hired in late summer 1865. Cato's former owner denounced

< *Driving the Last Spike* by Thomas Hill, 1881.

505

him as "a most insolent, indolent, and dishonest man." In response, Cato and his wife exercised their freedom in most fundamental sense—they left Liberty County altogether, moving to nearby Savannah. No longer able to control her former slaves, Cato's ex-owner lashed out by asserting that black people would not last: "with their emancipation must come their extermination."

Despite the rising anger among whites, many freedmen and freedwomen remained in Liberty and set about making contracts for their work. Porter and Patience stayed in the area, and in spite of the fluctuating labor agreements with area planters, they managed to buy their own farm outright. Patience's brother Stepney resided on Arcadia, a coastal plantation that supported two lucrative crops: rice and sea island cotton. He began to manage much of the former plantation land at Arcadia and helped coordinate the rental and purchase of land by freed people. The close family networks established among the Gullah people, as the black Southerners in this region were known, undoubtedly aided many in their transition to freedom.

Unfortunately, few freed people experienced the success they did. Peggy, who had lived on the same plantation as Cato, moved to Savannah but contracted smallpox and died. Some freed people began to labor for wages on the plantations that they had once farmed as slaves, but this rarely brought them the financial independence they desired. Others rented land or farmed on shares, splitting the proceeds from the yearly crop with the landlord. The sharecropper system, adopted widely across the South, trapped tenant farmers in cycles of debt and prevented the Southern agricultural sector from diversifying as the world cotton market collapsed. In Liberty County, as elsewhere in the South, the reintegration of the Southern economy into the larger global market reflected the efforts Southerners and Northerners made to reconstruct the nation. But Southerners' failure to build a sustainable and humane economy or a just social and political system represented one of the worst legacies of Reconstruction.

◼ THE YEAR OF JUBILEE, 1865

The dramatic changes underway in the South and the nation produced surprising outcomes. At the end of the Civil War, white Southerners were defeated and resentful, whereas black Southerners celebrated Jubilee, their deliverance from bondage. Northerners likewise celebrated because they had preserved the Union and extinguished slavery in the United States. But great questions remained: what role would recently freed slaves play in American life? What rights would they possess? What obligations did the federal government have to ensure a meaningful freedom? For Washington, the first order of business was reestablishing loyal governments in the South and bringing the region back into a normal relationship with the nation. No precedents guided this process and grand constitutional questions about the nature of the Union and the meaning of republican government acquired real political weight. Republicans and Democrats, Northerners and Southerners, and blacks and whites divided over the answers to these questions. The wartime task of reunion gave way to the postwar task of Reconstruction, which entailed reorganizing the Southern political system and rebuilding shattered public and private institutions.

African American Families

Of the nearly four million enslaved people in the South before the Civil War, approximately 500,000 fled to freedom during the war and the rest claimed their freedom at the war's conclusion. The most important task confronting freed people was reestablishing families broken by slavery. White Southerners wanted to restore what they considered normal labor relations, but for black Southerners the desire to reunite displaced family members outweighed even the desire for a steady wage. Sales often dispersed family members across states or even abroad, but in many cases, parents or siblings retained enough information to track down relatives. Through the late spring and summer of 1865, as white Southern soldiers headed home in defeat, black Southerners took to the road, following letters, reports, and rumors to track the exodus of children, parents, siblings, and loved ones as a result of slave sales. Black Union soldiers had a harder time

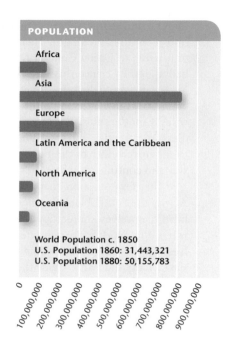

POPULATION

Africa

Asia

Europe

Latin America and the Caribbean

North America

Oceania

World Population c. 1850
U.S. Population 1860: 31,443,321
U.S. Population 1880: 50,155,783

0, 100,000,000, 200,000,000, 300,000,000, 400,000,000, 500,000,000, 600,000,000, 700,000,000, 800,000,000, 900,000,000

VICTORY FOR THE NORTH
After four long years, Northerners celebrated Union victory in the Civil War and the end of slavery. But the war's conclusion only began the struggle to define what freedom would mean in practice.

than most freedmen because they were kept in the service occupying Southern towns into 1866, thus prolonging their reunions with family members. As a South Carolina unit wrote to Union General Daniel Sickles, "the Biggest Majority of our mens never had a Home Science this late War Commence . . . the Greatist majority of them had Runaway from Rebels master & leave they wives & old mother & old Father & all they parent. . . . But General now to see that the war is over . . . we hadent nothing atall & our wifes & mother most all of them is aperishing." The army eventually released these soldiers from service, and they quickly sought out family members. This movement added to the uncertainty of the postwar period and alarmed whites who expected blacks to stay and continue the work they had done before emancipation.

The next question that confronted freed people was what work they would do. Across the South, black Southerners faced several choices: wage labor, renting land to farm themselves, sharecropping, or some combination of the three. But the question of where that work happened often took precedence. "If I stay here, I'll never know I'm free," explained one freedwoman as she left the plantation on which she had labored as a slave. Many thousands made the same choice, leaving behind farms and plantations on which they had been raised in favor of a new, if uncertain, life somewhere else. Often, they moved to cities, most overcrowded from the influx of refugees during the war (Map 15.1). Memphis and Nashville both grew by more than a third between 1860 and 1870, while Atlanta's population more than doubled. The movement of freed people into Southern cities created a labor glut, and the problem of unemployment exacerbated white fears of black criminality.

In rural areas, labor contracts and work were the most pressing priorities. Very few enslaved people owned any real estate before the war, which required them to work for

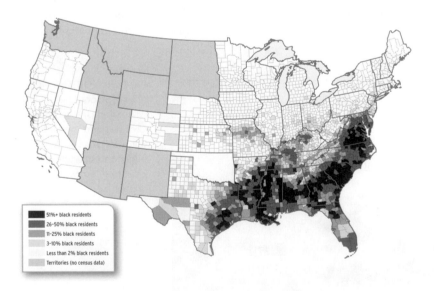

51%+ black residents
26–50% black residents
11–25% black residents
3–10% black residents
Less than 2% black residents
Territories (no census data)

MAP 15.1 ▲ Black Population of the United States, 1880 Despite the opportunities for movement created by emancipation, few former slaves had the resources to make a full relocation out of the region. As a result, black Americans continued to live predominately in the South until the second and third decades of the 20th century.

wages. The main challenge was working out fair and enforceable contracts with former masters or other whites. The Bureau of Refugees, Freedmen, and Abandoned Land (usually called the **Freedmen's Bureau**), established within the Army in early 1865, helped adjudicate labor disputes in the summer and fall of 1865. Led by former Union general Oliver Otis Howard, the Bureau also distributed food rations to blacks and whites during the hard winter that followed and initiated the building of schools, hospitals, and other communal institutions. Despite this important work, elite Southerners resented the intrusion of the federal government and joined with Northern Democrats to denounce the Bureau as an unnecessary federal imposition on states' rights. Even moderate Northerners expressed concerns about the freed people's work ethic. Because slaves had labored without incentive, whites did not expect them to understand paid work. In fact, most African Americans adjusted quickly, even when they could not rely on landowners to fairly fulfill the terms of labor contracts. One man, who had relocated to Ohio at the war's end, responded to a request from his former master to return to Tennessee by asking "you to send us our wages for the time we served you." "Here I draw my wages every Saturday night," wrote Jourdan Anderson, "but in Tennessee there was never any pay day for the negroes any more than for the horses and the cows. Surely there will be a day of reckoning for those who defraud the laborer of his hire."

Southern Whites and the Problem of Defeat

The spring and summer of 1865 exhilarated and bewildered Americans throughout the country. The most shocking event was the assassination of Abraham Lincoln. After celebrating the official surrender of Lee's Army of Northern Virginia on April 12, 1865, Lincoln attended a play on the evening of the 14th, Good Friday. John Wilkes Booth, a member of America's most famous acting family, organized a conspiracy to kill Lincoln and several cabinet members. Booth shot Lincoln in his box at Ford's Theater while a conspirator attacked Secretary of State William Seward in his home. Lincoln, unconscious but still alive, was taken to a house across the street from the theater, where doctors tried to save him. Cabinet members, generals, and other officials visited the room where he lay before Lincoln died just after dawn. Secretary of War Edwin Stanton summarized the grim morning and its effect on America's memory of Lincoln: "now he belongs to the ages." Booth escaped into Maryland before being killed by U.S. troops. Grief and anger flooded across the North, with many citizens blaming the conspiracy on Jefferson Davis, who fled south after evacuating Richmond in early April. Despite the controversies he stoked as president, Lincoln earned the deep appreciation of Northerners by steering the country through the crisis of disunion. Walt Whitman, who had seen Lincoln on his melancholy early morning walks around Washington, spoke for many when he lamented:

> O the bleeding drops of red,
> Where on the deck my Captain lies,
> Fallen cold and dead.

Some Southerners, Robert E. Lee among them, recognized Lincoln's generosity late in the war and regarded his murder as damaging to their interest. Others, however, could not help but exalt this final turn of events. "Hurrah! Old Abe Lincoln has been assassinated!" a South Carolina woman wrote in her diary. "Our hated enemy has met the just reward of his life." Northerners could not comprehend such an attitude. For them, the restoration of the Union brought relief and confirmation of God's favor over their society. Even as Southerners struggled to reconcile their religious understanding of defeat—many believed it was another test offered by God for his chosen people—they resisted the political consequences of Union victory. Some refused to accept the outcome and abandoned the United States rather than live under what they considered an enemy government. A number of high-ranking Confederate military officers fled to South America, fearful of punishment they might receive from the Union government. Edward Porter Alexander, Lee's chief of artillery, laid his plans on the retreat to Appomattox: "I had made up my mind that if ever a white flag was raised I would take to the bushes. And, somehow, I would manage to get out of the country & go to Brazil. Brazil was just going to war with Paraguay & I could doubtless get a place in their artillery . . . then for once I would be on the winning side." Several thousand white Southerners relocated to Brazil (although Alexander was not among them), where they created an expatriate community in one of the last two major slave societies remaining in the Western Hemisphere. More than 10,000 Confederates exiled themselves after the war. This exodus carried men, and sometimes their families, around the world. Many ended up serving as military advisors to foreign governments—including Britain, France, and Germany—and several were employed by the Khedive of Egypt.

Even as white Southerners lamented the war's outcome, they sought the easiest path toward readmission to the Union in hopes of restoring some measure of normality in the South and because it might allow them to retain authority over the freed people. So, despite their vigorous pursuit of independence and their wartime insistence that the Confederacy was a separate nation, many Southerners assumed that they could quickly and easily resume their old position within the United States. Northern Democrats largely agreed. They had long believed that Southerners could not leave the Union; so restoration of rights, especially property rights for Southern whites, would be a simple matter of affirming their future loyalty. Republicans resisted these easy terms but fought amongst themselves about the proper way to rebuild the nation's political system.

White Southerners also grappled with restoring order in their communities and explaining defeat to themselves. This proved particularly challenging for Southern men. In the prewar era, white men had claimed authority by promising to protect and care for members of Southern society they viewed as inferior to them, including women, children, and black people. Confederate defeat revealed the failure of paternalism. Southern women, in particular, had been forced to assume new burdens and responsibilities during the war. Many had worked in male occupations, including industrial enterprises, or they had managed plantations and household budgets. Would these wartime changes carry over to a new social order in the postwar period? On Virginia plantations, for instance, the economic consequences of defeat and emancipation forced men and women to share tasks and roles that were distinct before the war. The ethic of mutuality that developed in some rural communities around the South came more from necessity than ideology, but it still challenged one of the core aspects of prewar gender relations. In other places, the effects of the war compelled some women to reaffirm hierarchy rather than press forward with changes. To do this, white women relinquished their wartime responsibilities and advocated traditional gender relationships. As one editorial in a Georgia newspaper noted, "a married man falling into misfortunes is more apt to retrieve his situation in the world than a single one, chiefly because . . . although abroad may be darkness and humiliation, yet there is still a little world of love at home of which he is monarch."

Emancipation in Comparative Perspective

Americans followed neither an inevitable nor an entirely distinct path after emancipation. Both Jamaica and South Africa experienced similarly sudden and disruptive emancipation moments in the mid-19th century. Although both places functioned as British colonies when they freed their slaves, in all three societies, whites followed emancipation by vigorously pursuing racial supremacy. This pursuit took different forms. In Jamaica, white elites used the emerging scientific consensus behind racial hierarchy to abdicate local control to London. As a consequence, white property holders on the island were protected at the expense of black workers. In South Africa, local whites achieved greater autonomy from the colonial office, and although they allowed black voting, whites retained economic and social power. Unlike Jamaica, which had a society sharply divided between a small number of white elites and a high number of landless blacks, South Africa possessed a sizeable rural white population. Like its Southern counterpart in the United States, rural whites joined with elites to resist emancipation and, when resistance proved futile, worked to establish white supremacy.

A pivotal moment in Jamaican emancipation came 30 years after the start of the process. In the fall of 1865, as Americans struggled to devise the rules and goals of their own post-emancipation Reconstruction, word spread through the hemisphere of a rebellion of black farm workers in Jamaica. The Morant Bay Rebellion stemmed from inequities in post-emancipation Jamaica. The black laboring class continued to be denied access to land or political power, a consequence of policies designed by white leaders that restricted blacks to working as agricultural laborers. The rebellion consumed the eastern half of the island and left hundreds of black laborers dead and hundreds more beaten by state militia forces. American newspapers tracked the event and filtered it through the perspectives of the ongoing struggle over the role of the freedmen in American life. A Southern paper described "terrible massacres of the whites" by bands of deranged blacks. They "shuddered to think of what would be the effect of these incendiary teachings in the lately populous slave regions of the South." In contrast, American abolitionists used the event as an object lesson in why full equality and political rights were necessary for all Southerners. According to Senator Charles Sumner, the freedmen of the South "were not unlike the freedmen of San Domingo or Jamaica . . . and have the same sense of wrong."

The United States avoided a Morant Bay Rebellion, although it did not grant freed people the degree of freedom Sumner recommended. A key distinction between the three experiments in Reconstruction proved to be the nature of political change in each society. In Jamaica, a mulatto elite, composed mostly of the descendents of slaveholders and their slaves, entered into the political system, but they mostly sided with the white elite. When legislators granted blacks the right to vote in South Africa, they also enacted a property restriction that ensured white domination. In contrast, black Southern men received the vote without restriction. This helped make American Reconstruction the most radical of those slave societies that experienced emancipation in the 19th century.

■ SHAPING RECONSTRUCTION, 1865–1868

In 1865, a small group of Republican congressmen and senators had high hopes for a vigorous Reconstruction plan. These men—and a substantially more diverse body of black and white male and female reformers who urged them on—foresaw not just the expansion of free labor but a redistribution of Southern wealth and an egalitarian political order that included black male suffrage. Between 1865 and 1866, this group—known as the "radical Republicans"—went from the margins to the center of the political debate, and they did so largely because Northerners perceived President Andrew Johnson as currying favor with an unrepentant South. The fight that erupted between Johnson and his own party in Congress opened strange new rifts in American politics and propelled Republicans toward a surprising and dramatic shift in Reconstruction. In a series of clashes with Johnson, Congressional Republicans adopted increasingly radical measures meant to secure the fruits of Union victory in the war and protect the rights of the freed people.

Andrew Johnson's Reconstruction

As the uncertainty of spring gave way to summer, Southern whites confidently assumed they would be allowed to continue with "self-reconstruction." Under this theory, white Southerners reaffirmed their loyalty to the United States through existing political systems. With Congress out of session, Andrew Johnson, the Tennessee Unionist who had become president after Lincoln's assassination, set the terms. Despite radicals' hopes that Johnson would impose strict conditions on the reentry of Southern states, he set the bar low. Southerners needed to repudiate secession and state debts incurred during the war and confirm emancipation by ratifying the **Thirteenth Amendment**, which outlawed slavery in the United States. Johnson also extended amnesty to most of the high-ranking military and civilian officials of the Confederacy. Over the summer of 1865, Johnson restored voting and property rights to thousands of these men. In some cases, this process divested black families of land they had been given by the U.S. Army during the war. Before the war, Johnson was a bitter enemy of the plantation elite, championing the cause of the white artisans and nonslaveholding farmers of East Tennessee. But in his efforts to keep pace with the shifting political alignments of the postwar era, Johnson became a staunch defender of white supremacy and recast himself as the defender of embattled white elites.

In fall 1865, Southern states held new state elections. In the Upper South, a significant number of former Whigs and Unionists won; but voters in the Lower South largely reelected Democratic Party elites who led the region during the war. Alexander Stephens, the former vice president of the Confederacy, was elected U.S. senator from

Georgia. Most Northerners, and even some Democrats, reacted with shock and anger. Did the South really imagine it could send the very men who had led a bloody rebellion against the United States to serve in Congress? Andrew Johnson accepted the results as a product of the democratic process. Radical Republicans grew increasingly uneasy with Johnson's leniency.

Forced to accept emancipation, reconstituted state governments across the region adopted a series of laws known collectively as the "**Black codes**" in the fall of 1865, which proscribed both the extent and the limits of freedom for black residents in the region. The rights granted to freed people included the right to marry, to own property, and to participate in the judicial process through suing and being sued and giving testimony in court cases, but the legislators paid much more attention to restrictions on black freedom. The most nefarious of these were the "apprenticeship" laws, which gave county courts the authority to take children away from parents if those parents were not capable of providing for them. Children would be assigned a place to work by the court, with the "former master" having priority. Black Southerners and many Northerners perceived this as a blatant attempt to reimpose slavery. The codes also focused not just on ex-slaves but on "all freedpeople, free negroes, and mulattoes," effectively creating a new legal designation in Southern law that singled out black people where previously status (free or slave) had been the key distinction among residents.

For Northerners, the second half of 1865 proved nearly as disorienting as the first half. Just as they experienced the elation of victory and anguish over Lincoln's assassination, Northerners moved from supporting Johnson's initial measures to reconstruct the South quickly to anger at Johnson's capitulation to Southern arrogance. Carl Schurz, a prominent Civil War general and radical Republican, had been sent on a tour of the South by Johnson in late 1865 to assess the situation, but his findings undercut support for Johnson's policies. White Southerners did not think of themselves as Americans and did not trust black Southerners to work in a new free labor economy. Schurz concluded that "it is not only the political machinery of the States and their constitutional relations to the general government, but the whole organism of southern society that must be reconstructed, or rather constructed anew, so as to bring it into harmony with the rest of American society." As Congress reconvened in December 1865, its members weighed the merits and methods of reconstructing the South. After much debate, Congress slowed down the process of Reconstruction by refusing to seat the delegations recently elected from Southern states. As one constituent wrote to his congressmen, "Let these rebellious states know and feel that there is a power left that can reach and punish treason."

The Fight over Reconstruction

The desire to punish the South for its refusal to accept the verdict of war manifested itself in the first session of the 39th Congress. These were the men elected in fall 1864, at the moment of the Union's triumph at Atlanta, Mobile Bay, and the Shenandoah Valley. They came into office on Lincoln's coattails, and they were overwhelmingly Republican. They held more than a 2-to-1 advantage in the House of Representatives and a 3-to-1 advantage in the Senate. Further, as Johnson alienated himself from moderate Republicans, the balance of power in the party shifted toward the radicals. So it was with relative ease that Republicans overcame Democratic objections and refused to seat the delegations sent to Washington by the former Confederate states. Doing so amounted to a public challenge to Johnson's leadership and signaled a clear desire to slow down Reconstruction. Although Republicans would never have a free hand from their constituents, who worried about Reconstruction's costs and duration, a majority of Northerners and many Southern unionists wanted to reevaluate the purpose and direction of Reconstruction policy in late 1865 and early 1866.

Republican congressmen worried about the economic state of the former Confederacy. In the spring and summer, many freed people signed work contracts with former masters and others. Some of these promised weekly pay days, others by the month, and still others only once a year after harvest. Even if the contracts had been fairly conceived, conflict would have been likely. Union and Confederate forces alike had destroyed huge swathes of the Southern landscape, tearing down fence rails for firewood and tearing up railroads to weaken the Confederates' ability to fight. Most economically damaging of all was emancipation, which represented a capital loss of at least $3 billion for white Southerners. By one estimate, slave property comprised 60 percent of the wealth of the Deep South cotton states. The results of the Civil War in per capita terms were striking: the average total wealth of all Southern farm operators dropped from $22,819 in 1860 to $3,168 a decade later. Freed people thus entered the labor market during a period of severe contraction, with most farmers possessing little cash with which to pay workers.

Because of the immediate necessity for freed people to sign a contract of some sort and begin earning money, they were in a poor position to negotiate with landowners. Agents of the Freedmen's Bureau served as the only check on exploitative labor agreements. Freedmen's Bureau agents settled labor disputes when they arose, but the Bureau never fielded more than 900 agents in the whole South, which rarely amounted to more than 1 per county. Despite the importance of their work, Johnson and Congressional Democrats denounced the Freedmen's Bureau as an unwarranted extension of federal power. A typical political cartoon condemned the bureau as "an agency to keep the negro in idleness at the expense of the white man." White Southerners were much less subtle in their critique. Josiah Nott, an Alabamian and prominent prewar doctor, fumed against the reorganization of Mobile's public space to accommodate African Americans. "See how the damd Military, the nigger troops, the Freemen's Bureau spit upon us and rub it in." Republicans remained committed to a limited government, and many were concerned about the constitutional issues raised by the Bureau, but most regarded the work as too important to abandon. In 1866, Congress approved a one-year renewal of the Bureau. Johnson vetoed the bill and, in a sign of growing Republican solidarity, Congress overrode his veto.

Partisan politics played a large role in shaping the nature of Reconstruction. The Republican Party was only a decade old and had yet to establish any presence in the Southern United States, which it needed if it was to remain a viable entity. Democrats had alienated Northern voters by their opposition to Lincoln's policies during the war. Reconstruction occurred in this moment of fluidity. Republicans sought to build a coalition of "loyal" voters—drawing on former Unionists in the South and African Americans if they were enfranchised, along with their core base in the North. A key component of their rhetoric in the period focused on the "Bloody Shirt," a patriotic appeal to reward Republicans for steering the country through the Civil War. They condemned Democrats as traitors who abetted the Confederacy. Republicans benefited from the rise of the veteran as an American icon during this period. In previous wars, veterans had been honored, but only after the Civil War was military service promoted as the purest expression of civic pride. Veterans themselves played a key role in promulgating this idea. As the head of the Grand Army of the Republic, the Union veteran's association, Major General John Logan advocated this idea most forcefully. According to Logan, "it is wholly safe to say that in his [the veteran's] character of defender of right and justice, with no features of the despoiler and oppressor, and in his attributes of lofty patriotism, of unselfish, inflexible, and enduring courage, of patience under suffering, and of moderation under victory . . . he has no faithful counterpart in any age of the world."

Fresh from his defeat over the renewal of the Freedmen's Bureau, Johnson picked another fight with Congress, this time over the 1866 Civil Rights Act. The first instance of federal law designed expressly to protect the rights of citizens, rather than prohibiting the actions of government, the bill was authored by moderate Republican Lyman Trumbull of Illinois and was intended as a middle ground between radicals who wanted strong intervention in Southern states and conservatives who feared the centralizing nature of such action. The bill established a common national citizenship for all people born in the United States and promised the "full and equal benefit of all laws and proceedings for the security of person and property." It also empowered federal courts to hear violations of rights, but the bill principally protected people against state rather than private action. Johnson refused to accept even this moderate measure and vetoed the bill. Johnson's explanation, as with his earlier veto of the Freedmen's Bureau, conveyed his refusal to accept the "centralization" of power initiated by the bill. Johnson also made white supremacy an important part of his veto, arguing that by granting black Americans equal access to the law, it denied rights to whites. To Johnson's horror, the bill seemed to grant "a perfect equality of the white and colored races." Congress again overrode Johnson and enacted the legislation. Johnson's opposition to these two central measures and his intemperate veto messages isolated him politically and pushed the sizeable body of moderate Republicans closer to the radicals.

The Civil War Amendments and American Citizenship

After the Civil Rights bill passed, Republicans began debating a broader protection of individual rights. As they discussed what would become the **Fourteenth Amendment**, Republicans again quarreled among themselves about the propriety of creating federal safeguards for individual rights. And again, moderates won the day, this time crafting a broad guarantee of national citizenship and equality before the law but offering no specific protection of freed people's political rights. The second section of the amendment punished states that denied the vote to black men by reducing their representation in Congress. Under the prewar constitution, enslaved people counted as three-fifths of a free person for the purposes of apportionment; under the Fourteenth Amendment, if not enfranchised, they would effectively count as zero-fifths. This feature might compel Southern states to enfranchise black men, but it put little pressure on Northern states to do the same because ignoring their small black populations did not substantially reduce northern representation in Congress. The amendment also repudiated the debt accumulated by the Confederate and Southern state governments, leaving the millions of dollars issued during the war in bonds and currency worthless.

EMANCIPATION DAY African Americans held Emancipation Day ceremonies, like the one pictured at the center of this image, to commemorate Union victory and their deliverance from bondage. Despite the opposition of Southern whites, Southern blacks continued to celebrate emancipation and July 4th well into the 20th century.

A comparative framework is again useful. In post-emancipation Jamaica, the British had pursued a similarly bold plan for full civil equality, although imposed through the policies of the colonial secretary, Lord Glenelg, rather than through a constitution. In 1837, Glenelg explained that the "great cardinal principle of the law for the abolition of slavery is, that the apprenticeship of the emancipated slaves is to be immediately succeeded by personal freedom, in the full and unlimited sense of the term in which it is used in reference to the other subjects of the British Crown." Glenelg's policies held for a decade, but by the late 1840s, the government imposed restrictions on the right to vote and eventually suspended Jamaican self-government entirely. In Jamaica and the United States, the central governments issued broad grants of civil equality to recently freed slaves only to back away from these to give landholders more control over their labor force and to prevent black people from entering the political system.

The issue of black voting lurked just beneath the surface of the disputes among Southerners, Johnson, and Congressional Republicans. Radicals and even some moderates had long believed in the wisdom and justice of the measure. In 1864, as loyal representatives of Louisiana considered a new state constitution, Abraham Lincoln had suggested voting privileges for the men of color, "especially the intelligent and former soldiers." A partisan imperative was at work as well. Republicans knew that the end of slavery also meant the end of the three-fifths principle in the constitution, where five enslaved people were counted as three free people for the purposes of enumeration. If unmodified, emancipation would increase the South's representation in the House of Representatives and the Electoral College. Enfranchising black men would give Republicans the means to defend themselves and also ensure that the party could build a base of support in the South. Participants in the struggle to adapt political and civil frameworks in a post-emancipation world understood their effort in a global context. Henry Turner, a leading black minister, equated emancipation and the postwar amendments with "the almost instantaneous liberation of the Russian serfs, and their immediate investiture with citizens' immunities." Even as the amendment expanded rights for some, it contracted rights for others. Article I of the constitution refers only to "people" in sections on voting, but the Fourteenth Amendment set the minimum requirements as "male inhabitants" at least 21 years of age.

Shortly after passage of the Fourteenth Amendment, Republicans began work on the **Fifteenth Amendment**. Ratified in 1870, the amendment issued a blanket prohibition against denying the right to vote on the basis of race. The amendment's failure to enfranchise women incensed women's suffrage advocates who had been working since the 1830s to win women the right to vote. Leading suffrage activists, such as Susan B. Anthony and Elizabeth Cady Stanton, had essentially paused their work on this project during the war to help further emancipation. Congress's failure to consider women's suffrage created deep bitterness and led to tensions within the movement along racial lines. Elizabeth Cady Stanton railed, "think of Patrick and Sambo and Hans and Ung Tung who do not know the difference between a Monarchy and a Republic, who never read the Declaration of Independence . . . making laws for Lydia Maria Child, Lucretia Mott, or Fanny Kemble." Stanton's angry comparison of immigrants with the leaders of the women's rights movement underscored the personal nature of the issue. The Fifteenth Amendment also completed a fundamental shift in the language of the constitution and American conceptions of freedom. The first 10 amendments to the constitution all deny the ability of Congress to legislate on certain topics—they provide a "negative liberty" by protecting the people from government action. The Thirteenth, Fourteenth, and Fifteenth Amendments all concluded with the language "Congress shall have the power to enforce this provision." The postwar amendments relied on the idea of "positive liberty"—grants of power to Congress for it to protect the freedom of certain aspects of Americans' lives.

The fighting between the radicals and the president had long-term significance. It empowered Congress to act decisively when the president would not. Georges Clemenceau, the future prime minister of France, came to the United States in 1865 as a journalist. Clemenceau, an ardent liberal who had come to the United States to study democracy after the war, approved. "Congress may, when it pleases, take the President by the ear and lead him down from his high seat, and he can do nothing about it except to struggle and shout. . . . At each session they add a shackle to his bonds, tighten the bit in a different place, file a claw or tooth, and then when he is well bound up, fastened, and caught in an inextricable net of laws and decrees, more or less contradicting each other, they tie him to the stake of the Constitution and take a good look at him."

Irish Americans and the Fenian Struggle

Many of the Irish Americans who participated in the Civil War believed it was part of a broader liberal movement toward self-determination and democracy for all the world's people. In particular, they supported the Fenians, who aimed to end British control of Ireland. Not long after the South fell to defeat, the Fenians attacked the empire. In May 1866, an army of 800 men invaded Canada and captured Fort Erie. "We have taken up the sword to strike down the oppressor's rod," declared the army's leader, General John O'Neil, "to deliver Ireland from the tyrant, the despoiler, the robber." Although O'Neil's invasion soon faltered and casualties were few (less than a dozen), the attempt revealed Irish Americans as earnest foes of Britain, complicating the already strained diplomatic relations between the United Kingdom and the United States and demonstrating the revolutionary energy generated by the Civil War.

Within a few years of Appomattox, Fenians had organized hundreds of groups in 18 states and 3 territories, comprising perhaps 45,000 members. These men drew on their military training in the Civil War to design plans for emancipating Ireland. They were also emboldened by a change in American immigration law. During the debate over the Fourteenth Amendment, Maine Senator William Pitt Fessenden inserted two words into the first section. His change, adopted without a vote, granted citizenship to "naturalized" residents. This provision promised a conflict with Britain, which adhered to the idea of "perpetual allegiance," in which people owed loyalty to the sovereign under whom they were born for their entire life.

Congressional Reconstruction

Thaddeus Stevens, a Pennsylvania Republican, played a key role in the conflict with Johnson and the creation of federal protections for individual rights. Stevens helped lead the radical Republicans in Congress and served as perhaps the ablest and most dedicated white proponent of meaningful freedom for African Americans. Stevens owned a forge in Pennsylvania where he employed and paid equally both black and white workers. In Congress, Stevens used logic, rhetoric, and strong-arm parliamentary tactics to advance his agenda. Like other radicals, Stevens regarded the Southern states as having actually left the Union. He believed that Southern states could now be subjected to specific terms before they were granted reentry into the Union. For Stevens, the most important change—one compelled by humanity and justice as well as political necessity—was to diminish the clout of the white elites in Southern life and elevate the freed people. Stevens believed that this could only be accomplished if the government broke up the great landholdings of the prewar era and distributed the land to former slaves, but President Johnson killed a brief experiment with resettlement undertaken by General William T. Sherman in early 1865. Despite Stevens' urging, Republicans could not bring themselves to advocate the redistribution of property.

In early 1867, the British arrested 28 Fenians in Ireland, including two former Union Army officers. Secretary of State Seward reminded the American ambassador, Charles Francis Adams, that "faithful service in the armies or navy of the United States during the rebellion constituted an enhanced claim of persons so serving to the consideration of the Government which they have helped to perpetuate." Irish Americans in the United States inflamed the situation with massive rallies that called on Congress and the President to defend its naturalized citizens abroad. Seward pushed Adams more, noting that Britain's claim to perpetual allegiance "awakened a general feeling of resentment and deeply wounded our pride of sovereignty." As the two nations neared war over the matter, Congress passed a law (along with the 14th Amendment) guaranteeing the right of immigrants to naturalize and of the government to protect them as it would native-born citizens. The veterans and a host of Fenians were eventually released from jails in England, Ireland, and Canada in 1870 when Parliament passed a law allowing British citizens to renounce their native citizenship and naturalize abroad. The liberalization in American and British law stemmed from a most unlikely constituency—nativists in the United States had targeted Irish immigrants in the 1850s as unworthy of citizenship; but the Civil War and Reconstruction spurred a profound rethinking of the meaning and weight of citizenship.

- Why did the U.S. government protect American Fenians even when they took up arms against the British Empire?
- How did the naturalization of Irish immigrants as Americans relate to making freed people citizens at the same time?

For Stevens, the Southern reaction to the Fourteenth Amendment proved the necessity of radically reordering Southern politics. After quick passage by Congress, white Southerners overwhelmingly rejected the measure. The boldness of the Southern refusal to consider the Fourteenth Amendment and the increasingly violent racial politics of the region—whites killed dozens of African Americans in Memphis and New Orleans during riots in the summer of 1866—pushed Congress to seize control of Reconstruction completely. In March 1867, Congress passed the first of a series of Reconstruction Acts. Dramatic in their scope, the legislation consolidated the ex-Confederate states into five military districts, with former Union generals acting as military governors (Map 15.2). To return to the Union, Congress required states to ratify the Fourteenth Amendment and revise their constitutions to provide for black male voting.

The legislative changes of 1867 signaled the decisive shift of power within Washington to Capitol Hill. Angry Republicans hamstrung Johnson with laws of bewildering intricacy in the hopes of creating a pretext for impeaching him. The "Tenure of Office" Act, for example, restricted the president's ability to remove appointees that required Senate approval for their positions. After clashing with Congress over the constitutionality of this

ANDREW JOHNSON'S SENATE TRIAL
The impeachment of Andrew Johnson and his subsequent trial in the Senate (pictured here) established the clear dominance of Congress over the process and politics of Reconstruction.

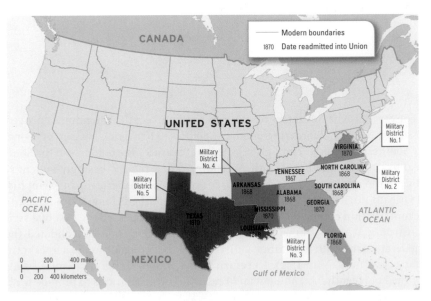

MAP 15.2 ▲ Military Districts Established by the Reconstruction Acts, 1867 One of the most radical pieces of legislation passed by the Reconstruction Congresses, these acts divided the South into five districts commanded by a military governor (usually a former Union army general). States had to revise their own constitutions to provide for universal manhood suffrage and ratify the Fourteenth Amendment before being returned to state status.

law in mid-1867, the House of Representatives impeached Johnson. The first U.S. president to ever be impeached, Johnson remained in office because the Senate failed to convict him by one vote. However, politically he was powerless. By the end of the year, Republicans turned with relief to selecting Johnson's successor, choosing the enormously popular Union general Ulysses S. Grant. Grant won the election easily in 1868, running on a platform of sectional reconciliation under the slogan "Let Us Have Peace." Despite his optimism, little sectional peace prevailed during Grant's presidency. White Southerners resented the changes forced on them through the Reconstruction Acts; but with no voice in Congress besides a few ideologically sympathetic Northern Democrats, they had little choice but to submit.

The first charge to the military governors now administering the Southern states was to hold elections to select delegates for state constitutional conventions. Black men participated in the election and helped produce a strong Republican victory, including the election of a majority of black delegates in South Carolina and Louisiana. In other Southern states, black delegates comprised only a small percent of the delegates, but even that small number invalidated the entire process for most white Southerners. The victories in the South confirmed that the Republican Party would stay competitive in the region as long as they could maintain the support of African American voters.

STUDY QUESTIONS FOR SHAPING RECONSTRUCTION, 1865–1868

1. Why did Republicans endorse a more radical Reconstruction policy than Andrew Johnson?
2. How did the changes made by Congress reshape the relationship between state and federal power?

■ RECONSTRUCTION IN THE SOUTH, 1866–1876

Even as Congress and the President fashioned and refashioned Reconstruction in Washington, black and white Southerners shaped the postwar world on the ground. They disputed the terms of work, housing, property, politics, and social relationships. For black Southerners, the first order of business was to create autonomous lives. True emancipation required not just free individuals but communities dedicated to uplifting and supporting its members. Politically, Reconstruction entailed creating Republican governments that would implement the policies articulated by Congress. Politics monopolized the public's attention; but the success of Reconstruction, and the ability of African Americans to make their freedom real, hinged on rebuilding the Southern economy.

African American Life in the Postwar South

The efforts that black Southerners made to reconstitute their families in the wake of emancipation laid the foundation for their postwar communities. The neighborhoods that defined the life of enslaved men and women in the plantation districts became the

VOTING EQUALITY The act of voting signaled a bedrock equality between white and black men that few on either side could have imagined at the beginning of the Civil War in 1861.

RECONSTRUCTION OPPORTUNITIES The political opportunities African Americans experienced during Reconstruction were not matched by economic opportunities. Across much of the Deep South, the only work available to black men and women continued to be agricultural labor in cotton fields.

basis for new free communities. Churches occupied the heart of these new communities. In some cases, they were new congregations; in others, they were biracial parishes from before the war that split into separate white and black churches after the war. By 1866, 62 percent of black Methodists had left their prewar churches. But more people came to the independent black churches after the war, and those who did joined a community that played a key role in reconstructing the South. As one Freedmen's Bureau agent noted in his survey of influential black leaders in his area, "Gibbons, a mulatto, is a farmer, and was formerly a slave. He, too, is a Baptist preacher. . . . As a preacher he is very popular, and has a large influence."

Another key change came with the Freedmen's Bureau and their drive to build schools. Before the Civil War, no Southern state maintained a public education system. Northerners viewed education as essential to both political and economic progress. Many Northerners believed that nonslaveholding whites supported secession because they could not dissect the misleading rhetoric of slaveholding elites. African Americans, in particular, viewed education as essential. Beginning in contraband camps during the war, freed people sought out literacy. Denied to them as slaves, literacy and higher education promised a life beyond the fields and satisfied many people's desire to read the Bible themselves. People of all ages lined up at churches and schools where instruction was available throughout the day and usually well into the evening. Despite complaints from white Southerners about the cost, public education proved one of the lasting accomplishments of Reconstruction-era governments.

The eagerness with which black Americans embraced their new lives as full citizens of the United States manifested itself in public celebrations of Emancipation Day and the Fourth of July. The first of these events began during the war itself, in Union-occupied territory on the Sea Islands of South Carolina where Union general Thomas Wentworth Higginson listened to a crowd of freed people spontaneously burst into the national anthem when the flag was raised. "I never saw anything so electric; it made all other words cheap . . . it seemed the choked voice of a race at last unloosed." Higginson captured the people's awareness of their fuller lives as free men and women. "Just think of it; the first day they had ever had a country, the first flag they had ever seen which promised anything to their people." Such celebrations formed the bedrock of an emerging black culture. The most enduring of these events, "Juneteenth," began in Texas as a commemoration of the war's end and evolved into a celebration of African American freedom that continues today.

The parades and festivals that accompanied these events provided an opportunity for community leaders—teachers, ministers, and politicians—to speak on themes both historical and contemporary. The messages they broadcast varied by place, gender, class position, and political ideology. Some emphasized cooperation with whites, whereas others preached self-help. **Martin Delaney**, the highest-ranking black officer during the Civil War, told a South Carolina audience in 1865, "I tell you slavery is over, and shall never return again. We have now 200,000 of our men well drilled in arms and used to War fare and I tell you it is with you and them that slavery shall not come back again." Some spoke through the language of religion and salvation, whereas others used the secular language of rights and law. Regardless of their differences, all of the speakers emphasized that black people would remain a permanent and progressive force for change and democracy within America. Rather than distancing themselves from the past, Southern African Americans proudly remembered the perseverance of their ancestors through generations of slavery. Anthropologists such as Zora Neale Hurston collected the stories that emerged in this era, a blending of old African motifs and legends in New World settings. The rabbit trickster so central to West African stories played a key role in the legends of the antebellum and postbellum South as "Brer Rabbit" before being incorporated into American culture as Bugs Bunny in the 20th century.

The festivals through which black Americans celebrated emancipation and Union victory also provided an opportunity for political organization. The Union League emerged as the most important institutional support for black politics. Started during the war by the Republican Party, Union League Clubs became social and political centers in many of the North's largest cities. After the war, the Leagues transformed into a grassroots movement that helped black Southerners organize themselves politically. Albion Tourgée, a Northern lawyer who lived in North Carolina during Reconstruction, wrote a famous novel, *A Fool's Errand*, that chronicled his experiences with Reconstruction. He described the Union Leagues as intended to "[cultivate] . . . an unbounded devotion for the flag in the hearts of the embryonic citizens, and [keep] alive the fire of patriotism in the hearts of the old Union element." The "fool" who comes South in the novel failed to appreciate the depth of hostility manifested by white Southerners against both their black neighbors and Northerners who came south. As Tourgée noted, a more farsighted man might have seen the organization of black citizens and voters as a "grim portent" of the conflict to come.

Even though the Civil War ended the split in the U.S. economy between free and slave labor, it did not equalize wages between the two sections or between the races. The South replaced slavery with a low-wage, free-labor system; and within that, African Americans consistently received lower pay for equivalent work done by white workers. Most black Southerners remained agricultural workers, but very few worked their own land. Instead, Southerners expanded a prewar practice called *sharecropping* in which landless workers signed contracts to take up residence and farm plots of land, often on property belonging to former slaveholders. In exchange for leasing land, property owners claimed 50 percent or more of the profits at harvest time. When sharecropping first came into use, it met the needs of property owners who required labor to farm the land but had no money with which to pay wages and workers who wanted more autonomy. **Sharecroppers** set their own schedules and supervised themselves in the field, but crucially it was usually landowners who chose the crop.

All across the Deep South and much of Arkansas, Tennessee, and North Carolina, that choice was cotton. Merchants, among the few actors in the postwar Southern economic system with access to credit, insisted on receiving cotton. The changes in the global cotton market, however, produced price fluctuations and great uncertainty for growers. Adding to the structural problems, white landowners exploited their laborers and merchants squeezed them on prices for goods and supplies. Egypt and India entered the global cotton market during the Civil War, adding competition and uncertainty for U.S. producers. As a result, sharecropping quickly trapped farmers in cycles of debt. Most signed the contracts hoping to produce enough to clear a surplus and over time accumulate the money to buy their own land. This rarely happened, and tenant farming dominated the South for the next 50 years. The results ensured overuse and poor treatment of Southern lands, a stunted regional economy, and little progress for African American farmers. As Georges Clemenceau, who toured the country in the late 1860s, observed, "The real misfortune of the negro race is in owning no land of its own.

There cannot be real emancipation for men who do not possess at least a small portion of the soil."

Republican Governments in the Postwar South

The Republican state governments established after the constitutional conventions in 1867–1868 were fragile and awkward alliances between groups with widely divergent interests. Black Southerners represented by far the largest component of the party. They wanted to receive a genuinely fair opportunity to perform work, buy land, gain an education, and live independent lives. White Northern Republicans, labeled "carpetbaggers" by conservatives because they assumed Northerners were only coming South to make quick money, focused on economic development. As the national party shifted to support black voting, its Southern wing did so as well, although this was never a priority for the leaders who represented the region in Congress and state houses. Native white Southerners proved the most troublesome part of the coalition. They had to brave the scorn of fellow whites when they joined the party. Usually prewar Whigs or wartime Unionists, white Southerners rarely came to the party with any interest in black voting or civil rights. Instead, they rejected the Democrats as the party that had led the region into secession and war and hoped that a Republican commitment to free labor would create a firm foundation for the new South. Democrats eagerly exploited the tensions within the Republican Party.

In those states with well-established free black communities before the Civil War, black voters demonstrated a diversity of political opinion. Charleston, Savannah, and New Orleans all included independent, educated, and prosperous communities of free people of color, many of whom carried into the postwar world conservative values on economics and community leadership. The split within black communities can be seen clearly in the case of Mobile, Alabama. After the Union navy captured the port city in August 1864, enslaved people flooded into it seeking freedom. Following the initial flush of enthusiasm in the late 1860s, a deep division opened within the black community. On one hand, well-educated, middle-class blacks pursued a moderate politics focused mostly on economic recovery and the protection of property. To achieve these goals, they advocated cooperation with white Southerners who worked with the Republicans. A larger group, mostly freed people, pushed more aggressively for the protection of civil rights and education, and they did so without white allies. At a volatile moment in summer 1866, a group of black leaders of "the better class," according to the city's conservative paper, approached the mayor to "place themselves on record as good law abiding citizens" and commit themselves to helping suppress any disturbances caused by "either Yankee agitators or New Orleans negroes."

In many places, white conservatives had initially boycotted elections that resulted from the constitutional conventions of 1867–1868. Hoping to undermine the legitimacy of these new governments, they succeeded only in hastening Republican dominance. In other states, some conservatives made alliances with Republicans to create coalition governments. But the 1872 national elections, in which Ulysses S. Grant was reelected despite substantial opposition within his own party, revealed a weakness that Democrats longed to exploit. Beginning in 1873, white conservatives returned to the political system and used charges of corruption and profligacy to defeat the Republicans. Both charges contained some merit—Republican legislators in the South, like those of both parties in state governments all across the country, were susceptible to the bribes and favors of the rich and well connected. The wide scale of corruption within Grant's administration had even threatened his reelection. Also, the policies that Republicans implemented—especially public education—required new taxes. Before the war, slaveholders and large property owners shouldered most of the tax burden; but with no slave property to tax, postwar state governments imposed property taxes on a much broader range of people. Even though the children of white property owners benefited from public education, they condemned the taxes required to pay for them. Democrats capitalized on these policy disputes and campaigned vigorously on the platform of white supremacy to retake state governments. In Virginia, the leaders of the "straight-out" ticket, which refused to compromise with moderate Republicans, explained that "to save the state, we must make the issue *White and Black* race against race and canvass red hot—the position must be made so odious that no decent white man can support the radical ticket and look a gentleman in the face." In Louisiana, Alabama, and other Southern states, this approach yielded electoral victories for Democrats in 1874, 1875, and 1876.

Cotton, Merchants, and the Lien

In 1865, the Southern United States was part of a region, extending south through Central America and the Caribbean and into northeastern Brazil, where plantation agriculture predominated. In the United States, cotton predominated; in the Caribbean, sugar; and in Brazil, coffee (Figure 15.1). This style of agriculture required huge plots of land, a large labor force, and high volumes of capital and credit. The plantation system changed but did not disappear after the Civil War. The major change entailed the use of tenant labor or sharecropping in place of the gang labor used under slavery, but land continued to be owned in large allotments and management functioned as it had before

COTTON PRODUCTION PROSPERED   Despite the numerous obstacles to cotton production, Southern river and ocean ports looked much as they had before the Civil War, with bales of cotton stacked and ready for transport, only now into an increasingly competitive global market.

FIGURE 15.1 ▲ **U.S. cotton prices, 1850–1900** The stable and lucrative cotton market changed significantly because of the Civil War. Responding to the Confederate embargo on cotton sales, England and France turned to new suppliers in Asia and the Middle East, which drove prices down for the remainder of the century.

the war. Even though many sharecroppers worked with some autonomy, landowners determined crop choices, fertilizer use, and harvest dates.

Even with the scattered residential pattern typical of the postwar era and the substantial effort made by sharecroppers to claim ownership of the crop, landowning planters continued to dominate Southern agriculture. They did so partly through the effective control of the **crop lien**, which represented farm workers' claim to ownership of the crops they raised. In Georgia, North Carolina, and Tennessee, the state supreme courts all ruled that the portion of crops given to a sharecropper constituted a wage. This removed from the sharecroppers any legal claim over the crops that they planted, raised, and harvested.

One of the few groups of workers to exercise some control over labor conditions and wages were sugar workers. Sugar's value had spurred Europeans' initial effort to import millions of Africans to the New World. Sugar growing and especially the process of harvesting earned an infamous reputation as the most deadly agricultural work in the Americas. It also required significant skill. Because the sugar cane had to be harvested at exactly the right moment and quickly processed, those workers with knowledge of the crop possessed more leverage to negotiate better terms with their employers. In the decade after emancipation, sugar workers—mostly in Louisiana's southern parishes—used politics and collective action to halt wage cuts and pursued the right to produce garden plots. Even after the Democrats regained power in the states, black sugar workers stayed their ground. Several large strikes in the early 1880s, some with white and black workers cooperating, laid the ground for the broader organization of workers under the **Knights of Labor** at the end of the decade. A white supremacist regime gained power in the state in the 1880s and used violence to crush black resistance. In the other major sugar-producing country in the hemisphere—Cuba—the post-emancipation story evolved differently. By the 1880s, when Cuba's emancipation took full effect, sugar work was not done exclusively by people of African descent. Black Cubans, mixed-race Cubans, and more recent Spanish immigrants all labored together, and their solidarity as workers undercut the use of racism that had been so effective in Louisiana. The comparatively stronger and more diverse community of Cuban sugar workers revealed another route that emancipation could take in the Americas.

Because sharecropping allowed white property owners to make their money from land, and related merchant work, it discouraged them from investing in industrial development. Nonetheless, between 1860 and 1880, the number of manufacturing establishments in the South increased from 30,000 to 50,000; and from 1880 to 1900, they grew from 50,000 to nearly 120,000, although this was still significantly lower than the Northern total from 1860. The failure to build factories in the Reconstruction-era South was not for lack of trying. The Republicans who assumed power in Southern states in the late 1860s and 1870s set economic development as their number one goal. The most important vital element of this plan was the railroad. Northern Republicans especially had a mystical faith in the railroad's ability to spur development of all sorts. As a Tennessee Republican asserted, "A free and living Republic [will] spring up in the track of the railroad as inevitably, as surely as grass and flowers follow in the spring." Unfortunately, Southern states and Southern investors could not meet the capital demands of new railroad construction. Northern and foreign investors found more lucrative and less risky places to put their money, and despite significant public attention, few new lines were built. What the fever for railroad construction did spur was corruption in state governments. Having perfected their skills on Northern legislatures in the prewar and wartime era—an old saying noted that the Pennsylvania Railroad could do anything with that state's legislature that it wanted except refine it—the lobbyists and agents who came South gained support among legislators by distributing discounted company stock. Frequent charges of corruption weakened Republicans at the polls. Other Republican policies did more to earn the support of their constituents, most importantly Republican efforts to give sharecroppers and tenant farmers control over crop liens.

STUDY QUESTIONS FOR RECONSTRUCTION IN THE SOUTH, 1866–1876

1. What was the experience of Reconstruction like for freed people in the South?
2. How did they protect their interests? How did whites seek to subvert those interests?

◼ THE END OF RECONSTRUCTION, 1877

For most of the 100 years following the end of Reconstruction, historians described the period as its contemporary white critics did—as the unconscionable elevation of blacks to positions of power from which they deprived whites of their rights. Sympathetic to

Southern whites and grounded in openly racist assumptions about the moral and intellectual inferiority of black people, these historians promoted a factually inaccurate and deeply compromised view of the era as one that attempted too much and failed. Thanks to a fundamentally different attitude about the meaning of race and a generation of research, historians today hold a nearly opposite view. They regard Congressional Reconstruction as well intentioned and appropriate to the situation. In their view, Reconstruction failed because the federal government did not persevere against Southern white resistance. The demise of Reconstruction—defined as the end of Republican governments in the region—came because of forces both internal and external to the South. The changes in how historians have accounted for that end and the meanings they have attached to it reveal how long it took America to outgrow the racial and political values of the era.

The Ku Klux Klan and Reconstruction Violence

The bitterest and most violent opponents of Reconstruction, and black freedom more generally, emerged at the very start of the era. In late 1865, a small group of men gathered in Pulaski, Tennessee, and organized the **Ku Klux Klan**. Membership in the group spread by word of mouth across the state and soon through the region. Klan members made denying African Americans any legitimate role in the public sphere their principle goal. As a white newspaper enthusiastically reported about the Memphis chapter in 1868, "it is rapidly organizing wherever the insolent negro, the malignant white traitor to his race and the infamous squatter are plotting to make the South utterly unfit for the residence of the decent white man. . . . It is purely defensive, and for the protection of the white race. . . . It will arrest the progress of that secret negro conspiracy which has for its object the

KU KLUX KLAN The Ku Klux Klan, a terrorist group bent on reestablishing white supremacy after the end of slavery, came to dominate many regions of the South. They pursued black leaders of all stripes—politicians, ministers, businessmen, and teachers—and their white allies with brutal violence.

THE LOUISIANA MURDERS—GATHERING THE DEAD AND WOUNDED.—[See Page 396.]

COLFAX MASSACRE   The Colfax Massacre embodied the ultimately successful strategy used in Louisiana, Mississippi, and South Carolina to drive the last Republicans from the region. The failure of local, state, and federal authorities to find any justice for the victims stands as one of the worst tragedies of Reconstruction.

establishment of negro domination." They also targeted white Republicans—especially native white Southerners who cooperated with the party—for their efforts to build an interracial democracy in the South. Klan members whipped, beat, burnt, and killed all manner of community leaders through the South. They targeted ministers, teachers, political leaders, and successful businessmen or farmers. The high point of Klan-related violence came in response to the Reconstruction Acts and to the prominent role played by Africans Americans in the reorganization of Southern life between 1868 and 1871.

Klan violence grew so public and so extreme that Congress finally took action. In 1870–1871, Republicans passed a series of laws, collectively known as the Force Acts, designed to impede the operation of the Ku Klux Klan. They did this by punishing as a federal crime any attempt to obstruct a person in the practice of a designated civil right. One of the Klan's most effective weapons was intimidation of black voters. The Enforcement Acts targeted this practice directly by designating as conspiracies any attempts to coerce black men at the polls or deny them access to the vote. Congress created the Department of Justice and tasked it with bringing cases against those men who used violence to enforce white supremacy. Finally, in 1871, Congress held hearings at which both victims and alleged members of the Klan told their stories to a national audience. Although the Justice Department was underfunded and less energetic in their prosecutions than Southern Republicans wished, they initiated thousands of prosecutions and secured hundreds of convictions across the South, driving the Klan underground.

Even with their success against the Klan, Northerners did not eradicate violence in Southern life. Klan members became, in effect, an arm of the Democratic Party. In Louisiana, the Knights of the White Camellia and the White League superseded the Klan. Mississippi saw the creation of "rifle clubs." Regardless of the terminology, after 1871, Southern whites reorganized their attack on Republican governments in the states. Louisiana saw a particularly bitter struggle. White conservatives in the state opposed the election of Henry Warmoth as governor, a northern lawyer and Civil War officer who operated mostly as a party of one, appointing men loyal to him alone and throwing the state into chaos. He was succeeded by William Kellogg, a radical Republican even more noxious to Louisiana Democrats. Kellogg was aided by a sizeable body of white Southerners, including James Longstreet, Lee's beloved Corps commander, and the most famous ex-Confederate Republican. Louisiana Democrats contested the election of Kellogg in 1872, setting up a rival government; and when the federal government recognized Kellogg as the duly elected state leader, they turned to violence as the means to unseat him.

All across Louisiana in 1873, conservatives began organizing themselves and forcing Republicans out of office. Sometimes, they simply intimidated the local sheriffs, judges, and tax assessors who comprised the body of local government in the state. Other times, they committed violence against officeholders or the families. The most notorious episode involved an attack on the northern parish town of Colfax. Residents of the town learned of the plan in advance, and perhaps 200 black men from the area converged on the courthouse on the morning of Easter Sunday, 1873. Armed with a variety of weapons, they came to protect the men they had elected. A white militia composed of several hundred men organized in neighboring Montgomery rode into town and drove the defenders back into the courthouse, which they set afire. The attackers shot men as they escaped and captured more, executing 37 that evening. By nightfall, they had killed around 150 in the worst racial massacre in U.S. history. The lesson to Republicans around the state was clear—white Democrats would stop at nothing to purge them from office. Although Kellogg hung on until 1876, Republican government around the state slowly gave way in the face of this terrorism. Whites in other Southern states observed the success of Louisiana conservatives and many adopted the same strategy.

Northern Weariness and Northern Conservatism

Governor Kellogg's metropolitan police force helped keep order in New Orleans, but without the support of the federal government, he could do little to protect fellow Republicans in outlying parishes. In a few isolated instances, President Grant sent U.S. troops back into the South to help quell disorder. Interventions such as these exposed Grant to the charge that his administration had failed to secure the peace he promised in 1868. It opened Republicans to criticism from fiscal conservatives about the continuing expense of Reconstruction and, more cynically, to those who felt that black Southerners needed to defend themselves from whites or suffer the consequences. White Southerners also mastered the art of spreading misinformation; they convinced many Northerners that black people could not be trusted to participate

WESTERN MIGRATION By settling the long-standing political conflicts over the future of slavery, the Civil War set in motion massive white migration into the Western states and territories. This process brought white Americans into more intimate contact, both benign and malignant, with native peoples all across the Western landscape.

in democratic governance. The violence in Mississippi in 1875 drove the governor, a young white Northerner named Adelbert Ames, to request federal troops. Grant had responded positively in 1874, sending a small contingent of troops to Vicksburg. The situation deteriorated even more the following year. Ames's telegram to the White House explained the dire situation: "I am in great danger of losing my life. Not only that, all the leading Republicans, who have not run away, in danger. . . . The [White] league here have adopted a new policy, which is to kill the leaders and spare the colored people, unless they 'rise'." This time Grant worried more about weakening Republicans at the polls in the North than with defending Republicans in the South. "The whole public are tired out with these annual autumnal outbreaks in the South . . . [and] are ready now to condemn any interference on the part of the Government," he told his attorney general. Grant, who had conquered Vicksburg, Mississippi, for the Union in 1863, sent no troops this time.

Federal courts likewise reflected Northern impatience with the duration and expense of Reconstruction in their increasing reluctance to support black or Republican plaintiffs. The most important of these cases revolved around the defendants arrested for leading the Colfax Massacre. Unable to secure justice in local courts, federal prosecutors sought a conviction on charges of violating the civil rights of the murdered officeholders. In *United States v. Cruikshank*, the Supreme Court ruled that the Fourteenth Amendment only protected citizens against official state actions and not private violence. Because the massacre's ringleader, William Cruikshank, operated without state sanction, the amendment offered no protection. Cruikshank went free, and in the process, the court dramatically narrowed the scope of protection offered by the Fourteenth Amendment. The *Cruikshank* case was decided in 1876, the same year that a new Republican won the presidency. Rutherford B. Hayes, a Union general like his predecessor Ulysses S. Grant, entered office under a storm of controversy. He secured the office after the contested election of 1876, when Republicans and Democrats clashed over the returns from Louisiana, Florida, and South Carolina (Map 15.3). Both sides agreed to count the presidential ballots for Hayes, but gave Democrats control at the state level. This ended the last three Republican state governments in the South and initiated an era

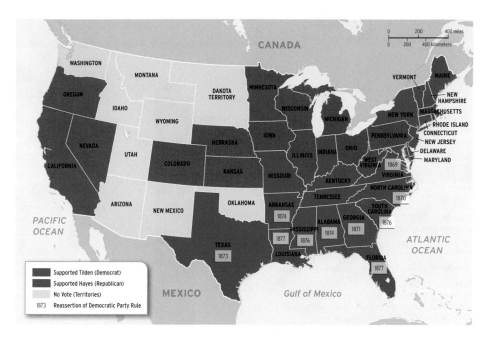

MAP 15.3 ▲ 1876 Presidential Election, by State Although the Republican presidential candidate, Rutherford B. Hayes, was credited with the electoral votes of Louisiana, South Carolina, and Florida, these states all elected Democratic governors and legislatures. This ended the presence of statewide Republican rule in the South and marked the end of political Reconstruction.

of Democratic dominance that lasted for most of the next century. Shortly after his inauguration, Hayes recalled the last few thousand U.S. troops out of the South, officially ending the period of Reconstruction.

Northerners' fatigue with Reconstruction also resulted from their preoccupation with the rapid changes happening in their own region. The wave of city building in the 1840s and 1850s that had developed during the technological boom of that era increased after the war. Immigrants continued to pour into Northern cities where their rapid incorporation changed the political contours of the region. Legislation passed by the dynamic wartime Congress also began to bear fruit. The most important of these was the **Homestead Act**, which allowed families to claim 160 acres of land if they improved it over five years of residence. The bill opened the Western United States—mostly land gained in the Mexican War or through the Louisiana Purchase—to white settlement. Accompanying settlers in the movement west was the nation's first Transcontinental Railroad, which had also been authorized by the 37th Congress. Congressmen, land developers, and businessmen regarded the railroad line, which reduced travel time between the Atlantic and Pacific coasts from months to days, as the nation's most important economic development measure.

As the Union Pacific laid track, Indian communities of the West resisted. During the Civil War, Indians exploited the opportunity of a distracted United States and undermanned forts to reestablish a position of strength. With the coming of peace in 1865,

TIMELINE 1865–1888

AMERICA	YEAR	THE WORLD
Jan Congress proposes 13th Amendment **Mar** Congress establishes Bureau of Refugees, Freedmen, and Abandoned Lands **Apr** Robert E. Lee's Army surrenders to Ulysses S. Grant at Appomattox, VA **Apr** Abraham Lincoln assassinated by John Wilkes Booth **Apr** Joseph Johnston's Army surrenders to William T. Sherman at Durham, NC **Oct** Morant Bay Rebellion in Jamaica **Dec** Ratification of 13th Amendment abolishes slavery in United States Southern state legislatures pass "Black Codes" Ku Klux Klan organized in Pulaski, TN	**1865**	
Feb President Andrew Johnson vetoes Freedmen's Bureau reauthorization bill **Mar** President Andrew Johnson vetoes 1866 Civil Rights Act **May** Memphis race riot **Jun** Congress proposes 14th Amendment **Jul** Congress overrides Johnson's veto of Freedmen's Bureau Act and Civil Rights Act **Jul** New Orleans race riot	**1866**	Austro–Prussian War
Mar Congress passes Reconstruction Acts Southern state constitutional conventions begin across the South with mixed-race delegates	**1867**	Karl Marx publishes *Das Kapital* Russia sells Alaska to United States Dominion of Canada established
Feb House of Representatives votes to impeach Andrew Johnson **Apr** Senate votes not to convict Andrew Johnson **Jun** Ratification of 14th Amendment establishes rights and due process for citizens **Nov** Republican Ulysses S. Grant elected president	**1868**	Meiji Restoration in Japan begins rapid modernization
Feb Congress proposes 15th Amendment **May** Transcontinental railroad completed	**1869**	Suez Canal, built by French, opens in Egypt
Feb Ratification of 15th Amendment prohibits discrimination in voting on the basis of race or previous condition of servitude **May** U.S. Congress passes "Force Act" giving it power to crack down on the Ku Klux Klan (followed by complementary legislation later in 1870 and 1871)	**1870**	Franco–Prussian War begins War of the Triple Alliance ends with at least 60% of Paraguayan population dead

a newly expanded, trained, and disciplined U.S. Army moved west. The Sioux, in particular, had challenged U.S. authority during the war, culminating in a wide-scale uprising in Minnesota that was violently suppressed by the army. Military tribunals had originally sentenced 303 men to death for crimes against settlers during the Minnesota conflicts, but Lincoln commuted the death sentences for 264 prisoners and allowed the execution of 39 others. After the war, Western Indians faced an emboldened army without the aid of a sympathetic executive. The shift away from Indians' hunting and low-impact farming practices to the more intensive style of American agriculture caused significant change throughout the Great Plains and the West, and within a few decades spurred a preservation movement aimed at balancing the development of the region and conserving its natural beauty.

Congress holds Ku Klux Klan Hearings to assess and publicize violence against freed people and their white allies in the South	**1871**	Brazil passes gradual emancipation law
		Rome declared capital of unified Italy
		Franco–Prussian War ends, Napoleon III overthrown, and Third Republic of France established
		Rising of the Paris Commune
		Germany victory in Franco–Prussian War yields unified Germany
Nov Republican Ulysses S. Grant reelected president First National Park created at Yellowstone in Wyoming Territory	**1872**	
Apr Colfax Massacre in northern Louisiana kills approximately 150 people	**1873**	
Nov Democrats gain control of U.S. House of Representatives	**1874**	
Mar Congress passes 1875 Civil Rights Act	**1875**	
Mar Supreme Court issues *United States v. Cruikshank* verdict, which restricted meaning of 14th Amendment to protection against actions taken by state actors George Armstrong Custer and his forces are defeated at "Battle of Little Bighorn"	**1876**	
Mar Rutherford B. Hayes inaugurated president; recalls last U.S. troops from the South Democrats seize control of last three Southern states (Florida, South Carolina, and Louisiana)	**1877**	
Albion Tourgée publishes *A Fool's Errand*	**1879**	
	1886	Cuba abolishes slavery
	1888	Brazil abolishes slavery

Legacies of Reconstruction

Before John Muir, one of the most important environmental activists of the era, gained fame as a protector and champion of the American West, he toured the South during Reconstruction. Leaving his home in Indianapolis in early 1867, Muir walked south to Florida, observing flora, fauna, and the human wildlife along the way. In addition to wry observations about the "long-haired ex-guerillas" of the Tennessee and North Carolina mountains, Muir chronicled the attitudes of the white and black citizens with whom he interacted on his trip. In Georgia, he observed, "the traces of war are not only apparent on the broken fields, burnt fences, mills, and woods ruthlessly slaughtered, but also on the countenances of the people. A few years after a forest has been burned, another generation of bright and happy trees arises. . . . So with the people of this war-field. Happy, unscarred, and unclouded youth is growing up around the aged, half-consumed, and fallen parents, who bear in sad measure the ineffaceable marks of the farthest-reaching and most infernal of all civilized calamities." The sadness that Muir observed in 1867 had changed to anger a decade later. Southern whites ended Reconstruction embittered against African Americans for the efforts they had made to claim civil rights; contemptuous of the federal government for assistance—however meager—they had given that effort; and deeply suspicious of the open, bipartisan politics that flourished briefly in the 1870s. All three of these attitudes weakened the South over time and encouraged whites to regard the most important political and social goal for their communities as the violent protection of white supremacy.

The unwillingness of federal authorities to enforce the civil rights laws and especially the Fourteenth and Fifteenth Amendments left Southern African Americans isolated, but blacks were never solely victims. From the earliest days of North American slavery, they had resisted the institution, and their actions during and after Reconstruction reveal a similar refusal to be defined by white actions. In early 1866, a group of "colored citizens" in Florida complained to then Secretary of War Grant that "the Civil authoritys here are taking from the Colord People all the fire arms that they find in their Persesion, including Dubble barrel Shot Guns, Pistols of any kind." Without the means of self-defense, they would be reliant on the government for their protection. Years before, Frederick Douglass had observed of black Americans, "It is enough to say, that if a knowledge of the use of arms is desirable in any people, it is desirable in us." As the Florida men who petitioned Ulysses Grant made clear, it remained desirable, sadly, imperative, after the war as well. Perhaps anticipating the day when Northerners would abandon the effort, they closed by noting that "if Congress Do not Stand Squarely up for us, and Make Laws that Will Protect us, over the heads of the States, We are Nothing More than Searfs." Congress did not stand up "squarely," but Southern African Americans forged ahead on their own. They pursued an egalitarian politics through the Republican Party, and many protected and used that vote until the end of the century. They also built communities, churches, schools, and businesses. These institutions and the networks of support and self-improvement that developed among them sustained black Southerners until another struggle against Southern violence produced America's Second Reconstruction—the Civil Rights Movement of the 1950s and 1960s—and the nation finally stood square.

STUDY QUESTIONS FOR THE END OF RECONSTRUCTION, 1877

1. Why did Reconstruction end in 1877?
2. What explains the Northern willingness to abandon the policies they initiated in 1867?

Summary

- In common with Brazil and Cuba, the two other major slave societies in the hemisphere, the American South struggled to reorganize its labor and landholding systems in the wake of emancipation.
- Unlike in those two nations, in America, blacks gained the vote and helped build new systems of public education over the opposition of Southern whites.
- Southerners needed money to rebuild and modernize the region's infrastructure, but stripped of capital by war and relying primarily on agricultural enterprises, Southerners had little success attracting American or European funds.
- Conservative Southern whites used both voting and violence, the latter formalized in the Ku Klux Klan and white militias, to defeat the Republican governments that represented such a sharp break with the region's past and end Reconstruction.
- Northerners, eager to develop the West and extend American influence within the Caribbean and across the oceans and weary of the expense and trouble of the South, consented to a return to Democratic rule, but the community building and education already enacted by African Americans created the networks that sustained them through the years of Jim Crow.

Key Terms and People

Black codes *513*

crop lien *527*

Delaney, Martin *523*

Fifteenth Amendment *517*

Fourteenth Amendment *515*

Freedmen's Bureau *509*

Homestead Act *533*

Knights of Labor *527*

Ku Klux Klan *529*

sharecroppers *524*

Stevens, Thaddeus *518*

Thirteenth Amendment *512*

Reviewing Chapter 15

1. How did the United States' experience of emancipation and nation building compare to other countries in the mid-19th century?
2. Was the Civil War and Reconstruction a "watershed" in American life? Explain what changed and what remained consistent.

Further Reading

Blight, David W. *Race and Reunion: The Civil War in American Memory*. Cambridge, MA: Belknap Press, 2001. The fullest account of changes in the memory of the Civil War, especially the willingness of white Northerners to marginalize the history of slavery and emancipation in the conflict.

Foner, Eric. *Reconstruction: America's Unfinished Revolution, 1863–1877*. New York: Harper and Row, 1988. A comprehensive history of Reconstruction with particular attention to labor and emancipation in the South.

Litwack, Leon F. *Been in the Storm So Long: The Aftermath of Slavery*. New York: Vintage, 1980. A vivid chronicle of the experience of emancipation for black Southerners.

Perman, Michel. *The Road to Redemption: Southern Politics, 1869–1879*. Chapel Hill: University of North Carolina Press, 1984. The clearest analysis of the national- and state-level politics that produced the end of Reconstruction.

Ransom, Roger L. and Richard Sutch. *One Kind of Freedom: The Economic Consequences of Emancipation*. Cambridge, England: Cambridge University Press, 1977. A comprehensive economic analysis of the effects of the Civil War on the South.

Silber, Nina. *The Romance of Reunion: Northerners and the South, 1865–1900*. Chapel Hill: University of North Carolina Press, 1993. An elegant study that emphasizes the cultural dimensions of the Northern shift toward reconciliation after the Civil War.

America In The World
PEOPLE, GOODS, IDEAS AND PRACTICES

CHAPTER 15: Reconstructing America 1865–1877

NORTH
AMERICA

to
EUROPE

ATLANTIC
OCEAN

from
BRAZIL

Cotton

Brazilian Coffee

Public education

Washington,
D.C.

Freedmen's Bureau

Industrialization

Chicago

Sharecropping

Ku Klux Klan
violence (1868)

Gulf of
Mexico

Omaha

Homestead Act settlers

Transcontinental Railroad

PACIFIC
OCEAN

↑	Goods
↑	Ideas
↑	People

500 miles

0   250   500 kilometers
0   250   500

PRIMARY SOURCES FOR CHAPTER 15
RECONSTRUCTING AMERICA, 1865–1877

SOURCE 15.1
Jourdon Anderson, Letter to P. H. Anderson (August 7, 1865)

Jourdon Anderson was one of the many ex-slaves who made their way north out of Tennessee and Kentucky into southern Ohio after the Civil War. The confused state of the labor market in the South led some masters to try to recruit former slaves back to their property to work as paid laborers.

Source: Lydia Maria Child, *The Freedmen's Book* (Boston: Tickenor and Fields, 1865), 265–67. Also see http://historymatters.gmu.edu/d/6369/.

Dayton, Ohio, August 7, 1865

To My Old Master, Colonel P. H. Anderson, Big Spring, Tennessee

Sir: I got your letter and was glad to find you had not forgotten Jourdon, and that you wanted me to come back and live with you again, promising to do better for me than anybody else can. I have often felt uneasy about you. I thought the Yankees would have hung you long before this for harboring Rebs they found at your house. I suppose they never heard about your going to Col. Martin's to kill the Union soldier that was left by his company in their stable. Although you shot at me twice before I left you, I did not want to hear of your being hurt, and am glad you are still living. It would do me good to go back to the dear old home again and see Miss Mary and Miss Martha and Allen, Esther, Green, and Lee. Give my love to them all, and tell them I hope we will meet in the better world, if not in this. I would have gone back to see you all when I was working in the Nashville Hospital, but one of the neighbors told me Henry intended to shoot me if he ever got a chance.

I want to know particularly what the good chance is you propose to give me. I am doing tolerably well here; I get $25 a month, with victuals and clothing; have a comfortable home for Mandy,—the folks here call her Mrs. Anderson),—and the children—Milly, Jane and Grundy—go to school and are learning well; the teacher says Grundy has a head for a preacher. They go to Sunday-School, and Mandy and me attend church regularly. We are kindly treated; sometimes we overhear others saying, "Them colored people were slaves" down in Tennessee. The children feel hurt when they hear such remarks, but I tell them it was no disgrace in Tennessee to belong to Col. Anderson. Many darkies would have been proud, as I used to be, to call you master. Now, if you will write and say what wages you will give me, I will be better able to decide whether it would be to my advantage to move back again.

As to my freedom, which you say I can have, there is nothing to be gained on that score, as I got my free papers in 1864 from the Provost-Marshal-General of the Department of Nashville. Mandy says she would be afraid to go back without some proof that you are sincerely disposed to treat us justly and kindly; and we have concluded to test your sincerity by asking you to send us our wages for the time we served you. This will make us forget and forgive old scores, and rely on your justice and friendship in the future. I served you faithfully for thirty-two years and Mandy twenty years. At twenty-five dollars a month for me, and two dollars a week for Mandy, our earnings would amount to eleven thousand six hundred and eighty dollars. Add to this the interest for the time our wages has been kept back and deduct what you paid for our clothing and three doctor's visits to me, and pulling a tooth for Mandy, and the balance will show what we are in justice entitled to. Please send the money by Adams Express, in care of V. Winters, Esq., Dayton, Ohio. If you fail to pay us for faithful labors in the past we can have little faith in your promises in the future. We trust the good Maker has opened your eyes to the wrongs which you and your fathers have done to me and my fathers, in making us toil for you for generations without recompense. Here I draw my wages every Saturday night, but in Tennessee there was never any pay-day for the Negroes any more than for the horses and cows. Surely there will be a day of reckoning for those who defraud the laborer of his hire.

In answering this letter please state if there would be any safety for my Milly and Jane, who are now grown up and both good-looking girls. You know how it was with Matilda and Catherine. I would rather stay here and starve, and die if it comes to that, than have my girls brought to shame by the violence and wickedness of their young masters. You will also please state if there has been any schools opened for the colored children in your neighborhood, the great desire of my life now is to give my children an education, and have them form virtuous habits.

P.S. —Say howdy to George Carter, and thank him for taking the pistol from you when you were shooting at me.

From your old servant,

Jourdon Anderson

WORKING WITH SOURCES

1. What do Anderson's comments reveal about the economic knowledge of former slaves?

2. What are the attributes of freedom that Anderson identifies as most important?

3. Explain the new power dynamic between Anderson and his former master. How would each of the participants have understood it?

SOURCE 15.2

Visual Document: Thomas Nast, Andrew Johnson's Reconstruction in Harper's Weekly (September 1, 1866)

During the summer of 1866, Memphis and New Orleans experienced horrible race riots, in which whites murdered dozens of blacks indiscriminately. Many Northerners felt that Johnson's lenient policies fomented a recalcitrant and unapologetic white South. Thomas Nast drew political cartoons for *Harper's Weekly*, the most widely read periodical in the country. He was an early critic of Johnson and a strong proponent for a Reconstruction that treated African Americans fairly.

Source: Ben and Beatrice Goldstein Foundation Collection/Library of Congress.

WORKING WITH SOURCES

1. What is Nast's critique of Johnson's Reconstruction policy?

2. What do the images around the margins of the cartoon portray as Johnson's responsibility for the riots?

3. Why does Nast portray the lone black individual as a wounded Union soldier?

SOURCE 15.3

José Inácio Barros Cobra, Excerpts from "Slave Property Is As Sacred as Any Other" (July 21, 1871)

After the emancipation of slaves in the United States, Brazilian and Cuban slaveholders began to consider ways to manage the end of slavery in their own countries (the last remaining slave nations in the western hemisphere). In Brazil, the parliament considered "Free Birth" legislation, which would have freed the newborns of enslaved women as a way to gradually transition to free labor. Even this modest proposal generated criticism from slaveholders, who worked to delay the process. Barros Cobra was a member of the Brazilian parliament who delivered the speech below opposing free-birth legislation.

Source: Robert Conrad, *Children of God's Fire: A Documentary History of Black Slavery in Brazil* (University Park: Pennsylvania State University Press, 1984), 436–46.

Gentlemen, it is true that in this country there exists a point of view that demands a solution to the great problem of slavery. The existence of this opinion is undeniable in the abstract, in principle; fortunately there is not one Brazilian who wishes the permanent preservation of slavery in the Empire; in this sense there is unanimous agreement: the cause of abolition is definitely decided upon.

To the honor of the Brazilian Empire, we do not need to overcome the difficulties, prejudices, and animosities against which the legislators of France and the United States had to struggle; the natural generosity of the Brazilian character, the religious spirit and the principles of morality and civilization decided the theoretical question a long time ago. . . . When we attempt to solve this great question, we should not be motivated by abstractions, philosophical concepts, or sentimental inspirations, but

rather by the high and venerable interests that are associated with it and that constitute the foundations of Brazilian society [*hear! hear!*]; much may be said, much may be desired in this regard, but a study and practical knowledge of our circumstances and of what can reasonably be done are what should guide us, in order that we may go forward securely. [*Hear! Hear!*] Gentlemen, I reflected very serenely about how we might most conveniently solve this important problem, which demands full attention and challenges the deepest meditation. I considered it with total calm, far from my legislative responsibilities, and with my mind uncluttered by other concerns. Momentarily the idea of freeing the womb seemed an acceptable method (to this chamber I confess the feelings of my inner conscience); however, further thought convinced me that this idea, which at first glance is so appealing, is the most dangerous way to go in this country. [*Hear! Hear!*]

History, that great preceptress of experience, shows us that almost all the nations that tried to abolish slavery gradually did not achieve this, but were instead forced to rush headlong and disastrously toward total abolition; this was the experience of England, France, and Portugal herself. A contrary example, such as that of the United States, may be mentioned; but none of those states had a tenth of the slave population which we have, and so cannot constitute an argument in favor of the government's bill.[1] The illustrious special committee asked in their report: "What reasons do we have to fear that in our country things will go differently from the way they did in countries where, after experiencing the same exaggerated fears, the same transformations were brought about?"

But those countries did not find themselves in circumstances identical to ours; they did not possess the number of slaves that we unfortunately possess, nor was agriculture almost the sole basis of their private and public wealth; nor like us did they have a free population spread out over an immense territory and, in terrifying contrast, a slave population concentrated in the main production centers. These different circumstances call for different ways to cure the evil. [*Hear! Hear!*] . . . Brazil's circumstances in this regard are very special, and we must not lose sight of them. . . . The slave born of a slave woman, who belongs to her master in virtue of principles sanctified in civil legislation, represents capital and is an instrument of labor; however, it is understood that the value of the slave is precisely dependent upon the services that he can perform [*hear! hear!*]; nobody would want an unused slave for the mere joy of possessing him. The capital here is represented by the instrument of labor, whose value is in direct proportion to the greater or lesser usefulness which as such he can render; in just the same way that the price of a slave is more or less, depending upon his capacity and fitness for work.

This being the case, which seems to me undeniable, it is entirely obvious that the intention here is to indemnify the masters with the identical thing that belongs to them by law, and which they cannot be deprived of without receiving full compensation. There is, however, a single difference: they are granted the use of the individual for thirteen years, a usufruct which, according to law, would otherwise belong to them for as long as the slave might live. It seems to me, therefore, that the right to property, sanctified and guaranteed by the Constitution of the Empire, which cannot be taken from the citizen of Brazil without prior indemnification, is in this case confiscated without any indemnification whatsoever, or with a false indemnification, which amounts to the same thing. . . .

It is known that, thanks to the generous and humane character of the Brazilians, slavery among us is so mild that the condition of our slaves is greatly preferable to that of the working classes of some European countries; on the largest agricultural establishments, order and subordination are maintained entirely by means of a prudent system of constant and severe discipline, in which careful preventive measures ordinarily make repression unnecessary. Once the proposed law is enforced, that system cannot be maintained, and it will be seriously and dangerously undermined by the simultaneous existence in those establishments of slave parents and free children, not as an exceptional or accidental situation, but as a regular and permanent reality, and by the unavoidable meddling of the

---

[1]This contention is false. In 1860, Georgia had a slave population of 462,000, which was more than any Brazilian province recorded during that country's entire history.

authorities responsible for enforcement of the law. This situation will awaken in those who remain slaves a dangerous impatience and a terrible hopelessness which must shatter all ties of subordination and respect for their masters....

WORKING WITH SOURCES

1. What lessons does the speaker draw from the American experience?

2. Can you identify any other influences of U.S. emancipation on the discussion here?

3. How does the speaker's treatment of slavery compare to the opinions of U.S. authorities on the subject, such as that of James Henry Hammond, presented in Chapter 13?

SOURCE 15.4

Ku Klux Klan, Letter to Mrs. I. A. Baldwin (1868)

Founded in 1866, the Ku Klux Klan was a terrorist organization devoted to driving black people out of positions of public authority in the South. Its members operated in secret and used all manner of threats and violence to break the political alliances between blacks and whites in the Republican Party and the social institutions built by black Southerners in the postwar years.

Source: Secretary of War, House Executive Document No. 329, 40th Cong., 2nd sess., 19.

Notice has been sent to Mrs. L. A. Baldwin, teacher of freedmen's school No. 1, Bowling Green, Kentucky, with post office dated April 27, 1868, of which the following is a copy:

Mrs. L. A. Baldwin, teacher colored school, Bonding Green, Kentucky:

KU KLUX KLANS!

BLOOD! POISON! POWDER! TORCH!

Leave in five days, or hell's your portion!

Rally, rally, watch your chance,

First blood, first premium K. K. K.

If ball, or torch, or poison fails,

The house beneath you shall be blown to hell, or move you.

K. K. K.

WORKING WITH SOURCES

1. Why would the KKK attack teachers?

2. What threat did education pose to the social order?

3. How would the anonymous nature of the threat delivered to Mrs. L. A. Baldwin affect the social fabric of the Kentucky community in which she lived?

Appendix A

HISTORICAL DOCUMENTS

The Declaration of Independence

When in the course of human events, it becomes necessary for one people to dissolve the political bands which have connected them with another, and to assume, among the powers of the earth, the separate and equal station to which the Laws of Nature and of Nature's God entitle them, a decent respect to the opinions of mankind requires that they should declare the causes which impel them to the separation.

We hold these truths to be self-evident, that all men are created equal, that they are endowed by their Creator with certain unalienable Rights, that among these are life, liberty and the pursuit of happiness. That to secure these rights, governments are instituted among men, deriving their just powers from the consent of the governed; that whenever any form of government becomes destructive of these ends, it is the right of the people to alter or to abolish it, and to institute new Government, laying its foundation on such principles and organizing its powers in such form, as to them shall seem most likely to effect their safety and happiness. Prudence, indeed, will dictate that Governments long established should not be changed for light and transient causes; and, accordingly, all experience hath shown, that mankind are more disposed to suffer, while evils are sufferable, than to right themselves by abolishing the forms to which they are accustomed. But when a long train of abuses and usurpations, pursuing invariably the same object evinces a design to reduce them under absolute despotism, it is their right, it is their duty, to throw off such government, and to provide new guards for their future security. Such has been the patient sufferance of these colonies; and such is now the necessity which constrains them to alter their former systems of government. The history of the present King of Great Britain is a history of repeated injuries and usurpations, all having in direct object the establishment of an absolute tyranny over these States. To prove this, let facts be submitted to a candid world:

He has refused his assent to laws, the most wholesome and necessary for the public good.

He has forbidden his governors to pass laws of immediate and pressing importance, unless suspended in their operation till his assent should be obtained; and, when so suspended, he has utterly neglected to attend to them.

He has refused to pass other laws for the accommodation of large districts of people, unless those people would relinquish the right of representation in the legislature, a right inestimable to them and formidable to tyrants only.

He has called together legislative bodies at places unusual, uncomfortable, and distant from the depository of their public records, for the sole purpose of fatiguing them into compliance with his measures.

He has dissolved representative houses repeatedly, for opposing with manly firmness his invasions on the rights of the people.

He has refused for a long time, after such dissolutions, to cause others to be elected; whereby the legislative powers, incapable of annihilation, have returned to the People at large for their exercise; the State remaining in the mean time exposed to all the dangers of invasion from without, and convulsions within.

He has endeavored to prevent the population of these States; for that purpose obstructing the laws for naturalization of foreigners; refusing to pass others to encourage their migrations hither, and raising the conditions of new appropriations of lands.

He has obstructed the administration of justice, by refusing his assent to laws for establishing judiciary powers.

He has made judges dependent on his will alone, for the tenure of their offices, and the amount and payment of their salaries.

He has erected a multitude of new offices, and sent hither swarms of officers to harass our people, and eat out their substance.

He has kept among us, in times of peace, standing armies without the consent of our legislatures.

He has affected to render the Military independent of, and superior to, the civil power.

He has combined with others to subject us to a jurisdiction foreign to our constitution and unacknowledged by our laws; giving his assent to their acts of pretended legislation:

For quartering large bodies of armed troops among us;

For protecting them, by a mock trial, from punishment for any murders which they should commit on the inhabitants of these States;

For cutting off our trade with all parts of the world;

For imposing taxes on us without our Consent;

For depriving us, in many cases, of the benefits of Trial by Jury;

For transporting us beyond Seas to be tried for pretended offences;

For abolishing the free System of English Laws in a neighbouring Province, establishing therein an Arbitrary government, and enlarging its Boundaries so as to render it at once an example and fit instrument for introducing the same absolute rule into these colonies;

For taking away our charters, abolishing our most valuable laws, and altering fundamentally the forms of our governments;

For suspending our own legislatures, and declaring themselves invested with power to legislate for us in all cases whatsoever.

He has abdicated government here, by declaring us out of his protection and waging war against us.

He has plundered our seas, ravaged our coasts, burnt our towns, and destroyed the lives of our people.

He is at this time transporting large armies of foreign mercenaries to complete the works of death, desolation and tyranny, already begun with circumstances of cruelty and perfidy scarcely paralleled in the most barbarous ages, and totally unworthy the head of a civilized nation.

He has constrained our fellow citizens taken captive on the high seas to bear arms against their country, to become the executioners of their friends and brethren, or to fall themselves by their hands.

He has excited domestic insurrections amongst us, and has endeavored to bring on the inhabitants of our frontiers, the merciless Indian savages, whose known rule of warfare, is an undistinguished destruction of all ages, sexes and conditions.

In every stage of these oppressions we have petitioned for redress in the most humble terms; our repeated petitions have been answered only by repeated injury. A prince whose character is thus marked by every act which may define a tyrant, is unfit to be the ruler of a free people.

Nor have we been wanting in attentions to our British brethren. We have warned them from time to time of attempts by their legislature to extend an unwarrantable jurisdiction over us. We have reminded them of the circumstances of our emigration and settlement here. We have appealed to their native justice and magnanimity, and we have conjured them by the ties of our common kindred to disavow these usurpations, which, would inevitably interrupt our connections and correspondence. They, too, have been deaf to the voice of justice and of consanguinity. We must, therefore, acquiesce in the necessity, which denounces our separation, and hold them, as we hold the rest of mankind, enemies in war, in peace friends.

We, therefore, the representatives of the United States of America, in general Congress, assembled, appealing to the Supreme Judge of the world for the rectitude of our intentions, do, in the name, and by the authority of the good people of these colonies, solemnly publish and declare, that these united colonies are, and of right ought to be free and independent states; that they are absolved from all allegiance to the British Crown, and that all political connection between them and the state of Great Britain, is and ought to be totally dissolved; and that, as free and independent states, they have full power to levy war, conclude peace, contract alliances, establish commerce, and to do all other acts and things which independent states may of right do. And for the support of this declaration, with a firm reliance on the protection of Divine Providence, we mutually pledge to each other our lives, our fortunes and our sacred honor.

The Constitution of the United States of America

We the People of the United States, in Order to form a more perfect Union, establish Justice, insure domestic Tranquility, provide for the common defence, promote the general Welfare, and secure the Blessings of Liberty to ourselves and our Posterity, do ordain and establish this Constitution for the United States of America.

ARTICLE I

Section 1.

All legislative Powers herein granted shall be vested in a Congress of the United States, which shall consist of a Senate and House of Representatives.

Section 2.

The House of Representatives shall be composed of Members chosen every second Year by the People of the several States, and the Electors in each State shall have the Qualifications requisite for Electors of the most numerous Branch of the State Legislature.

No Person shall be a Representative who shall not have attained to the Age of twenty five Years, and been seven Years a Citizen of the United States, and who shall not, when elected, be an Inhabitant of that State in which he shall be chosen.

Representatives and direct Taxes shall be apportioned among the several States which may be included within this Union, according to their respective Numbers, which shall be determined by adding to the whole Number of free Persons, including those bound to Service for a Term of Years, and excluding Indians not taxed, three fifths of all other Persons. The actual Enumeration shall be made within three Years after the first Meeting of the Congress of the United States, and within every subsequent Term of ten Years, in such Manner as they shall by Law direct. The Number of Representatives shall not exceed one for every thirty Thousand, but each State shall have at Least one Representative; and until such enumeration shall be made, the State of New Hampshire shall be entitled to choose three, Massachusetts eight, Rhode-Island and Providence Plantations one, Connecticut five, New York six, New Jersey four, Pennsylvania eight, Delaware one, Maryland six, Virginia ten, North Carolina five, South Carolina five, and Georgia three.

When vacancies happen in the Representation from any State, the Executive Authority thereof shall issue Writs of Election to fill such Vacancies.

The House of Representatives shall choose their Speaker and other Officers; and shall have the sole Power of Impeachment.

Section 3.

The Senate of the United States shall be composed of two Senators from each State, chosen by the Legislature thereof for six Years; and each Senator shall have one Vote.

Immediately after they shall be assembled in Consequence of the first Election, they shall be divided as equally as may be into three Classes. The Seats of the Senators of the first Class shall be vacated at the Expiration of the second Year, of the second Class at the Expiration of the fourth Year, and of the third Class at the Expiration of the sixth Year, so that one third may be chosen every second Year; and if Vacancies happen by Resignation, or otherwise, during the Recess of the Legislature of any State, the Executive thereof may make temporary Appointments until the next Meeting of the Legislature, which shall then fill such Vacancies.

No Person shall be a Senator who shall not have attained to the Age of thirty Years, and been nine Years a Citizen of the United States, and who shall not, when elected, be an Inhabitant of that State for which he shall be chosen.

The Vice President of the United States shall be President of the Senate, but shall have no Vote, unless they be equally divided.

The Senate shall choose their other Officers, and also a President pro tempore, in the Absence of the Vice President, or when he shall exercise the Office of President of the United States.

The Senate shall have the sole Power to try all Impeachments. When sitting for that Purpose, they shall be on Oath or Affirmation. When the President of the United States is tried, the Chief Justice shall preside: And no Person shall be convicted without the Concurrence of two thirds of the Members present.

Judgment in Cases of Impeachment shall not extend further than to removal from Office, and disqualification to hold and enjoy any Office of honor, Trust or Profit under the United States: but the Party convicted shall nevertheless be liable and subject to Indictment, Trial, Judgment and Punishment, according to Law.

Section 4.

The Times, Places and Manner of holding Elections for Senators and Representatives, shall be prescribed in each State by the Legislature thereof; but the Congress may at any time by Law make or alter such Regulations, except as to the Places of chusing Senators.

The Congress shall assemble at least once in every Year, and such Meeting shall be on the first Monday in December, unless they shall by Law appoint a different Day.

Section 5.

Each House shall be the Judge of the Elections, Returns and Qualifications of its own Members, and a Majority of each shall constitute a Quorum to do Business; but a smaller Number may adjourn from day to day, and may be authorized to compel the Attendance of absent Members, in such Manner, and under such Penalties as each House may provide.

Each House may determine the Rules of its Proceedings, punish its Members for disorderly Behaviour, and, with the Concurrence of two thirds, expel a Member.

Each House shall keep a Journal of its Proceedings, and from time to time publish the same, excepting such Parts as may in their Judgment require Secrecy; and the Yeas and Nays of the Members of either House on any question shall, at the Desire of one fifth of those Present, be entered on the Journal.

Neither House, during the Session of Congress, shall, without the Consent of the other, adjourn for more than three days, nor to any other Place than that in which the two Houses shall be sitting.

Section 6.

The Senators and Representatives shall receive a Compensation for their Services, to be ascertained by Law, and paid out of the Treasury of the United States. They shall in all Cases, except Treason, Felony and Breach of the Peace, be privileged from Arrest during their Attendance at the Session of their respective Houses, and in going to and returning from the same; and for any Speech or Debate in either House, they shall not be questioned in any other Place.

No Senator or Representative shall, during the Time for which he was elected, be appointed to any civil Office under the Authority of the United States, which shall have been created, or the Emoluments whereof shall have been increased during such time; and no Person holding any Office under the United States, shall be a Member of either House during his Continuance in Office.

Section 7.

All Bills for raising Revenue shall originate in the House of Representatives; but the Senate may propose or concur with Amendments as on other Bills.

Every Bill which shall have passed the House of Representatives and the Senate, shall, before it become a Law, be presented to the President of the United States: If he approve he shall sign it, but if not he shall return it, with his Objections to that House in which it shall have originated, who shall enter the Objections at large on their Journal, and proceed to reconsider it. If after such Reconsideration two thirds of that House shall agree to pass the Bill, it shall be sent, together with the Objections, to the other House, by which it shall likewise be reconsidered, and if approved by two thirds of that House, it shall become a Law. But in all such Cases the Votes of both Houses shall be determined by yeas and Nays, and the Names of the Persons voting for and against the Bill shall be entered on the Journal of each House respectively. If any Bill shall not be returned by the President within ten Days (Sundays excepted) after it shall have been presented to him, the Same shall be a Law, in like Manner as if he had signed it, unless the Congress by their Adjournment prevent its Return, in which Case it shall not be a Law.

Every Order, Resolution, or Vote to which the Concurrence of the Senate and House of Representatives may be necessary (except on a question of Adjournment) shall be presented to the President of the United States; and before the Same shall take Effect, shall be approved by him, or being disapproved by him, shall be repassed by two thirds of the Senate and House of Representatives, according to the Rules and Limitations prescribed in the Case of a Bill.

Section 8.

The Congress shall have Power

To lay and collect Taxes, Duties, Imposts and Excises, to pay the Debts and provide for the common Defence and general Welfare of the United States; but all Duties, Imposts and Excises shall be uniform throughout the United States;

To borrow Money on the credit of the United States;

To regulate Commerce with foreign Nations, and among the several States, and with the Indian Tribes;

To establish an uniform Rule of Naturalization, and uniform Laws on the subject of Bankruptcies throughout the United States;

To coin Money, regulate the Value thereof, and of foreign Coin, and fix the Standard of Weights and Measures;

To provide for the Punishment of counterfeiting the Securities and current Coin of the United States;

To establish Post Offices and post Roads;

To promote the Progress of Science and useful Arts, by securing for limited Times to Authors and Inventors the exclusive Right to their respective Writings and Discoveries;

To constitute Tribunals inferior to the supreme Court;

To define and punish Piracies and Felonies committed on the high Seas, and Offences against the Law of Nations;

To declare War, grant Letters of Marque and Reprisal, and make Rules concerning Captures on Land and Water;

To raise and support Armies, but no Appropriation of Money to that Use shall be for a longer Term than two Years;

To provide and maintain a Navy;

To make Rules for the Government and Regulation of the land and naval Forces;

To provide for calling forth the Militia to execute the Laws of the Union, suppress Insurrections and repel Invasions;

To provide for organizing, arming, and disciplining the Militia, and for governing such Part of them as may be employed in the Service of the United States, reserving to the States respectively, the Appointment of the Officers, and the Authority of training the Militia according to the discipline prescribed by Congress;

To exercise exclusive Legislation in all Cases whatsoever, over such District (not exceeding ten Miles square) as may, by Cession of particular States, and the Acceptance of Congress, become the Seat of the Government of the United States, and to exercise like Authority over all Places purchased by the Consent of the Legislature of the State in which the Same shall be, for the Erection of Forts, Magazines, Arsenals, dock-Yards, and other needful Buildings;—And

To make all Laws which shall be necessary and proper for carrying into Execution the foregoing Powers, and all other Powers vested by this Constitution in the Government of the United States, or in any Department or Officer thereof.

Section 9.

The Migration or Importation of such Persons as any of the States now existing shall think proper to admit, shall not be prohibited by the Congress prior to the Year one thousand eight hundred and eight, but a Tax or duty may be imposed on such Importation, not exceeding ten dollars for each Person.

The Privilege of the Writ of Habeas Corpus shall not be suspended, unless when in Cases of Rebellion or Invasion the public Safety may require it.

No Bill of Attainder or ex post facto Law shall be passed.

No Capitation, or other direct, Tax shall be laid, unless in Proportion to the Census or enumeration herein before directed to be taken.

No Tax or Duty shall be laid on Articles exported from any State.

No Preference shall be given by any Regulation of Commerce or Revenue to the Ports of one State over those of another; nor shall Vessels bound to, or from, one State, be obliged to enter, clear, or pay Duties in another.

No Money shall be drawn from the Treasury, but in Consequence of Appropriations made by Law; and a regular Statement and Account of the Receipts and Expenditures of all public Money shall be published from time to time.

No Title of Nobility shall be granted by the United States: And no Person holding any Office of Profit or Trust under them, shall, without the Consent of the Congress, accept of any present, Emolument, Office, or Title, of any kind whatever, from any King, Prince, or foreign State.

Section 10.

No State shall enter into any Treaty, Alliance, or Confederation; grant Letters of Marque and Reprisal; coin Money; emit Bills of Credit; make any Thing but gold and silver Coin a Tender in Payment of Debts; pass any Bill of Attainder, ex post facto Law, or Law impairing the Obligation of Contracts, or grant any Title of Nobility.

No State shall, without the Consent of the Congress, lay any Imposts or Duties on Imports or Exports, except what may be absolutely necessary for executing it's inspection Laws: and the net Produce of all Duties and Imposts, laid by any State on Imports or Exports, shall be for the Use of the Treasury of the United States; and all such Laws shall be subject to the Revision and Control of the Congress.

No State shall, without the Consent of Congress, lay any Duty of Tonnage, keep Troops, or Ships of War in time of Peace, enter into any Agreement or Compact with another State, or with a foreign Power, or engage in War, unless actually invaded, or in such imminent Danger as will not admit of delay.

ARTICLE II

Section 1.

The executive Power shall be vested in a President of the United States of America. He shall hold his Office during the Term of four Years, and, together with the Vice President, chosen for the same Term, be elected, as follows:

Each State shall appoint, in such Manner as the Legislature thereof may direct, a Number of Electors, equal to the whole Number of Senators and Representatives to which the State may be entitled in the Congress: but no Senator or Representative, or Person holding an Office of Trust or Profit under the United States, shall be appointed an Elector.

The Electors shall meet in their respective States, and vote by Ballot for two Persons, of whom one at least shall not be an Inhabitant of the same State with themselves. And they shall make a List of all the Persons voted for, and of the Number of Votes for each; which List they shall sign and certify, and transmit sealed to the Seat of the Government of the United States, directed to the President of the Senate. The President of the Senate shall, in the Presence of the Senate and House of Representatives, open all the Certificates, and the Votes shall then be counted. The Person having the greatest Number of Votes shall be the President, if such Number be a Majority of the whole Number of Electors appointed; and if there be more than one who have such Majority, and have an equal Number of Votes, then the House of Representatives shall immediately choose by Ballot one of them for President; and if no Person have a Majority, then from the five highest on the List the said House shall in like Manner choose the President. But in choosing the President, the Votes shall be taken by States, the Representation from each State having one Vote; A quorum for this purpose shall consist of a Member or Members from two thirds of the States, and a Majority of all the States shall be necessary to a Choice. In every Case, after the Choice of the President, the Person having the greatest Number of Votes of the Electors shall be the Vice President. But if there should remain two or more who have equal Votes, the Senate shall choose from them by Ballot the Vice President.

The Congress may determine the Time of choosing the Electors, and the Day on which they shall give their Votes; which Day shall be the same throughout the United States.

No Person except a natural born Citizen, or a Citizen of the United States, at the time of the Adoption of this Constitution, shall be eligible to the Office of President; neither shall any Person be eligible to that Office who shall not have attained to the Age of thirty five Years, and been fourteen Years a Resident within the United States.

In Case of the Removal of the President from Office, or of his Death, Resignation, or Inability to discharge the Powers and Duties of the said Office, the Same shall devolve on the Vice President, and the Congress may by Law provide for the Case of Removal, Death, Resignation or Inability, both of the President and Vice President, declaring what Officer shall then act as President, and such Officer shall act accordingly, until the Disability be removed, or a President shall be elected.

The President shall, at stated Times, receive for his Services, a Compensation, which shall neither be increased nor diminished during the Period for which he shall have been elected, and he shall not receive within that Period any other Emolument from the United States, or any of them.

Before he enter on the Execution of his Office, he shall take the following Oath or Affirmation:—"I do solemnly swear (or affirm) that I will faithfully execute the Office of President of the United States, and will to the best of my Ability, preserve, protect and defend the Constitution of the United States."

Section 2.

The President shall be Commander in Chief of the Army and Navy of the United States, and of the Militia of the several States, when called into the actual Service of the United States; he may require the Opinion, in writing, of the principal Officer in each of the executive Departments, upon any Subject relating to the Duties of their respective

Offices, and he shall have Power to grant Reprieves and Pardons for Offences against the United States, except in Cases of Impeachment.

He shall have Power, by and with the Advice and Consent of the Senate, to make Treaties, provided two thirds of the Senators present concur; and he shall nominate, and by and with the Advice and Consent of the Senate, shall appoint Ambassadors, other public Ministers and Consuls, Judges of the supreme Court, and all other Officers of the United States, whose Appointments are not herein otherwise provided for, and which shall be established by Law: but the Congress may by Law vest the Appointment of such inferior Officers, as they think proper, in the President alone, in the Courts of Law, or in the Heads of Departments.

The President shall have Power to fill up all Vacancies that may happen during the Recess of the Senate, by granting Commissions which shall expire at the End of their next Session.

Section 3.

He shall from time to time give to the Congress Information of the State of the Union, and recommend to their Consideration such Measures as he shall judge necessary and expedient; he may, on extraordinary Occasions, convene both Houses, or either of them, and in Case of Disagreement between them, with Respect to the Time of Adjournment, he may adjourn them to such Time as he shall think proper; he shall receive Ambassadors and other public Ministers; he shall take Care that the Laws be faithfully executed, and shall Commission all the Officers of the United States.

Section 4.

The President, Vice President and all civil Officers of the United States, shall be removed from Office on Impeachment for, and Conviction of, Treason, Bribery, or other high Crimes and Misdemeanors.

ARTICLE III

Section 1.

The judicial Power of the United States shall be vested in one supreme Court, and in such inferior Courts as the Congress may from time to time ordain and establish. The Judges, both of the supreme and inferior Courts, shall hold their Offices during good Behaviour, and shall, at stated Times, receive for their Services a Compensation, which shall not be diminished during their Continuance in Office.

Section 2.

The judicial Power shall extend to all Cases, in Law and Equity, arising under this Constitution, the Laws of the United States, and Treaties made, or which shall be made, under their Authority;—to all Cases affecting Ambassadors, other public Ministers and Consuls;—to all Cases of admiralty and maritime Jurisdiction;—to Controversies to which the United States shall be a Party;—to Controversies between two or more States;—between a State and Citizens of another State;—between Citizens of different States;—between Citizens of the same State claiming Lands under Grants of different States, and between a State, or the Citizens thereof, and foreign States, Citizens or Subjects.

In all Cases affecting Ambassadors, other public Ministers and Consuls, and those in which a State shall be Party, the supreme Court shall have original Jurisdiction. In all the other Cases before mentioned, the supreme Court shall have appellate Jurisdiction, both as to Law and Fact, with such Exceptions, and under such Regulations as the Congress shall make.

The Trial of all Crimes, except in Cases of Impeachment, shall be by Jury; and such Trial shall be held in the State where the said Crimes shall have been committed; but when not committed within any State, the Trial shall be at such Place or Places as the Congress may by Law have directed.

Section 3.

Treason against the United States, shall consist only in levying War against them, or in adhering to their Enemies, giving them Aid and Comfort. No Person shall be convicted of Treason unless on the Testimony of two Witnesses to the same overt Act, or on Confession in open Court.

The Congress shall have Power to declare the Punishment of Treason, but no Attainder of Treason shall work Corruption of Blood, or Forfeiture except during the Life of the Person attainted.

ARTICLE IV

Section 1.

Full Faith and Credit shall be given in each State to the public Acts, Records, and judicial Proceedings of every other State. And the Congress may by general Laws prescribe the Manner in which such Acts, Records and Proceedings shall be proved, and the Effect thereof.

Section 2.

The Citizens of each State shall be entitled to all Privileges and Immunities of Citizens in the several States.

A Person charged in any State with Treason, Felony, or other Crime, who shall flee from Justice, and be found in another State, shall on Demand of the executive Authority of the State from which he fled, be delivered up, to be removed to the State having Jurisdiction of the Crime.

No Person held to Service or Labour in one State, under the Laws thereof, escaping into another, shall, in Consequence of any Law or Regulation therein, be discharged from such Service or Labour, but shall be delivered up on Claim of the Party to whom such Service or Labour may be due.

Section 3.

New States may be admitted by the Congress into this Union; but no new State shall be formed or erected within the Jurisdiction of any other State; nor any State be formed by the Junction of two or more States, or Parts of States, without the Consent of the Legislatures of the States concerned as well as of the Congress.

The Congress shall have Power to dispose of and make all needful Rules and Regulations respecting the Territory or other Property belonging to the United States; and nothing in this Constitution shall be so construed as to Prejudice any Claims of the United States, or of any particular State.

Section 4.

The United States shall guarantee to every State in this Union a Republican Form of Government, and shall protect each of them against Invasion; and on Application of the Legislature, or of the Executive (when the Legislature cannot be convened), against domestic Violence.

ARTICLE V

The Congress, whenever two thirds of both Houses shall deem it necessary, shall propose Amendments to this Constitution, or, on the Application of the Legislatures of two thirds of the several States, shall call a Convention for proposing Amendments, which, in either Case, shall be valid to all Intents and Purposes, as Part of this Constitution, when ratified by the Legislatures of three fourths of the several States, or by Conventions in three fourths thereof, as the one or the other Mode of Ratification may be proposed by the Congress; Provided that no Amendment which may be made prior to the Year One thousand eight hundred and eight shall in any Manner affect the first and fourth Clauses in the Ninth Section of the first Article; and that no State, without its Consent, shall be deprived of its equal Suffrage in the Senate.

ARTICLE VI

All Debts contracted and Engagements entered into, before the Adoption of this Constitution, shall be as valid against the United States under this Constitution, as under the Confederation.

This Constitution, and the Laws of the United States which shall be made in Pursuance thereof; and all Treaties made, or which shall be made, under the Authority of the United States, shall be the supreme Law of the Land; and the Judges in every State shall be bound thereby, any Thing in the Constitution or Laws of any State to the Contrary notwithstanding.

The Senators and Representatives before mentioned, and the Members of the several State Legislatures, and all executive and judicial Officers, both of the United States and of the several States, shall be bound by Oath or Affirmation, to support this Constitution; but no religious Test shall ever be required as a Qualification to any Office or public Trust under the United States.

ARTICLE VII

The Ratification of the Conventions of nine States, shall be sufficient for the Establishment of this Constitution between the States so ratifying the Same.

The Word, "the," being interlined between the seventh and eighth Lines of the first Page, the Word "Thirty" being partly written on an Erazure in the fifteenth Line of the first Page, The Words "is tried" being interlined between the thirty second and thirty third Lines of the first Page and the Word "the" being interlined between the forty third and forty fourth Lines of the second Page.

Attest William Jackson Secretary

Done in Convention by the Unanimous Consent of the States present the Seventeenth Day of September in the Year of our Lord one thousand seven hundred and Eighty seven and of the Independence of the United States of America the Twelfth In witness whereof We have hereunto subscribed our Names,

G°. Washington
Presidt and deputy from Virginia

Delaware
Geo: Read
Gunning Bedford jun
John Dickinson
Richard Bassett
Jaco: Broom

Maryland
James McHenry
Dan of St Thos. Jenifer
Danl. Carroll

Virginia
John Blair
James Madison Jr.

North Carolina
Wm. Blount
Richd. Dobbs Spaight
Hu Williamson

South Carolina
J. Rutledge
Charles Cotesworth
Pinckney
Charles Pinckney
Pierce Butler

Georgia
William Few
Abr Baldwin

New Hampshire
John Langdon
Nicholas Gilman

Massachusetts
Nathaniel Gorham
Rufus King

Connecticut
Wm. Saml. Johnson
Roger Sherman

New York
Alexander Hamilton

New Jersey
Wil: Livingston
David Brearley
Wm. Paterson
Jona: Dayton

Pennsylvania
B Franklin
Thomas Mifflin
Robt. Morris
Geo. Clymer
Thos. FitzSimons
Jared Ingersoll
James Wilson
Gouv Morris

Articles

In addition to, and Amendment of the Constitution of the United States of America, proposed by Congress, and ratified by the Legislatures of the several States, pursuant to the fifth Article of the original Constitution.

(The first ten amendments to the U.S. Constitution were ratified December 15, 1791, and form what is known as the "Bill of Rights.")

AMENDMENT I

Congress shall make no law respecting an establishment of religion, or prohibiting the free exercise thereof; or abridging the freedom of speech, or of the press; or the right of the people peaceably to assemble, and to petition the Government for a redress of grievances.

AMENDMENT II

A well regulated Militia, being necessary to the security of a free State, the right of the people to keep and bear Arms, shall not be infringed.

AMENDMENT III

No Soldier shall, in time of peace be quartered in any house, without the consent of the Owner, nor in time of war, but in a manner to be prescribed by law.

AMENDMENT IV

The right of the people to be secure in their persons, houses, papers, and effects, against unreasonable searches and seizures, shall not be violated, and no Warrants shall issue, but upon probable cause, supported by Oath or affirmation, and particularly describing the place to be searched, and the persons or things to be seized.

AMENDMENT V

No person shall be held to answer for a capital, or otherwise infamous crime, unless on a presentment or indictment of a Grand Jury, except in cases arising in the land or naval forces, or in the Militia, when in actual service in time of War or public danger; nor shall any person be subject for the same offence to be twice put in jeopardy of life or limb; nor shall be compelled in any criminal case to be a witness against himself, nor be deprived of life, liberty, or property, without due process of law; nor shall private property be taken for public use, without just compensation.

AMENDMENT VI

In all criminal prosecutions, the accused shall enjoy the right to a speedy and public trial, by an impartial jury of the State and district wherein the crime shall have been committed, which district shall have been previously ascertained by law, and to be informed of the nature and cause of the accusation; to be confronted with the witnesses against him; to have compulsory process for obtaining witnesses in his favor, and to have the Assistance of Counsel for his defence.

AMENDMENT VII

In Suits at common law, where the value in controversy shall exceed twenty dollars, the right of trial by jury shall be preserved, and no fact tried by a jury, shall be otherwise re-examined in any Court of the United States, than according to the rules of the common law.

AMENDMENT VIII

Excessive bail shall not be required, nor excessive fines imposed, nor cruel and unusual punishments inflicted.

AMENDMENT IX

The enumeration in the Constitution, of certain rights, shall not be construed to deny or disparage others retained by the people.

AMENDMENT X

The powers not delegated to the United States by the Constitution, nor prohibited by it to the States, are reserved to the States respectively, or to the people.

AMENDMENT XI

Passed by Congress March 4, 1794. Ratified February 7, 1795.

Note: Article III, Section 2, of the Constitution was modified by Amendment XI.

The Judicial power of the United States shall not be construed to extend to any suit in law or equity, commenced or prosecuted against one of the United States by Citizens of another State, or by Citizens or Subjects of any Foreign State.

AMENDMENT XII

Passed by Congress December 9, 1803. Ratified June 15, 1804.

Note: A portion of Article II, Section 1, of the Constitution was superceded by the Twelfth Amendment.

The Electors shall meet in their respective states and vote by ballot for President and Vice-President, one of whom, at least, shall not be an inhabitant of the same state with themselves; they shall name in their ballots the person voted for as President, and in distinct ballots the person voted for as Vice-President, and they shall make distinct lists of all persons voted for as President, and of all persons voted for as Vice-President, and of the number of votes for each, which lists they shall sign and certify, and transmit sealed to the seat of the government of the United States, directed to the President of the Senate;—the President of the Senate shall, in the presence of the Senate and House of Representatives, open all the certificates and the votes shall then be counted;—The person having the greatest number of votes for President, shall be the President, if such number be a majority of the whole number of Electors appointed; and if no person have such majority, then from the persons having the highest numbers not exceeding three on the list of those voted for as President, the House of Representatives shall choose immediately, by ballot, the President. But in choosing the President, the votes shall be taken by states, the representation from each state having one vote; a quorum for this purpose shall consist of a member or members from two-thirds of the states, and a majority of all the states shall be necessary to a choice. [And if the House of Representatives shall not choose a President whenever the right of choice shall devolve upon them, before the fourth day of March next following, then the Vice-President shall act as President, as in case of the death or other constitutional disability of the President.—]* The person having the greatest number of votes as Vice-President, shall be the Vice-President, if such number be a majority of the whole number of Electors appointed, and if no person have a majority, then from the two highest numbers on the list, the Senate shall choose the Vice-President; a quorum for the purpose shall consist of two-thirds of the whole number of Senators, and a majority of the whole number shall be necessary to a choice. But no person constitutionally ineligible to the office of President shall be eligible to that of Vice-President of the United States.

*Superceded by Section 3 of the Twentieth Amendment.

AMENDMENT XIII

Passed by Congress January 31, 1865. Ratified December 6, 1865.

   Note: A portion of Article IV, Section 2, of the Constitution was superceded by the Thirteenth Amendment.

Section 1.

Neither slavery nor involuntary servitude, except as a punishment for crime whereof the party shall have been duly convicted, shall exist within the United States, or any place subject to their jurisdiction.

Section 2.

Congress shall have power to enforce this article by appropriate legislation.

AMENDMENT XIV

Passed by Congress June 13, 1866. Ratified July 9, 1868.

   Note: Article I, Section 2, of the Constitution was modified by Section 2 of the Fourteenth Amendment.

Section 1.

All persons born or naturalized in the United States, and subject to the jurisdiction thereof, are citizens of the United States and of the State wherein they reside. No State shall make or enforce any law which shall abridge the privileges or immunities of citizens of the United States; nor shall any State deprive any person of life, liberty, or property, without due process of law; nor deny to any person within its jurisdiction the equal protection of the laws.

Section 2.

Representatives shall be apportioned among the several States according to their respective numbers, counting the whole number of persons in each State, excluding Indians not taxed. But when the right to vote at any election for the choice of electors for President and Vice-President of the United States, Representatives in Congress, the Executive and Judicial officers of a State, or the members of the Legislature thereof, is denied to any of the male inhabitants of such State, being twenty-one years of age,* and citizens of the United States, or in any way abridged, except for participation in rebellion, or other crime, the basis of representation therein shall be reduced in the proportion which the number of such male citizens shall bear to the whole number of male citizens twenty-one years of age in such State.

Section 3.

No person shall be a Senator or Representative in Congress, or elector of President and Vice-President, or hold any office, civil or military, under the United States, or under any State, who, having previously taken an oath, as a member of Congress, or as an officer of the United States, or as a member of any State legislature, or as an executive or judicial officer of any State, to support the Constitution of the United States, shall have engaged in insurrection or rebellion against the same, or given aid or comfort to the enemies thereof. But Congress may by a vote of two-thirds of each House, remove such disability.

Section 4.

The validity of the public debt of the United States, authorized by law, including debts incurred for payment of pensions and bounties for services in suppressing insurrection or rebellion, shall not be questioned. But neither the United States nor any State shall assume or pay any debt or obligation incurred in aid of insurrection or rebellion against the United States, or any claim for the loss or emancipation of any slave; but all such debts, obligations and claims shall be held illegal and void.

Section 5.

The Congress shall have the power to enforce, by appropriate legislation, the provisions of this article.

*Changed by Section 1 of the Twenty-sixth Amendment.

AMENDMENT XV

Passed by Congress February 26, 1869. Ratified February 3, 1870.

Section 1.

The right of citizens of the United States to vote shall not be denied or abridged by the United States or by any State on account of race, color, or previous condition of servitude.

Section 2.

The Congress shall have the power to enforce this article by appropriate legislation.

AMENDMENT XVI

Passed by Congress July 2, 1909. Ratified February 3, 1913.

Note: Article I, Section 9, of the Constitution was modified by Amendment XVI.

The Congress shall have power to lay and collect taxes on incomes, from whatever source derived, without apportionment among the several States, and without regard to any census or enumeration.

AMENDMENT XVII

Passed by Congress May 13, 1912. Ratified April 8, 1913.

Note: Article I, Section 3, of the Constitution was modified by the Seventeenth Amendment.

The Senate of the United States shall be composed of two Senators from each State, elected by the people thereof, for six years; and each Senator shall have one vote. The electors in each State shall have the qualifications requisite for electors of the most numerous branch of the State legislatures.

When vacancies happen in the representation of any State in the Senate, the executive authority of such State shall issue writs of election to fill such vacancies: *Provided,* That the legislature of any State may empower the executive thereof to make temporary appointments until the people fill the vacancies by election as the legislature may direct.

This amendment shall not be so construed as to affect the election or term of any Senator chosen before it becomes valid as part of the Constitution.

AMENDMENT XVIII

Passed by Congress December 18, 1917. Ratified January 16, 1919. Repealed by Amendment XXI.

Section 1.

After one year from the ratification of this article the manufacture, sale, or transportation of intoxicating liquors within, the importation thereof into, or the exportation thereof from the United States and all territory subject to the jurisdiction thereof for beverage purposes is hereby prohibited.

Section 2.

The Congress and the several States shall have concurrent power to enforce this article by appropriate legislation.

Section 3.

This article shall be inoperative unless it shall have been ratified as an amendment to the Constitution by the legislatures of the several States, as provided in the Constitution, within seven years from the date of the submission hereof to the States by the Congress.

AMENDMENT XIX

Passed by Congress June 4, 1919. Ratified August 18, 1920.

The right of citizens of the United States to vote shall not be denied or abridged by the United States or by any State on account of sex.

Congress shall have power to enforce this article by appropriate legislation.

AMENDMENT XX

Passed by Congress March 2, 1932. Ratified January 23, 1933.

Note: Article I, Section 4, of the Constitution was modified by Section 2 of this amendment. In addition, a portion of the Twelfth Amendment was superceded by Section 3.

Section 1.

The terms of the President and the Vice President shall end at noon on the 20th day of January, and the terms of Senators and Representatives at noon on the 3d day of January, of the years in which such terms would have ended if this article had not been ratified; and the terms of their successors shall then begin.

Section 2.

The Congress shall assemble at least once in every year, and such meeting shall begin at noon on the 3d day of January, unless they shall by law appoint a different day.

Section 3.

If, at the time fixed for the beginning of the term of the President, the President elect shall have died, the Vice President elect shall become President. If a President shall not have been chosen before the time fixed for the beginning of his term, or if the President elect shall have failed to qualify, then the Vice President elect shall act as President until a President shall have qualified; and the Congress may by law provide for the case wherein neither a President elect nor a Vice President shall have qualified, declaring who shall then act as President, or the manner in which one who is to act shall be selected, and such person shall act accordingly until a President or Vice President shall have qualified.

Section 4.

The Congress may by law provide for the case of the death of any of the persons from whom the House of Representatives may choose a President whenever the right of choice shall have devolved upon them, and for the case of the death of any of the persons from whom the Senate may choose a Vice President whenever the right of choice shall have devolved upon them.

Section 5.

Sections 1 and 2 shall take effect on the 15th day of October following the ratification of this article.

Section 6.

This article shall be inoperative unless it shall have been ratified as an amendment to the Constitution by the legislatures of three-fourths of the several States within seven years from the date of its submission.

AMENDMENT XXI

Passed by Congress February 20, 1933. Ratified December 5, 1933.

Section 1.

The eighteenth article of amendment to the Constitution of the United States is hereby repealed.

Section 2.

The transportation or importation into any State, Territory, or Possession of the United States for delivery or use therein of intoxicating liquors, in violation of the laws thereof, is hereby prohibited.

Section 3.

This article shall be inoperative unless it shall have been ratified as an amendment to the Constitution by conventions in the several States, as provided in the Constitution, within seven years from the date of the submission hereof to the States by the Congress.

AMENDMENT XXII

Passed by Congress March 21, 1947. Ratified February 27, 1951.

Section 1.

No person shall be elected to the office of the President more than twice, and no person who has held the office of President, or acted as President, for more than two years of a term to which some other person was elected President shall be elected to the office of President more than once. But this Article shall not apply to any person holding the office of President when this Article was proposed by Congress, and shall not prevent any person who may be holding the office of President, or acting as President, during the term within which this Article becomes operative from holding the office of President or acting as President during the remainder of such term.

Section 2.

This article shall be inoperative unless it shall have been ratified as an amendment to the Constitution by the legislatures of three-fourths of the several States within seven years from the date of its submission to the States by the Congress.

AMENDMENT XXIII

Passed by Congress June 16, 1960. Ratified March 29, 1961.

Section 1.

The District constituting the seat of Government of the United States shall appoint in such manner as Congress may direct:

A number of electors of President and Vice President equal to the whole number of Senators and Representatives in Congress to which the District would be entitled if it were a State, but in no event more than the least populous State; they shall be in addition to those appointed by the States, but they shall be considered, for the purposes of the election of President and Vice President, to be electors appointed by a State; and they shall meet in the District and perform such duties as provided by the twelfth article of amendment.

Section 2.

The Congress shall have power to enforce this article by appropriate legislation.

AMENDMENT XXIV

Passed by Congress August 27, 1962. Ratified January 23, 1964.

Section 1.

The right of citizens of the United States to vote in any primary or other election for President or Vice President, for electors for President or Vice President, or for Senator or Representative in Congress, shall not be denied or abridged by the United States or any State by reason of failure to pay poll tax or other tax.

Section 2.

The Congress shall have power to enforce this article by appropriate legislation.

AMENDMENT XXV

Passed by Congress July 6, 1965. Ratified February 10, 1967.

Note: Article II, Section 1, of the Constitution was affected by the Twenty-fifth Amendment.

Section 1.

In case of the removal of the President from office or of his death or resignation, the Vice President shall become President.

Section 2.

Whenever there is a vacancy in the office of the Vice President, the President shall nominate a Vice President who shall take office upon confirmation by a majority vote of both Houses of Congress.

Section 3.

Whenever the President transmits to the President pro tempore of the Senate and the Speaker of the House of Representatives his written declaration that he is unable to discharge the powers and duties of his office, and until he transmits to them a written declaration to the contrary, such powers and duties shall be discharged by the Vice President as Acting President.

Section 4.

Whenever the Vice President and a majority of either the principal officers of the executive departments or of such other body as Congress may by law provide, transmit to the President pro tempore of the Senate and the Speaker of the House of Representatives their written declaration that the President is unable to discharge the powers and duties of his office, the Vice President shall immediately assume the powers and duties of the office as Acting President.

Thereafter, when the President transmits to the President pro tempore of the Senate and the Speaker of the House of Representatives his written declaration that no inability exists, he shall resume the powers and duties of his office unless the Vice President and a majority of either the principal officers of the executive department or of such other body as Congress may by law provide, transmit within four days to the President pro tempore of the Senate and the Speaker of the House of Representatives their written declaration that the President is unable to discharge the powers and duties of his office. Thereupon Congress shall decide the issue, assembling within forty-eight hours for that purpose if not in session. If the Congress, within twenty-one days after receipt of the latter written declaration, or, if Congress is not in session, within twenty-one days after Congress is required to assemble, determines by two-thirds vote of both Houses that the President is unable to discharge the powers and duties of his office, the Vice President shall continue to discharge the same as Acting President; otherwise, the President shall resume the powers and duties of his office.

AMENDMENT XXVI

Passed by Congress March 23, 1971. Ratified July 1, 1971.

Note: Amendment XIV, Section 2, of the Constitution was modified by Section 1 of the Twenty-sixth Amendment.

Section 1.

The right of citizens of the United States, who are eighteen years of age or older, to vote shall not be denied or abridged by the United States or by any State on account of age.

Section 2.

The Congress shall have power to enforce this article by appropriate legislation.

AMENDMENT XXVII

Originally proposed Sept. 25, 1789. Ratified May 7, 1992.

No law, varying the compensation for the services of the Senators and Representatives, shall take effect, until an election of representatives shall have intervened.

Lincoln's Gettysburg Address

Four score and seven years ago our fathers brought forth on this continent, a new nation, conceived in Liberty, and dedicated to the proposition that all men are created equal.

Now we are engaged in a great civil war, testing whether that nation, or any nation so conceived and so dedicated, can long endure. We are met on a great battle-field of that war. We have come to dedicate a portion of that field, as a final resting place for those who here gave their lives that that nation might live. It is altogether fitting and proper that we should do this.

But, in a larger sense, we can not dedicate—we can not consecrate—we can not hallow—this ground. The brave men, living and dead, who struggled here, have consecrated it, far above our poor power to add or detract. The world will little note, nor long remember what we say here, but it can never forget what they did here. It is for us the living, rather, to be dedicated here to the unfinished work which they who fought here have thus far so nobly advanced. It is rather for us to be here dedicated to the great task remaining before us—that from these honored dead we take increased devotion to that cause for which they gave the last full measure of devotion—that we here highly resolve that these dead shall not have died in vain—that this nation, under God, shall have a new birth of freedom—and that government of the people, by the people, for the people, shall not perish from the earth.

Appendix B

HISTORICAL FACTS AND DATA

U.S. Presidents and Vice Presidents

	President	Vice-President	Political Party	Term
1	George Washington	John Adams	No Party Designation	1789–1797
2	John Adams	Thomas Jefferson	Federalist	1797–1801
3	Thomas Jefferson	Aaron Burr George Clinton	Democratic- Republican	1801–1809
4	James Madison	George Clinton Elbridge Gerry	Democratic- Republican	1809–1817
5	James Monroe	Daniel D Tompkins	Democratic- Republican	1817–1825
6	John Quincy Adams	John C Calhoun	Democratic- Republican	1825–1829
7	Andrew Jackson	John C Calhoun Martin Van Buren	Democratic	1829–1837
8	Martin Van Buren	Richard M. Johnson	Democratic	1837–1841
9	William Henry Harrison	John Tyler	Whig	1841
10	John Tyler	None	Whig	1841–1845
11	James Knox Polk	George M Dallas	Democratic	1845–1849
12	Zachary Taylor	Millard Fillmore	Whig	1849–1850
13	Millard Fillmore	None	Whig	1850–1853
14	Franklin Pierce	William R King	Democratic	1853–1857
15	James Buchanan	John C Breckinridge	Democratic	1857–1861
16	Abraham Lincoln	Hannibal Hamlin Andrew Johnson	Union	1861–1865
17	Andrew Johnson	None	Union	1865–1869
18	Ulysses Simpson Grant	Schuyler Colfax Henry Wilson	Republican	1869–1877
19	Rutherford Birchard Hayes	William A Wheeler	Republican	1877–1881
20	James Abram Garfield	Chester Alan Arthur	Republican	1881

	President	Vice-President	Political Party	Term
21	Chester Alan Arthur	None	Republican	1881–1885
22	Stephen Grover Cleveland	Thomas Hendricks	Democratic	1885–1889
23	Benjamin Harrison	Levi P Morton	Republican	1889–1893
24	Chester Alan Arthur	Adlai E Stevenson	Democratic	1893–1897
25	William McKinley	Garret A. Hobart Theodore Roosevelt	Republican	1897–1901
26	Theodore Roosevelt	Charles W Fairbanks	Republican	1901–1909
27	William Howard Taft	James S Sherman	Republican	1909–1913
28	Woodrow Wilson	Thomas R Marshall	Democratic	1913–1921
29	Warren Gamaliel Harding	Calvin Coolidge	Republican	1921–1923
30	Calvin Coolidge	Charles G Dawes	Republican	1923–1929
31	Herbert Clark Hoover	Charles Curtis	Republican	1929–1933
32	Franklin Delano Roosevelt	John Nance Garner Henry A. Wallace Harry S. Truman	Democratic	1933–1945
33	Harry S. Truman	Alben W Barkley	Democratic	1945–1953
34	Dwight David Eisenhower	Richard Milhous Nixon	Republican	1953–1961
35	John Fitzgerald Kennedy	Lyndon Baines Johnson	Democratic	1961–1963
36	Lyndon Baines Johnson	Hubert Horatio Humphrey	Democratic	1963–1969
37	Richard Milhous Nixon	Spiro T. Agnew Gerald Rudolph Ford	Republican	1969–1974
38	Gerald Rudolph Ford	Nelson Rockefeller	Republican	1974–1977
39	James Earl Carter, Jr.	Walter Mondale	Democratic	1977–1981
40	Ronald Wilson Reagan	George Herbert Walker Bush	Republican	1981–1989
41	George Herbert Walker Bush	J. Danforth Quayle	Republican	1989–1993
42	William Jefferson Clinton	Albert Gore, Jr.	Democratic	1993–2001
43	George Walker Bush	Richard Cheney	Republican	2001–2008
44	Barack Hussein Obama	Joseph Biden	Democratic	2008–

Admission of States into the Union

	State	Date of Admission		State	Date of Admission
1	Delaware	December 7, 1787	28	Texas	December 29, 1845
2	Pennsylvania	December 12, 1787	29	Iowa	December 28, 1846
3	New Jersey	December 18, 1787	30	Wisconsin	May 29, 1848
4	Georgia	January 2, 1788	31	California	September 9, 1850
5	Connecticut	January 9, 1788	32	Minnesota	May 11, 1858
6	Massachusetts	February 6, 1788	33	Oregon	February 14, 1859
7	Maryland	April 28, 1788			
8	South Carolina	May 23, 1788	34	Kansas	January 29, 1861
9	New Hampshire	June 21, 1788	35	West Virginia	June 20, 1863
10	Virginia	June 25, 1788	36	Nevada	October 31, 1864
11	New York	July 26, 1788	37	Nebraska	March 1, 1867
12	North Carolina	November 21, 1789	38	Colorado	August 1, 1876
13	Rhode Island	May 29, 1790	39	North Dakota	November 2, 1889
14	Vermont	March 4, 1791	40	South Dakota	November 2, 1889
15	Kentucky	June 1, 1792			
16	Tennessee	June 1, 1796	41	Montana	November 11, 1889
17	Ohio	March 1, 1803			
18	Louisiana	April 30, 1812	42	Washington	November 11, 1889
19	Indiana	December 11, 1816	43	Idaho	July 3, 1890
20	Mississippi	December 10, 1817	44	Wyoming	July 10, 1890
			45	Utah	January 4, 1896
21	Illinois	December 3, 1818	46	Oklahoma	November 16, 1907
22	Alabama	December 14, 1819	47	New Mexico	January 6, 1912
			48	Arizona	February 14, 1912
23	Maine	March 15, 1820			
24	Missouri	August 10, 1821	49	Alaska	January 3, 1959
25	Arkansas	June 15, 1836	50	Hawaii	August 21, 1959
27	Florida	March 3, 1845			

Glossary

Abolition A pre-Civil War social movement devoted to the emancipation of slaves and their inclusion in American society as citizens with equal rights. (11)

Abu Ghraib Iraqi correctional facility near Baghdad that was widely publicized in 2004 for abuses of Iraqi prisoners of war by the U.S. military and CIA operatives. (31)

Act of Supremacy (1534) English parliamentary act that abolished papal authority over England, making King Henry VIII the head of the Church of England. (1)

Acts of Union (1707) Parliamentary acts that created the United Kingdom by merging the kingdoms and parliaments of England and Scotland. (4)

Adamson Act (1916) Congressional act that granted railroad workers an eight-hour workday and overtime pay. (21)

Affordable Care Act (2010) Health insurance reform legislation designed to cover millions of uninsured Americans. (31)

Agricultural Adjustment Administration (AAA, 1933) U.S. government agency created by the Agricultural Adjustment Act to provide credit, loans, and other subsidies to farmers. (23)

Alamo A mission outpost in San Antonio, Texas, that was defended down to the last man by American and Mexican separatists in the Texas War for Independence of 1836. (11)

Albany Congress (1754) A conference of representatives of seven British North American colonies, held in Albany, New York, to consider strategies for diplomacy with the Indians and dissuade Iroquois from becoming French allies. (5)

Alien and Sedition Acts (1798) Four congressional acts that severely restricted immigration into the United States, gave the president power to deport anyone thought to be dangerous, and restricted speech critical of the federal government. (8)

Alliance for Progress (1961) A multibillion-dollar aid program for Latin America aimed at establishing economic cooperation between the United States and South America. (27)

Al Qaeda A global militant Islamist organization founded by Osama bin Laden around 1989. (31)

American Anti-Slavery Society An abolitionist society organized by William Lloyd Garrison in 1833 with immediate abolition as its core objective. (12)

American Colonization Society (ACS) A society of antislavery whites, founded in 1817, that advocated the return of freed slaves to Africa. (9)

American Expeditionary Force (AEF) American armed forces, commanded by General John J. Pershing, sent to Europe during World War I to fight alongside British and French allied units. (21)

American Federation of Labor (AFL) A collective of craft unions, founded in 1886 and headed by Samuel Gompers, it was comprised of skilled workers and excluded most immigrants and women. (17)

American Indian Movement (AIM) Formed in Minneapolis in 1968, an activist organization devoted to protecting Indian rights and to upholding established treaties, particularly over land, with federal, state, and local governments. (27)

American Philosophical Society Scholarly organization founded in Philadelphia in 1743 to promote the dissemination of knowledge in the science and humanities. (5)

American Protective Association (APA) An anti-Catholic nativist organization founded in 1887. The APA advocated strict immigration laws and spread conspiracy theories about Roman Catholics. (18)

American Protective League (APL) Organization of private American citizens who worked with law enforcement agencies during World War I to identify and counteract the activities of German sympathizers and other antiwar advocates. (21)

American Railway Union (ARU) Founded in 1893 by Eugene V. Debs, the ARU was one of the first industrial unions in the United States. The ARU aimed to increase the power of railroad workers by organizing one industry-wide union. (17)

American Recovery and Reinvestment Act (2009) Congressional act allocating $787 billion in economic stimulus funds. The package combined government spending on infrastructure, unemployment benefits, and food stamps, with tax cuts. (31)

American System Senator Henry Clay's proposal of 1824 intended to spur domestic economic development as well as tariffs and currency regulation, also propounded recognition of Latin American independence movements. (10)

American Temperance Society Organization established in 1826 to advocate abstinence from distilled beverages. The movement did not end the consumption of alcohol in America, but it did help convince millions of people to rethink their relationship with drinking. (12)

Americans with Disabilities Act (ADA) Congressional act of 1990 that provided equal rights for people with disabilities. (30)

Anti-Imperial League American organization formed in 1898 by those who opposed American colonization of the Philippines. (19)

Articles of Capitulation (1664) English policies regarding Dutch residents of New Amsterdam, which granted them religious liberty, freedom from military conscription, property rights, the ability to leave New York within 18 months, and free trade and freedom of movement within the English Empire. (3)

Articles of Confederation The first written framework for a government of the United States, drafted by Congress and in effect from 1781 to 1788. (7)

Astrolabe A navigation instrument used to pinpoint and predict the location of the stars, Sun, Moon, and planets for determining longitude and latitude while sailing at sea. (1)

Atlantic Charter (1941) A joint policy statement issued by the United States and Great Britain that defined the goals and objectives of their alliance at the beginning of World War II. The charter called for disarming defeated aggressors and establishing a permanent system of general security. (24)

Atlantic slave trade The enslaving, trade, and transport of African people to Europe and the Americas, begun by the Portuguese in the early 1440s. (1)

Atlantic world Name given to the area of exploration bordering the Atlantic Ocean and including the five continents of North America, South America, Antarctica, Africa, and Europe. (1)

Baby boom The temporary but noteworthy increase in birth rate in the United States, Great Britain, and Europe in the years immediately following World War II. (26)

Bacon's Rebellion (1676) An uprising of poor white men, free blacks, and some enslaved people led by the English aristocrat Nathaniel Bacon that temporarily drove the Colonial Governor William Berkeley from Jamestown. Participants opposed the government's moderate policy toward local Indians and the concentration of landholding in elite hands. (3)

Balance of powers A model of governance in which authority is distributed to several different branches of government, providing checks and balances against one another. Also known as the separation of powers. (7)

Bank of the United States (BUS) The first federal bank, founded in 1791, that operated until 1811 and provided for the issuance of a national currency and centralization of federal tax collection. (9)

Barbados slave code (1661) English America's first slave code; it prescribed different treatment and contrasting levels of legal protection for enslaved Africans and white servants. (3)

Battle of Bunker Hill The first significant battle of the American Revolution. It actually took place on Breed's Hill, where colonial forces claimed victory and demonstrated that they could resist larger British forces. (6)

Battle of the Bulge The last major offensive by the German army in World War II, fought in Belgium in 1944. (24)

Bay of Pigs Invasion Failed operation approved by President Kennedy to invade Cuba with a small CIA-led military force of political Cuban exiles with hopes of liberating the country and removing Fidel Castro from power. (27)

Beaver Wars 70-year conflict between Iroquois and Huron over access to diminishing beaver hunting grounds in today's mid-Atlantic. (3)

Bill of Rights The first 10 amendments to the United States Constitution, ratified by the states in 1791. (8)

Black codes (1865–1866) Laws enacted by Southern state legislatures after the Civil War that granted limited rights to former slaves, including the right to marry, own land, and participate in the judicial process, but that also singled out black people under the law and imposed severe restraints on their occupations, mobility, and rights as parents. (15)

Black Legend Politically motivated, factually exploitative conviction that the Spaniards indiscriminately slaughtered Indians, tyrannized them, and imposed Catholicism on them during their 16th-century conquests in the Americas. (2)

Black Panther Party A radical civil rights organization founded in Oakland in 1966 by Huey Newton and Bobby Seale. Members of Black Panthers advocated black self-determination and armed self-defense against police brutality. (27)

Black Tuesday (October 29, 1929) The day that marked the start of the Great Depression, precipitated by a calamitous crash of the stock market. (22)

Blockade (1861–1865) Military policy of preventing an enemy from engaging in naval commerce by blocking ports and intercepting ships. (14)

Board of Trade (1696) An advisory council created by King William III of England that was charged to oversee colonial matters. The act testified to the colonies' growing significance to England's economy. (4)

Boston Massacre (1770) An altercation between occupying British troops and a Boston mob, resulting in the death of five colonists. This was a significant incident in the buildup of tensions between Britain and the colonies in the years leading up to the American Revolution. (6)

Boston Tea Party (1773) An act of defiance on the part of Boston colonists to protest the British Tea Act of 1773, a new tax on imported tea; 30 to 60 men disguised as Mohawk Indians stormed British tea ships and dumped 90,000 pounds of tea into Boston Harbor. (6)

Bracero Program (1942) Agreement between the governments of Mexico and the United States that granted annual entry to hundreds of thousands of seasonal agricultural workers. Control of the border was generally loosened and hundreds of thousands of other Mexicans were drawn north by growing opportunities in the greatly expanding U.S. economy. (24)

Bretton Woods agreements (1944) Multinational agreements that established a system for international trade and monetary values to promote economic recovery following World War II. (24)

***Brown v. Board of Education of Topeka Kansas* (1954)** U.S. Supreme Court decision that outlawed racial segregation in public schools. (26)

Bush Doctrine Foreign policy principles of President George W. Bush, the centerpiece of which was a policy wherein the United States had the right to engage in preemptive war to secure itself against terrorist groups and countries that harbored them. (31)

Bush v. Gore (2000) U.S. Supreme Court decision that determined the winner of the 2000 presidential race between Al Gore and George W. Bush. (30)

Calvinism A Protestant religion that followed the teachings of theologian John Calvin that was practiced by European and American Puritans. (1)

Central Powers Name given during World War I to the alliance of Germany, Austria-Hungary, and Ottoman Turkey. (21)

Charter of Freedoms and Exemptions (1640) A Dutch West India Company policy that granted 200 acres to whoever brought five adults to New Netherland and promised prospective colonists religious freedom and local self-governance; these offers attracted English Puritans from Massachusetts to eastern Long Island. (2)

Chinese Exclusion Act (1882) Congressional Act that barred the immigration of Chinese laborers. This law all but ended Chinese immigration and remained in effect until 1943. (16)

Church of England (Anglican Church) English Christian church established by King Henry VIII after his break from papal authority in 1534. (1)

Civil Rights Act of 1964 Congressional act that prohibited discrimination in employment or the use of public places on the basis of race, sex, religion, or national origin. (20)

Code Noir (1685) Slave code mandated by imperial France governing the rights and treatment of African slaves in their colonial territories from the French West Indies to Louisiana. (4)

Coercive Acts/Intolerable Acts (1774) Four British parliamentary decrees enacted in response to unrest and protests in Boston. The acts reorganized the Massachusetts government and placed more authority in the hands of royal appointees. The acts also imposed royal control over local courts and authorized troops to be forcibly housed in private homes and buildings. (6)

Coinage Act (1873) Congressional Act that made gold the nation's monetary standard and halted the making of silver dollars, later referred to by Populists, who wished to expand the nation's money supply with silver, as "the crime of 1873." (18)

Cold War Term given to the political, economic, and military tensions that existed between the United States and its allies and the Soviet Union between 1945 and the dissolution of the Soviet Union in 1991. (25)

Columbian exchange The historic movement of people, plants, animals, culture, and pathogens between the Americas and the rest of the world that began during the time of Columbus. (1)

Committee on Public Information Government agency created during WWI to promote war aims and distribute propaganda. (21)

Committee to Reelect the President (CREEP) Group organized by the Nixon White House to both promote the president's reelection and collect illegal funds to engage in "dirty tricks." (27)

Common law Law based on decisions previously made by judges and courts, as opposed to statutory, or written laws and statutes; the common law system was rooted in English legal practices. (2)

Commons Lands open to all residents. (2)

Compromise of 1850 Congressional measures created to resolve a series of regional tensions in the United States. The measures admitted California as a free state, organized the remainder of the New Mexico Territory, banned the slave trade in the District of Columbia, empowered the Treasury to assume Texas's debts from its independence struggle with Mexico, and gave the South a much stronger federal Fugitive Slave Law. (13)

Congress of Industrial Organizations (CIO) Umbrella group of labor unions, formed in 1935, to represent semiskilled workers in major industrial sectors. Unions within the Congress accepted black and other minority workers. (23)

Containment Name given to the foundation of U.S. foreign policy during the Cold War.

George F. Kennan argued that Soviet communism was "impervious to the logic of reason," inherently expansionist, and only controllable through "long-term, patient but firm and vigilant containment." (25)

Contraband Legal term denoting war materials that can be seized from an enemy during wartime. During the Civil War, northern leaders used the term to refer to enslaved people who fled to Union lines seeking freedom. (14)

Contract with America A document conceived by Republican Congressman Newt Gingrich in 1993 that promised to make Congress more accountable, balance the federal budget, reverse the tax increases passed in 1993, and reduce the capital gains tax. (30)

Contras Anticommunist guerrillas funded by the CIA to attack the Sandinista regime in Nicaragua in the 1980s. (29)

Conversion test An exercise developed by Massachusetts Bay Puritans to test prospective church members for membership in their congregation; prospects had to testify to their relationship with God and offer proof that God had saved them. (2)

Copper Borderlands Region in Southwest United States and northern Mexico where trade and labor networks transcended national borders. (16)

Copperheads Civil War era nickname for the faction of the Democratic Party that opposed the war. (14)

Counterculture In the 1960s and early 1970s, the name given to the subculture of college-age young Americans who developed distinctively liberal beliefs and practices regarding sexuality, race, gender, politics, and culture; these values stood in contrast to those of the dominant culture of their parents. (27)

Court packing scheme Abortive effort by President Roosevelt in 1937 to increase the number of justices on the Supreme Court. (23)

Covenant As practiced by New England Puritans, an agreement with God that required them to translate their faith into actions that obeyed God's will as revealed in the Bible. (2)

Coverture A principle of British and American law wherein a married woman lost her legal identity as an individual and in which her economic resources would be controlled by her husband. This law prevented married women from owning property. (7)

Crop lien A credit system widely used by Southern farmers from the 1860s to the 1920s. This was a way for farmers to get credit before the planting season by borrowing against the value for anticipated harvests. (15)

Cuban missile crisis A tense standoff between the United States and Soviet Union in October 1962 when the United States discovered that the Soviets had begun installing nuclear missiles in Cuba. The incident was the most dramatic nuclear standoff of the Cold War. (27)

Dawes Act (1887) Congressional act that divided two-thirds of Indian tribal lands to be sold off or confiscated. Many Indians who had lived on reservations became essentially landless. (16)

Dawes Plan (1924) Provided loan from U.S. banks to Germany to stabilize economy and reduce reparations burden. (22)

Declaration of Independence (1776) American revolutionary document that declared that the United States was free and independent of the British Empire and sought international recognition for the United States. (6)

Defense Advanced Research Projects Agency (DARPA) U.S. defense agency that created the Internet, originally founded in 1958 to counter Soviet advances in space science. (30)

Defense of Marriage Act (1996) Congressional act that decreed that no state would be compelled to recognize a same-sex marriage conducted in another state, nor would the federal government recognize the existence of such a marriage even if it were performed legally in a state. (31)

Desert Lands Act (1877) Congressional act, applicable in 11 Western states, that allowed for homesteading on 640-acre parcels of arid land at 25 cents per acre and provided title within three years for a dollar an acre for settled, irrigated land. (16)

Détente Term given to the U.S. relaxation of tension with the Soviets during the 1970s. (28)

Dollar Diplomacy Effort by Taft Administration to encourage U.S. bankers and businesses to expand into Latin America. (19)

Dominion of New England (1685–1689) A union of English colonies imposed by the English monarchy; it comprised eight contiguous colonies, from New England to New Jersey, under one governor, Edmond Andros, who dissolved representative assemblies, jailed dissidents, and imposed taxes on lands already owned outright. (3)

Dred Scott decision (1857) U.S. Supreme Court ruling that slaves were not citizens of the United States and were therefore unable to sue in a federal court of law. As a consequence, the federal government had no authority to outlaw slavery in the territories, leaving that choice up to the states. (13)

Dust Bowl Area in the West and Midwest plagued by drought and dust storms in the 1930s. (23)

Dutch West India Company (DWIC) Dutch trading company whose merchants were granted trade monopolies in parts of the New World, and whose activities included the acquisition of territories in the Hudson River Valley in New York. (2)

Earthrise First photo of the Earth from space captured by Apollo 8 astronauts on Christmas Eve, 1968. (27)

East India Company (EIC) Monopoly trading company of English merchants chartered in 1600 to trade in Asia and India. Influential in global British imperial policy into the 19th century. (4)

Edict of Nantes (1598) Proclamation by King Henry IV of France granting rights to Huguenots (French Calvinist Protestants). (2)

Eighteenth Amendment (1919) Constitutional amendment that barred the manufacture and sale of alcohol in the United States. Repealed in 1933. (20)

Emancipation Proclamation (1863) Proclamation by Abraham Lincoln that freed the slaves living in Confederate states. (14)

Emergency Banking Relief Act (1933) Congressional act that followed the market crash of 1929; it reopened banks and restored bank solvency under Treasury Department supervision. The act also removed U.S. currency from the gold standard. (23)

Emergency Economic Stabilization Act (2008) Congressional act that authorized the U.S. Treasury to budget up to $700 billion to bail out banks and other financial institutions affected by a crisis in subprime mortgage values. (31)

Emergency Immigration Act of 1921 Congressional act that created specific immigration limitations based on national origin. The act banned all immigration from Asia, but allowed free immigration from the Western Hemisphere, as the Southwest depended on Mexican and Central American labor. (22)

Encomienda System whereby the Spanish government granted land, villages, and indigenous people to its military leaders who conquered land in the Americas. (1)

Epic of Deganawidah Iroquois legend that explained the establishment of the Great League of Peace between Indian nations. (1)

Equal Rights Amendment (ERA) Proposed amendment to the U.S. Constitution that banned the denial or abridgment of rights on the basis of gender. (29)

Espionage Act (1917) Congressional act passed on the eve of America's entrance into World War I that expanded the definition of treason and defined a variety of acts deemed to comprise espionage. The Act was enacted to fight sabotage, spying, or interference with the war effort. (20)

Ethnic Cleansing The effort by government or private groups to remove or kill groups of people from land they traditionally occupied. (30)

Executive Order 9981 (1948) Order by President Truman that established equality in the armed services on the basis of race, color, religion, and national origin. (25)

Exodusters Freed slaves who fled the South in search of better opportunities and treatment in the West after the Civil War. (16)

Fair Deal Domestic programs for social reform proposed by the Truman administration. The 21-point program called for an increase in the minimum wage, comprehensive housing legislation for returning veterans, full employment and expanded unemployment benefits, permanent federal farm subsidies, expanded public works projects, and expanded environmental conservation programs. (25)

Federalism A system of government that divides powers between a centralized national administration and state governments. (7)

Federalist Papers A series of anonymously authored essays, published in newspapers, supporting ratification of the U.S. Constitution of 1787 by Madison, Hamilton, and Jay. (7)

Feitoria Portuguese name for a fortified trading post, early examples of which were first established in Africa in the 15th century during the early years of the Atlantic slave trade. (1)

Fifteenth Amendment (1870) Constitutional amendment that prohibited the denial of voting rights on the basis of race. (15)

Fireside chats Weekly radio addresses by President Franklin Roosevelt in which he explained his proposals, policies, and actions to the American people. (23)

First Continental Congress Representatives of the colonies (except Georgia) who met in Philadelphia for the first time in 1774 to articulate their positions and form policies against grievous British laws and regulations. The group charged committees in each colony to vigorously enforce boycotts; endorsed a declaration of rights and grievances on October 14, 1774; and then adjourned, hoping that the King would change the course of imperial policy. (6)

First Hundred Days President Franklin Roosevelt's first days in office, during which he prevailed on Congress to pass 14 major pieces of legislation including bills to raise agricultural prices, put the unemployed to work, regulate the stock market, reform banking practices, and assist homeowners and farmers in paying mortgages. (23)

Fordlandia Unsuccessful rubber plantation and company town established in Brazilian Amazon by Henry Ford in 1928. (22)

Fourteen Points Plan for peace and postwar order proclaimed by President Wilson in 1918. (21)

Fourteenth Amendment (1868) Constitutional amendment that guaranteed national citizenship and equality to former slaves, detailed changes related to the former Confederate states, but offered no specific protection of freed people's voting rights. (15)

Franciscans A Roman Catholic religious order, active in establishing Spanish missions in Southwestern North America in the 18th and 19th centuries. (1)

Freedmen's Bureau Shortened name for the Bureau of Refugees, Freedmen, and Abandoned Land, established within the Army in early 1865 to adjudicate labor disputes in the summer and fall of 1865. (15)

French and Indian War (1756–1763) Also known as the Seven Years' War, a conflict between Britain and France and their respective Indian allies in colonial America. This was largely a conflict between empires for territorial and economic control of the colonies and related trade routes. (5)

Fugitive Slave Act (1850) Congressional act that nationalized the process of slave capture and return by requiring federal judges to appoint "commissioners" to hear cases of accused fugitives and by requiring the active complicity of state officers. (13)

Fur trade The trading of furs, primarily through the St. Lawrence River region, that served as the primary gateway for European goods into North America into the 1600s. (2)

Gag rule Rule adopted by Congress in 1836 to block the discussion of slavery at the national as well as the state level. The rule was repealed in 1844. (11)

Gang system One of two general types of division of labor of plantation slaves, the other being the task system. The gang system involved the work of coordinated groups, supervised by a driver, to maintain an even level of productivity during the workday. (5)

General Allotment Act (1887) Congressional act that divided Indian reservation land into smaller parcels of property. (16)

Gentlemen's Agreement (1907) Agreement reached by President Theodore Roosevelt and the Japanese government that stated that the United States would no longer exclude Japanese immigrants if the Japanese promised to voluntarily limit the number of its immigrants to the United States, primarily adult male laborers. (19)

Glass-Steagall Banking Act (1933) Congressional act that established strict guidelines for banking operations and expanded the power of the Federal Reserve System. The act also founded the Federal Deposit Insurance Corporation. Some regulations associated with the original act were repealed in 1999, leading to mismanagement and scandals in the banking and finance industries, and the recession beginning around 2009. (23)

Globalization A term that was popularized in the 1990s to refer to the knitting together of the world's economies through new information technology and the end of the artificial political barrier of the Cold War. (30)

Glorious Revolution (1688) Uprising of the English Parliament against King James II that transformed the English system of government from an absolute monarchy to a constitutional monarchy and the rule of Parliament. (3)

Grand Settlement of 1701 A pair of treaties between Iroquois and the French that stabilized relations between the two in the Great Lakes and Northeast parts of North America. (4)

Grandfather clause Allowance created by Southern state constitutions in the 1890s permitting any person who had voted before 1867, or had a father or grandfather who had voted, to be exempt from the literacy test or other restrictions. The aim of this law was to increase the number of eligible white male voters while eliminating black voters. (20)

Great Depression International economic depression and the United States' worst economic downturn to date. Beginning at the end of 1929 and lasting for 10 years, the catastrophe spread to every corner of the country, wrecking lives and leaving people homeless, hungry, and desperate for work. (22)

Great Migration The large scale movement of African Americans from the South to the North during and after World War I where jobs were more plentiful. (21)

Great Railroad Strike of 1877 The first and largest general strike in U.S. history was sparked by wage and hour cuts of railroad workers in the midst of an economic depression. The strike was marked by violence as well as nonviolent sympathetic strikes by workers across the nation. President Hayes used federal troops to help break the strike after roughly a month. (17)

Great Recession An international economic collapse of 2008 where credit markets around the world froze and banks stopped lending to one another. Businesses dependent on lending began to downsize and fail. The meltdown affected financial institutions and governments throughout the world. (31)

Great Society President Lyndon Johnson's name for a series of social and economic reforms, begun in 1965, to end racial discrimination, expand educational opportunities, end hunger and poverty, and make health care available for all. (27)

Gulf of Tonkin Resolution Congressional authorization requested by President Lyndon Johnson in 1964 that gave him the power to escalate military action in Vietnam without additional congressional approval. (28)

Hard war Union's policy during the American Civil War that targeted the ability of Confederates to fight by destroying infrastructure, transportation networks, and food supplies for the army. (14)

Harlem Renaissance An African American cultural and arts movement of the 1920s centered in the Harlem neighborhood of New York City. (22)

Harpers Ferry (1859) Failed raid led by abolitionist John Brown on the U.S. arsenal in Harper's Ferry, Virginia. Brown's capture and execution led to greater regional tensions leading up to the Civil War. (13)

Haymarket Affair A violent conflict between protesting workers and police in Chicago's Haymarket Square in 1886 created antiunion hysteria that brought about the demise of the Knights of Labor. (17)

Helsinki Accords A set of principles that accepted the post-1945 division of Europe into East–West spheres. The accords recognized the right of all Europeans to seek peaceful change, and the Soviets agreed in a general way to respect human rights in their sphere. (29)

Holden v. Hardy (1898) U.S. Supreme Court decision that upheld Utah's law limiting the working hours of miners to 8 hours per day. (20)

Homestead Act (1862) Congressional act that allowed families to claim 160 acres of land if they improved it over five years of residence. The act opened the Western United States to settlement. (15)

Homestead Lockout In 1892, Carnegie partner Henry Clay Frick locked out workers at the Carnegie steel works in Homestead, Pennsylvania, when they refused a new contract, leading to violence and the destruction of their powerful union. (17)

Horizontal integration An innovation of the modern corporation, horizontal integration aimed to eliminate destructive aspects of competition by purchasing competitors or establishing agreements among them to share in profits. (17)

House of Burgesses The first representative government assembly and ruling body established in the English settlements in America; founded by the Virginia Company in 1619, this assembly replaced martial law with English common law, setting in motion the development of the county court system. (2)

House Committee on Un-American Activities (HCUA) Congressional committee formed in 1938 to search for communists and conspiracies within the United States including penetration into the labor movement and federal agencies. Although discredited during the 1950s for its investigations of entertainment and media figures, the committee was not abandoned until 1975. (25)

Hudson's Bay Company English trading company, formed in England in 1670, competed with the French in North America. (3)

Huguenots Name given to the French followers of Calvinism, a Protestant religion founded by theologian John Calvin. (1)

Huron A union of several tribes of Huron people, formed to established peaceful relations and trade. (1)

Immigration Restriction League An anti-immigration organization founded in Boston in 1894 that promoted legislation to restrict the immigration of Southern and Eastern Europeans. (18)

Indentured servitude An arrangement offered by various English enterprises to attract English people to the colonies, exchanging free passage by ship to America for up to seven years labor. (2)

Indian Removal Act (1830) Federal law that nullified 50 years' worth of treaties between the United States and many tribes. The law resulted in the relocation of more than 45,000 Indians living east of the Mississippi to points further west, opening up lands for white settlers. The law committed the federal government to creating an Indian Territory west of the Mississippi. (11)

Indian Reorganization Act (1934) Congressional act that slowed the division of reservation land into small plots, encouraged tribal self-government, and established Indian-run corporations to control communal land and resources. (23)

Industrial Workers of the World (IWW) Radical labor union, also known as "Wobblies," founded in 1905. The union embraced all workers in "one big union," called for the overthrow of capitalism, and advocated industrial sabotage. Especially active in the West up to WWI. (20)

Industrious revolution Preindustrialization period associated with 18th-century British North America during which there was a diversification of labor, development of a market-oriented society, and a labor shift from services to marketable goods. (4)

Initiative, referendum, and recall First proposed by Populists in the 1890s, the initiative and referendum, adopted originally in Oregon, made it possible for voters to place legislation directly before the electorate for a vote in general elections; the referendum allowed voters to repeal state legislation with which they disagreed; the recall gave voters the power to remove any public official who did not, in their view, act for the public good. (20)

Instant cities Urban areas such as San Francisco and Denver that grew rapidly from frontier outposts to major regional cities during the settlement of the West. (16)

Insular Cases (1901–1954) A series of U.S. Supreme Court cases that would be applied to all of the new territories added to the United States in which it was ruled that American constitutional rights and liberties did not extend to all lands under U.S. control. (19)

Interstate and Defense Highways Act (1956) The largest public works program in American history, approved by President Dwight Eisenhower, that facilitated the growth of suburban America and the businesses and industries that sustained them. (26)

Iran-Contra Scandal Scandalous effort by Reagan administration that involved ransoming hostages in Lebanon, selling arms to Iran, and illegally funding the Contras in Nicaragua. (29)

Iroquois League Also known as the Great League of Peace. A confederation formed c. 1400 and originally composed of five Iroquoian-speaking peoples of today's Upstate New York: Seneca, Cayuga, Onondaga, Oneida, and Mohawk. (1)

Jamestown The first permanent English settlement in America, founded in 1607 and located in what is today coastal Virginia. (2)

Jay's Treaty (1794) Treaty with Britain granting the United States trade rights on the Mississippi, in the British East Indies, and removing remaining British forts on American territory. (8)

Jesuits (Society of Jesus) A Catholic male religious order, founded in Spain in 1534, that was active in winning converts overseas. (1)

Jim Crow laws State and local laws that originated in the South in the mid 1880s and legally separated people according to race. These laws spread to many public facilities and established a policy of racial segregation that favored white citizens. (20)

Johnson–O'Malley Act of 1934 Congressional act that provided federal aid to improve health care and education to Indian tribes. (23)

Joint-stock companies An early form of shareholding company that was used by the British to finance development of the colonies. (2)

kachinas In Pueblo culture, ancestral beings believed to bring rain and communal harmony. (1)

Kansas-Nebraska Act (1854) Congressional act that repealed the Missouri Compromise. The bill's new policy of "popular sovereignty," intended to allow settlers in a territory to decide the status of slavery, initiated a strenuous debate about the future of slavery in the Western territories. (13)

Katsina Ancestral god spirits of Pueblo peoples. (3)

Keating–Owen Child Labor Act (1916) Law that banned interstate commerce in goods produced by child labor. Struck down by U.S. Supreme Court as unconstitutional in 1918. (20)

Kellogg–Briand Pact (1928) Also known as the "Pact of Paris," an agreement signed by 62 nations that agreed not to use war as an instrument of national policy. The pact was initiated by the United States and France. (22)

Kent State In the spring of 1970, the campus where the Ohio National Guard killed and wounded antiwar demonstrators. (28)

Keynesian Economics The idea that the government can boost the economy and counter recessions by increasing deficit spending on public projects. (23)

King Philip's War (1675–1676). Conflict between Indian inhabitants of the New England region, the English colonists, and their Indian allies. Named after the Indian leader Metacom, known to the English as King Philip. (3)

King William's War (1689–1697) The first of several colonial wars between English and French colonists in North America and their Indian allies. (3)

Kiva An underground chamber used by Pueblo Indians for religious ceremonies. (2)

Knights of Labor The first national labor union, founded in Baltimore in 1869. The Knights aimed to organize all laboring people into one large, national union, offering membership regardless of race, gender, or national origin. The organization rejected capitalism and wage labor and demanded a fair share of wealth for workers who produced it. (15)

Know-Nothing Party Antiforeign, anti-Catholic political organization established in 1854 and consisting of a network of secret fraternal associations, largely a nativist reaction against large-scale European immigration. The organization's name stemmed from its secrecy; if asked about the organization, members would essentially deny any knowledge of it, saying that they "knew nothing." (13)

Ku Klux Klan An organization associated with the bitterest and most violent opponents of Reconstruction and black freedom. Formed in Pulaski, Tennessee, in late 1865, Klan members devoted themselves to denying African Americans any legitimate role in the public sphere, stressing the superiority of white, Protestant, Anglo-Saxon citizens. Revived in the 1920s as an anti-immigrant, anti-Catholic, and anti-Jewish organization. (15)

Laissez-faire economics An economic doctrine that insisted that government should not interfere with businesses or the market. The term is from the French meaning "leave it alone." (17)

***Lawrence v. Texas* (2003)** U.S. Supreme Court decision that overturned most state antisodomy laws used to criminalize homosexual behavior. (31)

League of Nations Organization created after WWI to promote global peace and cooperation (21)

Lend-Lease Act (1941) Massive military and economic aid program to assist nations fighting Germany and Japan. (24)

Levittown The prototypical modern tract suburb of Levittown on Long Island, New York. First massive, planned subdivision created in New York suburbs after WWII. (26)

Limited Test Ban Treaty (1963) An agreement between the United States and the Soviet Union that ended above-ground atomic weapon testing but permitted continued testing underground. (27)

Linen Act of 1705 British parliamentary act that encouraged the export of Irish linen to North America. In turn, the act increased the demand in Northern Ireland for colonial flaxseed, the source of linen. (4)

Literacy Act (1917) Clause of the U.S. Immigration Act of 1917 that barred the entry of any persons unable to read in their own language on the grounds that this lack demonstrated their ignorance. (21)

Lochner v. New York (1905) U.S. Supreme Court decision that struck down a New York Law limiting the hours that male bakers could work. In the court's opinion, the state had no right to regulate their hours. (20)

Lowell Mill Girls Female workers associated with the textile mills in Lowell, Massachusetts. The mills had a large labor force of young women, who ranged between the ages of 15 and 35 and worked in one of the first large-scale, steam-powered industries in the United States. (11)

Ludlow Massacre (1914) An attack by local deputies and state militia on striking United Mine Workers in Ludlow, Colorado. At the request of mine owners, the militia attacked a camp of striking miners who had been evicted from company-owned housing, killing 14 people, including 11 children. Soon labeled the Ludlow Massacre, the killings sparked violent retaliation by the miners. (20)

Lusitania British passenger liner torpedoed by a German submarine in 1915 while sailing between New York and England. The attack killed 1,200 of the 2,000 passengers and crew, including 128 Americans. (21)

Lynching The murder of African American individuals by a mob, often by hanging, shooting, or burning, and was especially prevalent in the 1890s South. (20)

Malintzín A native Nahua woman from the Gulf Coast of Mexico who figured importantly in the Spanish conquest of Mexico by acting as the translator and advisor to Hernán Cortés, leader of a Spanish expedition. (1)

Maine (battleship) A U.S. battleship that exploded on February 15, 1898, killing 260 American sailors. Americans blamed Spain for the explosion, drawing the United States closer to war with Spain, which was declared two months later. (19)

Manhattan Project Secret U.S. scientific and military program during World War II dedicated to the development of an atomic bomb. The project was led by J. Robert Oppenheimer and employed 150,000 workers at numerous secret sites, including Los Alamos, New Mexico. (24)

Mann Act (1910) Congressional act that outlawed the transport of women across state lines for "immoral purposes." (20)

Manumission The freeing of slaves by their owners. (4)

Marbury v. Madison (1803) U.S. Supreme Court decision that firmly established the principle of "judicial review," the right of the U.S. Supreme Court to rule on the constitutionality of legislation and executive actions. (8)

March on Washington (1963) Civil rights demonstration in which Martin Luther King, Jr., delivered "I have a dream" speech. (27)

Marshall Plan (European Recovery Plan) (1948) A massive foreign aid program approved following World War II, it called for aid packages to help Western Europe, including West Germany, and Japan rapidly rebuild their devastated economies, restore industries and trade, and rejoin the free world. (25)

Massachusetts Bay Company A business enterprise founded by English Puritans and merchants in 1629 that founded the Massachusetts Bay Colony, resulting in a swell of English emigration to the colonies. (2)

Matrilineal A society in which social identity is based on kinship and descendency from the mother. (2)

Maysville Road Bill (1830) President Andrew Jackson vetoed this bill authorizing federal investment in a private turnpike company because he opposed using central power for infrastructure improvement. (10)

McCarran International Security Act (1950) Congressional act requiring the registration of American Communist Party members; the act reinforced perceptions of immigrants as a source of radicalism during the Cold War and set the tone for a contentious debate about immigration in the coming decade. (25)

McCarthyism Term named for Wisconsin senator who engaged in "witch hunts" against real and mostly imagined Communists inside the United States. (26)

McKinley Tariff (1890) Congressional act that ended the practice of allowing Hawaiian sugar to enter the United States duty free, ending Hawaii's favored status and threatening its sugar industry. (19)

McNary–Haugen Acts (1927–1928) Congressional acts that required the government to support crop prices by buying basic farm commodities. (22)

Meat Inspection Act (1906) Congressional act that required federal inspectors from the U.S. Department of Agriculture to inspect livestock in slaughterhouses and to guarantee sanitary standards. (20)

Medicaid A health care plan that originated with President Lyndon Johnson's Great Society program in which the federal government provided states matching grants to pay for medical costs of poor people of all ages. (27)

Medicare A health plan that originated with President Lyndon Johnson's Great Society programs that provided universal hospital insurance for Americans over 65. (27)

Medicare Modernization Act (2003) Congressional act that subsidized the cost of some, but not all, medication taken by seniors. (31)

Mercantilism An economic philosophy of English and French governments founded on the belief that control of foreign trade—including the acquisition of raw materials from their colonies—was key to securing the kingdom that ruled them. (3)

Methodists A Protestant evangelical sect, rooted in the 18th-century Anglican revival movement, that accepted slaves and freed blacks and opposed government intervention in religion. (5)

Minute men In Revolutionary War times, local militias in Massachusetts and Connecticut that went on alert in response to pending British military action. (6)

***Miranda v. Arizona* (1966)** Supreme Court decision that required police to tell suspects of their right to remain silent and to have access to legal counsel. (27)

Mississippi Bubble Name given the financial collapse in 1720 of the Company of the Indies, an investment scheme intended to finance the French colonization of Louisiana. (4)

Mississippian societies Name given to Indian societies of the Mississippi Valley, formed around 700 CE and peaking between 1100 and 1300. (1)

Model Cities Federal urban aid program created by President Lyndon Johnson to encourage physical and economic revitalization of the nation's poorest urban areas. (27)

Modern corporation Pioneered by railroads before the Civil War, the modern corporation developed in the last quarter of the 19th century, distinguished by its organization, massive scale, and forms of management. (17)

Modernists Religious leaders, influenced by the Social Gospel movement of the late 19th century, as well as Darwin's theory of evolution and archaeological discoveries, who believed Christianity should respond positively to new knowledge and social conditions. (22)

Monetarists Proponents of a conservative economic movement that favored a change to tax and spending policies. Led by Milton Friedman, these economists insisted that prosperity and freedom required reduced government spending along with more stringent control of the money supply. (29)

Monroe Doctrine (1823) Policy introduced by President James Monroe who declared that the United States shared common interest with other states in the Western Hemisphere and that the political system in Europe was "essentially different" from that of the democratic republics in North and South America. (9)

Montgomery Improvement Association An organization of black clergy and community leaders, formed in 1955, and led by Martin Luther King, Jr., who refined a philosophy of nonviolent protest for boycotters. (26)

Moral Majority Political lobbying movement organized by religious conservatives in 1979. (29)

Moravians (United Brethren) A Protestant religious sect, revived in Germany in 1727 and brought to Georgia in 1735, that sought to create closed, economically autonomous, sex-segregated communities in which Christian liturgical rituals and piety infused daily life. (5)

Mormons A Protestant religious sect, founded by Joseph Smith, who preached a conservative theology of patriarchal authority. (12)

Mourning wars Skirmishes associated with Eastern North American Indians to avenge the death of relatives by capturing or killing members of neighboring tribes. (1)

Muckraking An early form of investigative journalism. Believing that exposing facts

could rouse the public to demand change, "muckraking" helped bring about major reforms in the late 19th and early 20th centuries. (17)

Mudsill A sociological theory first proposed by South Carolina Senator James Henry Hammond in 1858 who stated that a division of upper and lower classes was the natural order of society, a view that was interpreted by many as a thinly veiled excuse for exploiting slavery. (11)

Mujahideen Islamic-inspired Afghan and foreign guerrillas who fought the occupying Soviets in Afghanistan during the 1980s. They counted among their ranks Saudi fundamentalist Osama bin Laden. (29)

Mulatto Mixed race people in the United States. (11)

***Muller v. Oregon* (1908)** U.S. Supreme Court decision that upheld an Oregon law limiting the workday of female laundry workers to 10 hours per day. (20)

My Lai massacre (1968) Massacre by American troops of 504 unarmed Vietnamese villagers during the Vietnam War. (28)

Natchez War (1729) Rebellion staged by Natchez warriors and African slaves against French colonists in Mississippi, suppressed by the French and their Choctaw allies. (4)

National American Woman Suffrage Association (NAWSA) Organization founded in 1890, headed by Carrie Chapman Catt, that sought a constitutional amendment to give women the right to vote. (20)

National Association for the Advancement of Colored People (NAACP) Civil Rights organization founded in 1909 that was innovative in establishing legal action as a powerful basis in the fight for African American rights. (20)

National Association of Colored Women (NACW) Organized in 1896, the NACW, made up largely of black middle-class women, addressed the needs of black neighborhoods, establishing hospitals, day nurseries, and kindergartens, and also attacked segregation and lynching. The organization's motto was "Lifting as we climb." (20)

National Organization for Women (NOW) Founded in 1966, this organization advocated an end to laws that discriminated against women, opportunity to work at any job, and equal pay for equal work. (27)

National Origins Act of 1924 Congressional act that established strict immigration ceilings and quotas favoring Northern European immigrants; the basis of immigration policy until 1965. (22)

National Parks Act of 1916 Congressional act that created the National Park Service and aimed, in part, to preserve national park lands and "leave them unimpaired for the enjoyment of future generations." (20)

National Recovery Administration (NRA) Early and unsuccessful New Deal effort to promote industrial recovery from the Great Depression. The NRA wrote "production codes" for each industry that encouraged cooperation among competing businesses to set stable prices and wages. (23)

National Security Act of 1947 This act consolidated the U.S. military command; a representative from each military branch would advise a newly created Secretary of Defense and the president through the Joint Chiefs of Staff Office. (25)

National Woman's Party (NWP) Founded in 1916 by Alice Paul and like-minded suffragists, the NWP conducted numerous protests to win women the right to vote, including marches and "silent sentinels," picketing outside of the White House. (20)

Nativism Name given to a strong anti-immigration, anti-Catholic activist movement that flourished in America from the 1830s to the 1850s and the 1890s to the 1920s. The term "nativists" was giving to those who strongly opposed the influx of immigrants into American society. (18)

Navigation Acts One of a series of English regulations and taxes on colonial trade dating from 1650 to 1775. (3)

"Neoconservatives" A small but influential coalition of Democrats and Republicans who rejected many of the tenets of liberalism and détente and called for more limited government at home and a more muscular military stance abroad. (29)

New Deal Name collectively given to President Franklin Roosevelt's programs to fight the Great Depression, first articulated during his 1932 presidential campaign. He pledged to use federal power to ensure a more equitable distribution of income and rebuild the economy from the bottom up. (23)

New Freedom Name given to Woodrow Wilson's 1912 presidential platform, which promised an attack on "bigness" in government and business, and his advocacy for small business and fair competition enforced by only minimal government interference. (20)

New Frontier Name given to President John F. Kennedy's phrase for a collection of programs to expand economic and social opportunities in the United States. (27)

New Left Counterculture protest movement of the 1960s whose young activists intentionally distanced themselves from the ideological infighting, Marxist leanings, and labor organizing of the Old Left of the 1930s and 1940s. (27)

New Look President Dwight Eisenhower's military reorganization of 1954 that established the central philosophy of the doctrine of "massive retaliation" as more economically feasible than containment alone. (26)

New Nationalism Name given to President Theodore Roosevelt's platform in 1912 that advocated expansive government activism and regulation for the public interest. (20)

New World Order George H. W. Bush proclaimed the dawn of a New World Order in 1989 in which the United States, the world's preeminent superpower, would lead multinational coalitions to enforce its standards of international behavior. (30)

Nineteenth Amendment (1920) Constitutional amendment granting women the right to vote. (20)

No Child Left Behind Act (NCLB) Program proposed by President George W. Bush in 2001 to improve educational outcomes for poor and minority children. It renewed federal funding for several existing school programs and provided some additional money for reading and math instruction. In return, all states had to implement "standards based educational reform," a term that in practice meant standardized testing of students in reading and math. (31)

Non-Governmental Organizations (NGOs) Independent groups that supported foreign relations and political programs and fostered the growth of global capitalism during the Cold War. (25)

Non-Intercourse Act (1809) Congressional act that reopened trade with countries other than Britain and France. (8)

North American Free Trade Agreement (NAFTA) Trade agreement approved by Democrats and Republicans in 1993 during the administration of President Bill Clinton. This agreement lifted barriers to trade between the United States, Mexico, and Canada; and nearly all conventional economists believed that it would lift living standards in these countries. (30)

Occupy Wall Street Protest movement active in 2011 that criticized predatory banks and corporations. (31)

Ohio Company of Virginia A group of land speculators composed mainly of well-connected British planters to whom the state of Virginia had granted over 300,000 acres by early 1745. They opened the door to British trade in the South, competing with the already established French traders. (5)

Olive Branch Petition (1775) Petition sent by the Continental Congress to King George III of England seeking his intervention in the conflict with Parliament over taxes. (6)

Open Door Policy Principles drafted in 1899 by Secretary of State John Hay requesting that European powers put an end to the further partitioning of China and open up areas of China claimed by each power to allow them to compete fairly for Chinese trade. These policies asked for unhindered access to markets where they could compete successfully against economic rivals. (19)

Organization of Petroleum Exporting Countries (OPEC) Cartel organized by major oil-producing nations to boost prices for crude oil. Became effective in the 1970s. (28)

PAC—see Political Action Committees. (29)

Palmer Raids Series of actions by Federal agents in 1919 and 1920 to arrest and deport radical immigrants. (21)

Panama Canal Opened in 1914, the canal, linking the Atlantic and Pacific Oceans, enhanced access to U.S. colonies in the Pacific as well as trade with Asia, but poisoned U.S. relations with Latin American countries because of the questionable way that the United States gained rights to build the canal. (19)

Parliament Legislative body of the British government. (3)

Peace Policy Organized by General Ely Samuel Parker, the Indian commissioners, and leaders of various Christian denominations provided Indians with food and clothing in exchange for promises to abandon cultural traditions and to assimilate into American society. (16)

Pendleton Civil Service Act (1883) Congressional act that established the modern Civil Service and initiated an examination for a classified list of federal jobs, including most government departments, custom house jobs, and post office positions. (18)

Pentagon Papers Popular name given to a collection of classified government documents that were illegally made public in

1971. The documents outlined decision making by the U.S. Defense Department during the period from World War II to the Vietnam War. (28)

People's (Populist) Party A third party, made up largely of rural people frustrated with the unresponsiveness of the Republican and Democratic parties to their pressing needs. The People's Party ran candidates for president in 1892 and 1896 on a platform demanding major reforms, including the government ownership of railroads, a graduated income tax, and the free coinage of silver. (18)

Pequot War (1636–1638) Conflict between the Pequot Indians of the Connecticut River Valley and British colonists and their Indian allies. (2)

Pietism A Protestant religious movement that linked North America, Britain, the Netherlands, and central Europe. Pietists promoted the personal piety of believers and the evangelization of all, including American Indians and enslaved Africans. (4)

Pinckney's Treaty (1795) A treaty with Spain that fully opened Mississippi River trade to the United States, provided tax-free markets in New Orleans, settled Florida border issues, and guaranteed Spanish help against Southwest Indians who moved to block U.S. settlers from expanding the West. (8)

Plantation Act of 1740 British parliamentary act that allowed non-Catholic aliens who resided for at least seven years in British North America, received communion in a Protestant church, swore allegiance to George II, and paid two shillings, to become citizens. (5)

Platt Amendment (1901) Amendment to the new Cuban constitution that gave the United States broad authority to intervene to preserve Cuban independence and required Cuba to sell or lease land for U.S. naval stations and coaling bases. (19)

Plessy v. Ferguson (1896) U.S. Supreme Court decision that upheld the legality of Jim Crow laws, declaring that segregation based on race was constitutional as long as "separate" facilities were "equal." It soon became clear, however, that facilities for black Americans, such as schools, railroad cars, and waiting rooms, were rarely, if ever, equal to those provided for whites. (20)

Political Action Committees (PACs) A private group dedicated to the election of a given political candidate or to influence a policy decision in government. (29)

Political machines Established in most major U.S. cities by the late 19th century, political organizations offered a variety of services to constituents, especially immigrants, in exchange for votes and party loyalty. (18)

Polygamy A marriage custom of having more than one partner at the same time, such as a man with more than one wife. (4)

Popular sovereignty A policy established in the mid-19th century that permitted settlers in newly established Western territories to decide on the policy of slavery for themselves. (7)

Prigg v. Pennsylvania (1842) U.S. Supreme Court decision that established federal protection to Southerners seeking to reclaim fugitive slaves who escaped to the North. (13)

Privateer A government contracted but privately owned warship used to attack foreign ships and disrupt trade. (1)

Proclamation of 1763 An order issued by King George III of England that prohibited settlements beyond a line west of the Appalachians running from the Hudson River south to Florida. (6)

Protestantism A Christian reform movement that arose in Europe during the 1500s and denied the authority of the Catholic Church. (1)

Pullman Strike Led by Eugene V. Debs and the American Railway Union in 1894 in response to massive wage cuts at the Pullman Palace Car Company, the strike and boycott of trains pulling Pullman cars froze rail service in the Midwest and slowed it elsewhere until federal troops helped crush the strike. (17)

Pure Food and Drug Act (1906) Congressional act that outlawed adulterated or mislabeled food and drugs and gave the federal government the right to seize illegal products and fine and jail those who manufactured and sold them. (20)

Puritans Europeans who followed the Christian teachings of theologian John Calvin, defied the Catholic Church, and sought to place the governance of church affairs in the hands of local officials, ministers, and elders. (1)

Queen Anne's War (1702–1713) Fought between the British and French for control of North American colonies, simultaneous with a war in Europe over the Spanish monarchy. (4)

Quitrent A land tax or rent imposed on colonists by their European governing body. (3)

Reaganomics Informal term for policy of cutting taxes on the well-to-do and reducing government regulation of business to promote growth. (29)

Reconquista Expansion of western European Christian nations during the 1400s into Muslim settlements on the Iberian Peninsula. (1)

Reconstruction Finance Corporation (RFC, 1932) Federal program of President Herbert Hoover to loan money to struggling banks, railroads, manufacturers, and mortgage companies during the Great Depression. (23)

Redemptioners In the 18th century, indentured servants who paid for their passage across the Atlantic by selling their services when they landed. (5)

Rerum novarum A papal encyclical from Pope Leo XIII, issued in 1891, condemning the exploitation of laborers and supporting state intervention to promote social justice. (20)

Revivalists Leaders and advocates of various evangelical Protestant campaigns of the First Great Awakening (18th century). Revivalists sought to rekindle widespread religious enthusiasm in the American colonies. (5)

Roe v. Wade (1973) U.S. Supreme Court decision upholding a woman's constitutional right to terminate a pregnancy. (29)

Roosevelt Corollary Articulated by President Theodore Roosevelt in 1904, this corollary to the Monroe Doctrine declared that the United States had the right to intervene in the affairs of Latin American nations to ensure order. (19)

Rough Riders Colonel Theodore Roosevelt and his First Volunteer Cavalry Regiment, known as "The Rough Riders," became national heroes for their daring exploits during the Spanish-American War (1898). (19)

Royal African Company A British mercantile firm that received the royal monopoly on trade in Africa. Active in the gold trade, by 1663 the company possessed exclusive rights to buy and transport slaves across the Atlantic for sale in British colonies. (3)

Royal Orders for New Discoveries (1573) Decree by King Philip II of Spain that missionaries should play the principal role in exploring, pacifying, and colonizing new territories and mandated that baptized Indians should live on missions, learn to speak Spanish, keep livestock, cultivate European crops, and use European tools to master European crafts. (2)

Royal Society An elite organization founded in London that connected colonists and residents of the capital in the pursuit of scientific evidence and investigation. (3)

Russo-Japanese War Rival imperial claims in Asia sparked this war between Russia and Japan in 1904. President Theodore Roosevelt brokered a peace treaty between the two countries in 1905, earning him the Nobel Peace Prize. (19)

St. Augustine First Spanish settlement in North America, founded in 1565. (1)

Salutary neglect Name given to the practice of colonists to defy or ignore British laws that they found onerous, often with the complicity of those charged to enforce them. (4)

Science Lag Term used to describe perceived disparity between U.S. and Soviet education programs during the Cold War. (26)

Scopes Trial Highly publicized 1925 trial of Tennessee high school science teacher John Scopes, who was found guilty of teaching the theory of evolution in violation of state law. (22)

Secession The act of withdrawing formally from an existing union with another political state. (14)

Second Bill of Rights List of "economic bill of rights," proposed by President Franklin D. Roosevelt in 1944, that guaranteed every citizen a job, a living wage, decent housing, adequate medical care, educational opportunity, and protection against unemployment in postwar America. (24)

Second Great Awakening Religious revivalist movement of the early 19th century that echoed the Great Awakening of the 1730s. The movement linked evangelical Christians on both sides of the Atlantic to exchange ideas and strategies that inspired a broad set of social, cultural, and intellectual changes. (9)

Securities Act of 1933 Congressional act that required companies selling stock to the public to register with a federal agency and provide accurate information on what was being sold. (23)

Securities Exchange Act of 1934 Congressional act that created the Securities and Exchange Commission to regulate stock markets and activities by brokers. (23)

Sedition Act (1918) Amendments to the Espionage Act of 1917 that added a variety of offenses to the list of prohibited acts, including the use of "disloyal, profane, scurrilous, or abusive language about the form of government of the United States, or the Constitution of the United States." (20)

Separation of powers Political concept as articulated by French Enlightenment philosopher the Baron de Montesquieu that each state establish a balance between executive, legislative, and judicial powers. (7)

September 11 Shorthand for attacks on the World Trade Center and Pentagon that took place on September 11, 2001. (31)

Settler Societies Collections of immigrants from foreign places who used their numbers to gain control of territory and resources from indigenous peoples across the globe. (16)

Seventeenth Amendment (1913) Constitutional amendment that mandated the direct election of U.S. senators. (20)

Sharecroppers Farmers who rented land or farmed on shares, splitting the proceeds from the yearly crop with the landlord. (15)

Shays' Rebellion (1786–1787) An armed insurrection by indebted Massachusetts farmers, led by Daniel Shays, to prevent the state government from seizing their property. (7)

Shelly v. Kraemer (1948) U.S. Supreme Court case outlawing racial housing covenants. (26)

Sherman Antitrust Act (1890) Congressional act aimed at dismantling combinations and trusts that restrained trade. It was the first U.S. law to restrict business monopolies, but loopholes and court decisions rendered it largely ineffective. (17)

Sixteenth Amendment (1913) Constitutional amendment that authorized a federal income tax on both personal and corporate income. (20)

Smoot–Hawley Tariff of 1930 Passed in 1930 at the onset of the Great Depression, the tariff made it especially difficult for international manufacturers to sell their products in the United States, resulting in retaliatory tariffs that worsened the international economy. (22)

Social Darwinism A theory, popularized by Herbert Spencer, which purported that Charles Darwin's theory of evolution could be applied to human society as well. This belief that society evolved and improved through competition in which the "fittest" survived justified non-interference by the government in the economy and workplace as well as the massive fortunes amassed by industrialists. (16)

Social Gospel A broad, multidimensional and international movement among Protestants in the late 19th and early 20th centuries that insisted that Christian principles needed to be applied to social problems. (18)

Social Security Act (1935) Congressional act that established a federally administered retirement system for workers at age 65, funded primarily by contributions—payroll taxes—from workers and employers, not general tax revenues. (23)

Society for the Propagation of the Gospel in Foreign Parts (SPG) Anglican reform organization founded in 1701 for sending missionaries to North America and the West Indies. (4)

Society of Friends ("Quakers") A Christian religious sect that broke from the Church of England and established itself in America during the 17th century. (3)

Sons of Liberty Groups of colonial protestors, originating with the 1765 Stamp Act, who spread anti-British sentiment between colonies. (6)

Stagflation A slowly growing economy with high rates of unemployment and inflation. (28)

Stamp Act (1765) British parliamentary act that required many forms of colonial printed materials and products be affixed with revenue stamps, or taxes, paid to the British. (6)

Sunbelt Band of warm climate states of the Southern and Southwest United States that grew in political, cultural, and economic significance after massive post-WWII migrations. (27)

Tariff A tax on imported goods. (10)

Task system One of two general types of division of labor of plantation slaves, the other being the gang system. The task system assigned individuals with specific tasks. Rather than being part of a group that worked continuously to the day's end, the task system allowed individuals to end their work day when their task was done and thus granted them more autonomy. (5)

Tea Party Movement Grassroots conservative movement active from 2010 that called for limited government. (31)

Teapot Dome Scandal Bribery scandal, uncovered in 1924, implicating Secretary of the Interior Fall, a member of President Harding's cabinet who took bribes in return for lucrative leases to drill for oil on government-owned land. (22)

Teller Amendment (1898) An amendment to Congress's declaration of war in April 1898 that stated that the United States would not colonize Cuba. (19)

Tennessee Valley Authority (TVA) Federal agency created in 1933 to construct a network of dams and hydroelectric projects to control floods, generate power, and promote growth in a chronically poor area of the South. (23)

Third World Term used to classify mostly non-white nations considered inferior to "First World" nations such as the United States and Western Allies. (25)

Thirteenth Amendment (1865) Constitutional amendment that outlawed slavery in the United States. (15)

Townshend Acts (1767) British parliamentary acts that taxed commons goods in the colonies such as tea and other commodities. The acts represented Britain's resolve to control and regulate the colonies. (6)

Trail of Tears Cherokee name for the United States' forced removal of their people from the Southeast to other lands. In early 1838, few Cherokee had prepared for the trip; contaminated water, inadequate food, and disease killed many of those restricted in stockades, and many more perished on the 800-mile journey west. (11)

Transportation Act (1718) British parliamentary act that mandated the exile of convicted criminals to North America, mostly those who had committed property crimes such as theft. (4)

Treaty of Paris (1763) The treaty ending the French and Indian War. The terms of the treaty transformed eastern North America's political geography. France surrendered North America, swapping Canada for the return of Guadeloupe. France ceded Louisiana to Spain, and Spain traded Florida to the British to regain control of Havana. The British Empire claimed almost all of North America east of the Mississippi. (5)

Treaty of Tordesillas (1494) Treaty signed by Spain and Portugal that divided newly discovered lands between them, specifically those in Africa (to Portugal) and those associated with Columbus (to Spain). (1)

Treaty of Versailles (1919) The treaty that ended World War I and created independent Poland, Czechoslovakia, Yugoslavia, Hungary, Finland, and the Baltic states of Latvia, Lithuania, and Estonia. (20)

Triangle fire In March 1911, a raging fire swept through the Triangle Waist Company in New York City, killing 146 workers, mostly young women, leading to a series of workplace reforms. (20)

Truman Doctrine Policy announced by president in 1947 whereby the United States pledged to defend allies against Communist threats. (25)

U.S. Colored Troops Black troops consisting of freed black men and former slaves, enlisted for the Union Army after the Emancipation Proclamation of January 1, 1863. (14)

United Colonies of New England (1643) Union of the Massachusetts Bay, Plymouth, Connecticut, and New Haven colonies to bolster their mutual defenses and negotiations with Indians. (2)

United Fruit Company A Boston-based company originally established for importing bananas to the United States from Latin America, it was known as "The Octopus" for its involvement and influence in the affairs of Honduras, Guatemala, and Costa Rica. (19)

United Mine Workers (UMW) Founded in 1890 as an industry-wide union for mine workers. (17)

United Nations Organization (UN) An organization open to all nations, established in 1945, for maintaining world peace. It is headquartered in New York. (24)

United States v. E. C. Knight Co. **(1895)** U.S. Supreme Court decision that weakened the Sherman Antitrust Act by declaring that the federal government could only regulate monopolies engaged in interstate commerce. (17)

Universal Negro Improvement Association (UNIA) Pan-African organization founded by black Nationalist leader Marcus Garvey that emphasized black separatism and "Africa for Africans." (22)

USA PATRIOT Act (2001) Congressional act that expanded the Justice Department's powers to conduct surveillance on terrorist suspects at and home and abroad. (31)

Vertical integration A hallmark of the modern corporation, vertical integration cut costs and guaranteed a flow of raw materials by controlling both the production and distribution processes. (17)

Vice-admiralty courts Colonial courts established by the English Board of Trade to enforce the Navigation Act of 1696. (4)

Virginia Company of London English joint-stock company established in 1606 by a royal charter that gave it exclusive rights to colonize from New England south to Virginia. (2)

Voting Rights Act (1965) Congressional act that outlawed literacy tests to vote and gave the Justice Department the power directly to register voters in districts where discrimination existed. (27)

Watergate Scandal Composite term of illegal political acts by Nixon Administration that culminated in the 1972 burglary of the Democratic Party headquarters and subsequent cover-up. (28)

Whig Party American political party formed in 1834 that supported government investments in infrastructure to stimulate business, and, in some parts of the North, endorsed moderate antislavery politics. (6)

Whiskey Rebellion (1794) Violent uprising in western Pennsylvania by farmers who refused to pay a federal tax on liquor. (8)

***Williams v. Mississippi* (1898)** The U.S. Supreme Court decision that upheld Mississippi's disfranchisement amendment aimed at eliminating the black vote. (20)

Women's Christian Temperance Union (WCTU) Formed in 1874, the nation's largest female reform organization of the 19th century, specifically dedicated to the banning of intoxicating beverages. The WCTU also sought the vote for women. (18)

XYZ Affair (1797–98) Name given to a scandal caused by French diplomats demanding bribes from American diplomats, leading to a rise in tensions between the United States and France. (8)

Yellow journalism Name given to sensationalist newspaper journalism of the late 19th century. This type of journalism provoked widespread public support for the Cuban rebels. (19)

Yeomen The term applied in the 18th and early 19th century to self-sufficient farmers who owned small plots of land, an idealized type. (9)

Credits

MAP, FIGURE, AND TABLE SOURCES

Maps by International Mapping.

America in the World (Population) Source(s): United States Population Division; United Nations, Department of Economic and Social Affairs, Population Division (2011). *World Population Prospects: The 2010 Revision*; Massimo Livi Bacci, *A Concise History of World Population* (Wiley-Blackwell, 2001).

Chapter 1

Map 1.1   Source(s): Helen Hornbeck Tanner, ed., *The Settling of North America: The Atlas of the Great Migrations into North America from the Ice Age to the Present* (New York: MacMillan, 1995), 29; Mark C. Carnes, ed., *Historical Atlas of the United States* (New York: Routledge, 2003), 20–21.

Map 1.2   Source(s): Michael Coe et al., *Atlas of Ancient North America* (New York: Facts on File, 1986), 44–45.

Map 1.3   Source(s): Mark Kishlansky et al., *Societies and Culture in World History* (New York: Harper Collins, 1995), 414; *The Oxford Atlas of Exploration*, 2nd edition (New York: Oxford University Press, 2008), 34; Patrick K. O'Brien, gen. ed., *The Oxford Atlas of World History*, concise ed. (New York: Oxford University Press, 2002), 116–17.

Map 1.4   Source(s): D. W. Meinig, *The Shaping of America: A Geographic Perspective on 500 Years of History: Volume 1: Atlantic America, 1492–1800* (New Haven: Yale University Press, 1986), 5; Alfred W. Crosby, *Ecological Imperialism: The Biological Expansion of Europe, 900–1900* (New York: Cambridge University Press, 1985), 110; Albert C. Jensen, *The Cod* (New York: Thomas Y. Crowell, 1972), 3; Patrick K. O'Brien, gen. ed., *The Oxford Atlas of World History*, concise ed. (New York: Oxford University Press, 2002), 116–17.

Map 1.6   Source(s): Peter Bakewell, *A History of Latin America*, 2nd edition (Malden, Mass.: Blackwell, 2004), xxii.

Map 1.7   Source(s): *The Oxford Atlas of Exploration*, 2nd edition (New York: Oxford University Press, 2008), 34, 124; Patrick K. O'Brien, gen. ed., *The Oxford Atlas of World History*, concise ed. (New York: Oxford University Press, 2002), 120.

Chapter 2

Map 2.1   Source(s): *The Cambridge History of the Native Peoples of the Americas: Volume 1: North America: Part I*, eds. Bruce G. Trigger and Wilcomb E. Washburn (New York: Cambridge University Press, 1996), 345, 346; *The Oxford Atlas of Exploration*, 2nd edition (New York: Oxford University Press, 2008), 124.

Map 2.2   Source(s): *The Cambridge History of the Native Peoples of the Americas: Volume 1: North America: Part I*, ed. Bruce G. Trigger and Wilcomb E. Washburn (New York: Cambridge University Press, 1996), 341.

Map 2.3   Source(s): *The Cambridge History of the Native Peoples of the Americas: Volume 1: North America: Part I*, ed. Bruce G. Trigger and Wilcomb E. Washburn (New York: Cambridge University Press, 1996), 405; *The Settling of North America: The Atlas of the Great Migration into North America from the Ice Age to the Present*, ed. Helen Hornbeck Tanner (New York: MacMillan, 1995), 42; James Oakes et al., *Of the People: A History of the United States* (New York, Oxford: Oxford University Press, 2010), 77.

Map 2.4   Source(s): Jenny Hale Pulsipher, *Subjects unto the Same King: Indians, English, and the Contest for Authority in Colonial New England* (Philadelphia: University of Pennsylvania Press, 2005), 78.

Chapter 3

Map 3.1   Source(s): *The Historical Atlas of Canada*, ed. R. Cole Harris (Toronto: University of Toronto Press, 1987), Volume 1, Plate 35.

Map 3.2   Source(s): David Eltis and David Richardson, *Atlas of the Transatlantic Slave Trade* (New Haven: Yale University Press, 2010), 18–19; Assessing the Slave Trade. 2009. *Voyages: The Trans-Atlantic Slave Trade Database.* http://www.slavevoyages.org (accessed November 29, 2011); Gregory O'Malley, "Beyond the Middle Passage: Slave Migration from the Caribbean to North America,

1619–1807," *The William and Mary Quarterly*, 3rd Series, 66 (January 2009), 141–42, 146, 160–61, 163.

Map 3.3   Source(s): Mark C. Carnes, ed., *Historical Atlas of the United States* (New York: Routledge, 2003), 48.

Map 3.4   Source(s): *The Cambridge History of the Native Peoples of the Americas: Volume 1: North America: Part I*, ed. Bruce G. Trigger and Wilcomb E. Washburn (New York: Cambridge University Press, 1996), 416, 426; Andrew K. Frank, ed., *The Routledge Historical Atlas of the American South* (New York: Routledge, 1999), 20.

Figure 3.1   Source(s): Assessing the Slave Trade. 2009. *Voyages: The Trans-Atlantic Slave Trade Database.* http://www.slavevoyages.org (accessed November 29, 2011).

Figure 3.2   Source(s): David Eltis, *The Rise of African Slavery in the Americas* (New York: Cambridge University Press, 2000), 9.

Figure 3.3   Source(s): David W. Galenson, *White Servitude in Colonial America: An Economic Analysis* (New York: Cambridge University Press, 1981), 83, 84.

Table 3.1   Source(s): Assessing the Slave Trade. 2009. *Voyages: The Trans-Atlantic Slave Trade Database.* http://www.slavevoyages.org (accessed November 29, 2011).

Table 3.2   Source(s): Richard Middleton, *Colonial America: A History*, 3rd edition (Oxford, England: Blackwell, 2002); Charles M. Andrews, *The Colonial Period of American History, Volume 4: England's Commercial and Colonial Policy* (New Haven: Yale University Press, 1938).

Chapter 4

Map 4.1   Source(s): Carl Waldman, *Atlas of the North American Indian*, 3rd edition (New York: Facts on File, 2009), 79; Colin G. Calloway, *First Peoples: A Documentary Survey of American Indian History*, 3rd edition (Boston: Bedford/St. Martin's, 2008), 295.

Map 4.2   Source(s): Paul Kelton, *Epidemics and Enslavement: Biological Catastrophe in the Native Southeast, 1492–1715* (Lincoln: University of Nebraska Press, 2007), 201.

Map 4.3   Source(s): David Eltis and David Richardson, *Atlas of the Transatlantic Slave Trade* (New Haven: Yale University Press, 2010), 18–19; Assessing the Slave Trade. 2009. *Voyages: The Trans-Atlantic Slave Trade Database.* http://www.slavevoyages.org (accessed November 29, 2011).

Map 4.4   Source(s): Mark C. Carnes, ed., *Historical Atlas of the United States* (New York: Routledge, 2003), 73.

Figure 4.1   Source(s): Assessing the Slave Trade. 2009. *Voyages: The Trans-Atlantic Slave Trade Database.* http://www.slavevoyages.org (accessed November 29, 2011).

Table 4.1   Source(s): Aaron S. Fogleman, "Migrations to the Thirteen British North American Colonies, 1700–1775: New Estimates," *Journal of Interdisciplinary History* 22 (1992), 691–709; Assessing the Slave Trade. 2009. *Voyages: The Trans-Atlantic Slave Trade Database.* http://www.slavevoyages.org (accessed November 29, 2011).

Chapter 5

Map 5.1   Source(s): David Eltis and David Richardson, *Atlas of the Transatlantic Slave Trade* (New Haven: Yale University Press, 2010), 18–19; Assessing the Slave Trade. 2009. *Voyages: The Trans-Atlantic Slave Trade Database.* http://www.slavevoyages.org (accessed November 29, 2011).

Map 5.2   Source(s): Mark C. Carnes, ed., *Historical Atlas of the United States* (New York: Routledge, 2003), 59.

Map 5.3   Source(s): Mark C. Carnes, ed., *Historical Atlas of the United States* (New York: Routledge, 2003), 58; Andrew K. Frank, ed., *The Routledge Historical Atlas of the American South* (New York: Routledge, 1999), 20.

Map 5.4   Source(s): Robert H. Ferrell and Richard Natkiel, *Atlas of American History* (New York: Facts on File, 1987, 1993), 30; Mark C. Carnes, ed., *Historical Atlas of the United States* (New York: Routledge, 2003), 58.

Map 5.6   Source(s): Robert H. Ferrell and Richard Natkiel, *Atlas of American History* (New York: Facts on File, 1987, 1993), 16; *Historical Atlas of Canada*, R. Cole Harris, ed. (Toronto: University of Toronto Press, 1987), Volume 1, Plate 30.

Map 5.7   Source(s): *Historical Atlas of Canada*, R. Cole Harris, ed. (Toronto: University of Toronto Press, 1987), Volume 1, Plate 30.

Figure 5.1   Source(s): Assessing the Slave Trade. 2009. *Voyages: The Trans-Atlantic Slave Trade Database.* http://www.slavevoyages.org (accessed November 29, 2011).

Figure 5.2   Source(s): Jay Coughtry, *The Notorious Triangle: Rhode Island and the African Slave Trade,*

1700–1807 (Philadelphia: Temple University Press, 1981), 34.

Figure 5.3   Source(s): Jacob Cooke, ed., *Encyclopedia of North American Colonies* (New York: Scribner's, 1993), 1, 470.

Table 5.1   Source(s): Aaron S. Fogleman, "Migrations to the Thirteen British North American Colonies, 1700–1775: New Estimates," *Journal of Interdisciplinary History* 22 (1992), 691–709; Assessing the Slave Trade. 2009. *Voyages: The Trans-Atlantic Slave Trade Database.* http://www.slavevoyages.org (accessed November 29, 2011).

Table 5.2   Source(s): Richard Middleton, *Colonial America: A History*, 3rd edition (Oxford: Blackwell, 2002); Jack P. Greene, ed., *Settlements to Society: A Documentary History of Colonial America* (New York: W.W. Norton, 1975).

Chapter 8

Figure 8.1   Source(s): *Historical Statistics of the United States Millennial Edition Online*, eds. Susan B. Carter, Scott Sigmund Gartner, Michael R. Haines, Alan L. Olmstead, Richard Sutch, and Gavin Wright (Cambridge University Press, 2011). http://hsus.cambridge.org/HSUSWeb (accessed November 29, 2011).

Chapter 10

Map 10.2   Source(s): Steven Dutch, University of Wisconsin–Green Bay; C.O. Paullin, *Atlas of the Historical Geography of the United States* (Carnegie Institute, 1932, reproduced in facsimile by Greenwood Press, 1975).

Chapter 11

Map 11.3   Source(s): Nathanial Philbrick, *Sea of Glory: America's Voyage of Discovery, the U.S. Exploring Expedition, 1838–1842* (New York: Viking, 2003).

Figure 11.1   Source(s): *Historical Statistics of the United States, 1789–1945.* Dept. of the Census, 1949. Series B 304–330—Immigration—Immigrants by Country: 1820 to 1945.

Figure 11.2   Source(s): *Historical Statistics of the United States, 1789–1945.* Dept. of the Census, 1949. Series B 13–23: Population, Decennial Summary—Sex, Urban-Rural Residence, and Race: 1790 to 1940.

Chapter 12

Map 12.1   Source(s): John H. Thompson, *Geography of New York State* (New York: Syracuse University Press, 1966).

Map 12.2   Source(s): Kenneth Greenberg, *The Confessions of Nat Turner* (Bedford/St. Martins, 1996).

Figure 12.1   Source(s): Eighth U.S. Census. Schedule 1.

Figure 12.3   Source(s): Lyn Ragsdale, *Vital Statistics on the Presidency* (Washington, DC: Congressional Quarterly Press, 1998), 132–38.

Chapter 13

Figure 13.1   Source(s): Campbell J. Gibson and Emily Lennon, "Historical Census Statistics on the Foreign-Born Population of the United States: 1850–1990." Population Division, U.S. Bureau of the Census, Washington, DC 20233–8800. February 1999, POPULATION   DIVISION

WORKING PAPER NO. 29, Table 4. Region and Country or Area of Birth of the Foreign-Born Population.

Chapter 14

Map 14.1   Source(s): Aaron Sheehan-Dean, *Concise Historical Atlas of the U.S. Civil War* (New York: Oxford University Press, 2008).

Map 14.2   Source(s): Aaron Sheehan-Dean, *Concise Historical Atlas of the U.S. Civil War* (New York: Oxford University Press, 2008).

Map 14.3   Source(s): Aaron Sheehan-Dean, *Concise Historical Atlas of the U.S. Civil War* (New York: Oxford University Press, 2008).

Map 14.4   Source(s): Aaron Sheehan-Dean, *Concise Historical Atlas of the U.S. Civil War* (New York: Oxford University Press, 2008).

Figure 14.2   Source(s): Douglas B. Ball, *Financial Failure and Confederate Defeat* (Urbana: University of Illinois Press, 1991); J. G. Randall, *The Civil War and Reconstruction* (Boston: D.C. Heath, 1937); Richard Cecil Todd, *Confederate Finance* (Athens: University of Georgia Press, 1954).

Chapter 15

Map 15.1   Source(s): Aaron Sheehan-Dean, *Concise Historical Atlas of the U.S. Civil War* (New York: Oxford University Press, 2008).

Map 15.2   Source(s): Aaron Sheehan-Dean, *Concise Historical Atlas of the U.S. Civil War* (New York: Oxford University Press, 2008).

Map 15.3   Source(s): Aaron Sheehan-Dean, *Concise Historical Atlas of the U.S. Civil War* (New York: Oxford University Press, 2008).

Figure 15.1   Source(s): James L. Watkins, *King Cotton: A Historical and Statistical Review, 1790–1908* (New York: James L. Watkins and Sons, 1908).

PHOTO CREDITS

Chapter 1 Page 2: *Monumenta Cartographia,* 1502 by © Royal Geographical Society, London, UK. p. 5: Courtesy of The Bancroft Library, University of California, Berkeley, xE51 C76 v. 3 p. 350; p. 8: Ira Block/National Geographic/Getty Images; p. 10: Library and Archives Canada; p. 14: The Stapleton Collection/The Bridgeman Art Library; p. 18: © The Trustees of the British Museum; p. 19: Museo de America, Madrid, Spain/The Bridgeman Art Library; p. 25: Courtesy of Library and Archives Canada; p. 29: © The Trustees of the British Museum/Art Resource, NY.

Chapter 2 Page 38: © The Trustees of the British Museum. p. 41: Private Collection/Archives Charmet/The Bridgeman Art Library; p. 43: © Cindy Miller Hopkins/DanitaDelimont.com; p. 47: National Museum of American History, Kenneth E. Behring Center; p. 50: Virginia Historical Society; p. 55: Art Resource, NY; p. 57: Library and Archives Canada/C21404; p. 62: Virginia Historical Society, Richmond, Virginia, USA/ The Bridgeman Art Library.

Chapter 3 Page 72: Portrait of Elsie (Rutgers) Schuyler Vas, 1723. Albany Institute of History & Art, 1957. 104. p. 75: Centre Historique des Archives Nationales, Paris, France/Giraudon/The Bridgeman Art Library; p. 77: © The Huntington Library, Art Collections & Botanical Gardens/The Bridgeman Art Library; p. 78: British Library, London, UK/© British Library Board. All Rights Reserved/The Bridgeman Art Library; p. 83: © The British Library Board; p. 94: Courtesy, National Museum of

the American Indian, Smithsonian Institution [23/9269]; p. 97: Danita Delimont/Alamy; p. 101: New York State Archives.

Chapter 4 Page 110: Library and Archives Canada, acc. No. 1977-35-4. Acquired with a special grant from the Canadian Government in 1977. p. 112: The Historic New Orleans Collection; p. 117: State Library of Louisiana; p. 122: © Trustees of the British Museum; p. 128: Courtesy Houghton Library, Harvard University EC7.A100.709s2; p. 132: The Granger Collection, NYC — All rights reserved; p. 133: Portrait of an Unidentified Woman (oil on canvas), American School, (18th century)/© Collection of the New-York Historical Society, USA/The Bridgeman Art Library International; p. 140: The Granger Collection, NYC — All rights reserved; p. 141: Mary Evans Picture Library.

Chapter 5 Page 148: George Whitefield by John Wollaston, oil on canvas, circa 1742. © National Portrait Gallery, London. p. 150: Newport Historical Society; p. 155: Document opposing the re-election of Benjamin Franklin to the Assembly, 1764 (print), Weiss, Lewis (1717–96)/New York Public Library, USA/The Bridgeman Art Library; p. 159: Courtesy of Texas Archeological Research Laboratory, University of Texas at Austin; p. 161: Courtesy Florida Museum of Natural History-Historical Archaeology Collections; p. 164: Courtesy American Antiquarian Society; p. 166: The Gansevoort Limner, Susanna Truax, Gift of Edgar William and Bernice Chrysler

Garbisch. Image courtesy of the National Gallery of Art, Washington; p. 178: The Death of General Wolfe (1727–59), c.1771 (oil on panel) (see also 105409, 119752 & 124902), West, Benjamin (1738–1820)/Private Collection/Phillips, Fine Art Auctioneers, New York, USA/The Bridgeman Art Library; p. 178: A View of the Plundering and Burning of the City of Grimross, 1758 by Thomas Davies (1737–1812), National Gallery of Canada (6270); p. 181: © Look and Learn/The Bridgeman Art Library.

Chapter 6 Page 190: Yale University Art Gallery/Art Resource, NY; p. 193: George III, 1761–62 (oil on canvas), Ramsay, Allan (1713–84)/The Royal Collection © 2011 Her Majesty Queen Elizabeth II/The Bridgeman Art Library; p. 201: Library of Congress; p. 201: Samuel Adams (colour litho) by John Singleton Copley (1738–1815) Private Collection/Peter Newark American Pictures/ The Bridgeman Art Library; p. 205: Image copyright © The Metropolitan Museum of Art/Art Resource, NY; p. 206: The Granger Collection, NYC — All rights reserved; p. 208: Boston Tea Party, 16th December 1773 (engraving)/Private Collection/Bridgeman Images; p. 214: Courtesy of United States National Archives and Records Administration; p. 215: © Christie's Images/The Bridgeman Art Library International; p. 216: Lebrecht 3/Lebrecht Music & Arts/Corbis.

Chapter 7 Page 222: Image copyright © The Metropolitan Museum of Art/ Art Resource, NY; p. 224: Courtesy of Historical Society of Pennsylvania

Index

Italicized page numbers indicate a table or figure. Page numbers followed by m indicate a map.

CANADA

MINNESOTA

Lake Superior

Minneapolis
St. Paul
Mississippi

WISCONSIN

Green Bay

Madison ★ • Milwaukee

Lake Michigan

MICHIGAN

Lansing ★ • Flint
Detroit •

Lake Huron

Lake Ontario

St. Lawrence

MAINE

• Bangor
Augusta ★
• Portland

VERMONT

Montpelier ★

Concord ★ **NEW HAMPSHIRE**

NEW YORK
Albany ★   Boston ★ **MASSACHUSETTS**
Buffalo •   Hartford • • Providence
          Hudson • **RHODE ISLAND**
                  CONNECTICUT

Lake Erie

Erie •

IOWA

• Cedar
Rapids
Des Moines ★

maha
• Omaha ★

ILLINOIS

Peoria •

Chicago •

Fort Wayne •

INDIANA

Indianapolis ★

Toledo • Cleveland •

Allegheny

PENNSYLVANIA

Harrisburg ★   Trenton ★ **NEW JERSEY**
Pittsburgh •   Philadelphia •
Susquehanna   Dover •

New York •

Springfield ★

Wabash

OHIO

Columbus ★

Cincinnati •

Ohio

Baltimore •

Washington D.C. ⊛ • Annapolis **DELAWARE**

MARYLAND

Kansas
City
Topeka ★
ichita

St. Louis •

Jefferson
City ★

MISSOURI

Louisville •

KENTUCKY

Frankfort ★

**WEST
VIRGINIA**

Charleston ★

Potomac

VIRGINIA

Richmond ★

Norfolk •

Roanoke

Tulsa •

homa
Fort Smith •

Memphis •

Nashville ★

TENNESSEE

Knoxville •

Asheville •

Raleigh •

NORTH CAROLINA

• Charlotte

Tennessee

Pee Dee

Wilmington •

Little Rock •

ARKANSAS

El Dorado •

Tupelo •

Birmingham •

Columbia •

**SOUTH
CAROLINA**

Charleston •

Dallas

Shreveport •

MISSISSIPPI

Jackson ★

Montgomery ★

ALABAMA

Atlanta ★

GEORGIA

Augusta •

Chattahoochee

Savannah •

Savannah

**ATLANTIC
OCEAN**

co

LOUISIANA

Baton Rouge ★

Natchez •

Mobile •

New Orleans •

• Pensacola

ALABAMA

Valdosta •

★ Tallahassee

Jacksonville •

Houston •

Gulf of Mexico

Orlando •

Tampa •

FLORIDA

Miami •

BAHAMAS

Christi

ville

**PUERTO
RICO**

San Juan
Bayamón ★ • Carolina
Ponce •

0   30 miles
0   30 kilometers

Caribbean Sea

ARCTIC OCEAN

Beaufort Sea

Baffin Bay

Greenland
(Denmark)

Greenland
Sea

ICELAND

Mackenzie

Hudson
Bay

Davis Strait

UNITED
KINGDOM

Gulf of
Alaska

Peace

CANADA

Labrador
Sea

IRELAND

N

BELGIU
LUX
FRANC

Missouri

NORTH PACIFIC
OCEAN

UNITED STATES

NORTH ATLANTIC
OCEAN

PORTUGAL

ANDORRA

SPAIN

Mississippi

MOROCCO

ALGERIA

Gulf of
Mexico

MEXICO

BAHAMAS

CUBA

DOM.
REP.

BELIZE   HAITI

JAMAICA

GUATEMALA   HONDURAS

EL SALVADOR   NICARAGUA

COSTA RICA

PANAMA

SAINT KITTS AND NEVIS
ANTIGUA AND BARBUDA
DOMINICA
SAINT LUCIA
SAINT VINCENT AND
THE GRENADINES
BARBADOS
GRENADA
TRINIDAD AND TOBAGO

Caribbean Sea

WESTERN
SAHARA
(Morocco)

CAPE
VERDE

MAURITANIA

MALI

THE GAMBIA   SENEGAL

GUINEA-BISSAU

BURKINA
FASO

GUINEA

BENIN
TOGO

GHANA

SIERRA LEONE

LIBERIA

COTE D'IVOIRE

EQUATORIA
GUINE

VENEZUELA

GUYANA

SURINAME

FRENCH GUIANA
(France)

SAO TOME
AND PRINCIPE

COLOMBIA

KIRIBATI

ECUADOR

Amazon

PERU

BRAZIL

BOLIVIA

PARAGUAY

Parana

SOUTH PACIFIC
OCEAN

SOUTH ATLANTIC
OCEAN

CHILE

URUGUAY

ARGENTINA

Weddell Sea